Social
Administration

FOUNDATIONS OF SOCIAL WORK KNOWLEDGE
Frederic G. Reamer, Series Editor

Foundations of
Social Work Knowledge

Frederic G. Reamer, Series Editor

Social work has a unique history, purpose, perspective, and method. The primary purpose of this series is to articulate these distinct qualities and to define and explore the ideas, concepts, and skills that together constitute social work's intellectual foundations and boundaries and its emerging issues and concerns.

To accomplish this goal, the series will publish a cohesive collection of books that address both the core knowledge of the profession and its newly emerging topics. The core is defined by the evolving consensus, as primarily reflected in the Council of Social Work Education's Curriculum Policy Statement, concerning what courses accredited social work education programs must include in their curricula. The series will be characterized by an emphasis on the widely embraced ecological perspective; attention to issues concerning direct and indirect practice; and emphasis on cultural diversity and multiculturalism, social justice, oppression, populations at risk, and social work values and ethics. The series will have a dual focus on practice traditions and emerging issues and concepts.

DAVID G. GIL, *Confronting Injustice and Oppression: Concepts and Strategies for Social Workers*

GEORGE ALAN APPLEBY AND JEANE W. ANASTAS, *Not Just a Passing Phase: Social Work with Gay, Lesbian, and Bisexual People*

FREDERIC G. REAMER, *Social Work Research and Evaluation Skills*

PALLASSANA R. BALGOPAL, *Social Work Practice with Immigrants and Refugees*

FREDERIC G. REAMER, *Tangled Relationships: Managing Boundary Issues in the Human Services*

Social Administration

Roger A. Lohmann and Nancy Lohmann

COLUMBIA UNIVERSITY PRESS
NEW YORK

Columbia University Press
Publishers Since 1893
New York   Chichester, West Sussex
Copyright © 2002 Columbia University Press
All rights reserved
Library of Congress Cataloging-in-Publication Data

Lohmann, Roger A., 1942–
    Social administration / Roger A. Lohmann and Nancy Lohmann.
        p.   cm. — (Foundations of social work knowledge)
    Includes bibliographical references and index.
    ISBN 0-231-11198-3 (cloth : alk. paper)
    1. Social work administration. I. Lohmann, Nancy. II. Title. III. Series.
HV41.L633 2002
361.3′068—dc21   2001028098

∞ Casebound editions of Columbia University Press books are printed on
permanent and durable acid-free paper.

Printed in the United States of America
10 9 8 7 6 5 4 3 2 1

*To Melissa Lohmann
and
Andrew and Lisa Lohmann*

Contents

Foreword

For student readers, book sections such as forewords are often quickly skipped over, while to authors, such sections are laden with statements of intentions and implications. We are aware that many readers of this work will skip this particular section and leap directly into chapter 1. Even so, we wish to say a few words here about the title, direction, and focus of this book.

A number of years ago, a group of social work faculty in the United States who were teaching in the macro practice areas of community organization, management, administration, planning, and policy formed a new association called the Association for Community Organization and Social Administration (ACOSA). In naming the new group, they gave increased visibility to the two-word term that forms the title and principal subject of this book. For many people in the profession, community organization and social administration (COSA) forms the core of their professional interests and commitments, just as it has for many from the earliest days of the profession. This is a book about the practice of social work from that vantage point.

One of the genuine curiosities of the naming conventions of American social science is the durability of the adjective *social*. Combining it with suitable nouns, you can form an astounding variety of disciplinary names and subdisciplinary specialties. Dictionaries and encyclopedias of social science, university departmental course listings, and other standard sources are full of such examples. One can find everything from *social anthropology* to *social zoology* formed in this way. The field of social work has been an active participant in this naming process. Not only the general name of the profession, but such specialties within it as social casework, social psychiatry, social group work, social planning, social action and social policy, and several more are all prominent on the list. The social work profession was one of the earliest entrants in this language game, signaling in the earliest years of the twentieth century the collective intent of transforming charitable endeavors from leisure-time avocation to *work* or paid occupation.

More recently, social work educators have moved in different directions for the names they have chosen, using such universal and misleading adjectives derived from Latin as micro, mezzo and macro and such references to intent as direct and indirect. One of the recurrent puzzles along the way has been what to call the serious business of planning, creating, operating, and evaluating social agencies. Many people have tried many different solutions. In naming this book, our solution is to apply the rule of parsimony: simplest is best; why use three words or more when two will do as well? So, *social administration* it is.

Now, a brief word about direction and focus. We have sought to present in this work a suitable mixture of the theoretical and the practical aspects of social administration practice. One of us has been engaged in the actual practice of administration for most of the past two decades, while the other has been interested for many years in the state of theory in social administration and related practice topics, together with having extensive experience with boards, teaching, and conducting training workshops. We have sought to bring together in this book our interests in the knowledge, values, and skills of social administration, with greater attention to knowledge and values and relatively less on skill development.

Social work students, in our experience, often show a definite partiality for the apparent certainty of practice skills. They often display a strong belief that knowledge and skill are one and the same thing, and indeed sometimes in social work practice they are. These students believe that they already know what to do; they just need to know how to do it better. Such an approach can work well when one is considering settled practice approaches within established programs, clearly defined services, fixed routines, and standardized expectations.

In the case of social administration, however, social work students usually have little real-world experience with practice of administration and a very limited understanding of what administration is really all about. In this case, immediate focus on the certainty of skill building serves quite another purpose. When faced with the many uncertainties of any largely new subject matter, it can be tempting to seek out and grasp onto the few certainties that one encounters, including the techniques that those with mastery of the subject employ. In many learning situations such a strategy works well. In learning computer programming, for example, the task is made easier by the knowledge that whatever else you encounter, some version of *If . . . then . . .* conditional logic (usually known as the feedback loop) will arise in some form. Learning to write proper if-then statements is thus a major part of learning any program.

Learning social administration, however, is not like learning computer programming. A learning strategy built heavily around the certainty of discrete skills is not functional in the introduction to social administration. In this case, students unfamiliar with the topic must come to grips not only with their own uncertainties but also with the fact that *uncertainty* as a general condition is one of the defining characteristics of administrative situations. In administration, the practitioner is frequently concerned with establishing programs that do not presently exist, defining services that are currently undefined, creating and establishing routines, and standardizing expectations. In such situations, premature concern for the concrete certainties of skill building without a prior understanding of the broader situation can easily lull the learner and the practitioner into a false sense of certainty where none is warranted. Knowing computer programming or how to write a job description or any of the other technical skills associated with administrative practice does not translate easily into an understanding of the role, scope, and purposes of administration.

In administrative situations, the practical question of what to do is both logically prior to *and more important than* the technical question of how to do it. We do not wish to suggest that the practice of social administration is not filled with the application of discrete skills; quite the contrary. We do wish to suggest however, that much of the technical knowledge of social administration is based on highly subjective preferences and situation- and organization-specific expectations. Mastery of the techniques of a planning-budgeting schema known as Program Planning Budgeting System (PPBS), for example, is of little use today, when almost no one uses it and the practice model of budgeting it embodies can be highly misleading besides. In that rare agency that has implemented a PPBS system, however, technical mastery of these skills is essential.

Stanley L. Witkin (2001), editor of *Social Work,* described this issue in his valediction for Howard Goldstein. He described Goldstein as "chagrined by the trend in some quarters of the profession toward training (rather than education) that reduced social work practice to a contextless grab bag of skills and techniques" (p.105). We share Goldstein's concern and designed this book to provide the context for social administration as well as to introduce a few basic practice skills. As such, our goal is to contribute to the education of the book's readers.

processes (communications, information, authority, and power). In the final chapters of the book, discrete topics of fundamental importance in contemporary social administration are considered.

Roger A. Lohmann and Nancy Lohmann

Social
Administration

CHAPTER 1

Social Administration:
An Overview

Organized social services face greater challenges now than at any time in the past half century. Movement away from a grants economy has been coupled with the spread of managed care, the increasing growth and legitimacy of the social work profession, and the proliferation of a new breed of social administrators who must be part entrepreneur and part technocrat. The implications of those challenges for social agencies and the social work profession are many and far-reaching. One important practice arena in which many of the challenges and opportunities facing social work and social services come to bear most directly is in social administration, which is the study and practice of management, leadership, decision making, and institution building in social service.

This book provides an introduction to the study and practice of social administration. The term itself is not new, but it may be unfamiliar to the reader. Several decades ago, the British scholar David Donnison (1961) defined social administration as "the study of the development, structure and practices of the social services." To this we would add "and the methods used to initiate, develop, foster, and maintain them." Within the United States, Simon Slavin (1978), the founding editor of the journal *Administra-*

tion in Social Work, was among the foremost advocates of this term. We appreciate not only Slavin's use of the term, but also his intent. Slavin and Perlmutter (1980) wrote that "executive leadership in social administration must be grounded in the fundamental values and historical concerns of the social work profession." Archie Hanlon (1978) wrote that

> social administration moves toward the opinion that knowledge and skills of the (social work) profession are interrelated not only with the social sciences but also with the values, priorities, and resources of the larger social institutions. Thus, social administration focuses on the policies, planning, and administration of social welfare goods and services in relation to the political, social, and economic institutions and to the determinants of the distribution of national[1] resources to social welfare needs. (p. 55)

Any adequate conception of social administration is not merely instrumental, concerned with completing the task at hand, but also clearly normative, concerned with judgments about whether the task is worth doing. As Abels and Murphy (1981) stated, "The purpose of administration is to provide the resources and structural and psychological supports necessary to insure that the agency will function in a manner leading to positive consequences for the client served and, ultimately, to a more just society" (p. 9). Social administrators are not technicians and tacticians, but moral actors. It is in this concern for building and maintaining the institutions of a just society where much of the distinctive content of social administration is grounded.

More than two decades ago, Dumpson, Mullen, First, and Harder (1978) noted the

> absence of systematic frameworks or models for organizing existing social welfare administrative practice knowledge. While considerable potentially relevant knowledge has been developed by various disciplines around what administrators in social welfare settings should know, it has not been systematically organized or utilized in ways that will promote effective social welfare administrative practice. (p. 33)

Since that time, there has been a substantial body of work devoted to laying out various partial frameworks and detailed models, and it can truly be said that administrative practice knowledge in social work has expanded considerably. (Compare, for example, Slavin [1978] with Patti [2000].) To date, however, an up-to-date general framework for encompassing the entire topic of social administration has been notably absent. There have been a number of management textbooks, to be sure, but generally these have offered only partial coverage of the topic. The premise of several is the alluring but highly misleading notion that effective social administration involves the mastery of a limited range of skills and techniques. We believe that there is value in a single viewpoint alongside the plurality of diverse views.

In writing this book, we set out to provide a comprehensive introductory overview that emphasizes the conceptual and theoretical aspects of social administration. The most basic framework of this book is a four-part model of social administration. The term *social administration* is used throughout this book to refer to these related phenomena:

1. Management of social services[2]
2. Efforts to encourage, develop, and exercise leadership of social services at all levels
3. Organizational and institutional policy making and other decision making affecting the purposes, strategies, and direction of social services[3]
4. Institution-building efforts to ensure the continuation of viable social services

Throughout the book, the terms *administration* and *management* are often used interchangeably. This is in marked contrast to a number of earlier social work sources that have sought to make a major distinction between the two terms. For example, Abels and Murphy (1981) quote former National Association of Social Workers (NASW) Executive Director Chauncey Alexander: "Administration is viewed as focusing on efficiency—the direction and improvement of existing systems—while management is thought to encompass the additional responsibility of obtaining or redirecting resources or markets for new opportunities and thus to effectiveness" (p. 9). Others have attempted to make similar distinctions without notable success. We believe that concern for efficiency, systems improvement, resource development, exploiting new opportunities, and effectiveness are part of a single bundle, and within the broader practice community, sometimes it seems clearer to call that bundle administration; sometimes, management.

Although the terms *management* and *administration* are frequently used interchangeably, we hold to one consistent and rather subtle difference. Management refers to internal concerns of existing organizations, whereas social administration also encompasses the full sweep of leadership, decision making, and institution building. Thus, social administrators must, of necessity, also be managers. One would hope that managers in the social services also have the breadth of vision and incisive judgment to be social administrators as well.

One of the major points of emphasis in our perspective is the integral relationship between social administration, social services, and the social work profession. It continues to be the case, as Slavin noted in 1980, that

> the current national emphasis on efficiency, cost containment, and quantifiable objectives often mythologizes management and its power, and tends to lead to a narrow technicism which will "set matters right." The reliance on technically trained managers, drawn from disciplines often removed from the experience of the social services in many of the public bureaucracies dealing with human need, has created as many problems for client service integrity as it has solved. (p. xx)

In our view, this statement should not be read simply as a matter of disciplinary preference. Trained social workers have proved to be as capable of their own types of narrow technicism as managers from accounting, management, or public administration backgrounds. The challenge for anyone seeking to manage and lead social services is to transcend such limits.

In this chapter, we examine the issue of where knowledge of the four basic components of social administration properly fits in the social work curriculum and within the general practice of social work. This issue involves a number of questions that have troubled social work educators and practitioners for a long time and with which every student taking a course in social administration must grapple.

Foremost among these questions is this: Why is it necessary and how is it possible to connect the seemingly straightforward wish to help others with the seemingly remote, arcane, and esoteric concerns of organizing, programs, strategies, budgets, costs, efficiencies, and the other exotic topics that arise in social administration? Why can't we just simplify things? The honest answer, of course, is that it may not be necessary to deliver social services using professionals in formal organizations. There certainly are other ways to approach the solving of social problems. However, organized, professional social services were the medium of choice throughout most of the twentieth century and continue to be so in the early years of this millennium. Within the institutional context of social welfare thus laid down, the simplest explanation for both formal organization and professionalization may be found in the twentieth-century phenomena of the rationalization of social relations, which interested and troubled Max Weber and a host of other social critics.[4]

Organized and administered social service delivery is a fact of life in all human services. As many a caseworker or therapist who has gone into private practice has learned, the concerns and details that are the special province of social administration cannot easily be wished away in the real world.

Contracts and budgets must be negotiated, plans must be drawn up, strategy and purpose must be clear, and reports must be completed and submitted to funders for the service enterprise to continue. Various external constituencies must be dealt with. The real world of social service practice involves complex and tricky resource, decision, and evaluation issues, and these issues are realities that must be confronted. The daily demands of social administration—in such diverse forms as supervision, reporting requirements, and coping with resource limitations—are part of the practice experience of all social workers, no matter what else it may say in their titles or job descriptions.

The concerns of social administration that we present here are among the major preoccupations of professional leaders and most MSW-level social workers. One school of social work recently polled the members of its faculty about their actual practice experience as opposed to their practice preferences or teaching interests. It was discovered that all of them—100 percent—had prior administrative experience as supervisors, program managers, budget managers, or executives in managing inventories of supplies and equipment, in managing cases, or in some other capacity. Many recent MSW graduates move into administrative support positions early in their professional careers (Sherwood, 1979). The stereotype of the independent therapist alone in her cozy office, giving solace to troubled clients who are hers exclusively, and free from the demands of contracts, budgets, and schedules is largely a pipe dream far removed from the realities of contemporary social work practice. Social work practice is still largely agency practice—even if the agency is very small—and agency practice is not possible without some measure of social administration.

Even as students are adjusting their gaze to fit these realities, however, these daily realities of social administration are changing before our eyes. Just as the global economy has changed the rules of the management game in business management, it is also exercising subtle but profound influences upon the practice of social administration (Mitroff, Mohrman, & Little, 1987). Devolution, managed care, welfare reform, the private practice of social work outside the traditional community agency, the growth of multidisciplinary nonprofit management: these and a score of other contemporary influences are changing the rules of the game for social administration practice. No one can say for sure what the implications for social services may be ten years from now. However, five things are clear:

1. A large and growing number of tasks of the type we associate in this book with social administration will be involved in making whatever transition may be necessary. This may involve hiring qualified people, planning and directing new and innovative programs, establishing adequate infor-

mation systems, negotiating contracts and provider agreements, and a good deal more.

2. Large measures of creative, flexible, and decisive leadership will be demanded in the continuing assault on social problems by the profession, agencies, and programs. If social workers no longer wish to provide that leadership, then others must and will rise to the occasion.

3. Present trends are (as always) paradoxical and difficult to interpret. It is within the realm of possibility that the social agency as it evolved during what we call the "age of grants" (roughly 1965–1980) will soon be a thing of the past, rendered obsolete by the new economics of limited public funding, increasing donations, and the exigencies of managed care. It is equally possible that the renewed emphasis on service contracting during the 1990s signaled the beginning of a genuine renaissance of the social agency, if only we had been able to read the signals more clearly. No one can say for sure what the future of social service will be.

4. When we look back years from now, it will probably be clear that a small number of key or critical decisions were decisive in determining the strategic directions that social agencies and the social service field actually took. Passage of a single piece of legislation, the Social Security Act, for example, marked the end of a 300-year-old local poor law system in the United States and defined much of the modern structure of social services.

5. Social agencies and other institutions of American social welfare will have been shaped and molded by events and joined by additional, new, as-yet-unknown institutions designed to deal with emerging new problems and new ways of viewing old problems. All this will not have happened randomly or automatically but through the deliberate, continuous efforts of those engaged in social administration.

The four constant elements in these observations—management, leadership, critical decision making, and institution building—are the essential concerns of social administration as we approach it in this book.

There are at least 300,000 nonprofit social service organizations in the United States as well as public social services bureaucracies in all fifty states (Salamon, 1992). There are also an uncounted number of social service units in commercial[5] corporations (hospitals, nursing homes, day care centers, and a broad range of general businesses).

Independent nonprofit social agencies continue to be a major venue for social service delivery. A study of MSW graduates in twenty-one programs found that more than 50 percent were employed in nonprofit settings; about 25 percent, in public settings; and 18 percent, in commercial organizations (Beaucar, 1999). The vast majority of these public and private organizations are administered organizations, that is, they are (1) social groups character-ized by planned and orderly social relations grounded in rules (2) with staffs of employees hired and paid for their expertise in social problem solving and (3) led by paid, appointed officials designated as leaders empowered to make critical decisions using criteria such as quality, efficiency, and ef-fectiveness and (4) expected to create, nurture, and maintain these orga-nizations as enduring social institutions at least until such times as the social problems they are to address may be resolved.

SOCIAL ADMINISTRATION DEFINED

In general, as noted earlier, we use the term *social administration* through-out to designate the full range of concerns in this book. The phrase is short and easy to remember. Social administration is an organizational reality in all administered organizations and concerned principally with the four do-mains of management, leadership, decision making, and institution build-ing. Management is concerned primarily with creating viable organizations and programs, maintaining order and guiding change, facilitating the as-signment and completion of social work and related social service tasks, discovering and utilizing human and financial resources, maintaining worker morale and client/consumer satisfaction, and making organiza-tional policy and enforcing rules. Leadership is personal behavior and or-ganizational roles that guide and direct the purpose and meaning of the efforts of others. Leadership in social administration is generally of five prin-cipal types: community, policy, agency, program, and professional. In social administration, critical decisions address issues of policy, strategy, program, operations, and resources. Institution building is a long-term concern for creating and sustaining vision, defining mission and strategy, and public representation of community, agency, program, and professional purposes.

Social administration has long been understood to be an important as-pect of social work practice and one that inevitably shapes, molds, and reaches deep into the domain of micro or clinical practice. Weissman, Ep-stein, and Savage (1983) perhaps spoke for the entire profession when they said, "The everyday activities of most clinical social workers involve the performance of a variety of helping roles that in varying degrees require both administrative and therapeutic knowledge and skill." Yet, much of the social work curriculum does not truly reflect this. Attempts to operationalize this dualistic nature of social work practice have often attempted to recon-struct administrative knowledge and skills within the dominant models of therapeutic language and imagery. We are proceeding instead from the as-sumption woven throughout the human services management movement of the past thirty years that administrative situations must be understood in themselves for what they are.

Administration has been important in the social services since before the Elizabethan Poor Law of 1601 institutionalized the concept of overseers of the poor in English law.[6] Yet, administrative content has never played a particularly large or important role in the social work curriculum. Social administration was, in fact, a rather late arrival in social work education. A course in administration was first offered in a school of social work in 1914, nearly two decades after other training courses for social work first appeared. The first social work courses offered in the 1890s were directed at preparation of what today are called direct service workers. It seems to be the case that the social administrators responsible for setting up such training programs did not at first judge themselves to be as much in need of training as their workers.

It was not until 1944 that the curriculum statement of the American Association of Schools of Social Work included administration as one of eight basic methods defining social work.[7] Since that time, many schools of social work have tended to offer small clusters of social administration courses at the graduate level that include only limited or no coverage of administrative topics in introductory practice courses. Social administration topics are often not covered at all in undergraduate programs. Despite this rather limited coverage, all the recent approaches to the definition of social work emphasize the pervasive role of social administration in social work practice. For example, the 1992 Curriculum Policy Statement issued by the Council on Social Work Education identified the following four purposes of professional social work:

1. The promotion, restoration, maintenance, or enhancement of the functioning of individuals, families, groups, *organizations and communities* by helping them to accomplish life tasks, prevent and alleviate distress, and utilize resources
2. The planning, development, and implementation of social policies, services, resources, and programs needed to meet basic human needs and support the development of human capacities and abilities
3. The pursuit of such policies, services, resources, and programs through organizational or administrative advocacy and social or political action, including the empowerment of groups at risk
4. The development and testing of professional knowledge and skills related to these purposes. [emphasis added] (Commission on Accreditation, 1994)

The first purpose could be seen as a predominantly direct practice objective, although enhancing the functioning of organizations and commu-

nities certainly falls at least partially within the domain of social administration as we deal with it here.[8] The fourth purpose relates most closely to
research and scholarly activity and thus to all other practice specialties
equally. The remaining two objectives are both purposive statements in
which the predominant accent is social administration.

Examination of the NASW's definition of social work as a profession with
three basic objectives will support much the same conclusion. The portion
of the statement identifying the importance of meeting basic human needs
is arguably a clinical practice statement. However, the remaining two basic
purposes of social work (promoting effective/humane operations and linking people with resources) have clear social administrative dimensions.
Thus, despite the minor role sometimes assigned to social administration
in the curriculum, the distinctive concerns and interests of social administration loom large in contemporary definitions of social work by practicing
professionals and by educators.

The importance of social administration in social work can also be
gauged by examining the practice experience of past and present professional leaders in the field. Although those with job titles as administrators
are always a minority of all the social workers involved in organized helping
efforts, a close examination of social work leadership reveals a very different
picture. Virtually the entire leadership of American social services throughout the twentieth century has come from the ranks of social administrators.
And in both past and present, much of that social work leadership has been
engaged directly and primarily in the practice of social administration. One
of the icons of the field, Jane Addams, was not only the founder of Hull
House settlement and a leader in the settlement house movement in the
United States for more than forty years but also the treasurer (for ten years),
and she served as president of the Hull House Association and head resident
(roughly the equivalent of executive director today) of Hull House throughout her entire career.[9] Addams was preeminently a manager, leader, decision maker, and institution builder.

Less known, perhaps, but equally telling is the important social administration role of one of the icons of clinical practice, Mary Richmond. Usually accorded a role as the founding mother of social casework, Richmond
never actually worked as a caseworker or direct practitioner of any other
kind. She simply could not have developed her perspective in social casework from personal experience alone. Richmond was, like so many others
in the social work leadership pantheon, primarily a social administrator.
She began her career with the Baltimore Charity Organization Society
(COS), not as a friendly visitor but as assistant treasurer. She later became
director of the COS in Baltimore, then directed the Philadelphia COS, and

moved to the Russell Sage Foundation as director of the Charity Organization Department, where she remained for the rest of her career.

That Addams and Richmond were deeply involved in defining aspects of social work practice goes without saying. Much the same can be said for Robert Hartley, Homer Folks, Edith and Grace Abbot, Harry Hopkins, Paul Kellogg, Florence Kelley, Wilbur Cohen, and countless others typically included among the social work leadership pantheon. Indeed, in recent decades, academics (faculty members in schools of social work) and social administrators are the two most consistently visible groups among the national leadership of professional social work; much the same is true in many states. Social administrators may not be a representative cross-section of the profession as a whole, but they have always been heavily represented among the leaders of the profession—so much so that it is reasonable to define leadership as one of the components of social administration practice.

In keeping with these historical realities, we wish to suggest that social administration is, in fact, the most inclusive form of social work practice. It is a mode of practice that by its very nature encompasses, incorporates, and embraces the highest aspirations of the profession and the concerns of all other aspects of practice of social work within its view. This is the primary reason why social work has been correct in its long-term assertion that the administration of social agencies should be in the hands of social work professionals. Such a view is not a simple expression of professional hegemony.

Far from being an occult specialty practiced indirectly in remote, obscure corners of the profession, social administration is concerned with creating the very conditions of social service that make professional and paraprofessional service delivery possible. It is the task of social administration to mobilize the people and other resources necessary to carry on that activity and to create and sustain assorted critical processes of judgment, deliberation, and evaluation to keep that activity viable in a world of many other possible interests and concerns.

Given the importance of social administration to the field of social service and to the profession of social work, it is genuinely surprising how many introductory social work texts and survey-introductions to the profession devote so little or no attention to its unique tasks. It is even more surprising how many social work management texts also begin with humble acceptance and elaborate acknowledgments for the rather tenuous and peripheral place of social administration at the indirect outer fringes of the social work curriculum.

As a teaching device this is understandable, even if it is not an accurate statement of practice reality. Professional training is in large part preparation for entry-level practice, and social administration is not an entry-level concern. Although a great many MSWs may eventually make their way into administrative practice, most begin at the bottom. Indeed, this pattern of promotion up through the ranks is one of the most enduring characteristics of social agencies during the past seventy-five years.

Beginning practitioners should expect to only gradually become fully engaged with the particular issues and concerns of social administration that are the principal concerns of agency executives and the most senior, experienced staff members. However, there is currently no level of professional education available to those moving up in this manner at the time and place when they may need it most. This entry-level emphasis of social work education can easily create a distorted picture of real professional practice. In general, the concerns of social administration assume a far larger portion of professional energy and attention than the current entry-level concerns that the social work curriculum recognizes.

One of the perspectives in social work education that contributes to perpetuating this false picture of the role of social administration in the social agency is the conception of administration as a narrowly specialized enabling method or form of indirect practice.[10] The notion of administration as indirect practice has proved to be an extremely unfortunate and counterproductive one, carrying as it does possible implications of being circuitous, devious, roundabout, and perhaps even manipulative, dishonest, and misleading.[11] In more extreme forms, such claims may even go so far as to contrast social administration with real social work! Clearly, there is an important difference between working face-to-face with clients and working on budgets to enable such face-to-face encounters to occur. The difficulty is that there is no genuinely suitable term currently in widespread usage to express this difference. We believe that social administration as we have developed it offers such a substitute. But keep in mind that social administration is no less a form of practice than case work or group work. Like them, it is social work.

The whole notion of indirect practice confronts the reality of practice in the social agency exactly backward. Despite some movement toward independent private practice, social work practice is still predominantly agency practice, and agencies (including most schools of social work) are organized hierarchically. In such hierarchical contexts, there is no coherent reason to define the essential professional core of social work as uniquely centered only in the lowest level professional positions to the subordination or even partial exclusion of those at the upper levels. It is also contrary to any vision of a close relationship among social work, social agencies, and social services to suggest that those most responsible for the mission of social agencies are somehow indirectly or tangentially related to the mission of the profession. Social administration is not a supportive activity to enable social work. It is the principal professional concern and activity of a substantial portion of the most senior members of the professional social work community and the pivotal force in agency-based practice.

To emphasize the centrality of social administration takes nothing away from the equally skilled and in many cases equally senior clinical professionals engaged in defining, modeling, and carrying out client service delivery. Nor does it necessarily represent a dismissal of the idea of indirect practice per se. Social planning, social work research, and social work education may be three genuine forms of indirect practice. To suggest that social administration is a similar activity, however, is in error. In matters of administrative justice, for example, social administrators must be as concerned with specific, individual clients as any caseworker. To suggest, however, that because social administrators must sometimes be concerned with large aggregates of clients they are not directly concerned with clients stretches the limits of both credulity and the language.

Much the same conclusion is suggested by the ordinary pattern of career progression in social work. In social work, as in most occupations, career progression is a matter of promotion from entry-level positions to positions of increasing responsibility and authority. To our knowledge in the entire history of the field, no one has ever been rewarded for successful social administration by promotion to an entry-level clinical position. In contrast, the research literature clearly documents that substantial numbers of clinicians move into administrative positions as promotions. It seems equally plausible that at least some social administrators move back into senior clinical positions at some point, but this matter has received little or no attention. The main point here is that social workers fought long and hard to attain a measure of professional standing. The notion that those victories would purposely be compromised by taking some of the most senior and experienced people out of the lines of authority and responsibility and directing them into indirect administrative and leadership positions is not reasonable.

In short, there is nothing at all indirect about social administration. Executives supervise and direct the work of supervisors who supervise and direct the work of workers who work face-to-face with clients. Each has different roles and responsibilities, but nowhere in that chain of authority and responsibility is it possible to identify a cusp or cut point where direct delegations of mission, authority, or responsibility become in any meaningful sense indirect. Indeed, to draw such a line would cut both ways. If upper-level administrators are only indirectly engaged in service delivery, then lower-level workers must also only indirectly be carrying out the mission of the agency and the purposes of the profession. Both views are nonsensical, and any indirect service conception of social administration deserves to be abandoned entirely.

Social Administration as Management

Management is the term that applies to the first essential element of social administration practice that addresses the internal governance of an organization. Social administration strives to guide and enhance the operation of social services in part through use of the broad perspectives of general management and by selecting from the range of tools from the emergent disciplines that call themselves *management sciences.* Classic management science applied to social service embraces a number of interesting updates and approaches, explored more thoroughly in chapters 6 and 7.

Any consideration of management in the context of social work poses an interesting dilemma. Traditional approaches to administration in social work prior to 1970, such as those of Arthur Dunham (1947), Harleigh Trecker (1971), Sue Spencer (1970), John Kidneigh (1950), and Nathan Cohen (1957), constructed the topic of social work administration as an integral component of general social work while bootlegging in a rather motley assortment of management concepts. Unfortunately, adherents of this position were too few, and their writings reached too limited an audience within the profession to prove fully persuasive. This approach was downplayed and eventually abandoned by many because of the seeming inability to incorporate many of the technical advances of the contemporary management sciences into a rapidly changing body of knowledge. The 1970s were a decade of tremendous technical advances in social administration knowledge, and the label "human services management" became a banner held high by the advocates of those advances.

Beginning in the 1970s, and largely coinciding with the initial publication of the journal *Administration in Social Work,* a new management perspective in social administration began to evolve with greater ties to the main interdisciplinary body of management theory. At first largely centered on a concern for applications of organization theory to social work, more recently this has evolved into a full-bodied management perspective (Edwards, Yankey, & Altpeter, 1998; Ginsberg, 1995; Ginsberg & Keys, 1995; Sarri, 1971).

Social Administration as Leadership

The second important dimension in social administration is the phenomenon of leadership (Perlmutter & Slavin, 1984–85). In some management science conceptions, administration *is* leadership. William H. Newman (1951) defined administration as "the guidance, leadership, and control of the efforts of a group of individuals toward some common goal." In dealing with leadership, we are concerned with the full scope of the topic: board leadership as well as policy leadership; community leadership as well as professional leadership; unit and departmental leadership by supervisors as well as executive leadership.

Leadership in the field of social services is inherently wrapped up in the activities and particular skills associated with social administration. This is true not only in professional circles but also in policy, identification of needs, innovation and creation of new services, and a thousand other venues. When the governor asks for a representative from social services for a task force on welfare reform, chances are that person will be a social administrator. When the press interviews for the "social service perspective" on a health care reform proposal, chances are they will interview an administrator. The Accreditation Commission and the Council on Social Work Education's Board of Directors, which set the standards that this book was written to reflect, are composed predominantly of administrators. There are countless other examples showing that the people who decide critical questions about social work constitute the visible public leadership profile of the profession, and those most frequently held up as exemplars of the best in professional practice are disproportionately administrators.

Leadership in social work has always had a very strong social administrative connection. A majority of the officers and committee chairs of the Council on Social Work administration at any given time are likely to be administrators. They are deans and directors, undergraduate program directors, directors of field instruction, and the like. The same was true for early psychiatry. It was eighteenth and nineteenth century state hospital superintendents—not psychotherapists or pharmacologists—who formed the core of the psychiatric profession long before the term *mental health administrator* came into use.

Social administrators continue to make up a disproportionately large share of the day-to-day leadership of the social work profession, social agencies, and programs even as they continue to be an integral part of the profession. For example, in 1965, an anniversary symposium was held to celebrate the founding of NASW ten years earlier. Fifteen of the sixteen members of the planning committee for that event were either administrators or faculty members, as were forty-one of the forty-nine presenters at the conference (Alexander, 1965). This pattern of leadership has been repeated over and over again throughout the entire history of the profession.

Social Administration as Decision Making

Beginning with the pioneering work of Herbert Simon (1947/1997) in the 1940s, the importance of decision making to administrative practice began to be recognized. More recently, with advances in the strategic paradigm, such as strategic management and strategic planning, understanding of the central importance of critical decisions has also reached a new high in business management. Decision-making theory is important to social administration in part because of its integrative capacity. It brings together attention to the interplay of rational (economic), political (interactional), and socioemotional factors that affect decisions and their outcomes.

The decision-making perspective is also important in social administration because it offers two additional ways to link social administration into the main body of social work theory and practice. Administrative decision making and generalist social work share an underlying perspective in problem solving. The more important, indeed overriding, reason is because of the manner in which a concern for the most important, key, or critical decisions in social services offers the strongest point at which to tie the social work profession and social administration together. It simply makes no sense whatsoever to develop a professional infrastructure in which the key decisions are by design left to outsiders.

In the 1940s, political scientist and later cognitive scientist Herbert Simon (1947/1997) focused attention on the importance of decisions. Since then, decision-making theory has gone in two highly divergent directions that are extremely difficult to apply directly to general perspectives on social administration but that are nonetheless important to keep in mind. One of these is rational choice theory, in which decisions are approached largely within the rubrics of microeconomics and analytical philosophy. This approach, referred to variously as *rationalism* and the *synoptic approach*, has as its essential feature a largely futile quest for certainty often referred to in terms of replacing decisions based on politics with scientific, rational, or objective decisions. The rational choice approach to decisions often moves in very mathematical directions and is the basis for most economic approaches to administration.

The second direction is a less technical and more interactional concern for the strategic importance of key decisions found woven throughout the writings of journalists, political commentators, political scientists, historians, sociologists, and others. In general, much of this work is informed by recognition of the importance of uncertainty as a condition of all administrative decision making and the tradeoffs between evidence and opinion that must be part of every real-life decision.

One of the key terms that occurs repeatedly throughout this book arises from the incremental decision-making perspective originated by Simon, Charles Lindblom (1957, 1979), and others. This is the idea of strategy. The term *strategy* usually refers to an active orientation toward the environment of an organization or community and also to a deliberateness and reflectiveness that transcends simpler, ad hoc problem-solving responses to issues and problems arising in the environment.

Social Administration as Institution Building

A full understanding of our topic requires that we consider also the role of social administration in building and promoting social welfare institutions. After several decades of primary preoccupation with behavioral concerns and considerations, organization researchers have begun to return to a concern with the institutional level of organizations (Scott, 1995). This is fortunate. One of the misadventures of the influence of studies of organizational behavior on social administration was the mistaken advancement of an ultraconservative image of the manager as institutional conserver. This view, put forth as the "maintenance perspective," suggested that the manager was the self-interested protector of organizational turf, interested primarily either in building empires or in creating a safe and comfortable work environment that avoided risk taking at all costs. Although studies have often found that such people do exist in social service and other organizations, such behavior is hardly deserving of the label professional or worthy of emulating under any label.

In our experience, the actual practice of social administration is equally well populated with risk takers on a mission. These persons are institution builders and less interested in building personal fiefs than in establishing, building, maintaining, and expanding viable programs and services that make real differences in clients' lives. The notion that social administrators generally seek only to serve their own career and economic interests is a false and misleading one that deserves the scorn of professionals everywhere.

When people have in mind considerations such as "serving the community" and "advancing the social work profession," it is generally institution building and not the simple pursuit of individual and organizational self-interest that is uppermost in their minds. Some of the studies of organizations notwithstanding, no very strong normative case can be made for the view that professions *should* exist merely as organized fronts for the pursuit of empire building and personal aggrandizement by their members. Any profession that seeks advancement purely on such grounds is likely in the long run to succumb to its own cynicism. However, any profession that does not pay careful and continuous attention to building and maintaining the institutions within which it may flourish is giving up an important measure of self-control and self-direction. For a profession such as social work, which is barely a century old, to ignore issues of institutionalization is virtually to ensure that its existence may be a short one.

CONCLUSION

Social administration as it is articulated in this book may well be the highest form of social work practice. It is a form of practice in which one not only does professional social work but enables others to do social work at the same time. Effective social administration requires highly advanced and sophisticated practice skills. It incorporates the broadest possible range of practice skills and knowledge. This positioning of social administration embraces and sheds light upon the most complete history of the social work profession and not merely upon the enthusiasms of most recent decades. In addition, it matches the existing reward structure within the profession, within human service organizations, and in society.

The best approach to social administration is to see it as the epitome of advanced practice in social work and not as a peripheral afterthought or indirect practice. However, with this position also go major obligations. Because of its importance to the profession and to social services, social administration must remain thoroughly integrated into the values and ethics of the profession. Insistence on a handmaiden role for administration and the continued loss of social administration positions to those without social work training are merely two sides of the same coin. What is needed in the longer view is an approach to administration that is both process oriented and deeply grounded in the ethics and values of the profession. The epitome of the organizational and community leadership exercised by social administrators is the type of behavior that Manning (1997) termed *moral citizenship:* "The responsibility to determine right and good behavior as part of the rights and privileges social workers have as members of a community that includes clients, colleagues, agencies and society" (p. 24). Throughout the book, we explore aspects of such a perspective.

We live in an administered world, and administration/management is one of the fundamental determining factors in the world today. Nowhere is this any more true than in the nature and direction of the social services. In addition, the core of what we might call the administrative paradigm is relatively simple and straightforward, built around a few basic concepts of decision making, leadership, and organization. Following through on the full practice implications of these seemingly simple ideas, however, can be the professional journey of a lifetime.

And so, let the journey begin.

The Ecology of Social Administration

This book introduces the study and practice of social administration, which we believe deserves to be recognized as one of the distinctive major subdisciplines of the social work profession, along with social casework and groupwork (the so-called direct practices), social work research, and community practice. The three chapters in this introductory unit lay the groundwork for an understanding of the important role of administration for social work practice in social agencies. Social administration as presented here is not simply management, as conventionally conceived. It also encompasses leadership, critical decision making, and institution building in communities and social agencies.

Throughout this book, we discuss this broad conception of social administration and set it squarely within the context of the profession of social work and the social services. The broad approach taken in this book is in marked contrast to most introductory social work methods texts. These typically locate the core of social work practice in the "direct" practice methods and treat social administration as an "indirect" or supportive method, of interest primarily for its role in enabling the practice of real social work or direct practice.[1] Our conception is that social administration is social work equally as much as the other forms or modes of practice.

In making this distinction, we wish to call attention to a genuine division within the practice of social work that is currently not well reflected in the professional literature. We believe it is a more accurate reflection of the realities of contemporary agency-based practice to cast social administration and social administrators in a unique historic and contemporary role of leadership and institution building both in the profession and in social services, including advocacy and legislative policy change. Administrative leaders are involved in most of the major decisions affecting the role, scope, and direction of both the social work profession and the social services. Moreover, social administrators are also the primary agents who have taken upon themselves responsibility for building strong, stable, and effective social service programs. Social work students need to understand that delivery of services to clients is not an act done in isolation. Management, leadership, decision-making, and institution-building tasks of social administration are integral components of modern social service delivery. Without them, professional direct services simply would not happen.

In chapters 2, 3, and 4, we explore specific aspects of the social environment of social service practice as they are experienced in social administration practice. Community, organization, and social agency are just three of the many important social environments that affect social administration. They are, however, among the most important. In chapter 2, we examine selected comments from the vast literature on communities to explore the critically important place of community in contemporary social services and the role of social work administration in the community. As we approach the topic, community is important because it is the primary locus of stakeholders who care about and influence the social agency. In an age of social policy devolution, community has again become the primary locus within which the personal troubles of clients are defined as social problems and attract the attention of service agencies.

In chapter 3, we focus on the concept of the social agency and examine the range of public, commercial, and nonprofit social agencies. We also explore questions of incorporation, tax exemption, and other related issues. In doing so, we seek to restore to a place of prominence in social work practice the earlier perspectives on the centrality of the social agency as the central institution for organizing the delivery of social services in the community.

In chapter 4, we build upon this agency perspective and focus selectively on a number of perspectives from the equally vast literature on organizations to explore the administrative niche within organizational ecosystems. Perspectives presented throughout the rest of the book are based in the basic frameworks laid out in this section.

CHAPTER 2

Social Administration
and Community

The key premise of chapter 1 was that social administration is the epitome of professional social work in the social agency and that the social administration skills of management, leadership, decision making, and institution building are essential to the success of the profession and social services in this new millennium. In this chapter, we hope to redeem one part of that claim by addressing certain connections among three aspects of contemporary social work: social administration, community organization, and clinical social work practice. Indeed, we would like the reader to understand the importance of attention to the ongoing problem of the legitimacy of social service activity. Closely associated with the idea of community, legitimacy is not some vague, abstract theoretical quality but the ever-present possibility of raising social work activity from simply the proper execution of defined methods or technical prowess to the high art of professional practice.

In this chapter, we examine the importance of various community impacts on social administration. This chapter serves three important purposes:

1. To introduce the concept of community as the matrix of stakeholder relations
2. To identify the practice of social administration as responsive to the specific social environment of community
3. To highlight the importance of the local community context for the practice of social administration in an era when other contexts such as the nation–state may be receding in importance and when the antiscience and antiprofessional arguments of postmodernism are openly challenging the foundations of professional activity as science based

Typically, social service delivery occurs in a social agency within a preexisting community defined functionally as all those who are concerned or interested in what happens. Later, in discussions of constituency building and marketing, we examine the special case of those that, in the view of social administrators and other social workers, should care but do not appear to at present. A great many people not only are interested, but also are willing to act on their interests by renting and selling, appealing and suggesting, demanding and donating, volunteering, working, and so on. When they are willing to act, whether for or against the service, their interest takes on additional meaning. In this case, we can say that they have a stake in what happens, and the term *stakeholder* is widely used to refer to any members of the community with a particular interest in what happens with an agency or program (Barry, 1992).

We can define community more formally as a stratified resident population living together in a locality with at least household and family institutions, economic markets, some level of government or policy, and a civil society of additional social institutions such as churches, schools, membership associations, and the like.[1] The term *community* embraces many different types: place communities, communities of interest, and dialogical or speech communities where people "speak the same language" in various ways.

A COMPLEX CONCEPT

Note that in the context of social administration, community is always approached from the particular vantage point of a specific agency, program, or service with its own unique information, interests, assumptions, and biases. There is simply no reason for administrators to approach it any other way. One should never presume to take the role of the community or approach issues from the point of view of the community as a whole since it is clearly not possible to do so. As a result, administrative understanding of any community is always partial and incomplete. One cannot expect to develop a total or complete understanding of any community.

Communities are among the most complex and constantly changing phenomena in the social world. It is difficult enough to gain a full understanding of half a dozen people in direct, face-to-face interaction within a single room. In attempting to understand communities, one is frequently dealing with hundreds, perhaps thousands, of discrete individual persons, organizations, and institutions. They may or may not know each other personally. Because communities are often aggregates of large numbers of people, it is sometimes useful to think of them also as distributions of particular, selected attributes, such as the statistical distributions of the normal curve and scattergram. It is physically impossible to know of all possible interactions among them. The inherent complexity of community is further complicated by the frequent treatment of vast urban complexes and even entire regions with millions of residents as communities.

One can never measure or know everything about a community. And, when it is said that "the community is very supportive of this program" one must always think very closely about what that means. It may mean, for example, that everyone in the community is highly enthusiastic about the program, although in fact such universal enthusiasm is relatively rare. The greater likelihood in most instances is that there are those in the community who are indifferent or even opposed. More likely, it might mean that there are more people who support the program than oppose it or that the supporters are more active, vocal, or organized. It may also mean that when a few key community leaders speak up in behalf of the program there is no voiced opposition. One of the challenges in the latter case is determining whether such silence represents simple indifference or quiet resentment.

Community has always been important as a primary environment of social service activity. Local community is also taking on entirely new or perhaps revitalizing traditional meanings in the context of the new federalism and policy devolution to the state and local levels. After several decades of pursuing the distinctive vision of national community associated with the welfare state, social administrators find themselves once again facing the reality expressed by the Speaker of the House Tip O'Neill's reminder that "all politics is local." Thus, after several decades of relative neglect, community practice and community organization are once again terms that are uttered with some confidence and that arouse considerable interest in social work practice.

What is the role of community in social work administration in this new postwelfare state? There are both very narrow and very broad answers to this question. One narrow answer is, as already suggested, that the local community forms the environment of the administered social service organization. The broader answer is that real community is never located or found in some objective sense. It is made in the day-to-day social reality of people's lives, and the skills and methods of community practice, including social administration, are important in the making.

Communities in the sense of networks of caring relationships and the concern of dependencies are built up bit by bit over entire lifetimes. This kind of community development is one of the consistent never-ending challenges of social administration as institution building. A major part of the challenge of community represents the ongoing effort necessary to ensure that community institutions exist not merely in principal or in the abstract but as concrete realities in people's daily lives. Such institution building is essential to care for the homeless, mentally ill, elderly, abused and neglected children, and other dependent populations who may have fallen out of traditional family or neighborhood care fields. In order for such institution building to be successful, it is necessary for social administrators to assume roles as community leaders (Skidmore, 1995).

COMMUNITY ORGANIZATION

The term *community organization* has at least three distinct meanings in social work practice. In the first sense, community organization is a method of social work practice that some of its most vocal adherents see as the cutting edge of social change. Many take their cues from work by Saul Alinsky (1946) and Franz Fanon (1963) (neither of whom had any visible connection to professional social work) and work by Cloward and Piven (1974, 1975; Piven & Cloward, 1971, 1979, 1982, 1988, 1993), Bertha Reynolds, and others.They may also adopt a fundamentally oppositional stance toward established institutions, which sometimes include social administration and organized social services.

A second, older, quieter, and less rambunctious meaning of community organization practice in social work is much more important for social administration. It is one equally committed to fundamental social change and to working with disempowered populations and increasing social justice. This is an approach generally more committed to attaining limited results of social improvement in the short turn. Community organizing in this sense is more generally directed at proximate targets like landlords and rents and at proximate objectives like increasing school attendance.[2]

As a practice method, George Brager and Harry Specht (1973) said, "Community organization is a method of intervention whereby individuals, groups, and organizations engage in planned action to influence social problems" (p. 27). In this sense, Jack Rothman (1977, 1996) identified three distinct types or modalities of community organization practice: locality development, social action, and social planning. Within this definition, social administration should be seen as closely related to this form of community practice. Many notions of locality and community development are consistent with the type of institution building advanced in this work, and the methods of social action and social planning are, in principle, as readily employable in the social agency context as in any other.

During the 1970s, interest in community organization methods in social work declined dramatically while interest within other fields, such as environmental issues and politically conservative causes, increased just as dramatically. A small band of devotees kept the flame alive, and there is currently a resurgence of interest in community methods in social work education and practice.[3] Community organization in this second sense is of primary interest to social administration as one of the increasingly broad range of community and clinical practice methods that social workers can bring to bear on community problems through social agency practice.

A third sense that emerged earlier, fell into relative neglect, but is still fundamentally important for an adequate understanding of social administration is community organization in the sense of the organization of communities. It is a descriptive label for the organization of the local community social services network or the organization of the community field. On a day-to-day basis, social workers tend to view communities less as the complex social organisms portrayed by sociologists than as clusters of locality-based networks or fields of sentiments, interests, power arrangements, or interagency structures (Martinez-Brawley, 1990). A fundamentally important dimension of this view was the adoption, during the 1940s, of some of the abstract concepts of field theory developed by Kurt Lewin (Lewin & University of Michigan, 1975) and their later application in community and social work practice.

According to Scott (1994), "The notion of field connotes the existence of a community of organizations that partake of a common meaning system and whose participants interact more frequently and fatefully with one another than with actors outside the field" (pp. 207–208). This is the exact sense in which social worker curricula usually use the phrase *fields of practice,* for example. This is also the sense that social work curricula ordinarily intend by referring to internships and practicum experiences as field placements.

Placing students *in the field* ordinarily refers to arranging work experiences within the community of organizations that share the common meaning systems we call social work and social services. Much of the primary educational value of such placements is expected to grow out of the frequent and fateful interactions expected to occur as a result. Those interactions are referred to by terms such as practice experience, supervision, gate-keeping, modeling, mentoring, and the like. Likewise, most references in social work to service delivery systems also typically have similar implicit field and community parameters to them. For example, in social services it might make sense to include fast food restaurants, dry cleaners, and used car lots as part of the field of social services. However, this would only make sense if it could be shown that there were shared meanings, frequent and fateful interactions, or other similar and apparent connections that brought these forms of human service into the field of social service.

A social service field is likely to be shared by the employees of a group of agencies who share a common sense of a social service enterprise and its need by a community. The same field might be shared with all of the clients, volunteers, board members, actual and potential donors, supporters, local powerbrokers, and others who share some part of that common sense of meaning and purpose. Later, we define the full set of those who share the common meanings and expectations that collectively define the field of a particular social agency as stakeholders; how inclusive this total group of stakeholders may be is one of the measures of the success of social administration institution building.

Community as a field has three principal dimensions that are of greatest interest to the practice of social administration:

1. Specific, identifiable client populations living in geographic proximity (most important, reasonable travel distance and times) to an agency and potentially interested in receiving services from the agency
2. Specific, identifiable patron populations also living in geographic proximity to the same agency and potentially interested in providing time, support, or other resources to enable the agency to provide services to selected client groups within its identified client populations
3. Specific, identifiable networks of agents or intermediary groups and organizations also working with those client and patron populations

After World War II, social administration theorists formulated an increasingly sophisticated field theory of community, first by themselves and later with the assistance of community sociology.[4] Sue Spencer (1970), for example, formulated a kind of early ecological perspective on social administration through her view that the locus of the social agency is community and that administrative process should be concerned with community-level needs, resources, and services. More recent published approaches to management have to some extent ignored or obscured this perspective even as policy devolution, the shrinkage and collapse of social planning activities by both public and voluntary agencies, and other developments have brought it into increasingly sharp focus.

Though Spencer linked social work into the community through the social agency, others tied social agency programs directly to community needs and resources. Arthur Dunham (1958) wrote, "Community organization for social welfare (or community welfare organization) is the process of bringing about and maintaining adjustment between social welfare needs and social welfare resources in a geographical area or a special field of service" (p. 23). Dunham also said, "The term is not entirely satisfactory."

One important issue that advocates of community organization in this third sense have never adequately resolved is the normative challenge this view poses. What are good communities, and what community features are most worth preserving and protecting? Community organization approaches in social work have generally been content to answer such questions strictly in terms of reducing individual needs. The concept of aggregating individual needs into community needs through surveys and related research methodologies referred to grandly but ambiguously as *needs assessments* has been a standard community planning method. Recently, wellness, asset-based, and strengths approaches have challenged the traditional need and problem models without fully encountering the thorny normative issues involved. Where the moral basis for promoting the wellness or encouraging the strengths of a community resides is no more clear than how to assess or define community needs.

In her ecological theory of social work, Carel Germain (1991) offered a somewhat novel approach to this matter. She uses the concept of the competent community defined as one that "manifests a collective capacity for dealing with the wide-ranging needs and problems in communal life" (p. 42). Germain relied upon the definition of community competence set forth by Leonard Cottrell (1976). Cottrell spoke of the ability to "collaborate effectively in identifying the problems and needs of the community; achieve a working consensus on goals and priorities; agree on ways and means to implement the agreed-upon goals; and collaborate effectively in the required actions" (p. 197). It seems largely unproblematic and rather useful to extend Cottrell's collective abilities from problems and needs to strengths, assets, and well-being. However, to our knowledge, methodologies of competence assessment that go beyond the rather limited opinion survey approaches or epidemiological studies of conventional needs assessment have yet to be promulgated.

Germain's competent community displays a continuity with the earlier era represented by Spencer and Dunham in which there was assumed to be a uniform social work interest consistent with the general interests of the community. In this view, there was thought to be a single, unified view of the common good or community interest. It was the principal task of community practice to identify and work toward that end. However, Germain's notion of the competent community, though descriptively useful, does not fully resolve the issue of where and how such competent communities distinguish between multiple or pluralistic community goods. It does not resolve how such decisions are made, how action is staged and carried out authoritatively, or, most important, how the distinctly political aspects of deciding are handled, especially when there are strong disagreements. The conventional social work formula of meeting community needs to the best of one's ability with available resources does little to solve the matter theoretically or conceptually. However, a division of professional labor in the social agency in which one cadre of social workers (namely, social administrators) assumes the burden of responsibility for assessing and mobilizing community competence, organizing effective community decision making, and exercising power, authority, and influence to resolve disagreements goes a long way toward resolving these issues in practice.

Recently, the human services management literature has tended to downplay these issues, largely concentrating instead on the manager as a tactician. The literature of social work has placed greater emphasis on the diversity and conflict among the multiplicity of interests. The picture that has emerged has been less that of the competent community than of the community as a battleground of competent agencies, each in pursuit of its own interests. Fisher and Karger (1997) identify six major divergences that impinge upon contemporary community practice:

> The dissonant strands in the community organization literature in social work revolve around tensions such as: (1) the importance of representing social agencies as opposed to empowering communities and constituents, (2) the collaborative versus conflict model of community organization, (3) the emphasis on administration versus grassroots community organization, (4) the procurement of resources versus systematic resource distribution, (5) the social worker as expert versus the social worker as grassroots community organizer, and (6) the social worker as social planner as opposed to grassroots community organizer. (p. 122)

The responsibility for creating more competent communities will involve what Arthur Dunham (1970) called "the process of bringing about and maintaining adjustment between social welfare needs and social welfare resources in a geographical area or a special field of service" (p. 23). It is far from clear that single-minded pursuit of agency self-interest will ever accomplish that end, but at the moment there are no clear institutional alternatives either in the social work literature or in day-to-day practice. One thing is abundantly clear. Whether we approach the community issue as a matter of representing agency interests or of empowering communities, whether we approach it as an organizational or a grass-roots issue, or whether we approach it from any of the divergent views Fisher and Karger point to, social administration will continue to have a major role in community practice and locality development efforts to create more competent communities.

SOCIOLOGY OF COMMUNITY

The essential point for social administration of the earlier social work view of the organization of communities was to view communities as networks of services operating within programmatically unified fields of service. This grew out of the original organizational challenge of community organization first posed by the aptly named charity organization society movement of the late nineteenth century. Those in the movement sought a more rational, efficient, and effective "scientific" basis for organizing those community networks of charities. Such organization was to be rational in its linkage of means to ends, efficient in its use of resources, and effective in achieving results. These scientific charity organization objectives were taken over by the emerging social work profession and others, with impressive long-term results.

Some of the early achievements of this concern for the organization of community fields were quite dramatic and long lasting. Community-wide charity organizations, social surveys or needs assessment studies, federated financing plans, community foundations, community service roundtables and forums, community service planning agencies, and social service exchanges are some of the major community institutions that arose from this applied spirit of community. Local federated financing organizations for fund raising to support multiple agencies were first called community chests. Later they became United Ways and have more recently proliferated into many different plans. Community foundations allow pooling of multiple small, independent donations, trusts, and bequests into larger, more effective donative bodies. Community service roundtables and forums, which bring social service providers together to discuss issues of mutual concern, operate under a staggering variety of different names, such as coalitions, networks, etc. In recent decades what were once called social service exchanges have tended to be known as information and referral programs producing community service directories and one-stop information sources on available community services. Most of this was done by social administrators on a purely pragmatic basis, with minimal dependence on community theory.

The gradual introduction of the ecological perspectives of community sociology extended and broadened common understanding of the task of community organization considerably.[5] The contemporary community literature in social work and in sociology is vast. Our principal concern in this discussion is with a few selected aspects of modern community theory that impact most directly on social administration practice.

By the late 1960s, there was an evident shift toward theory that took community organization practice increasingly out of the realm of day-to-day social service delivery in social agencies and into the more abstract realms of social criticism and social reconstruction. This shift appears to be related to several things. Roland Warren's *The Community in America* (1963) made the vast and diffuse sociological literature on community readily available for the first time to an entire generation of social work students.[6] Likewise, the publication at about the same time of the works by Alinsky (1946) and Fanon (1963) outlined a new (for social work) vision of community methods of radical social change. Since that time, however, sociological community theory has been of limited immediate use to community organization in the Spencer–Dunham sense. It is of use primarily as a basis for organizing inventories of community resources and typologies of community institutions.

Horizontal and Vertical Integration

This transition in the social work literature from the concrete, day-to-day experiences of community services to more abstract concern for community structure and process has unfolded since the early 1960s. In the process, community institutions of social service, coordination, and exchange were transformed from local objects important in themselves to symbols, markers, or indicators of abstract ideas and theoretical categories like community integration. Roland Warren (1963, 1966, 1967) was at the theoretical vortex of the transition in community perspectives in social work during the 1960s. A sociologist at the Florence Heller Graduate School for Advanced Studies in Social Welfare at Brandeis University, Warren sought not simply to apply sociological community theory to social work but to make community theory a tool for social change.

In one influential construction, Warren identified the horizontal and vertical integration of community. By horizontal, Warren (1956) referred to those factors that emphasized locality, whereas vertical referred to specialized interests, especially those shared across community boundaries. This distinction has become very important for situating organizations in communities and also for linking to the concept of national or functional communities. Horizontally, we are concerned with the issue of how various community institutions like business and labor or social services and religion interact and relate. Vertically, we may be concerned both with how institutions in a particular community relate to similar institutions in other communities and with how local affiliates relate to state, regional, and national organizations, for example, how a local Red Cross or United Way relates to the national Red Cross or the United Way of America.

The Devolution Revolution

Looking back beyond the sociology of community to earlier social work perspectives on community arises from the devolution of services in recent years from the national level to the local community level. The funding and reporting arrangements of what we refer to as the "Age of Grants" tended to emphasize the vertical integration of specific agencies into national networks and funding streams. By contrast, decentralization of services and block grants tend to place much greater emphasis on the horizontal linkages of community.

Warren's distinction has recently taken on powerful and unexpected implications in explaining changes in the health care delivery system. Brown and Kornmayer (1996) characterize the effects of managed care and the expansion of investor-owned hospital and nursing home firms as major factors driving the industry toward consolidation into vertically integrated, regional systems of health services that have transformed the industry from a charitable, community (that is, horizontal) orientation to a business orientation, concerned with market shares and profits. Health care, in other words, is losing its traditional horizontal community focus.

Community theory perspectives in social work seemed to reach something of an impasse after Warren. The older empirical traditions have not returned, but further theoretical development has also largely stagnated. In the 1970s and 1980s, one might suggest that social work in general lost interest in community as such, largely replacing it with interest in individuals on the one hand and formal organizations on the other. Only in the 1990s was there a resurgence of interest in community practice in the social work literature. For many social workers today, community appears to offer a context for practice (see Germain, 1991, chap. 2) as well as an environment within which to integrate the rich perspectives on support systems into the main body of social work theory (see Germain, 1991, chap. 3).

INSTITUTIONALIZATION

Social services are not simply the activities of organizations, nor are they merely the environments in which the activities of individual workers are conducted. They are, in an important sense, community institutions whose existence and continued operation demonstrate, symbolize, and actualize the community as certainly as neighborhood schools, youth baseball and soccer leagues, central business districts, and places of worship. In many cities, the annual United Way campaign is one of the most visible of community institutions. Testaments to the general importance of community institutions in peoples' lives are easy to locate. Rural residents everywhere can recognize the sentiment expressed by an Appalachian woman who observed at the closing of the local elementary school, "Without our school, its not the same. We're not a community anymore." Former residents of urban areas now living in the suburbs often feel similarly about the definitive nature of the corner market, the parish church, the synagogue, and other institutions in the old neighborhood. After an initial period of transition, many alumni feel the same way about their college days. One of the perpetual challenges facing social administration is the prospect of engendering similar strong feelings of identity and attachment to social service institutions on the part of clients and stakeholders.

Part of the difficulty for social services in generating stakeholder loyalty may, in fact, be due to the way in which social services define themselves. In general, many social work community practitioners define themselves and their services as dissident forces within their community. In the so-called residual perspective on social welfare, for example, social services are usually said to be alternatives to or substitutes for more "normal" social institutions like families and communities. As residuals, social services only come into play when the normal community institutions have demonstrably failed. This residual perspective, then, defines social services as a kind of perpetually alienated counter-culture existing within but also outside of communities. Subcultures of the poor and those who work with them have always had elements of this alienated posture. The radical tradition in community organization has sought to transform it into a rallying cry. More recently, community subcultures that have grown up around substance abusers, the homeless, and the deinstitutionalized mentally ill also have similar potential for alienation. Thus, one of the principal challenges for social administration is to create institutions that bring these alienated populations into the community in meaningful ways.

MANY INSTITUTIONS: FOUR SECTORS

An important political dimension to the relative loss of interest in community in social work existed during the 1970s. Following the heady optimism of the 1960s and the radical import of the perspectives of Alinsky, Fanon, and others, social workers across the country appeared to become disenchanted with the assorted community action strategies and moved gradually back to more traditional social service orientations. In doing so, they largely ignored the earlier presociological perspectives on community that were part of the earlier social work view. Even as social work gradually lost interest in community, social administration moved strongly to embrace organization studies and newer models grounded in the new political economy, which shifted attention away from the spiraling list of community institutions as the basis of organization structure. Rather than abstraction continuing to facilitate greater and greater complexity, within this *theory of the middle range* in this new approach even higher levels of abstraction served to further simplification and parsimony (Ilchman & Uphoff, 1968; Lindblom, 1977).

What makes the political economy approach particularly relevant for the practice of social work administration is the way in which it encapsulates and synthesizes an extremely broad range of institutional options and arrangements for organizing and delivering social services into four basic types. David Austin, who has been one of the most articulate advocates of the new political economy approach to social administration, made this point clear. In laying out the case for administrative practice in the social work curriculum, Austin (1983) identified four basic societal frameworks:

> An analysis of political economy concepts relevant to the development of an administrative practice curriculum starts with several general assumptions. . . . The first is that voluntary, philanthropic organizations and governmental organizations constitute two of the four basic societal frameworks for the provision of helping services among human beings. The other two are primary groups such as the family and the marketplace. A second assumption is that the administrative functions in human service organizations involve two major objectives: the provision of effective and efficient services and the maintenance and development of the organization as an essential instrument for service provision. A third assumption is that the key function in administrative practice is decision making, including decisions dealing with the process of service provision, decisions dealing with the internal operations of the organization, and decisions dealing with the relation of the organization to its environment. (p. 343)

Using this approach, the horizontal organization of communities can be characterized not in terms of its surface complexity but of an underlying simplicity and order. Rather than a vast array of discrete, functionally autonomous institutions, community can be seen in terms of relations between four basic sectors or institutional clusters encompassing any number of discrete institutions. The economic or market sector is made up of the institutions of production, consumption, and trade. It is composed of factories, warehouses, retail stores, and other marketplaces. The political or state sector is made up of the multiple executive, legislative, judicial, and administrative branches of government. The nonprofit or third sector consists of nonprofit organizations, voluntary associations, and philanthropy. The household sector is composed of families, friendships, and peer groups and the multiple institutions of our private lives, which are sometimes taken for granted and sometimes explicitly identified.[7]

The purely formal, logical genesis of this schema is easy to reconstruct. One of the stock theoretical dichotomies of liberal social theory during the past two centuries has been to dichotomize communities and societies into public and private realms (Bahrdt, 1966). Another stock dichotomy is to talk of rational action in terms of means and ends. Robert Payton's (1988) definition of philanthropy as "private action for the public good" is essentially a contrast of private means and public ends.

It is possible to use this simple notion to bring together the insights of Warren and like-minded researchers with those of Austin and Payton. Table 2.1 illustrates public and private means and ends. Public means to achieve public ends captures the essence of what is ordinarily meant by governmental or state action, whereas private means in pursuit of public or social or societal ends is what has traditionally been meant by philanthropy, one of the key third sector objectives.[8] By contrast, the household (the locale of home, family, intimacy, etc.) is the domain of private means to private ends. It is the very archetype of privacy. In an economy in which the publicly traded stock corporation is increasingly the dominant actor and retail stores are open to anyone caring to walk in, it is not too overreaching to define market activity in terms of the pursuit of private ends through public action. To those accustomed to the social liberal tradition of the New Deal, the notion of defining business as public rather than private in this way may appear the very opposite of good sense. Yet, there is an underlying publicness to shopping malls and other markets. Although it is very different from the public–governmental, it is nevertheless public in its own way. It can be argued, for example, that the public nature of widely available and advertised published prices of products and services like televisions and automobiles contrasts with the personal and private use of market purchases and the utility they serve. Even so, the model allows us to differentiate public in this sense from the public qualities of government.

There is a strong empirical and historical content underlying the emergence of the sectors paradigm. It is related first to the subsidy by government of nonprofit or—as they were once known in the United States and still are known in Britain—voluntary organizations, through the tremendous proliferation of grant programs during the Kennedy–Johnson years. Communities in the community organization sense were vertically integrated within the national society through the interaction of the two sectors of state/government and nonprofit/voluntary/commons.[9] A key dimension

Table 2.1 The Four-Sector Model of Community

Ends	Means	
	Public	*Private*
Public	Polity (state)	Commons*
Private	Market	Household

*The term "Commons" is generally to be preferred to the more ambiguous "Third Sector" for reasons spelled out in R. Lohmann (1992, 1993). The term is not intended to suggest that all forms of third sector organization conform in all respects to the ideal-type of the commons, but rather that the archetype of the commons (voluntary participation of individuals pursuing common, joint, or shared purposes, with common or shared resources, experiencing a sense of mutuality, community, or communion and feeling bound by an indigenous sense of justice) exercises a strong normative, or moral, constraint on all activity within this sector. Thus, nonprofit social services, educational, or health administrators acting in an excessively entrepreneurial manner will, at some point, come under criticism for being "too commercial."

of this growing verticalization was the sudden and dramatic increase in social service grant programs during the Great Society years. With the transition during the Nixon years from grants to contracting and the inclusion of for-profit alongside nonprofit service vendors, vertical integration of social services became a three-sector model of state, commons, and market. And at any point that one chooses to not merely examine the supply side and remember where clients are located, the household or family sector appears.

As the earlier Austin quote suggests, this model of community segmented into four principal sectors is useful as a way of extending the community insights of the Dunham tradition of community organization and the sociological literature on community. It provides a single, unified perspective while avoiding many of the theoretical muddles of the "nested boxes" approaches. It takes rather commonplace empirical observations and extends them into powerful insights.

Likewise, the sector model amplifies the insights of Warren's horizontal and vertical integration. We can examine not only the vertical linkages of each sector within regional, national, and perhaps international society, but also the vertical linkages of nonprofit community services with the broader polity through public purchase of service contracts and the horizontal linkages between sectors such as social services relations with the business community. The model also points us to the multiple possibilities for horizontal and vertical integration within community sectors, such as the subordination of commercial subsidiaries to nonprofit or public services.

Further extensions of the four-sector community model are also suggested. For example, Henry Hansmann (1987) makes dichotomies between the donative and commercial resource bases and mutual and entrepreneurial styles of nonprofit organizations, which results in the classification shown in table 2.2. By breaking each of the four cells of the basic table into an additional distinction of more and less, it is possible to derive a sixteen-cell table descriptive of many of the major nonprofit social service options. This approach suggests a basic classification scheme for social service institutions and many bases for comparison between sectors. For example, capitation-based programs appear roughly as commercial a strategy as professional associations but more entrepreneurial.

THE SOCIAL SERVICE TRANSACTION

The sectoral approach to community of the new political economy represents an advance in community theory in another respect as well. It helps us to see the fundamentally triadic (public, nonprofit, commercial) nature of all social service delivery that is the ultimate justification for why communities matter in social services. One of the serious limits of the prevailing exchange theory that has been a feature of the social work service delivery model for several decades is the dualistic model of economic exchange in which it is grounded.[10] All service provisions are presented as simple two-

Table 2.2 Expanded Typology of Nonprofit Social Services (Resource Base by Management Style)

| Resource Base | Management Style | | | |
| | Mutual | | Entrepreneurial | |
	More	Less	More	Less
Donative				
More	Charity societies	Collabora-tories	Donation-funded social services	Grant-funded social services
Less	Membership orgs.	United Way	Sliding-scale fees for service	POS contract services
Commercial				
More	Professional associations		Fee-based social services	Capitation payments
Less		Trade associations		Market pricing of social services

Source: The four basic categories of this table are from Hansmann (1981). The examples listed in each cell are illustrative only.

part transactions. That is, from an exchange view, there are dyadic transactions between supervisor and worker, and there are separate transactions between supervisor and executive and between worker and client. Each of these is seen as a separate, more or less autonomous exchange relationship. The effect of seeing everything in these dualistic terms is a form of reductionism that drops the community out of everything but the most overt group transactions such as neighborhood meetings. This dyadic model is a major reason why many clinical social workers have real difficulty seeing any place for social administration and agency stakeholders in service delivery: "I am helping my client, who needs only me. Why should we need you?"

In reality, such a view abstracts out of the picture the full range of circumstances that led up to the moment of service delivery and make it possible (as well as define it in important ways). Those are the authorizations by legislation or board action that made it possible to employ this particular worker and to authorize the particular program of service under which she is operating. They are also the resources that enable the program to be carried out and all the rest of the legitimate community interests and concerns that make up the particular environment of any particular service exchange. Where the community connection is not lost entirely in the reductionism of the worker–client dyad, it is at least very difficult to trace the reality of community to the level of the individual service transactions. As a result, interactions between worker and client, especially when surrounded by a necessary blanket of confidentiality, appear to be purely private exchanges. But if social service were truly a private matter, there would be no reason for any norm of confidentiality. It is only because of the ever-present possibility of the interest and involvement of significant others in the community that norms of confidentiality are necessary. Moreover, if social service were purely private, how could the claims of generations of social workers that social services are or ought to be community concerns have any validity?

We can recognize more clearly the legitimacy of the community in social service transactions by viewing them as parts of a fundamental service triad; a relationship involving three parties rather than two. The basic service triad concerns the relations among those we call in this book patrons, agents, and clients. Omit any one of the three and the very idea of delivering a social service becomes impossible. The very fact that social administrators and social workers (the agents) find it necessary to invoke and defend a veil of confidentiality screening out patrons from client-related information is evidence of the vitality of this triad. Otherwise, patrons, whether wealthy donors, legislators, or others, might easily claim—and in the past, they have—that in exchange for the money or legitimacy provided they have a right to know the full details of what clients disclose to workers. These are not, in fact, separate transactions at all but can only be understood relative to one another.

STAKEHOLDERS

This model of triadic transactions is a useful way to think about the most important stakeholders for social service agencies. Based on this model, we can say that there are three principal classes of stakeholders in the typical social service: those who provide the support and legitimacy for social service activity (patrons); those who carry out patron wishes or preferences and provide the services (agents and the social agency), and clients, who are the recipients of the services. With only patrons and clients, you may have traditional personal charity, and perhaps a new form of feudalism. You do not have social services or a social agency. The same is true when you have only agents and clients. With only patrons and agents, but no clients, you may have a basis for pretense, but not for service. Only when you take into account all three classes of actors does anything resembling a social service or social agency come clearly into view.

It is inevitable that doing any type of social service activity will draw responses from a host of significant others. The significant others may be the parents of young children or a child of elderly parents. They may be the friends and neighbors of the clients. They may be the building owners from whom office space is rented, bankers from whom to obtain short-term loans while a grant is being processed, or lawyers who assist with incorporation and taxes and contracts. They may be the physicians, teachers, and clergy members who welcome the social worker as a solution to their problems even as they challenge her legitimacy. They may be the enthusiasts and supporters of various sorts who welcome social service as a good idea, a blessing, an opportunity to volunteer, or an improvement in the business climate. They may be the officials who see affiliation with social service as improving their chances of re-election. They may be the staff of cooperating agencies willing to make a place for a service in their referral lists or the staff of competing services who quietly hope that the same service will fail and go away. The lists of possible significant others could be continued for pages. The point is that social service is never a strictly private act between workers and clients, and there will always be significant others to contend with. This is the very essence of the triadic transaction at the core of all social services.

Patricia Yancey Martin (1985) identified seven distinct external constituencies that have relevance to the social service organization:

1. The general public (including the media, civic groups, private contributors, churches, ordinary citizens, public opinion, etc.)
2. Legislative and regulatory bodies (including federal, regional and state
   funding and oversight agencies)
3. Local funding and regulatory bodies (such as city and county government policies and laws, United Fund standards and grants, etc.)
4. Employee unions, professional associations, licensing and accreditation bodies
5. Client referral sources and targets, (including human service organizations, private and public employers, business, industries, etc.)
6. The personnel resource pool (including educational and professional
   schools, employment agencies and private citizens seeking employment)
7. Clients (not merely as individuals to be recruited, served and dis-
   charged, but also as collectivities, such as parents and friends of the
   retarded) that organize for purposes of advancing or publicizing various concerns or for lobbying and pressuring organizations to be more
   responsive to particular interests and demands

No one in social services should ever feel they are in it alone. The number
of people who may have an interest in social agencies and are potential
supporters of social services is extremely broad and diverse. The main challenge of constituency building is to bring as many of them as possible into
the tent—to neutralize active opposition into indifference, to convert the
indifferent into active supporters, and to give active supporters reasons to
remain so and to do even more. As the leadership perspective of Mary
Parker Follett (explored in chapter 6) suggests, the point here should always
be not to encourage personal support for you or for your organization. Support should be sought for the common cause that you, your organization,
other organizations with which you share common cause, and all of your
constituents jointly support. There are several simple but very demanding
rules of thumb to observe in furthering such common efforts:

1. *Always be receptive to potential new support.* When people show an
interest in your social agency, program, or institution, reciprocate by showing an interest in them and encouraging their involvement. Answer donations with thank-you letters or notes, find meaningful activities for volunteers, keep interested community groups informed about what the agency
is doing, answer questions, and so on.

2. *Never go out of your way to reject support.* There can be an almost
infinite number of ways to inadvertently or unavoidably alienate or turn off

supporters. They include phone calls missed, letters unanswered, and decisions that must be made even though some people will be angry or alienated as a result. There is simply no need ever to add to your opposition by insulting, snubbing, or deliberately ignoring potential supporters.

3. *Go out of your way whenever possible to build additional support.* A vital part of constituency building is community outreach. This is not hard. It's actually fun to do, but it can be very demanding on your time and energy. Give speeches, talk with groups, write letters, join others in community service campaigns, and generally be visible in your community wherever and whenever possible.

4. *Concentrate on the young.* Social workers need to remember the sixties are over, but so are the eighties! All of the media hype in recent decades about the self-centered me generation, yuppies, generation Xer's, and the like points to changes that are very real. Even so, many potential volunteers, donors, and stakeholders are available.The support of future generations for social services should not be taken for granted. Take every opportunity to encourage college, high school, and even grade school students to volunteer, donate, engage in community service, and consider careers in social services.

5. *Build and encourage career ladders for a lifetime of support.* Don't treat support as a one-time thing. Give people reasons and ways to stay involved and committed to your cause for as long as possible and find ways for them to assume different roles with the organization as their time, energy, and interest permit.

CONCLUSION

Community is one of the centrally important concepts of social administration. Indeed, community continues to be perhaps the single most powerful organizing concept and context in the worldview of social administration. In an American culture still largely defined in terms of the individual, community is the primary social nexus for organized action as well as the single most important element in defining the social environment of practice. This is as true for the social agency administrator today as it was for seminal figures in the development of professional social work practice during the nineteenth and early twentieth centuries.

Community is important for all of social work because it is the location in which clients reside and the social environment that has an important formative influence on their behavior. Community is also critically important because it is the location of many other of the most important agency constituencies or stakeholders. The concept of vertical and horizontal linkages is especially important for social administration. It explains both how communities are integrated into the larger society and how important supportive linkages within the community arise. The concept of the competent community also brings both of these dimensions to bear on social administration theory and practice. Part of the practice of any competent community will be adequate support for social agencies and other caring institutions.

Though institutional theories of community emphasize the complexity and diversity of community institutions, a measure of order and simplicity can be brought to our understanding of community by visualizing networks of community institutions as components of four broad sectors. These are the marketplace or economy, government or the state, the third sector or the commons, and the family or household sector. Not only do clients usually come from the latter, but this is also the locus of most individual mutual aid and self-help efforts. Organized mutual aid and self-help groups as well as most social agencies are part of the third sector.

Closely associated with this four-sector model of communities is a distinctive trilateral pattern of exchange or transactions that is characteristic of organized social services. Social services are organized as a three-way transaction among patrons, those who supply the necessary resources for service delivery; clients, whose needs provide the rationale for patrons to offer those resources; and social administrators, social workers, and other service providers whose activities link the interests of patrons with those of clients.

These core ideas provide the essential framework for understanding the importance of community in contemporary social administration.

CHAPTER 3

The Social Agency

The commonsense notion of referring to any organization delivering social services as a social agency goes back to the early decades of the twentieth century. The essence of the term is to be found in the legal concept of agency as the representation of the interests of others. In this case, both clients and other stakeholders are represented. In recent years, social work scholars have generally accepted the reality of the social agency as a given and sought to delineate ever more precisely the particular organizational traits most characteristic of social or human service agencies. At the same time, the evolution of private practice is premised partly on escaping the responsibilities and burdens of agency-based practice. Much of the recent attention to social agencies has centered on two overlapping conceptions of the *human service organization* and the *nonprofit organization.* The first underlines social service agencies as part of a larger class of service-delivering organizations and the second emphasizes the elevation of service over profit in the agency's mission. Although a significant amount of social service activity actually takes place in state and local governmental agencies and in private, for-profit settings, these public bureaus and firms have been of considerably less interest to the human services research community or have been simply lumped in as "agencies."

The continuing central importance of the social agency was outlined by Weissman, Epstein, and Savage (1983): "The agency is the hidden reality of social work. Agency decisions determine, among other things, which clients will be served, how they will be served, by who, for how long, and at what cost" (p. 3). They might have added that it is primarily social administration by executives and boards making such decisions in social agencies. In this chapter, we will endeavor to isolate at least some of the essential characteristics of social agencies and their role in social work practice.

The legal concept of agency with its implications of representing the interests of others is more than incidentally important in understanding the form taken by attempts to organize and deliver social services at the community level. In fact, that notion of agency as expressed in the three-way transaction of clients, workers, and stakeholders introduced in chapter 2 is an ever-present reality of social administration. Managers and workers interact daily on the job fully aware of the impact of the various stakeholders' opinions on what they do. Managers define the work environment of workers through policy and rules, a significant portion of which are imposed on the organization by stakeholder authorities. The exercise of transformational leadership to change the environment and circumstances of work is subject to various limitations imposed by workers, clients, board members, courts, and others. All of these images fit neatly within the broader metaphor of social administration as an activity occurring in organizations. But organizations don't just happen; creating and maintaining viable organizations are major tasks of social administration.[1]

Most social administrators are likely to perceive organizations as the natural environment of their day-to-day working life. With the exception of some recent forms of private practice, social work practice was primarily agency-based practice throughout the twentieth century, although contemporary concerns about managed care have the potential of changing that (discussed in later chapters). Use of the term *agency* originally arose in the community context in which organized groups of charity workers were employed as the direct agents of patrons engaged in charitable actions helping clients. It is wise to remember, therefore, that in the context of agency-based social work practice, the term *organization* always means *organization-in-community*. In other words, there is always an external as well as an internal dimension to the organization of social services. As such, social services are also always community institutions. In recent decades, this aspect of agencies as community institutions has been enhanced and extended with detailed internal views of social agencies as formal organizations. However, the external dimension of community relations remains of great importance. As the model of triadic exchange suggests, stakeholders in the community are an important and vital part of any organized social service agency.

THE RIGHT OF ASSOCIATION

Any effort to track the history of the modern American social agency will eventually end up in the voluntary social service membership associations of the nineteenth century, from which the more recent voluntary sector social agency and even later the public and modern publicly funded nonprofit arose.

Social services throughout the twentieth century were in the forefront of a number of significant social movements in the practices affecting the management of organizations. One of the most significant of these was the evolution of the nonprofit social agency that gradually evolved from the non-staff voluntary-membership charity societies of the late nineteenth century into the managed nonprofit corporation of today. A central element in that transition was the gradual evolution of the voluntary association into the modern professionally staffed nonprofit organization. Nonetheless, an essential dimension of the modern social agency remains in traditional doctrines of the right of free association.

The right of association was explicitly declared by the U.S. Supreme Court in *NAACP v. Alabama* in 1958 and confirmed in *NAACP v. Button* in 1963, but it had been evolving at least since the English Statute of Charitable Uses was adopted in 1601. Under this doctrine, associations or groups of people are entitled to assemble and pursue together virtually any lawful purpose that they might pursue individually (Lohmann, 1992). The practical import of this right of association is clear in the case of social services. Any time a group of social workers and others identifies a major unmet need or social problem in an American community, at least two general courses of action are open to them.

They may organize for political action or what the First Amendment of the Constitution refers to as "petition for redress of grievances" to try to pressure Congress or a state legislature, county commission, or city council into action. Or, with or without concluding that such redress may be futile, unnecessary, or ill-advised, they may organize a private action or organize a social service entirely on their own and seek to enlist others to help support this activity. In so doing, they may create a new social agency or a new program within an existing agency. Those "others" may be donors, in which case the organization is more likely to take a nonprofit form, or paying clients or customers, in which case a more classic business enterprise is

suggested. Or they may represent some mix of donor support and customers, in which case any form of organization is possible.

This organizing response is closely associated with the tradition of civic
republicanism[2] in American public life. Civic republicanism is the political
doctrine of self-governing or autonomous individuals within self-governing
communities. According to Michael Sandel (1996), civic republicanism is,
along with liberal individualism, one of the two dominant political ideologies of American history. Although the rhetoric of civic republicanism had
limited impact on social work from the New Deal to the Great Society, it
was clearly a major element in earlier social work and in the formation of
voluntary social agencies.

It is also clear that civic republican ideals have a continuing importance
in social work. One could even argue that the civic republican ideal of individual self-governance is the political or civic dimension of all clinical
social work. Although most clinicians would be more comfortable with
terms like *growth and development,* it is clear from the traditional uses of
developmental models like those of Erikson (1959) and Maslow (1959) and
more recent models of empowerment that personal autonomy or self-
governance are the ends toward which most such models point.

Furthermore, firmly grounded in the civic republican tradition are the
idea of social work as a self-governing profession, with institutions such as
governing boards, delegate assemblies, and local and state chapters, and
major social work ideals such as the dignity of *all* people. These connections
were well explored by such pioneers as Jane Addams (1902/1964, 1893/1970).
Contemporary social work and social policy are amalgams of a range of
widely different political and social theories. Yet, there can be little doubt
that policy and practice in the areas of governing and advisory boards
are deeply grounded in principles of personal and organizational self-
governance generally and are externally reinforced by the doctrine of free
association in particular (see Kramer [1973], for example).

In social administration, we typically assume that persons are capable
of self-governance. Indeed, this may be a fundamental point of demarcation
between clinical social work and social administration. In social administration, we assume personal autonomy as the normal condition until further notice, whereas clinical social work often deals with persons whose
personal autonomy is damaged or impaired. Up to the point at which any
board or staff member may demonstrate seriously impaired judgment, we
assume that they are capable of rational or intelligent action. It is only when
someone involved in social administration, such as a board member, staff
member, or volunteer or other stakeholder, is demonstrably not able to
function autonomously that their behavior becomes a clinical issue.[3] This
can lead to some interesting and complex issues of role incongruity, such

as when individuals under treatment for substance abuse, schizophrenia, or other serious mental illnesses are also members of board or advisory groups. The complexity of sorting out such issues, however, should not detract from the essential importance of the underlying principle of assuming personal autonomy. The capacity for self-governance that in its more modern sense might better be termed self-control or self-efficacy is thus a precondition for social administration. Implications of this issue when talking of empowerment are explored in chapter 17.

CONTEMPORARY FORMS OF SOCIAL AGENCY

Although it once was considered a distinctive form of organization, the *social agency* in contemporary social work is generally considered today as any organization capable of the delivery of social services through office work, outreach, and the employment of social workers. Generally speaking, we can identify three principal forms of such agencies per se and a fourth form of a quasi-public agency. Consistent with our four-sector model (see chapter 2), the four principal forms are the *public* social service bureau, the *commercial* firm engaged in the retail sale of social services, the *nonprofit* or voluntary sector social service organization, and a vast array of *mutual aid, self-help* and social caring arrangements. The latter arrangements currently deliver a sizeable portion of social care services using volunteer care providers largely through nonadministered informal organizations. Mutual aid and self-help efforts are not widely discussed as "social agencies" in either organization studies or the sociological subfield of mutual aid and self-help even though an important kind of self-agency is involved (Borkman, 1999). Therefore, they are not discussed. We do, however, examine briefly a fifth hybrid category (to which we attach the label QUANGO [quasi-nongovernmental organization], after recent British practice) that appears to many authorities to be arising from a kind of convergence of commercial, public, and nonprofit types.

Public agencies are part of the public bureaucracy and thus part of the *polity* or political system. Commercial agencies are part of the market sector or the business community. Nonprofit agencies and organized mutual aid and self-help groups are both part of the vast third sector, and informal helping by family and friends may most appropriately be seen as part of the household sector, although the use of volunteers in formal organizations also points toward the third sector. QUANGOs display some of the characteristics of all three of these nonhousehold types. Interestingly, regardless of the legal organizational form adopted, social agencies all tend to be organized into the particular physical workspaces known as offices, much like other human services such as insurance and medical offices.[4] Before considering other aspects of the social agency, therefore, it serves us well to take a close look at the modern social work office.

The Social Work Office

The single most salient physical fact about the social agency is that it is an office in the modern life sense of a particular type of dedicated workspace.[5] Although we tend to take it for granted, the modern office is as distinctive in its features and characteristics as the farmstead, factory, medieval monastery, or Renaissance artisan's atelier. Social work was not in any of its multiple points of origin an office-based profession. The friendly visitors of the charity organization society were more inclined toward home visits than to asking clients to visit them in the office. Settlement workers were much more likely to be found in classrooms, community meeting halls, sewing rooms, recreation centers, or kitchens than in any office, as such. School social work began with visiting teachers that worked in the homes of shut-in children, and medical social work began on the wards of public hospitals.

However, in the early decades of the twentieth century, factors internal and external to the profession converged to create the underlying office culture of the contemporary social agency. The evolution of the medical model after 1920 underlined the necessity of private treatment rooms even for social treatments. At the same time, the demands of accountability and professionalism converged in the necessity for documented case records and integrated filing systems like those found in legal, accounting, and other professional offices. The professional emphasis on supervision and coordination brought further need for co-located offices and discouraged the development of solo practices. Further, rule-bound and policy-based bureaucratization of professional practice was a direct consequence of both the growing standardization of practice methods and the demands of public and community accountability.

As a result, since the Great Depression social work has been predominantly an office-based profession, and social service today contends with the office organization problems that are also experienced in legal firms, business corporations, and government bureaus. Like other office-based professions, social workers make forays outside the office into the world (outreach) but, in general, information about the world comes to the social worker via a broad range of information media such as the telephone; such intelligence is processed, stored, and acted upon in the office environment.[6]

Contemporary social service typically occurs within generally recognized office space that is not markedly different from similar space employed by other commercial or nonprofit service establishments. Social work practice also relies upon generic office equipment and supplies. The basic office requirements of the typical social agency can be precisely identified, which is precisely what faculty often do, for example, in setting up new programs and in spelling out minimal requirements for students in field placement. Students must have access to an office, a desk, a telephone, secretarial services, and so on. Further, because of the reliance on generic, widely available office practices and the absence of specialized equipment or technology, a social service office is comparatively easy and inexpensive to set up. This is in contrast, for example, to a dentist's or radiologist's office, both of which require specialized and expensive equipment and supplies. Setting up social work offices is often one of the tasks of social administration. The same is true for the more complex task of attempting to organize relationships and interactions in the office.

The Human Service Organization

In chapter 1, we explicitly rejected the term *human services* as overly general for our purposes. Much of the recent social work literature on organizations uses that broad term in ways that suggest or apply only to social services. Therefore, in this section (only) we adopt this usage as the most accurate way of reflecting a body of important work.

In general, we concur with Burton Gummer (1995b), who suggested that even though the management literature is replete with articles on "empowering employees," "satisfying customers," "working smarter, not harder," "decentralization," and a host of other forward-looking management practices, in reality most social service organizations are more like the bureaucracies that Max Weber described than anything else. This point is crucial in understanding the notion of social administrators at the apex of professional agency hierarchies discussed in chapter 1. Social service work is generally not just office work; it is usually hierarchically organized office work at that.

More than forty years ago, Robert Vinter (1959) differentiated one category of social agencies, which he called people-changing organizations, into two types: treatment organizations and others. Vinter also attributed the two primary social functions of socialization and social control to such organizations. Using Vinter's distinction, Hasenfeld and English define a human service organization as "an organization whose primary function is to define or alter a person's behavior, attributes, and social status in order to maintain or enhance his well being" (Hasenfeld & English, 1974, p. 1; Hasenfeld, 1992).

Two things can be said about this definition. First, it appears to define more clearly the particular human service organizations we call social services than some of the other organizations included in the broader conception of human services noted in chapter 1. It is difficult to envision the behavioral change dimensions of an insurance broker or even an unemployment compensation program. Second, their definition appears to be more appropriate to what Hasenfeld and English call *people-changing* organizations than to what they call *people-processing* ones. Altering behavior is more clearly the function of a mental health program, for example, than of income maintenance or insurance sales. The mission of people-processing programs, they note, is principally to confer statuses that will maintain or enhance well-being (in either the weak sense of eligibility-status or the stronger sense of client, patient, or inmate). People-changing activities have as their mission altering the social attributes or behavior of clients. Thus, there should be no problem in interchangeably referring to the organizations identified as human services by Hasenfeld and English as social agencies.

In addition to attention to the social-agency-cum-human-service-organization as a distinct form of organization, Hasenfeld and English emphasized the importance of the concept of task environment, introduced into the organizational literature by James Thompson (1967). Hasenfeld (1983) defined the task environment as "a specific set of organizations and groups with which the organization exchanges resources and services and with whom it establishes specific modes of interactions" (p. 51). This task environment renders the task of goal definition problematic in social services because of disagreements and conflict among these organizations and groups (Hasenfeld & English, 1974, p. 10). There are at least six classes of such groups in the human services task environment (Hasenfeld, 1983, pp. 61–62):

1. Providers of fiscal resources
2. Providers of legitimization and authority
3. Providers of clients
4. Providers of complimentary services
5. Consumers and recipients
6. Competing services

Here, we have yet another list of possible constituencies or stakeholders. The development of multiple goals and strategies is thus an effort to appeal to these multiple interest groups and enhance the organization's legitimacy, reflecting adaptation to and manipulation of the organization's environment (Thompson & McEwen, 1958).

One implication of the Hasenfeld and English approach that has remained largely implicit is the way in which it accounts for the fact of a good deal of private practice in therapy and clinical services and almost no private practice in eligibility determination! This is the apparent relationship between the different style and type of work groups that result from the different task environments of people-changing and people-processing organizations. People-changing activities are almost always intimate, private, and surrounded by a cloak of confidentiality. Thus, they are easily associated with small, autonomous work groups in which workers have very little dependence on other workers to carry out their tasks. By contrast, people-processing activities (admissions, loans, eligibility determinations, discharge planning, etc.) often involve complex matters of contract, external accountabilities, and control concerns. Confidentiality is at odds with accountability. The division of labor is often designed so that no single worker can fully understand or control the process, and many different hands carry out pieces of the full task. Individual work groups in this case are highly interdependent, and intermediate layers of authority and decision making are explicitly required to coordinate all the complex pieces.

These definitions and conceptualizations have brought additional specificity to the task of identifying and characterizing the social agency. However, at some level it becomes useful also to attempt to differentiate among subtypes of social agencies and human service organizations. In the following sections, we look at the distinctive characteristics of four distinct subtypes of social agency: the public bureau, the commercial firm, the traditional nonprofit or voluntary organization, and the recently emergent hybrid, QUANGO.

The Social Service Bureau

Public organizations are organizations that are enacted, enabled, and appropriated by legislative acts. A public agency, such as those in public welfare and public health, is not created by groups of citizens who band together for joint action but is explicitly enacted by specific legislative directives. In general, one can locate specific statutes or laws creating public agencies and defining their powers.

Traditionally, public agencies in this sense are also explicitly empowered and limited only to those powers mentioned in the act. Thus, although a nonprofit social service agency created to serve children might occasionally serve an elderly client with little fear of recriminations, a public agency that did so might be in violation of its mandate and could be subject to serious legal recriminations.

The formal method of funding public agencies generally differs from both nonprofit and commercial organizations in that public agencies are also funded by legislative action or appropriations bills. Usually this occurs within ceilings or funding limits (authorizations) established in the original legislation creating the agency.

Such limitations are part of the traditional American vigilance against big government, which is a set of concerns that goes back to the founding fathers. Thus, for example, the furor created in 1998 by evidence that the Internal Revenue Service had exceeded its powers is part of a much longer legacy of vigilance against government tyranny. This is a legitimate concern not only in the case of federal but also with state and local governmental agencies.

Indeed, in the case of social welfare it may be more of a concern at the state level since few federal agencies have anything approaching the kinds of broad police powers possessed by many state agencies. Thus, for example, before the practice was struck down by the Supreme Court in 1967, state and local welfare agencies were empowered to conduct "man in the house" night raids against recipients of Aid to Families with Dependent Children. Further, generally only state child welfare agencies and their agents are empowered to legally remove children from their homes. However, in recent years, there has been considerable blurring of these traditional federal–state and even private–public distinctions.

Federal agencies in social welfare are a special case. Before it was broken up and the process of federal devolution began, the federal Department of Health, Education, and Welfare (HEW) was the largest single civilian or nonmilitary organization in American history, with more than 100,000 employees. Even with huge amounts of money to spend, the HEW department and its successors, including the Department of Education and the Department of Health and Human Services, are virtually powerless in most social policy arenas to do anything more than fund, advise, train, and admonish others. With a few notable exceptions, such as the Veterans Affairs medical system, federal agencies are constitutionally prohibited from engaging in direct service delivery.

Social Services and Commercial Firms

The involvement of social work with commercial forms of organization is the most recent and, for many veterans in the field, the strangest and most tenuous of arrangements. A number of sources in social work are still inclined to call such organizations "private, for profit." The term *commercial* is not only shorter but it is also easier to use and encompasses all the major implications of the longer neologism. The *Random House Dictionary* defines *commercial* as characterized by a "sole or chief emphasis on salability or profit."

Business accounting texts usually identify three principle types of commercial firms: sole proprietorships, partnerships, and corporations. There are currently no good data on which to rely, but it would appear that two generalizations are true of the involvement of social workers in the commercial practice of social work. Where social workers themselves have entered into private practice through creating new commercial organizations, they generally tend to organize as sole proprietorships (that is, practice alone) or enter into group partnerships. These practice groups may be with other social workers or in multiprofessional partnerships that also involve physicians, nurses, psychiatrists, psychologists, and others. This variety is in marked contrast to social workers' entry into the nonprofit arena, where the section 501(c)(3) (tax-exempt) nonprofit corporation is the universal organization of choice.[7] It is not just the interest in profit that characterizes social service firms, but also the fact that their services are for sale.

By contrast, when social workers join existing private practice organizations, they are most likely to join existing commercial corporations: nursing homes, hospitals, day care centers, and all manner of professional corporations organized by physicians, lawyers, and others. The reasons for this are relatively straightforward and both historic and strategic. Probably most important is the nearly complete lack of a coherent base of knowledge and experience within the profession of how to create and operate anything beyond the most simple types of businesses. Because of the long-standing history of involvement of the profession with the nonprofit and public sectors, little exists in the way of organized knowledge or technical know-how for corporate organization in the field, and there are few ways to develop such knowledge.

The Nonprofit Organization

One of the original and still distinct forms of social agency is what was originally referred to as the voluntary agency and has since come to be known as the nonprofit organization.

The term *nonprofit* is a residual one, delineating a class of organizations by what they are not or by characteristics that they do not possess. It is a bit like defining vegetables as nonanimals (Lohmann, 1989). According to Robert Anthony and David Young (1984), "A non-profit organization is an organization whose goal is something other than earning a profit for its owners. Usually its goal is to provide services" (p. 35). Alone, this approach is a distinctly unhelpful one.

Anthony and Young went on to identify seven additional basic criteria of such organizations that set them apart from business firms:

1. Absence of a profit motive
2. Service orientation
3. Constraints on goals and strategies

4. Less dependence on clients for financial support
5. Domination of professionals
6. Differences in governance
7. Differences in top management
8. Importance of political influences
9. A tradition of inadequate management controls

Through these criteria, Anthony and Young detail a rather common view of nonprofit organizations as deficient or incomplete forms of ordinary business firms. "The absence of a single, satisfactory, overall measure of performance that is comparable to the profit measure is the most serious problem inhibiting the development of effective management control systems in nonprofit organizations" (p. 39). Newman and Wallender (1978) say that nonprofits

> differ from firms in the profit-making sector because objectives are often intangible; employees have dual commitments, being as loyal to their professions as to their employing agencies; the influence of consumers or "customers" is weak; and rewards, punishments, and funding are not fully under the control of internal management. (quoted in Lewis & Lewis, 1983, p. 87)

In general, all of these characteristics of nonprofit organizations are on the mark. The principal issue is the (usually negative) connotations (or "spin") attached to so many of them. It should be noted that this view of nonprofit organizations as deficient forms of commercial or business organizations is an interpretation originating primarily among business and accounting writers and not an established fact. The implications of this opinion on accountability are discussed further in chapter 12.

Other writers have taken the term *nonprofit* less residually and attempted to state positively what is involved, rather than what is missing. Lester Salamon (1992) says that the *nonprofit sector* is a collection of organizations that are

- Formally constituted
- Nongovernmental
- Not profit distributing
- Self-governing
- Voluntary
- Of public benefit (p. 6)

These models of the nonprofit organization define certain essential characteristics (see below), but they provide no real basis for identifying social agencies as unique organizations. By concentrating more on the voluntary association origins of social service, the importance of community ties, and the links with mutual aid and self-help networks, disciplines, and professions, Roger Lohmann (1992) identified five defining characteristics of an ideal type called a *commons:*

1. Voluntary (noncoercive) participation
2. Shared purposes
3. Shared resources
4. An evolving sense of mutuality
5. Indigenous norms of justice

Such organizations, it is suggested, are engaged in the prosumption[8] of common goods including social services.[9] Most American nonprofit organizations at the community level only approximate the characteristics of the ideal type of the commons in the same way that organizations only approximate the ideal type of Weber's bureau.

The perspective of the commons is fundamental to understanding what social workers have traditionally meant by a social agency and why the triadic transaction discussed at the end of chapter 2 is important in the definition of social service. The commons view of the social agency also helps explain why the Newman–Wallender perspective quoted earlier by Lewis and Lewis is wide of the mark. Under the circumstances envisioned by earlier generations of social workers discussed in chapter 2, triadic transactions involving patrons, professional social workers, and community clients defined social agencies that would voluntarily share a sense of common purpose, shared resources, mutuality, and situationally informed norms of fairness (such as criteria for the eligibility for service).[10] Thus, any sense in which equal loyalty to profession and employing agency might be problematic does not result from the model of the nonprofit, community-oriented social agency. It comes from retroactively applying a completely different perspective to the same circumstances. The problem stems from the familiar dyad of buyer and seller as adversaries imported from economic market theory.

We may legitimately accuse earlier generations of social workers of naïveté or of failure to follow through sufficiently on their vision of the voluntary social agency as a commons. We can also accuse them, after the fact, of not living up to our more recent visions of entrepreneurial nonprofits. (Of being, in effect, poor vegetables because they look and act so much like animals!) However, it is both unfair and inaccurate to accuse them of not having a clear, coherent, well-thought-out view of the world.[11] The real question facing social administration today is not whether theirs was a false view of their social world of communities and agencies, but whether any of that earlier view is still useful today.

In one sense, social administration is concerned with all organizational behavior in social agencies and at least with the relevant behavior of stakeholders in communities. But what about those people specifically designated as managers or administrators? Who are they? Rosemary Sarri (1971) used Talcott Parson's model of organizations to identify the different functional expectations of three distinct levels.

1. *Institutional level* administration is concerned with "activities in the translation and implementation of social goals into social action" (p. 44). Such institutional concerns in the ideal nonprofit organization are a shared concern of the board and the executive. In the case of professional service organizations, however, it may be the executive that carries the primary burden of institutional administration (whether the executive is an individual executive director or chief executive officer or there is an executive group).

2. *Managerial level* efforts "involve mediation between the consumers and the technical suborganization" (p. 44). In the typical small social agency, these managerial concerns will also be the domain of the executive. In larger organizations, such concerns are commonly the domain of division and department heads and office managers.[12]

3. *Technical level* efforts "includes the suborganization concerned with the technical activities" of service delivery by the organization (p. 45). In the smallest social agencies (of which there are many), the lone executive officer may also have to absorb technical level administration. In even moderate-sized organizations, however, technical administration in this sense is the domain of supervisors.

Notably absent from this classification are staff support positions such as accounting, fund-raising, planning, and human resources. In the smallest organizations, a most essential staff position is typically a lone bookkeeper that, like any department heads or supervisors, reports directly to the chief executive officer. The largest organizations may have an assistant director or vice president for administration to whom all staff units report.

We can identify up to five distinct levels of management one might expect to find in the human service organization: executive, staff–support, departmental, office manager, and supervisor. A sixth category, which becomes important to the degree that the organization is professionalized, is some notion of the senior professional staff, defined as those with the highest levels of training and most experience who can be counted on for leadership. One finds this particular model well developed in hospitals and higher education where physicians, social workers, and other professionals are commonly expected to play quasi-managerial roles in leadership and decision making. This role is also in evidence in a number of other professionalized social service agencies, such as community mental health agencies. The administration of a particular social service agency might embrace employees in one of these categories or in all of them.

The Quasi-Nongovernmental Organization

From the sector perspective introduced earlier, many researchers active in nonprofit and public sector studies today have serious questions about the descriptive accuracy of the three ideal types of organizations—public, commercial, and nonprofit. The suggestion of organizational convergence of the sectors, and primarily public and nonprofit organizations becoming more profit-like, has been made repeatedly in the research literature during the past decade. What appears to many to be emerging is an entirely new form of cross-sector organization that is legally a nonprofit, financially public, and managerially entrepreneurial in nature. The trouble is that there is no agreed upon name for such organizations.

QUANGO is the term used in Great Britain and a number of other countries to identify and describe this distinctive category of organization that is a mixture of traditional governmental organizations (as described above) and traditional *private* nonprofit organizations with an essentially entrepreneurial managerial style. In the United States, it appears that this new form is a modification of private nonprofit organizations. In most of the rest of the world, it is the nonstatist nature of these organizations that is deemed most important, and they are termed *nongovernment organizations* (NGOs). It is from this context that the term QUANGO arises. Legally, the status of such QUANGOs is straightforward: they are nonprofit corporations. However, organizationally, they appear to many people to span two sectors—the public and the voluntary—and to display a mix of characteristics of governmental and nonprofit entities.

Some authorities would characterize a number of different social service organizations, such as community action agencies (originally funded by the Office of Economic Opportunity), local aging agencies (funded under Title III of the Older Americans Act), and community mental health centers as QUANGOs. Others might also include a host of other, similar grant-created and funded nonprofit agencies. Some might even be inclined to extend the term to include the type of nonprofit service vendors, funded through purchase of service contracts, described by Susan Bernstein (1991a, 1991b) in New York City.

It is important to point out that such QUANGOs are presently a purely analytic category, with no legal or operational standing. The legal form of such organizations, regardless of the degree of public funding and control, is almost universally identical with the traditional 501(c)(3) nonprofit corporation. Yet, there is often also some measure of explicit empowerment of legislative action involved.

Though the majority of voluntary and nonprofit social agencies have traditionally arisen from and been aligned with nonprofit community groups, contemporary QUANGOs may or may not have such affiliations. The category, however, is an increasingly important one in those cases where legislatures or the courts have given specific mandates and powers to such QUANGOs—to investigate cases of abuse and neglect of children or the elderly, to remove children from the home, to incarcerate juvenile offenders, and so on. Recent initiatives have also extended the category to commercial service vendors, such as those empowered to exercise traditional police powers in operating prisons, or involuntary holding juveniles, mental patients, or others.

THE WELL-MANAGED AGENCY

Although the modern social agency arose originally in the nonprofit/voluntary form, the range of contemporary social agencies also includes public and commercial agencies and the increasingly important hybrid called the QUANGO. Much of the existing social work research on organizations has sought to use the category label of the human service organization to generalize across these types. Despite important differences in form of organization, there are a variety of commonalities that this work has revealed.

A key question is what do we expect of social administration in all types of social agencies? One answer to this question comes from the normative model of the *well-managed* social agency set forth by Sugarman (1988). He identifies six criteria for organizational health:

1. A clearly defined mission as well as goals and plans based on that mission
2. Appropriate organizational mechanisms and programs for accomplishing its goals
3. Carefully selected, oriented, supervised, and developed staff
4. Effective leadership at all levels
5. Regular evaluation and corrective action when needed
6. Proactive management of relationships with other organizations and forces in the environment

CONCLUSION

In this chapter, we attempted to go beyond the conventional organizational literature and to highlight the emergence over the past century of a distinctive form of organization known colloquially within social work and the social services as the social agency. The social agency emerged in the late nineteenth century from the voluntary associations of the charity organization society movement and the complex groups of the settlement house movement. More recently, it has taken four principal forms: the public bureau, the private nonprofit organization, the commercial firm, and the QUANGO. All three of the pure types as well as QUANGOs tend to be organized utilizing the model of the modern office. (The only exceptions to office-based practice, it would appear, are the mutual aid and self-help networks, and even some of these have adopted office-based approaches.) The private nonprofit, commercial, and QUANGO forms all tend to be corporations. Solo practices or partnerships are much less common. Private nonprofits, governments, and QUANGOs all tend to be subject to the nondistribution constraint.[13] All four forms of social agency are part of a larger class of organizations that we labeled benefactories, characterized by distribution of intangible benefits in the form of a three-way economic transaction termed *prosumption*.

In chapter 4, we examine more closely perspectives from organization theory and practice as they apply to the social agency in its multiple forms.

Social Administration and Organization

The problem of how to best organize social service delivery is complex and multifaceted. It often goes well beyond the simple choice of bureau, firm, commons, QUANGO, or self-help group. On the one hand, *organization* refers to certain recognizable social relations and expected patterns of interaction or to how people relate effectively to one another on the job. On the other hand, virtually all assignments of work assume a technical or technological dimension. The ever-present challenge for social administration is balancing these two diverse concerns. Those who have struggled with questions of the organization of social services have dealt extensively with both questions of relationships on the job and the technological questions of the best way to organize to get the job done.

If you are in charge of seeing that a particular job gets done, the most immediate issue of organization becomes one of shaping and structuring the work situation. If you are not in charge, the issue is a four-part challenge, consisting of

- Recognizing and adapting to the expectations of your boss, at least to the extent he or she is entitled to speak for the organization.

- Negotiating arrangements and understandings with your fellow workers about how best to carry out these expectations. It is a fact of organizational life that those same negotiated agreements can also be used to resist, frustrate, nullify, or overturn any publicly stated official or formal expectations.
- Organizing social services to ensure that the work of the agency is carried out properly and in a timely manner.
- Acknowledging unavoidable value and ethical dimensions of organization, also in part because of the fundamental social service triad. These dimensions focus on how to organize in ways that are consistent with professional ethics and that do not harm or endanger clients or workers.

Each of these elements is a source of its own ongoing problems. A large part of the interest in organization theory in social services stems from a continuing search for better ways to structure work and improve the work-based interactions between people on the job. Because of this, there is a long-standing interest in how others such as managers in factories, business offices, and government bureaus have approached similar tasks of organization.

Gareth Morgan (1997) identified eight primary images or metaphors of organization. These include organizations as machines, organisms, brains (capable of learning and self-organization), cultures, political systems (shaped by the agendas of their members), psychic prisons (determined by favored ways of thinking and unconscious processes), logics of change (flux and transformation), and instruments of domination. Rice and Bishoprick (1971) identified a range of variations of the machine model and the egalitarian model of human relations and federation, collegial, decentralized, three humanistic models, bureaucracy, corporate, systems, and modular organizations.

Organization became a major issue in general management during the latter decades of the nineteenth century. The earliest approaches to the problem of organization in general management dealt with the problems of how to organize the multiple work activities of large-scale projects such as transcontinental railroads and assembly line production in factories. In some respects, factory production may have been one of the simpler problems arising out of the industrial revolution. At least as complex were the problems of organizing free labor in mines, transcontinental railroads, transoceanic steamship lines, new forms of retail trade such as the department store, and the modern business firm and government bureau. As noted in chapter 3, problems of the organization of social service delivery were seen primarily in community terms until the second half of the twentieth century.

These approaches generally took for granted what appears in retrospect to be an idealized, two-class organization built upon command-and-control in which managers were in control and workers were expected to fully and completely carry out management commands and not bring any personal interests or concerns to work with them. The legacy of this model of organization as a machine to carry out management direction still has great appeal in some quarters. When real workers in real settings fail to carry out management directives or when the results are different from expectations, ineffective organization such as a machine in need of repair is one of the principal suspects for many people.

WHY ORGANIZE?

It is pretty easy to see that cars would not get built, coal would not get mined, and railroads, buses, and airlines could not operate without large-scale organizations. But why are organizations for social service necessary? Why can't we all just go out and help people simply and directly? Why complicate things?

There are many possible approaches to answering this question. We have already seen part of the answer in the division of labor of the three-part transaction among patrons, agents, and clients. For clients to get help from workers and agencies, resources and legitimacy[1] must be secured from patrons. In this simple fact alone there is already the germ of a complex organization.

But there are additional reasons that explain why social service organization did not halt at the level of these three roles and the voluntary charity associations of the nineteenth century. We will consider five such reasons: historical, economic, political, technological, and informational. Each approaches the problem of organization in social agencies from a slightly different angle. From a historical view, social agencies may have arisen to allow social workers greater control over their work. The economic concept known as transaction costs addresses the most fundamental question of whether there is a need for organization at all in particular circumstances. But transaction costs alone offer a necessary but not sufficient explanation for social service organizations. Thus, we will turn to the problem of legitimacy and the political theory of constituency. Though transaction costs may dictate the existence of organized social service, the particular wishes and desires of various constituents in the community go a long way toward explaining much else that occurs in defining programs, strategies, and missions. The evolution of the social work profession is in part a history of the evolution of a distinctive set of technologies for helping people cope with their problems, and formal organizations have become an important way

of developing, focusing, and refining the expanding repertory of social work problem-solving tools. Finally, a major part of the case for professionalized service delivery organizations may be attributable to the existence of particular information asymmetries anchored within the social service task environment.

Historical Continuity

One possible explanation for why social service organizations arose is a purely historical one involving the efforts of social workers to control the circumstances of their work. Baghadi (1975) notes, for example, that in response to the dramatic urban growth of the early nineteenth century, charity workers in Boston and New York attempted to organize and control the distribution of charity. These efforts at control culminated in the creation of charitable bureaucracies with regular rules of administration, self-consciously professional administrators, and supervision of volunteers.

But even if charity workers in Boston, New York, and elsewhere sought what was, in effect, a measure of self-control, we are still left to wonder why this was necessary. Several decades ago, the sociologist Harold Wilensky and others fashioned this historic insight into a model of the development of social services grounded in the historic urbanization and industrialization of American cities (Wilensky & LeBeaux, 1965). This thesis has become a stock feature of social work discussions of the development of social services even though the underlying model of unilinear urban/industrial development has been largely discredited. Although the Wilensky model accurately summarizes the actual historical experience of the development of agency-based social service, it does not offer any particularly convincing explanations for why this development may have occurred. Urbanization, industrialization, and bureaucratization are not explanations as such. Instead they merely offer convenient labels for descriptions of complex, macrosocial processes that actually occurred. To explain the process by offering up only a label for the process is what philosophers call a tautology and others call circular reasoning.

Transaction Costs

One set of explanations for social service organizations is to be found in the economic theory of transaction costs. The economic answer to the question of organization was first posed by Ronald Coase (1937) in the late 1930s. The issue he raised is why organizations or firms in microeconomic theory arise

within markets when the economic theory of the market would seem to predict that the most efficient forms of production, distribution, and exchange of economic goods are those based upon contracts between individual buyers and sellers. Why, for example, do you buy your groceries from a large corporate chain store rather than directly from individual producers who grow, raise, or manufacture food? Coase's colorful metaphor was to ask why in an economic sea of buttermilk there were lumps? Why, in other words, does a capitalist economy include large and small producer and consumer organizations rather than simply individual producers and consumers interacting directly in markets?

Coase's answer centered upon what have come to be known as *transaction costs* and the resulting *economies of scale*. Organizations exist, he said, when negotiating employment and/or production contracts can lower the transaction costs of acquiring necessary commodities, for example, when it is cheaper for consumers in both time and money to shop at the grocery store than to contact each farmer or dairy. At the same time, each food producer can ensure a more secure income by contracting to sell large quantities to a grocer than to wait for customers to call directly.

The Coase model applies directly to explain how social service organizations arise out of the triadic social service transaction. The transaction costs of helping in money and time are lower for both clients and patrons if an organization is created and remains in place with a publicly advertised address and programs. Where agencies exist neither clients nor donors need to conduct elaborate searches when they require services or wish to make charitable donations. In its simplest and most fundamental form, a social agency might consist only of a single person—an agent as it were. This agent accepts donations and requests for services and contracts out the work with individual social workers on an hourly or job basis as resources and demand for services allow. It is in fact this position of brokerage between clients and other workers that also offers one of the strongest evidence of social administration as an integral part of social work in the agency model.

At some point, the transaction costs of contracting out each case with independent social work contractors will be such that it will be cheaper to hire one or more employees and keep them working than it would be to continually search out and contract with independent contractors. Likewise, whenever the demand for services exceeds the resources coming in, as in reality it nearly always does, our erstwhile agent will find it necessary to spend some portion of her time in what economists call search activity. That is, she will find it necessary to seek out additional support and resources through fund-raising, grant writing, legislative advocacy, or whatever or, if resources permit, to hire someone to do this task. In either case, it would be expected that hiring an employee to do these tasks might reduce the total time our broker spent searching out and contracting for these services.

The savings would represent what is known as an *economy of scale*.[2] An equally clear case of scale economies would arise if our broker hired twelve workers and discovered that she could keep track of all twelve in the same time it took to keep track of one. This she might do if she made supervision of the other ten workers part of the workload of two workers who report directly to her. She would, thereby, also have discovered the fundamental organizational principals of the *division of labor* and *task specialization*. Thus, following Coase's simple but elegant approach, it is possible to build up an entire social agency or any other type of organization as a sequence of "do-or-buy" decisions by our broker, who has both created an organization and transformed herself into a social administrator through her decisions.

The simple but elegant explanation offered by transaction costs provides a remarkably durable explanation for much of the actual composition of organizations. This is particularly the case when allowing for certain amounts of *time lag* in decisions. Sometimes it takes agents/administrators a while to realize that the point has come when it would be cheaper to hire a full-time worker than to contract out cases by the hour. Thus, the theory of transaction costs offers us a reasonable and clear explanation for understanding how social service organizations might arise out of the several simple related facts. A group of donors may be willing to give support and legitimacy but not know where best to give. At the same time, groups of clients in need of service may also be lost without at least one agent willing to link them with necessary resources.

The realities of most situations are obviously much more complex than this. However, it is relatively easy to see how the transaction costs model abstracts out some key elements that go a long way toward explaining how organizations might arise. We can also see from this approach how several enduring institutional qualities of social service organizations might begin to emerge. As donors, other supporters, and clients discover that it is easier and more convenient to keep going back to the same agency than to seek a new one each time and as habits are built up over time, relationships are formed, and loyalties are established; this is how institutions are built.

Constituency

The single greatest strength of the transaction costs explanation is also its greatest weakness. At times it is simply necessary to cry out, "But people

aren't like that!" They are not all that rational, coherent, informed, and ce-
rebral. Patrons don't just give to causes that offer them the lowest transaction costs. Sometimes they give for no coherent reasons at all. They act
on pure intuition and gut feelings. Sometimes clients haven't got a clue
where to look for help and seem to be merely floundering. Many of the
appeals for social service support to legislators and others are purely emotional. And sometimes agency efforts not only generate support, they create
opponents and enemies as well.

Each of these objections is well taken, and there are more that might be
raised as well. There is an underlying plausibility to the theory of transaction
costs that is immediately recognizable to anyone who has ever started or
built up a social agency. But it is the reality of a partial explanation. If we
follow our erstwhile agent a bit further, we can begin to see that she is also
faced with some other decisions and factors that will undercut the reality
of the purely rational economic model without any need to dismiss it entirely.

Let's look again at our agent/administrator and her ten employees and
two supervisors, all of whom have taken to calling her "the director." They
are concerned because their agency has identified far more clients than they
can serve, so they approach an important local wealthy community leader
to request help in getting some additional funding for their activities. They
learn very quickly that this person has never heard of their agency and tells
them that he never gives his hard-earned money to any charity with which
he is not already familiar. They approach a second wealthy community
leader who has heard of them but finds all efforts to aid the poor ill conceived and unjustified. Rather than simply turning them away, this person
promises to oppose the agency at every turn and do everything he can to
put them and others like them out of business. Finally, they decide to approach a local political figure for help. It really doesn't matter who they
approach—the mayor, the city or county manager, their local legislator or
congressman. They learn very quickly that this particular politician would
like to help but expects to be opposed in the next election by a candidate
who is already one of their major patrons.

In these three brief encounters, our agency staff have transcended the
purely rational calculations of transaction costs and entered the particular
domain of the *theory of constituency*. In this context, donors, clients, and
agents appear far less interested in reducing their costs than in simply having their way. In this approach, which is the traditional province of political
science, we are concerned less with the question of economic resources
than with the question of legitimacy and, for reasons that will be explored
later, with the twin problems of limited information and uncertainty. In the

real world, sometimes people can't make informed decisions except in such contentious environments, where measuring support and opposition is more fundamental than measuring costs.

The theory of constituency tells us that organizations can only exist in an environment where there is at least enough support to overcome the effects of indifference and opposition. The environments of particular organizations are likely to be made up of actual and potential supporters, actual and potential opponents, and people who simply don't care one way or the other.

For more than three decades, system-oriented thinking about organizations has relied upon the abstract concept of an *open system* first set forth by Daniel Katz and Robert Kahn (1966) to link organizations to their environments. Such open systems "maintain themselves through constant commerce (read, interaction) with the environment, i.e., a continuous inflow and outflow of energy through permeable boundaries" (p. 17). This open systems concept, although useful and durable, has a strongly and unnecessarily mechanistic undertone: the boundaries involved are largely defined by the employment contracts of workers. The border is largely a differentiation of who is employed by the organization and who isn't. Many times the location of organizational offices in a single building gives a physical dimension to the notion of organizational boundaries that can at other times be grossly deceiving. Also, it is not, in any meaningful sense, anything as vague or abstract as energy that flows in and out of organizations to and from their environments. Rather, the flows are those of communications, information, resources, power, and the like. In the case of the theory of constituency, these can be thought of most clearly in the political terms of *demands* and *constraints:* explicit expectations of organizational action by specific actors in the environment and situational limitations constraining the possible actions of the organization.

Measuring the demands and constraints of constituencies is not at all like the exact measurement of costs. In fact, there is typically a huge measure of uncertainty associated with them. In a classic study, James Thompson (1967) suggested that *uncertainty* is the key characteristic of organizational environments and that organizations seek predictability in their environments as a means to enabling ongoing, rational action. We will return to the strategic importance of uncertainty in subsequent chapters.

Thus, the theory of constituency suggests that organizations will be created when a supportive coalition or *constituency* has enough interest in creating them and the power to create them even in the face of opposition. In other words, organizations can arise and continue only when effective demands for them exceed constraints upon them. This is one of the most fundamental dynamics of institution building. Organizations can continue even in a hostile environment in the face of very direct opposition so long as support for them is stronger than the opposition. A rather famous case of this involves the organization of the embattled federal Children's Bureau. The bureau was organized in 1912, after years of struggle, when its supporters overcame strong congressional and interest group opposition. The bureau continued in operation long past the time that it served any useful purpose simply because opposition to the bureau in Congress was unable to generate the necessary votes to do away with it. Many congressmen were afraid or unwilling to be portrayed as opposed to the interests of children even when no one had any particularly good idea what interests of children were served by the bureau. (As an aside, the Children's Bureau also represents an example of an agency that clearly lost its initial mission after the passage of state and federal child welfare legislation and never successfully found another.) At the same time, opponents were able to finally overwhelm and eliminate the children's pension program created by the Sheppard–Towner Act, which didn't last beyond the decade of the 1920s.

Constituency support is a two-way street that explains a great deal that social workers sometimes find confusing. Just as support can maintain programs such as the Children's Bureau even in the face of no apparent purpose, the loss of constituency support can result in the elimination of programs even in the face of evident need for them. Thus, we have known for quite some time that it is less a matter of declining need than general dissatisfaction with administrative performance in human service programs that has contributed to the broad political support for reducing the role of the federal government in many social programs (Austin, 1983). According to the theory of constituency, social agencies and programs will only grow and expand to the extent that support capable of overcoming the organized opposition can be mobilized.

Technology

The fourth approach to the question of why organizations exist to be considered here is to look at what organizational theorists call the technology or know-how involved. The transaction costs argument necessarily assumes technology as a constant. Assuming that we know all the steps involved in making an automobile, is it less costly to assemble all the necessary know-how in a single organization or to contract parts of the process out? Likewise, technological know-how is an implicit but largely unrecognized aspect of most constituency arguments.[3] Technology explanations offer the answer that organizations exist to bring together the know-how to get a particular job done. The underlying knowledge necessary to tackle particular problems may be scattered among a group of different individuals, each of whom holds a piece of the answer. Only when there is some way to bring all the pieces together does it become possible to tackle the problem as a whole.

Technology explanations of organizations are typically less a matter of explaining why organizations exist than pointing toward the particular shape and form the organization requires to achieve its goals. Perhaps the first group of management thinkers to draw the link between technology and the organization of work were the adherents of scientific management under the leadership of Frederick Taylor. Scientific management in general is a distinct expression of American individualism and lacks any particularly coherent model of organization as such. However, the detailed time-and-motion study of work that characterizes the scientific management approach is suggestive of a view of organizations in which the nature of the array of tasks is allowed to dictate the organizational structure.

Several decades later, British management researcher Joan Woodward was among the first to follow up on the implications of this simple insight for organization.[4] Woodward and associates (1965) established a relationship between organizational form and technology. They determined that the most successful firms in each of three categories of manufacturing tended to be organized similarly. She classified organizations as (1) unit or small batch production (e.g., a cabinet shop), (2) large-batch or mass production (e.g., aircraft and ship manufacturers), and (3) long-run continuous production (e.g., automobile or toaster manufacturing). She found that organizations with small batch or long-run continuous production processes, for example, typically need to be able to adjust quickly to changes in customer's expectations and advances in technology. By contrast, large batch and mass production operations can afford to be more formal and less responsive. In most respects, the distinction made by Hasenfeld and English (1974) between people-processing and people-changing organizations is as fundamental to social services as this unit production/mass production distinction is in manufacturing. However, the full implications of this basic distinction (discussed further below) for social agency organizations have not yet been fully explored.

James Thompson developed what is probably the most universally recognized and applied model of the role of technology in organizations. Thompson (1967) described three levels of organization: the *technical core*, made up of the structures and processes necessary for carrying out the organization's mission; the *managerial system*, for managing and directing the work of the technical core, and the *institutional system*, which defines the interactions between the organization and its environment. Shortly thereafter, Rosemary Sarri (1971) applied these levels to social agencies in a major redefinition of social work administration for the *Encyclopedia of*

Social Work, and the idea has been widely used in examining human service organizations since that time.

Thompson placed particular emphasis on the technical nature of organization–environment relations as opposed to the more political emphasis on demands and constraints in constituency theory. The concept of the *task environment,* from which inputs of money, materials, clients, and information including feedback information flow, is said to peculiarly define and shape the work of the organization. The task environment of most social agencies is defined largely within the interaction of four such "inputs" classes: (1) social policies (laws, regulations, guidelines, etc.), (2) social work methods (e.g., case management, family therapy, community organization), (3) specific social programs (e.g., outreach and counseling), and (4) what might be termed the generalized constraint of the possible (available resources, existing know-how, community support).

Thompson's managerial and institutional layers are themselves important factors in defining the task environment of social services. Yet, one of the major lessons of organizational research is that a suitable task environment may not be enough to bring organizational change. Enabling legislation backed up by reasonable funding combined with professionals appropriately trained in suitable methods and working in clearly defined programs may not be sufficient in themselves. Needed changes can as easily be held back by an over-cautious or hostile management or the crushing burden of institutional traditions as by lack of sanction, employee resistance to change, or resource limitations. Yet, the task environment and the underlying idea of organizational technology remain important tools for understanding social service organizations.

Emery and Trist (1966) set forth a framework for categorizing task environments in terms of five dichotomous pairs of labels that are fairly self-explanatory: placidity versus turbulence, homogeneity versus heterogeneity, richness versus paucity, organized versus unorganized, and certainty versus uncertainty.[5]

Charles Perrow (1973) summarized the technology tradition in organization studies:

A fair amount of variation in both firms and industries is due to the type of work done in the organization—the technology. We are now fairly confident in recommending that if work is predictable and routine, the necessary arrangement for getting the work done can be highly structured, and one can use a good deal of bureaucratic theory in accomplishing this. If it is not predictable, if it is nonroutine and there is a great deal of uncertainty as to how to do a job, then one

had better utilize the theories that emphasize autonomy, temporary groups, multiple lines of authority and communications and so on. (reprinted in Carroll, Paine, & Miner, 1977, p. 13)

Some types of social service activity such as eligibility determination clearly fall into Perrow's category of the predictable and routine, whereas other social service activities such as emergency services are highly non-routine and unpredictable. Richard English and Yeheskel Hasenfeld (1974) transformed this distinction into a very useful theoretical perspective on social service organizations.

The essential insight of the technological approach is that work should be organized to reflect our understandings of the best ways of carrying out the particular tasks and jobs involved. In the context of social services, achieving consensus on the repertory of these best ways is one of the principal responsibilities of social administration and the social work profession, and disseminating that consensus should be one of the chief tasks of education programs in social work.

Information Asymmetry

A fifth general argument that has arisen recently in the emerging field of nonprofit economics goes a long way toward explaining why some organizations might be more reasonably organized as nonprofits (Weisbrod, 1988). This argument is generally known as *information asymmetry* and refers to a condition whereby information is systematically available to some members of an organization and not to others. In the case of social agencies, the most fundamental asymmetries would be those involving patrons, agents, and clients. Following the Simon–Lindblom premise that rational actors in organizations typically act not on the basis of complete knowledge but on the basis of partial knowledge, it would seem likely that such asymmetric information distribution would have very real consequences in an organization.

One of the clearest examples of asymmetric information distribution is the classic case of adoptions. At one time, nonprofit and public social agencies had a virtual monopoly on handling adoption cases. This monopoly position was premised in large part on an information asymmetry argument that neither birth parents anxious to resolve a problem nor adoptive parents anxious to obtain a child were in a strong position to identify the best adoptive arrangements for a particular child; this determination was best left to a neutral third party who could take into account the best interests of both sides and who didn't have any financial or other vested interest in the outcome. The knowledge on the part of workers and the lack of knowledge on

the part of birth mothers and adoptive parents is a clear case of information asymmetry with major program and policy implications.

More recently, other groups, primarily lawyers, have attempted to redefine an emerging market in placement of infants premised on the familiar principles of consumer demand. Those principles suggest that the adoptive parent is a kind of consumer who knows best what is desired or what kind of infant is wanted and that caveat emptor (let the buyer beware) is the proper standard by which to judge the transaction. The information assumption here contrasts markedly with the asymmetric assumption and also has program and policy implications. By assuming that birth mothers and adoptive parents both have sufficient knowledge to make informed decisions, the model dissolves away the rationale for limiting adoptions to nonprofit and public agencies without a vested or profit interest in the adoption decision. By changing assumptions, advocates of this view seriously undercut the information asymmetry aspects of the adoption process, including the idea of the neutral intermediary who should not stand to gain from the transaction.

Following out this example, one might suggest that social agencies rise as organizations under conditions where there are clear information asymmetries between workers and patrons over what to do with resources and with clients over where to find and use problem-solving resources. If patrons were clear and definite on how best to "help the poor" with their donations, for example, why would they need social workers? In the same vein, if clients already know where to find help and how to solve their own problems, why would they need social workers? The case for social service emerges when social workers and social agencies have, if not an outright monopoly, a strong relative advantage in their ability to locate clients in need and provide them with the assistance needed. Information asymmetry, in other words, may offer a useful tool for thinking through problems of organization in particular situations.

Some element of information asymmetry is present in virtually all organization technologies. There is always a difference between those who know how to do the job and those who do not. Information asymmetry is particularly evident in all arguments for professional service delivery. If your social worker does not know more than you—the client—about where and how to get help with your problems, then why exactly do you need a social worker? Likewise, if you aren't confident that an agency has a better handle on the needs of the community than you do, why would you donate your money to them, give them a grant, or endorse them to your legislator?

Each of these five approaches sheds a different kind of light on the problem of organization in social agencies. Organization never occurs in a historical vacuum; events always precede and follow from it. The transaction

cost argument addresses the fundamental question of whether there is a need for organization at all in particular circumstances. The constituency argument addresses the important issue of feasibility of organization in those same circumstances. Technology arguments address the effectiveness issue of whether what is cost effective and feasible may also be doable (that is, whether it falls within Thompson's generalized constraint of the possible). Finally, information asymmetry arguments examine the important question of whether organized service interventions are really necessary or the best way to proceed. These questions are vital to addressing the basic issues or organization in social agencies. Keeping them in mind, we next examine in greater depth the contributions of a number of different sources to understanding the general problem of organization and the important question of whether professional interventions are called for.

HOW TO ORGANIZE

There are a number of reasons for the strong upsurge in sociological interest in organizations since the middle decades of the twentieth century. Part of this interest is purely descriptive. Researchers and practitioners alike find satisfaction in the process of naming and exploring familiar aspects of organizational life. For decades, graduate students have shown great interest in applying labels such as co-optation, goal displacement, trained incapacity, and structural conflict to describe phenomena they recognize from their experiences with organizations. The study of organizations has produced more than simply a grab bag of useful labels, however.

Perhaps the single most important theoretical or conceptual reason was the translation of Max Weber's work on bureaucracy from German into English and the resulting increases in awareness and familiarity among American social scientists. The seminal work of Weber on organizations is extremely difficult to fit comfortably in any larger scheme of social or management theory. Although Weber was certainly cognizant of at least some of the practical implications of his bureaucratic ideal type (discussed below), his was a much more pure scholarly approach of formal sociological theory. It was written in a Germany that lagged seriously behind the United States, Britain, and France in its level of industrialization and still encompassed many of the medieval elements he denoted as traditional. Moreover, Weber wrote in German and is generally the only German-language source regularly included among the American management pantheon.[6]

Discussions of Weber in the social work management literature seldom do justice to these contextual realities or to the power and originality of his ideas. Social work sources are most likely to quote his three types of legitimate authority. Less commonly cited are the characteristics of bureaucracy

that he also identified. In the following section, we attempt to clarify and elaborate Weber's full model of bureaucracy. We emphasize not only its connection to legitimate authority but also the importance of rules, offices, qualifications, hierarchy, records, and careers. In general, we do not speak of a *bureaucracy* as an organization; instead, we use the simpler term *bureau* and reserve the term bureaucracy for a regime or social order characterized by bureaus, just as democracy refers to a regime of the people (demos).

Characteristics of Bureaucracy

According to Weber, bureaus consist of systems of fixed and official jurisdictions ordered by rules or laws or administrative regulations. Within a bureau, regular activities are distributed in fixed ways as official duties. Thus, a set of regulations is typically used to spell out standard operating procedures. A bureaucracy often covers a number of bureaus that relate like Warren's (1963) communities—horizontally and vertically—and also laterally. Within the bureaucracy, authority to give commands is distributed in a fixed way and is limited by rules concerning its uses. Such fixed distribution of authority in a bureaucracy often contrasts markedly with power and authority distributions in communities where such distributions are often more fluid and unpredictable. Within a bureau, provision is made for regular and continuous fulfillment of duties and execution of corresponding rights. This dual theme of rights and duties of everyone involved, including clients, is one of several fundamental and interrelated characteristics of bureaus in social service settings.

Weberian bureaucracy was grounded at least partly in Weber's historical studies of Chinese and ancient administration and emphasizes moral and merit criteria over power. Only persons having the regular qualifications are employed. Levels of authority in a bureaucracy are arranged so that higher levels of officials supervise the work of lower levels. According to Weber, effective functioning of the bureau relies upon files consisting of written records.

Bureaucracy in the Weberian sense also presupposes thorough and expert training. Management of the bureaucratic office follows general rules that are more or less stable, are exhaustive, and can be learned. Moreover, bureaus are not the habitat of dilettantes or sinecures. Bureaucratic activity, he says, "demands the full working capacity of the official irrespective of the fact that his obligatory time . . . must be firmly delimited." Further, from the viewpoint of the official, a bureaucratic position is a vocation or career. Thus, it is of interest here that the transition from charity organization societies into social service agencies was accompanied by the development of paid, full-time social service positions for social *workers*.

From the vantage point of the practice of social administration, the central characteristic of Weberian bureaucracy as a model of organization is the importance of rules, goals, and positions. There is also a strong anti-nepotism aspect of the Weberian model of bureaucracy that has been particularly important in the context of state and local governments once riddled with political patronage and corruption. The social administrator seeking to create an organization from a purely Weberian perspective would, therefore, seek first to establish a body of rational, coherent, and just policy and procedure much in the manner of what is known in social work today as *policy practice* (Flynn, 1992; Jansson, 1990).

The Neo-Weberians

The original partial translations of Weber's work into English in the 1940s increased familiarity among American sociologists, public administrators, and management scientists with Weberian ideas of organization. These ideas also provoked major new initiatives on the problem of organization by an interdisciplinary body of American scholars who have come to be identified as neo-Weberians, and who in many respects resemble the schools of management discussed in chapter 6. Most of the writings on organization in the social work literature fall within this purview. There is no clear, precise meaning to the term neo-Weberian. Different authors use it in different ways. Some have sought to identify with and elaborate upon Weber's basic model of the bureau as an organization within a bureaucracy or a large system of organizations, whereas others have sought to overturn and revise certain fundamental Weberian ideas. Others have applied it to the quest to get beyond hierarchical organizations.

Weber's model of bureaucracy as a legal–rational organization based upon rules is in marked contrast to the usual images of bureaucracy prevalent in American public life. In the United States, the concept of bureaucracy has long had negative connotations, unlike anything in the Weberian model. For serious study of all that can go wrong in bureaus, sometimes called *bureaupathology*, we must look to other neo-Weberian sources and in particular to Robert Merton. Merton (1952) published a now-classic essay, "Bureaucratic Structure and Personality," in which he addressed the dysfunctional side of bureaucratic organization. *Goal displacement*, he argued, is a more-or-less inevitable process in bureaucratic organizations by which means are transformed into ends in themselves. Thus, for a bureaupath, the proper completion of paperwork may be transformed from a necessary means to the key task of the job. Another enduring concept of Merton's work is the idea of *trained incapacity*, which refers to the ways in which organizations not only selectively encourage and socialize the learning of certain skills but discourage other learning. Merton also suggested a link between organizational characteristics and personality type, whereby submissive people may be more inclined to be concentrated in the lower echelons of organizations, and less competitive people may be more inclined toward government and nonprofit organizations.

Other possible connections between personality type and bureaucracy have been a fascination since Merton's time. The economist Anthony Downs (Downs & Rand Corporation, 1967) constructed a model of five ideal types of organizational role performers based on three factors: the nature of the position occupied, the probability of goal attainment, and psychological predispositions of personality:

1. *Climbers,* whose principal motivations are seeking additional income, power, and prestige
2. *Conservers,* whose primary orientations are a bias against any type of change in the status quo
3. *Zealots,* who are intensely loyal to a narrow set of particular interests
4. *Advocates,* who are loyal to a broader set of functions
5. *Statesmen,* who are proponents of the general welfare

The difficulty with applying the Downs model to real organizations, of course, is that one must take into account who is doing the reckoning. Within social work it may appear, for example, that advocates of particular interests are functioning as statesmen even as the same advocacy may appear to others in the community as zealotry. Moreover, in an age characterized by funding cutbacks, advocacy of the general welfare, other strenuous advocacy, and even zealotry may come across as a conserver's bias in favor of the status quo.

Classic Management

Management writers in the classical management tradition had been aware of and interested in organization as a method of domination through command and control since before Weber's work became widely known in the United States. Beginning in the 1870s, executives and management consultants, who were frequently engineers, developed a relatively large body of writings on organizations as command-and-control networks. In general, because of the consistent and narrow viewpoint of organizations as machines, this literature is seldom consulted today.

Chester Barnard was a management practitioner (chief executive officer of New Jersey Bell) writing in the late 1930s whose work departed dramatically from the classic, mechanistic tradition.[7] Barnard's best known work,

The Functions of the Executive (1938), was based on a series of lectures given in Boston in 1937. In that seminal work, Barnard defined organizations as "system(s) of consciously coordinated activities or forces of two or more persons" (p. 72). Formal organizations were "that kind of cooperation among men [sic] that is conscious, deliberate and purposeful" (p. 4).

The reader should take careful note of two aspects of these definitions. First, there is a very heavy social action dimension to Barnard's definition. Organizations are not machines. They are not merely environments or "structures." They are instead "consciously coordinated activities" involving "two or more persons." Second, as in Weber, the formality of formal organizations is said to arise from conscious awareness, deliberation, and purposefulness. There is also a strong component in Barnard's model of organizations that resonates with current ecological thinking in social work: "maintenance of an equilibrium of complex character in a continuously fluctuating environment of physical, biological and social materials, elements and forces" (p. 6).

Interestingly, in light of more recent developments in organization theory, Barnard's original conception of the formal organization included not only employees but also such stakeholders as investors, customers, suppliers, and others whose actions contributed to the goals as part of the organization per se. The original reviewers and later critics of Barnard's work greeted this view with criticism and suspicion. Even so, his solution has not been improved upon. One still faces the choice of either including stakeholders as members of the organization, as Barnard did, or excluding them as outsiders, as others have done.

Barnard is also the primary source in management theory of the emphasis on organizational goals and of related notions of efficiency and effectiveness. Discrepancies between individual motives and officially proclaimed organizational goals led Barnard to the notion of efficiency and effectiveness as central administrative concerns, although his approach to these two seminal ideas was somewhat different than contemporary approaches. If cooperation was successful and goals were attained, effectiveness in Barnard's sense was said to result. Efficiency, as defined by Barnard, was the degree to which individual motives were met. This was something that only individuals could determine. Note that although the words are the same, these definitions are miles apart from the quasi-engineering perspectives that inform parts of the accountability debate today.

Barnard (1938) also introduced the concept of informal organization, which he defined as "the aggregate of the personal contacts and interactions and the associated groupings of people" (p. 115). Virtually all writers agree that the informal organization is an important management consideration. However, there is little agreement over the exact nature of the role of informal relations in social administration. At least one source has attempted to use dramaturgical concepts to recast the informal organization as the "interpersonal underworld" (Kuypers & Alers, 1996). A notion of informal ties on the job subverting or undermining executive or managerial intent is an idea students will encounter frequently in various guises.

In his original formulation, Barnard attributed three functions to the informal organization: (1) communication among workers, (2) maintenance of cohesiveness by regulating willingness to serve, and (3) maintenance of workers' feelings and self-respect. Thus, if one is employed in an organization but feels largely out of the information loop, dissatisfied, and unwilling to take steps to get further involved, Barnard's perspective would implicate the informal organization of others around you.

Barnard (1938) singled out the executive function or executive work that "is not of the organization, but the specialized work of maintaining the organization in operation. . . . The executive functions serve to maintain a system of cooperative effort. They are impersonal" (p. 216). Three specific executive functions were singled out: (1) to provide a system of communication, (2) to promote the securing of essential personal efforts, and (3) to formulate and define purpose.

Central to Barnard's ideas of formal and informal organization, the executive, and his other insights on management was the process of communication. All activity in an organization was based on communication grounded in five principles:

1. "Channels of communication should be definitely known." (p. 175)
2. "Objective authority requires a definite formal channel of communication to every member of the organization." (p. 176)
3. "The line of communication must be as direct or short as possible." (p. 176).
4. "The line of communication should not be interrupted." (p. 179)
5. "Every communication should be authenticated." (p. 180)

Rational Choice Theory

Theoretically speaking, all of the administrative and decision sciences, including organization studies, social administration, the broader field of human services management, business management, public administration, and hospital administration all evolved out of a common theoretical base ultimately derived in part from Adam Smith's *Wealth of Nations* (1981). The real clue to this common origin, as distinctive in its own way as a set of DNA markers, is the continuing presence of several aspects of Smith's invention. The most relevant of these for our purposes is the signature influence of rational choice theory, sometimes labeled exchange theory, which is one of its main branches. Just as most psychosocial clinical perspectives betray their common origins in, or near, or in reaction to Freud, all administrative and decision sciences share this common origin in the work of Adam Smith.

The most immediate manifestation of rational choice assumptions for our purposes is the tendency to see all issues and decisions as involving tradeoffs between the advantages they bring (or the benefits) and the obligations (or burdens or costs). You know you have become a social administrator when your first thought in response to a long recitation of the advantages of a proposed change in organizational structure (or anything else) is to wonder what it will cost and whether the costs will outweigh the benefits.

Beginning in the 1940s and continuing up to the present day, public administration and other scholars have built upon and extended the Barnard view of organizations following the rational choice model. This approach later became the basis of the incentive theory of organizations, a view that has been influential among social work writers into the present. In this view, the organization as such is downplayed except as a behavioral environment in which self-interested organizational participants respond to incentives and disincentives. In the incentive theory tradition of rational choice theory, users are also likely to speak of burdens and benefits.

Rational choice in the 1950s was also the basis of efforts by George Homans (1961, 1968), Peter Blau (1962, 1967), and others to bring behavioral psychology to bear upon problems of organization. The exchange theorists generally worked within the behavioral psychology paradigm of rewards and punishments, thereby transforming the incentive theory paradigm subtly but importantly. There is a fundamental but subtle distinction to be made here. Rational choice theories generally are concerned with the notion of fair or just exchange in which, for example, a buyer and a seller exchange money for a good at an agreed-upon price. In this context, both are concerned with cost and benefit. Exchange theories since Homans (1968) have generally been built upon an operant conditioning model developed by B. F. Skinner that shifts the equation subtly but dramatically to a concern for rewards, such as benefits, and punishments that are not at all the same as costs. If they apply at all in rational choice, punishments might be thought of as extremely high costs. Ask yourself: If you have the money to buy a new car, do you think of yourself as being punished because you had to pay for it? Of course not, unless you paid way too much. Therein lies the essential difference between rational choice theory, concerned with costs and benefits, and exchange theory, concerned with rewards and punishments.

At the same time, exchange theorists have introduced several important new quasi-economic concepts into the discussion of organizations, including

- *Satiation,* or the diminished marginal utility that arises from repeated use of a reward and that diminishes its motivational appeal.
- *Scarcity,* or the inverse relationship between a good and its value and the principle of least interest, which suggests that the person least motivated to maintain a relationship is in the best position to control it. This is because they have the least to lose by the relationship's dissolution.
- *Norm of reciprocity,* which assumes that all giving people expect something in return, whether a material benefit or a symbolic benefit such as gratitude, allegiance, or support (Homans, 1968).
- *Power,* which was introduced into organization theory by Peter Blau (1956, 1962, 1967); French and Raven (1968), who are discussed briefly in chapter 17, later followed this up.

Exchange theory has been both directly and indirectly influential in organization theory. However, in recent years it has been largely abandoned in favor of other, more sophisticated brands of rational choice theory grounded in economics. The legacy of Adam Smith remains vital. In general, all academics and most practitioners of the administrative sciences today speak the lingua franca of rational choice theory whether or not they have any conscious awareness of its theoretical origins. It is in part because of this legacy and its remarkably strong dualistic tendencies toward seeing everything in pairs of exact opposites, such as costs and benefits, rewards and punishments, buyers and sellers, and so on, that we placed so much emphasis on the triadic exchange in chapter 3. Administrators do balance costs and benefits, and concepts such as the norm of reciprocity are also extremely useful. However, effective social administrators simply cannot make choices in an organization only by taking their own preferences into account. Such an administrator would be, in fact, an antisocial creature in that particular context, which Adam Smith, moral philosopher that he was, would have been the first to admit. Thus, a purely dualistic behaviorism is a completely inappropriate basis for understanding the rational choices involved in social service organizations.

A social behavioral or interactional model along the lines of George Herbert Mead's notion of role taking is a much more satisfactory way to approach social service decisions than the simple dualities of behaviorism.

Such an approach posits that administrators choose by taking the role of the other, by weighing the potential costs and benefits for those significant others alongside the potential costs and benefits for themselves and the agency: How will this affect patrons? How will this affect clients? How will this affect the agency? How will this affect me? In this way, although both patrons and clients *may* see things in dualistic terms (e.g., What can this agency do for me?), social administrators cannot. It is usually highly inappropriate and in at least some cases literally impossible in this situation to make decisions affecting social services and social agencies without considering the impact for patrons, clients, the agency, and the decision maker. All must be considered if decisions are to be rational choices.

Human Relations

At roughly the same time that Barnard was developing the view of organizations as systems of cooperation based in communications and before Weber's social action model was well known among American social scientists, another major management perspective was taking shape. Generally known as the human relations school or approach, it was an approach that sought to understand the problem of organization as a matter of organizing social relationships among workers rather than dictating the proper movements of the machine that is the human body.

Although the human relations approach to management is usually set in sharp contrast from classical management and scientific management, the human relations model of organization shares a great deal with Barnard. According to Bernard Neugeboren (1985), the human relations approach to organization is distinctive in four respects:

1. As in classic management, productivity is important, but productivity in the human relations view is socially determined. That is to say, individual performance is determined more by social norms that arise in the organizational context than by individual capacities, as in the scientific management approach.

2. Workers respond as much to symbolic and social rewards as to economic incentives. Individuals are motivated more by social approval, recognition, and status than by economic rewards.

3. There may be major limits on the role of the task structure of an organization that restrict its ability to achieve its mission. In particular, high specialization and very narrowly defined tasks may be dysfunctional. Satisfactions in work are more likely to come from performing and completing more integrated tasks.

4. As in Barnard, human relations holds up the importance of communication and leadership. Organizations are social units in which influences occur through participation and social processes. In contrast to classical and scientific management approaches, problems are solved not by ordering and forbidding or by study and redesign but through group process and consensus building.

ORGANIZATIONAL DESIGN

The quasi-military approaches of classic management would emphasize issuing detailed orders and closely controlling their implementation. In the Weberian model, the central accent is on rule making and following. In scientific management, organization flows organically from detailed study of the tasks to be completed and the rational recombination of those tasks into the most efficient forms. In the human relations approach, the importance of commands and rules is downplayed in favor of discussion and consensus. Each of these approaches is suggestive of particular approaches for managers to take in organizations: ordering and forbidding, making and enforcing rules, communicating, exercising incentives, and achieving consensus.

Mintzberg

One of the most thoroughgoing attempts to redirect organization models was formulated by Henry Mintzberg (1979). The structure of organizations, in his view, reflects both the division of work into tasks and coordination of these tasks necessary to get the work done and achieve the organization's mission. Mintzberg saw five distinct coordinating mechanisms at work in formal organizations: direct supervision, standardization of work, standardization of output, standardization of skills, and mutual adjustment or what others frequently call organizational politics. These coordination mechanisms, in his view, also linked to an environmental dimension. In particular, as the external control of an organization decreases, internal centralization and formalization tend to increase (Hasenfeld, 2000, p. 94). The traditional model of professional social work arising as it did out of the progressive era has tended toward a three-mechanism approach to coordination. Standardization of work and of output were recognized early to be difficult to achieve, and so the emerging profession of social work opted instead for emphasis on direct supervision and standardization of skills, which accounts for the strong emphasis on methods in social work education. At the same time, the progressive element in the social work model continues to encourage some types of mutual adjustment or coordination while discouraging others that get labeled organizational politics. Group cooperation is seen as a good thing when one is included, but indicative of cliques and conspiracies when one is left out.

One of the conventional approaches to internal differentiation within classic organization theory was the line-staff distinction that arose in the U.S. Navy between officers of the line who commanded ships and staff officers who coordinated services. Mintzberg argues for a five-part model instead, dividing organizations into their operating core, middle line, technostructure, support staff, and strategic apex. In the modern hospital, for example, the majority of physicians and nurses would be considered part of the operating core, and nursing supervision would largely define the middle line. The technostructure of the modern hospital is defined by the complex array of X-ray, magnetic resonance imaging, and computed tomography machines and other technology and the highly skilled workers necessary to operate them. Social work services along with various other allied health professions and clerical, janitorial, parking, and other services fall into the support staff category; hospital administration generally defines the strategic apex of the hospital organization.

The Mintzberg organizational model also identifies four analytical issues or design parameters. Organizations, he says, are divided into two distinct levels, positions and superstructures, and two distinct types of linkages, lateral linkages and vertical linkages. This latter distinction closely parallels the horizontal/vertical one by Warren noted in chapter 2. Positions are said to be made by specialization, formalization, and training. However promising, the Mintzberg approach to organizations appears to have had little demonstrable impact on how social administrators go about thinking about, planning, creating, or changing social agency organizations.

Departmentation

Alongside other more elegant approaches to organization is a long-standing commonsense perspective. One of the products of classical management approaches to the problem of organizing work is what might be termed the problem of departmentation, or devising an overall plan or scheme for dividing a large organization into meaningful subunits. Much of basic theory is not terribly useful in this regard. For example, it would hardly make sense to divide organizations along Weberian lines into those governed by rational authority, tradition, and charisma. So in many organizations, the following commonsense approaches have been used to deal with the problem of departmentation.

Departmentation by Numbers

The simplest form of organizational subdivision is to create a unit for each fixed number of employees. An example of this is the infantry squad composed of a specific number of riflemen, a radio operator, and a squad leader. Departmentation by number is probably only useful at the lowest levels of an organization when all of the major organizational problems are resolved at higher levels. The concept of departmentation by numbers corresponds well with the management research tradition of span-of-control research, which has generally held that there must be an ideal number of workers under direct supervision and has attempted to find that number. If, for example, six is the optimum number of workers for a supervisor to oversee, then that would be a good candidate for the ideal department size. As of the moment, the search for that ideal number goes on.

Departmentation by Function

The next-simplest approach to organization is to cluster, group, or relate people by similar activities, job, and task assignments. Thus, in the social service organization, the therapists, case managers, community organizers, and group workers might similarly be organized into special-function units.

Departmentation by Profession/Occupation

A variant on departmentation by function is grouping units by profession or training. The typical placement of social work services and many other allied health professions within health care is generally on the basis of departmentation by profession/occupation. In these cases, the social services unit is where the social workers are, and so on.

Line and Staff

There is a great deal of practical problem solving and common sense that enters into many departmentation schemes. For example, one of the most basic and universal is to divide organizations into those most concerned with the major goals of the organization, often called program or line units, and those providing various sorts of supportive services, often called support or staff units. It is important to note that there is no fixed designation of line and staff functions depending on the purpose of the organization. Thus, for example, a casework unit in a family service agency may be a programmatic or line unit closely related to the basic purposes of the organization. At the same time, a casework unit dealing with employee stress, for example, in a manufacturing corporation will almost certainly be seen as a staff or supportive unit. The line–staff distinction is a particularly important one in public agencies, where it is sometimes inscribed in public law. Although there is only a limited body of research evidence for this point, extensive experience with large state agencies suggests that line–staff conflict between in-house consultants and subject-matter experts in the central office and disbursed workers and supervisors "in the field" is a major issue in social administration (Dalton, 1950).

Departmentation by Territory

Public social service organizations with legally defined mandates within specific geographic boundaries are often subdivided into territorial units as well. Thus, agencies of the federal government are divided into ten standard, multistate federal regions, and state governments are basically territorial units with some measure of political sovereignty. What may not be obvious is that most nonprofit community social services also operate with some explicit or implicit territorial notions. This may be most obvious in the case of community mental health centers, where the 3,000-plus counties of the United States were divided into approximately 600 multicounty catchment areas. If you check the articles of incorporation and by-laws of most non-profit social services, however, you will probably find an explicit territorial mandate spelled out: "to provide services in the Roxbury neighborhood," "to serve the city of Morgantown," "to operate in the four counties of Washington, Adams, Jefferson and Madison," and so on. In the case of nonprofit organizations, however, those territorial distinctions seldom extend to departments.

Departmentation by Client Group

It is also possible to use client groups as the basis for organizing different work units within a social work organization. Thus, for example, there might be an aging department, an adolescent department, a children's department, a department for mentally retarded persons, and a department for chronically mentally ill persons.

Departmentation by Process or Technology

The simplest example of a social work organization organized by process would be one in which there was a management department and community organization, groupwork, and casework departments. More complex examples might incorporate units for adoptions, therapy, marital counseling, and so on.

Departmentation by Program

Most distinctive social service processes and technologies are freestanding. That is, the organization is not structured on the assumption that clients will ordinarily flow from adoptions to crisis intervention to marital counseling. As a result, departmentation by process in the above sense ordinarily translates into departmentation by program by default.

Departmentation by Product

This is one of the more common forms of departmentation in business. For example, the Chevrolet Division of General Motors makes cars and trucks and the Frigidaire Division makes refrigerators. This approach has been one of the least likely to appear in social services. However, it may be occurring more frequently in response to managed care, as social agencies strive to define their product lines more clearly. Applications of departmentation by product are dependent on determinations of what the "products" of particular services may be, and in the past most such distinctions easily broke down into distinctions of function, profession, client group, programs, or processes.

Ideas of departmentation taken from classic management in business have proven difficult to apply to social services settings. This has resulted in two additional forms of organization worthy of note.

Multiplex Organization

The multiplex organization is the organization design in which two or more of the above ideas have been combined. The larger the organization, in fact, the more likely it is that some combination will be necessary. Thus, a large public social services organization might use a line staff distinction to organize the executives in its central office into operating and consultative offices combined with a territorial organization of regional or county offices, each of which is subdivided into program units.

Constant Reorganization

Many social service settings, particularly in the public sector, have been in an almost constant state of reorganization at least since the 1970s. Managers continue to cast about for some elusive organization plan that will bring permanent harmony, justice, and prosperity to the organization. More recently, politicians have picked up on the political advantages of appearing to bring order to the chaos fostered by their predecessors, and health and human services units have often been singled out as easy targets for such symbolic reorganizations. As a result, each new administration in some states brings with it an allegedly dramatic new and improved model of organizations, which often looks suspiciously like an earlier model by the same political party several administrations earlier.

Matrix Organization

A matrix organization is like a multiplex organization in which two distinct principles of organization are operating simultaneously. One of these is the conventional organizational hierarchy of authority and responsibility. The other involves a pattern of task organization by project. The multiplex approach usually involves an ad hoc, custom-tailored solution to the organizational demands of a specific situation for which no theory, standards, or general principles have been identified. By contrast, there is significant literature detailing matrix organization, its justification principles, and uses (Benedetto & Benedetto, 1989; Delbecq & Filley, 1974; Kerzner & Cleland, 1985; Kingdon, 1973; Knight, 1977; Ryan & Washington, 1977; Venable, 1999; Walden, 1981).

The simplest way to visualize what a matrix organization might look like is to project the familiar phenomenon of multidisciplinary treatment teams on an organization-wide basis. The various professionals involved in such teams (social workers, psychiatrists, nurses, etc.) might all have a primary assignment with a disciplinary department (e.g., social services). However, whether or not the organization formally recognizes their involvement, participation in such a team constitutes a second dimension of organizational structure not easily accommodated by the conventional model of departmental hierarchies. The model of matrix organization, with its associated theories, constitutes an alternative organizational universe within which to talk and think about such possibilities. The model of matrix organization is especially suitable for highly professional organizations in which work groups built up around multidisciplinary or multidepartmental tasks or other project-based or time-limited work groups occur frequently. Matrix organizations must be seen along with the ubiquitous idea of nonhierarchical organizations as constituting major alternatives for debureaucratizing social agencies.

ORGANIZATIONAL CHANGE

Although we posed the problem of organizations in terms of creating new organizations, it is more often experienced in practice as a matter of changing existing ones. Charles Perrow (1973) summarizes this challenge rather nicely:

> If we cannot solve our problems through good human relations or through good leadership, what are we then left with? The literature suggests that changing the structures of organizations might be the most effective and certainly the quickest and cheapest method. However, we are now sophisticated enough to know that changing the

formal organization by itself is not likely to produce the desired changes. (reprinted in Carroll et al., 1977, p. 14)

How is such change to be effected?

According to the neo-Weberian bureaucratic model, as it has been influenced by work on decision-making and behavioral psychology, we should find out how to manipulate the reward structure, change the premises of the decision-makers through finer controls of the information received and the expectations generated, search for inter-departmental conflicts that prevent better inspection procedures from being followed, and after manipulating these variables, sit back and wait for two or three months for them to take hold. (reprinted in Carroll et al., 1977, p. 14)

Perrow goes on to say:

Management should be advised that the attempt to produce change in an organization through managerial grids, sensitivity training, and even job enrichment and job enlargement is likely to be fairly ineffective for all but a few organizations. . . . Of course managers should be sensitive, decent, kind, courteous and courageous, but we have known that for some time now, and beyond a minimal threshold level, the payoff is hard to measure. The various attempts to make work and interpersonal relations more humane and stimulating should be applauded, but we should not confuse this with solving problems of structure, or as the equivalent of decentralization or participatory democracy. (reprinted in Carroll et al., 1977, p. 13)

CONCLUSION

Much of the management interest in organizing might be characterized as the search for the one best way to organize particular activities. However, as Perrow suggests, not all organization researchers are convinced that there is a single best way of organizing. Reacting to the Woodward findings discussed earlier, Lawrence and Lorch (1967) concluded that there was no one best way. It depends on the organizational environment, including its market, technology, and other external demands from stakeholders. We refined this list somewhat into the five factors of historical legacy, transaction costs, constituency demands, available technology, and the distribution of information discussed above. Taking these five factors into account it is possible to generate many possible plausible solutions to just about any known organizational problem.

The sheer diversity of possible organizational models and approaches raises an interesting and troubling question, which has yet to receive a satisfactory answer. If, indeed, there is no one best way to organize social services and people manage on their own to find a variety of equally workable solutions through trial-and-error, what is the nature of the possible scientific contribution of the vast and rapidly growing body of organization studies? One plausible answer is simply interest. Large numbers of people in and around social administration find description and analysis of organizations an interesting topic to consider, and others find it interesting to research and write about them. Another answer is heuristic. The process of problem solving involved in each organization finding its own best ways is undoubtedly furthered by comparison and discussion of the experiences of others. Finally, it is important to note that there is a very powerful scientific argument involved here as well. Although we suspect Lawrence and Lorch are correct that there is no one best way to organize, no one can say with any scientific certainty that such a null hypothesis is correct. It is, in fact, only by subjecting the possibility of such best ways to continued testing that we can have any certainty that the best ways have not yet been found.

In light of the limit suggested by Lawrence and Lorch, it may be well to end this chapter with a note of caution and, perhaps, a cautious prediction. The social service agency—the nonprofit organization or public bureau with a mandate for social service delivery—was *the* distinctive form of social service delivery throughout most of the twentieth century. Whether it will remain so in the twenty-first century is a very open question. The economic and political conditions associated with managed care, welfare reform, devolution, private practice, and technology all have the potential for bringing about massive changes in the organization of social services. Whether they will do so or not remains to be seen. What is at issue in each case is the question of whether traditional forms of social agency will be sufficient for the new century. Or will social administration need to develop greater concern for finding more appropriate organizational and institutional forms and structures for organizing social service practice in a new age? And whether that question has one answer or many depends on the results of further study.

Elements of Social Administration

In the next three chapters, we examine in greater detail three of the four major elements of social administration as they were identified in chapter 1. Chapter 5 discusses the elements of leadership and decision-making. Chapter 6 examines the basic process of management and a number of conventional approaches to management thinking known as classic management, scientific management, human relations, and an eclectic mixture of more recent management ideas. Chapter 7 is also devoted to management, looking at a number of self-contained models that we call the *management-bys*. The fourth element of social administration, institution building, is the subject of chapter 8, which introduces part III on institution building topics.

Leadership and Decision Making

In chapter 1, we noted that a large part of the historic and contemporary leadership of the social work profession and social welfare came from social administrators, but only Jane Addams and Mary Richmond and a few others were mentioned. That list might also have included at least the following names (and a great many more recent names besides):[1] Edith and Grace Abbott, Charles Loring Brace, Z. R. Brockway, Frank Bruno, Bradley Buell, Ida M. Cannon, Wilbur Cohen, Edward T. Devine, Arthur Dunham, Ophelia S. Egypt, Martha Eliot, Fedele Fauri, Ruth Fizdale, Homer Folks, Lester Granger, Jane Hoey, Harry Hopkins, Donald Howard, Wallace Kuralt, Julia Lathrop, Katherine Lenroot, Richard Lodge, Josephine Shaw Lowell, Leonard Mayo, Frances Perkins, Mary Switzer, Graham Taylor, Lillian Wald, Forrester Washington, Ernest Witte, and Benjamin Youngdahl.

Given such a list of social work leaders who were also social administrators and the history of community and professional leadership they represent, it seems fair to ask, What do social administrators actually do as leaders? A major part of the answer to that question is to provide organizational and community leadership, but what exactly does this mean? Leaders are engaged in defining the vision, mission, and goals of social services. They

work in strategy formulation within communities, and in the policy arena, they work within organizations and programs and in the social work profession. Another important part of that answer is that such leaders also identify and facilitate critical decision making on matters of policy, strategy, program, and operations.

There are close relationships among all of the key terms of administrative practice theory. This is a situation that can sometimes be confusing for beginning students. Perhaps no greater confusion is to be found than between the terms *administration* and *leadership*. This is one of those cases (that seem to abound in the social sciences) where a lack of careful definition is combined with a large community of teachers, researchers, and practitioners who appear to know what they mean and seem able to function in the midst of ongoing semantic confusion. Thus, there is very little incentive to clear things up, and the novice student has little choice but to try to come to terms with the underlying ideas in all their unruly profusion. In this case, there is little to be done about the major overlaps between the leadership and management literatures except to recognize and come to terms with it.

In the opening chapters of this book, we suggested that social administration was closely associated with leadership in the social work profession and social services in communities and organizations. In this chapter, we try to tease out the distinctive place of leadership in an administered organization led by social administrators and its environment.

The task will not necessarily be easy. For at least some people, administration and leadership are quite different entities. For others, leadership is synonymous with administration. For example, William H. Newman (1951) defined administration in terms of "the guidance, *leadership,* and control of the efforts of a group of individuals toward some common goal" [emphasis added] (p. 1). Ralph C. Davis (1951) spoke for a good portion of management professionals when he defined management even more forthrightly as "the function of executive leadership."

More recently, Peter Drucker, Peters and Waterman, and others have popularized a similar conception of management in which executive leadership is conceived principally in terms of the unique role of defining and holding organized institutions to their mission (Drucker, 1990; Peters, 1997). There is some research support for this connection. A study of executive leadership in nonprofit organizations by Heimovics, Herman, and Coughlin (1993) found that effective executives work to revitalize the missions of their organizations. Henry Mintzberg (1989) specifically spoke of "missionary zeal" in nonprofit leaders as an element in maintaining workforce commitment to the organization's mission. The question of whether the good administrator is a technical wizard, conversant with budgets and schedules;

a legal sage, conversant with policies and procedures; or a spell-binding zealot, able to dispense ample doses of that missionary zeal (or all of the above) is anything but an idle one. A study of leadership by Charles Glisson (1989) involving 319 individuals in forty-seven workgroups of twenty-two different human service organizations supports the view that the primary purpose of leadership is to affect the climate of the organization so that workers are empowered, excited, and inspired about the goals and mission of their organizations.

This is not to suggest that leadership is merely cheerleading or that social administrators are the only locus of leadership in social services or the social work profession. We can identify at least four other important groups that figure prominently among social work leaders:

1. *Community elite members.* Those who serve on boards of directors, as trustees for foundations, and in other key roles are in a position to influence the future and direction of social services. In many communities today, social work and social services attract relatively little interest or support from the very rich, old line families, large-corporate chief executive officers, and others of the highest levels of community elites. Those elites are nonetheless still found in support of museums, symphonies, and other vaguely identified "charitable" causes (Ostrower, 1997). What elite support for social services there may be tends to come mainly from business, educational, religious, labor, and other such "second tier" community leaders.

2. *Senior clinicians.* Because of their extensive experience, specialized training, sound judgement, or other qualifications, senior clinicians are regularly consulted or included in the making of critical decisions about personnel, programs, and other important matters. Social work is relatively lacking in institutional supports and recognition of the leadership role played by nonadministrative senior staff. Yet it is clear that many clinicians routinely perform such leadership roles.

3. *Social work educators.* Because of their involvement as consultants, planners, and evaluators and expectations of community or public service, combined with their prior work experience, social work educators can be found among the leadership of many contemporary social services.

4. *Client populations.* There is a genuine leadership dimension to ongoing efforts toward empowerment that is responsible for a constant, if small, pool of clients; former clients as well as some of their friends, neighbors, and family members are among the ranks of social service leaders. As most social work educators quickly become aware, a significant minority of social work students—and, therefore, professionals—are former clients whose prior experiences with social work were one of the factors that influenced their career and professional choices.

The focus here on involvement of social administrators in social service and professional social work leadership is not intended to disparage or downplay the importance of any of these other categories of leaders, who are often ranked among the most important stakeholders of social agencies. It is important to point out, however, that so long as there is the kind of commitment in the social work profession to the central role of the social agency in service delivery, social administrators will continue to be included regularly among the leadership of the profession and of social services at all levels.

Interestingly, social work education has paid only limited attention to leadership studies arising from many different directions. Leadership studies in social science were first undertaken by management researchers in an attempt to isolate the elements of successful administrative leadership. Somewhat later, social psychologists interested in group leadership as an element of small group behavior also began studying leadership. The overlaps between these two research traditions are not always easily resolved. One of the clearest cases of this involves the strong preference that has arisen in social work for democratic over laissez-faire or autocratic leadership. Yet, ironically, the principal studies from which this terminology and preference are both derived are from the small group and not the organizational literature (Lewin, Lippitt & White, 1939). It is far from clear that behavior considered democratic in the limited-term, face-to-face context of small groups will be appropriate, feasible, or even legal as administrative leadership in many large organizational settings.

More recently, the issue has been addressed from many additional angles, including anthropological, political science, and psycho-historical, and other perspectives (Bargal & Schmid, 1989). The result has simply been a profusion of leadership research with unreconciled outcomes; one of the principal issues at present, as in the case of organizational studies, is attempting to make sense of this plethora of contradictory material. One approach to making sense of it has been to distinguish those studies that have identified situational traits or theories of leadership from personal trait studies that have focused on the personality traits of leaders.

One key aspect of the professional leadership challenge facing social administrators in social work in the new millennium is tension between what might be termed *administrative realism* and *clinical romanticism*.[2] Although social administrators have tried to perfect their use of the tough-minded realism of general management, most clinical practitioners prefer to speak what Brown (1989) calls "the discourse of romanticism and humanism." The latter appears to be a language well suited for describing subjective feelings and moral obligations in ways that the discourse of macro practice often cannot reach. Nevertheless, clinical discourse also appears singularly ill suited to address the issues necessary to effectively guide policy and practice beyond the level of the individual case. This is as true of vigorously psychosocial perspectives and the recent dialogues over empowerment as it is of the most traditional intra-psychic "depth psychologies."

The challenge facing social work leadership is not one of rejecting either the flinty realism of social administration or the romantic–humanism of clinical practice. Instead, it is necessary to critically understand both and to find ways of combining them into what Brown (1989) calls "a more comprehensive language of public life that respects systems efficiency as well as moral agency, and thereby allows persons to act responsibly as citizens governing their politics" (p. ix). This is perhaps a fair summary of the central leadership challenge facing social administrators as leaders in the profession in the near term future. But this is not a unique challenge for social work in striving to bring together macro and micro perspectives within a unified profession. It is also a general challenge for public life.

LEADERSHIP AS DEFINING PURPOSE

For the classic management and scientific management approaches of the late nineteenth century, leadership was not a particularly important or even a mildly interesting issue. Within their mechanistic models of organization, secure domination, and class privilege, leadership referred simply to the exercise of command. To the extent it was considered at all, leadership was typically conceptualized in quasi-military terms, easily summed up in the phrase "command and control." Beginning in the 1920s and gradually coming to maturity in the human relations studies of the 1930s and later group process research, however, was a completely new vision of administrative leadership. Daniel Wren (1994) neatly summed up this change as follows: "Leadership would no longer be based on power but on the reciprocal influence of leader on follower and follower on leader in the context of the situation. The primary leadership task was defining the purpose of the organization" (p. 263).

One of the key figures in this transition away from the power–control–domination model of leadership was Mary Parker Follett, a celebrated business management and political theorist whose career began as a vocational counselor at Boston's Roxbury Neighborhood House.[3] According to Follett, a leader should

> make his[4] co-workers see that it is not his purpose that is to be achieved, but a common purpose, born of the desires and the activities of the group. The best leader does not ask people to serve him, but the common end. The best leader has not followers, but men and women working with him. (Follett, Fox & Urwick, 1973, p. 262)

This task of translating the leader's purposes into group purposes or, conversely, of adoption of the group's purposes by the leaders remains one of the essential components of leadership and organization. This new model of leadership, for which Follett became the voice, had built into it a fairly heavy training burden akin to the many burdens of teaching new ways of relating that social work has faced in the past century. If managers were to come to understand that the exercise of leadership involved more than simple command and control, they would have to learn entirely new ways of relating to one another and to their workers. Implicitly, the need to train managers in this new approach also recognized the limits of the approach. Follett understood that simply exhorting business executives to give up the old ways of command and control and adopt a completely new style of leadership was unlikely to succeed. So she called for more research on leadership and decision making and for development of a new "motive of service to the community." Follett's model of leadership became an essential component of the "management is management" viewpoint. Together, she thought, the combination of scientific knowledge and service would form the basis of a new profession of management that would serve the best interests of society (Wren, 1994, p. 263). Follett's ideas of the importance of community service were influenced by and, in turn, an influence on the practice of social administration.

Follett's distinction of domination and leadership became one of the standard reference points of modern leadership studies. The style of leadership she advocated has become known variously as participative, democratic, and group-centered. It is ordinarily contrasted with the domination approach of command and control that is also known as directive, authoritarian, and autocratic. Perhaps no single issue has attracted greater attention from researchers on leadership than the contrast of these two leadership styles.

A good deal of research on administrative leadership in the past several decades has addressed primarily the internal organizational perspective and has done so in the wake of the transition away from models of leadership by domination pointed to by Follett nearly seventy years ago. Explorations of leadership outside the organization—and in particular studies of community, policy, and professional leadership—have generally fallen outside the paradigm of social administration. Although a large body of interesting and potentially relevant work exists in these areas, it is outside the parameters of this work.[5]

Much of the existing management research on leadership can be organized under two headings: behavioral theories and situational theories. There is another body of work that addresses traits of the leader, such as height, physical appearance, or intelligence, that has produced little worthy of note here. Much of this latter tradition is derived from the nineteenth-century essay by Thomas Carlyle that laid out his "great man" theory of history. Most of the leadership traits research suffers from methodological problems associated with predicting a variable from a constant. For example, even if leaders are more likely to be highly intelligent, tall, and good-looking, we are still faced with the task of explaining why all intelligent, tall, good-looking people aren't leaders as a result of these characteristics. Friedmann (1973) was reacting specifically to the Carlyle tradition of leadership traits when he observed that an administrative leader is not a great man imposing his will upon an organization, but a facilitator who stimulates others.

In the late 1950s, Tannenbaum and Schmidt proposed a continuum of behavioral leadership styles from "boss-centered" to "subordinate-centered." At one end was the familiar autocratic leader attempting to lead by domination that Follett had sought to relegate to the dustbin of history, and at the other end was the employee-centered leader that she had endorsed (Tannenbaum & Schmidt, 1958, 1973). In between was moderation. Within the social work management literature, Lewis and Lewis (1983) interpret the 1973 Tannenbaum–Schmidt continuum as moving toward greater recognition of environmental factors and downplaying the contrast between authoritarian and participative leaders in favor of a more behavioral approach of managers who make decisions single-handedly and those who favor group decisions.

Discussions of leadership have continued to vacillate between the contrast of polar opposite types in Follett's original distinction and proposed continua where the opposites shade into each other, as in the Tannenbaum–Schmidt approach. In a somewhat different recent contrast, Bombyk and Chernesky (1985) call the control option the alpha style of leadership that emphasizes rationality, task orientation, hierarchical structures, and direct manipulation of the environment. The alternative model, which they call the beta style, is characterized by a concern for sharing resources, collective problem solving, and interdependent, cooperative relationships. Another common approach to much the same set of issues involves distinguishing between *instrumental leadership* that like Bombyk and Chernesky's alpha is task oriented, and *expressive leadership* that is more relationship oriented. There is also a frequently remarked upon tendency in the social work literature that is very supportive of an expressive view of leadership, which views leadership as an extension of direct service provision (Applegate, 1988).

Another well-known series of leadership studies by Ralph Stogdill and colleagues (1974) that began at Ohio State University during the 1940s replaced the continuum with two discrete leadership factors, each of which could be high or low. One factor was termed *initiating structure* to delineate the leaders' clear organizational patterns and methods, and the other was *consideration,* or the use of supportive, relation-oriented behavior. The Stogdill approach projected leadership in terms of a linear regression line across a two-by-two table such that high initiating structure was directly proportional to low consideration and vice versa.

One of the somewhat ironic effects of Stogdill's work was to intensify the search for the personality traits associated with leadership: Stogdill associated leadership with the capacity for judgment and the verbal skill of the leader. Others pointed to intelligence and a host of additional personal factors as equally important. Additional others have pointed to physical traits like height and physical appearance. Despite great searching, however, no one has yet definitively identified the traits or characteristics of the successful leader, for reasons already noted. That there are huge ranges of interesting traits that provide partial correlates of leadership, however, is not to be doubted.

By the late 1970s, Hersey and Blanchard (1977) proposed in the third edition of *Management Effectiveness* what may be the ultimate situational leadership model to date. They offered a complex situational model in that leadership effectiveness was said to have a curvilinear relationship with both high relationship and high task orientations. Producing effective leadership, then, depended on the "maturity" (that is, willingness to cooperate with the leader) level of the followers. The implications of this train of thought are, of course, completely subversive of the entire tradition of leadership studies: Leadership may be entirely dependent on characteristics or actions such as the willingness of followers to follow. It may simply be the case not only that leaders are made rather than born, but also that they are not self-made but are made leaders by their followers. The issue may not be as simple as that, but leadership studies in the wake of Hersey and Blanchard have clearly found room to accommodate the impact of followers upon leaders into their perspectives.

By the 1960s, the linear approach of Stogdill had evolved in another direction into the managerial grid theory of leadership put forth by Robert Blake and Jane Mouton (1964, 1978). Blake and Mouton termed their two leadership factors *concern for production* and *concern for people* and used these two dimensions as the core of a management theory of organizational leadership presented in the form of a nine-by-nine grid. Although the grid produces an overwhelming eighty-one theoretical gradations of leadership, most interpretations concentrate on only five: authority–obedience (9,1 or high production/low people), impoverished management (1,1 or low production/low people), organization man management (5,5 or moderate production/moderate people), country club management (1,9 or low production/high people), and team management (9,9 or high production/high people).

Within social work, leadership continua have often been interpreted as similar to task versus process orientations of leaders or as job-centered and employee-centered leadership (Lewis & Lewis, 1983, p. 119). Reddin (1970) proposed a third situational dimension of effectiveness. He argued that in some situations, task- or job-centered leadership may be called for, whereas in others employee- or relationship-centered leadership may be more appropriate.

Lewis and Lewis (1983) summarize the situational approach as one in which "the leader should adapt his or her style to the follower's needs" (p. 123). Fred Fiedler's (1967) contingency theory of leadership offered up one pathway to such adaptation. According to Fiedler, leadership is dependent upon three situational variables: leader–follower relations, the structure of tasks or work to be completed, and the positional power of the leader. Fiedler concluded that task-oriented leaders are most effective at the extremes: very good or very poor relations with followers, very structured or very unstructured tasks, and a very strong or very weak power position. By contrast, employee-oriented or relationship-oriented leaders are likely to provide more effective leadership in between the extremes.

The Hersey–Blanchard focus on maturity may have encouraged Hasenfeld and Schmid (1989) to propose a life cycle perspective of organizational change and adaptation in that one of the key purposes of administrative leadership is to harness the forces of growth and arrest the forces of decline. At any rate, they concluded that the success of administrative leadership depends on its ability to make necessary adjustments in relations with the environment, the internal structure, and the service delivery system.

Taken together, these and literally hundreds of other leadership studies suggest that one of the fundamental aspects of leadership upon which social administrators should concentrate involves efforts toward the shaping and molding of a work environment that is conducive both to achieving the purposes for which the organization was created and to maintaining employee morale. They also suggest, however, that the exercise of real leadership may be a maddeningly elusive task for which no cookbook recipes or exact behavioral guidelines exist.

Decades ago, Charles Perrow (1973) noted:

> The burning cry in all organizations is for "good leadership," but we have learned that beyond a threshold level of adequacy it is extremely difficult to know what good leadership is. The hundreds of scientific studies of this phenomenon come to one general conclusion: Leadership is highly variable or "contingent" upon a large variety of im-

portant variables such as the nature of the task, size of the group, length of time the group has existed, type of personnel within the group and their relationships with each other, and amount of pressure the group is under. (reprinted in Carroll, Paine & Miner, 1977, p. 14)

Things have not changed dramatically in the ensuing decades.

Bargal and Schmid's (1989) recent review of this and other leadership research found four recent themes:

1. The leader as the creator of organizational culture
2. The leader as a creator of vision and a strategic architect
3. Leadership and followership as distinct organizational "moments"
4. An emphasis on what they called transformative and transactional types of leadership

However hard it may be to isolate, the primary task of leadership remains defining the mission and purpose of the organization (Wren, 1994, p. 263). In chapter 6, we describe how this process of definition is the crucial first step in a long chain of institution-building actions. In chapter 8, we examine how more recent management thinkers, particularly Peter Drucker, wove this basic insight into the model of management by objectives.

MULTIPLE ROLES OF LEADERSHIP

Chester Barnard, whose work on organizations was examined earlier, was one of the first to concentrate upon the role of leadership in management. According to Barnard (1938), moral leadership is the moving creative force in organization. By focusing on morality, Barnard's view is ultimately quite compatible with Follett's view. The problem has always been (and remains) discerning how such moral leadership is to be exercised and determining the status of morality under conditions of conflict or controversy. Some progress is made on this score in the model of moral entrepreneurship set forth by Rapp and Poertner (1992). Hasenfeld (2000, p. 100) interprets their view as consistent with the new institutionalism in organization theory.

Much of the leadership literature has evaded such difficult questions entirely through various functional or efficiency-oriented perspectives. Boris and Fiedler (1976), like many others, distinguished between task- and relationship-oriented leaders. Baumheir (1982) spoke for the task-centered perspective, when he concluded that factors that promote staff efficiency and effectiveness are directly related to leadership behavior.

Executive Group as Institutionalized Leadership

In smaller organizations that are plentiful in social services, leadership responsibility is likely given to a single administrator. Whether in the small organization or large, the position of chief executive officer in human service organizations is critically important for the development of effective social services. Yet, the requirements and expectations of this position have received little attention in the social work literature. In one study, Michael Austin (1989) identified motivation of personnel, production technology, resource mobilization, and goal-oriented planning and organizational development as key expectations of chief executive officer leadership.

In larger organizations, such leadership roles are likely to rest with a group that can be termed the *executive team* or *executive group*. The function of an executive group, according to Chester Barnard, is to reconcile conflicting individual interests, ideas, and purposes in order to ensure the survival of the organization as a whole. Iain Mangham (1986) argues that such a reconciliation is a complex matter of interactions within the group, involving subtle forces of individual and collective power, passion, and performance.

Leadership from Middle Management

Within the social service organization, leadership is seldom the exclusive preoccupation of top management. Realistically, defining the mission and direction of an organization is not as simple as the board passing a resolution or the chief executive approving a memorandum. What might be termed the message of the mission must be communicated effectively throughout the organization, translated into operational terms in each of the various units, and understood and accepted by all employees. Those tasks are the unique province of leadership by middle management.

Michael Austin (1988) captured much of the essence of middle management leadership in the concept of *managing up*. The premise here is that helping the executive to perform his or her job is one method for gaining help and appropriate recognition in carrying out the middle management job. Five basic components are said to define managing up:

1. Advocating for the needs of subordinates in relationship to career development, meritorious performance, and environmental and social needs
2. Influencing agency policy by proposing changes in the way the organization functions
3. Influencing agency program development by proposing new program directions and identifying implementation strategies
4. Influencing agency leadership and providing constructive feedback
5. Enhancing the capacity of top management to receive and utilize input from middle managers who seek to manage up as well as the

capacity of middle managers to view the managing up process as enhancing their career development

CREATION OF ORGANIZATIONAL CULTURE

A good deal of recent work has addressed the issue of organizational culture (Boisot, 1995; Cole, 1996; Erve, 1993; Johnson, 1998; Smith & Peterson, 1988; Westoby, 1988; Zucker, 1988). Yet, there is no exact methodology for creating or changing organizational culture. Everything that is said and done within the organization has a potential impact, but some things are clearly more important than others. Over time, organizations come to be characterized by certain ways of doing things. Some of these considerations are matters of uses of the informal organization such as special luncheons on staff members' birthdays or rotating responsibility for bringing in doughnuts. In such cases, there may be little the astute social administrator can do beyond encouraging or discouraging such activities and participating in others. Other ways of doing things are matters of direct administrative concern. For example, it is a point of pride in a number of social service organizations that meetings must operate informally without parliamentary procedures and with decisions reached only by consensus. But when that informality extends to meetings regularly beginning ten to fifteen minutes late because one or two key staff members cannot get there on time, while the rest of the staff must sit and wait for them, there may be important issues of productivity involved that require administrative leadership.

Long experience with the social services suggests that social workers almost always express an interest in a warm, supportive organizational culture where clients feel welcome and workers feel valued. The challenge that this brings to the social administrator is that of realizing the mission and purposes of the organization within such a supportive environment.

CREATION OF VISION AND STRATEGY

Organizational culture and the internal environment of an organization generally can become an overwhelming, almost oppressive, influence upon workers and block out awareness of other factors. The community environment can easily recede into the background. Operational routine takes over, and people find themselves "just doing their jobs," almost mindlessly indifferent to the larger issues that are always of greatest concern to the various stakeholders in the community. Thus, one of the constant challenges for social administration leaders involves reminding social service workers and volunteers of the continuing importance of the outside world of clients, supporters, opponents, and the full range of significant others. In particular in social services, where educational, social class, and other factors can have corrosive effects on workers and volunteers, who can come to believe that the agency exists to serve their needs, constantly holding up the vision of "a service orientation" and the strategic standard that "the needs of the clients come first" can be particularly important.

It is sometimes said that without followers, there are no leaders. One of the surest signs of good leadership in social administration is to have workers who feel supported by the organizational culture and are supportive of the vision and strategic direction of the leadership. However, the leader–follower relationship is not entirely unidirectional. Administrative leadership is much easier to deploy in situations where workers are already accustomed to responding to effective leadership. By contrast, providing administrative leadership will be equally difficult in chaotic situations where leadership and direction have been missing and in those situations characterized by domination and tight control.

Leadership in social service organizations can be particularly crucial under conditions of sudden and dramatic change, such as those posed by managed care and welfare reform. Indeed, it is well understood that an administrator's response to crisis can determine whether the crisis will be a disastrous or strengthening experience (Alwon, 1980). Yet, there is no clear consensus in the leadership literature on what types of action represent the most effective forms of leadership under conditions of change.

LEADERSHIP AND DECISION MAKING

Programmatic or goal-oriented leadership oriented toward defining and operationalizing an organization's mission is, however, not a sufficient conception of leadership in social services. A second major component of leadership is identification of critical decisions and facilitation of satisfactory decision making. One of the key leadership tasks in decision making is seeing that issues get fully identified and defined. Terry (1998), for example, contends that leadership depends on framing issues correctly and calling forth authentic responses. Michael Austin (1989) frames this issue in terms of Drucker's (1974) distinction between managers who focus on efficiency by "doing things right" and leaders who focus on effectiveness by "doing the right things." Effective leaders, he argued, appear able to put seeking to "know why" ahead of "knowing how" and to engage in both problem finding and problem solving.

What distinguishes decision making from other forms of human behavior and social action? An example of immediate relevance in any management context might be differentiating decisions from the announcements and directives through which those decisions may be implemented. In an important behavioral sense, making decisions is simply answering questions. Such a view of decisions as questions is directly applicable to the leadership perspective. A good leader will ensure that good decisions get made, and one way to ensure good decisions is to ask good questions. Sometimes both in groups and in agencies the single most important element in the quality of decision making can be making sure that the group or organization is asking the right question. Should we hire this person? Does she deserve a raise? Is this program effective? The first two of these questions will almost inevitably result in decisions, one way or another. Though there may be no obvious decision immediately connected to the third question, if the answer is that the program is not effective, it is likely to set in motion a chain of further questioning about what should be done to make the program effective.

One of the most important practice abilities that good social administrators have is an ability to recognize the circumstances when decisions are necessary, to formulate decision points or questions out of general discussion, and to stick with issues until decisions get made. More than anything else, this requires an ability to ask the right questions and to ask them at the right times and of the right people.

Timing is another important element in decision making. A question that is merely a matter of idle interest at one moment may become a matter of great urgency at a later date. Generally speaking, in social administration earlier is better than later, and learning to anticipate the need for a decision goes with the territory. Some of the literature on decision making refers to such moments as *decision points*.

In another sense, however, administrative decisions are more than simply answers to questions. It is this sense that allows us to differentiate, for example, between the question of whether to hire a job applicant and the question of whether board members like jelly doughnuts. Generally speaking, in social administration decisions are those questions whose answers have real or potential consequences for stakeholders. Simply speaking, stakeholders are the people who matter or should matter to decision makers. It is for this reason that many people like to refer to decisions as addressing or resolving *issues* rather than simply questions. Issues in this sense are questions in context, whose answers have consequences (or different stakes) for others. Thus, the term *stakeholder*.

The work of Herbert Simon, beginning with the publication of the first edition of *Administrative Behavior* in 1947, was a hallmark in the development of understanding the role of decisions in administrative leadership. Simon placed decision making at the forefront of administrative behavior, placing administration in a dynamic, proactive, action-oriented posture.

Even as he did so, however, he seriously undercut the rationalist model of decision making as necessarily following careful definition, complete fact gathering, and full identification and consideration of all alternatives. In doing so, Simon pointed toward a revised psychological model of administrators. What might be called the "all-wise" model of classic rationality, as found in the economic model of maximization, was replaced with a view of administrators as chronically short of the necessary knowledge, information, time, money, and mental ability to make perfect decisions and able to make only the best decisions their limited intellects and resources would allow under a specific set of circumstances.

"Whereas economic man supposedly maximizes—selects the best alternative from among all those available to him—his cousin, the administrator, *satisfices*—looks for a course of action that is satisfactory or 'good enough'" (Simon, 1997, p. 119). Simon called the selection of good-enough or satisfactory alternatives *satisficing*, in contrast to the pursuit of the best possible alternative known in economics as maximizing. Since the time of the first edition in 1947, there has been nearly universal agreement that Simon made an accurate behavioral finding. Real administrators in all fields do, in fact, typically act in precisely this manner. They tend to choose the first "good enough" alternative they are able to identify, rather than holding out for the very best alternative.

More controversial, however, was Simon's suggestion, unfortunately termed *muddling through* in a later journal article by Charles Lindblom (1959), that choosing the satisfactory solution rather than holding out made good administrative and human sense. In fact, full-blown rational decision making was probably not possible in most administrative cases since it was beyond the mental capabilities of mere humans, and even when it appeared possible, it might not produce noticeably better results than satisficing. In fact, it might simply produce inconsistent or conflicting results.

It is now more than half a century since Simon first put forth this view of administrative decision making and the resultant form of decision-making behavior it encourages. In that time, it has been complained about, objected to, and argued against, but his initial premise that this is how decisions are actually made (and since repeated by countless others, with important refinements by James Thompson, Charles Lindblom, James Brian Quinn, and many others) has not been directly refuted. The essential Simon insight—that the key administrative act is decision making—remains.

H. Igor Ansoff divides what he terms *total decision space* into three classes or domains: strategic, administrative, and operating. Strategic decisions address selection of product-market opportunities. Administrative decisions are concerned with the organization, acquisition and development of resources, and operating decisions have to do with budgeting, scheduling, supervision, and control of resources (Moore, 1992, p. 18). Derek F. Abell found in studies of businesses that a unit's strategic plan comprises three classes of decisions: definitional decisions that in social services would involve mission and goals, but also client groups, anticipated outcomes, and the like; decisions about objectives; and functional strategy decisions (how to do it) (Moore, 1992, p. 108).

Not every decision is of equal importance. This was made clear in one of the most important works on administrative leadership, by Philip Selznick (1957). In this slim volume entitled *Leadership in Administration,* Selznick introduced the idea of *critical decisions,* which he says are "decisions affecting institutional development" that "help to shape the key values in an organization, and especially the distribution of power to affect those values" (pp. 56–57). Critical decisions are distinguished from routine ones, in part, by the important matter of *precedent.* Thus, policy-making decisions that set precedents for future decisions are distinguished from policy-serving ones (that follow or adhere to those precedents).

Selznick cites four particular examples of such critical decisions:

1. Recruitment of key personnel
2. Training of key personnel
3. A system for representation of internal group interests
4. Cooperation with other organizations

CONCLUSION

When these ideas of critical decisions are combined with those of the previous section, what emerges is a model of administrative leadership in which leadership is focused upon the mission, goals, vision, and strategy of the organization as realized through the making of critical decisions. In a very real sense, the essential core of organizational leadership in social agencies can be captured through this lens of critical decisions. Leadership isn't a question of who speaks first at meetings or loudest or longest. It isn't a matter of who orders people around or is most visible at professional meetings or in the media. Real leadership comes from among those willing and able to recognize which decisions among the many hundreds of decisions being made in every organization all the time are the most critical.

Recognition alone is not the answer, however. The real leaders in any organization are those who not only recognize the critical issues, but who rise to the occasion. Not every routine decision requires careful study and thoughtful consideration. Critical decisions do. They are the decisions in which the heart and soul of the organization hang in the balance. They are the decisions that determine an organization's mission, goals, vision, or strategy and set the stage for its legitimacy and long-term viability. It is primarily at such points that the management concern for decision making rises to the level of institution building.

CHAPTER 6

The Processes of Management

Although leadership as we have presented it involves critically important tasks in social administration, there are no defined professional roles in social work leadership or paid positions in social services in which such leadership is the major task assignment. Instead, responsibility for these major roles generally falls to those professional staff members with executive, managerial, and supervisory roles. In this chapter, we examine several baseline perspectives on managerial roles as they were developed within the management sciences literature, with an eye toward their implications for the practice of social administration. In particular, we will look at three general management approaches often called "schools": classic management, scientific management, and human relations perspectives. In general, we adopt a rather eclectic approach to the topic of defining management, bringing in a number of different perspectives along the way.

The legacy of management can be read as a history of movement from machine models of organization and an emphasis on command and control to more relational models of organization as systems of interaction.[1] We explore in later chapters how and under what conditions that interaction may be politicized.

ADMINISTRATION AND MANAGEMENT

George Terry (1972) defined management as "the activity which plans, organizes and controls the operations of the basic elements of men [sic], materials, machines, methods, money, and markets, providing direction and coordination, and giving leadership to human efforts, so as to achieve the sought objectives of the enterprise" (p. 1). One of the trickier semantic issues in introducing the term management in a work on social administration involves the distinction, if any, to be made between the terms *administration, management,* and *governance.* In large part, variations of this type can be traced to two principal sources:

1. A long-standing disciplinary inconsistency in use of the terms business *management* and public *administration* and the highly variable use of both terms in social administration/management to refer to approximately the same guidance processes in commercial and public organizations, respectively
2. Problems with translation into English of key terms in the French classic management tradition that originated largely with Henri Fayol

Fayol (1841–1925) was a French mining engineer who is generally credited as an originator of the classic management tradition and the first to formulate a complete set of management principles intended to guide the practice of managers. Although Fayol's principles are commonly known, somewhat less clearly understood (for good reason!) is his attempt to distinguish management (*gouverner*) as a general process from administration (*administrer*) as a narrower, more specialized part of overall management.[2] When social administration, public administration, and such other institutionally specific fields as school administration, hospital administration, nursing home administration, and higher education administration came into being, they tended to make Fayol's distinction in English but to reverse the order of the terms. Management became the narrower term. More recently, a distinct "management" literature has emerged in several of these disciplines. Although the terms vary, the underlying distinction between a general overall guidance process (in our case called social administration) and some associated narrower technical specialties (including one that we are calling management) remains remarkably constant. As we saw in chapter 1, one of Slavin's concerns was precisely with social administration being supplanted by a narrower more technical management. That also was Fayol's exact point decades earlier.

To make matters even more confusing, in social services, the terms administration and management along with administrator and manager are frequently used interchangeably. The 1970 edition of the *Encyclopedia of*

Social Work speaks only of administration, whereas the 1995 edition speaks only of management, even though they discuss the same topics! Thus, in social services to be an administrator is to be a manager, and vice versa. (See also the distinction made in Patti [1983].)

To the extent any distinction can be drawn, the one we most wish to make is between a general process of institutional oversight and direction (which we will call social administration) and a number of specific subprocesses (one of which we call management). There is a strong case to be made that such a distinction has been recognized for more than a century in those disciplines that call themselves administrative or management sciences. However, there is no strong logical or theoretical case to be made for this or any other particular choice of terms. Our particular choice of terms seems to make sense in light of the fact that scientific management, case management, financial management, and time management are all concerned with relatively narrow, precisely defined technologies.

In a strange turn of events, there is also a rather curious support for our usage to be found in Fayol's original. Fayol's original management functions—production, manufacturing, commercial exchange, the optimum use of capital, protection of property and persons, financial reporting—are all of somewhat secondary importance in the social service agency. By contrast, those functions that he associated with administration—planning, organizing, command, coordination, and control—are much more centrally important in contemporary social administration. Thus, even such usage as financial management as a subfield of social administration may be justified.

There is yet another reason for our distinction between the more general social administration and the more technical management and that is to highlight the view that social administration is not most fundamentally a technical practice but a broadly social and political one in the specific social development sense previously noted (and discussed more fully in chapter 8). It reflects a concern for translating community desires and concerns into specific institutions and programs. Cost analysis is a technical management process: It has definite rules that can be followed in a precise, routine manner to achieve a certain result. Program planning and implementation are administrative processes, with no definite rules, no exact procedures, and few certain results. Both types of activity are essential parts of the challenge of social administration.

The Lure of Management Methods

In examining management, one of the things to avoid (as in any practice discipline) is excessive devotion to the seemingly magical powers of particular methods and technologies. In fact, there are hundreds of management techniques available, many with colorful and alluring names like goals analysis, time and motion study, and total quality management and wonderful graphic devices like Gantt and PERT charts and break-even charts. The certainty they promise can be very reassuring to students mucking about in the vagaries of planning or decision theory and levels of social administration they have seldom, if ever, actually seen in operation. It is vitally important, however, to keep in mind at all times that however useful such techniques may be, they are merely tools, and each is based on a set of assumptions. They may be useful for certain purposes and completely inappropriate at other times. In no sense do these tools define the essential content of the practice of social administration.

Several decades ago, the philosopher of science Abraham Kaplan (1964) encouraged keeping a proper perspective on the limits of technologies with his very graphic example of the "law of the hammer." Give a little boy a hammer, Kaplan noted, and he will find things that need pounding. The same is true of management and all methods. The concern is that if one teaches administrators total quality management or management by objectives, for example, they will try to apply those techniques to every problem or situation, whether applicable or not.

Challenge them with efficiency and effectiveness and possibly they will learn to ask critically, with Peter Drucker (1964), whether they are doing the right things and whether they are doing things the right way. Or, they will keep looking for some holy grail of an efficiency or effectiveness scale that is so powerful that it will remove all uncertainty from their decisions and allow them to be right every time. One of the first luxuries to abandon in the study of social administration is the notion that anyone *can* be right all the time. Administrative decisions are made in real time, and momentous choices must often be made with insufficient time for full consideration or review. Under such conditions, no one should expect to always be right. The critical difference between effective and ineffective administrators is not so much a matter of who is right most often, but of who has learned to recognize, confront, and correct their mistakes. Management tools can be very helpful for many things, but they can do little to eliminate an essential core of uncertainty in administrative decision making.

SCHOOLS OF MANAGEMENT?

One conventional textbook approach to the presentation of basic management models is to divide them into basic schools of thought: Weberian bureaucracy, administrative management, scientific management, human relations, and so on. Yet, as David Austin (1989) notes, such models as scientific management and human relations management, developed in for-profit industrial firms, have been introduced into the social administration literature with very little examination of their applicability to social service programs. The approach we take here is to suggest that though many of the traditional business management perspectives offer interesting insights useful for social administration, none offers a comprehensive enough perspective to serve as the basis for a school of social administration. It should be possible, therefore, to consider many different perspectives for their potential contributions to understanding the problems of social administration without the necessity of treating any as a complete and total package. There is, rather, a role for a purely eclectic and pragmatic approach by social administrators to any management approaches and technologies that anyone anywhere has found useful.

In saying this, we wish to question any need for social administrators to distinguish among separate schools of management thought or practice in existing management theory while at the same time do justice to the diversity of approaches to concrete problems, approaches, and issues. There can be no doubt that particular groups at particular times and in particular countries and languages have concentrated on and emphasized one aspect of management over another. For the early engineers concerned with managing large organizations to build and operate railroads and factories, for example, a good deal of the challenge of management was mechanistic. Much of the difference in management approaches is attributable to contextual or environmental differences in the particular problems being faced.

By dismissing the idea that "schools" of management are important for social administration, we hope also to dismiss some of the baggage this idea has accumulated in social work. One of the stock clichés that appears as an undercurrent in the social work literature, for example, is that scientific management is a highly oppressive management style, whereas the human relations approach is much more humanistic and person centered. Both of these appraisals have a grain of truth, but are seriously wide of the mark. For example, Henry L. Gantt (1916), developer of the Gantt chart and one of the leading innovators (and therefore, one of the alleged oppressors) of scientific management uttered this rather humanistic message in 1916: "The general policy of the past has been to drive (that is, force workers to work harder); but the era of force must give way to that of knowledge, and the policy of the future will be to teach and lead, to the advantage of all concerned" (p. 148). That surely is a sentiment that a humanist like Mary Parker Follett easily could and did endorse.

It is equally anachronistic to characterize scientific management as unduly promanagement and antilabor in outlook. To the contrary, Frederick Taylor and his followers initially saw themselves, and were seen by others, as reformers in much the same vein as the progressives and human relations advocates. Gantt said in the same work, "The only healthy industrial condition is that in which the employer has the best men obtainable for his work, and the workman feels that his labor is being sold at the highest possible market price" (p. 33). The emphasis on the qualifications of workers and the accent on worker satisfaction are consistent with the views and aspirations of Elton Mayo and the human relations approach as it evolved a couple of decades later. Likewise, the renowned European historian and social theorist Max Weber, working on histories of Byzantine and Egyptian bureaucracies in a preindustrial Germany not yet modernized, emphasized the universal, timeless characteristics of the bureaucratic ideal type. To call the lone Weber a "school of management" borders on the comic.

Henri Fayol, who was a French mining engineer, and Frederick Taylor, who was an American time and motion expert, were both absorbed by practical problems of factory production, although the answers they developed are quite distinct. The American academic social psychologists associated with the later human relations movement were as much concerned with the Hawthorne effects conventionally taught today in the research curriculum as they were with the management implications of their data.[3] Likewise, it was primarily social service administrators who first paid much attention to the problem of community and the environment of management beyond the organization because they were the first to deal extensively with stakeholder problems.

To suggest that those who still find meaning in Weber's ideal type represent one "school" of management theory and that the practitioners of Taylorism or scientific management represent another is to seriously risk misreading selective attention as theoretical disagreement. Littler (1982) suggested that management ideas should not be thought of as ideologies, along the lines of schools of management, but rather as "forms of work organization" or "sets of principles underlying work organizations" (p. 215). Following Littler, Huczynski (1993) said, "Scientific management, human relations, classical management and similar idea systems can be considered as significant sets of design criteria which are used to structure work" (p. 215). This in no way detracts from their importance, as Huczynski noted. "As such, they have continued to exert a major influence on managerial thinking and organizational design right through to the present day."

ELEMENTS OF MANAGEMENT PROCESS

Henri Fayol originated the idea of a general management process in organizations and was the first to attempt to spell out a set of general management principles. According to Wren (1994), Fayol did not use the term *pro-*

cess to describe the manager's functions but spoke instead of "elements of management" (pp. 184–85). Fayol identified as the central concerns of the manager (1) planning (*prévoyance*); (2) organizing (which many later writers split into organizing and staffing); (3) command; (4) coordination "to harmonize all the activities of the concern so as to facilitate its working, and its success"; and (5) control, "verifying whether everything occurs in conformity with the plan adopted, the instructions issued, and the principles established."

Based on his experience with these elements, Fayol identified fifteen principles that he said were the basis of all management:

1. *Specialization* of effort and division of labor are part of the natural order. In general, related things should be together and different things should be apart.
2. *Authority* is the right to give orders and be obeyed, and responsibility is the obligation to obey at the risk of sanctions. The key characteristic of management is its authority; the key characteristic of workers is their responsibility to obey.
3. *Discipline* is the obligation to obey. It is the obligation of management to impose discipline on workers.
4. *Unity of command.* Each worker in an organization should receive orders from one, and only one, superior.
5. *Unity of direction.* There should be only one head and a single plan for any group of activities with a common objective.
6. Work organizations should be characterized by a *subordination* of individual interests to the general interests of the company.
7. *Remuneration* of workers should be fair and satisfactory.
8. *Centralization* of authority is part of the natural order. Others were later to argue equally vigorously for decentralization and teamwork.
9. Each organization is characterized by a unique *hierarchy* or *chain of authority* from highest to lowest.
10. *Social order.* Effective management is characterized by having the right man for the job in the right place.
11. *Material order.* As your grandmother used to tell you, "There is a place for everything, and everything belongs in its place."
12. *Equity.* Management should ensure the fair and even-handed treatment of employees.
13. *Stability of tenure.* Managers should be around long enough to carry projects through to fruition.
14. *Initiative* should be encouraged.
15. *Esprit de corps.* Harmony and cooperation should prevail.

A point-by-point comparison will show that several of Fayol's principles of management also figure importantly in Weber's description of bureaucracy, which we treated in chapter 3. For example, the thirteenth principle, stability of tenure, corresponds with Weber's lifetime tenure and vocational premises. It is important to note also that it was Fayol, and not Weber, who was the more important transmitter of essentially medieval ideas of hierarchy into modern organizational theory. Though scalar hierarchies are closely associated in the popular imagination with bureaucracy, there is little in the Weberian model of rational–legal organization quite as clearly suggestive of hierarchy as Fayol's scalar principle.

In interpreting these management principles, we must allow for the problems of anachronism and the language differences discussed at the start of this chapter. Even taking such considerations into account, however, may not be enough to fully preserve the usefulness of such management principles, for reasons noted by Herbert Simon and others and discussed below. In general, we are far enough removed from nineteenth-century industrial corporations to see some of their principled inconsistencies, although we would certainly have a great deal more difficulty seeing our own quite as clearly. For instance, Fayol makes clear that management should treat workers fairly—but reserves the right of management to determine for itself what fair treatment involves—and should pay them fairly but only *if* it feels that it can. This is clearly at odds with twentieth-century labor legislation and policy. Moreover, to the modern ear, Fayol appears to be suggesting that once you have subordinated your employees to lifetime commitment in a singular chain of command, you should encourage them to transcend that chain of command with their individual initiative and encourage in them a sense of harmony and spirit of cooperation. It can be difficult for subordinated workers to demonstrate initiative.

Perhaps the best that can be said of such matters is that these and other issues raised by the principles are still important management issues and concerns in social administration today. Therefore, rather than offering the simple guide to practice for which most authors of principles strive, Fayol has given to modern management in social administration and other fields a checklist for where at least some likely trouble spots may occur and some general guidance about directions in which desirable practice may be sought.

There have been a number of attempts to derive sets of distinctive management principles for social administration. For example, Abels and Murphy (1981, pp. 14–16) sought to ground their normative model of administration in seven principles:

1. Administrative actions should lead to just consequences.

2. The agency structure should ensure a democratic, minimally stratified environment.
3. Decisions need to be based on rational inquiry.
4. Agency social interactions within and among agencies need to be synergistic.
5. Administration should foster independence for staff and clients through mutual support and growth.
6. The administrator promotes mutual accountability to ensure the highest ethical level of practice.
7. The administrator is a guide.

Like other principles, these are probably most useful as guides to anticipated trouble spots than as definitive guides for action.

From Principles to Methods

While Fayol and European management thought sought to anchor practice deductively in principles, another emerging American perspective sought to ground management inductively in experimentalism. There is little doubt of the origins of the scientific management of Frederick Taylor (1856–1915) in Adam Smith's work and the nineteenth-century American market revolution (Sellers, 1991; Stokes, 1997). Taylorism also contains a strong measure of the Puritan work ethic (Weber, 1947a). Moreover, Taylor's ideas of "scientific management" probably rank with Puritanism and manifest destiny as major influences on contemporary American culture. Scientific management, with its individualism, optimism, and empiricism could, almost certainly, have developed nowhere else but in the United States. It was Taylor, for example, who worked with Henry Ford in perfecting the assembly line method of production for automobiles.

Unlike the management writers working in the tradition of Fayol, adherents of scientific management were little concerned with discovering or purveying principles. Yet, scientific management is fundamentally an approach grounded in a few simple methodological principles. At its core, scientific management is a simple, rigorous empirical (fact-gathering) methodology for practical investigation and work–redesign that can be summed up in four terms: study–recruit–train–organize:

1. Collect and study detailed information of time and motions of work activities.
2. Select workers carefully and see to their development.
3. Induce workers to do things in the most efficient way.
4. Reorganize the division of labor appropriately.

Follow this simple method, it is said, and everything else will fall into place. The fundamental principles of scientific management are, at heart, empirical. Human decision makers are mental clean slates who can know nothing without careful study and data collection. Time-and-motion studies are the proverbial scientific management tool. In many respects, Taylor's classic work was on the science of efficient shoveling and the bodily movements involved.

The impact of scientific management on the practice of social administration has been twofold. First, the general milieu of economizing legitimated by scientific management has had an enduring effect on the organization of work in American society. Members of the general public agree that social services should be delivered efficiently and effectively even when they haven't a clue of precisely what an efficient or effective social service should look like or what characteristics would give it these economizing qualities. Second, a rich variety of scientific management approaches and results have been incorporated into the very warp and woof of modern office culture. One of the most pervasive and influential application of scientific management approaches in human services are the "error-reduction" strategies employed by the federal government to reduce the level of erroneous claims in public assistance. Studying samples of completed forms to determine rates of error by workers and then revising procedures accordingly is a pure form of the scientific management approach.

THE DISCOVERY OF THE SOCIAL

Although it is seldom noted as such, the initial studies out of which the human relations approach to management grew began as pure applications of scientific management. The first study was an experimental design investigation of the impact of differing lighting conditions on worker productivity, with an eye toward improving worker productivity, but that discovered the impact of social conditions (observability) on workers' productivity.

The underlying principles and general outlook of the human relations approach to management are best illustrated by the contrast evident in Douglas McGregor's (1960) theory X and theory Y. Theory X as described by McGregor included the following elements. Theory X is almost certainly meant to refer to Fayol's approach or the best management practices of the day, which often amounted to the same thing:

1. Management is responsible for organizing the elements of productive enterprise for economic ends—money, material, equipment, and people.

2. This is a process of directing people's efforts, motivating them, controlling their actions, and modifying their behavior to fit the needs of the organization.
3. Without management intervention, workers are passive or even lazy and need to be persuaded, rewarded, punished, controlled, or directed.
4. The average worker
   a. Is naturally indolent
   b. Lacks ambition
   c. Dislikes responsibility
   d. Is self-centered and indifferent to the organization's needs
   e. Is resistant to change
   f. Is gullible, not too bright, and easily duped

As an alternative to this, McGregor offered the theory Y of the human relations approach:

1. Management is, indeed, responsible for organizing the elements of productive enterprise for economic ends—money, material, equipment, and people.
2. People are not naturally passive or resistant to organizational needs. They only become so in light of their experiences with the organization.
3. Motivation, potential for development, capacity for responsibility, and readiness to direct their individual behavior to larger organizational goals are present in all people. Management does not instill such values; it is the responsibility of management to create the circumstances for people to recognize and develop these characteristics for themselves.
4. The essential task of management is to arrange organizational conditions so that people can achieve their own goals best by directing their efforts toward organizational objectives.
5. Steps in the right direction include decentralization and delegation of authority, job enlargement, participative and consultative management, and regular performance appraisal.

In placing its emphasis on the "human relations" between management and workers, McGregor and his associates permanently modified the way all of us view organizations and the way people treat one another in the workplace. This is entirely in keeping with transitions in the nature of work that were not fully realized until several decades after their original work in the 1930s. Nonetheless, the image of a work organization not as a human-augmented machine for handling materials but as a complex set of intentional human relationships is one of fundamental importance in the evo-lution of social administration.

THE CASE AGAINST MANAGEMENT PRINCIPLES

Although he might be seen as a collaborator in one of the most lively and innovative debates over contemporary management principles, Herbert Simon is also noted for making the strongest case against management principles approaches. Simon (1947/1997, pp. 20–44) launched a head-on assault on Fayol's or any approach to principles, which at that time still had a strong foothold in management thinking. Gulick and Urwick (1937) had held, for example, that if there was to be a science of public administration worthy of the name, it must be based on an articulation of Fayolian or other management principles.

Simon identified four common principles that he said were really "prov-erbs" and showed that they were mutually and internally inconsistent. In what may be an acknowledgment of the importance of economizing, all four of the proverbs he chose were related to efficiency, although his point is no less valid when applied to other management principles, or for that matter, other statements of practice principles in general. It has been said, according to Simon:

1. Efficiency is increased by task specialization.
2. Efficiency is increased by arranging members of a group in a deter-minate hierarchy.
3. Efficiency is increased by a small span of control.
4. Efficiency is increased by grouping workers by purpose, process, cli-entele, and place.

The problem, Simon noted, is that task specialization is inconsistent with any of the groupings in proverb four, and hierarchy is inconsistent with small span of control, just to name two of many conflicts. And when prin-ciples conflict there is no way to resolve the differences, short of identifying another set of higher meta principles, which when they conflict will require even higher meta-meta principles and so on and so on.

One can understand Simon's point equally well using Fayol's list of prin-ciples. Following the principle of specialization, for example, will produce an organization of many experts in particular areas, whereas the principle of obedience will require these experts generally to obey those who know less than they do about their particular areas of expertise. Thus, strict ad-herence to Fayol's principles would seem to endorse hiring people for their expertise and then creating an environment designed to frustrate them in which such unique expertise can be suppressed. This is a seemingly absurd circumstance and an invitation to certain failure but one altogether too common in hierarchical organizations. It does not appear possible, as Simon argued, to create a rational or logically consistent model of organization in which both the principles are observed. Yet both are intuitively important to Fayol's approach.

MANAGEMENT PROCESS MODELS

The other major approach to organizing management ideas evident in the history of management thought arose out of the muddle created by the search for principles that Simon pointed up. If it is not possible to identify the unique practice principles that define management, perhaps it will be possible to point to the list of unique processes that together define management practice.

In the process tradition, one finds two very distinct types of writings. Some authors have identified a single process as the critical moment in management. Max Weber's focus on rationalization can be viewed from this perspective. Others have identified communications (Barnard), decision making (Simon), cooperation (Barnard), leadership (Newman and Davis), planning (Fayol), mission (Drucker), and co-optation (Selznick) as central processes. Consistent with our rejection of applying the notion of "schools" of management to social administration, it is possible to read these various assertions of central process as a series of devices used by various authors to organize and present their ideas and not as competing master processes or functions.

How many management functions are there and what are their names? Various authors have identified different sets, and each brings something to the overall discussion. In 1937, Luther Gulick arrived at his famous formulation of seven basic management functions that have guided the study of public administration ever since: planning, organizing, staffing, directing, coordinating, reporting, and budgeting (POSDCORB) (Gulick & Urwick, 1937). Following and adapting Fayol's ideas, Harold Koontz and Cyril O'Donnell (1978), in the business school tradition, divided management functions into five: planning, organizing, staffing, directing, and controlling. George Terry's (1972) version of the management process included planning, organizing, directing, coordinating, controlling, and leading. Littler (1982) had a three-level framework that he termed *the levels of structuralization*: (1) employee relations, (2) structure of control, and (3) work design or the division of labor and technology. It is less important for the student of social administration to memorize any particular list of management functions than to know something of the rich variety of attempts to capture the essence of management through this approach.

The Simon–March Principle

Herbert Simon is one of the genuinely original management thinkers of the twentieth century. We have already commented on some of his contributions to organization and institutions theory in previous chapters and his rejection of management principles just above. Simon is also one of the originators of the field of cognitive psychology. In 1947, he made a major contribution to management theory that focused on the importance of decision making in the management process and offered detailed analyses of communications and information, authority, efficiency, and organizational goals. Another of the concepts in that study, the idea of satisficing or accepting the first plausible alternative, was later reformulated by Charles Lindblom (1977) into the concept of strategy.

At the core of Simon's work was a model of organization and administration cognizant of both the desirability of rational organization and behavior and the human mental limitations.

Neo-Weberian Practice

A decade after publication of the first edition of *Administrative Behavior* in 1947, Simon and James March (1958) wrote *Organizations*, in which they advanced beyond what they saw as the Weberian view of organizations as rule-bound social organizations in two important ways.[4] In the Weberian view, humans are rule-following creatures and rules control and direct behavior. Grounded in enlightenment rationalism, this view has at its core a rather simple or straightforward rational model of practice: change the rules and you change the behavior. This is the same view that social workers typically adopt toward social policy, for example.

Beginning from his earlier rejection of management principles and a model of administrative process grounded in partial rationality and satisficing, Simon and co-author March set out a non-rule-based approach to changing behavior in organizations. The Simon–March model identifies three non-rule-related mechanisms, in particular, as worthy of note: (1) limiting and channeling information flows as a way of controlling the premises upon which decisions are made, (2) deliberate emphasis—or de-emphasis—of aspects of situations can be used to change the definition of the situation, and (3) recognizing that limits placed on the search for alternative solutions to a problem can affect the outcome. They set out to show how the majority of efforts in organizations fit this neo-Weberian view more closely than the classical, Weberian rule-following model.

The provocative message for social administration arising from this approach is that it isn't always necessary or sometimes even desirable to change the rules in order to change an organization. This may also apply to a change in the organization's incentive scheme. Changing the premises of decisions can have a salutary effect as well. This is the sort of approach that has come to be called "thinking outside of the box."

One of the implications of the Simon–March perspective is a view of administration as a quasi-political process. Despite its rather obvious (to the modern eye) political content and social class implications, the command and control perspective of the classical management school was seen by its developers as a fundamentally apolitical, scientific, and technical approach. Organized labor, not surprisingly, seldom made the same benign interpretation. In a similar vein, the social work community perspective prior to the 1960s typically viewed the process of representing community needs and interests in largely apolitical, scientific, and professional terms. At least since the Civil Rights movement, such apolitical and political models of community and administration have existed side by side in the profession.

Richan (1983) sought to articulate a "politicized" model of social administration in response to the New Federalism and devolution of power to the local level, which he argued was insufficiently responsive to the twin legacies of localism: social irresponsibility and racism. His model posited three equally important dimensions of administration, which he termed management, policy, and service delivery. Few would argue with the notion that all of these are important. Indeed, we treat the relationship between social policy and administration in a subsequent chapter as part of the overall process of institutional development. Some in social work might question such a project of politicizing administration. As should be clear, the legacy of management is a history of movement from machine models of organization and an emphasis on command and control to more relational models of organization as systems of interaction. We explore in later chapters how and under what conditions that interaction may need to be politicized.

WHO ADMINISTERS HUMAN SERVICES?

Who really runs human services? It is often taken for granted that the answer to that is administrators or the chief executive officer (CEO), and our archaic ideas of organizational hierarchy often support such a predisposition. In the narrowest sense, of course, it is likely to be true that boards and administrators administer all existing social services. However, in another sense, there are a few cases in which it is also clear that effective control has been wrested from agency managers by a number of outside forces. It is possible to find woven through the contemporary social services management literature a range of suggestions along this line. In particular, four such perspectives are explored briefly below: the ideas that judges, lawyers, insurance companies, and workers actually control and operate human services.

Judicial Administration?

Judges play a seemingly ever-larger role in administering schools, mental hospitals, prisons, and other institutions (Chambers, 2000; Glazer, 1978). A small number of judicial decisions involving fairly elaborate provisions for supervision and administration specify in detail how existing agencies are to operate and that almost inevitably provide for continued oversight for an indeterminate period by the court. In at least a few cases, such decisions have been broad and sweeping enough to overturn entire service delivery systems, as in the case of the court cases that forced de-institutionalization of mental patients or mandate particular service provisions over an entire state. For several decades now, judicial decisions, remedies, and interventions have been a major factor in shaping the warp and woof of American social policy. According to Glazer, the overall effect of judicial intervention in social-policy administration can be to reduce the responsibility and discretion of administrators and workers; to reduce their authority; to give greater weight to theoretical than to practical considerations; to give greater weight to speculations, considerations, and research of social scientists in policy formulation; and to increase the legal power of the profession and the power of the more theoretical professions in each branch of social service over that of professionals dealing directly with service clients.

Ironically, however, administration by judicial fiat does not pose any fundamental problems for the social agency or social administration as it has evolved throughout the twentieth century. Carrying out the mandates of courts as stated in judicial orders is not fundamentally different from carrying out congressional or legislative policy, nor is it fundamentally different from carrying out bureaucratic intent as expressed in regulations, grants, and contracts or the will of boards of directors in nonprofit organizations. Judiciary fiat becomes merely one more authoritative voice that must be obeyed.

Management by Lawyers?

A more complex and potentially sinister challenge comes from the growing necessity for legal advice prior to undertaking an increasingly broad range of professional actions. Following judicial directives is ordinarily far more clear-cut than the kinds of legal negotiation that arise in the current litigious environment, in which avoiding lawsuits becomes an important objective of management decision making. Legal services for the poor have significantly increased litigation against public agencies. Employees, other service providers, and clients have challenged rules and regulations adopted by many agencies. Commercial corporations providing contract services such as home health care may seek to exert their influence, using the best legal talent available (Page & St. John, 1984). These and other legal challenges have made it necessary that legal general counsel be included among the regular staff and consultants of many agencies, and most agencies will have at least occasional need of professional legal advice.

In some types of agencies such as state welfare agencies and some fields of practice such as child welfare, the need for legal counsel may, at times, surpass these more or less normal bounds and leave administrators feeling that they simply cannot act on anything without seeking prior legal advice. We are not speaking here of the normal concerns of professionals with being sued. Most social workers are, in fact, terrified of the prospect of being sued. It is well to remember, therefore, that anyone can sue an agency or its workers over just about anything. Community organizing efforts, for example, may be uniquely vulnerable to the Strategic Lawsuit Against Public Participation (SLAPP) suits intended for the specific purpose of silencing opposition (Pring & Canan, 1997). The real question with all cases is whether the plaintiff has a case.

This new age of legalism poses serious and fundamental challenges for social agencies. Will a volunteer board and an in-house executive still direct the social agency of the future or will that direction come by default from law firms and judicial chambers?

Management by Insurance Companies

The emergence of managed care has also raised the specter of management by yet another external influence: insurance companies. Although many discussions of vision, mission, focus, goals, and policies continue to project an image of fully autonomous management decision makers, the reality is that in many instances the focus and direction of social services are being imposed from the outside by funding sources.

This, of course, is not really new. During the age of grants that began in the 1960s, similar concerns were raised about management decision making devolving, in effect, to an assorted variety of public and private grant makers. And, it must be noted, subsequent experience has often confirmed that such influences can indeed be pervasive. However, the threats posed to agency autonomy by insurance companies in the managed care environment are of an entirely new and different order. The most typical conflict between grant makers and agencies in the past have been over differing or rival interpretations of policy or practice. By contrast, the conflicts with insurance companies are often within an issue frame that appears to question whether the actual focus of services is to be service delivery or profit.

Worker Autonomy

One of the long-standing ideals for social administration supported by many social workers has been the idea of a fully democratic social agency in which everyone has an equal voice and is more or less free to pursue their own agendas. This is the normal connotation of "democratic" leadership styles, for example. It is also the interpretation given to theory Y. Many social administrators have clung to the notion that such expectations are simply unrealistic, and to an important degree they are right. However, in the case of the fully professionalized agency where all staff members have approximately equal experience and credentials, most of the traditional arguments for management hierarchies don't carry a lot of weight. It is interesting, therefore, that the long-standing vision of nonhierarchical social agencies appears to have been largely abandoned at the very time when increased numbers of professionally trained workers entering the field make it more feasible.

The most commonly perceived danger in nonhierarchy is anarchy. Everyone doing his or her own thing implies inconsistent treatment of clients, differing interpretations of policy, dilution of agency mission, and the like, and this is truly something to be feared. Even anarchy would not be an entirely unacceptable situation among professionals if it were an accurate and complete reading of the situation. The greater difficulty with the idea of complete worker autonomy in reality is that granting everyone the right to do his or her own thing in any employment setting may not be legally possible or organizationally realistic. Doing so may have the result that actions by any particular free-wheeling staff member may put the board, executive director, department heads, or others in the organization at risk of liability, prosecution, or malpractice. In many technical areas of social administration, such as contracts, borrowing funds, wage and hour regulations, affirmative action, and clients' rights, it is simply not possible to structure an organization such that board members or principal executives can be freed of all measure of the responsibilities imposed from the environment by law, government regulations, purchase of service agreements, or other circumstances.

In principal, the idea of a democratically administered agency, whereby everyone has an equal voice, sounds great. In reality, however, few of us would care to be put in the position it implies: everyone gets to decide what will happen, but only some of us will be held responsible if something goes wrong. Until this problem can be solved, the concepts of complete worker autonomy and the fully democratic social agency are likely to remain largely pipe dreams.

CONCLUSION

In this chapter, we introduced some of the range and diversity of management thought without seeking to classify different figures as representatives of different "schools" of management. It is easy for purposes of scholarly activity to accentuate the differences between them, so that they fall into neat categories. Yet, in the reality of social administration it is equally plausible to see them as representatives of a greater community, as diverse parts of a unified whole. Like a great many early and more recent social work authors, Henri Fayol sought principles as fixed reference points to serve as justifications for management action. Max Weber looked beyond simple principles to reason as the great agent in establishing a precedent or a policy as well as a tradition and a law. The radical individualism of the Taylorists saw administration as not simply a concern for the collectivity but, like the early caseworkers, discerned the morally autonomous individuals who made up the parts of the whole. Just as importantly, the human relations researchers and Mary Parker Follett (whose ideas are discussed more fully in chapter 7), saw the limitations of the machine model and grasped the importance of real genuine communication (not command and control) as the vital link between the individuals and the organization.

One important distinction has become somewhat muddied over the past two decades as the management perspective in social work has unfolded and organizational studies of social services have expanded. This is the distinction between models of organizational process (as discussed in chapters 3 and 4) and models of executive and other managerial processes (as discussed in this and the next chapter). The questions of what an organization *is* and what its managers must *do* to fulfill their role and duties within the organization are distinct and separate, albeit related, issues. In this light, this chapter can be seen as a report of historic efforts in general management science to clarify what, exactly, management is all about.

In most general terms, the Weberian answer is that the central activity of management involves rule (or, as we are more inclined to say, policy) making. The answer provided by classic management perspectives of Fayol and others involved principle-guided command and control. To the Taylorists of scientific management, the manager was a kind of scientist/technician, whose role involves as its major task careful analysis of work task assignments and careful reengineering of jobs. To the human relations writers, the manager was a kind and compassionate therapist, responsible for rules and effectiveness certainly, but even more responsible for structuring a supportive work environment in which employees could find satisfaction in their work. From these assorted behavioral perspectives, the manager emerges as a kind of philosopher–king (a governor in the original sense or a leader), using carrots and sticks to govern in the best way possible. The neo-Weberian perspective of Simon and March brings this into particularly sharp focus. Management theorists such as Fayol, Gulick and, more recently, Koontz and O'Donnell have sought to define comprehensive typologies of management processes. The search for an optimal list of such continues, yet suffers much the same fate as the search for the perfect organization. In chapter 7, we will consider a number of other approaches to the topic of general management with important implications for social administration.

Management Models

This chapter is largely a continuation of chapter 6, with one important difference. In chapter 6, we approached some of the basic issues of management through the lens of certain orientations so broad and encompassing that some writers have distinguished them as different "schools" of management. In this chapter, we concentrate instead on a larger number of different perspectives that are, by their nature, less comprehensive and inclusive than the so-called schools but that offer in most cases equally fundamental orientations and overviews to the nature of the management process. These various approaches are, in many respects, as fundamental as the "schools" in forming basic outlooks or ways of viewing social administration today. We begin with a perspective we call "self-management" and move through a variety of perspectives we call the "management-bys," ending with a discussion of the ideas of an assorted collection of management "gurus."

SELF-MANAGEMENT

An approach we call self-management (an application of the general social work notion of use of self) is very important to note here because it ties so directly into social work goals and professional aspirations on one hand and with American culture on the other. The concept of self-management or personal autonomy has a rich tradition in American life, associated as it is with ideas of individualism and civic republicanism. Ideas of self-management of workers have been important in recent management history and in social work. Two writers in particular, both of whom we have encountered in other contexts, are especially important in exploring this idea of self-management. First, the idea arose in the work of Mary Parker Follett that we discussed in chapter 5. Within social administration, the self-management ideal is an important part of the group approach to management laid out by Harleigh Trecker (1946, 1961, 1965, 1971). Peter Drucker (1954, 1964, 1973, 1987, 1990, 1992, 1993, 1996) is important in part because of his contribution to the self-management approach through his focus on management by objectives, considered later in this chapter. Drucker is generally considered one of the giants of modern management thought. He is credited as inventing the concept of the manager, and in the later phases of his career, he concentrated heavily on nonprofit management.[1]

Although largely ignored for a period of time, Mary Parker Follett, whose early work experience included a stint as a social worker, is a key figure in modern management thought. In her radical rethinking of the subject during the 1920s and 1930s, management would no longer be seen in mechanical terms as an issue of command and control, but of the reciprocal influences of leader on follower and follower on leader in the context of a particular organizational setting. According to Follett, a leader should "make his co-workers see that it is not his purpose which is to be achieved, but a common purpose, born of the desires and the activities of the group. The best leader does not ask people to serve him, but the common end. The best leader has not followers, but men and women working with him" (Follett, Fox, & Urwick, p. 262).

Since its inception, the Follett model of self-management has struck some people as hopelessly idealistic and utopian. One major exception to this has been the social work tradition of management associated most closely with the postwar vision of social services. One of the most articulate spokesperson for self-management in social work was Harleigh Trecker, who, in the three books published between 1946 and 1971 cited above, laid out his vision of the "group process of administration." Curiously, even as Trecker's approach has been progressively incorporated into general social work practice theory, his distinctive contributions to social administration have been largely ignored or forgotten.

That the self-management perspective appealed to emerging social work professionals of the postwar period should surprise no one because of the direct link between professional autonomy and self-management. Clearly, the more professionalized a social agency or any other organization became, the easier it was to visualize it as a network of self-managers collaborating on joint projects, rather than either as a bureaucratic hierarchy of rule followers or a command network of order followers. The opposite is also true, however. To the extent that social services personnel, whether degreed and licensed or not, are unable or unwilling to function effectively as self-managers, Follett's collaborative vision remains largely empty rhetoric, and professional autonomy is threatened.

Social work remains caught in a kind of middle world on this issue. In reviewing patterns in mental health, for example, David Mechanic (1998) offered the following assessment: "Psychiatric social workers, the weakest politically of the mental health quartet,[2] most often work on a salaried basis in clinics and social agencies, although many aspire to be individual therapists. Attracting independent reimbursement is a major difficulty" (p. 8). Although Mechanic does not explore the issue of self-management directly, his contrast of "work on a salaried basis in clinics and social agencies" with the "independent reimbursement" of "individual therapists" speaks directly to one major aspect of the self-management issue.

One should not view the issue raised by Mechanic as only a dichotomy of private practice versus agency-based practice. Models of self-managed practice proffered by traditional medical practice not withstanding, there are certainly many cases of essentially self-managed professionals operating within large organized settings. Researchers, college and university professors, law firm partners, and others illustrate this practice. Thus, the model of self-managing social work professionals operating in social agencies run essentially as professional collaboratives—a truly group basis of administration—remains one of the possible futures of the social agency. It is, in fact, the view of the future on which most of the insights offered in this book are premised.

However, it must be acknowledged that under the present circumstances the reigning vision of professional self-management points in at least two directions beyond the social agency as well. One of these is the health care based vision of professional self-management as independent practice. The other and more disturbing vision is the complete loss of the self-management ideal and the disappearance of the social agency through the subordination of social work within the hierarchies of host institutions such as hospitals, nursing homes, schools, and business corporations and the control of the state.

THE "MANAGEMENT-BYS"

A number of management writers have sought to address the issue of management principles by singling out and focusing on one central critical process in order to explore its implications more generally. Chester Barnard's (1938) communications approach to management as cooperation is among the best known early examples of this approach. Within a category we call "management-bys," a number of different attempts to organize understandings of management around a central issue are introduced and discussed in this chapter.

Management by Principles

Henri Fayol and others sought diligently to isolate a set of management principles that could serve as a firm basis for modern management (see chapter 6). Herbert Simon voiced the skepticism that all such systems of principle are inherently self-contradicting. Simon's objections are part of a larger climate of uncertainty about the wisdom of principles approaches in general. Yet, the search for an adequate principles approach to organizing practice disciplines remains a popular idea. It remains to be seen whether some future management thinker will rise to the challenge of articulating a set of logically consistent principals of management by which the actions of social administrators in concrete situations can be guided. Since Simon's objection in the 1950s, management writers have generally preferred other approaches.

Management by Objectives

Probably the best known, most complete, and widely used "management-by" during the past three decades has been *management by objectives* (MBO), which is sometimes also known as *management by objectives and results* (MBOR).[3] The essential idea of the MBO model is a performance- and outcome-based schema, intended to maximize the autonomy of the individual manager. Koontz and O'Donnell (1978) see three principle advantages to managing by objectives: better managing, clarified organization, and improved employee commitment.

Within the business arena where it arose, the MBO model was intended primarily to undermine the command-and-control model of management.

As a refugee from European authoritarianism and oppression in the 1940s, Peter Drucker's formulation of MBO was strongly animated by his apparent sympathy for a model of management by self-control to replace the still widely practiced domination model of management by command and control. By establishing objectives and linking them to measurable outcomes, Drucker argued, each manager should be able to measure performance against a goal, leading to an organization driven by evaluative self-control. In highly professionalized organizations such as scientific laboratories, medical clinics, and colleges and in highly professionalized social service agencies, such a model is actualized.

Even in a regime of self-managers, however, some measure of an overall management role will remain. Drucker (1987) wrote that the fundamental task of management in this larger sense is "to make people capable of joint performance by giving them common goals, common values, the right structure, and the ongoing training and development they need to perform and to respond to change" (p. 65). That is the task that the MBO model sets for itself.

Within social services, however, the Follett tradition of collaborative effort was already well entrenched, and MBO has had greater impact on developing models of accountability. For this reason, the application of the MBO model in social services is discussed in greater detail in the context of accountability in chapter 12.

Management by Authority and Rule Making

Even though we discount the notion that Max Weber had set out to develop a theory of management (see chapter 6), it is possible to view the Weberian model of bureaucracy as a management theory. Indeed, that is precisely what many previous writers have done in setting Weber's ideal type of bureaucracy up in contrast with classic management, scientific management, and human relations. To the extent that Weberian bureaucracy offers or implies actual management models suggesting what administrators are to do, two candidates seem most likely.

One such management approach that is logically consistent with the Weberian model of authority might be termed *management by the reasonable use of power*. From this view, managers should use their legal authority to establish rational processes in organizations and attain reasonable ends. Given Weber's rather pessimistic mood of concern about the iron cage of rationality gripping modern humanity, however, it seems extremely doubtful that he would have seriously advocated such an approach to management practice. However, a great deal of day-to-day social services management behavior does appear to fit this description, including perhaps the unending rounds of departmental reorganization to which federal and state social service agencies have been subjected. These are almost always efforts to establish rational processes through the reasonable use of power.

The more likely candidate as Weber's preferred management style would be *management by rule making.* In this approach, the primary role of the manager, like that of the ancient kings, is that of wise lawgiver. The manager is the person who sets boundaries and limits on human behavior within the agency, *ordering* that employees, clients, and others must engage in certain activities and practices (being at work on time, attending staff meetings, updating their case notes in a timely manner, etc.) and *forbidding* that employees engage in other activities and practices (no sexual relations with clients, no use of company vehicles for personal travel, no disclosure of business practices to competitors, etc.). In the Weberian variant, it is the policies and rules and not the personal expressions of the manager that form the basis for command and control.

A key issue in management by rule making and one that is of great concern for women and minorities becomes whose rules are being made and how they are enforced. If rules are fair, are public, and have the authority of the organization behind them, it is one thing. If they are the personal rules of an individual manager, appear to be based on mere personal whim, or lack publicity (publicness), it is quite another matter.

Until very recently, there was a strong tradition of suspicion of rules in social services. Indeed, Weberian rule making has often been seen as an expression of personal command and control. This is unfortunate, because it suggests that rules can only be formulated by controlling authorities. In reality, a great many organizations including many social agencies operate today on the basis of rules formulated by the kind of collaborative process first suggested by Follett and the human relations approach. Such an approach to rule making appears to bring together advantages of both approaches.

Management by Exception

One of the foremost management-by models is called *management by exception* (MBE). Management by exception is an old idea, particularly well used in accounting texts, but not often included in management texts. It is an idea that is especially appropriate for mid-level management or what Mintzberg (1979) calls the middle line and technostructures. In essence it results from the merger of the idea of management by rules or by principles with the notion of autonomy. The basic stance is: "These are the rules or principles or operations or procedures. Generally, you know what to do. If you run into a problem where the rules or principles don't apply or for some other reason you don't know how to solve, call me."

Management by exception is a common way for technical experts and consultants, accountants, lawyers, and other members of the technostructure to relate to employees dependent upon their expertise, but not directly under their command or control. It is also an important way for supervisors and other middle managers to grant levels of autonomy to their subordinates.

Management by Walking Around

Another important management-by model really amounts to a kind of communication principle. It is called *management by walking around*. The essential idea is for managers, particularly middle managers and members of the technostructure, to improve communications, problem solving, and morale among workers by being readily available to them in their work setting. An important variant on this idea, usually presented as the *open door policy,* is one that is probably part of the inaugural presentation of all new social administrators: "I want all of you to know that my door is always open to you." There may, of course, be certain reasonable limits that can be imposed on this practice without eliminating its basic intent. All 700 employees in a large agency should not expect to be able to drop in on the executive director at any time without appointment. The poor woman would never be able to get anything else done. However, all practitioners of an open door policy need to be constantly alert to the damage to their reputations that can be done by the manifold possibilities for unintentionally or covertly subverting such a policy. It can be subverted, for example, by a secretary who makes employees jump through all kinds of hoops to "get in to see the boss," limits appointments with the boss to the times when those employees already have the greatest demands on their time, and engages in similar controlling behaviors. Getting out and walking around the office can, in itself, be a way of transcending such subversions.

Management by Reengineering

Management by reengineering is the application of the business and industry concept of altering business processes to improve products and services. It is described by its proponents as a way of achieving gradual, incremental improvement. Reengineering is, in effect, an updating of the methods of scientific management. The process typically includes documenting an existing process, identifying measures of that process tied to what customers are seeking, testing the process against the measures, and identifying improvements in the process that might result in better performance in terms of the measures. These steps are then repeated over and over again. It is the repetition of the process that results in it sometimes being called a "continuous process improvement" technique.

An example of this application from the business world would be a grocery store owner's wish to reduce the time customers spend in the checkout lane. The owner would identify the existing steps involved in checking out, such as putting the groceries on the counter, the checker manually entering each item, and so on. The owner would then identify a measure such as total time spent in line waiting to check out. She would measure the times that a sample of customers spend in line. She would then identify ways in which the process could be improved to reduce the time spent in line. Such changes might include changing from a counter to a cart from which the checker could directly pull items to using bar code readers to enter items and prices. After implementing those changes, she would again measure the times customers spend in line and again attempt to identify additional ways the time could be reduced.

Reengineering does have applications to the delivery of social services. They could range from efforts to reduce the time clients spend in waiting rooms to efforts to improve the agency's record-keeping processes. The approach, at its core, involves looking critically to identify incremental changes that might be made in improving the processes used to deliver services.

Managing Quality

Total quality management (TQM) is a management approach that emphasizes the quality of the product or service delivered and the role of customers and workers in identifying ways in which quality could be improved (Gummer, 1996; Martin, 1993). Some would argue that the difference between TQM and reengineering is only the term that one chooses to use and that the application of both is identical. Others see TQM as placing more emphasis on employee and customer involvement in identifying the changes that may be needed if improvement is to occur.

Prasad and Sprague (1996) indicate that three fundamental TQM principles are customer or client focus, continuous improvement, and teamwork. TQM efforts are most often characterized by extensive employee involvement in identifying the ways in which processes might be improved. Thus, in the example above, it is not the grocery store owner who would decide how to reduce the time spent in line at her store, but the employees, who would work as a team to identify the ways in which time in line might be reduced. However, when the process is completed, it is most often the owner, not the employees, who select the alternative(s) to be introduced.

Total quality management as an approach has been popular in governmental and nonprofit organizations. Berman (1995) reported that more than thirty states had TQM efforts underway in state welfare agencies. Beinecke, Goodman, and Lockhart (1997) indicated that Medicaid managed care programs were increasingly using TQM. Kaplama and Varoglu (1997) suggested that social service agencies, like educational institutions, are convenient environments for applying the TQM philosophy because of their strong emphasis on learning and self-improvement.

The application of TQM is not without its critics. TQM requires time for employees to work as teams, and it is not always clear that the benefits from the process outweigh the costs of the time involved. A part of the organization may come to be devoted to implement TQM reviews and outcomes, reducing worker involvement and making its approach not all that different from usual approaches. The fact that those recommending changes to existing processes are often not in a position to decide to implement the changes leads some to see TQM as a form of co-optation of employees.

Performance Management

One of the most recent management innovations might be summed up with the phrase management by performance (Kettner & Martin, 1995). In a general sense, of course, performance measurement is a component of all management systems. What were scientific managers all about, for example, if not measuring performance? Currently, however, this phrase is a specific reference to activities associated with or inspired by passage of the federal Government Performance and Results Act of 1993 and several other related initiatives that are discussed more extensively in chapter 13.

Performance measurement as currently understood is an inherently neoconservative management perspective primarily concerned only with assessment of the status quo. The broader concerns of social administration associated with leadership and institution building do not figure into the perspective at all, and decision making is seen entirely through the lens of accountability for current activities.

There is an unmistakable ideological aura of neoconservatism associated with the performance measurement movement. At first glance, there appears to be nothing ideological about the measurement of performance, and efficiency, effectiveness, and quality are not, in themselves, criteria biased for or against any political position. The connection is most evident in the origins and context of contemporary performance measurement.

Within a few years of the origin of the age of grants in the 1960s, it was clear to a great many people of all political persuasions that a number of the new Great Society programs were not working. Effects to "fix" welfare programs and eliminate poverty were also seemingly responsible for huge growth in the beneficiary population and ultimately for the decline of New Deal liberalism. Political scientists such as Theodore Lowi (1969, 1995) and Robert Binstock and Katherine Ely (1971) saw the issue in terms of a transformation from "old welfare" to "new welfare" programs. Many other social scientists saw the problem apolitically in terms of the need for ongoing program evaluation.

Political conservatives quickly recognized in the accountability concerns of professionals and social scientists a golden opportunity for an attack on the legitimacy of the welfare state. Terms like "fraud" and "waste" and "privatization" became code words for an all-out assault on public social programs that have literally redefined the public culture in recent decades. In this highly charged political environment, advocates of performance measurement approaches have generally continued to address the issue from the vantage point of autonomous public administrators and politically neutral bureaucracy. In doing so, they have made themselves the pawns of larger conservative political interests for whom "effective performance" is merely another proximate objective like tax cuts on the way to total downsizing of government.

It is not the political naïveté of the performance measurement approach, however, that is of greatest concern. Everyone in social administration is susceptible to being used politically from time to time. The real problem that should be cause for concern in social administration is the incompleteness of the performance management model. At the very least, it needs to address the institutional implications of various performance outcomes. Is it really the case, for example, that clients are better off left unserved than being served ineffectively? Are no services always preferable to poor quality services? Can anybody even really know what makes a particular outcome effective and another ineffective in the social arena (or is that belief a by-product of surviving models of organizations as machines) (Lohmann, 1999)?

What, in other words, are the appropriate criteria, standards, and benchmarks that can be associated with performance appraisals? Until such questions can be answered, the approach merely supplies fodder for witchhunting. In the absence of definite criteria, scare words such as "waste," "inefficiency," "lack of effectiveness," and "poor quality" provide cover for what may be a political goal unrelated to the desire to help those in need.

MANAGEMENT BY THE BOOK

Something that everyone associated with management practice, research, and teaching quickly learns is to expect the question, Have you read [fill in the name of the latest popular management best-selling book]? Popular works on management dispensing advice crowd the shelves of mall bookstores and airport newsstands. One of the cultural phenomena of the 1980s in America was the transformation of certain corporate chief executive officers (CEOs) into something approaching cult figures; another was the meteoric rise of the management book. We saw the emergence of the management category on lists of best-selling books. As this trend was building, *Publishers' Weekly* noted that "dieting, sex, whimsy, food and gossip are no longer first in the hearts of bibliophiles. With no near competitors, business was the strongest selling subject in the United States in 1983" (Maryles, 1984, cited in Freeman, 1985, pp. 345–50).

There was, of course, important precedent for this. In the first decades of the twentieth century, Frederick Taylor's ideas about efficient performance on the job and their astonishing application in the Ford Motor Company assembly line production of the Model T (named for Taylor) represent such a precedent. Scientific management actually struck such a chord that it became an enduring part of American culture. Similarly, Chester Barnard, who was CEO of New Jersey Bell Telephone, and Mary Parker Follett, Herbert Simon, and Elton Mayo were also very widely read in their time.

Further, there is an interesting tradition of management humor anchored in such classics as Parkinson's law, Murphy's law, and the Peter Principle. Robert Townsend, CEO of the Xerox Corporation, achieved best-seller status with an irreverent work that, among other things, recommended that CEOs abolish their personnel departments and other similarly "audacious" claims. In fact, the topic of administrative and bureaucratic humor has its own scholarly journal, *The Bureaucrat*.

From Taylor forward, American culture seems also to periodically single out a few individuals (management "gurus") who are particularly adept at packaging and marketing their own interpretations and extensions of general management ideas. These management gurus tend to write best-selling books and collect huge fees for lecturing and consulting. This phenomenon of the management consultant/guru is very pervasive in contemporary life. It has even produced its own small body of theory: guru theory, as characterized by Huczynski (1993), is a popular (nonacademic) approach that he says is based in five beliefs:

1. The innovation that leads to improved products and services cannot be planned, but is largely dependent on trial and error.

2. Managers are more likely to "act into a feeling" than "feeling yourself into action."
3. Value systems and organizational cultures are more reliable guides to co-ordination than rules and commands.
4. Customers are the main source of innovations.
5. A strong customer orientation is fundamentally important.

He sees four distinct types of books being produced in this area:

1. Books aimed at lower-level executives, intended to show them how to move up the corporate ladder.
2. What-we-can-learn-from business books that purport to reveal the inner workings of large, multinational corporations.
3. Books striving to explain the complications of the stock market, finance, export trade, and so on.
4. Survival guides.

Huczynski also categorizes three classes of gurus, whom he calls academic gurus (Mintzberg, Warren Bennis, and Rosbeth Moss Kanter), consultants (John Naisbitt, Thomas Peters, Robert Waterman), and hero-managers (Harold Geneen, Donald Trump, Lee Iacocca, and John Scully).

Part of Huczynski's (1993) concern with this phenomenon should be of general concern in social administration, also, especially the way in which the guru aura renders certain ideas impervious to testing and falsification:

Certain ideas, such as those of Herzberg et al. (1959), continue to be popular even after other writers have demonstrated flaws in the research methods and have challenged them. The fact that newer and methodologically sounder ideas have become available has not reduced the popularity or discussion of older ideas like those of Abraham Maslow (1943), Douglas McGregor (1960) or Rensis Likert (1961). These continue to have a profound effect on management teaching. (p. 3)

Oversimplification is also near the core of Huczynski's case against the management gurus.

In *In Search of Excellence* Peters and Waterman demonstrated that they believe that the acronyms, logos and memory hooks were all necessary to the marketing of ideas to a managerial leadership who had serious intellectual difficulties to overcome. Whether any popular management writer has ever failed by underestimating the intellectual ability of his audience is not known. However, the ISOE formula of reducing ideas to easily remembered steps to success may have been a decisive factor in enticing such a large number of managers to read and discuss ideas which previously they had not considered to be particularly interesting. (p. 66)

It is, of course, very easy for those who are much less well known and lower paid teachers and researchers to overstate the dire threat to civilization posed by these popular and well-paid figures. To their credit, most gurus have successfully breached the sometimes formidable chasm between popular culture and the ivory tower world of traditional management theory. Yet the "quick fix" nostrums preached by some of the management gurus may not work quite as promised. However, this body of popular work has provided entry into the rich world of management ideas for many lower-level organizational employees, a useful guide for many social workers promoted into management, and continuing reading interest for experienced managers. Within the social administration systems of often insufficient education and promotion through the ranks, the easily understood writings of the gurus are often a key part of the education of social administrators.

CONCLUSION

The interest in management ideas that has overtaken the earlier concerns of social administration in social work has brought a rich vein of new ideas and practices into the traditional practice field and integrated social services administration or human services management more deeply into the general world of management. In particular, the MBO model has had a large and an enduring impact on social services. The MBO logic of mission, objective, and action statements is fundamental to many grant applications, for example. Likewise, the continuing influence of the other ideas discussed in this chapter and the newest and latest effusions of the management gurus have been important in the careers of many social administrators.

However, there are dangers associated with the emphasis on management and organizational leadership as it has evolved in the past two decades. The risk is that the equally important concerns of community leadership, the impact of critical decisions, and the general state of social service and professional social work institutions are in danger of being defined outside the perimeters of management concerns. At the same time, the contemporary fixation of managers in all sectors with short-term results and quick fixes to problems shows signs of infecting managers of social services at the very time that momentous changes are occurring as a result of managed care welfare reform and policy devolution. As this occurs, there are few fixed or reliably established roles in most communities for community organizers, social planners, or social action specialists, and clinical social workers in most settings are increasingly tied to a daily schedule that allows time only for client appointments. By default, leadership of social services and the profession will continue to fall more and more on these same managers. In part III, we take up these themes of institution building and the role of social administrators in that process.

The Processes of
Institutionalization

The discussion of institutionalization in social agencies up to this point has, by necessity, been somewhat vague, abstract, and theoretical. We attempt to clarify a number of those questions in part III. Through a series of chapters on the nature of institutionalization in organizations, planning, implementation, operation, and evaluation, we endeavor to flesh out these abstractions and show their relationship to the practice of social administration.[1]

That institutionalization is a major macrosocial process in human affairs there should be no doubt. In the modern world, institutionalization is the process whereby the habits, rituals, and routines of daily life (in the case of this book, work life) give meaning and structure to our lives. When, in discussing human behavior, we speak of social structure, it is largely the products of such institutional development that we recognize and relate to. Institutionalization comes in two principal forms in social administration. First, there is the steady, gradual, unplanned accumulation of habits, rituals, and routines (portions of which are called by such labels as policies and procedures, informal organizations, and task environments). Second, there are those deliberate, intentional efforts at creating, changing, or eliminating established and meaningful behavior patterns, which we sum up here with the term *institution building*. The term deliberately subsumes many related aspects of planning, program development, policy practice, and social change as these are experienced in the administrative setting.

Indeed, institutionalization is in many respects a living, organic process, as the many references to the "life cycles" of institutions attest. We can easily speak of the birth, death, development, and reincarnation of institutions, in almost human terms. We need to exercise care, however, in drawing too many close parallels between the cycles of human institutions and the life cycles of human beings. Individual humans generally live a relatively fixed life cycle, shortened only by disease and accident, up to a more or less absolute maximum physical limit somewhere above age 100. Even though social institutions may appear to be similarly finite in nature, some have proven themselves remarkably capable of cycles of renewal and change quite unlike any known forms of human longevity. The institutions of enduring major religions such as Judaism, Christianity, Buddhism, and Islam have long histories stretching over many centuries and characterized by many cycles of degeneration and renewal that often transcend the lives of many generations of human participants. Though social services in their modern, twentieth-century form have yet to attain such long-lasting status, some forms of social service institutions, such as residential care facilities for children, infirm old people, and various other categories of socially dependent populations, have been around for many centuries. From the perspective of institutional history, twentieth-century professional social services may turn out to be simply the product of a particular cycle of institutional renewal sparked by the social conditions of late nineteenth-century industrial society.

Be that as it may, we know also that some institutions, such as families, have built-in means of renewal and replacement of members, whereas in others, such as formal organizations, the problem is one of *telesis*, or the conscious, deliberate use of knowledge to attempt to renew or improve them.[2] Family systems such as traditional villages appear capable of existing for many hundreds of generations without outside interference. By contrast, formal organizations do not even get formed, much less have any hope of continuing, without some measure of social telesis.

In the first five chapters, we explore the general process of institutionalization in organizations and four moments or phases in the cycle of institutionalization of social agencies: planning, implementation, operations, and evaluation. The reader should take note that these four phases form a *logical* cycle but not necessarily an empirical one. There are no great, universal laws of institutional development whereby this cycle must proceed in any particular serial order, and there are not likely to be any.[3] However, there does appear to be a certain elemental logic to the notion that you plan before you do, and you can't judge the value or worth of something until you at least know what it is and probably know how it works as well.

CHAPTER 8

Policy, Institutions, and Strategic Action

In chapter 5, we examined research on organizational leadership and concluded with Charles Perrow that research in this area is rather inconclusive. In this chapter, we explore further a perspective on leadership introduced in chapter 1 but found only infrequently in the existing social work management literature. We begin with the assertion that one of the unique and important responsibilities of social administrators, and one that transcends management as such, is to provide institutional leadership for social welfare institutions. In this sense, we are in agreement with both Gummer (1979), who defines the primary objective of administration as defining the mission of institutions, and Reamer (1993), who argues that the social work profession should provide leadership in social welfare institutions. There is also an important element of social development in this view of social administration. This is evident, for instance, in Spergel's (1977) definition of social development as creating institutions to meet needs.[1]

However, there is little or no discussion in the practice literature of *who*, precisely, among social work professionals should take the initiative in institution building or *how* they should do it. One partial answer to the question of who is that much of the institutional leadership in social welfare and the profession of social work will almost certainly continue to come from social administrators, as it has for the past century. With respect to how that leadership will be done, the model introduced below identifies and details several of the major steps in that process.

REPRESENTATIVE SOCIAL SERVICE INSTITUTIONS

The reader still may not be clear on what we mean in this book by social service institutions and, therefore, why we suggest social administrators have a role in defining, creating, and maintaining them. Social agencies can be seen as consisting of clusters of interlaced social institutions in much the same way that buildings consist of unique combinations of architectural elements. Thus, a particular service *program* might be made up of a unique blend of *intake* and *discharge interviews, case recording practices, supervisory conferences, referrals,* and the like. Each of these sets of conventional behavior and various recognizable combinations of them (e.g., the particular interviews, recording practices, conferences, and referral practices of a hospice program) constitute institutions in the sense that we are using the term here.

The topic of institutionalization in social administration is not, as it may first appear, identical with the topic of social work methods. This is in part because one of the constant challenges in the social agency institutionalization process involves deciding when to use exclusively social work services and when to combine them with other professions and practices. For example, certain characteristic things will happen if professional social workers are used in making home visits, such as conducting social history assessment of the family, and slightly different things will happen if nurses are used, such as obtaining blood pressure readings. Movements, programs, rules, policies, sets of procedures, and other objects may also be institutions. The challenge of institutionalization in its simplest sense is deciding which combinations of such known elements, and perhaps which elements of novel or new methods, should be combined and continued.

An Example

There is little question that institutional leadership in social welfare and elsewhere *does* make a difference in the long run. In one exceptionally clear example, a historical case study by Broadhurst (1978) shows that Johns Hopkins University in Baltimore was quite likely *the* preeminent American institution in social reform and the emerging social professions during the late nineteenth century. Hopkins was also a leading training center for one of the social reform movements most closely associated with the emergence of social work as a profession. The students and professors of Johns Hopkins University had established relationships with the Charity Organization Society of Baltimore (the agency later directed by Mary Richmond), which was then an employer of graduate students in social science. Broadhurst notes that at the 1894 International Congress of Charities and Correction in Chicago, four of the eight reports were edited by faculty associated with Hopkins. But in the new century, university leaders at Johns Hopkins turned away from social reform. Johns Hopkins failed to establish a school of social work during the first decade of the new century when other institutions in New York, Boston, Cleveland, and elsewhere did so (or later). Subsequently, Johns Hopkins lost both its preeminent position in social science and also ceased to be a training ground for social workers (Broadhurst, 1978). The crucial turning point for all of this was the changing vision of the role of Johns Hopkins University and a change in strategy by the institutional leadership of the university.

Institutional leadership is anything but an exact science, but the point seems clear nonetheless: Had officials at Johns Hopkins acted differently at the turn of the century, the entire history of social work and that university could easily have been altered. Success or failure is not the point here. The issue is the role of administrative leaders in establishing the direction and focus of organized and ongoing institutions. The Hopkins case might be described using current jargon as a win-win situation: An institution as distinguished as Johns Hopkins can hardly be said to have been harmed by this fateful choice, and social work education certainly survived and prospered at other institutions. However, this vignette illustrates clearly the role of institutional leadership in decisions affecting the direction and vision of a particular university and the profession. After a promising start quite near the center of the emerging profession of social work, the institutional leadership of Johns Hopkins opted to move in other directions and yielded what would almost certainly have been a preeminent role in the evolution of American social welfare.

The postwar period (1945–1960) generation of social administrators and professional social work leaders did precisely this again as they pursued a vision of the United States as a "reluctant welfare state" and established a professional mission in which publicly funded, professionally delivered social services were to become a major component. The institutional testaments to that vision have been many, including the 1962 and 1967 social service amendments to the Social Security Act and local implementations of dozens of Great Society, Title XX, and other federal grant programs. Many of these programs were eliminated or changed into social service block grants during the Reagan–G. H. W. Bush years, and the drumbeat of conservative rhetoric consistently disparages the approach that these programs represented. Nevertheless, the vision of a national welfare state with state and local social services supported by national financing remains a strong one for a great many people in social work today. The coherence of this vision did not happen by accident, and it did not happen simply because the United States became a fabulously wealthy, urban-industrial superpower in this period. Moreover, it did not happen because of some inexorable laws of social development.

Publicly supported social services did not evolve as completely as these social work leaders originally envisioned for a variety of reasons, including the normal measure of strategic and tactical blunders, opposition, unintended consequences, and a host of other factors. The overriding point here is that these leaders set forth an institutional vision embracing the social work profession, social services, community leadership, and government at all levels. It was a vision that has served the social work profession and social service community well for roughly a half-century. But it is one that is currently much in need of updating. A major institutional leadership challenge facing social services today and for the foreseeable future involves dissemination of a new, updated vision that incorporates the roles of professional and community institutions. At minimum, this would involve translating the bipartisan New Federalist agenda of lower taxes, a smaller federal government, and policy devolution to the states and local communities into a meaningful vision of the future for social services or into identifying believable, feasible alternatives.

Although institutional leadership in this sense is not an exact science, it is nonetheless possible to identify four principal sets of tasks for institutional leadership:

1. Defining purpose and the broad parameters of policy
2. Establishing workable strategies for achieving those goals
3. Symbolizing and representing the institution(s)
4. Managing the process of institutionalization
    a. Establishing careful and deliberate planning processes
    b. Overseeing the implementation of policy
    c. Establishing and directing day-to-day operations
    d. Evaluating the results of operations

These tasks are suffused throughout the study of social administration. Some aspects of this topic are dealt with in this chapter, and others are dealt with in those that follow. Defining purposes and strategy is discussed in chapter 9 on administrative planning, symbolizing the institution is a concern of chapter 18 on marketing, and institutional representation is a theme of other chapters on leadership (chapter 5) and boards (chapter 27). Overseeing implementation is discussed in chapter 10 on implementation, and establishing and directing day-to-day operations is dealt with in chapter 11 on managing operations. The remaining aspects of this model of institutional leadership are taken up in the rest of this chapter.

SOCIAL POLICY

In the most general sense, social policy is the portion of the social work curriculum most directly concerned with issues of basic organizational and community purpose. In the context of institution building, social policy is the vehicle through which most social service institutions are defined, formed, and maintained.

As they have evolved within the social work curriculum, social policy and practice methods including social administration are treated as discrete and distinct subject matters studied in different classes and often in different semesters. Students can easily get the impression that subject matter in one course does not hold or carryover into the domain of another in the same way that speed limit laws in one state do not apply to other states. As a result, students may sometimes leave classes with the impression that practice and policy are less interwoven than they actually are in the real worlds of practice. Nowhere is this separation more unfortunate than in considering the role of policy in institutional leadership. What social work *is* and what social workers *do* at any particular moment is largely policy driven. Leslie Leighninger and Phil Popple found just this accent when they termed social work a "policy based profession" (Popple & Leighninger, 1997). Current conceptions of social work are very much grounded in that post-war vision of professional leaders. It is possible to take any of several views on the issue of institutional leadership.

For a great many people in social work, prior policy enactments, such as the *service strategy*[2] of the 1962 and 1967 Social Security Amendments, the *community*[3] approach of the Community Mental Health Centers Act, and the *opportunity theory*[4] approach to poverty, have settled once and for all the large questions of purpose, strategy, and direction in social services. From this view, the primary challenge facing institutional leadership in social welfare in the recent past and future might best be termed *fidelity* or, as it is sometimes termed, institutional maintenance. Like the Marines whose motto *semper fidelis* means "always faithful," this view projects that social work leaders must encourage their workers and professional colleagues to remain forever faithful to the vision of a comprehensive and coordinated national system of efficient and effective, federally funded, state-regulated, and locally administered social services.

For holders of other more radical visions, the larger questions are also settled, and fidelity is also required. In this case, fidelity is owed to the vision that the contradictions of advanced capitalism will sooner or later bring revolutionary movement toward social justice, and prerevolutionary praxis involves efforts at consciousness raising and abetting the downfall of capitalist hegemony. The challenge of social services is not to become a force of reaction in the meantime.

From other vantage points, fidelity is seen as a much-overrated virtue, and what is needed is precisely the kind of activities that are often called *revisioning, repurposing, rethinking,* and *reinventing.* These represent reconsiderations of the basic missions, directions, goals, objectives, and strategies of social welfare activity (Adams & Nelson, 1995; Gummer, 1995a; Morris & Morris, 1986; Osborne & Gaebler, 1992). From these viewpoints, social welfare is a case of Peter Drucker's guideline that institutions need to rethink themselves and their purposes periodically. Drucker (1993) observed that "any organization, whether a business, a nonprofit, or a government agency, needs to rethink itself once it is more than forty or fifty years old. It has outgrown its policies and its rules of behavior. If it continues in its old ways, it becomes ungovernable, unmanageable, uncontrollable" (p. 290). That is somewhat less than the amount of time that has passed since the formulation of the public social services institutional model.

The problem of revisioning social services might be seen as a largely theoretical task, in which case primary responsibility will be left to the intellectuals: writers, teachers, researchers, theorists, and others. Some of that kind of revisioning work goes on continually in academia. For example, the social work literature is filled with proposals for reconceptualizations of various aspects of policy and practice.[5] Also, in recent decades within sociology there was residual interest in a vision of social work first raised in the debate over income versus services strategies for dealing with poverty in the 1960s and later seized upon by the Nixon administration in the welfare reform efforts of the early 1970s. In this negative vision, social workers are seen as interested in social services only because the services provide jobs for social workers little concerned for the benefits to clients.[6] Likewise, managers are seen as narrowly focused only in the self-interests of their organizations. Given the degree to which new social work undergraduate programs were gaining enrollment from among former sociology majors during the time, one might add that sociological writing on this vision was anything but disinterested. In fact, it often read like sour grapes. This did not minimize the effect, however, when neoconservative advocates of family values also seized upon these arguments as further evidence of the problems of bureaucratization and big government. The bottom line here is the need for revisioning the social service goal of a national service state.

A good deal of revisioning work goes on within social work education. The kind of rethinking of the causes of poverty done by Richard Cloward and associates in the Grey Areas Project during the 1960s represents such revisioning (Cloward & Ohlin, 1960). The challenge posed during the 1970s by Joel Fischer's (1973) evaluation work that concluded that casework was largely ineffective is another example. Robert Morris's (Morris & Morris, 1986) *Why Care for the Stranger* and Michael Sherraden's (1991) innovative work on the assets and capital of the poor are among the better known examples nationally. At the local level, social work educators and social work professionals have been involved in literally thousands of innovative projects, a significant portion of which have sought to take the profession in new directions and toward new visions of the future.

The problem is that much of this local effort has been highly fragmented and tailored to local circumstances, and almost all of it has taken place within the now threadbare postwar vision of a gradually unfolding American welfare state. In social work today there is nothing approaching a consistent, coherent national vision for the coming decade to either update or supplant the comprehensive community services vision of the late 1940s. Perhaps the closest we have come to such an institutional vision of social services through most of the 1980s and 1990s might be the metaphor of "a thousand points of light" used by President George H. W. Bush or the individualistic residue of the 1960s "do your own thing."

Social work and social service leaders everywhere have moved energetically and opportunistically into dozens of new fields with hundreds of new forms of service, and the social work literature is abuzz with proposals for yet more innovative ventures. This overall strategy of simply adding more and more innovative community services may be increasingly threadbare, however, without an up-to-date vision of what it all means in the new millennium.[7] As a result, the institutions of social welfare may appear fuzzy, out of focus, and lacking direction to a great many people who might otherwise support those efforts.

Strategy as Environmental Response

One of the general points of the preceding discussion is that the environment of social administration practice is anything but fixed and immutable. Changes in policy, historical trends, a sometimes contingent relation with the social work profession, social problems, social science, and the liberal arts, along with the earlier noted influences of community and organization all work together to shape and mold social administration practice. All of these influences, however, share the common characteristic of being environmental forces that *act upon* social administration. In the remainder of this chapter, we reverse the view and consider the ways in which the practice of social administration acts upon its environment. We do so within the general paradigm of strategy. The general issue involved is how organizations, programs, and services can best be directed in a changing environment. The answer we suggest is through thoughtful, deliberate development and strategy to implement policy.

Strategy Defined

According to James Brian Quinn (1980), *strategy* "is the pattern or plan that integrates an organization's major goals, policies, and action sequences into a cohesive whole" (quoted in Moore, 1992, p. 256). Well-formulated strategy "helps to marshal and allocate an organization's resources into a unique and viable posture based on its relative internal competencies and shortcomings, anticipated changes in the environment, and contingent moves by intelligent opponents" (quoted in Moore, 1992, p. 256).

For the social administrator, goal-oriented thinking on strategy may be said to be deliberate, thoughtful action in response to opportunities, limits, and commitments. Competitive market and political opportunities, grant announcements and requests for proposals, available resources and unused competencies, all offer *opportunities* for action. At the same time, limits on resources, knowledge, time, and energy all establish *constraints* upon strategic action. And, finally, values and ethics, beliefs, personal and professional obligations, and human needs bring forth binding *commitments* that shape and mold action. Social administration is, in Erving Goffman's (1969) phrase, strategic interaction: a use of self and groups to organize and carry out our intentional strategic projects, enlisting others in the process through consent, coercion, and other possible means. Careful, conscious, deliberate selection of strategies is a key aspect of this process.

An example should suffice to illustrate the role of strategy. As noted in the previous section, the challenge taken up by the postwar generation of social work leaders was one of building a genuine national system of community-based social services and a cadre of trained professionals capable of staffing the system. That objective has to a considerable degree been accomplished.

One of the principal strategies employed to that end was to opportunistically seize upon available funds for a broad range of purposes and tailor them to fit the overall objective of creating community-based social services staffed by professional social workers. Was there ever a specific national meeting of social work leaders at which an explicit decision was made to deliberately pursue such a "soft money" strategy? We are not aware of any such meetings, although there easily could have been. It is just as likely that the strategy emerged gradually in response to grant opportunities as they became available. It is difficult to fault these leaders for this strategic choice. It clearly appeared to be the best option available at the time.

To avoid blame, however, does not require being blinded to one obvious, if unanticipated, consequence of pursuing the soft money strategy. Significant portions of the existing social service system in the United States are built on a very soft financial base. This represents a major institutional weakness of the system. Soft money in the form of grants is almost always also short-term money, and the Nixon-era transition from grants to contracts, the Reagan-era transition to block grants, and the current transition to managed care have done little to allay the problem. Along with the greater certainty offered by contracts has come the long-term uncertainty caused by the political environment of reducing public expenditures.

As a result, the national social services system at times resembles a network of Gold Rush mining camps. It is the most tentative of communities. It is clusters of jerrybuilt shacks, with no permanent foundations, easily swept away in the frequent flash floods of political change. The foremost challenge facing the institutional leadership of social services in the current century may well be one of shoring up the institutional foundations. That challenge is one of finding a more secure financial base, increasing the constituency support, rethinking the mission, revisioning the idea of social services, and recommitting to those ideals. Reaffirming or modifying basic strategies of funding, service delivery, and so on may be a fundamental aspect of that challenge for institutional leaders. Because of the strong durable connection between social welfare leadership and social administration, much of the burden of this institutional challenge will fall squarely on the shoulders of current and future social administrators.

The Theory of Strategy

Whereas policy is primarily concerned with answering the question "What are we going to do?" the related question of "and how are we going to do it?" is the province of what has become known as strategic theory. The theory of strategy, as it is outlined here, is fundamental to the practice of social administration in this task of institution building and renewal. Modern strategic theory has emerged only slowly into the management mainstream over the past half-century and is not yet fully formed. As we saw in chapters 6 and 7, management theorists in the wake of Herbert Simon sketched out a psychology and sociology of organizational decision making. One of the further directions that this work has taken is the development of the theory of strategy.

Charles E. Lindblom has been a major contributor to strategic theory in this sense. In an early publication, Lindblom (1959) amplified on a number of the themes already highlighted by Herbert Simon (1947/1997). Administrators in the public sector typically don't have the time, the resources, or any other particularly compelling reason to carefully define their problems, identify, and investigate all of their alternatives and choose only the best possible options. Instead, Lindblom noted they tend to "muddle through," not infrequently "satisficing" or seizing upon the first workable alternative, as Simon had suggested. Lindblom's interest, however, was not merely in reporting that this was how managers behaved. He actually set out with the aid of the philosopher David Braybrooke to make the case that this was the best way to operate in the practical contexts of policy and strategy (Braybrooke & Lindblom, 1963). Decision makers, they said, made strategic choices that were remedial, serial, and incremental. That is, they sought to correct mistakes, which seldom occurred in isolation but rather a part of a long (serial) chain of related decisions, no one of which could be singled out as unique or definitively important. Together, these three characteristics of decisions define the interactional framework on which the cycle of institutionalization—planning, implementation and evaluation—is based.

A number of years later, James Brian Quinn applied this insight to strategic theory when he discovered

> the same paradox which C. E. Lindblom had come across before him: that large, well-managed organizations changed their strategies in ways which bore little resemblance to the planning prescriptions usually found in management literature; and that the rationale for what they were doing—"incremental strategy formulation"—was not an instance of failure, but probably constituted "the best normative model" for this type of decision making.[8] (Moore, 1992, p. 258)

In seeking to explain this paradox, Quinn turned to the literature on military–diplomatic strategy formulation and drew four essential insights:

1. "Effective formal strategies contain three elements: the most important goals, the most significant policies, and the major programs (or action strategies)."
2. "Such strategies develop around a few key concepts and 'thrusts' or emphases that provide cohesion, balance, and focus."
3. Strategy doesn't just deal with the unpredictable, but with the unknowable. "The essence of strategy, therefore is to 'build a posture' that is both strong enough and flexible enough to allow the organization to attain its goal regardless of the unforeseen interactions of external events."

4. Like the military, civil organizations should have a hierarchy of strategies appropriate to each of its spheres of operations (grand, theater, area, and battle) and appropriate to its level of decentralization. A similar hierarchy is evident in social services in national or state policy, agency mission, program objectives, and daily assignments. (Moore, 1992, p. 260)

It is possible, Quinn argued, to identify nine critical factors and structural elements that should be present in good strategy:

1. *Clear, decisive objectives.* Again, we are back to this most fundamental of leadership concerns: *What are we doing, and why are we doing it? When the funding of the agency is threatened, and new funding must be found, will the agency bend with the wind and adopt whatever purpose is fundable? Or, is there a clear sense of mission for which funding is sought?*

2. *Maintaining initiative* through proactive selection of courses of action and timing. In other words, it is not a strategy if it just happens, and it is opportunism not strategy just to react to events as they occur. *If an agency knows in advance that it will be singled out for criticism at the next legislative session, because it is always criticized, then a strategic approach involves working out in advance how to deal with such criticism.*

3. *Concentration.* One of the purposes of strategy is to concentrate the attention and energies of a large number of people on the same objectives and use of the same tactics. *Can all of the major employees (executives, department heads and supervisors) and most of the rest of employees indicate to anyone who may ask for whatever reason that the agency is in transition from a general-purpose outpatient mental health center to a resource base specifically supporting persistent and chronic mentally ill persons living independently in the community? Is the strategy clear? Can it be clearly communicated?*

4. *Conceding selected positions.* When one is clear on the objectives and the strategy, it is not necessary to be right all the time, strong in every area or to win every point. *All of our professional staff have training and credentials and interest in counseling activity, so we will contract out any community-outreach work that needs to be done. Community work isn't our strong suit.*

5. *Flexibility.* When the overall strategy is clear, rigid adherence to particular tactics for achieving that strategy are unnecessary. *It's clear that our tactics last year to overcome legislative criticism didn't work. What do we need to do differently this year?*

6. *Coordinated and committed leadership.* The theory of strategy, in fact, identifies one major source of coordination in social administration. This

strategic point is sometimes characterized as "making sure that everyone is singing from the same page." *If anyone from our organization talks with a legislator, they need to make sure to emphasize that we have addressed their concerns in the following ways. . . .*

7. *Surprise.* Use of speed, secrecy, and industrial intelligence. This is not an endorsement of industrial espionage. In most cases, merely paying attention to the public record will be sufficient. *Every year, every agency goes to the county commission with the same request for an increase as the previous year. The economy is so strong, and our funding is holding up. We know from what our board members tell us that the commission really likes our service consolidation initiatives, and would undoubtedly support another increase this year. But we really don't need the money right now, so let's be honest, ask for a decrease and bank the credibility instead.*

8. *Security.* A matter of knowing what opponents, competitors, and supporters may be seeking and what you plan to do about it. *We know the legislative committee has no real problem with us, except that the vice chairperson's daughter once had a bad experience with our agency and she's out to get even. Now we hear that she's starting a petition drive to remove our funding.*

9. *Communications.* Develop broad, clear, and uncomplicated plans for conveying the strategy to the appropriate audiences. *Our friends and supporters throughout the community need to know that we are uncompromisingly committed to making our support program for independent living work, and we would like their help in communicating this message.*

Although Quinn was primarily concerned with very large, strategically dynamic, diversified multinational corporations, many of his insights are equally applicable to small nonprofits and medium-sized public social service bureaus. Quinn argued for the displacement of formal planning systems by "the realities of logical incrementalism" (Moore, 1992, p. 260). Organizations, he said, that allegedly engaged in synoptic (comprehensive) planning "rarely write down their complete strategy; and typically, construct it with processes which are 'fragmented, evolutionary, and largely intuitive'" (p. 260). What Quinn calls "the real strategy" usually evolves out of the decision situation: "Consensus among top management which is created by an interaction between internal decisions and external events" (p. 257).

It is precisely because of the evolutionary character of the postwar social service vision and strategy, for example, that we cannot presently point to the specific planning documents in which it is written down and to the exact meetings at which it was decided. When, for example, was the decision made by the federal government to extend grants in aid, which had traditionally been reserved only for other levels of (state, local, and regional) government to nonprofit social service organizations? And in what policy was that decision first spelled out?[9] It is only with the kind of detailed ferreting out of facts that characterizes good historical research that this picture will eventually emerge. In the meantime, we must go on with only a very hazy picture of that period and the choices that were made.

Other terms that are important in Quinn's model include goals and objectives, policies, programs, tactics, influence, power, authority, political behavior, process, and subsystems. *Goals and objectives* "state what is to be achieved and when results are to be accomplished." *Policies* "are rules or guidelines that express the limits within which action should occur." *Programs* "specify the step-by-step sequence of actions necessary to achieve major objectives." *Tactics* "are the short-duration, adaptive, action-interaction realignments that opposing or competitive forces use to accomplish limited goals after their initial contact." In the Quinn model, formal authority is "the delegated right to use legitimate power" and is distinguished from informal authority that arises from the individual personality. *Political behavior* is "normal for any ambitious person" and "consists of activities undertaken primarily to increase an individual's or group's referent or legitimate power." *Process* is "the sequence of steps, relationship transformations, and interpersonal or intellectual transactions needed to reach an end state or outcome" (Moore, 1992, pp. 256–57).

Quinn is emphatic that despite appearances, this process should not be characterized as Lindblom did as "muddling through." It is, by contrast, a "conscious, purposeful, proactive, executive practice." In the end, strategies are really only judged by their success. For example, the soft-money strategy of social service funding has clearly been a successful one over the medium term. Agencies have been founded, built up, and maintained in this way. The soft funding base that this has produced for much of the existing service delivery system is better seen as an emergent consequence than as a failure of the strategy. How the strategy will play out in the long run, however, remains to be seen.

INSTITUTIONALIZATION

How are policy and strategy translated into services? We take up part of the answer to that question in chapter 10. In this section, we explore another part of that answer by examining the social process of institutionalization in organizations. Busy administrators, hard-pressed to locate increasingly scarce sources of funding and striving to stay abreast of even the most minute changes in policy, are not always well tuned into their role in visioning, strategy formation, and other aspects of the institutionalization of services and programs. But that role is theirs nonetheless.

The process of institutionalization can be initially understood by looking briefly at the McDonald's hamburger chain and community mental health centers network. One is clearly commercial and the other is predominantly, although not exclusively, nonprofit. Both trace their establishment to roughly the same period (1959 and 1963, respectively). And, over the past four decades each, in its own way, has become an important community institution in most American communities. Crisis intervention, community treatment, and short-term treatment are as much social services institutions today, because of the work of community mental health, as junk food is in general American culture because of the influence of McDonald's. Part of the difference between the place of McDonald's and the place of social work and mental health social services as community institutions, however, is wrapped up in the universal recognition and visibility of the former and the near-invisibility of the latter for large segments of the community.[10] It is also not *merely* a matter of public relations, advertising, and marketing, although these are genuinely important, as discussed in chapter 18.

In fact, an underlying problem that plagues virtually all of social work and social services today is the incomplete realization of the aspirations of social policy and lack of public recognition because of what will be termed *incomplete institutionalization*. In the context of policy implementation, institutionalization is the social process that explains how particularity and individuality arise out of the generality and abstraction of policy. In the case of social services, policies have been laid down, strategies mapped out, organizations structured, and institutions founded and built up, but there has been insufficient attention to the challenge of fully incorporating those institutions into the daily life of the communities in which they are located. Everyone in a community will recognize the local elementary school, the senior center, the police station, the United Way, Red Cross, and Salvation Army and a host of other local community institutions. But what about the homeless shelter? The adolescent halfway house? The adoption agency that has existed there for 100 years? Many social agencies are little short of completely unknown in their home communities.

Institutions are also basic to understanding how real organizations are actually constructed in the day-to-day relations of their members and also explain why their shared social worlds are not infinitely malleable and indeterminate or subjective. The sociologist Richard Scott is one of a group of organization researchers who have been promoting a new institutionalism. Scott (1995) said, "Institutions consist of cognitive, normative, and regulative structures and activities that provide stability and meaning to social behavior. Institutions are transported by various carriers—cultures, structures and routines—and they operate at multiple levels of jurisdiction" (p. 33).

Philip Selznick (1949), in Scott's view, was the first organization theorist concerned with the transformation of organizations into institutions as "the structural expression of rational action" (p. 25). According to Selznick, "Institutionalization is a process. It is something that happens to an organization over time, reflecting the organization's own distinctive history, the people who have been in it, the groups it embodies and the vested interests they have created, and the way it has adapted to its environment" (p. 16). Institutionalization, in brief, is the process by which people come to know about, care about, and feel involved with and committed to an organization.

The new institutionalism in organization studies also brings in the concepts of field and stakeholder. As Paul DiMaggio and Walter Powell (1983) note, an *organizational field* refers to "those organizations that, in the aggregate, constitute a recognized area of institutional life: key suppliers, resource and product consumers, regulatory agencies and other organizations that produce similar services or products" (p. 143). Thus, we can speak of the field of community mental health, for example, as the aggregate of organizations providing mental health services together with those aspects of law enforcement, support services, health care, state regulators and monitoring agencies, and others engaged in activities and services that bear upon the delivery of those services.

One of the reasons why the concentration on institutionalization processes in this book is important is due to a deficit in attention to institutional concerns. Social work in recent decades has seldom attended closely to institutional concerns and issues with predictable and sometimes discouraging results. One of the best ways to begin to understand the importance of institutional perspectives is to compare the present politically invulnerable position of the social security program, for example, with thousands of other lesser known programs and services. When social security is threatened, as it frequently has been, millions of people can and do show concern and spring into action. One of the most dramatic facts about many community social services is how few people other than employees know about them or care what happens to them. In some cases, even clients don't care! This is not a natural circumstance or an inevitable condition. It is not due to something inherently unpopular or unappealing in the nature of social services. It is due to the ways in which these institutions have been (or more likely not been) nurtured and tended.[11]

There are, certainly, important ambiguities in the public image of the social work profession as a social institution that accurately reflect professional self-understandings. Much of the public understanding of social work in American culture in recent decades, for example, might well be summed up in the social worker character portrayed in Leonard Bernstein's *West Side Story*. In the song "Officer Krupke," one of the soloists is portrayed as a confused, harried, and befuddled social worker who is one in a series of referrals for a troubled adolescent gang member. After an attempt to summon up compassion, the social worker concludes:

This boy don't need a job.
He needs a year in the pen!

The tendency among social workers familiar with this characterization has been to see it as a case of poor public relations and to bemoan lack of public understanding of the role of social work. Both, of course, are partially true. Almost nowhere has there been any professional recognition that Bernstein artistically captured one side of the legitimate ongoing professional debate between the impulse for *social control* and more compassionate responses of *social support.* For better or for worse, the depiction of the social worker in *West Side Story* is—as it was four decades ago—what social work looks like for much of the modern world. Therein may lie a large portion of the problem of institutionalization for the profession, and it is not unlike the problems faced by most social services.

CONCLUSION

In this chapter, we introduced the concept of social institutions and suggested it and the related idea of institution building as suitable subjects for the practice of social administration. To the previous dimensions of leadership discussed in chapter 5 we added the important dimension of leadership as institution building and preservation. Social work, it was noted, is truly a policy-based profession, in that the dictates of social policy have a strong impact on the shape and form of what is perceived as proper social work practice at any given time. This conception of policy-based practice led us into a discussion of the role of strategy and strategic decisions. The particular model of strategy that we focused on articulates closely with the incrementalist models of decision making and policy development and suggests a role for social administrators as the architects and builders of lasting social service institutions.

In the next four chapters, we continue exploring the somewhat complex topic of institutionalization. The notion of social agencies and programs as well as the broader notion of organizations as institutions is a very familiar one in social administration and yet one that is not often subjected to the kind of careful examination or scrutiny that we offered in this chapter. Institutional leadership is the process of defining purpose and the broad parameters of policy, working out strategies for goal attainment, symbolizing and representing the institution, and managing the process of institutionalization through the cycle of planning, implementation, operations, and evaluation. A key element in this cycle is the development of effective and sound strategy, and in this chapter recent management contributions in the area of strategy were examined closely. Finally, contributions from the sociology of knowledge, like the resurgence of institutionalism in organizational studies, point up the ways in which individuals become engaged in and committed to institutions. In the next four chapters, we examine in greater detail the four moments in the unique cycle of institutionalization for social agencies that begins in social policy and ends in evaluation and reconsideration of what has gone on before.

CHAPTER 9

Administrative Planning

In this chapter, we concentrate on administrative and organizational planning, paying particular attention to the daunting task of defining and keeping fresh the agency's purposes, missions, objectives, and strategies in constantly changing environments. Management by objectives, discussed in chapter 7, examines this issue narrowly in terms of procedures for linking statements and texts. The planning literature examines many associated questions and perspectives arising out of that attempt to construct a management by objectives statement or a standing plan of any type.

In our experience, students often find much of the social planning literature frustratingly abstract, vague, and unapproachable. It is often unclear why one ought to engage in planning or precisely how to go about it. Assorted laundry lists of procedures and operations do little to clarify the underlying dynamics. Thus, it is not at all surprising that Cnaan and Rothman (1986) found that practitioners were not able to perform community practice roles to the extent they believed it was appropriate to do so and that the disparity was particularly sharp in the case of social planning.

The origins of such difficulties may be due in part to the way the subject is approached. In actuality, there are a relatively small number of occasions that call for an extended and deliberate planning process. As James Brian Quinn noted (see chapter 8), formal planning processes are less relevant to ongoing administration than logical incrementalism. In the commercial arena, entrepreneurs may even discourage planning as a barrier to timely responses to unforeseen opportunities (Mintzberg, 1994). To be sure, planned, deliberate thoughtful responses to the future are one of the universal expectations of all choice or decision-making and a day-to-day reality for social administrators. Yet planning conversations almost always begin with or attempt to embrace the totality of some particular conception of a planning process—to discover, as it were, the planning aspect of all human behavior and social relations rather than concentrating on the particulars of the special occasions.

OCCASIONS FOR PLANNING

In this discussion, rather than presenting the usual detailed discussion of an overall planning process, we focus instead on identifying some of the common situations in which planning arises or where planned responses are needed.

Many present planning in these and other situations as one phase or moment in a general cycle or system of social action that also involves implementation, evaluation, and feedback (Banerjee, 1979). Indeed, that is how we present it here, as part of the cycle of institutionalization that also includes implementation, operations, and evaluation as a form of accountability.

Organization

Although seldom discussed as a planning problem, the formal organization as discussed in chapter 4 is also the planned organization. The principal thing that distinguishes formal or rational organization from the informal is the planned, deliberate character of the former. For the social administrator, formal organizations can be planned; informal organization can only be anticipated.

Resource Allocation

Any major change in the pattern of the flow of resources through an organization will be an occasion requiring planning. Thus, for example, budgeting is a form of planning that is discussed separately in chapter 23. Likewise, the hiring of any new staff person or the departure of existing staff will also be the occasion for planned responses.

Program Change

Creation of new programs or modifications of existing ones will also require some planning, whether the change results from internal initiatives (board or executive action) or external demands (new legislation or regulations). Affirmative action, block grants, devolution, managed care, and welfare reform are just a few of the occasions requiring planned responses by social agencies.

Facilities

In the smallest social agencies, facilities planning is a matter of renting an office space, installing desks and chairs, a phone line or two, and you are off and running. As organizations increase in size, the problem of facilities planning gets increasingly complicated. For large hospitals, residential treatment facilities and other large establishments, facilities planning may require an entire full-time staff.

Initiatives

Bright ideas, flashes of insight, and unmotivated or unanticipated proposals for change arise with great regularity in organizations. When they are yours, they can generate tremendous enthusiasm. Less predictably, this may also be true when they are someone else's. Typically, however, initiatives proposed by nonsignificant others or outsiders tend to be simply ignored in organizations that have their own agendas and that develop very proprietary senses about who can tell them what they ought to be doing. Initiatives proposed by outside stakeholders, however, may demand responses regardless of their merits and thus work themselves onto the agency's planning agenda.

PLANNING DEFINED

Planning has been part of overall models of management since the nineteenth century. Henri Fayol identified planning (*prévoyance)* as the first element of management. Logically, it is not hard to see how this is the case. We must plan before we act and evaluate or reconsider afterward. For Fayol, managing means "looking ahead," and a good plan of action was one that included

- *Unity,* or one general plan that informed the specific plans for each activity

- *Continuity,* or a concern for both the short and long range implications of planned actions
- *Flexibility,* or adjustments for unforeseen events
- *Precision,* or eliminating as much guesswork as possible (Wren, 1979, p. 241)

Luther Gulick, director of the Institute of Public Administration at Columbia University and a member of President Franklin D. Roosevelt's Committee on Administrative Management, and his coauthor Lyndall Urwick defined planning as "working out in broad outline the things that need to be done and the methods for doing them to accomplish the purpose for the enterprise" (Gulick & Urwick, 1937, quoted in Wren, 1979, p. 382). Noted management scholar William H. Newman (1951) said that planning "provides the basis for organization, assembling resources, direction and control" (p. 17). Planning, he noted, involves recognizing the need for action, investigation and analysis, proposing action, and decisions.

Newman's model emphasized three types of plans:

1. Goals, objectives, and other expressions of the purposes of organized action
2. Single-use plans that establish a course of action to deal with a specific situation and are "used up" when that situation has been dealt with
3. Standing plans that endure and are changed only as circumstances warrant

According to Peter Drucker (1990), planning in nonprofit organizations "is quite different from what business people usually mean by the term" (p. 111) and embraces concern for the impact upon the organizations multiple constituencies now more commonly known as stakeholders.

These have been some of the universally recognized elements of planning for decades. Looking ahead to the future. Recognizing the need for action. Establishing a course of action. Working out details of purpose, strategy, and tactics in advance. Assembling the resources necessary to accomplish desirable tasks. Establishing relationships between general strategy and specific courses of action. Making adjustments for unforeseen events. Eliminating guesswork where possible. Establishing an agenda of needed decisions and actions. And having a standing plan that among other things takes into account the impact of plans on stakeholders. To this list might easily be added a sense of empowerment sufficient to overcome feelings of futility, a concern for feasibility, a sense of proportion, and a host of additional considerations.

Planning means different things to different people and in different situations. In the broadest sense, planning can be seen as a way of life generally associated with professionals and other educated people of higher socioeconomic status—an interest in and concern for anticipating and preparing for the future. Professionals, for example, plan for their careers and take appropriate steps like attending graduate school to prepare themselves. Family planning is now an accepted part of family life for many people. At some point later in life (one hopes not too much later), they also begin planning for their retirement, and a growing number of people make preparations later in life for their own death, such as funeral planning, estate planning, living wills, and so on.

According to Edward Banfield (1970, p. 54), in a study that was highly controversial at the time but is now widely accepted, one of the defining characteristics of people in poverty is an inability or unwillingness to plan, most likely associated with a general sense of futility and lack of empowerment. Banfield's premise does not rest upon imputing differences in intelligence or any cognitive ability to plan between poor and nonpoor people nor does it rely upon differences in education. The reasoning here is relatively simple to understand and is grounded in a lack of futurity. If you don't believe that you have a future, or if your future offers little to look forward to, why anticipate or plan for it?

At times, *social* planning, which Rothman (1977, 1996) suggests is one of three change-oriented approaches to community practice, has been posed as an alternative outlook to management that is seen as very maintenance oriented. Yet, planning in the context of social administration is not really a debatable alternative. Formal organizations engage in planning in the above senses because they must. In constantly changing environments, the issue is not whether or not to plan. It is whether to plan poorly or well. In the administrative context, planning can be said to be the *executive and organizational problem-solving processes of preparing a set of decisions for action in the future.*[1]

TYPES OF PLANNING

The planning theorist John Friedmann (1959, 1973) identified two principal forms of planning. The first he called *allocative* planning, concerned with preparing for decisions to change the allocation of resources, such as setting apart resources for particular purposes or then assigning them to particular objectives. The second type he called *innovative* planning, which is literally concerned with preparing for decisions to implement social change. Planning theorists typically also make distinctions between long-range (e.g., five-year) and short-range (e.g., quarterly) planning. The distinction is largely theoretical, except in the sense that some types of planning involve immediate results and some involve results that will not be known for some time into the future. If one is the parent of a five-year-old child, educational planning for kindergarten involves a much shorter time frame than planning for college for the same child. And the answer to whether you chose the right day care program will probably be known long before the college choice issue even arises. Much the same commonsense logic arises in social agency planning.

Most administrative planning, by necessity, involves relatively and often artificially short time horizons of often a year or two at most (e.g., Bryson, 1995). However, most short-term planning also has long-term consequences, whether or not they are taken into account in the planning. Programs and decisions, once in place, can be very difficult to amend, modify or undo, and thus decisions made for short-term considerations turn out to have permanent long-term implications by default. Myron Weiner (1990, p. 110) differentiates *long range* from *incremental* rather than short-term planning. The implication of his distinction is that change is ordinarily accomplished in small increments as opportunities present themselves. It is important to note that this notion of the increment as opportunistic small change is different from the uses of the term as employed in strategic management, as discussed in chapter 8.

In the business environment, Richard Hamermesh developed the commonly used notion of portfolio planning, defined as "those analytic techniques that aid in the classification of a firm's businesses for resource allocation purposes, and for selecting a competitive strategy on the basis of the growth potential of each business and of the financial resources that will be either consumed or produced by a business" (Moore, 1992, p. 120). This portfolio model has applications in social service planning and budgeting. They begin to unfold by substituting the term *agency* for *firm* and *program* for *business* in the Hamermesh quotation above.

Social Planning

There is a rich and substantial body of social planning literature in social work. Yet a large portion of it is obsolete in today's more opportunistic, market-oriented world of the social agency. We concur generally with Capoccia (1981) that the established conceptual basis for the practice of social planning no longer applies in the particular environment of social services and has not at least since the early 1980s. It is truly the case that planned responses by social agencies have in considerable degree been replaced by competitive, market responses. Social planning in the public sector is primarily an exercise in complying with prescribed protocols and regulations to legitimize the expenditure of funds for social programs. At the same time, social planning in the nonprofit sector is primarily an exercise in legitimizing various revenue-generation activities such as grant writing, contract negotiation, and fund raising. Much of the community social service planning network established during the 1960s in Office of Economic Opportunity, model cities, community mental health, aging, rehabilitation, retardation, and other service fields has been defunded and disestablished (Lohmann, 1981, 1991a; Lohmann, Locke, & Meehan, 1984). As a result, a national network of community social service planning capability and the development of a cadre of trained social service planning professionals are probably even farther from reality today than they were two decades ago.

Interagency Planning

One of the most stable features of social planning thought has been the idea of coalitions of social organizations and agencies banding together to serve the general interest of the community. A study of model cities coordination efforts found (1) an inverse relationship between the number of agencies involved in planning and implementation and the rating of success achieved in coordination and (2) a positive relationship between commitments of funds and estimates of coordination by federal observers (Gilbert & Specht, 1977). The decline of social planning systems has resulted in less and less of this type of planning in many communities and a kind of defaulting of social planning responsibility to individual agencies.

The result of this is a somewhat paradoxical community service planning system at present. On the one hand, we have social administrators, who are charged formally by corporate law with fiduciary responsibility for serving the interests of their corporations. Those portions of the organizational research literature that emphasize seemingly inevitable self-interest and maintenance tendencies in organizations reinforce them in this. On the other hand, we have the demands and expectations for social service planning in the interest of the needs of the community. Social administration is not presently well equipped to reconcile these irreconcilable tendencies, and simply being aware of the dilemma does little to point up its solution. However, it does appear fair to say that throughout the 1980s and the 1990s, social administration was the main front of social planning in most American communities. If social administrators representing specific service institutions (either individually or in coalition) did not address issues of community social service planning and institution building and renewal, these issues did not get addressed.

What this means in a community composed entirely of entrepreneurial, self-interested agency managers is that certain issues are not being addressed. This planning deficiency has been not only reconciled, but actually extolled in quasi-market terms, suggesting that consumer demand should control what social services emerge and survive. Yet, this approach simply fails to acknowledge the long-known limitations of market strategies in dealing with low income and special needs clients, demand for public goods, and other special circumstances that apply here. One of the target areas for institution-building activity related to social planning could be to construct new alternatives to the social surveys, community forums, and other community planning mechanisms of the past.

MODELS OF ADMINISTRATIVE PLANNING

The decline of community social planning approach, however, is quite distinct from the need for planning in the social agency. Even in the most entrepreneurial agencies, the question arises of who is to carry out administrative planning? Who, in other words, is "the planner?" Clifton and Dahms (1993, p. 127) argue that a board of directors exists primarily to plan the policies of the agency it governs. Others locate planning in the executive, and earlier social planning work in the late 1960s thought they saw the emergence of a formal new social planner roles in the union of urban and social service planning (Frieden & Morris, 1968; Kahn, 1969a, 1969b; Mayer, 1972, 1985). The best available answer is, it depends. Planning a new program usually requires resources available within an existing organization. At the same time, planning a major capital (fund-raising) campaign or building a major new building requires skills and talents not found in most social services and can only be done effectively with the aid of outside consultants. This is perhaps why much of the planning literature addresses surveying or identifying the resources available to do planning as one of the preliminary steps in preplanning, or the first step in carrying out a planning process.

How is administrative planning to be conducted? Though there are a wealth of planning process models for use in the formal organization, six will concern us in this chapter. In addition, financial planning is a major theme of the chapters on budgeting (chapter 23) and revenue sources (chapter 22). Institutionalization aspects of planning are also a major consideration in chapter 18 on marketing.

- *Organizational planning* is concerned with the details of organizational arrangements such as supervisory, directive and reporting responsibilities and prescribing the circumstances under which separate work groups are expected to relate to one another.
- *Financial planning* is concerned with budgeting, but also with resource identification, with planning fund-raising campaigns and activities, and a host of other financially related issues and concerns.

- *Program change planning* is concerned with identifying and informing decisions on organized or coordinated programs of action.
- *Strategic planning* is concerned with anticipating management decisions specifically associated with the strategic positioning of an organization in its environment—its niche in a larger ecosystem.
- *Contingency planning* might be thought of as identifying alternative scenarios, including at times worst case scenarios and considering what to do if the unexpected occurs.
- *Facilities planning* is generally concerned with "bricks and mortar" issues involving the rental, purchase, construction, repair and maintenance of space and physical facilities, including computers and wiring, for the social agency.

Organizational Planning

Rational organizations are planned organizations. One of the earliest and most widely used planning techniques for dealing with problems of organization is the *organization chart,* a two-dimensional schematic drawing, usually a set or rectangular boxes connected by lines representing reporting lines or lines of authority, as shown in Figure 9.1.

Figure 9.1 Organization Chart

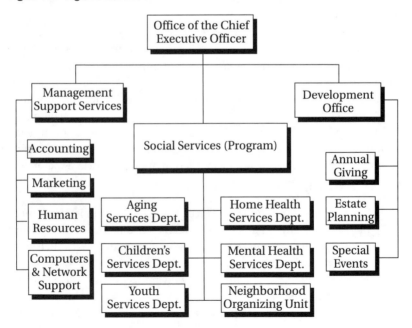

In management, this desire to "see" representations of the whole organization has been most commonly expressed in the organization chart. The urge to convey the complex networks of relationships that make up social organizations is seemingly very human and very strong. Over several decades, Jacob Moreno laid out a plan for a research and group therapy approach he called *sociometry* (Miller, 1970; Moreno, 1956, 1960; Moreno, Jennings, Whitin, & National Committee on Prisons, 1932; Price & Mueller, 1986). In social work, we have had additional assorted sociometric proposals for systems diagrams, genograms, and ecomaps.

Daniel Wren (1994) says that to the early management theorists,

> Organization charts were a *sine qua non* of every enterprise. The preparation of a formal organization chart enabled one to visualize the organization as a whole, specified lines of authority, provided channels of communication, prevented the overlapping or encroachment of departments, avoided dual command situations, and clearly assigned duties and responsibilities. The chart itself was a managerial instrument for analyzing relationships between departments, for specifying individuals and their tasks, and for making modifications in the organization. (p. 190)

Planned realignments of organizational arrangements, or reorganizations, are fairly common events in social services, especially in the public sector, where in some states they occur predictably with the election of each new administration. Cynics might even conclude that the standardized outcome of all social service planning ventures, regardless of original intent, is reorganization. This fits with the wisdom that one wag has called the First Law of Management: when all else fails, redraw the organization chart. In general, such reorganizations work within fairly prescribed boundaries laid out by the principles of departmentation discussed in chapter 3.

Financial Planning

Financial planning in social agencies is almost always short term and occurs on a year-to-year, or annual, basis. Financial planning is almost always also strongly incremental in nature, as planners consider and decide upon future financial availabilities for next year and perhaps the year after based on recent past actualities (last year and perhaps the year before). Yet, fees, third-party payments, managed care, and the drive of the new public management to make social agencies more business-like have brought entirely new approaches ever more clearly into focus. Some aspects of this transformation were already clear more than two decades ago, such as the growing importance of fees and contracts (Lohmann, 1976, 1980a). Others are not yet clear today. However, it is clear that in this context, the traditional fixed annual budget cycle and once-a-year budgeting have become increasingly less important and are being replaced by ongoing or rolling budget processes in which budget assumptions are adjusted and calculations are revised to reflect changing environmental conditions for the agency. This makes financial planning today much more of an ongoing operation for agency executives, department heads, supervisors, and others involved in the budgetary process. Additional aspects of this question are taken up in chapters 21 to 23.

Program Change Planning

Planning for program change is a term used here to embrace the full range of major changes in social service programs that may require planned responses: initial development of new programs, major modifications, or even phasing out of existing programs. Total quality management and management by objective techniques discussed in chapter 7 rightfully deserve to be recognized as parts of the planning arsenal for program change.

Such program change is sometimes the result of a process like total quality management or may simply be the result of agency personnel brainstorming about their programs. In such instances, the change is a desired one and the consequences of its implementation have been considered. Such program changes are most often the modification of an existing service, expansion of an existing service, or creation of a new and complementary service. For example, an agency might decide to reduce the number of hours of adult day care provided because of limited demand for the full range of hours provided, to provide the day care at an additional site, or to begin a new special day care program for Alzheimer's victims.

Not all program change, however, is sought by the agency. Sometimes such change occurs as a result of external forces. Such changes may occur when a grant funding a service is not renewed or changed rules mean the agency is no longer qualified to provide a service. An example of the latter type of change is a modified state rule about the staffing of a day care center, which may mean that one of the agency's sites must either add to its staff or close. In such instances, the agency may find itself forced to respond very quickly and in a less planful way to such external demands.

Planning has been described as "an integrated and iterative process" in that planning of programs and strategies must necessarily be "undertaken in tandem" (Weiner, 1990, p. 248). When program change occurs without much advance planning, as is often the case when it results from forces external to the agency, services may no longer operate in tandem or may lead to other unanticipated consequences. Thus, it may become necessary for further rounds of planning to consider the impact that a change in one aspect of the agency's services has for its other services.

In large agencies, there may be formal policies in place describing the processes to be observed when engaging in program change, especially when such change may result in the loss of employment. Such policies are also more likely when employees are unionized. Policies, for example, may require that displaced workers be given top priority for other vacancies occurring in the agency at the time. Those policies may also address other protections for such areas as retirement, health care, and other fringe benefits that are to be provided long-term employees when program changes impact them.

Strategic Planning

One of the most useful management perspectives to come along in quite some time is the model of strategic planning, which has been borrowed largely from the business world and depends heavily on models of strategic management like the one discussed in chapter 8. Strategic planning is a term with military origins, where it is differentiated from tactical planning. Thus, for example, the principal strategic objective of the D-Day invasion of Normandy involved establishing an Allied beachhead on the European continent. One tactical objective that furthered this strategy was the amphibious assault upon Omaha Beach. Likewise, in the social agency, the strategic objective of successfully launching a new program may be accompanied by the tactical objective of grant funding for the program.

It has been argued that the most important generic skill of future administrators will involve strategic planning, especially in forecasting patterns of emerging technologies and their implications (Broskowski, 1987). This is as true with respect to strategies for the selection and adoption of social service technologies as it is of computer and information technology. Some of such forecasting is a matter of common sense and experience. For example, there are large residuals of dissatisfaction in the practice community over the sudden and complete abandonment of virtually all types of long-term treatment in recent years. Thus, it is not hard at all to predict from the vantage point of today that long-term treatment approaches of some sort will make a comeback in the foreseeable future. The only real questions are strategic ones. Where and how this comeback will occur and what will have to be given up or changed to make it possible?

According to John Bryson (1995), *strategic planning* is "a disciplined effort to produce fundamental decisions and actions that shape and guide what an organization (or other entity) is, what it does, and why it does it" (p. 5).

Interestingly, Bryson (1994) characterizes the principle methodology of strategic planning not as conceptual/analytic or mental in any way, but rather as interactional: "Its most basic formal requirement is a series of discussions and decisions among key decision makers about what is truly important for the organization" (p. 155). This emphasis on interaction over analysis is another reason for downplaying the importance of planning process models, which are usually built on some type of cognitive process model.

When key decision makers gather for such discussions, Bryson (1994) notes, attention should be paid to eight steps of an orderly process "in order to provide for order, deliberation and participation":

1. Development of an initial agreement or a plan for planning
2. Identification and clarification of mandates
3. Development and clarification of mission and values
4. External environmental assessment
5. Internal environmental assessment
6. Strategic issue identification
7. Strategy development
8. Description of the organization in the future (visioning)

The emphasis in strategic planning on environmental assessments is a novel and important contribution to general planning theory and practice.

Examples of Strategy

In the area of knowledge development, for example, survey research is a particular strategic response. It addresses a carefully limited set of questions (the questionnaire) to a carefully selected group of people (the sample) and tabulates the results using procedures of descriptive and inferential statistics to summarize and interpret (the findings).

It will probably take some careful thinking, in most cases, to tease the strategy of an agency or program apart from its mission; management by objectives models that begin with mission have exercised a powerful influence on social service program theory for nearly a generation. In part, strategy is often more a matter of positioning or responding to other stakeholders, whereas the mission of most 501(c)(3) nonprofit services is usually stated in terms of client relations. Thus, the mission of the agency may be something like offering a program of high-quality services to clients. At the same time, the overall strategy of a social service agency in a time of welfare reform, devolution, and so on might involve shifting the resource base of the agency away from federal funds and increasing local donations, the use of volunteers, and the support of local patrons (Lohmann, 1999).

Although the concept of strategy is vitally important, perhaps the key departure of strategic planning from more traditional models of social planning is the emphasis on environmental assessment. There have been isolated movements in this direction for decades such as Morris and Binstock's (1966) emphasis on feasibility. However, the systematic incorporation of various environmental considerations into strategic planning puts it in a unique position among planning models. Thus, for example, considering the impact of plans upon stakeholders is usually a sensible and significant thing to do.

Contingency Planning

Another important form of administrative planning is preparing for contingencies, particularly for possible undesirable consequences, outcomes, or occurrences. Contingency planning might best be described as planning for alternative possibilities. For example, police departments and other public services routinely engage in planning and preparations for disasters, civil disturbances, and other possibilities. The hope is that such events will never occur; but the reality is they might and it is better to be prepared. In social agencies, cutback management and program elimination are often approached primarily as questions calling for contingency planning.

Significant contingency planning occurred in a range of social service agencies, businesses, and other organizations in preparation for the change of dates associated with the new millennium to address what was referred to as the Y2K problem. This became a popular joke, and much of the media treatment suggested a kind of carnival atmosphere. Yet the problem was a serious and expensive one that required a great deal of careful planning for many organizations including social agencies providing emergency mental health services. The problem arose as an unanticipated consequence of early computer programming mostly in the COBOL language from the 1950s that simply did not anticipate dates beyond the end of 1999, and it was unclear whether such programs would freeze, fail, or produce erratic results. Thus, industry, business, and social agencies and many individual households were forced to consider how they would continue to function if heat, food supplies, banking, and other basic services were disrupted. In doing so, they were engaging in contingency planning.

Many models of administrative planning are premised on optimization strategies directed at finding the best solutions to problems in terms of cost, effectiveness, and other factors. Most experienced administrators will tell you that the best is not always an achievable ideal, however. One of the most important ideas of contingency planning, and one that is closely associated with ideas of Banfield and Simon discussed elsewhere, is the idea of planning for the "second best" alternative. Herbert Simon's notion of satisficing introduced in chapter 6 is another example of an approach to contingency planning not directed at optimizing. Often, particularly under conditions like those offered by program change, cutback management, and Y2K, administrators deliberately choose the first available solution that offers an acceptable number of advantages rather than engaging in the additional time and effort necessary to find "the best" solution.

Facilities Planning

For a profession laying claim to the central importance of environment, social work in the twentieth century has proven to be remarkably indifferent to effects of the built environment on human behavior. The point where this is most evident is in the almost complete absence of any detectable architecture of social work or social service. However, it also is evident in the almost complete lack of any consideration of facilities planning in the social administration literature.

We may have church architecture, school architecture, and commercial architecture, but the idea of a recognizable architecture of social work or social service architecture is so unfamiliar as to seem almost an oxymoron. It is so strange that one cannot even pose the question of its nonexistence very exactly. For example, even when taken from their environments, one instantly recognizes the couches and sofas of a home as typically different in subtle ways from the similar furniture found in offices, the bench seating of churches and synagogues, the carpeted floors without seats in mosques, and the tablet seats of a classroom. Yet, even to ask the question of what kinds of seating are most appropriate for social services seems somehow strange. The same is true of lighting, layouts, equipment, and most other facilities. As noted earlier, the social work office is a quite generic space!

For the most part, social services everywhere are delivered in spaces converted from other uses—environments built as homes, offices, shops, garages and in at least a few cases, factories, and now used by social workers to deliver social services. While it was still "the social work foundation," the Russell Sage Foundation built a specially designed office building in Manhattan. However, surviving photographs of it suggest nothing special at all; a conventional, brownstone ten-story office building suitable for any type of "human service" paper processing in the modern mode. Likewise, photos and site maps of the Hull House physical plant that was bulldozed in the 1950s show that it was mostly generic spaces of an entirely different kind: apartments and meeting rooms, a theater, dining room, and so on.

Even if facilities planning in social agencies is limited completely to the redesign and retrofitting of existing buildings and spaces, asking what kinds of spatial environments are most appropriate to the practices of social work is a question that grows directly from the ecological perspective, generally, and the institutional perspectives laid out in this book. Distinctive institutions (schools, churches, hospitals, homes, stores, etc.) are recognizable in part because of the distinctive qualities of their physical spaces. Social services and social work can, currently, lay claim to no such distinctiveness.

The field is not entirely without distinctive architecture albeit none of it in the United States. Perhaps the most distinctive social service architecture in the world is Filippo Brunelleschi's (1377–1446) foundling hospital or orphanage in Florence, Italy. With its distinctive loggia of columns, round arches, and domed bays and its proportions, it has stood among the most recognizable architectural hallmarks of Medicean Venice for more than five centuries. Likewise, Christopher Wren's Royal Hospital at Chelsea, designed at the request of Charles II, is still home to the "Chelsea pensioners," retired British military men. As an "old age home," it features a distinctive design, suitable for retired military accustomed to dormitory accommodations. It has nine-by-nine foot (originally six-by-six) cubicles on the inside of hallways, with sunlit windowed commons areas on the outside. Also of interest is Wren's Greenwich Palace, once designated Greenwich Hospital and used as a home for retired sailors from the time of William and Mary. Queen Anne reportedly gave the captured treasure of the pirate Captain Kidd to a foundation for support of the hospital.

In general, the failures of social service architecture are much more notable than the achievements. Although they have little to do with social service practice theory or the social work profession, they do provide instructive lessons nonetheless. Studies of the policy failures of public housing, for example, came up with concepts of personal space, observable space, and controllable space, all of which have important implications in the context of empowerment.

PLANNING AND CHANGE

The notion of *planned change* was first introduced into the social planning literature by a social worker, Robert Morris (1964), in a book published by National Association of Social Workers. Since then, the metaphors of planned change have become fixed features of planning discussions. It is fair to say that there are two general, philosophical approaches to change in organizations. The model of planned change is based on what might be called the *theory of flux.* This approach is that organizations are constantly changing and that change is inevitable and constant. Planned change, in this context, is differentiated most meaningfully from *unplanned,* which is to say accidental or unanticipated, change. The notion of nonchange never really enters into consideration on philosophical grounds that it is impossible to prove a negative (that nothing changed). *Structural change theory*, on the other hand, tends to view organizations as characterized by states of equilibrium and change as a special circumstance or occasion, bracketed or preceded and followed by nonchange or structural stability.

From either approach, one can readily see the three principal change strategies identified by Chin and Benne (1976): *empirical–rational* change, involving appeals to individual and organizational self-interest; *normative–reeducative*, in that change occurs through modification of attitudes, values, skills, and relationships; and *power–coercive* change, in that change comes about only through the exercise of power or force. In much the same vein, one can approach Holloway and Brager's (1977) identification of the three major types of organizational change that they term alterations in behavior, technology, and structure from either vantage point. A study of planned change in public and nonprofit organizations by David Billis (1992) concluded that the core problems faced by public agencies were those of *role confusion* or questions of who will do what, whereas those of nonprofits involved *status ambiguity* or questions of whether the organization was the right one to do something.

One approach to change that has been particularly evident in social services for several decades is what Everett Rogers called the *diffusion of innovations*. According to Rogers and Shoemaker (1971), the diffusion process moves through five states: awareness, interest, evaluation, trial, and adoption. They also classified adopters of innovation as five types, depending upon which stage they first adopted the change: innovators, early adopters, the early majority, the late majority, and laggards. One should expect to find each of these types in response to most administrative planning initiatives.

PROCESS PLANNING

One of the principal forms of administrative planning has always been preplanning of standardized processes and operations. In the earliest days of the Industrial Revolution, industrial innovators such as Robert Owen, Richard Arkwright, and the firm of Boulton and Watt provided such planned standardized procedures in textile manufacturing and other fields (Wren, 1979, p. 516). In social agencies, policy and procedures manuals, standardized forms, service protocols, and professional methods all strive for such standardization. Process planning in the social agency is often directed at searching for such standardization.

In 1956 and 1957, the DuPont Company developed a computerized arrow diagram or network method for planning and controlling processes that acquired the name Critical Path Method (CPM). This was later refined by the U.S. Navy and its contractors (Booz, Allen Hamilton and the Lockheed Missile Systems Division) into the Program Evaluation and Review Technique (PERT) (Wren, 1979, p. 516).

More recently, a variety of applications of systems analysis in social services have brought a range of process planning insights to social services. These approaches are often coupled with scientific management–inspired close examinations of social work processes that have revealed a great deal about how things are done in social services. However, most process planning in social work occurs within existing paradigms and operating procedures. There is little evidence that any major systematic redesigns of social services practice or process technologies have occurred as a result of such planning ventures.

CONCLUSION

Formal organizations are planned organizations, and social agencies are formal agencies. The need for planning in social administration varies directly with the rate of change in social agencies. Thus, most social agencies are engaged in almost constant processes of planning and adapting to planned change. At one time, it seemed clear that there was a definite planning method, which allowed clear distinctions between "rational" and "nonrational" preparations for change. It is increasingly clear today that most of those models of social planning are, in fact, adaptations of models of rational thinking, problem-solving, and decision-making.

In a very real sense, to be a social administrator is also to be a planner in numerous senses. Not only is there an ongoing need for planning activities and operations, there are also more-or-less continuous responsibilities for reconsideration of programs and policies. These grow out of the necessity to review and revitalize visions, missions, goals, objectives, strategies, and the other aspects of the organization's mission and relations with its various stakeholders. One of the major additional reasons that social administrators must also be planners is the relative decline of free-standing social planning institutions and the devolution of such planning responsibilities to individual social agencies. It truly is a case today in many communities that if social administrators do not initiate and engage in social planning who will?

CHAPTER 10

Implementation

The topic of implementation that is the focus of this chapter is a key, together with the previous discussion of planning, to unlocking a complex paradox at the core of social administration practice. If the manager of social services concentrates her attention only on following the rules and pressing the buttons and on tactics and procedures and day-to-day schedules and routines, then the leadership and institution-building challenges of social administration will remain unfulfilled. Conversely, if the social administrator concentrates only on the grand scheme of things—on purpose and mission, goals and objectives—social administration and social planning easily becomes a kind of parlor game, an armchair exercise in the construction of ivory towers. It is really only when strategies are used as visions that can be translated into programs, when missions become policies, and when objectives become rules and protocols that the concern for visions, strategies, missions, and objectives transcends intellectual exercise and becomes social administration practice. Broadly speaking, it is this translation of plans into action that is the unique concern of any discussion of implementation.

The problem of implementation as a separate issue or problem of social administration rather than an integral aspect of the cycle of planning, operations, and evaluation is, in one respect, an artifact of enlightenment rationalist thinking in management. Thus, it represents one of the very ideas that Follett, Simon, Lindblom, Quinn, and many others have been struggling against. Through the rationalist lens, planning, decision making and implementation are seen as separable moments in a discrete series of separate events. First we decide *what* we would like to do by agreeing upon purpose, mission, and objectives and only then do we go about the task of deciding *how* the agreed-upon task is to be done. Such a division, of course, is not only arbitrary but also quite artificial. As Follett, Simon, Quinn, and others have attempted to demonstrate, talk of how to accomplish our purposes and objectives can never be completely separated from talk of what those objectives are or how we evaluate past performances. The fact that we see any type of separation at all is a testament to the powerful hold rationalist thinking still has on contemporary practice thought.

We are, of course, all rationalists in our ability to perceive distinctions between goals, ends, or purposes, such as family preservation, and the means necessary to achieve them, such as family counseling. If we were truly Weber's *traditionalists* or even *charismatics* there would be no talk of "implementation" apart from goal definition—separating what we wish to do from how we want to do it. Indeed, for some parts of the social work profession this is exactly the case. For those most uncritically under the spell of the charisma of social work professionalism, for example, there can be no problem of strategy and purpose. The general problem of implementation is simple. Apply the law of the hammer to any social problem: hire a social worker and let her do what social workers do! The problem will be solved. Likewise, as the social work profession has matured we see increasing appeals to traditional authority in fields that once abhorred any appeal to the traditional. Mary Richmond, Jane Addams, and others are increasingly invoked in a manner not entirely unlike that of the community of saints of medieval Christianity. Under the spell of traditionalism, the problem of implementation likewise becomes simple: hire a social worker and let her do what social workers have always done.

For the main body of the profession, however, implementation is a serious pragmatic consideration of problem solving and intelligent action. Given what we seek to do, how is it best to do it, and what are the particular details that must be looked after?

TERMINOLOGY: IMPLEMENTATION, PROGRAMMING, ACTION PLANNING

What we call implementation in this chapter carries a number of other labels as well. Curiously, despite the fact that there is virtually no significant volume of published literature on the subject, some practitioners and beginning students continue to use the phrase *program development*. There is also a tradition, probably traceable to broadcasting, for calling this set of concerns *programming*. Finally, John Bryson (1995), in his work on strategic planning for nonprofit organizations, refers to this same set of concerns as *action planning*. Bryson's use of this term in particular should remind us that drawing any lines between planning and implementation is always arbitrary. Whatever it is called, follow-up action is necessary in all types of planning and decision-making activity if plans that have been developed and decisions that have been made are ever to be put into effect. Putting any plan into action requires answers to a number of interrelated questions.

1. What? The specific steps or actions required.
2. Who? Who will carry out the plan and who will be accountable for seeing that each step or action is carried out.
3. When? Timing and scheduling issues.
4. With what enabling issues? A number of financial, human capital, social capital, and other resource questions will arise.
5. What feedback mechanisms are needed to monitor progress within each action step?

Some approaches (e.g., Below, Morrissey, & Acomb, 1987, pp. 63–64) suggest that resources need to be allocated in order to carry out a plan. This is surely true, but it is also an insufficient response that fails to take into account the challenge of feasibility (Morris & Binstock, 1966). If resources haven't been considered before this point, your plans may very well not be particularly feasible, and you've wasted your time! The concern with resources in implementation are generally not with resource-identification questions as they are in planning, but rather with making specific arrangements, commitments, and contracts for use of the identified resources. Thus, planning efforts for a new program may identify and even write a grant to fund the effort for a five-year period. The unique challenge of implementation is attention to the series of steps necessary to ensure that arrangements have been made to receive the grant funds to comply with the terms of the grant.

THREE KEY PROBLEMS

There are three key problems associated with implementation that require special attention and brief consideration. They are administrative discretion, unanticipated consequences, and self-fulfilling prophecies. One of the general issues in the implementation of public policy in public organizations that always seems to arise is the issue of *administrative discretion*.

This refers to the latitude that those responsible for implementing plans may have for ignoring, overturning, or undermining the chances for success of aspects of plans with which they disagree or that they view as less important. In part, this is because of the way in which planning and implementation typically move in a grand sweeping movement from the most general visions and missions to the most specific rules and regulations, and there is room at every step along the way for subverting original intent.

Implementing policy must always allow a huge role for discretionary judgment in the decisions necessary to transform the words and phrases of a law, court ruling, set of administrative regulations, or board motion into action. Although the management by objectives model makes the most explicit effort to deal with this issue by forcing progressively greater specificity, no model of planning can be freed of this problem. Instead, the discretionary judgments involved usually consist of negotiating between three general issues:

1. What did the framers of this law, or this rule, or this policy really intend? This is the issue of original intent.
2. What are we really trying to accomplish here? This is the issue of immediate intent.
3. What is feasible and possible to achieve under present or foreseeable circumstances? This is the issue of constraint.

The exercise of administrative discretion is ordinarily carried out by interpreting the original intent of rule makers, establishing the immediate intent of management and assessing the situational constraints that limit actions.

The second key problem of implementation is generally known as "unanticipated consequences." No matter how carefully planning is done, and no matter how detailed the plans may be, it is inevitable that things will occur that were not thought of in the planning process. One of the most important forms of unanticipated consequences is *self-fulfilling prophecies:* predictions that come true, in part, simply because they were made. In implementing plans and programs, social administrators must always be particularly wary of unanticipated consequences of this type because they are usually avoidable. Thus, a prediction spoken publicly by top management that workers aren't going to like a particular policy change may well have the effect of producing precisely that result! Even if workers were previously inclined to be positive or indifferent to the policy, a forewarning that they aren't going to like it is often enough to alarm people.

We might note parenthetically that the somber intoning of the insight that organizational actors always oppose change as though it were somehow a law of nature has frequently had this effect in social services. There are, of course, a number of important variations on the basic idea of such prophecies, such as the *self-negating prophecy*, which fails to come true precisely because it has been made. Thus, to say to one's teenaged children, "We know that you're going to like this," is often to set up such a situation.

Sometimes self-negating prophecies can have enormous consequences. For example, in introducing the concept of unanticipated consequences, the sociologist Robert Merton (1940/1952, 1957) noted that at least some of the predictions that Karl Marx made about the dire consequences of capitalism may have failed to come true because of an unanticipated consequence. Business, labor, and governmental and other leaders of industrial societies took actions to forestall the predicted effects in reaction to those predictions and, as a result, proved them wrong. Most writers on subjects such as the effects of automation on unemployment are clearly hoping to provoke precisely this type of self-negating effect. We are, of course, dealing here in the very iffy realm of metaphysics and alternative realities, unfamiliar territories for the hard-shell realism of most management thinkers. Nonetheless, the idea of circumventing or forestalling an otherwise likely possibility simply by calling attention to it is an idea with strong intuitive appeal because it genuinely appears to fit a significant number of situations in social administration.

Merton extended much the same view to his analysis of "bureaupathology," which Richard Scott (1995) calls "a lucid discussion of processes within organizations that lead officials to orient their actions around the rules even to the point where primary concern with conformity to the rules interferes with the achievement of the purposes of the organization." The essential idea here is that, whether or not they intend to, officials in organizations whose careers are built upon the observance of rules and policies may come to regard, over time, the following of rules as more central than obtaining results. Probably more than anything else, this intuitive notion, for which there is little more than anecdotal evidence, is at the base of the modern negative attitudes toward the bureaucracy of nonprofit and public organizations. When people today say bureaucracy, bureaupathology more than anything else is what they are likely to be alluding to. They may not stop to examine closely why such behavior should be more characteristic of employees of public or nonprofit organizations than of private or commercial ones. In fact, it may not be. Stockholders and top management in commercial corporations may have a profit motive. Lower-level employees in all kinds of organizations seem instead to share a wage-and-salary motive regardless of the type of organization.

The reality of unanticipated consequences arises in part from the fact that the future is, in principle, unknowable and in part from the fact that humans are as capable of reacting to predictions of future consequences as they are of reacting to actual consequences. Thus, for example, the very prediction that a shift to managed care will result in different personnel needs and work patterns may itself be enough to bring about the predicted changes! A recent reminder of this phenomenon can be found in the apparent manner in which devolution of social policy to the states appears instead to be increasing federal involvement in micromanagement of state and local programs, according to a recent report:

> Devolution, which was supposed to allow greater freedom for states to work out the details, has instead, says the report, led to additional federal micromanagement, a threefold increase in federal reporting requirements and other burdens on states already struggling with Y2K conversion and the loss of technical staff to the private sector. (Singer, 1998, p. 34)

Like this example, some of the most surprising and disturbing recent perspectives on unanticipated consequences of policy implementation have arisen in close analyses of recent public sector initiatives such as reinventing government and the new public management. This is evident in an extensive recent analysis of the actual extent of adoption of reforms associated with government reinvention. In *Reinventing Government,* Osborne and Gaebler (1992) set out to make the case for what has been characterized as a postbureaucratic paradigm of public services, including social services marked chiefly by greater emphasis upon being more entrepreneurial and business-like in attitude and behavior. In an award-winning study, however, Brudney, Hebert, and Wright (1999) determined that though some states are more active than others in attempting to implement eleven specific reforms associated with the reinvention movement, they could find little evidence of a concerted reinvention movement across the states through 1998. They conclude that

> while the results indicate that agencies are selectively adopting specific reinvention reforms—most notably strategic planning—and some reforms addressing customer service—and that a few states are more active than others, the principal conclusion is that a concerted reinvention movement does not appear to be underway across state governments. (p. 19)

Such rhetorical approaches to reforms are generally consistent with earlier management reform movements that were proclaimed but never appeared, such as Program Planning Budgeting Systems (PPBS), zero-based budgeting, and a great many others. Many such reforms have the similar unanticipated consequences of being selectively adopted by a few innovators, but otherwise primarily only transform the way managers talked about their traditional activities. In fact, this leads to what appears to be a viable generalization. Proposals for comprehensive management reform in public and social services are most likely to produce the unanticipated consequence of partial and selective adoption. Such a consequence is, of course, truly unanticipated only by the true-believing reformers who advance these types of comprehensive visions. It is entirely to be anticipated by the Simon–Lindblom view of incomplete information and the partial, remedial, and incremental nature of administrative change.

Although the substitution of rhetorical reform-speak for actual changes may or may not be surprising to individual readers, the implications of a recent study of the new public management (NPM) appear equally surprising and somewhat more sinister (Maor, 1999). In a study of NPM in Australia, New Zealand, Canada, the United Kingdom, Austria, and Malta between 1980 and 1996, Moshe Maor concluded that NPM has produced something of a paradox: "What were intended to be solutions to managerial problems have developed into solutions to political problems." About NPM, Maor says:

> Borrowing from the world of private-sector management, the vocabulary of the new public management has so far shown a remarkable degree of consensus among the political leadership and opinion makers in various countries about the desired nature of change. Change is to be primarily organizational: its goal is to strengthen management capacity in government operations. New public management thus conjures up images of debureaucratization and depoliticization. (p. 5)

In each of the countries studied, Maor found that rather than producing improved management, by giving career professional public managers greater authority to manage programs, NPM was, in fact, weakening their authority and giving political appointees greater incentive for setting central directions and priorities and intervention in personnel matters. That was, in this context, a genuinely unanticipated consequence. Although the matter has not been studied from this vantage point in the United States, it seems entirely plausible that a number of political reforms of the past two decades have had approximately that same result.

MODELS OF IMPLEMENTATION

There are distinctive models of implementation embedded in the four main approaches to general management that we examined in chapter 6. We refer, in roughly chronological order of their appearance, to the management principles approach of Henri Fayol and others; the scientific management approach of Frederick Taylor (known commonly as Taylorism); the human relations approach of Elton Mayo and others; and the more recent behavioral and quasi-economic applications of incentive or inducement theory. In addition, there are a growing number of specific models of implementation applied specifically to social administration. Under this heading, we refer also to the model of implementation as an outgrowth of social planning set forth by Alfred Kahn and Shiela Kamerman (1977), John Flynn's (1992) model of agency policy, and Bruce Jansson's (1990) model of policy practice, all of which are adequately examined elsewhere in the social work literature. Each of these examples offers embedded theories of implementation in that they offer distinctive approaches to what to do within an organization to enact or implement an agreed upon goal or purpose.

In the remainder of this chapter, we briefly consider the implementation models embedded in each of the four main approaches as well as some other issues related to implementation.

Fayol and General Principles of Implementation

The implementation approach offered by Fayol and others is known as "the general principles" approach to implementation. The exact principles identified by Fayol for business corporations (scalar organization, unity of command, etc.) need not concern us particularly, since they have, in fact, exercised only slight direct influence upon social administration. What is more important here is his general approach.

Fayol's appeal to principles in implementation has exercised a powerful influence upon social work thinking both directly and indirectly. One finds strong evidence of a general principles approach in the conventional teaching of social work methods in schools of social work, for example. On the one hand, we recognize a general set of problems—poverty, homelessness, stress, family violence, and so on. On the other hand, we recognize a general set of methods—interviewing, assessment, diagnosis, and so on. To make this approach work, there must be general principles that tell us when and how to apply which methods to the solution of which problems. For some reason, the "confidentiality" principle always seems to come to mind first, but there are others: individualization, for instance, "situational/contextual sensitivity." The essential point here is that from a Fayolian principles perspective, the task of implementation is largely one of locating methods or organizational technologies most consistent with the appropriate principle.

The most critical problem with implementation using a general principles approach in administration was identified by Herbert Simon more than fifty years ago. General principles can easily overreach in their generality and overlap one another, yielding inconsistent prescriptions for what to do.

The implementer is then left with the problem of which principle(s) to apply and how to choose among inconsistent guidelines for implementation. The issue raised by the *Tarasoff* decision,[1] for example, represents a clear case in which confidentiality conflicts with other strong principles, and, under the law, must yield to those other principles, that is, identifying murderers is a greater public good than protecting the privacy of the individual. Yet, stating in general terms suitable for a theory of implementation exactly what those other principles are, without totally abandoning a commitment to confidentiality, is no easy task and likely to yield uncertain results rather than clear, definitive principles. In general, social problems are too complex and practice principles too general to make this a particularly useful approach to the challenges of implementation.

There is a second approach to implementation growing out of classic management. It might be called "implementation by control," or the cybernetic approach. As noted in chapter 6, a punitive model of control by domination through ordering, forbidding, and punishment was an important element in early management thinking. This was supplemented and to some degree replaced by later, more sophisticated models of social control emphasizing group influences, incentives, and a variety of other factors articulated by Barnard, Follett, Simon, and a host of others. Yet, control as an element of management thought certainly has not disappeared. It is important to note, however, that a major part of the control perspective in modern management relates to control over tangible objects and not people.

Within the classic management tradition, Koontz and O'Donnell (1978) spelled out what might be termed the classic theory of control. They begin with a single assumption: primary responsibility for control rests with the manager charged with execution of a plan. Control, they argue, is essentially the same whether what is being controlled is cash, behavior, quality, and so on. It consists of three basic steps: (1) establishing standards that need not be quantitative, but may involve qualities such as loyalty; (2) measuring performance against those standards; and (3) correcting deviations from standards.

According to the Koontz–O'Donnell general theory of control, there are ten general requirements of adequate controls:

1. Controls must reflect the nature and needs of the activity to be controlled.
2. Controls should report deviations promptly.
3. Controls should be forward looking or future oriented.
4. Controls should point up exceptions at critical points.

5. Controls should be objective and subject to high levels of intersubjective agreement.
6. Controls should be flexible.
7. Controls should reflect organizational patterns such as supervision.
8. Controls should be economical.
9. Controls should be understandable.
10. Controls should lead to corrective action.

The possibility of rational control is implicit in the management theory of control, and it is assumed that effective controls will depend upon the ability to establish criteria or standards against which to measure, or benchmark, performance. The engineering origins of these ideas should be obvious, and their importance in manufacturing is undoubted. The types of critical standards identified by Koontz and O'Donnell are

1. Physical standards (weights, measures, temperature, etc.)
2. Cost standards
3. Capital standards (return on investment, administrative costs, etc.)
4. Revenue standards
5. Program standards (worker–client ratios, length of wait for interview, etc.)
6. Intangible standards ("good," "efficient," "ethical conduct," "quality," etc.)
7. Goal-related standards (goal attainment scaling as a control device)

The extent to which these materialist conceptions can be applied in social administration remains to be seen. Even so, the performance measurement approach and the government performance initiative discussed in chapter 13 are premised in large part on a very similar theory of control (Martin & Kettner, 1997).

Taylor and the Metaprinciple of Scientific Management

A radically different approach to implementation was proffered by Frederick Taylor in the approach he termed *scientific management*. Taylor's approach has proven particularly important well beyond its core implementation in time and motion studies. This is because of its handling of another limitation of general principles not often recognized in the management literature. Scientific management offers ways for choosing appropriate action in new or unprecedented circumstances that exceed the bounds of agreed upon knowledge. This is precisely the case Henry Ford was dealing with in the establishment of the automobile assembly line, for example. Taylor's

experimental method of close scrutiny of problematic situations, definition of likely procedures, observation, and redesign helped Ford do what he sought and made Taylor an international celebrity.

It has been relatively easy in many industrial labor contexts of management deception and worker distrust to dismiss Taylor's methods as applicable only to the problem of worker exploitation. And there was ample evidence of their actual use in this long before the Lordstown, Ohio, controversy over speed-ups of the assembly line in the 1970s. It is important to remember, therefore, that some of Taylor's most famous work on the science of shoveling, which involved close study of the physical motions involved in human operation of a sand shovel, has important humanistic as well as efficiency implications. Industrial workers have at least as great an interest in prevention of unnecessary back injuries through faulty shoveling technique as management does in the efficiencies reflected in more sand shoveled per hour. Probably the most widely recognized application of principles to human service administration is the controversial measurement of recording errors in completion of welfare eligibility applications. Implementation in the Taylorian mode is a sequence of careful study or planning, provisional implementation, restudy, and corrective action.

Mayo and Human Relations Approaches

Approached from a scientific management perspective, the human relations approach to implementation offers a caution backed up by extensive research and empirical support. The caution is that what you find may not be what you were looking for. The human relations tradition also offers a single central variable around which to measure the effectiveness of implementation: morale, or worker happiness on the job. The biggest difference between the scientific management and human relations approaches is that while scientific management typically leads to redesign or redefinition of an individual job or task or of a group of related jobs, human relations approaches often lead to redesign of the work environment. That redesign may be either of the physical environment where work is completed or a reordering of the work organization. Thus, in choosing between a scientific management approach and human relations approach to implementation, one of the key considerations is whether it is more likely that detailed attention should be given to the job or task definition or to the situation and circumstances under which the work occurs.

Social researchers today are almost universally aware of the Hawthorne effect as a threat to the validity of findings, but its corollaries for implementation are frequently ignored and regularly forgotten. People really do benefit from attention and suffer from neglect! This is as true on the job as

elsewhere in life. One of the biggest insights of the rediscovery of Japanese management styles in the 1980s (which had been human relations management styles in the 1940s), for example, was that if you really want to know whether a procedure or operation works, ask the worker who completes it. That such worker–management collaboration not only yields impressive results but also contributes to improved worker morale was an insight of the original human relations studies in the 1940s long forgotten by American management until the Japanese miracle of the 1980s.

Social Control Theory

A concern for control is not altogether lacking in the human relations approach. Perhaps the social science perspective most congruent with the human relations approach to social control is that loose affiliation of sociological insights that can be grouped together under the heading of *social control theory.* It is important to note that we are not speaking now of the Marxian doctrine of class domination and its various modern manifestations that involve fundamental issues of power, domination, and alienation. Instead, we are referring to the much more elusive tendencies that arose in twentieth-century social science that might well be seen as attempts to detail the characteristics of Adam Smith's "invisible hand." As Mary Parker Follett (Follett & Graham, 1995) noted, there has been growing awareness of this phenomenon since the 1920s. Where Follett saw it as control by the situation, others have concentrated on culture, small group influences, values, and similar variables. Amatai Etzioni's (1961a) theory of compliance lumps these assorted processes together under the heading of *normative compliance.* In chapter 17, we examine in some detail Edward Banfield's (1961) theory of social influence. The group process literature was the basis for a fairly sophisticated "social control" perspective highlighting at least three types of normative compliance: group control of members through the establishment of group norms, the reciprocal control of leaders and followers, and individual self-monitoring and control. Erving Goffman's (1986) writings on stigma as well as the general literature on deviance also fit within this overall framework, as do the organizational perspectives that emphasize the informal organization. The essential insight in all these cases is the importance for management of the ways in which people influence or control the behavior of others in work situations.

Much as Follett predicted in the 1920s, one of the principal imports of these various social control perspectives has been to undercut notions of domination and command as effective means of administrative control. Indeed, many have come to see domination and command as the last resort of scoundrels, fools, and the psychological defense mechanisms of those

whose organizational authority or personal integrity is threatened. Materials, physical processes, equipment, and finances can indeed be effectively controlled in this sense. Proper management of human resources requires a different approach. Even to speak of controlling behavior is to use the term in an entirely different sense from that which is used in the control of materials. The challenge posed by social control is a profound one. It is how best to achieve organizational missions and purposes without undue harm to the personal integrity and well-being of subordinate employees.

Incentive and Exchange Theories

Part of the contemporary approach to social control as a major component of the modern science of social administration can best be understood on intellectual and theoretical grounds. The apparent failure of control/domination theory and the modest successes of social control theory, combined with the undercutting of rationality, create something of an intellectual vacuum that explains in part the rise of modern organization theory. Theories of class control extended to managers simply lacked believability.

Theories of social control have had great and growing credibility in the social sciences generally and in social work in particular. However, they have the serious drawback of complexity—a situation made even worse when one remembers the social work environment of Freudian influence and models of human growth and development. If behavior is actually as complicated as these models imply, how can it ever be possible to talk realistically about plans in the future perfect tense? How can our plans be implemented if all these complexities must be taken into account?

One answer to this challenge has been to resort to rational models that reduce the complexities of behavior to simple cause–effect chains. This approach results in constructing behavior as series of cause–effect relations in response to definite rules and/or established consistent principles: If the manager does this, it will cause this effect, and so forth. Indeed, there is some question as to whether theories of intervention can be organized in any other way. Unfortunately, the Simon–Lindblom challenge as well as many other parts of contemporary social science seriously undermines the credibility of this approach. Organizational actors (in this case, the planners and implementers) simply lack the mental capacity to process all the information needed to make this a reality. There are simply too many variables to take into account and too many relations among them.

Yet, something approaching the promise of this kind of rational behavioral control has been an important consideration in two important and related but distinct approaches to management thinking implementation. Incentive theory and its corollaries, exchange theory and the new political

economy, are all premised upon implied promises of rational control. The underlying element in all of these approaches is a kind of elegantly simple social economics. Human social actors in organizations are seen as consistently self-interested and will, therefore, respond in predictable ways to incentives, which are preferably rewards but may also be punishments.

One elegant statement of this view is to be found in the psychology of George Homans (1961). Within public administration, as in political science, the resulting behaviorism was a departure from the earlier institutionalism to which we now seem to be returning. In organization theory and sociology generally, Homan's extreme psychological reductionism and various partial rejections of it resulted in the distinctive perspective known as "exchange theory" (Blau, 1967; Homans, 1968). It has been a small step from Blau and Scott to the emergence of the full-blown rationalism of the "new political economy" perspectives of Gary Becker (1976) or Warren Ilchman and Norman Uphoff (1968).

Exchange theory should already be familiar to most students of social administration. Robbins, Chatterjee, and Canda (1998) have written an interesting and thorough discussion of exchange theory that we need not repeat. The essential point here is that as perspectives on implementation, exchange theories and a host of related models are built on ideas of the implementer as provider of incentives and inducements (sometimes called carrots and sticks) to secure the compliance of others.

MANAGEMENT BY OBJECTIVES AND RESULTS

One of the most serious weaknesses of the various incentive, inducement, and exchange approaches is their collective inability to account for or anchor implementation more deeply than the personal discretion or even the whims of managers. They fail to explain how it is that managers are justified in assuming a right to manipulate others in this way. In this, they are of a piece with the earlier command-and-control perspectives of classic management theory: Managers have a right to command and demand compliance, and that's that! The approach known variously as MBO (management by objectives) and MBOR (management by objectives and results) offers an approach to implementation grounded in such carrot and stick psychology that also addresses this issue.

Although he was not the first to use the term, management guru Peter Drucker (1954) was most likely the originator of the fundamental ideas of MBO. Drucker placed heavy emphasis on setting objectives and then using them to measure performance. As noted previously, he argued that objective setting allows managers to control their work and dampen the pressures of hierarchy. In both of these cases, Drucker was moving beyond traditional command-and-control perspectives toward his own unique synthesis of the problem of social control first raised by Follett.

Drucker's (1954, p. 63) emphasis on objectives signaled a profound shift in management thinking also supported by a variety of sociological studies of organizations from what might be termed an *other-control* orientation to an orientation that sees workers as engaged in *evaluative self-control.* Guy and Hitchcock (2000) see this as the first appearance of *empowerment* thinking in management. They note also that Drucker—in an argument reminiscent of Follett—states an important caveat: "It is not a great step forward to take power out at the top and put it in at the bottom. It's still power. To build achieving organizations, you must replace power with responsibility" (p. 17).

The problem may not be quite as simple as that (see chapter 17). Power may not be an inherent factor in organizations, but the transition away from power is also not something as easily wished away as Drucker, Follett, and others may suggest. Power has its own ways of creeping back in. However, the immediate point here is to explain further how implementation occurs through the complex process of social or, as Follett called it, situational control in ways that workers will embrace ends (goals and objectives) identified by others in ways that will exercise evaluative self-control over their behavior. A good deal of the answer to this question is to be found in the set of related social processes known as institutionalization.

INSTITUTIONALIZATION

We spoke earlier of institutionalization in relation to planning in chapter 8. In order to examine further the role of institutionalization as it relates to implementation, we will have to look more closely at some basic perspectives of human behavior and the social environment as they relate to social administration. Specifically, the perspective known as "the social construction of reality" or social constructivism gives us a base from which to see how social institutions can and do arise in the day-to-day lifeworld of social administration and enable this kind of evaluative self-control.

Scott (1995) defined institutions as "the formal rules, compliance procedures and standard operating practices that structure the relationships of people in various units of the polity and economy" (p. 19). Thus, for example, the institution of *payday* gives structure and meaning to the lives of many workers. Institutions not only empower and constrain but also shape, form, and give meaning to actors. A paycheck is for most people part of the meaning of working. Decades ago, the sociologist Everett Hughes (1936) defined an institution as an "establishment of relative permanence of a distinctly social sort made up of (1) a set of mores, or formal rules, or both, which can be fulfilled only by (2) people acting collectively in establishing complimentary capacities or offices" (p. 180). It would take many pages to describe all the rules associated with paying employees. "Institutions," he said, "exist in the integrated and standardized behavior of individuals" (Hughes, 1939, p. 319). In this sense, "all institutionalized conduct involves rules" (Berger & Luckman, 1966, p. 74). Knowing how to receive your paycheck and what to do with it is very much part of "getting paid."

"Institutions, Durkheim writes, are a product of joint activity and association, the effort of which is to 'fix,' to 'institute' outside us certain initially subjective and individual ways of acting and judging. Institutions, then, are the 'crystalizations' of Durkheim's early writing" (cited in Scott, 1995, p. 259). Alexander's comment suggests a fourth dimension to the trio of cognitive, normative, and regulative aspects of institutions suggested by Richard Scott: the evaluative, as concerned with value creation and judgment. His comment also points directly to Herbert Blumer's interpretation of social interactions as "joint lines of action" mediated by communication. Thus, when one member of the family deposits a paycheck, a second may proceed to buy groceries and a third to pay the phone bill. Payday for each may have a slightly different meaning.

Much of the work on social work administration and community practice prior to 1970 had a very strong institutional flavor to it. From about that time, concern for institutions was largely overcome by a behavioral turn in which the analysis of micro-organizational behavior and motivations took precedence over the traditional concerns. Other aspects of this shift toward behavioral explanations were discussed in the chapters on communities, organizations, and management. Our interest here is less in turning away from the behavioral perspectives of the past thirty years than in bringing together the earlier institutional foci with the more recent behavioral emphasis for a more complete, composite perspective.

Why do humans create culture and social institutions such as payday? The theory of administrative rationalism offers an answer in terms of some prior aspiration: goals, or profits, or self-interest, or needs, or some such. Berger and Luckman (1966) note that humans are unique in the animal kingdom in that we have no species-specific environment, structured and fixed by our own instinctual organization (p. 47). A formal organization is not such an environment, for example, because all people are not in organizations all the time. Yet, becoming fully human "takes place in relationship within an environment" (p. 48) and human "self-production is always and necessarily a social enterprise" never carried out by individuals alone (p. 51).

As a result, the human instinctual environment is underdeveloped by comparison (p. 48), and the human social environment is peculiarly open and indeterminate (a condition that they call *world openness*). In marked contrast to the rest of the natural world, *human nature* refers only to anthropological constants that hold across cultures (Brown, 1991).

"The human organism lacks the necessary biological means to provide stability for human conduct" (Berger & Luckman, 1966, p. 51). The stability we observe in human behavior is derived from our social and not our physical environment. A given social order, they indicate, precedes any individual organic development. As a result, for each of us, our biological world-openness is at least partially preempted by the particular social world into which we are born (p. 51). That particular social world, like every other social order, is an ongoing distinctive human production, subject to "habitualization" (pp. 52–53). Habits retain their meaning for the individual even as they become embedded as routines in our general stock of knowledge (p. 53). Through habitualization, choices are narrowed, and the mental burden of "all those decisions" is reduced. All of those decisions are the result, in the first place, of no pre-given instinctual environment. Something of the same sort of habitualization occurs over time in organizations as a basic process of institutionalization. It has positive effects such as policy consistency and negative effects such as the stultifying impact of bureaucratic routine.

Habitualization, in this sense, precedes and grounds institutionalization that they define with the grandiose phrase as "reciprocal typifications of habitualized actions by types of actors" (p. 54). Employees come to expect certain things of the employer, and the employer expects certain things of them. In organizations, such typifications involve various forms of role-taking behavior, beginning with the largest role sets of patron, agent, and client. Each has ideas about and expectations of the other. As typifications, institutions are (1) always shared, (2) available to all members of a reference group, (3) "always have a history of which they are the products" (p. 54), and (4) impossible to understand except in light of their historical production.

A particular social world or existing set of social realities like social administration is made up of "thick" concentrations of such institutions that have "hardened" or become habituated or routinized for those involved (p. 59). These expectations are not merely subjective. An institutional social world of this type is "experienced as an objective reality" (p. 54), although its objectivity is humanly produced and constructed. Few, if any students sitting in a class, for example, seriously question the objective reality of the other students, the instructor(s), the assignments, and the classroom they inhabit. All situations in social administration have similar compositions, and it is the institutions involved that gives each situation a ring of familiarity.

Such social realities also have a continuity or an ongoingness that predates any individual's birth or joining and will probably postdate his or her death or departure (p. 60). It is possible, in this context, to take a purely fatalistic and noninterventionist approach to the reality of institutionalization, grounded in the human need for meaning. It occurs, and that's that. So what? The general impulse in social administration is to recognize that these familiar processes of institutionalization are directly involved in both the structure and process and in the implementation of change. Each time a new agency, program, or service is created, the cycle begins anew, and each time an agency or program or service is downscaled, changed, or eliminated, old, familiar meanings are disrupted or destroyed. Completely rational, unemotional, and thoroughly alienated creatures would be unaffected by such disruptions in the ongoing meanings of their lives, but humans are affected, often deeply, personally, and profoundly.

CONCLUSION

The problem of implementation is a consequence of the problem of rational, deliberate, or thoughtful action. It is also a topic that falls within generalized concern for the problem of change. Once you have decided what to do, the next obvious question is how to go about doing it. In organizations, implementation almost always involves changes in conventional ways of doing things. It goes by several different names such as action planning, program development, and programming. These various approaches, however, share a concern for what specific steps are needed, who is responsible for acting, what are the timetables for various actions, what resource issues will arise, and how to monitor progress in the implementation.

There are three key problems that are particularly important for social administration and of which students need to be aware. First is the problem of administrative discretion. Finding just the right combination of policy direction and professional autonomy for those involved with the implementation can be complex and difficult. Administrators engaged in implementation often find themselves guided by a concern for the original intent of the policymakers, a concern for the immediate intent of what makes sense in the situation, and a concern for feasibility or what is possible in the situation. The second key problem is unanticipated consequences. Unexpected things happen in all situations, and implementation needs to be flexible enough to respond and adapt to these surprises without losing the original intent or focus. One of the most perplexing of such consequences are the self-fulfilling prophecies. It appears that any plan that is genuinely expected to fail will fail, if only to succeed in attaining that prediction. The challenge for social administrators, therefore, is to create a climate of positive expectations. This task may be made harder today than it once was if only because of a large and growing body of research on organizations detailing the various bureaupathologies through which organizational participants can retain things as they are. These findings can easily become normal expectations and defenses for those seeking to forestall effective implementation of change. The third problem is the substitution of rhetorical change, or reform-speak, for actual change. Adoption of new terminology often serves as a substitute for real change and is certainly easier to implement.

Many approaches to general management incorporate distinctive models of implementation. For the intuitive command-and-control approach, giving and following orders offers a clear model of implementation. In the principles approach, implementation is often primarily a matter of following the blueprints suggested by those principles. Thanks to Simon, however, we've known for more than half a century that the blueprints offered by management principles are often contradictory and inconsistent. In the case of material processes, in particular manufacturing, theories of control are a major implementation concern. Application of such perspectives to nonmaterial services usually involves efforts to articulate performance standards of some type.

Taylorism, or scientific management, embodies the distinctive implementation sequence of study, implement, and revise. Applications of the Taylorist model using the distinctive and humanistic standard of increasing worker morale or job satisfaction were fundamental to the early human relations approaches, which in turn contributed to understanding of the problem of implementation as a problem of social control.

Recent models of implementation have often relied heavily on exchange and incentive theories and other quasi-economic approaches, with a characteristic emphasis upon implementation as a problem in inducing desired behavior in employees by offering them appropriate inducements or incentives. One of the most comprehensive of these approaches is termed MBO, which seeks to frame inducements in an overall pattern of goals and objectives and to emphasize the issue as one of evaluative self-control. In a larger perspective, the problem of implementation is a key part of the overall problem of institution building, of which the problem of habit formation or habitualization forms a key step. In chapter 11, we examine one key type of such organizational habits or routines, usually known as standard operating procedures.

CHAPTER 11

Operations

The viability of programs and activities planned and implemented must still be established on a day-to-day basis within organizations, policies, programs, and institutions as ongoing concerns. Most first-time administrators, as well as students doing field placements, find themselves entering into ongoing operations that have already been planned and implemented and are up and running by the time they arrive on the scene. Many of these same operations are completely institutionalized and will probably continue in operation long after they depart. The initial experience can be a whirl of rather confusing activities taking place. A good deal of what is happening can at first appear entirely random and unrelated and remain very confusing for a good long while. The explanations for some things that go on in almost any organization are never quite clear, and a small number of events may always appear downright mysterious. At the same time, management textbooks like this one are almost always written with an eye toward clarity in the big picture. They focus on organizational missions and strategies, planning, and the making of major decisions, with little concern for the confusing day-to-day experience in administration. The student and new manager are left largely to their own devices to try to figure out what is going on any given day and how it relates to the big picture.

In organizations of any size at all, social administrators do well to remain focused on the broader perspective and to leave most of the details to others. This is as true within a department or large unit as it is in an entire organization. Typically, there will be plenty of "worker bees" ready and able to concentrate on those details, but only a limited few interested in, or willing to assume responsibility for the whole package or the bigger picture. Nevertheless, the link between the overall panorama and any particular set of details can be a vital one, and consequently most administrators find themselves enmeshed in details from time to time. In this chapter, we shall be concerned with what we are calling *organizational operations* or *operations management*. By this we mean concern for the specific actions, processes, and day-to-day routines through which the "grand plans" of social administration have already been implemented and are experienced as ongoing operational realities on a day-to-day basis. This is a huge topic, and one not very clearly marked out in the existing social administration literature. Others use terms such as *scheduling* and *time management* to refer to parts of this domain.

STANDARD OPERATING PROCEDURE

Organizational culture is full of colorful expressions and acronyms describing and summarizing the particular concerns of operations. Some of these express a certain irreverent humor: SNAFU (situation normal—all fouled up), KISS (keep it simple, stupid!), Murphy's law (whatever can go wrong, will), Parkinson's law (work expands to fill the time available), the Peter principle (people rise to their highest level of incompetence), and even such gems as the alligator's principle of reengineering (when you are up to your waist in alligators, it's hard to drain the swamp!).

Other acronyms carry more straightforwardly serious messages. The most general management acronym is probably SOP, or standard operating procedure(s). Much of the day-to-day reality of virtually all administrative organizations is defined by its institutionalized routines; procedures that may also be recognizable as norms, folkways, mores, conventions, traditions, or informal rules or by other terms and labels. In a large number of higher education institutions, for example, it is SOP that on the first day of class, the instructor will hand out a syllabus and, at the end of the semester, distribute a course evaluation form for students to fill out. Likewise, prior to the start of class, the instructor will have sent a list of required and recommended books to the appropriate bookstore(s) and will have received a listing of students registered for the course. Further, the class schedule will make allowances for appropriate holidays and include a listing of assignments. We all know this and can anticipate it because of our prior experiences with the SOPs of higher education. SOPs can be highly localized. If one were a student in higher education in Britain, France, or Japan, for example, distinctly different sets of such expectations would be in force. Likewise, in a social agency SOP may involve an informal case conference first thing in the morning, weekly informal staff lunches, or a six-month follow-up call for all clients.

In some cases, SOPs can be translated into what amount to unstated organizational policies. For example, it is almost universal for those concerned with accounting systems to employ the discretionary concept of *usual and customary* rather than to spell out long, complex, and redundant descriptions to characterize how certain conventional problems are handled. Thus, the usual and customary practice of many agencies is to reimburse employees after the fact for use of their own vehicles in traveling to in-state meetings.

Many of the day-to-day routines of organizations have the character of such SOPs, and one should anticipate that only part of these procedures will be clearly spelled out in the policy and procedures of any agency. A great deal of the daily reality of administered organizations is, contrary to expectations, taken for granted by those involved. One of the unfortunate aspects of habituation is that some (perhaps many) SOPs may survive long after their original reasons for being have changed. Thus, employees may be required to report odometer readings when filing for travel reimbursement even though there is no practical reason for such information.

POLICY AND PROCEDURES

A phrase closely related to SOP is *policy and procedures*. This compact phrase explicitly brings together concern for the big picture or policy and operating details or procedures. It also explicitly suggests one of the major concerns of operations management. This is sometimes referred to as "the way we do things around here" and combines the notions of usual and customary with the suggestion that such customs may be so taken for granted that they aren't even written down. Efforts to capture such taken-for-granted procedures can take a number of forms, usually when the conventional wisdom has become problematic in some respect. Thus, an agency of all professionals might get along quite well without an explicit procedure for taking compensatory time off until this becomes an item in a major conflict between two employees, at which time a policy spelling out a formal procedure may become necessary.

KEEPING RECORDS AND REPORTING

Perhaps the single most durable and widespread SOP in all organizations throughout history is the keeping of records or files.[1] All organizations keep records. It is particularly important to keep those records that are most closely associated with major commitments, decisions, or policies. However, many organizations err on the side of caution and keep a great deal beyond what is legally or prudently necessary. "You never can tell," it is often said, "when this may be needed." Often, the answer to that is that it never is. It should have been thrown out initially. In general, three reasons for keeping records are of utmost importance: institutional memory; justification of decisions, sometimes also known as keeping a paper trail; and retaining the necessary raw materials for later preparation of reports.

Institutional Memory

One of the principal reasons for keeping records is what is sometimes referred to as the problem of institutional memory. In a certain sense, organizations are not made up of people but rather of the offices held for brief periods of time by those people. From time to time the people change, even as the requirements, expectations, and commitments of the offices and the organization do not. At other times, the people remain the same while the expectations of them change. Thus, it may be important to keep records of actions taken, descriptions of processes followed, details of routines, and other information to avoid major disruptions in the event of staff turnovers. Much of the material of policy and procedure handbooks is often of this nature. The handbook is intended to indicate to new employees, "Be aware that this is how we do things around here."

In some cases, such descriptions of SOPs also contain an implied message for new managers: "This may not be the best way of handling these matters, and it may not be the way you would prefer but it's the way we do things around here. We've gotten used to doing them this way, and if you plan on changing them, be prepared. We may resist those changes, and you must deal with us."

It is often the case that long-time employees of the organization may serve some of this role of institutional memory simply through individual recall. In even the most complete recording systems, it is not possible to write down everything, and at some point, the individual recollections of long-time (and sometimes not-so-long-time) employees become a part of the agency record for some purposes. However, for an organization to rely solely on the memories of long-term employees is to run the risk that the loss of those employees may produce chaos in the organization. It is for this reason that paper—and more recently, computer chips—were invented.

Paper Trails

Another major reason for keeping records in organizations is to maintain what are sometimes called paper trails, or documentary evidence justifying or explaining certain decisions, actions, or events that are part of a larger complex or chain of events. It is largely because of the sequential, remedial, and partial nature of decisions that terms such as *trail* and *chain* apply here.

As a routine matter, for example, the paper trail for a grant may contain the original grant application as submitted, letters and telephone logs of conversations with the granting agency discussing the proposal, the letter of award, the letter of transmittal and check stubs for payments received, the journal entries for grant-related expenditures, and a copy of the final report sent to the granting agency. This particular paper trail could serve several purposes. It could be used to remind those involved or should there ever be a dispute about what the agency had agreed to do in return for the grant funding. It could also be used to orient a new employee or an employee new to the grant of the actions that the agency should be taking with regard to the grant.

Keeping a paper trail explaining and justifying actions by workers on behalf of clients is probably the most important *management* dimension of case recording, although clinicians may, quite legitimately, surround such records with a host of other justifications and rationales. In the event of investigations, formal complaints, lawsuits, or even criminal proceedings, the case record itself may become an *evidentiary record* (a.k.a. paper trail) of great importance. In such cases, most lawyers are likely to stress the *contemporaneous* nature of such records, that is, their close proximity in time to the events involved. Because of their proximity to actual events, they are presumed to yield a more accurate record of the actions taken and reasons for those actions than someone's recollection of these several months or years after the event.

Reports

Everyone in organizations must "do reports" from time to time on their activities, decisions, and results. This is the most fundamental level of accountability. Activity reporting is in some sense inherent in the concept of a division of labor since that concept suggests that different employees will be engaging in different activities. Activity reporting consists of describing the activities that an employee has been engaged in and enables others to review how an employee has spent her time. Although result or outcome reporting is not yet widely practiced in social services, the basic idea is an inherently sound one. In outcome reporting, the employee reports not only what activities they have engaged in but what the outcomes or results of those activities have been. Even if ordinary notions of hierarchy completely disappeared and no one was responsible or reported to anyone else, some measure of activity and outcome reporting would still be necessary and desirable for the purpose of coordination of activities. We all occasionally do exactly that: "I wanted to let you know what I (we) have been doing. . . ." we say, because we know that our actions affect the actions of others and vice versa.

Modern bureaucratic models often dress up this basic reporting impulse with fancy and elaborating phrasing. The reporting may be called monitoring, process recording, quality assessment, and so on. Many of these models do bring additional dimensions into account. In the case of social services, most of these models have arisen as demands or contract requirements associated with the receipt of federal funds. In such cases, practice wisdom usually suggests that just doing the reports is an absolute necessity, no matter how long this takes or how absurd or impossible to accurately report the information requested may be. However, we all do well to remember that the basic, underlying purpose of all reporting in organizations is to inform others of our efforts, decisions, and results. Accountability is a fundamental, operational reality of everything from minutes and financial statements to the most elaborate, quantitative activity reports and the most sophisticated outcome reporting. Indeed, accountability is of such importance as an operational notion that we devote the entire next chapter to it.

One final point on reporting is worth mentioning here because of the tremendous expansion of reporting expectations in social service programs in recent years. One of the simplest yet most profound insights into the limits of reporting is the principle that reporting activities should never consume more time than the activities they report upon. If they do, then the question can legitimately be asked: Why are you not reporting on the activity that takes the majority of your time (reporting) and concentrating only on the minority of your time? It is always surprising how difficult it is for organizations to take this into account.

Organizing the Files

A large number of reports are written, which means that they must be stored or filed. There are probably as many approaches to organizing filing systems as there are office personnel. Generally the social administrator is well advised to set the expectation that the filing system should be systematic, logical, and orderly, that filing should be done regularly, and that it should be possible to retrieve documents from the system with a minimum of effort. Beyond that, it ought to be possible for the social administrator to forget about the filing system and leave it to others.

For literally hundreds of years in the past, maintaining a set of files was largely a task of filing sheets of paper in some system involving subsets (folders) in drawers. In recent decades, however, electronic technology has revolutionized this basic, physical store-and-retrieve arrangement. Sometimes this produces startling and unexpected results, as the lawyers in the Microsoft antitrust suit learned in 1999. Stored and forgotten E-mail messages between Microsoft executives were retrieved and became key evidence in the federal government's antitrust case.

Throughout the 1970s and 1980s, models of structured management information systems were held up as the standard for information storage and retrieval in social services. Entirely new approaches to record keeping and retrieval are emerging, such as data warehousing, which involves procedures for retaining old electronic records, and data mining, which involves searching for information across software formats.[2] In the near term, some additional management attention will be required to identify, install, and implement adequate data warehousing procedures and suitable data mining strategies for social agencies. After successful implementation, one should expect that these devices will become the domain of specialists within virtually all organizations. We should expect also, however, that the levels of administrative access to information may be raised considerably, whereas the time and outlay cost of information retrieval may be considerably reduced.

Over and beyond the general responsibility to ensure that their organization has adequate systems in place for record keeping, social administrators must also attend to managing their own personal information caches. Many administrators will keep working files that may have detailed information about particular projects with which they are involved. Those files may include draft materials and other materials that do not need to be kept in the organization's files. At the conclusion of a given project, the organization will be well served if the administrator reviews her working files to identify any materials that should be made a part of the organization's permanent files.

Chronological Files

In cases where there is a high volume of independent communications as opposed to case-related information that fits readily in case files or a great deal of material that is time sensitive, it may be advantageous to establish a secondary "chron" (for chronological) file. In many offices, a chron file is kept of the formal communication of major administrators in addition to keeping a copy of the communication in the appropriate subject file. The chron file, sometimes maintained in notebooks, has an index that indicates that date of the correspondence and the person to whom it was addressed. The chron file often makes it easier to retrieve correspondence relevant to a particular matter quickly.

Tickler ("To Do") Files

The other case in which the social administrator may wish to take a personal interest in filing would be in establishing some form of "to-do" or tickler file as a periodic reminder of unfinished or impending tasks. Many people find their appointment books adequate for this purpose, others use assorted personal digital assistant hardware or software, and others use specialized notebook systems with clever names such as Day-Timers to keep track of such tickler information. Others keep notices, correspondence, announcements, and other reminders of upcoming events in a special file drawer. If such a system is going to work, you have to remember not just to file things there, but also to check it regularly!

A large number of software programs to perform calendering and tickler file functions for individuals are available, and many organizations have moved to integrated groupware solutions such as Lotus Notes or Groupwise.

Throwing Out Files

In addition to creating files, files need to be periodically reviewed and materials that are no longer needed should be thrown out. Unless this is done, agencies will find that they are investing scarce resources in an ever-growing number of file cabinets and the cost of additional space in which to house the cabinets.

With the passage of time, some things found in the files will simply no longer be needed. A copy of a final grant application, for example, will be needed, but copies of the drafts leading up to the final version will not. Once a grant-funded project has been concluded, some of the correspondence about the project may no longer be needed.

In some instances, there will be federal or state laws governing how long certain filed materials should be retained. Public agencies, for example, often cannot destroy financial records until the agency's records have been audited. Application materials for vacant positions are often kept for three years after the position has been filled to ensure their availability for audit and so the agency can respond to any complaints about a given hiring decision.

Before investing in additional file cabinet or space, any administrator would be well served by first ensuring that the agency is not continuing to keep records that are no longer needed simply because keeping them is easier than reviewing them to determine what might be discarded.

One of the longer-term considerations in determining what files should be discarded involves establishing procedures for archiving valuable historical records (Lohmann & Barbeau, 1992). The social work profession, for example, has benefited from the fact that so much is available about its early history in the archives. However, in considering whether materials need to be archived for historical purposes, the administrator would do well to reflect on how great the interest may be in the future in the records and how historians in the future will access them. Uncataloged material about an agency that is not particularly distinguished will likely be of limited future interest.

Logging Information

In large offices, logs need to be kept of information received because of the volume of incoming information and its critical nature. In medium-sized and smaller offices, logs may not be kept or may only be kept of the most important mail received. A log usually is a chronological listing of the date a piece of mail was received, the person from whom it was received, and the disposition of the item or to whom it was forwarded for response.

Even when a log is not needed, it is a good idea to date stamp mail that is received. Doing so enables the administrator to determine how long it may take the agency to respond to both critical and routine mail. Logs may also be kept of those within the agency to whom mail is forwarded for a response. In such instances, it is also helpful to have a space on the log where the date a response has been returned can be noted so the administrator can ensure that all needed responses are received.

THE USE AND MISUSE OF COMMITTEES AND MEETINGS

One of the critical operational topics associated with the effective use of time by social administrators is the knotty problem of attendance at meetings. There is a small but interesting published literature on committees in social services (Edson, 1977; Epstein, 1981; Guetzkow, 1950; Tropman, 1977; Tropman, Johnson, & Tropman, 1992). The limited size of this literature is somewhat surprising given that so much of the work of social administration takes place in committee and small group settings. It is equally surprising given the pervasiveness of meetings that Harleigh Trecker's (1946) group process approach to social administration, which deals with many of these operational concerns, has largely disappeared from the social work knowledge base. This has occurred despite the enormous growth of small group studies in the past four decades.

When social work students describe their images of administrators on the job, they often point to lone-figures sitting behind large desks pondering the weighty affairs of the organization and, from time to time, issuing authoritative pronouncements. Perhaps the most inaccurate aspect of these images is the notion of the administrator as a lone figure. These images are often nourished by such conventional wisdom as "it's lonely at the top." However much this may refer to the psychology of responsibility, it has little to do with the daily experience of administration.

Anyone who has ever had to make a difficult decision will remember clearly the feeling of the loneliness of command. It doesn't matter whether the decision involved terminating a popular but impractical program, transferring a well-liked employee to another office, raising fees when it is clear that this will deprive some clients of service, or any of a host of other unpopular but necessary choices. The same is true of taking responsibility for decisions that were wrong. It is said, with some justification, that success has many parents, but failure is an orphan.

In general, however, there is good reason for believing that it is only lonely at the top on certain occasions. For the most part, the experience of social administration is a highly social one. In small organizations, social administration is generally carried out in close proximity to the clerical, clinical, and other workers. All of the assorted activities of social administration described in this book may be carried out on a day-to-day basis through an uninterrupted series of informal conversations with other employees and stakeholders. In large organizations, the burden of administration is typically subject to a division of labor spread over a large number of people who must inevitably communicate with one another and with outside stakeholders to carry out their responsibilities. In the large organization, the informal, face-to-face communications of the small organization is usually supplemented with endless rounds of formal communication events or meetings.

MEETINGS, MEETINGS, MEETINGS

There are as many different types of meetings as there are people in organizations. Without any pretense of offering a comprehensive or exhaustive typology, we have selected six different types of meetings for discussion: regular business meetings, planning meetings, decision meetings, calls to account, informal group therapy, and the nonmeeting. This list is admittedly incomplete. There are many other types, such as meetings for the purpose of networking, that might be added.

Regular Business Meetings

Probably the most familiar type of meeting for most people is the business meeting held periodically and characterized by a fairly standardized routine. *Robert's Rules of Order,* for example, suggests an agenda consisting of a formal opening, reading and/or approval of the minutes of the previous meeting, old business, and new business. Such a meeting may be attended by the stakeholders in an organization, as is the case when a nonprofit organization holds an annual business meeting as specified in its articles of incorporation. More often, however, such a meeting serves as a periodic staff meeting for the organization, and attendance is limited to the organization's employees.

Business meetings serve multiple purposes, including dissemination of information; making decisions; planning; acknowledging accomplishments of units, individuals, and groups; and a variety of psychosocial considerations. The regular business meeting is an extremely flexible small group format, and the term itself covers an incredible range of gatherings in organizations. In different agencies and at different times, they may range from highly formal to very informal, from very focused to quite diffuse, and from very contentious to peaceful to the point of boring.

As the use of the term *regular* suggests, this type of meeting occurs periodically. It may occur every Monday morning or the third Thursday of every month. The regularity in its scheduling allows participants to plan on this event and to identify in advance issues that they wish to make certain are raised with the group.

Planning Meetings and Retreats

Another special form of meeting commonly found in social administration is the planning meeting, devoted to various types of planning activities, especially the kind of vision, mission, and strategy considerations that are difficult to adequately consider in the grind of daily operations. The basic idea of such planning meetings is to set aside a block of group time in which otherwise busy people can discuss, reflect, and focus on questions of what ought to be done or done differently. This may involve broad, philosophical discussions of weighty issues, or it may involve attention to the minutest details of operations, such as the color of chairs to be purchased, layout of forms, or policies on the distribution of office keys.

Some organizational cultures have developed forms of planning meetings known as retreats, which includes in-house and living room retreats (Hughes, 1999). The original concept of a retreat is a special meeting of the board, executive committee, senior administrators, department heads, supervisors, or some other similar group. Such retreats are usually held at remote locations, such as resorts, conference centers, or religious retreats. The most important consideration is that the retreat be away from telephones and the insistent demands of daily operations. For some organizations, the retreat also becomes a corporate perk with ample time for golf, tennis, and informal networking built into the retreat schedule.

Phrases such as "creativity" and "thinking outside the box" and other au courant notions are frequently heard at such retreats, and it is relatively easy for cynics to dismiss retreats as useless. Retreats can prove very useful, however, if there is an organizational need that justifies holding the retreat and the agenda for the retreat is carefully planned.

Decision Meetings

Another fairly common meeting in administrative contexts is one called for the express purpose of reaching a decision on a pending matter or issue. In general terms, decision meetings are the exact opposite of planning meetings. The focus is on action, decisiveness, and clarity. Meetings for the explicit purpose of decisions are usually reserved for major or critical decisions such as creation of new programs, hiring major or critical employees, the adoption of highly innovative, controversial or risky practices, and so on.

Decision meetings as opposed to ordinary business meetings in which decisions are made are usually characterized by tightly limited agendas of one or two items. They usually occur late in a planning-and-decision process and often represent the terminus of particular planning initiatives. "We've planned. We've examined all the alternatives. We've carefully examined the implications of both acting and not acting. Now it's time to decide. Do we want to do this or not?"

Particularly if the planning has been done well and the principals involved are ready to resolve the issues, decision meetings may often be quite short. As Herbert Simon and others suggested long ago, such decision meetings are often as much for the purposes of ratifying what has already, in effect, been decided as for exhaustive consideration of an issue. In many respects, the ease with which such meetings unfold may be directly related to the adequacy of planning that preceded them.

Calls to Account

Another common form of administrative meeting is what might be termed the call-to-account or "remember where the buck stops" meeting. One sub-form of this can be called the "I am the boss" or "who's in charge here?" meeting, since conveying that message is the principal purpose of the meeting. In this type of meeting, a supervisory or administrative boss will gather a group of employees together for the express purpose of reminding, lecturing, or just plain haranguing them. Often the motivation for such a meeting is the sense of the administrator that his or her authority is not being taken seriously enough. The supervisor may believe that directives are being ignored, policies undermined, or managerial directions not followed. New bosses should remember that this type of meeting almost certainly always has costs as well as benefits associated with it and should approach it with caution. In our experience, such meetings often arise more out of the boss's insecurities and uncertainties than out of the workers' behavior and often do not have the effect desired by the supervisor.

Other forms of call-to-account meetings may involve such matters as dealing with issues of contract noncompliance, individual and group non-performance, dismissals, and a host of other themes and issues where "calling someone on the carpet" is advisable and necessary.

Informal Group Therapy

Not all of the meetings one encounters in social administration go "by the book" or conform closely to rational actor models of organization. Some types of social work involve serious high-stress activities, and most forms of social work intervention involve at least moderate levels of stress. Yet very few social agency organizations have established procedures for dealing with these stresses, and most social agency offices have few physical facilities for coping with employee stress either. Partly as a result of these deficits in organization and physical setting and partly because it has become part of the professional subculture of social work, many social work meetings take on an important quality that looks very much like a type of informal group therapy. This is one of the most interesting institutions of the social agency in many ways.

In such meetings, the purpose may nominally be on conducting business, planning, making decisions, or calling people on the carpet. However, the real purpose of the meeting may be to vent frustration and perform stress reduction activity. Such meetings are often a necessary and important part of the social agency operation. Even as workers may complain of unnecessary or useless meetings, they may also attend and participate fully.

The danger is that what is a very desirable climate for such meetings—a kind of freewheeling free association exercise with no formal structure and lots of opportunity for people to express themselves—can endanger or even completely overwhelm the quite different purposes of other types of meetings, which may throw the day-to-day operations of the agency into a state of limbo.

The Nonmeeting

At an operational level, organizational life is often an unending round of meetings. Unfortunately, people become so accustomed to sitting in meetings that their critical faculties can become seriously eroded, often resulting in nonmeetings, meetings that serve no discernible purpose whatsoever. One is reminded here of a television commercial in which a number of people are shown sitting quietly around a table, obviously awaiting the start of a meeting. After several moments of silence, someone asks, "Who called this meeting?" Everyone looks at the others silently for a moment or two and then they all get up to leave as they realize that no one present called it and there is no reason for them to stay, because they don't know why they are there. Much of the poignancy of this message comes from the fact that we've all attended meetings that had no reason for occurring; except that, in most cases, no one raised such basic questions. We all just sat and endured the meeting, pointless though it was.

At one such moment of particular frustration with faculty meetings a number of years ago, a group of us came up with four "principles of organizational inaction" that were subsequently published in an administrative humor magazine (Lohmann, 1979):

1. *The time theorem:* The present is too soon or too late to discuss any important issue.
2. *The subject matter theorem:* The topic is too narrow or too broad to be considered.
3. *The group size theorem:* The group is too small or too large for effective action.
4. *The excitement theorem:* The topic is too controversial or too dull to deal with.

Ultimately, there is no complete protection from dreary, tedious, or pointless meetings, especially when they are called or run by someone else. However, one should always strive to ensure that the meetings you call and the meetings you arrange do have a clear purpose and that the meeting is conducted in a manner consistent with that purpose. Decision meetings that deteriorate into group therapy sessions probably should not have been called in the first place, or the group leader should have exercised more skill or control in introducing the issue for decision.

ORGANIZATIONAL CHANGE

Most discussions of organizational change implicitly assume the ongoing nature of organizations. Yet, the experience of change is approximately as common as the experience of stability in most organizations. People, programs, grants, policies all come and go, and yet life must go on! As a general rule, it is typically far easier to participate in making major decisions involving sweeping changes and fundamental reforms than it is to live through the experience of those changes unfolding day after day in the organization.

In general, the literature on organizational change tends to paint a rather dreary picture of bureaucrats resistant to change. For a great many people in organizations—both management and nonmanagement—SOPs over time come to define "the" organization, and even relatively minor disruptions in these conventional ways of doing things can be extremely upsetting and threatening.

In general, however, much of the social work literature on social change fails to differentiate adequately between changes at the operational level and deeper change of a more fundamental, profound nature. Operational changes are taking place all the time in most organizations, and a good deal of the *angst* associated with such changes can be overcome by sensible, intelligent preparation for such changes. At an absolute minimum, this seems to involve:

- Seeking the opinions of those affected by the change at all stages of the process whenever and wherever possible. However, administrators need not feel apologetic for the fact that, even in the best managed organizations, it is not always desirable to consult everyone about everything.
- Announcing changes in sufficient time to allow people to adjust to the idea.
- Accepting the initial reactions, which may range across the board, as normal without over-reacting. Every complaint and expression of opposition to an operational change is not a sign of incipient revolt.
- Deciding when corrective action may be needed. Not every negative reaction requires corrective action. Sometimes just listening is enough. In other cases, it may be necessary to explain patiently but firmly that the change is necessary and people will just have to accept it. Adopting a tone of "if you don't like it, leave" is almost never a good idea, but in some extreme cases that *is* the message.

TIME MANAGEMENT

Another of the most universal experiences of administration and one of the aspects that sets administrative experience apart from other human affairs is the strong sense that time must be used effectively, which includes the sense that

- Things will or can occur only at certain times
- Tasks can only take so much time to complete
- Certain things must be begun or completed at particular times (deadlines)
- Some types of activities can only be completed between particular times (office hours)

These are all unique concerns of the administered organization. In all these cases, there is the sense that time is a scarce and valuable resource not to be misused. It is a resource to be managed. In all these senses, time management is an important part of managing an organization as an ongoing operation.

A great many workshops, handbooks, and other materials are available on the general topic of effective time management and cultivating the work habits that support effectiveness on the job (see, for example, Covey [1997]).

Hours of Operation

In most organizations, the established routine or SOP includes listed or published hours of operation—times during which the office will be open for business. One of the genuine curiosities of contemporary social service operations has been the extent to which they conform more to the traditional operating schedules of business (nine to five, Monday through Friday) than to the periods of greatest availability of clients (e.g., after work, on weekends) or the periods of greatest frequency of problems or crises, such as evenings. This remains the case even as businesses have moved to be more flexible in their hours to better meet the needs of the contemporary family.

In terms of client availability, a transition to shopping center hours (e.g., 10:00 A.M. or later to 9:00 P.M. or later) might make more sense. A study of crisis episodes reported to the mobile crisis team of a community mental health center, for example, found that the largest incidence of crisis reports occurred in the late afternoon and early evening hours, up to about midnight. After that, reports dropped off dramatically until mid-morning the following day (Lohmann, 1991b). There are additional considerations. For example, these extended hours might initially raise havoc with agency budgets and staffing plans and could even trigger new shortages of trained personnel. However, in at least some agencies, client availability only during these later hours is already being accommodated informally or on a crisis basis. And it is unclear in most cases what the real cost of these accommodations for the agency may be. Thus, the costs of extended hours may not be as great as is assumed.

Scheduling Tools

In much of the human services management literature, techniques of time management have typically been designated as planning tools. This may be a somewhat misguided designation, since many of the techniques are much more commonly used in coordinating implementations and guiding ongoing operations than in extensive program development or planning. For example, it takes careful time scheduling of workers, material deliveries, the arrivals and departures of specialty contractors, and a host of other factors to build automobiles or submarines. It has yet to be shown that anything more complicated than the coordination of one group of people (clients) with another group of people (workers) and the occasional involvement of supervisors and consultants is involved in time scheduling in the social agency. Thus, in the social agency, scheduling tools are most likely to be deployed to assist individual workers in developing their daily schedules. As such, they are also very useful as training tools in highlighting the need for effective scheduling and performance habits and modeling aspects of effective time management. The actual use of these tools in the coordination of agency-wide programs in social services is relatively limited.

Gantt Charts

The earliest attempt at actually plotting time and work flows on paper was the Gantt chart, named for its developer, Henry Gantt, one of the major early contributors to scientific management.[3] Time management (often labeled *time and motion study*) was a major consideration for the scientific management movement.

Gantt's innovation was to envision a linear time line and to break it into segments, each devoted to a particular activity or task. If each task were listed in order on a chart together with a bar indicating its segment, any viewer wishing to do so could get a quick and relatively easy grasp of the job. The chart showed not only in what order things were to occur but also proportionately how much time each task was expected to take. Figure 11.1 is an example of such a Gantt chart.

Figure 11.1 Gantt Chart

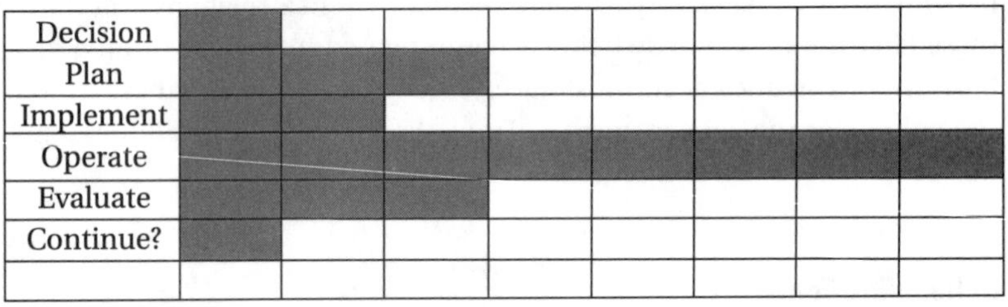

Decision								
Plan								
Implement								
Operate								
Evaluate								
Continue?								

Gantt charts can be very useful representations of relatively simple processes with only a small number of steps and few activities occurring simultaneously. A good rule of thumb is that Gantt charts work well for those sets of activities that would fit together with explanatory material on a single sheet of paper. This is generally why it is so helpful for mapping individual and small group projects. For more complex processes of greater duration, however, Gantt charts have a number of major drawbacks. The most important limitation is the linear sequencing they imply: The bars are line segments and the implication would appear to be that as one event or period ends another begins. There is little provision in the Gantt chart for overlapping sequences or simultaneous events. In some cases, a simple sense of sequencing can be obtained by spreading the bars across the page (Figure 11.2).

PERT Charts

The Program Evaluation and Review Technique (PERT) is an approach developed by the RAND corporation for the U.S. Navy that solves many of the weaknesses of the Gantt approach. PERT embraces a simple, but powerful, mathematical model from graph theory. Lines are defined as time se-

Figure 11.2 Gantt Chart

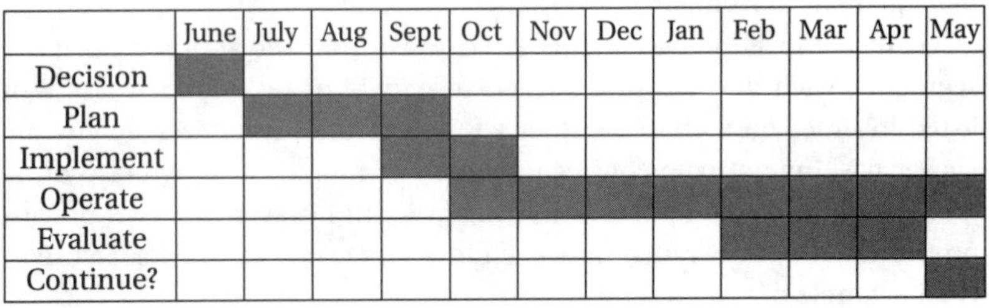

	June	July	Aug	Sept	Oct	Nov	Dec	Jan	Feb	Mar	Apr	May
Decision												
Plan												
Implement												
Operate												
Evaluate												
Continue?												

quences, processes (or, for our purposes, operations) and the points or nodes where lines intersect are defined as events. Thus, in PERT each operation is defined by two events: its beginning and end. Noting when it began and ended allows relatively simple determination by subtraction of the interval between beginning and end of its duration. For tasks of any complexity at all, the typical PERT chart quickly becomes a large, complex, network of connecting line segments, as in Figure 11.3, together with an accompanying table of time values, as in Table 11.1. Unless one wishes merely to savor the complexity of events, it is not clear that it is always necessary or worth the time and cost involved to model social service processes or programs in this way.

The PERT techniques are sometimes also known as PERT-CPM (for Critical Path Method). The critical path is the central aspect of PERT modeling. It involves determination of the single irreducible path, or sequence of events and activities, that marks the shortest possible time in which the job could be completed. This is the so-called critical path around which the appropriateness of all other time sequences in the job can be determined and has a number of important and sometimes highly technical uses in constructing the optimum operational schedule. For complex tasks like building submarines or jet fighters, around which literally thousands of

Figure 11.3 PERT Chart of Events and Activities

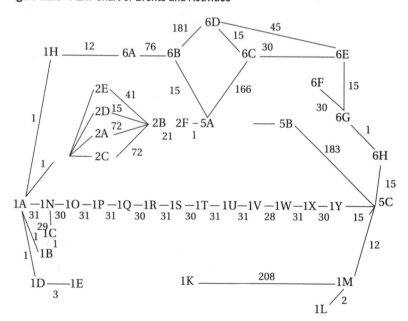

Table 11.1 Table of Events and Activities

Event/Activity	Start	ID	Finish	ID
Board Decision to Start Program	6/17/01	1A		
Press release no. 1	6/18/01	1B	6/19/01	1C
Press release no. 2	9/15/01	1J	9/20/01	1K
Press release no. 3 (if needed)	5/16/02	IL	5/18/02	1M
Notify stakeholders	6/18/01	1D	6/21/01	1E
Name planning team	6/18/01	1F	7/1/01	2C
Name evaluation team	6/18/01	1H	7/1/01	6A
Monthly progress reports to board	7/15/01	1N	5/15/02	1Y
Planning Phase				
Develop policies	7/1/01	2A	9/10/01	2B
Establish procedures	7/1/01	2C	9/10/01	2B
Contact other agencies—referral plans	7/15/01	2D	9/10/01	2B
Develop client outreach plan	7/31/01	2E	9/10/01	2B
Planning phase completed			9/30/01	2F
Implementation Phase				
Select and appoint program leader	6/18/01	3A	9/1/01	3D
Define jobs and hire staff	7/1/01	3A	9/15/01	3B
Advertise positions	7/15/01	3A	7/25/01	3C
Interview candidates	8/15/01	3D	9/5/01	3E
Check references	8/7/01	3F	9/7/01	3G
Target date for staff all hired			9/15/01	3H
Train staff	9/25/01	3I	9/30/01	3J
Arrange Space				
Relocate existing staff in new space	6/18/01	4A	7/15/01	4B
Arrange reconstruction contracts	6/18/01	4A	7/1/01	4C
Repair and repaint walls	7/15/01	4D	7/31/01	4E
Recarpet	8/1/01	4F	8/15/01	4G
Install furniture and fixtures	8/10/01	4H	9/1/01	4H
Operations Phase				
See first clients	10/1/01	5A		
First monthly staff meeting	10/15/01	5B		
Suspend operations or enter year two			6/1/02	5C
Evaluation Phase				
Identify outcomes/design monitoring	7/1/01	6A	9/15/01	6B
Data collection	10/1/01	5A	3/15/02	6C
Analyze first year data	3/1/02	6D	4/15/02	6E
Write first year evaluation report	4/1/02	6F	4/30/02	6G
Evaluation report send to board	5/1/02	6H		
May board mtg.—decision to continue?			5/15/02	5C

interrelated tasks are clustered, PERT is a highly useful management device. For the example in Figure 11.3, another kind of critical path is evident. This is the sequence of monthly board meetings shown from 1N to 1Y. The scheduling of many other events is determined in part by when they will be reported to the board.

Because it is relatively straightforward to move from the PERT chart and its table of times to estimates of the cost of each element in the chart/table, PERT can also be a highly effective means of estimating the costs of particular projects as well. This has resulted in a procedure known as PERT-Cost.

One of the most useful features of PERT has been the development of sophisticated software programs like Microsoft's Project that enable even relatively unsophisticated users to construct highly sophisticated PERT and PERT-Cost studies. Not only does this software make it relatively easy to construct PERT charts and identify critical paths, it also allows for inclusion of highly sophisticated cost estimates of project costs. Because of its ease of use and availability, social administrators need to be alert to the previously discussed law of the hammer in evaluating the use of PERT software:

1. Would the time and cost of conducting a PERT study in a social agency be justified by the results such a study would produce? Or, is it merely a fun toy capable of producing some gee-whiz graphics and esoteric time and cost estimates?
2. Does the agency have or can it readily develop the expertise necessary to understand and evaluate the results of a PERT study and incorporate them into more intelligent decision making?

TACTICAL DECISIONS AND METHODS SELECTION

Time is, of course, not the only consideration in operations planning. Another major concern is the selection and use of what might be called tactics. Tactics might be defined as the microstrategies within macrostrategies. Tactical concerns are generally of a how-to-do-it nature. They address how to best carry out a particular task or procedure that has already been decided upon. Many social work methods are, from an administrative standpoint, elaborated at the tactical level. The decision to deal with particular social problems, and to address those problems through the delivery of services as opposed, for example, to the delivery of income, modification of the built environment, or the like, is a strategic choice. Within such grand strategies, the choice of what to do and how to do it is the arena of tactics.

One of the least developed aspects of social administration practice theory is any consideration of how social agencies ought to go about the tactical selection of the actual methods to be used by workers. Because of the breach between management and direct practice discussed in chapter 1, the literature of social work seldom reflects serious consideration of a role for social administration in the selection of methods. In the textbooks, the choice of methods is a matter of professional discretion. In actual practice, much may be dictated by agency policy or SOP. The most common tactical approach used in social agency operations would appear to be simply to hire good people you trust, give them an outline of policies to work with, and let them do their jobs. This approach is purely surmise; there are actually no research data whatsoever to indicate actual administrative behavior in this area. If one assumes, as advocates of the indirect practice approach often do, that social administrators are a foreign, invasive presence in the social agency, such a hands-off approach makes sense. If on the other hand, you assume as we do that social administration is an encompassing, all-embracing mode of practice, there would appear to be a strong case for administrative involvement in the selection of methods. This would most likely be reflected in the planning process, in the definition of tasks and jobs, and in the recruitment, hiring, and development of workers as well as in ongoing operations.

TECHNOLOGY AND OPERATIONS

There are a variety of technological devices that can assist with the operational management of an agency. If the agency has a local area network (LAN), electronic calendars can be used to facilitate scheduling meetings that involve multiple employees. A domain of devices that might be termed *information appliances* is becoming more important every day at the operational levels of social administration. As recently as two decades ago and for at least some social agencies even today, pens and pencils, notepads, typewriters, and desktop telephones exhaustively defined the information appliance domain. Today, there are literally hundreds of new devices and gadgets for generating, storing, retrieving, moving, organizing, and in other ways processing information in records.

Personal digital assistants (PDAs), for example, allow the social administrator to carry detailed information with her about her schedule, important phone numbers, to-do lists, and even provide access to the Internet. PDAs permit uploading and downloading of such information from the administrator's computer. Though their adoption has tended to be limited to the more technologically savvy, as costs decline they are being more widely adopted.

Laptop computers also permit the administrator to carry with him needed information and, with a modem, provide easy access to the Internet and E-mail. Some administrators are choosing to have only a laptop computer and are forgoing a desktop one because they like the portability made possible by a laptop.

Cell phones have become so ubiquitous that there is a growing backlash against them and the lack of manners that appears to go with their use. Though it may be annoying to observe a driver paying more attention to his cell phone than his driving or a fellow restaurant patron chatting during dinner, there is no denying the added convenience. They are especially convenient in settings like crisis management agencies, where a staff member must be accessible by phone at all times.

The technology that can assist with organizational operations is changing quickly and, as it changes, costs usually come down as well. Administrators are well served by keeping track of technological advances and adopting those that will meet their needs and fit within their budgets.

CONCLUSION

Organizational operations consist of the things needed to keep a social agency functioning on a daily basis. In large organizations, the social administrator may not need to focus much on these operations. There will be other specialized employees to whom responsibility for them has been delegated. However, in smaller agencies concern for operations may consume considerable amounts of the administrator's time. In all agencies, administrators are served by having some knowledge of operational procedures so they may ensure that those procedures are consistent with and supportive of the agency's mission and goals.

This chapter discusses a variety of techniques that might be used to assist in managing daily operations. In some instances, those techniques are labeled as planning approaches. In other instances, they deal with the processing of paper. The most rapidly expanding area is that of technological applications to organizational operations.

CHAPTER 12

Accountability

Among the major considerations that bring the cycle of institutionalization into alignment with the relations of patrons, agents, and clients in the community are issues of accountability. The term *accountability* is derived, in the first instance, from the process of "giving an account" or offering an explanation or justification.

The concept of accountability is often identified with being fiscally accountable (Greenlee, 1998). The underlying idea is that a social agency should provide an accounting or explanation of how it has spent the funds that it received. Although such fiscal accountability is important, there are other forms of accountability that agencies need to consider as well. In social agencies, the concept of accountability is usually used both in a narrow sense, such as the successful completion of timely financial reporting, and in a broader sense, such as embracing concerns for reports of effectiveness, efficiency, performance, and quality. All of these forms of accountability are discussed in this chapter and chapter 13.

In this chapter, we examine six distinct approaches or dimensions to social service accountability:

1. The accounting theory of accountability
2. The nonprofit corporate theory of accountability
3. The theory of accountability arising out of management by objectives and results
4. The political theory of accountability implicit in democratic governance
5. Contract or legal accountability.
6. Emerging new concepts of accountability associated with managed care

In chapter 13, program evaluation is discussed. Program evaluation is one of the methodologies often used by social service agencies to demonstrate their accountability and can be used to address issues of effectiveness, efficiency, performance, and quality.

ACCOUNTABILITY IS NOT A NEW IDEA

Accountability has been a major concern for public and private nonprofit social services for centuries. For example, the following excerpts from accountability reports were published in the *Pennsylvania Gazette* more than 200 years ago, on November 13, 1782. They show clearly that some measure of accountability was a concern under the American poor law system just as it is today. They also show that many of the contemporary concerns with reporting and outcome measurement are of very long standing. Just as important, they show that (because the fiscal year reports for 1780, 1781, and 1782 were all published at the same time) the question of what constitutes timely reporting was no more settled then than it is today.

> GENERAL STATE of the Accounts of the CONTRIBUTORS to the Relief and Employment of the POOR, in the City of Philadelphia (particularly for Cash, received and expended for Support of the Poor, in the House of Employment) from the 25th of March, 1779, to the 8th of May, 1780.
> . . .
> We, James Wharton and John Mease, appointed by the Managers of the Contributors for the Relief and Employment of the Poor of the City of Philadelphia, to examine the Steward Books, Accounts and Vouchers, and to prepare a general State of the Accounts of this Corporation, do report, That, having gone fully and regularly through such Examination, we find his Accounts, full, clear and just, and that as it appears by the above general State, &c. (taken from them) he is £ 3006 14 6, (3,000 pounds, 14 shillings and 6 pence) now in Advance,

for Necessaries purchased for the Poor, and that he hath not received any Thing for or in Consideration of his Salary during the Space of the above Account.

That on an Average there has been 91 Persons (in almost every Stage of helpless Distress) supported and relieved in the House, for the Time above mentioned, particularly for the late severe and heavily expensive Winter, when Provisions and every Necessary has been so extravagantly high, and therefore run up our Expences [sic] to a most amazing Appearance, besides which we are now heavily in Debt for many Kinds of Provisions and Necessaries long since expended and consumed, to the Amount of many Thousand Pounds.

JAMES WHARTON, Philadelphia, May 8, 1780.

JOHN MEASE.

GENERAL STATE of the Account of the CONTRIBUTORS, &c. from May 8, 1780, to May 14, 1781, in Continental Currency. . . .

Yet we have to remark, that altho' there now is so large a nominal Sum in the Hands of the Treasurer, yet it is but lately paid in, and the Depreciation is now so very rapid, that it will go but a little Way in Support of 110 poor, helpless Objects (which has been the average Number supported in the House for the Year past;) had the Poor Funds been sooner collected and paid, their Support might have been less expensive, though more comfortable.

ANNUAL STATE of the Accounts of the CONTRIBUTORS, &c. from May 12, 1781, to May 11, 1782. . . .

We the Committee appointed to examine the Accounts of the Treasurer and steward for the Year past,. . . . Your Committee have farther to observe, that although the last and present Year Poor Taxes have been considerably burthensome to the Community, yet, from the Time and Manner of their having been paid in, particularly by the District and Townships connected in this Corporation, the Managers have not been enabled to discharge the Debts of the Corporation, or to lay in Wood, Provisions, &c. on the most advantageous Terms; . . . The average Number of poor Persons supported in the House for this Year has been at lest 118, and under every Disadvantage, but by the Assistance obtained from the laudable Vigilance of the Flour Inspector, they have been well supplied with Provisions, Firewood, Bedding and Cloathing, for abut £ 15 each per Annum, which, considering the advanced Price of those Necessaries, is, we apprehend, full as low as can be expected, consistent with the benevolent Purposes of a charitable institution. With almost an empty treasury we are sorry to report, the Institution remains considerably incumbered for want of a fuller Support, by more punctual Compliance with the Poor Law.

Clearly, the expectation that social administrators must be accountable for their efforts and programs is anything but a new phenomenon. The same is true of running short of funds when need is high. As these and many comparable examples show, the overseers of the poor were already expected to be publicly accountable for their actions in the late eighteenth century. It is very unlikely that overseers Warton, Meese, and others would have taken the extraordinary step of publishing this information in the newspaper were there not some legal mandate or very strong social obligation to do so. In fact, such expectations had already been in place for at least two centuries by the time these notices were published. So accountability to the patrons is anything but a new phenomenon. Yet, clearly something else is afoot today. Contemporary concerns for accountability are something more than the time-honored public accountings of such financial reports. Accountability today means something more than simply publishing perfunctory legal notices in the local newspaper. And these reports are indeed perfunctory. All three of these annual reports were published in the same issue in 1782, even though both of the overseers who signed the first report were apparently no longer serving by that time.

In part, there is a generalized sense today that traditional means of accountability may have failed to keep pace with rapid development of new administrative technologies. Thus, Davidson, Schlesinger, Dorwart, and Schnell (1991) conclude that though purchase of service contracting (POSC) has expanded quickly for mental health services, accountability mechanisms have lagged behind. There is also a general sense of unaccountability. Kettner speculated in 1985 that most government human service contracting agencies would be unable to produce data that demonstrate either efficiency or effectiveness of services provided through POSC (Kettner & Martin, 1985). This may be attributed, in part, to the absence of well-developed POSC monitoring systems. Well-designed monitoring systems should (1) ensure accountability, (2) ensure contract compliance, (3) identify problems, and (4) provide decision makers with information for future planning.

As these examples show, the practice of accountability through financial accounting and reporting has evolved over a long period of time into concern for a highly specific set of practices for developing reports (giving an accounting) of the condition and changes in a set of financial records (known as accounts).[1]

Accountabilities are multiple in just about every modern organization: In the business corporation, management is generally accountable to shareholders or stockholders first and foremost with respect to returns on their investment. However, as assorted protest movements have made clear in the case of plant closings, for example, the question of the community accountability of business corporations is a much-debated subject. Much of the energy of the current accountability movement in social services builds off encouragement to be more businesslike, a notion that keys on the idea of management being more accountable to stakeholders. Many of the problems arising from this basic notion are related to the questions, Accountable to whom? And for what?

The most fundamental purpose of accounting in business is to determine the precise amount of profits available for distribution to shareholders. This occurs within its own triad: customers buy, businesses sell to them, and shareholders profit.[2] Government and nonprofit accounting have traditionally been done for quite different reasons. Governments and nonprofit organizations do not have shareholders or stockholders and are less concerned with income and profit calculations. Instead, they typically account in detail for expenditure or what has been done with any money they have received. This style of accounting has traditionally been characterized as stewardship accountability and differentiated from income accountability of businesses.

It is more than a little ironic that in fields of practice like social services in which those involved pride themselves on both their practical natures and lack of familiarity with economic theory that the accountability issue has arisen. This is so at least in part because of a rather obscure implication of a not very widely known economic theory known as public choice theory (Downs, 1957; Downs and Rand Corporation, 1967; Niskanen, 1968, 1998; Tullock, 1965). To its adherents, the economics of public choice suggest that oversupply and inefficiency occur when government officials have a monopoly on service delivery (Blais & Dion, 1992; Boyne, 1998; Jackson, 1982; McMaster & Sawkins, 1996). On this basis alone, there is widespread suspicion and concern that social service "public utilities" may be susceptible to the twin problems of oversupply and inefficiency. Some authorities have even taken the doctrinaire stance that if it is public and the only service of its kind, it must be oversupplied and inefficient. This was part of the underlying case for the need for welfare reform and reducing caseloads, for example.

In the case of nonprofit organizations, this has led to so-called government failure theory, which states that nonprofit service vendors have arisen in large part out of the failure of government to solve the problem of monopoly (Salamon & Anheier, 1998). The most telling applications of public choice theory, however, have been the broad range of developing commercial social service vendors, whether private nursing homes, day care facilities, or prisons. It is ironic that the present practical concern for accountability may have resulted from an economic theory. It may be true as John Kenneth Galbraith once noted that the activities of the most practical sort are guided, almost unconsciously, by some obscure and long-forgotten theorist.

THE ACCOUNTING THEORY OF ACCOUNTABILITY

Businesses have been keeping records for thousands of years. Some of the earliest examples of writing are, in fact, business records, such as lists of customers, prices paid for goods acquired, and revenue received from goods sold. As the modern accounting procedure known as determining the cost of goods sold demonstrates, it is impossible to talk meaningfully about any notion of business profit without accurate and timely record keeping and reporting.[3] Modern accounting practice is built upon systems of *double-entry* bookkeeping, first codified by a fifteenth-century Italian monk, Luca Paciola.[4] In double-entry accounting systems derived from Paciola, *original entries* of financial *transactions* are entered as pairs in two of five categories that vary depending on the nature of the transaction. The basic categories are *assets*, or things owned; *liabilities*, or amounts owed to others; *income*, or resource inflows; *expenditures*, or resource outflows; and *capital*, or the current net worth or economic value of the business. *Profit* can only be determined by standardized calculations within the accounting system, the results of which are shown in financial reports.

Although governments and nonprofit-like organizations have existed for many centuries, most have done so with only a very hazy idea of where they stand financially.[5] The development of suitable variations of standard business accounting in the form of accurate, dependable government and nonprofit accounting systems is remarkably recent. Definite nonprofit accounting standards were not agreed to until the 1970s. The key to advances in both governmental and nonprofit accounting is a departure from ordinary business accounting in what accountants call the *entity*. In business, the real purpose of accounting is determining income and profit, and the key aspects of the processes of manufacturing, transportation, sales, and delivery can all be expressed in financial terms as costs and prices. Thus, a single entity ("the firm" or "the business") is ordinarily a satisfactory unit of analysis.

In the case of governments and nonprofit organizations, however, accounting reports based on the equivalent of the firm (ambiguously either the government as a whole or the particular organization or bureau) are seldom sufficient. Thus, if the federal government or a foundation or an individual gives a grant to a nonprofit organization for a specific purpose, they should not see it as an investment for which they expect a return.

Moreover, they are unlikely to be satisfied with accounting reports that show only total inflows from all sources and how much was left unspent at the end of the accounting period. Yet that is all that the direct application of business methods of accounting could show.

What most funders or donors are really interested in is what the organization did with their money and whether those activities made a difference. This is the essence of the accountability question for governments and nonprofits. There are a number of indications, including a national survey of donors by Independent Sector (Hodgekinson, 1993) suggesting that the fundamental issue of accountability in the case of donated funds may be trust. It is at this point that the image of social administrators as stewards of resources put forth by others becomes the dominant metaphor. If and when stakeholders trust agents, the issue of accountability is likely to be fully institutionalized and handled completely by routine reports.

These concerns for stewardship accountability, however, run directly into an annoying characteristic of financial reporting. Money is *fungible;* that is, as soon as any particular sum is deposited in your accounts any given dollar (or peso, franc, pound, lire, or rupee) looks pretty much like any other, and there is no simple way to keep track of what came from whom or where it in particular went. To illustrate this concept, check the change in your pocket or purse. Can you identify the source of any coin or bill that you find? Unless they bear a distinctive mark of some sort, it is unlikely that you will be able to tell which dollar you got as change at the grocery store and which at the drug store. Fund accountability was literally invented as a solution to that particular stewardship problem: How can we best tell our donors, particularly the largest and most important ones, what we did with their donations? The eighteenth-century reports noted earlier reflect much of what is still the emphasis in efforts to provide such feedback.

ACCOUNTABILITY

The concept of accountability has received a great deal of attention in donative organizations, in which it is usually used in a narrow sense as the successful completion of timely financial reporting and in a broad sense embracing concerns for reports of effectiveness, efficiency, performance and quality.[6] By general consensus, the fundamental questions of accountability are those of "efficiency," or whether resources were appropriately used, and "effectiveness," or what good resulted from use of a resource obtained from patrons. More recently, major concerns with performance and quality have also arisen. In its present state, social service accounting is far more adept at answering the first question than in dealing with any of the others.

In order to compensate for the loss of information and other tracking problems arising from fungibility, accountability for donated or given funds about which donors wish to know how they are spent, requires sophisticated systems for tracking expenditures by funding source. To do so, governments and nonprofits typically resort to *fund accounting systems* in which separate accounting records are maintained for each major source and financial reports are prepared separately for each of these entities and summarized for the organization as a whole. Ways of showing the necessary detail for separate funds together with an overall statement of the position and activity of the whole organization were the most recent major pieces of the puzzle to be solved. In the case of fund accounting for nonprofit organizations, hospitals, and educational institutions, suitable accounting standards were not agreed upon until 1974, nearly 500 years after Pacioli.

One of the most fundamental lines of development in the area of accountability in recent decades has been the promulgation of accounting standards for nonprofit services (Gross, Warshauer, & Larkin, 1991; Sorensen, Hanbery, & Kucic, 1983; Sumariwalla, 1989). This began with the promulgation of audit standards for nonprofit health and welfare services by national accounting bodies in the mid-1970s and may well continue until the accounting profession achieves its long-sought objective of a single, unified set of accounting standards for all types of organizations.[7] A broad range of scholarly inquiry has also been devoted to the examination of various possible ratios, measures, and tests that might be used to extend organizational accountability in social services (Drtina, 1982; Elkin & Molitor, 1984; Hairston, 1985; Hall, 1981). One tangent of this effort has been work by Tuckman and Chang (1991) and Greenlee and Trussel (2000) on indicators of financial distress in nonprofit organizations.

Financial accountability in the business firm is a very simple concept. Owners and investors would like to know on a regular basis the amount of the return on their investment they can expect. As we saw in chapter 4, the nondistribution constraint prevents accountability in this "income" sense from being an issue for nonprofit and public organizations. The problems of stewardship have resulted in the development of fund accounting procedures and general accounting standards that allow the preparation of accurate, standardized financial statements. However, just to know that the dollars you devoted to a service or cause were spent for the broad purpose you intended and reported according to "generally accepted standards of accounting" is really to know very little. It is precisely because of stakeholder concerns about these limits of financial accountability in nonprofit and public social services settings that additional concerns for accountability have arisen.

THE THEORY OF NONPROFIT CORPORATE ACCOUNTABILITY

In modern corporation law, whether nonprofit or commercial, there is a second level of concern for ensuring the accountability of management, whether to investors or, as in the case of nonprofit social services, stakeholders. We might call this *process accountability* or, perhaps, accountability by association, because it is generally concerned with ensuring accountability by establishing lines of reporting and responsibility and various process and procedural safeguards and by enforcing at least minimal protections and guarantees that patrons and agents will communicate with one another. The ordinary theory of corporate accountability is built on the business dyad of relations between management and investors. It ordinarily omits from consideration any systematic concern for including third parties, whether community residents, as in plant relocation and environmental issues; customers, as in product quality and consumer safety discussions; or clients, as in social services. Even customers are relatively peripheral in the accountability sense.

The modified theory of nonprofit corporate accountability is built around four principal requirements of relations between management and stakeholders:[8]

1. *Board of directors.* The board in the commercial corporation serves (at least theoretically) as the representatives of the shareholders, not the customers, whereas the trustees of a nonprofit corporation are often presented as representing "the community" in the sense discussed in chapter 2. In the nonprofit corporate theory of accountability, the board of directors (or trustees) is typically charged with managing the affairs of the corporation. Thus, as a matter of legal principle, it is the board that is the real "management" of a nonprofit. Under this model, executives serve by express delegation of responsibilities as "agents" of the board, highlighting yet another aspect of the agency model discussed in chapter 3. Thus, it is the board and executives together that function as agents of the patrons and act on behalf of the clients.

2. *Annual meetings.* Articles of incorporation or similar founding documents and by-laws (operating rules for the board) typically must spell out the requirement of an annual meeting of the board, open to all stakeholders or interested parties. In the most general terms, the purpose of annual meetings is much like the proverbial New England town meeting. It is an opportunity for the management and board of the corporation to give an

account of themselves and their performance during the past year to those with an interest in the affairs of the corporation.

3. *Annual reports.* In conjunction with the verbal reports presented at the annual meeting, many corporations (both nonprofit and commercial) find it to their advantage to publish a written report in conjunction with the annual meeting. Such reports typically include both financial and program information.

4. *Evaluation studies.* In the traditional corporation, cost studies and inventories are examples of special accountability studies. More recently, evaluation, performance, and outcome studies have been added to that list (Mullen & Magnabosco, 1997). We look more closely at this topic in chapter 13. The important point here is that such studies are special. That is, they are not a part of the standard operating procedure of most social agencies at present.

Contemporary nonprofit social agencies, although they are covered by the general doctrines of free and private association discussed in chapter 3, are usually not membership organizations in which support for the organization comes in the form of dues in the way, for example, charity societies once were. Thus, some very large issues of accountability arise when a self-constituted group of individuals take upon themselves the responsibility of interfering in the lives of others the way social services inevitably do and assert that they will hold themselves accountable to a perhaps indifferent and reluctant community. Both commercial and nonprofit laws hold boards of directors to be the actual parties with the greatest burden of accountability. They are the ones charged officially with managing the affairs of the corporation. Legally, administrators and workers are seen as paid agents of the board, working under their direction. In the case of nonprofit organizations, this same relation is assumed, with much less certainty about whom exactly it is that the board is accountable to. Indeed, part of the reason for the community and institutional discussions in this book is to try to strengthen the answers to this question of accountability, which remain weak both in law and in practice.

In part because of these legal weaknesses, the theory of the social agency as developed by social administration theorists during the 1940s and 1950s evolved a "community stewardship" stance that continues to exercise a powerful influence over social work thinking today. As Holland and Jackson (1998) state the matter, "The governing boards of nonprofit organizations are groups to whom the community entrusts power and resources so they can act as fiduciaries and guide their organizations with caring, skill and integrity." This delegation of stewardship responsibility can be equally strong whether the obligation is active as in the case of the Poor Law reports cited earlier or merely implicit. It can even be quite strong when no express community delegation of responsibility occurred and board members merely assume for themselves a burden as agents of the community.

THE MANAGEMENT THEORY OF ACCOUNTABILITY

It is not entirely accurate to portray the theory of financial accountability as satisfactory in the case of ordinary commercial (for-profit) activity. We mentioned the vexing problem of plant closings and losses of jobs. Although financial statements are sufficient for reports by the firm to its investors, managers may go beyond the purely financial. They may also ask for an accounting from lower level management of what the organization theories discussed in chapter 3 called the concerns of technology and of its plans: What does this company (or your division) intend to do next year and in the future to continue to make money? Make cars? Sell insurance? Sell groceries? Grow vegetables? This is another way of approaching the particular set of problems and concerns of the internal accountability of management within the organization. It is one that seems to have led to the development by Peter Drucker and others of the management by objectives (MBO) approach discussed in chapter 7. Drucker and others were quick to detect also that the MBO model easily generalized from commercial manufacturing to nonprofit, governmental, and service organizations.

In social services, there is a long tradition of stating our intentions for services in Panglossian rhetoric and lofty ideals. There is an equally long tradition of failing to measure such intentions against achieved results. This can easily become problematic in the context of accountability issues and concerns. Most of us would agree, for example, with the executive who says that "the purpose of our agency is to help those in need." Objectives such as eliminating poverty, achieving community, and even just reaching consensus often have much this same idealistic edge, which often fall well short of being fully "realistic" and which also have few explicit, concrete indicators or measures. Accountability also raises the question of what exactly do we mean when we set our objective as helping those in need.

By the very nature of concepts of human need, almost everyone is in need of *something* at any particular moment, and thus an agency with a mission this broad simply can't go very far wrong. Literally, anything it does, including such things as allowing employees to stay home from work, meets *someone's* needs and could therefore be construed as achieving the agency's mission. However, meeting the needs of employees for greater leisure time at home would probably not fall within the scope of what donors, contractors, and others had in mind when they provided the money to pay employees of the agency. Struggling with the dual challenge of stating purposes in the form of visions, missions, goals, and objectives that are appealing enough to attract and hold support while realistic enough to actually guide action may be the fundamental management accountability challenge in the present.

The greatest long-term value of the management by objectives and results (MBOR) approach in social services, therefore, has been to provide a systematic methodology for considering these questions of management accountability; specifically for answering the question, "What do you mean by that?" The key concepts in the management by objectives regimen are mission, goals, objectives, and plans. *Mission* describes the overall purpose and direction of an agency—preventing child abuse, for example. As Wiehe (1978) terms it, mission is the "reason for existence." *Objectives*, then, are particular results the agency must achieve in order to remain viable in terms of its mission, such as teaching better parenting skills to potentially abusive parents. Within the MBO model, goals are subordinate to objectives, whereas in other more traditional planning and problem-solving models objectives are subordinate to goals. In MBO, *goals* are said to be the end results to be achieved in a particular time period, for example, twenty parents are to be instructed in parenting by the end of the month. Finally, in the MBO model, *plans* are the set of steps, discrete acts, projects, and tasks that must be undertaken to complete a particular goal. For twenty parents to be instructed, they must be identified, a trainer hired, a curriculum on parenting skills developed, a classroom located, and so on. More recently, the strategy theorists have added the additional dimensions of vision, strategy, and tactics to this list.

A final stipulation usually incorporated into applications of MBO and outcome measurement is the idea that at some level these dimensions should be *measurable;* in the most general sense, this means that objectives should be stated in such a way that it is possible to determine whether they have been achieved. In social administration, this often will involve *quantification* (transformation into quantities) and *enumeration* (counting), simply because the administrator will be dealing with large numbers, and counting quantitative units is the simplest way to do that.

Note, however, that quantification and enumeration are not ends in themselves. They are merely means to the end of measurability, which in turn is a means to the end of determining answers to basic accountability questions. In many cases, it is quite possible to measure the objective or determine if it has been achieved without quantification. The essential characteristic of measurability here is not quantification, but rather what philosophers of science call *falsifiability.* Is the objective stated in such a way that it is possible to determine definitely when it has not been achieved? If not, quantification by itself is little more than an exercise in rubber-ruler measurement. The measuring stick can expand and contract to fit the wishes of those taking the measurement.

Interestingly, the fact that the MBO model speaks of mission and objective while traditional problem-solving models speak of defining problems and identifying goals has produced interminable (but largely unnecessary) confusion for many in the field. Such confusion over terms should not blind one to the fact that like most renderings of the problem-solving model of planning, MBO bespeaks a synoptic model of enlightenment rationality in which the mental processes of rational thought and the social process of rational organization are said to produce satisfactory results. Despite the best efforts of Drucker and others, MBO thus remains a *reconstructive logic* in the sense of how we might like people to approach matters, and not a model of the logic of how people actually think or how groups actually solve problems.[9] In the context of social administration, however, it has proven to be a particularly useful reconstruction in precisely the same sense that Aristotle's beginning-middle-end reconstructive logic of rhetoric is still a useful model for writers and speakers. It may be artificial and inaccurate as a model of how people actually speak, but it is a useful model for constructing intelligible speaking and writing.

THE POLITICAL THEORY OF ACCOUNTABILITY

In social services and other contexts where major use is made of public funds that originate in tax collections from citizens, accountability also has a major political edge to it. Our system of government after all is not a direct democracy but a representative one in which we elect chief executives and legislators to represent us, and they in turn appoint judges, cabinet officers, and a host of other public officials and empower them to carry out the public will. In this case, representation implies accountability. Accountability of appointed and elected officials to those who elected them is a fundamental feature of the system, although we generally have erected civil service and other barriers, protections, and limits on the accountability of appointed officials to those who appointed them.

It is one of the stock features of discussions of social service accounting to note that accounting reports do not present "the whole picture" of what may be going on. It is extremely difficult (until recently, in fact, completely impossible) to convey meaningful information about social services in financial terms, and meaningful ratios are a long way from being standard or generally recognized practices. The whole picture from a political standpoint is more concerned with issues of public trust and authority along these chains of delegated responsibility than with any financial data.

Political accountability is unlike other forms of accountability in one important respect. Whereas both financial and management accountability are primarily reconstructive (reconstructing post hoc accounts and explanations after events have occurred), political accountability is best practiced preemptively. To be politically accountable is to be sufficiently candid, forthright, and savvy that major issues or questions about the performance of your agency never come up and that your agency and program continue to be viewed either favorably or indifferently by politicians and the media. This is a critically important aspect of institution building and maintenance.

One of the worst positions for any public entity to be in is to become a political football publicly tossed about by different political factions, members of the media, and others, any of whom may choose to use you for their own purposes. In such cases, "the facts of the matter" often and readily take a back seat to appearance, possibility, rumor, and innuendo. The cardinal rule of political accountability, therefore, is to preempt the need for giving an account of particular events or occurrences that may be difficult to explain or justify by avoiding the *appearance* of impropriety. In most such cases, it quite literally doesn't matter whether you did anything wrong. If it appears that you may have, you are vulnerable. One standard or rule of thumb for social administrators to apply in such cases is whether the matter is something you would like to see discussed on CBS's *60 Minutes* or discussed by the equivalent local investigative reporter for your newspaper. If your answer is "definitely not," you may have a potential political accountability problem that may need to be addressed.

CONTRACT ACCOUNTABILITY

It is important to note also that quite apart from all other considerations of accounting, nonprofit governance, management, and political accountability, there is one very elementary consideration that can be termed the accountability of contract, or *contract accountability*. In its simplest form a contract is an agreement—an offer and an acceptance. The point of contract accountability is that such agreements are legally enforceable, and this suggests that parties to a contract are accountable to one another, and potentially to the courts, for their actions.

The third edition of Barron's *Law Dictionary* includes a number of related definitions of the term contract that note that contracts involve a promise or a set of promises for which the law offers remedies if breached. It says also that a contract is "a transaction involving two or more individuals whereby each becomes obligated to the other, with *reciprocal rights to demand performance of what is promised by each respectively*" (Gifis, 1991,

p. 97). It is really the transformation of the moral obligations and mutual expectations of any or all parties to a trilateral social service transaction into legally actionable issues that is the unique domain of contract accountability.

Contracts are usually specific as to what is to be done and sometimes even specify the way in which tasks are to be completed. Thus, some of the ambiguities that arise from trying to be accountable for achievement of an agency's mission, as has been discussed above in terms of other forms of accountability, are often avoided.

ACCOUNTABILITY AND MANAGED CARE

Managed care has the potential for fundamentally transforming the traditional agency relationships on which modern social work was built (Lohmann, 1997). In the agency model, individual social workers provided service free from the practical burdens of finance, which were isolated as separate administrative responsibilities. Administrators, in this traditional model, were the intermediaries who explained and justified the actions of social workers to stakeholders and negotiated continued support for services. Managed care introduces a completely new division of labor in which greater financial accountability is an assumed characteristic of workers and administrators alike.

CONCLUSION

Concern for accountability is an ancient and honorable part of the social contract between clients, service providers, and stakeholders that we have defined as the distinctive tripartite transaction of social service. If clients are going to place themselves in the hands of social service providers, they want some assurance that they will be well served in doing so. And, if patrons are going to contribute resources to these service ventures, not only do they need assurances that their contributions will not be used to harm or disadvantage clients, they also require assurances that their resources will not be squandered, misused, or wasted. It is the responsibility of social services providers to offer these respective assurances, and it is the particular obligation of social administration to see that these obligations are met.

This chapter presented several approaches to accountability, some of which are more developed as theories and in practice than others. In doing so, it has not been our intent to suggest that the approaches are mutually exclusive and that using one approach does not mean an agency may not also use a second or third approach. Most agencies engage in practices that would fall under several of the theories described. They may, for example, practice standard accounting forms of accountability and have contracts that require contract accountability while also being aware of the need to be politically accountable. Thus, the theories and approaches are presented not to suggest that an agency select one and utilize only it but to indicate the various approaches that may be taken to accountability.

CHAPTER 13

Program Evaluation

In chapter 12, we discussed accountability and the expectations of donors and stakeholders that social service organizations be accountable. Accountability has come to be seen as more than financial reports; it is a concept that could include reports of effectiveness, efficiency, performance, and quality. This chapter discusses program evaluation as a methodology often applied to social programs and social agencies to assess their accountability in terms of effectiveness, efficiency, performance, or quality.

Program and practice evaluation has become a primary accountability mechanism for all social programs within a relatively short time frame. Before the late 1950s, a review of a social administration or social work practice text would have revealed few, if any, references to the concept of program evaluation. Today, nearly every text makes reference to this approach, and it is expected that all social work curricula prepare social work graduates to evaluate the outcomes of their practice.

The importance of program evaluation comes from the increased emphasis on accountability in social programs. The accountability is to several constituencies. Funding sources want to know that their funds are resulting in programs that produce the desired results. A more general public accountability, growing out of the community–agent relationship, is needed. Many social services are delivered by nonprofit organizations, and the public at large is interested in whether the services produce the desired effect in a way that justifies the organization's nonprofit status. Clients want to know that the services provided to them will have the effect that they desire. There is also the need to be accountable to the profession and to establish that the methods used by a profession are professionally responsible and have the desired impact on clients.

Although there are a variety of ways in which such accountability could be provided, the use of scientific methodology to establish the impact of social programs is a widely embraced accountability mechanism. It has the advantage of the neutrality that is assumed to be part of scientific methods. Though the application of scientific methods is not as neutral as is often assumed, there is enough public confidence in the methods that their application is seen as positive. Thus, program evaluation allows one to embrace the need for accountability and the positive good of the application of scientific methodologies in justifying the existence of one's program.

The focus of this chapter is on the issues and challenges that program evaluation creates for the agency administrator. We review the approaches associated with program evaluation and the administrative issues and problems associated with those approaches. This chapter touches on the methodology associated with program and practice evaluation, but it does not examine those methodologies in detail.[1]

HISTORY OF PROGRAM EVALUATION

Though we referred above to the relatively recent emphasis on program evaluation, in fact there is some evidence that program evaluation extends back over several centuries.[2] Rossi and Freeman (1985) indicate that social experiments and their evaluation have been identified as far back as the eighteenth century. The origins of contemporary interest in program evaluation are largely in efforts to evaluate the New Deal social programs of the 1930s, many of which represented large-scale social experiments. Some social work studies predated this time period, however. Zimbalist (1977) describes Sophie van Senden Theis's 1924 report, "How Foster Children Turn Out," as an example of some early social work research that embodied some of the characteristics of evaluative research.

Rossi and Freeman describe the 1940s and 1950s as the "boom period" in evaluation research, with programs on delinquency prevention, public housing, and community organization among the programs evaluated. Zimbalist identifies the Cambridge–Somerville Youth Study, which was an experiment in the prevention of juvenile delinquency, as one of the more important studies of this period for social workers.

With the growth of social programs during the time of President Lyndon Johnson's Great Society, there was an accompanying growth of interest in program evaluation during the late 1960s and 1970s. Many federal grants and other funding sources required program evaluation as a condition of award, and several significant books on the topic were written (Caro, 1971; Suchman, 1967; Weiss, 1972), and firms specializing in program evaluation were created. This general emphasis on program evaluation was accompanied by an emphasis on preparing social workers to engage in evaluation. More recent developments, especially the passage of the Government Performance and Results Act of 1993 (GPRA), have the potential to have significant further impact on social program evaluation.

Poister and Streib (1999), when discussing local government evaluation, indicate that the increased use of result-oriented management tools has required better measurements systems so as to provide baseline information and evaluate effectiveness. They indicate that such management approaches as strategic planning, quality management programs, and reengineering, benchmarking, and reformed budgeting processes all require better measurement.

GOVERNMENT PERFORMANCE AND RESULTS ACT

The GPRA, which was adopted with overwhelming bipartisan support by both houses of the U.S. Congress, requires executive agency heads to submit to the Director of the Office of Management and Budget (OMB) and to Congress a strategic plan for performance goals of their agency's program activities. The plan is to cover at least a five-year period and is to be updated at least every three years. The plan is to cover each program activity in the agency's budget. Agencies are to focus on program results, service quality, and customer satisfaction (Radin, 1998). The act does have some implications for social agencies, which are discussed below.

The act also requires federal executive agency heads to report annually to the president and the Congress on program performance for the previous fiscal year, setting forth performance indicators, actual program performance, and a comparison with plan goals for that fiscal year. The first agency strategic plans were issued in September 1997, and the first pilot performance plans were issued in February 1998. The first performance plans for all agencies were due March 2000. Radin (1998) reported that the Washington press and others expressed unusual interest about the GPRA reports because of the information they contain about agency performance.

A survey of nonprofit organizations conducted by the OMB Watch in 1998 demonstrates the importance that this act may have in the evaluation of agency performance, including that of social agencies.[3] Some of the major findings of that survey that speak to attitudes with regard to performance evaluation include

- A high level of awareness among nonprofit agencies with regard to performance measurement generally but a low level of awareness with regard to GPRA as a specific application of performance measurement
- A generally positive attitude toward performance measurement with respondents generally responding that such measures would improve government agency accountability, program management, and program performance
- Concern that not all program impacts can be measured in numerical terms and that the task of conducting performance measurement may require staff time or other resource expenditures that are unreasonable

The concerns expressed by nonprofit administrators are common. Caputo (1988) reports that administrators are often reluctant to invest in program evaluation because of concern about the expense of such evaluations, the length of time that they may take, and the possibility of negative findings.

The strategic plan to implement GPRA in the federal Department of Health and Human Services (DHHS) may serve to illustrate some of the challenges posed with this act and with program evaluation generally.[4] DHHS identified six goals in its strategic plan, one of which was to improve the economic and social well-being of individuals, families, and communities. A strategic objective for this goal is that of increasing opportunities for seniors to have an active and healthy aging experience. DHHS indicates that success in meeting this objective will be met through the following measures:

1. Average age of onset for the chronic diseases of old age
2. Disability rates for the elderly
3. Proportion of older people who are nutritionally healthy
4. Proportion of older people with access to preventive health services
5. Number of years of functional independence for the elderly
6. Number of persons older than 65 receiving preventive and primary care in Health Resources Services Administration programs

The measures of this strategic objective are used next to illustrate the issues associated with program evaluation in the social agency.

ISSUES ASSOCIATED WITH PROGRAM EVALUATION

What Is Being Measured?

The first issue faced when conducting program evaluation in a social agency is that of deciding what will be measured so as to assess program impact. Depending on the complexity of the program, that can be a very difficult decision. Consider, for example, the six measurements chosen for the DHHS objective of providing an active and healthy aging experience.

Those six measurements address largely the issues of health, although active aging is also a part of the objective. One supposes that the reasoning behind the selection of those measures is that an older person cannot enjoy an active aging experience unless he or she is healthy. Not all would agree that health is needed for an appropriate level of activity. Further, while assuming that the reasoning is likely valid, being healthy does not guarantee an older person an active aging experience. Health thus may be a necessary condition for active aging, but it is not a sufficient condition.

Others might identify far different measures of active and healthy aging. They may conclude that access to transportation is important to measure, because it is difficult to be active if an older person is confined to home. Or they may determine that the number of self-reported friends and family members with whom an older person regularly interacts is important, reasoning that interaction with others is important to activity. They may conclude that the only important health measure is that of functional independence, because an older person may be active even if he or she has a chronic disease or disability.

The issue of what is measured is often guided by what is easiest or cheapest to measure, even though those factors may not be the critical ones in the program. When that happens, the agency administrator may find that program evaluation results are not especially helpful.

If what is being measured are not the factors that the program was intended to influence or change, it may appear that the program is having little impact. Such a result, however, would not be helpful because the program may actually be having an impact. That impact may have been evident if the factors that were intended to be changed had been measured. The results may also be unhelpful because, though they demonstrate change, the change is around the fringes of the program and not in the factors on which the program is focused. For example, a program intended to reduce infant abuse may decide to use attendance at a well-baby clinic as an evaluation measure because it is cheap and easy to measure. After time, though attendance at the clinic may have increased, the agency may find that abuse is unchanged. Rather than selecting a measure that went to the primary goal of the program (reduction of abuse), the evaluation focused on something that may have a relationship to the goal (clinic attendance) but was not a good measure of goal accomplishment. Thus, it may appear that the program has had no impact.

The danger for the agency administrator if the program evaluation does not measure what the program was intended to impact is that the evaluation results will produce either an inaccurate sense of the impact of the program or results falsely suggesting an indifferent response to the program. In the latter case, funding agencies and others may decide that the program is not worth funding if it doesn't produce results demonstrating a greater impact. Thus, it is important that the administrator ensure that the evaluation is measuring the central objectives of the program, not merely those elements that are easy to measure.

What Measurements Are Used?

Once there is agreement as to which program impacts need to be measured, there is the need to decide how to measure those impacts. There are typically a number of ways that any given impact can be measured. Some of those ways will be more valid and reliable than others. Some will be easier and less costly to administer than others will. If the administrator is lucky, the most valid and reliable measures will also be the easiest and cheapest to administer. Often, however, program evaluation results in a series of tradeoffs among those factors.

A valid measure is one that truly measures what the measurement purports to measure. For example, a room thermometer that accurately measures the temperature in a room is a valid measurement. To be valid, the thermometer would need to always show 68 degrees when, in fact, it is 68 degrees in the room.

A reliable measure is one that consistently measures a characteristic. For the thermometer to be reliable, it would need to show 68 degrees every time the room was at that temperature and not 68 degrees one minute and 55 degrees the next when, in fact, the room temperature had not changed. It is possible for a measure to be reliable but not be valid. A valid measure, however, is always reliable.[5]

Using the DHHS example cited above, the measurement of the average age of onset of chronic diseases might be used to illustrate the concepts of validity and reliability. Arthritis is one of the chronic conditions typically associated with aging. With certain types of arthritis, however, it can be difficult to accurately assess whether arthritis is the cause of the symptoms experienced or some other condition is the cause. For this measurement goal to be accomplished, there must be a valid way to measure the onset of arthritis. That is, it must be clear that a person's lower back pain is caused by arthritis and not an orthopedic problem, such as a slipped disc or other cause. In addition, the measure must reliably determine the onset of arthritis as a chronic condition and produce comparable results in different individuals with similar conditions.

Valid and reliable measures are not always the easiest to administer. The best way to determine the onset of arthritis, for example, may be through the use of X-rays and blood tests. However, these invasive procedures require an older person's cooperation, and not all older people will undergo the procedures just so DHHS will better know whether it is accomplishing one of its strategic objectives.

Even if easy to administer, the measurement may be costly. Continuing with the arthritis example, X-rays and blood tests are costly procedures. Not all programs could afford the cost of these measurements, even if they are the most valid and reliable way to measure the onset of a chronic disease.

The challenge for the administrator, then, is not only to ensure that the core purposes of the program are being measured but to ensure that the measurements used are appropriate. Determining appropriateness usually involves some compromises with regard to measurement instrument validity, reliability, ease of use, and cost of use.

Ethics of Evaluation

Program evaluation also challenges the social administrator with some ethical questions. The ethical issues come from the potential conflict between what represents good research methodology and the commitment of the agency to deliver services.

Generally, an experimental design is viewed as the best research methodology to confirm that a program is having the intended impact. An experimental design is one in which some randomly assigned prospective clients receive service and others, who form a control group, do not. The design helps ensure that the differences between the two groups are due to the service or program and not to some other factor. To avoid selection bias in determining who receives services, prospective clients are randomly assigned to either the experimental group receiving services or the control group.[6]

Agencies and their administrators, however, often have difficulty making use of the strongest designs to evaluate programs. In many instances, these difficulties are the result of ethical misgivings about denying services to potential clients. Sometimes these misgivings are the results of the administrator's commitment to the program: an administrator might firmly believe the program produces positive results and finds it inappropriate to exclude anyone who could benefit from the program, even if the reason for the exclusion is to demonstrate the program's positive impact. Other times, difficulties arise when potential clients learn why they cannot receive services from the program; the esoterica of research methods and program evaluation does not matter much to them.

It is interesting to note that experimental design is almost always used in the assessment of new medical treatments or prescription drugs, with few ethical misgivings expressed. Research on the effect of one approach to an illness or health issue, such as the use of aspirin at the onset of a heart attack or the effect of fiber in the diet, is almost always reported in terms of the impact on the experimental group as opposed to the control group. This is the case when such reports appear in the popular press, although the terms *experimental* and *control* may not be used. Prescription drugs cannot be granted a license unless they have been tested through the use of experimental design.

It seems somewhat ironic that there is widespread acceptance of experimental design in potential matters of life or death but far less acceptance in social services, where death is less often a consequence of the denial of service. Cynics will suggest that this lack of acceptance results from uncertainty as to whether social programs have the desired impact and from the wish to not establish impact with much certainty. However, it is probable that the misgivings about experimental design are more lofty than the cynical attitude suggests. An agency's employees might have intellectual and moral commitment to the services being delivered as well as genuine concern about the potential negative impact that could result when services were denied to individuals in a control group.

Resources Required for Program Evaluation

The final issue faced by the administrator in deciding to carry out program evaluation is conflict over the resources that may be required to conduct such evaluation. This concern is among those found in the OMB survey of nonprofit agencies described above. Agencies reported concern that the conduct of performance measurement may require staff time or other resource expenditures that are unreasonable.

This concern comes from the limited resources available in most social service agencies. Given those limited resources, there is interest in using existing resources in the most effective way possible. The assumption is that those resources are better used to deliver services than to assess the effectiveness of the service delivered.

The reasons for this view are much like those that influence the use of experimental designs to assess program impact. Agency employees tend to believe that the services they deliver do have a positive impact. If they did not believe this, it would be difficult for them to continue to engage in the delivery of services. Thus, any evaluation of the impact of service is seen as taking resources away from positive activities and expending them on activities whose utility is uncertain and may even be destructive.

Evaluation does require resources. It may require staff time to complete paperwork about clients and services that they would not ordinarily complete. It may require that a portion or all of one or several staff members' time be devoted to the collection and analysis of data. It may require that measuring instruments be purchased or duplicated. The challenge for the administrator is to determine what resources are appropriate to apply to program evaluation.

It would be helpful if guidelines existed as to the standard percentage of an agency's budget that should be devoted to program evaluation, similar to the guidelines that do exist regarding the portion of donated funds that should be devoted to fund-raising activities. As program evaluation becomes a more standard practice, it may be that such benchmarks will be developed.

In the absence of such benchmarks, agency directors need to use common sense. For the reasons discussed at the start of this chapter, program evaluation is an important component of accountability and needs to be supported. However, the amount of support provided needs to be considered in the overall context of the mission of the agency.

EFFICIENCY AND RATIO ANALYSIS

Program evaluation methodologies are most often used to assess program effectiveness, quality, and client satisfaction. However, efficiency is also something often assessed as a part of the concern with financial accountability. Ratio analysis is a point of overlap between the interests of those concerned primarily with fiscal matters and those concerned with program evaluation.

Ratio analysis is one of the techniques that modern business analysis has invented for extending the range and power of financial reports. In this approach, two financial terms (a numerator and a denominator) are compared via division of the numerator by the denominator to determine a decimal fraction or ratio. Thus, if we know the additional amounts owned or liabilities payable in the current period and the additional inflows received by an entity in the same current period, we can compute the *current ratio:* current liabilities/current income. A current ratio of 2:1 is a short-hand way of noting that we have borrowed twice as much as we have taken in during the current period—a situation that obviously cannot continue indefinitely!

More than two decades ago, one of us outlined a suggested scheme of ratios for human services (Lohmann, 1980a). The following year, Mary Hall (1981) laid out a proposed set of ratios, and two years later, Ralph Drtina (1982) laid out a refined set of proposed indicators. Robert Elkin and Mark Molitor (1984) took on the whole area in a project funded by one of the big eight accounting firms (Elkin, 1985).

One of the most interesting recent discussions from the vantage point of the application of ratios to social services is the treatment of the issue by Howard Tuckman and Cyril Chang (1991). They approached ratios from the vantage point of the financial vulnerability of nonprofits defined as their ability to withstand financial shocks. Their ratios were designed to measure the adequacy of equity balances, the concentration/diversity of revenue sources, administrative costs, and operating margins (defined as revenues less expenditures, divided by revenues). Those agencies with the least equity relative to revenues (in the bottom quintile) are said to be at the greatest risk. The revenue concentration is computed as the sum of the squares of the percentage share that each revenue source represents of the total. The closer the resulting sum is to 0, the more diverse the agency's revenue base and the closer to 1, the greater its financial vulnerability. Administrative costs are computed as the percentage of administrative costs to total costs. The higher the percentage, the greater the vulnerability. Finally, a nonprofit with a negative operating margin is, they say, already likely to be engaged in reducing its program offerings, and agencies with the lowest operating margins are most at risk.

Perhaps the most general and, in many respects, the most deceptive proposals for ratio measurement are the so-called efficiency ratios: the ratio of inputs to outputs. The engineers (e.g., Fayol and Taylor) concerned with the management of manufacturing first introduced efficiency as a management consideration. In engineering, efficiency—subject to the second law of thermodynamics—is used to exactly measure the ratio of energy inputs to work output in machines. Thus, most of us are familiar with measures of horsepower and calories, both of which are this type of efficiency measure. The rhetoric of efficiency was first applied to social service problems at about the same time, and various sources have been trying ever since to make something of it, with lots of continuing rhetoric but very little result.

The problem in social services is complex but clear. If by inputs and outputs are meant financial inflows and outflows, the results are purely trivial and meaningless or utterly misleading. An efficiency ratio of 1:1 shows only that the amount spent equals the amount taken in, whereas a negative ratio suggests proportionately greater spending or savings. The adequacy of equity balances outlined by Tuckman and Chang (1991) is a far more precise and superior measure of this phenomenon than any vague notion of "efficiency," for which the results are hardly earth shattering, and, in comparative terms, meaningless. What can it mean that program A spent all it took in, while program B didn't and program C spent more than it took in? The answer is that it can mean just about anything or nothing at all.

Although this notion of efficient services has become a staple of political rhetoric, its scientific and technical measurement value is almost nil. In point of fact, there has never been a single valid and reliable study of the efficiency of social services that could be used to guide policymaking or decision making published in the entire literature of social administration. Efficiency in human affairs isn't in fact, anything more than a broad moral guideline: the challenge to do more and better with less.

OVERCOMING BARRIERS TO EVALUATION

There are approaches that administrators can use to overcome some of the perceived barriers to implementing an effective evaluation program. Briar and Blythe (1985), for example, suggested that administrators may need to think of existing data as a source of evaluation information that may not have previously been considered rather than assuming new data needs to be collected to evaluate a program. They suggested, for example, that case-specific outcome data, when aggregated over many cases, can provide evidence of the agency's effectiveness.

Briar and Blythe also suggested some specific actions that agencies might take to enhance the amount of program evaluation undertaken. Agencies might provide support services that will reduce the amount of time practitioners need to devote to the evaluation process since practitioners often identify limited time as one of the barriers to evaluating practice. Developing a package of assessment tools available in the agency for use with the typical agency client is one such action. Doing so reduces the amount of time that each practitioner must devote to identifying appropriate tools. They also suggested exploring whether paraprofessionals or secretarial support staff might administer some of the instruments; those personnel could be provided with the training needed to administer the selection instruments.

Briar and Blythe also suggested that the agency explore whether its management information systems (MIS) can be used to support evaluation activities. This assumes, of course, that agencies have such systems already in place. They indicated that data routinely entered into such systems for other purposes may be relevant for evaluation purposes if analyzed differently. Finally, they suggested that practitioners be involved in the design and implementation of program evaluation programs. Such involvement may help practitioners to understand the reasons for certain activities that are part of the evaluation and result in greater cooperation.

Caputo (1988) suggested another way in which barriers could be overcome. He reported on a service/research demonstration project dealing with domestic violence that suffered from some flawed research methodology. However, he indicated that the research proved useful in that it identified some unanticipated consequences, such as police officers failing to make referrals to a treatment program of incidents they verified as representing domestic violence. As a result of the research, such counterproductive actions were corrected. Thus, he concluded that even when it turns out that the research methodology used was faulty for a particular environment, some insight that will be of benefit to the program may result.

CONCLUSION

Program evaluation receives considerable attention in the social work profession today, and it does so because the methodologies associated with it can be an important way to demonstrate accountability. Its methods can be used to demonstrate the effectiveness, efficiency, quality, and/or client satisfaction with a program. The emphasis on the GPRA at the federal level is likely to result in increased attention to program evaluation.

An administrator must deal with several issues when evaluating a program. Issues described in this chapter include questions about what is being evaluated, what measuring instruments are used in the evaluation, the ethics of evaluation, and the resources required for evaluation. Involving the agency personnel in the program(s) to be evaluated may help resolve some of these issues, achieve greater understanding of what is being evaluated and why it is being evaluated, and ensure their cooperation in the evaluation process.

We believe it is important that all agencies be involved in continuous or periodic evaluations of their programs and the programs' impacts as a means of providing accountability. Fiscal accountability, which is the form of accountability most fully developed, is important and needed. However, the accountability of social agencies needs to go beyond fiscal accountability, and program evaluation is one way to ensure that it does so.

PART IV

Communications and Information

Effective communication is essential to a well-run social agency. Communication occurs in a variety of oral and written forms. Most administrators spend the bulk of their working days involved in communication using the range of modalities available to them.

Organizational communication moves in a variety of directions and may be deemed either formal or informal.

The conversation is the most common form of communication found in organizations. Meetings are also common and may be seen as a series of structured conversations that have certain elements in common. Written communications may be a basic medium of communication, or they may serve primarily to confirm and record messages delivered orally.

Some of the most startling and impressive developments of twentieth-century social science have been advances in our understanding of the twin concepts of communication as a social process and information as the stuff of human communications. Communications presents a double challenge for social administration. One the one hand, communications theories are at the heart of virtually every advancement beyond the rather limited rational man approaches of early administration theorists and the even more limited machine models of organization. On the other hand, communication as a socioemotional process as that idea is understood in modern clinical social work practice is a set of ideas to which it is difficult to give adequate attention in social administration. Generally speaking, administrative theories of communication tread lightly when they enter at all into such areas as communication of affect and nonverbal communication. In fact, communication is generally treated largely as a cognitive information-transfer process throughout most of the management sciences. Thus, what is presented in chapters 14 and 15 may not touch upon a variety of communications topics held to be of interest or important in clinical practice, such as nonverbal communication. The chapters do, however, offer a faithful rendition of the state of the art as it is practiced in contemporary social administration.

CHAPTER 14

Administrative Communication

Among the most innovative aspects of twentieth-century social science is the attention given to the role of language as a medium and to communication as a process at the center of virtually all forms of human interaction. The effects and implications of this communications revolution appear throughout this book. Management theory would be very different today if it were not for the impact of communications theory, as seen through the work of Max Weber, Chester Barnard, Mary Parker Follett, Elton Mayo, the neo-Weberians, and a host of other researchers. Contemporary perspectives on communications and social interaction are at the theoretical core of the movement away from machine models of organization and command and control as the essential management practices.

In this chapter, we examine the ways in which we communicate in administrative settings. We look at bureaucratic communication and the particular implications of the human relations approach for communications, and we discuss meetings as one of the primary ways communication is carried on in many organizations.

Assorted definitions tend to emphasize different aspects of the communication process, but there appears to be widespread general agreement on the nature of the process itself and of its impact on organizations. One management writer in the 1940s referred to it simply as "the fateful process of A talking to B." In a purely mechanical sense, communication is the process of transmitting a signal or message from a sender to a receiver. Many of the sophisticated developments in communications technology as well as general systems theory and the institutional cycle presented in this work are grounded in the cybernetic model of sender-signal-receiver-feedback loop. A goodly portion of the communications challenge in social agencies arises out of the responsibilities and expectations of accountability (see chapter 12).

From a social standpoint, the sender becomes a speaker or writer and the receiver becomes a listener or reader in an audience. Signal and feedback become forms of interaction within institutions. Speaker-message-audience-feedback defines a social system and the essentials of communication theory are opened to numerous possibilities. Yet, as an illustration of the theoretical power of the communications paradigm, almost all of the essential elements of any particular communication or interaction can be captured as answers to a single question: Who said (or did or in some other way communicated) what to whom by what means and with what effects?

We answer some or all of these questions every time we talk about our communications: "We (whom) received a fax (what means) from the executive director (who) that says to stop working on the United Way proposal (what) and to concentrate instead on getting the quarterly reports done for the board meeting next week (what effects)." In social administration the entire content or meaning of management, leadership, decisions, and institutions must be communicated to patrons, clients, and staff.

The emphasis on communications arose in the shift from mechanical to relationship models of organization. Although classic nineteenth-century management thinkers placed stress on control, planning, and coordination processes, they appear to have given little attention to the complex and subtle communications those processes encompass. This is particularly surprising in that the management of railroads, mines, and long factory assembly lines required dramatic innovations in communications. The revolutionary technologies of telegraph and telephone opened amazing new possibilities for larger and more dispersed organizations. However, classic management theorists were largely silent on the subject of communications prior to the 1930s.

In large part, it was the influence of the Weberian model of bureaucracy and the neo-Weberian organizational theories following from the work of Chester Barnard that first brought communication into management theory. Undoubtedly, one of the influences that resulted in emphasis on communication was the important twentieth-century discovery of signal theory associated with the growth of mass communications media, such as telegraphy, telephony, radio, television, and the Internet. It is probably not too much of a stretch, for example, to suggest that Barnard, a telephone company executive, was ideally suited to grasp the importance of communication in his theory of administrative organization. Indeed, Barnard's views on the centrality of communication to organizations were probably influenced, at least in part, by the cybernetic model in which his company's core technology was grounded.

Not everyone agrees that the purpose of formal means of message transmission in organizations is communication. Lydall Urwick (1943) suggested that formal channels of communication in organizations functioned, in fact, not to convey messages but primarily to "confirm and record" (p. 47) decisions arrived at by more personal and informal means. Although this conception places a somewhat different slant on the importance of communication in administrative interaction, it in no way disparages the importance of communication as an administrative process. Whether they carry messages or merely confirm and record messages conveyed in other ways, communication channels are an important aspect of the organizations of social agencies.

COMMUNICATION IN SOCIAL ADMINISTRATION

The term *communication* is used in three identifiable approaches in talking about social administration: First, it may be used to indicate a basis of interaction. Thus, one might ask the question, "Can you hear me?" This usage is very common throughout the social and behavioral sciences. The second approach is to use communication to indicate information or knowledge transfer, as in the question, "Did you receive my message?" This type of question has become more common with the increased use of E-mail and voice mail, when the sender does not always know whether the message sent has been received. This approach is quite common in discussions of engineering, technology, and communications media. The third approach is to indicate the genesis of understanding, as in the plaintive question, "Do you see what I'm saying? Are we together on this?" Such concern for understanding is common in discussions of communications by philosophers, by therapists, and in the so-called *verstehen* (understanding) approaches of the social sciences. Ensuring that various audiences receive, hear, and understand the communications of social administration is one of the most fundamental challenges facing social administrators.

Each of these distinctive meanings of communication enters into social work administration in different ways. In a purely physical sense, ensuring that an organization is capable of getting messages from one point to another has been a constant concern of management since the age when the process depended on telegraph and human voice-to-ear messengers. In an information-transfer sense, information technology, such as management information systems, data bases, and decision support systems, are fundamental to contemporary administration. As Max Weber noted in his theory of bureaucracy, records are one of the essential, defining characteristics of bureaucratic organization. In the interactional sense with its concern for meaning, communication patterns such as who talks to whom most frequently about the most important questions are the basic elements of organizational structure. Whom we communicate with most immediately and directly on the job goes a long way toward identifying both formal and informal organizations.

How Do We Communicate?

How do social workers communicate in social service organizations? What are the channels of communication? One way to approach this question is to survey a brief inventory of communications techniques and media:

- *Meetings.* A very large part of the information exchange and communication that occurs in and around social administration involves group communications of some form.
- *Speeches* by the organization's administrator or others to organizational employees or stakeholders represent a relatively formal means of communication.
- *Telegraph.* From the Civil War until after the turn of the nineteenth century, a good deal of communication by emerging national organizations was carried on by telegraph. Even as recently as the early years of the age of grants in the late 1960s announcements of grant awards were still sent by telegram.
- *Telephone* conversation has been a stable element of communications technology for most social workers throughout the twentieth century. Unlike the telegraph, it remains a backbone of social work practice today.
- *Interview.* The structured, face-to-face interaction of the interview is probably the most common form of communication between workers and their clients.
- *Memoranda,* including those specialized memoranda known as policy bulletins, are in common use in larger organizations, in which face-

to-face interaction is too time consuming for the necessary communications.

- *Letters* are most often used in administrative settings of all types to communicate new information or to certify or document messages or information that has already been conveyed in a less permanent, verbal form.

In the 1990s, fax, E-mail, voice mail, beepers, electronic schedulers, personal digital assistants, and a host of other technological enhancements revised and extended these earlier forms of communication. In most office contexts today, memos, letters, and other written communications are prepared and distributed in a variety of ways: typewriter, word processor, laser printer, fax machine, E-mail, voice mail, and so on. A note of caution about the use of E-mail as a means of communication may be in order. E-mail is quick and easy and is already the preferred means of communication in many agencies. However, the informality of an E-mail message, as opposed to a memo or letter, means that writers are often not as careful about what they say and the way in which they say it as they might otherwise be. Bill Neukom, an attorney for Microsoft in its defense against a government antitrust suit, indicated that E-mail "is written in haste, is often full of bluster, and is not necessarily an accurate reflection of what people think and do" (Auletta, 1999, p. 49). As much care should be taken with regard to what is said in an E-mail message as would be taken in a more formal memo.

Much of the attention to communication in the general management literature has addressed barriers to communication. Koontz and O'Donnell (1974) included a list of ten such barriers in their management text:

1. Badly expressed messages.
2. Faulty "translations."
3. Loss by transmission and retention. As much as 30 percent of the information they say is lost in every message. Employees are said to retain as little as 50 percent and supervisors only slightly more of information transmitted.
4. Inattention. Failure to read memos, notices, and so on. Selective inattention (some people are just not heard).
5. Unclear assumptions. This is especially clear in cross-group and cross-cultural settings where assumptions can be expected to vary.
6. Insufficient adjustment period. Complex or ambiguous implications of particular messages may require some time to think about the message before fully understanding it. Emotion-laden messages such as announcements of layoffs, downsizing, and so on may bring out common human defense mechanisms.

7. Distrust of the communicator. "That's what he says now; but will he change his mind tomorrow?" "Is he just using us?"

8. Premature evaluation. More commonly known as jumping to conclusions. We have already seen in the considerations of Simon, Lindblom, and others that decision making in administration is usually based on incomplete information. Knowing how much is enough is one of the premier management skills.

9. Fear. Fear on the part of the communicator of the reaction of the receiver may result in selection bias about what is presented, presentation of partial, or "half truths," omission of key facts, or other distortions.

10. Failure to communicate. Often we tend to assume that everyone knows what we know, and therefore there is no reason to tell them. Several theories of organizations argue that all bureaucratic organizations have tendencies toward secrecy.

BUREAUCRATIC COMMUNICATION

Conventional bureaucratic viewpoints woven into modern management theory and practice frequently tend to emphasize three types of communication and two modes. In the bureaucratic organization, communication takes for granted a stratified, hierarchical social world in which communications can be upward, downward, or lateral, any of which may be formal or informal.

Upward

Upward communications involve messages from subordinates in positions defined by the organizational plan as lower in the hierarchy to superiors in positions higher in the hierarchy. Examples of such communications might include intelligence or feedback from the environment, such as word of the activities of competitors or other stakeholders; strategic information on the effects of decision on employees, clients, or others; and reactions to policy proposals and the like. Common barriers to such communications might include physical distance, accessibility or attitude of the superior, the status of the subordinate, or office traditions that encourage/discourage particular communications.

One of the most valuable of communications skills in social administration is learning to read, listen, and watch for *meta-messages*—the messages behind, before, or surrounding the actual message before you. Literary scholars sometimes also refer to meta-messages as subtexts. What prompted this memo? Should I interpret that comment as sarcasm or poor word choice? I know she's unhappy, but what can I do? What does she expect me to do about this? How am I supposed to respond to this? Like reading body language, reading meta-messages is hardly an exact science, but it is certainly an essential managerial art.

The difficulties of correctly reading meta-messages are compounded by the multiple ways in which workers in a hierarchy can distort communication, either deliberately or inadvertently. This actually adds a whole level of additional questions to all such efforts: "Can she be that naïve or that cagey?" Although this is a constant problem, it is especially evident in vertical communications up and down the hierarchy. Filtering and distortion of messages is common in all types of bureaucratic communication. The sender of a particular message may color it to curry favor with the boss, seek to become popular with subordinates, or a host of other reasons.

Downward

One of the constant challenges for social administrators is anticipating the unintended subtexts that others may read into their messages. Downward communications in bureaucratic organizations tend to be easily influenced by the impact of authority. This may be because so many authoritative and official communications, orders, directives, policies, and rules move in this direction, flowing from organizational superiors to subordinates. Indeed, the ways in which official communications flow from person to person go a long way toward defining the official hierarchy of any organization. In most cases, official communication channels are probably much more important than any organizational charts in establishing the official hierarchy of authority and responsibility. Common barriers involved with downward communications include misinterpretations along the way, whether inadvertent or deliberate, and interruptions. Care must always be taken in official communications to ensure that word will reach everyone who needs to receive the message being communicated.

Lateral

It is fairly common in bureaucratic settings to characterize any communication that isn't overtly upward or downward as *lateral*. Within the general hierarchical terms in which administrative communication is usually broached, lateral messaging is perhaps best defined as communication among peers. This may involve an extremely wide variety of types of communication. The communication could be between persons at the same hierarchical level or at different levels in different command chains in the organization or with persons in different organizations. The basic barriers to lateral communication are those most closely associated with problems of coordination.

Networks

The upward, downward, and lateral communications channels of bureaus define distinctive types of communication networks. They certainly do not exhaust the topic, however. There are, in fact, an almost unlimited number of different communication networks that enter into the social administration arena at various times and places. They may be

- Networks of executives or workers in similar positions in different agencies
- Networks of patrons, agencies, and clients
- Networks of competitors and opponents that rise to awareness and consideration
- Informal networks of peer, neighbor and friendship groups

In social work education, for example, the communications networks formed by classes of students who were in school together are one of the enduring characteristics of community and social agency life. General models of communications that take into account the various elements of the basic communications question are a useful way to approach defining and understanding all types of communications networks.

One of the most basic forms of communication networks in bureaucratic organizations is that defined by the chain of command. One of the most basic forms of professional communication is peer to peer. Conflict between these two is a fundamental dynamic of social agencies. Can a worker, who is a professional peer, talk to the director, for example, without going through a supervisor?

INFORMAL COMMUNICATION

The concept of informal organization, introduced in chapter 3, has a natural corollary in the idea of informal or unofficial communication. One of the critical dimensions of informal organization ("work groups," peer and friendship groups on the job) is their role in communications. Spread of rumors, leaks of formal announcements, and many other types of communication are all part of the informal communication of an organization. More excessive interpretations of the command-and-control orientation of classical management have typically taken the stance that informal communication on the job simply ought not to occur. (There are several amusing parodies of the idea of stamping out informal communications in movies such as *9 to 5*.)

In small nonprofit and community social service organizations, *all* internal communications tend to be informal. In large organizations, there may also be a tendency for communications within the work group to be informal. Skillful administrators need to be aware of and know how to make use of the informal organization for communications. Dropping hints, testing out ideas, listening to office gossip, and many other examples of informal communication can be helpful to the administrator.

IMPLICATION OF WEBER'S THEORIES FOR COMMUNICATION

Communication in the Weberian mode has had the strongest practical impact in defining the legal and political environment of large organizations and a great many smaller organizations as well. Because bureaucracies consist of fixed and official jurisdictions, ordered by rules (laws or administrative regulations), certain formal communications are essential to the effective operation of bureaucratic organizations. For example, a bureau must be able to communicate its jurisdictions (boundaries) to its various *reference publics*.[1] This is one of the important purposes of mission statements, goals documents, and vision statements. To a lesser extent, certain limitations on jurisdiction may be spelled out in *foundation documents*,[2] such as enabling statutes in the case of public agencies, articles of incorporation in the case of nonprofit and for-profit corporations, or letters of gift in the case of foundations.

In addition, bureaus must also be able to communicate the rules that order or regulate its existence and operations. Policy and procedures manuals are useful for that purpose. Because its regular activities are defined as fixed official duties, the organization must communicate the specific obligations of each office to the appropriate officeholders. Policy and procedures manuals are also useful for communicating such obligations, as are organization charts.

Because the authority to give commands is distributed in fixed ways and limited by rules concerning its uses, the "pattern of authority" must also be communicated. In addition to policy manuals, letters of appointment that specify supervisors and supervisory responsibilities and job descriptions typically convey such information. Because provision is made for the regular and continuous fulfillment of duties and the execution of corresponding rights, the rights and duties of all employees must be made clear.

In bureaus, changes in any policy or practice are typically also communicated in writing. Indeed, willingness to commit such changes in written form is sometimes a test of the seriousness of intent of the official proposing the change. "Will you put that in writing?" is an oft-heard question in bureaus everywhere.

Because offices (positions) are open only to persons having the regular qualifications, those qualifications must be communicated to potential officeholders (job applicants). The procedures for communicating such notices are frequently spelled out in great detail in public bureaus and may include formal position announcements, job advertising, and posting of notices, as well as detailed instructions on the contents and/or form of such announcements.

Because levels of authority in a bureaucracy are arranged so that higher levels of officials supervise the work of lower levels, communication frequently occurs along the chain of command. In addition, a vast array of additional messages is communicated about the particular hierarchies of specific organizations. For example, higher offices are frequently located on higher floors or even in separate buildings. On university campuses, for example, the president's office may, in fact, be a separate building.

Because management of the modern office is based on files or written records, provision must be made so that selected communications made in other forms are ratified in writing. Thus, it is extremely common to ratify or formalize agreements reached verbally in meetings with a memorandum of understanding from one of the parties involved (not infrequently, the one with the greatest stake in the agreed upon outcome.) Equally common are what have come to be known as CYA (cover-your-ass) memos. One party to a conversation may have some concern about the sincerity of an agreement reached verbally. Or, some dubious or questionable action may be ordered by verbal instructions. An employee who feels in jeopardy may find it necessary to write a CYA memo, either to the person who ordered them to carry out the questionable action or to the file for future reference in case a problem arises.[3]

The memorandum or memo is probably the most universal form of written message in all types of organizations. An example of a memo appears in appendix 1. Because bureaucracy presupposes thorough and expert training, there must be provision for communication of expert knowledge both among and between experts and between experts and nonexperts. Remember that in the contemporary social agency, *legal expertise trumps all other forms of expert knowledge, including scientific and professional.* The reason for this may simply be that most judges and hearing examiners are lawyers.

In a bureaucracy, work activity demands the full attention of the employee for a carefully defined period of time. This requires communication confirming that officials are working to capacity during their work time and that they are meeting their obligatory time commitments. Time cards, professional service contracts, policy statements about working hours, and a host of other documents may communicate bureaucratic intent in this area.

Management of the bureaucratic office follows general rules that are more or less stable, exhaustive, and can be learned. Some aspects of that learning may be formalized and codified through orientation sessions for new workers, job-training workshops and manuals, and so on. Much of it can only be learned on the job and over time.

IMPLICATIONS OF SCIENTIFIC MANAGEMENT FOR COMMUNICATION

There is no systematic conceptualization of communication in scientific management to match that of the Weberian or neo-Weberian models. Even so, scientific management has had a limited, but important, impact on the practices of administrative communication in human services, both directly and by inspiration.

Just as early scientific managers believed, along with Frederick Taylor, that a science of shoveling could determine the one best (that is, single most efficient) set of motions in shoveling sand, so do contemporary organizational designers in human services frequently act as though they believe that communication is an exact science. The "error rate" calculations in completion of public welfare forms are probably the high point or, some might argue, the low point of scientific management attempts to direct communications in human service offices.

Under the inspiration of the scientific management example, it would appear at times that there is a belief in many social work offices that if there is a standard communication problem, there should be a report or form for communicating it! It is not enough to supply the standard information in a conventional form through a memorandum or note. Many people in social agencies need boxes and tick marks to convey information. The conventional assumption here is that forms are a more efficient means of conveying standardized information. Although this may or may not be true, the belief that forms are preferable is widespread in social agencies.

IMPLICATIONS OF HUMAN RELATIONS FOR COMMUNICATION

There is no formalized theory of communication evident in the human relations approach, although the socioemotional overtones of this approach are clearly traceable to the influence of psychosocial perspectives in Elton Mayo's work. Thus, it might be said that communication in the human relations mode has had a strong if somewhat indirect impact on social work. Perhaps more than anything else, this approach suggests that the communication of feelings becomes a preeminent concern, and informal communications are emphasized. Thus, the great importance many in social work attach to nonverbal communication, for example, falls readily within the human relations perspective, broadly conceived.

Another of the many reasons for the links between social work and social administration is a proper appreciation for the important dimension of communications in the social agency. Sometimes it is not what you say but how you say it that conveys the real message.

COMMUNICATION THROUGH MEETINGS

Given the importance of communication in management theory in recent decades, it is very curious that conversations, interviews, conferences, meetings, and other communication events[4] play almost no role in that theory. In social administration, the simplest level of such events is the *conversation* or one-on-one, voice-to-voice communication. Such direct communications can be what we tend to call face to face, via phone calls or by memos, faxes, telegraphs, or any other technologically enhanced media. In recent decades, a host of social psychologists of interactionist, phenomenological, and dramaturgical orientations have closely studied numerous aspects of conversations as strategic or purposeful interactions.[5]

Conversations are universally human and can occur between any two or more humans speaking the same language and not experiencing profound communications difficulties. A great deal of attention in social work has been devoted to the particular forms of conversations between professionals and clients that we call *interviews*. In social administration, we are often more concerned with a second kind of interview, conducted with someone other than a client, usually for the basic purpose of information gathering. Thus, a contract monitor or an auditor may gather information on the compliance of an agency both through written reports and through interviews with key staff. The term conference is applied to a broad range of distinct communication events from the parent-teacher conference to the national meeting of a membership association such as the National Association of Social Workers or Council on Social Work Education, attended by thousands. In all cases, the use of this term suggests the importance of conversations to the mission of the event.

Along with the conversation, the most interesting and important form of communications event from the vantage point of social administration is the meeting: a structured set of conversations called at a specific time and place for a specific set of purposes. Meetings, which are discussed more fully in chapter 11, are ordinarily characterized by four factors:

1. There is recognition of the special role of one participant as a convener, president, or chair.
2. There is a topical list or agenda used to guide the meeting.
3. The meeting participants use formal and/or informal rules of order.
4. Minutes or a record of topics discussed and decisions made is kept.

The principal thing that differentiates a meeting from any other small group is the role of one participant in beginning or convening the meeting, controlling the order of topics discussed, recognizing participants who wish to speak, terminating specific discussions, and closing or adjourning the meeting. An agenda consists of written or verbal information detailing the time, place, and the anticipated set of topics for the meeting. Agendas are frequently distributed in advance to inform participants of subjects to be considered and allow them to make any needed preparations in advance.

Rules of order are simply agreed-upon guidelines and standards for conducting meetings. Both houses of Congress and state legislatures have their own rules of order, specifically tailored to the needs of the legislative process. The most universally familiar reference work on conducting meetings is *Robert's Rules of Order* (1999), written by a nineteenth-century British military officer in his retirement. Major Robert's ideas on meetings are by turns charming and frustrating but they do have one major advantage. They are the standard against which meetings are judged. *Robert's Rules* spells out suggestions on matters such as agendas, structuring decisions by formal motion, and other items that are universally recognized throughout the English-speaking world as *the* way to conduct a meeting.

For some peculiar reason, it is a point of pride with some people in social work that meetings "do not follow Roberts." If this means that the group has their own formal or informal agreements on workable ways to get their collective business done, there is certainly no problem with that. However, as in the case of some social work faculty meetings we have participated in, it may also mean that

- Meetings are conducted in a disorderly and disorganized manner
- Minutes (particularly a record of decisions made) are not kept
- Some speakers unfairly dominate conversations and others never have a chance to speak
- It's really not possible to know when an issue has been resolved
- The group is continually forced to revisit and reconsider the same issues over and over again

It is important to note that with an effective chairperson, the methodology of meetings typically unfolds smoothly and almost transparently regardless of whether the meeting is conducted informally or following a highly structured agenda and close attention to rules of order. However, it is when there are substantial disagreements or conflicts that close attention to the items mentioned above such as rules of order becomes essential. If everyone is speaking (or perhaps shouting) at once, the role of an effective chairperson becomes critical in recognizing speakers in an orderly fashion, silencing the disorderly or those attempting to speak out of turn, and ruling or determining specific conversations to be relevant or irrelevant to the particular item on the floor.

Clarifying proposals in the language of motions, amendments, and the like can be one of the most effective ways to focus on specific issues and proposed actions. And just as importantly, having minutes that accurately record actions taken can, under conditions of conflict, be an absolute legal necessity: Did the board authorize the staff to start this program or not? Was this employee fired for cause? If questions like this come before the courts, board and committee minutes become important legal evidence. This can cut both ways. If an executive attempts to argue in court that an employee was fired only after careful discussion with the board, that claim will be considerably weakened and probably dismissed entirely if board minutes show no evidence of such a discussion.

In larger organizations that stress openness in communication and a participatory management style, the practice of social administration may be largely synonymous with attending meetings. As one practitioner told us: "My career is just one unending series of meetings!" Research tends to support this view. Mintzberg (1973) found oral communication of overwhelming importance to managers. He concluded that up to 80 percent of their time is spent in oral communication (face to face, on the phone, and in unscheduled and scheduled meetings). A study of British social service offices by Wilson and Streatfield (in Lohmann, 1983) found that meetings were the single most important medium used to disseminate information in British social service offices.

THE NEED TO KNOW

One of the most influential principles guiding modern administrative communication grew out of the context of government security and classified information and goes under the heading of "need to know." The idea is generalizable well beyond the news media, where it originated, and beyond government security and the military-industrial complex, where it arose as a management principle. The answer to the question, "Who needs to know this?" will in specific situations usually offer a basic guideline for information distribution that applies particularly well in social service agencies that routinely work with sensitive, confidential, and potentially damaging information about clients, patrons, and others.

Many practical communications problems can be solved simply by asking this basic question: "Do I (we/they) need to know this in order to carry out my (our/their) job or role in this situation?" A new executive director may need to know many things about a predecessor who was fired, for example, but in most cases a detailed review of the circumstances leading up to the firing will not be part of that necessary knowledge. In other cases, important questions of strategy and policy can be resolved by examining closely the tentative answers. One important set of answers to this question *prescribes* or defines the target or appropriate *audience* for particular messages: call, memo, letter, report, fax, or whatever. Equally important, however, is the way in which answers to this question *proscribe* or define who does *not* need to know particular bits of information.

CONCLUSION

Effective communication is important to a well-managed organization. Most administrators spend the bulk of their working days involved in communication using the range of modalities available to them.

Communication may be upward, downward, or lateral. It may involve informal networks outside the organization. Often the informal communication within the organization and with those in different organizations is as important as the formal communication.

The conversation is the most common form of communication found in organizations. Meetings are also common and may be seen as a series of structured conversations that have certain elements in common. Written communications may be a basic medium of communication, or they may serve to confirm and record messages delivered orally.

CHAPTER 15

Administrative Information Systems

As noted in preceding chapters, various theories of information figure prominently in modern management theory and knowledge-based models of organization. The cost of information is the central consideration underlying Coase's transaction cost approach to organization and in Simon's and Lindblom's qualifications on the limits of synoptic rationality that form the basis of strategy theory. In another vein, Peter Drucker and a host of others have been developing the implications of postindustrial arguments for an emerging knowledge economy, one of which is the information theory of poverty. In a knowledge economy, it is suggested that it is a lack of access to information even more than limited financial resources that defines real poverty (Haywood, 1995; Lang & St. John's University, 1988). Although the social work administration literature has made limited note of these points, there has been little systematic attempt to tie these findings together with current developments in information technology, such as the widespread use of management information systems. In this chapter, we attempt to explore management perspectives on information and use them to explain, in particular, the otherwise curious lags in social service applications of electronic information technology.

INFORMATION DEFINITIONS

Throughout this chapter, we will make repeated use of terms such as *information, information system,* and *information revolution.* We will also discuss *knowledge* as it may be differentiated from information.

It is straightforward to define *information revolution* as a summary term used to refer to the broad class of changes in information handling practices and social changes currently impacting upon virtually all aspects of American society. At its very core, the essence of the information revolution involves entirely new ways to capture, store, process, and retrieve all manner of information in the form of human speech, sounds, images, encoded data, words, and many other forms. Together they have already added up to a revolutionary change in the way a great many things are done, including social administration.

Information systems are generally acknowledged as organized computer and other electronic systems and programs for collecting, storing, and retrieving information. Information processing technology has generally identified ten basic functions of an information system: capture (collection or recording), verification (checking or validating), classification (categorizing), arrangement (sorting), summary (data reduction), calculation, storage, retrieval, reproduction, and dissemination.

However, it is extremely difficult to state exactly what *information* is and how it differs from *knowledge.* In a certain behavioral sense, information is the content of cognition, the stuff of behavior and the topics of communication. Knowledge is what is known or, perhaps, understandable.

There is an important process dimension to information. To inform someone is to apprise them of a set of facts or circumstances of possible interest. It is to reveal, disclose, or impart something of which the informant is aware but the recipient was previously unaware. By definition, if an informant informs someone of something they already know, it is not information. It is repetition or redundancy. Information, like communication, is in this sense a name of the process of informing or disclosure. This important sense of novelty or revelation is actually retained in the technical, mathematical theory of information upon which all modern information technology is based. As Darnell (1972) notes, "The technical, mathematical concept of information corresponds to *surprise* and *uncertainty*. It is a mathematical function of the number of things a system (an information source, for example) can do and of the possibilities of occurrence of those different possibilities. It is the inverse of predictability" (p. 158).

A fundamental connection exists between this mathematical definition of information and another of the easily observed qualities of information— its lack of exclusivity or *unalienability*.[1] If one has information such as where a piece of equipment is located or whom to see about gaining admission to a program or service, it can be imparted to others without being lost to the original person whose information it was. Thus, we often speak today not of owning or possessing information but of having access to it. This is in marked contrast to tangible objects. If I give or sell my car, bicycle, or computer to someone else in another neighborhood, for example, I am by law and physical reality *alienated* from it. It is now theirs to possess, not mine, and parked in their driveway, not mine. Not so with information, which, if it is to be controlled at all, must not only be retained but be retained in secret or in confidence. Thus, information can never really be exchanged; it can only be disseminated. The implicit promise of any ordinary exchange cannot be fulfilled in the case of information. Even the possibility is rather whimsical: "If you can tell me where the nearest family service agency is located I'll pay you for the information, but only if you forget where the agency is once I've paid you!" Information would be a far different thing if it were subject to alienation in this sense.

Many notions of the concept of information used in discussing its organizational and management implications fail to retain this important sense of surprise and uncertainty and its accompanying unalienability that are at the core of the concept. For example, Alvin Toffler (1990) defines information in purely operational terms as "data that has been fitted into categories and classification schemes or other patterns" (p. 18). Such an approach merely shifts the issue back another level by raising the question of what is data. In recognition of the difficulty, Gregory Bateson once defined information as "a difference that makes a difference," referring most likely to the patterned variations by which meaning is encoded in many media and the impact of information upon behavior.

Everyone, it seems, knows what information is but can't quite say what they know.

Murray Edelman (1971) perhaps came closest to the original and mathematical meaning when he explored the political implications of information as novelty and knowledge as certainty. Edelman's approach points toward a more concrete treatment of information consistent with the perspectives on decision making and policymaking outlined in chapter 8. The informative content or information in any message is what is experienced as new, what was not previously known, what surprises and is "news" to us. Knowledge, by contrast, is the result of prior information; that of which we already are aware, that which we know.

In an important sense, there is a large gap between information in this theoretical sense and information as it is meant in the phrase *information technology*. In terms of technology, it is probably appropriate to define information as any form of novelty *or certainty* that can be digitized and stored in electronic form: words, letters, numbers, visual or auditory images, and so on. Thus, information in terms of technology may consist of both information and knowledge because it may include both the novel and the certain. This is so because information technology is presently capable primarily of treating what Michael Buckland calls "information-as-thing" (Wresch, 1995, p. 7).

Photographs, voice recordings, maps, and drawings all may contain information. The same may be said for written texts of all types, agency reports and records, and even information-bearing objects such as fossils, archeological artifacts, and forensic evidence. But to consider such data sources uncritically without attempting to recognize or evaluate the information of such data runs the risk of simply accelerating the inundation of data overload that is assaulting us all. The technical challenge remains: how to extract information—the novel or unknown element capable of reducing our uncertainties—from the accelerating flow of data.

Computer operating systems and software share the unalienability of information. This is one of the things that makes dealing with their legal and economic consequences so complicated. For example, a consumer doesn't actually buy a software program; only the medium (disk, etc.) the copy of the software resides on and the limited right to use it are what is purchased. Moreover, the rules against illegal copying of software are necessary precisely because of its unalienability. Copying a disk just makes an additional copy and leaves the original intact. This is dissemination, not exchange.

Yet another fundamental characteristic of information noted previously by Herbert Simon is that information is not free. There are costs for someone associated with the collection and organization of information. As such diverse phenomena as the fantastic financial success of a number of major computer companies and software piracies attest, with information it is relatively easy to let someone else pay those costs. It is also precisely around the reduction of uncertainty and the diffusion patterns of case and resource information and knowledge resulting from group learning that the strongest case for the continuing need for social agencies is to be made.

One of the most fundamentally important and frequently overlooked points of Weber's model of the bureaucratic organization regards the novelty reduction resulting from organized systems of records. In at least one important sense a social agency *is* its records. Who was served? Why? With what results? What resources are available to clients and where? It's all in the records and the memories of individual workers. Without the communication and coordination inherent in a set of well-kept client and program records and colleagues who inform and support one another, a social agency would be little more than a collection of independent and unrelated entrepreneurs occupying the same office space.

As a result, an appropriate concern for information management has been central to social work for more than a century. One of the principal points of the Charity Organization Society (COS) movement, for example, was the emphasis on *eliminating duplication* and *improving efficiency.* Much of the "duplication" COS managers were interested in eliminating was duplicate or redundant *information* in client records maintained by two or more charity societies. Closely related to this were "unnecessarily" redundant awards of relief to the same individuals or families by two or more societies because of the absence of adequate record sharing.

Relatively few unique information processing conditions or require-ments of social work offices have been identified as information manage-ment issues, although there appear to be a number of candidates, such as the constant demand for updates in referral directory information. One way to view the social work office, built as it is on the triad of relations among patrons, clients, and agents, discussed in chapter 2 is as a locus of infor-mation flows within a community. In general terms, the social work office is the intersection of three independent information channels. The *needs channel* is the flow of information from clients and informants about the personal troubles and social problems of those in need. Interviews, referrals, inquiries, and case records are all part of this channel. Within each social agency, a unique needs channel intersects with a similarly unique *resources channel,* bringing a flow of information about self-help groups, services, equipment, prostheses, and all manner of other available problem-solving resources. It is important to note here that in the arena of financial re-sources, in particular, agencies handle remarkably few tangible resources. Social agencies primarily process financial *information* in the form of checks, letters of credit, electronic payments, grant award notifications, fi-nancial reports, and so on. There is no reason for false modesty here. Social workers in social agencies also excel at the gathering and systematic orga-nization of resource information (albeit sometimes only in worker's heads!) and the transformation of information on available service and community resources into a store of knowledge of the community.

To fully appreciate this point, one must take into account Edelman's distinction of information as novelty and knowledge as certainty. Based on this distinction, it is possible to project a third *knowledge channel* that is also important to information flow in the social agency. An agency staff with no present knowledge of how to maintain client records or financial record keeping must discover everything for themselves or find some systematic way to acquire the knowledge, for example, through strategic staff hiring. An agency with experienced, trained, or professional staff will almost certainly have such knowledge in its repertory. Taken together, these three channels—needs information, resources information, and knowledge in all its many forms—uniquely define the information system of social agencies.

Information processing in social agencies began as a paper and pencil technology. COS friendly visitors, early hospital and school social workers, and settlement houses maintained a good deal of information on index cards and tablets of paper. Indeed, the image of the social worker with her clipboard and pad is still something of a stock character in American folklore, and real social work has evolved only slightly in its typical, or modal, information processing capability. Telephones, electrical typewriters, dictation equipment, the copy machine and in some agencies, videotaping equipment have been the only important technological advances in the social work office from these modest beginnings. Paper folders containing inexact combinations of handwritten slips of paper, completed forms, and typed sheets of paper are still the core of the information storage system in many social agencies.

This model of a social agency as intersecting channels of information offers a way to tie information perspectives directly into the organizational concerns raised in chapter 3. It suggests a way, for example, to raise important questions about the relative advantage of agency-based social services in comparison with corporate and solo-practitioner models of delivering social services. In chapter 4, we noted the importance of Coase's model of transaction costs in the economic theory of organization. Coase's approach is often linked with the determination of *relative advantage:* A particular organization may be economically justified by the relative advantages of efficiency, effectiveness, safety, or other considerations that it brings over alternatives or competitors. Thus, the relative advantage of large, integrated corporations over networks of independent operators in the railroad industry are fairly clear.

The question that Coase's perspective should raise for the social service office is what relative advantage the social agency brings to the delivery of social services, in terms of transaction costs. Since the time of the COS movement social workers have acted as though the answer was to be found in terms of reducing the costs of information processing at the intersection of the three information channels noted above. If a worker or a unit of workers together have both detailed information about the needs of a particular set of clients and exacting information about resources available to meet those needs, when combined with knowledge distilled not only from their combined practice wisdom but also from the wider profession, they should be ideally positioned to get the best results with the least expenditure of resources. This is, in fact, the theory of professional social services delivered in social agencies in a nutshell.

In social service organizations, each of the three channels is made up of separate identifiable individual subchannels for each worker who possesses particular information on resources, knowledge of particular interventions, and awareness of particular client needs. Moreover, the costs of combining three separate channels are often formidable.

At the same time, various media of storage, dissemination, and retrieval can dramatically reduce the costs of needs and resources information collection. This is, for example, one justification for the case record. Not only does it store information that the individual worker would otherwise have to remember or collect each time it was needed, it also enables several workers to have access to the same information about a case. By contrast, if each worker were an independent operator, as in the case of many private practitioners, the relative advantage arising from pooled resource and need information and knowledge of interventions would be lost. Social service exchanges, multiservice centers, and numerous other experiments in the history of social service delivery seem to fit within this model as attempts to find the optimum relative advantage of various forms of social service organization in the community.

One of the aspects of the question of relative advantage of various forms of information processing that is difficult to assess in the case of social services is the role of individual memory and mental process. Individual social workers not only collect information about particular clients and particular agency and other community resources, they routinely remember and recall a great many things and make evaluations of the importance, reliability, consistency, and other characteristics of all the information at their command. What else could they be expected to do, given the unalienability of information?

This doesn't mean that workers must have perfect recall or that they always will or can make the right decisions. Highly publicized cases of workers not taking action in abuse cases where children were later killed or workers failing to pursue commitment of mental patients that later committed violent acts serve to show the risks of being wrong in such determinations. It does mean, however, that the distribution of information in the heads of workers as well as the files lends a dramatically egalitarian quality to the social agency consistent with what we have seen of the organizational perspectives of Mary Parker Follett and others. No one is in a position to control or alienate all of the information essential to the operation of a social agency. It is simply too widely distributed and in too many inaccessible places, such as workers' memories. A social agency can truly function effectively only if everyone involved is willing to use what they know and share what they learn.

Another of the relative advantages of agency-based information flows thus arises out of the distinction of formal and informal organization and a kind of two-step flow of communication. As Simon, Lindblom, and others have noted, it would be literally too costly and impossibly time consuming for a worker to note everything about a case. However, contemporary approaches of case recording associated with concerns for liability and managed care seem to be testing the limits of this assumption more and more each year. In all cases of needs, resources, or knowledge, the worker may form impressions, hunches, hints, and other subjective findings that would be inappropriate to include in the official record or that only become significant in light of the information of later events. Even so, these impressionistic data may be a valuable part of the information base from which effective service delivery arises.

The unalienability of information combined with the genuinely revolutionary cost implications of at least some information processing technologies has contributed to the well-known mantra of the free Internet movement: "Information wants to be free." What this statement might just as well have said is "Information wants to be known."

Not all types of information raise these complex issues of alienation, however. Certain types of information are inherently *public goods*, in the dual economic and political sense that they are indivisible and irretrievably in the public domain. Public information *may* be sold once, but from that point on it uncontrollably enters the public domain. News of Paul Revere's ride, the discovery of the Americas, and news that a human astronaut walked on the moon are examples of such cases. Other types of information are inherently saleable *private goods,* often more because of their immediacy and novelty than any desire for exclusivity. Minute-by-minute stock quotations from a month ago have very little value in any stock market. Although they may be quite valuable to a prosecutor seeking evidence of illegal manipulations or to a historian, such secondary value is quite limited.

INFORMATION POVERTY

One of the interesting ideas to have emerged from information studies in recent years is the notion of defining poverty in terms of information access rather than in terms of income. Given the previously noted difficulties of defining information, there is a certain genuine audacity to any suggestion of defining anything else in terms of it. However, the notion of information poverty also has some very sensible implications. The idea first arose in the context of the cost of personal computers and restrictions on Internet access. The concern was that only the rich would be able to benefit from the information revolution. This idea reached its apogee in the suggestion of House Speaker Newt Gingrich and others that poor families be given portable computers in lieu of welfare benefits.

More serious approaches to the subject have noted the strong correlation between poverty and lack of education and the important role of education in teaching what might be called techniques of information gathering (Haywood, 1995; Lang & St. John's University, 1988). Thus, it is likely that an educated upper income client with a particular form of cancer will have access to a greater amount and variety of information about the nature of the disease and its implications than a low-income high school dropout. It is also likely that the educated client will also be more likely to make more effective use of any information that is equally available. Something very much like the information theory of poverty has been operative in social work for a long time. With programs like information and referral services and community service directories, social workers have sought to increase the flow of information to the poor and to increase the information resources that poor people could bring to bear on their daily lives. Also, information and knowledge dissemination is arguably one of the fundamental roles of all casework and group-work activity and of many community organizing efforts.

THE EMERGING DIGITAL ECONOMY

The long-promised information revolution took a great leap forward in the mid-1990s with the popular acceptance of the Internet on top of the popularity of personal computers at home and at work for a large portion of the emerging class of knowledge workers. In April 1998, the U.S. Commerce Department released a report[2] entitled *The Emerging Digital Economy* that showed that in the previous five years, information technologies were responsible for more than one-fourth of the real economic growth in the United States. Investments in technology accounted for more than 45 percent of all business equipment investment in the 1990s—up from 3 percent in the 1960s. In some industries such as communication, insurance, and brokerage, information technology constitutes more than 75 percent of all equipment investments. Moreover, computer and communications industries were found to be growing at more than double the rate of the economy, according to then Commerce Secretary, William M. Daley.[3]

Where do social services fit in this brave new world? One of the issues raised by the emerging digital economy is whether social work is truly a knowledge-based profession or a service occupation. In an article entitled "The Post Capitalist World," Peter Drucker (1996) foresaw two future classes of employees: knowledge workers and service workers. Service workers are defined primarily as those who lack the necessary education to be knowledge workers. He predicts that service workers will make up the majority of the labor force, which poses the important policy problem of how to ensure the dignity of service work and workers. Jeremy Rifkin (1995) takes this same argument in an entirely different direction and predicts the demise of ordinary employment as we know it and the rise of nonprofit service organizations as a possible core of future employment.

In terms of its aspirations, social work is clearly a knowledge-based profession, and professional social services are clearly the preferred approach. However, in terms of the responsiveness or, more accurately, lack of response of the profession and of social services to the emerging digital economy, the issue is somewhat cloudy. Are social work and the social agency merely vestiges of the bygone age on industrialization? It has long been understood that social services are far back from the cutting edges of the information revolution. It is increasingly clear, however, that reliance on the marketplace alone is resulting in social services falling farther and farther out of the electronic network each year. From the vantage point of information poverty, it is no longer just clients who are affected; social agencies are also to be counted among the information poor. Some new and more effective forms of leadership in bringing the profession and social services more directly into the digital economy will be necessary. As noted in chapter 1 and elsewhere in this book, one of the places to look for that leadership would be from social administrators. However, current evidence suggests such leadership is largely lacking in both the public and the nonprofit sectors.

In a 1998 study of state governments funded by the Progress and Freedom Foundation, and published in *Government Technology News*, information technology achievements in social services were ranked absolutely last among state government service areas two years in a row. Social services were well below the overall average state scores with scores of 33 and 48 out of a possible 100 in eight categories of technological progress ("States Progress Toward Digital Nation," 1998). Table 15.1 shows the categories, two-year scores, and percentage change.

Six states—Indiana, Kansas, Minnesota, South Dakota, Washington, and West Virginia—earned perfect scores in the ongoing information technology commitment category. Washington state government earned the highest rankings overall both years, well ahead of eight other states (Wisconsin, Missouri, Pennsylvania, Florida, Michigan, Arizona, Minnesota, Kansas, and Maryland, ranked in that order). California state government, despite the vaunted presence of the computer industry there, only ranked near the middle of the states.

Table 15.1 Information Technology Achievements in State Government

Category	1998 Average	1997 Average	Change (%)
Digital democracy	59	51	+16
Higher education	62	44	+40
K–12 education	67	44	+52
Business regulation	59	42	+64
Taxation	59	42	+41
Social services	48	33	+45
Law and the courts	52	37	+40
Ongoing IT commitment	84	70	+20
Total	61	44	+39

The study found that many states still rely on paper records for most social service programs, and eleven states reported that they did not use any digital systems at all for social service record keeping. On the other hand, in the second study, thirteen states were found to offer benefit forms online or via kiosks, up from five in the first. Oregon, Connecticut, and other unnamed states were developing on-line job banks to help people find employment. Alaska rated highest on the survey, followed by Washington, with Florida, Oklahoma, Vermont, and Wyoming tied for third.

In the remainder of this chapter, we explore two principle themes: the hidden cost of information technology and organization responses to technology adoption.

THE HIDDEN COST OF INFORMATION TECHNOLOGY

However the bill is to be paid, by whom, and over what period of time, the costs involved in creating an electronic world have been and will continue to be enormous.[4] National Information Infrastructure (NII) proposals to date have adopted a fundamentally commercial posture by which those costs will ultimately be born by information "consumers" in the form of various competition-based user charges. Therefore, a key question—perhaps *the* key question—regarding the social service response to the Internet, the information superhighway, and NII must be what it will cost and what we can expect to get for the money. The answers to those questions remain anything but clear.

The *cost of* anything is ordinarily measured in one of two ways. *Outlays* correspond most closely to purchase prices and represent the amount paid or "laid out" for a particular good or service. Although this is ordinarily an adequate retrospective measure for detailing costs that have already been incurred, when examining the future, *opportunity costs* are a more fundamental measure of the cost of an entity or objective in terms of the alternatives given up in order to realize it (Lohmann & Lohmann, 1997).

Also relevant to the outlay and opportunity costs is the concept of *hidden costs*. Hidden costs are those that are not revealed or apparent. In the case of the opportunity costs of network technology adoption, at least two distinct classes of hidden costs should be distinguished. *Overlooked costs* can easily result from excessive enthusiasm, inadequate planning, poor quality consultant information, and other sources, including deliberate attempts to understate the costs of a project. Many a networking project has doubled in cost when someone discovered that the original estimates did not include the cost of copper wiring or routers or software.

Also important hidden costs that are particularly important in the adoption of new technology are *discovery costs*, which cannot, in principle, be known ahead of time. After all of the hoopla over the "paperless office" that occurred roughly between the first wave of desktop computers and the introduction of laser printers, many a social service budget manager must have been chagrined at what actually happened to paper costs. Instead of being paperless, most offices have found themselves in an unprecedented deluge of paper flow, most of it well printed and attractive, but still clearly and costly paper. The laser printer was a genuinely new development, and it would have been impossible in principle to predict its cost or any other implications with any degree of accuracy. The full cost of laser printing in any office is not simply equipment, electricity, and toner, but also the large and increasing quantities of paper consumed and ultimately the additional time that employees must put into reading that additional print output.

AN "IRON LAW" OF SOCIAL SERVICE TECHNOLOGY ADOPTION?

Social service organizations have been struggling—not very successfully—to catch up and then to keep up with the rate of technology adoption in business and higher education, two generally acknowledged leaders in this area. In this milieu, the outlay costs of equipment acquisition have sometimes appeared to act as the only major constraint upon adoption. Longer-term consideration of the hidden costs of training, maintenance, and upgrading and other costs have not always been carefully considered. It is extremely difficult to make reasonable policy in this context because of the many unknowns. Employees using their computers to play games or entertain themselves on the job are ordinarily assumed to be the exception and not the rule. Social service computer use is expected to allow conventional work to be done more quickly and easily, and the same number of workers to do more or fewer workers will be necessary to do the same work.

Despite the dramatic movement to revenue-based community service delivery in the past two decades, many nonprofit community services still operate in a relatively fixed-budget environment. Decision makers assume they will have a fixed if unknown amount to spend in any given fiscal period, and they operate by adjusting their expenditures to that amount. As one example of this, the United Way in most communities still allocates on fixed-budget assumptions. Public purchases of service contracts also include fixed ceilings as well as a contracted fee rate. All of these factors tend to create a situation whereby funds for technology adoption can only be acquired by diverting funding away from some other, existing expenditure.

At the same time, there are real and severe limitations on the ability of administrators in many settings to dramatically increase revenues or decrease costs. An administrator with most funds committed to full-time salaries, for example, may be able to adjust spending in any significant way only by laying off employees. Yet, in a fixed budget environment, it is a certainty that escalating costs in one area such as information technology will necessitate cutbacks in other areas.

This brings us to what appears to be an iron law of technology adoption in social service settings. Because most social service organizations are heavily service oriented and their abilities to increase revenues to offset increased costs are limited, at some point the added costs of technology *must* begin to compete with other costs. Thus, technology that does not result in bona fide economies of scale or scope for the organization—allowing workers to perform services more efficiently or to perform a broader scope of services in the same time—must inevitably diminish the ability of the organization to perform its primary mission of service delivery.

THE COST OF UNDERESTIMATING COSTS

At the institutional level, the impact of understating the true costs of technology, whether done intentionally or unintentionally, can be devastating. In one case, we were aware of a decision to introduce a new statewide system of electronic conference rooms, whose initial cost seemed reasonable. The purpose of the rooms was to engage in state-wide training and conferences at distant sites as well as to have electronic features available for local training. Only after it had been announced and received widespread favorable comment was it learned that the software would also require a dedicated server ($400,000), workstations with which to access the system (another $200,000), full-time personnel to get the system up and keep it running (at least $80,000 a year), and additional personnel not fully dedicated to the project but spending substantial amounts of time with it (another $80,000), as well as temporary personnel to bring the program up

($110,000 for the first year) and the ongoing cost of consultants. Physical renovations to the space in which the seminar room would be housed were also required ($100,000). Thus, what looked like a software bargain actually wound up costing the organization more than a million dollars, including more than $150,000 in ongoing personnel commitments.

None of these costs were part of the original estimate, and no special or dedicated funds were available for this purpose. As a result, decision makers were faced with the classic rock-and-hard-place choice of simply absorbing this amount in the ongoing operating budget or facing a hostile public reaction to the apparent reversal of a popular and seemingly sensible decision. Unfortunately, absorbing this cost could only be done by delaying or denying other worthwhile objectives. Many of the initial participants withdrew from the project because the costs outstripped their ability to participate.

The larger the organization, of course, the greater its ability to absorb such problems. One of the facts of life in the smallest social service agencies is that they have virtually no leeway for dealing with such complications. In the case of a small nonprofit community service, even a $5,000 oversight of this type could be catastrophic. Yet the problem remains, regardless of the scale at which it is acted out.

THE INFORMATION CRITERION

Referring back to the discussion of Coase's buttermilk metaphor in chapter 4, we wish to suggest here that it is in fact information and the communications process that binds the various "lumps" of an organization together in market firms and social service organizations. Information, in the context of coordination, may be a *factor of production*—raw material, as it were, in the production of goods and services or *products*. All kinds of examples illustrate information as a factor in the technology or know-how that defines and makes sense of production processes. You may have all the raw materials for mixing auto paint that will stick to metal and remain bright through various weather conditions, but information on how to mix them properly (the formula) is the key ingredient, without which all of the raw materials are useless. In the context of the modern economy, information may also be a commodity in itself. How else may we better describe modern banking based as it is on electronic funds transfer? Isn't it simply information exchange?

From a social service viewpoint, it is possible to suggest that coordination and cooperation are in fact two ends of an extensive continuum of possibilities and that it is the manner of sharing information that differentiates them. At one end of the continuum is *purely competitive coordination*, in which information sharing is always and only based solely on demonstrable mutual advantage. At the opposite end of the continuum is *pure coopera-tion,* in which mutual advantage is not an issue and unreserved sharing of information is always and only based on full trust and mutuality and the absence of calculated advantage.

Both ends of this continuum are, of course, ideal types. The calculated lumps in Coase's buttermilk correspond closely with the perspective of mi-croeconomics as it has come to be applied to the social service sector, and the mushy lumps of trust at the other end of the continuum correspond just as closely with the perspective outlined in the theory of the commons. For most existing social service organizations, reality is generally to be found somewhere along the continuum, with different organizations plac-ing themselves at different points through their information handling practices.

WORKGROUPS

One of the most revolutionary developments to come out of the information revolution was reaffirmation of the importance of the workgroup in orga-nizations, something that had long been working knowledge in social ad-ministration (see Trecker [1946], for example) and a component of organi-zation theory. When social administrators working on implementation of the newly developing public welfare program in the late 1930s confronted the limitations of available funds and such other realities as the need for information sharing and confidentiality, they learned that the best form of organization on a day-to-day basis was the agency, with some measure of overall control through policy organized as a kind of loose confederation of workgroups that came to be known as "units."

Since that time, public social service agencies have most typically been organizations in the sense that they are networks of loosely coupled work groups or units. As Trecker noted long ago, it is really these small, distinctly hierarchical groups made up of supervisors and experienced and novice workers (and perhaps volunteers and clients) who form the essential service core of the social agency. As we noted in chapter 3, Hasenfeld and English (1974) laid an elegant theoretical basis for further understanding the feder-ated workgroup nature of social agency organization in their theory of human service organizations. Their distinction of people-processing and people-changing technologies combined with a Joan Woodward (1965)–inspired distinction of long-link and short-link technologies is directly sup-portive of a model of social service units engaged in people-changing ac-tivities as quasi-autonomous workgroups. And, the unique information flows of needs, resources, and knowledge in these workgroups give shape and form to these units.

LEAD USERS

The experience of information technology adoption has added at least one additional key role to the workgroup. One of the major insights to come out of the experience of technology adoption in higher education was the concept of the *lead user.* This term refers to the staff member who out of personal interest and enthusiasm, individual self-interest, or some other personal motive assumes the role of advocating, introducing, and supporting the introduction of technology into the workgroup. During the 1980s, leadership provided by higher education administration was relatively nonexistent, and in departments all across campus, individual faculty members assumed the role of lead users. Although no hard data on this phenomenon in social agencies exists, it appears that those social agencies that have advanced furthest into technology adoption have also done so under the leadership of these lead users. In a narrow sense, it may be the lack of such lead users that accounts for the pattern of technology nonadoption in social agencies.

CONCLUSION

Many contemporary discussions of information in social work management operate under the short-sighted view that the tactical issues of the deployment and use of digital information technology should be the central questions of concern to administrators or the equally short-sighted view that there need be no concern for information except as the contents of communications. As we have shown in this chapter, there is much more to the subject than that.

Human limitations on information processing ability, models that define information in terms of novelty and difference, and the cost of information as a factor in organizational structure are all part of the intricately interwoven fabric of information theory that is becoming an increasingly important part of an overall understanding of social administration theory and practice.

Empowerment

One of the most fascinating and enduring elements in social work knowledge is the ongoing dialectic between the rational and irrational elements of human behavior. Humans, in the social work view, are neither wholly rational creatures as portrayed in classic economics, nor wholly irrational as in some erroneous interpretations. In clinical practice, this is most evident in the interplay between reason and emotion. In social administration this is evident in the interplay between a wished-for rational choice in planning and decision making and the seemingly mundane realities of authority, power, influence, and image. In this section, we devote three chapters to unraveling some of the dimensions of this broad set of concerns.

In the wake of Weberian and neo-Weberian models of bureaucratic organization like those considered in chapter 3, and classic models of management like those considered in chapter 6, the topic of authority always looms large in social administrative thought. In chapter 16 we examine this interesting phenomenon from several vantage points, including the view of Max Weber, the somewhat eccentric but insightful view of Chester Barnard, and the powerful view of Mary Parker Follett. This latter has had an enduring, if largely unrecognized, impact in social work approaches to authority even during the years when the subject was completely out of fashion in general management.

In chapter 17, we look a step further beyond the purely rational and the more sophisticated psycho-social bases of authority, at the associated dimensions of power and influence. There is a widespread perception today among members of the profession that social work is becoming more political (Haynes & Mickelson, 2000). In an age as ideological as the present such a development is perhaps unavoidable. The concern in this chapter is with several narrowly constrained approaches to the vast topic of empowerment. We begin by differentiating administrative concern with empowerment and influence by a broad range of organizational and political theorists.

Perhaps most challenging of all are the views of Goffman and Banfield regarding social influence, which open the possibility that sometimes decisions get made that cannot easily be ascribed to the motives of particular individual or group decision making. As Follett suggested decades earlier, sometimes, the situation did it!

Chapter 18 may at first appear out of place in a section with authority, power, and influence. Marketing, public relations, and advertising may, on the surface, appear more properly placed with discussions of other management techniques, like those in the sections that follow. Or, given their underlying communications theory basis, they might alternatively be placed along with chapter 14. In many respects, the discussion of the dialectics of authority and power in chapters 16 and 17 makes the placement of this topic at the end of this section and immediately before the next quite appropriate. If social administration were approached on a purely rational basis, the topics of marketing, public relations, and advertising would best be omitted entirely, dealing as they do with image, positioning, and other seemingly irrational appeals and persuasion techniques. However, as the prior discussions of authority, power, and influence and the long and fascinating record of emotional appeals on behalf of needy clients show, social administration is never a purely rational activity. We show in chapter 18 how these approaches are appropriate for use by social administrators to shore up legitimacy and improve the accountability of controversial or unpopular social services.

CHAPTER 16

Administrative Authority

In this chapter and in chapter 17, we try to unravel the complex skein of ideas associated with the notion of power as an administrative phenomenon. Power, authority, influence, compliance, control, empowerment as well as stratification, oppression, and inequality are some of the major terms that will be introduced and discussed. The cornerstone of this whole discussion in conventional administrative theory is what might be termed the authority-responsibility dyad. This set of ideas came into organization theory through Max Weber and into American management theory by Chester Barnard and Mary Parker Follett. A close reading of Follett's comments quoted in chapter 3 will support the view that the problem of authority and the associated problems of legitimacy and trust as issues in social administration arise in the wake of the shift away from domination. After considering the contributions of Weber and Barnard to our understanding of authority, we will examine more closely Follett's distinctive contributions to contemporary understandings of the role of authority in social administration. Each of the approaches to authority reviewed in this chapter brings to light different aspects of the problem of authority.

This chapter discusses authority, power, legitimacy, and influence. Two of these four interrelated concepts are routinely discussed in the management literature; two are heavily implicated in those discussions. In the next section, a hypothetical situation illustrates some of the most important differences in these ideas.

TERMS AND DEFINITIONS

Imagine a social agency with a clear service program and stable funding. For some reason, all of the service delivery staff—none of whom had degrees, licenses, or professional training—suddenly decided to quit at the same time. An entirely new and more professional staff was hired. At their first meeting on the second day on the job, one of the new staff members, who had spent her first day perusing the policy and procedures manual, asked the others a question: "Do we have to be bound by the practices and policies of the old (and nonprofessional) staff, even when we think they don't make sense?"

Most of the assorted answers one might provide to such a seemingly simple question point toward our cluster of four concepts. For example, a member of the clerical staff (who didn't quit) or a client might pose this answer: "Well, you'd better because that's the way things have always been done here." That would be a resort to what Max Weber called traditional authority. By contrast, if the answer was, "Well, yes, but only if and when they make sense to us," that would be a reference to rational authority. Or, if the answer was, "We'd better until we find out what our contracts call for and government agencies like the Internal Revenue Service demand," that would be a reference to a closely related type that Weber called legal authority. If the agency's program was part of a national or international social movement and the new workers elected to consult the movement's guru or charismatic leader, they would be responding to what Weber called charismatic authority.

If the new workers' answer to this simple question was, "We'd better consult the Board President. We wouldn't want to get fired in our first week!" they would be somewhere in the domain between authority and power. And, if one of the clients who happened to be passing by the room and heard the question responded, "You'd better, or I'll see to it that all the clients from my neighborhood refuse to come in for their appointments," they would be in the clear domain of power.

But this does not exhaust all the possible answers. The answer might also be something like, "We will need to make clear to clients from the start that we know what we are doing." This would still be a reference to professional authority, but with a particular emphasis on the legitimacy of that authority. When the initial question was posed, if all the others in the room (including the initial questioner) had turned, in unison, to one worker in particular and asked what she thought, this would be a demonstration of her influence.

There is a tendency in the contemporary context of empowerment in the social professions to see all of these variations as manifestations of power, and in a certain limited sense that may be true. Certainly, these responses are all related in that they are different responses to the same question. However, rather than collapsing them all into a single category, conventional practice in social administration and management science has been to see power, authority, legitimacy, and influence as related but distinguishable concepts.

Initially, authority can be defined as legitimate or formal power to achieve one's ends under either of two conditions: (1) in the face of illegitimate, inappropriate, or stigmatized opposition; and (2) in the face of latent or unorganized opposition. Thus, when a physician's diagnosis is questioned or challenged by a managed care clerk with no medical training, we may have a clear case of professional authority versus illegitimate power. In the same vein, responsibility is the state or quality of being accountable or answerable for something within one's control or domain. In the classical formulations of public administration, where the sphere of authority of the public official is a foremost concern, the concept of administrative authority is usually offset against the counterbalance of responsibility (Block, 1987). Relatively few published sources in the management sciences make clear, however, what is the exact nature of the relationship between authority and responsibility, simply presenting the matter as obvious and self-evident.

In social administration and elsewhere, one of the temptations of most new administrators is to reduce the complex problem of authority to a simple problem of contract rights and obligations. "As long as I work here and accept payment for my work," new workers generally say, "I will do what they tell me to do." The problem for administrators is often that it is unclear whom the "they" to be listened to may be. What's more, "they" may offer contradictory messages. One hears much the same thing from time to time from boards of directors and public agencies whose authority has been challenged. This is an authority claim that is grounded in simple economic power and very much encouraged by the trend toward incipient managerialism.

Most experienced observers recognize, however, that this issue is not as simple as it may at first appear. This was, for example, the basis for one of Slavin's objections to managerialism quoted at the beginning of this work. The behaviorism and reductionism inherent in such raw appeals to economic self-interest and the quid pro quo is not only a generally ineffective response, as the discussion of Mary Parker Follett in chapter 6 pointed up; it also fails to adequately resolve the real issues raised by administrative authority.

A minor example of this situational dilemma is built into the model of the social agency staffed by professional social workers. It offers one of the foremost arguments for the model of social administration as the epitome of social work professionalism presented in chapter 1. If social work is ethically based practice and if prescribing the ethical basis for practice is a primary professional responsibility, then one genuine limitation on the contract authority of a social administrator (regardless of profession or discipline) to issue orders to any social worker would be that those orders must be consistent with the ethical norms of the profession. However, the ethical claims of the social work profession do not and cannot have the force of law for everyone. If they did, they would be public law and not professional norms. A social worker cannot be held to the ethical standards of a surgeon or lawyer, or business ethics and vice versa, and the nonprofessional can be held to none of these. Thus, only if the social administrator giving the orders is also a social worker can this claim on the ethical limits of administrative orders be fully enforceable. Even then, the same problem would appear to extend to voluntary boards, although the traditional standard—that the executive or other employee who cannot carry out board policy is expected to take the path of honor and resign—may be adequate in this case.

All of this only speaks to the limits imposed by professional norms on giving orders: what social workers may not be ordered to do and, if ordered, must not comply with. Make no mistake: this is a powerful, encompassing, and troubling domain in the present environment, an important consideration in an era when welfare reforms are premised on the rationing of scarce services. The discretionary judgments of policy and administrative decision may lawfully turn away those in need in this managed care environment where the ability to pay has been set up as a trump card to overrule need.

To some extent, nontreatment of the problem of authority by early management theorists and their attempts to rely on the power and tacit authority of command must be seen as efforts to transform the traditional authority of class and church of medieval Europe to the changed circumstances of the industrial age.[1] The degree to which contemporary conceptions of administrative authority are an offshoot of the taking up of the mantle of traditional European aristocratic prerogatives by a rising European and American class of industrial managers is a complex question. Haber (1991), for example, argues that the value that the modern professions of medicine, law, and the ministry in America placed upon "authority and honor" reflect a borrowing of the class positions and occupational prescriptions of eighteenth-century English gentlemen. Perhaps because of its complexity and upper-class associations, social work writers on management have mostly elected to steer clear of the issue entirely. It may also be the case that at least some social administrators strive to adopt the prerogatives of an aristocratic class within the profession.

A direct link of some sort between the authority of managers to direct and the responsibility of workers to obey is one of the standard assumptions to come down to us from classic management theory. Our favorite French expert Henri Fayol is the nominal source of this linkage, although it is more likely to be found deep in the practice wisdom and class consciousness of nineteenth-century factory managers. In all likelihood, the authority-responsibility link was, in its original form, an assertion on the part of a rising middle class of industrial managers of their own version of the ironic noblesse oblige of the European ancient regime: These industrial managers, like their aristocratic forebears, assumed a right to be served and a right to expect that workers would serve them faithfully and without question! The degree to which American industrial managers identified with and sought to assume the mantle of European aristocracy is remarkable.

This would seem to be a rather clear case of theory following practice. Any notion that industrial-age managers in organizations did not understand command and control until Henri Fayol introduced them into management thinking simply lacks plausibility. Instead, Fayol was probably voicing the conventional wisdom of industrial managers of the 1880s when, as one of his principles of management, he defined authority as the right to give orders and be obeyed. Responsibility, he added, is the obligation of workers, under the threat of sanctions, to obey orders given. By introducing the necessity of possible sanctions into the basic definition/principle of authority, Fayol acknowledged, however obliquely, the conflict between management and worker interests and the necessity of the use of coercive power by management that we now know was such an inherent part of classical management. To some degree, this same conflict and coercion are similarly inherent in social administration today.

The effort by Fayol and the classic management tradition to isolate the principles of authority and responsibility that are the moral basis for the command-and-control tactics at the core of classic management tells us a great deal about the problematic nature of authority in modern management generally. The overall situation in which factory managers and government bureaucrats found themselves in the late nineteenth century was not new. The concern Fayol and Weber had with authority, however, indicates a rather profound change in one aspect of that situation. In the past, even when the workers refused to follow orders or worse, rioted—as European workers often did (Hobsbawm, 1998, pp. 9–10)—the moral basis of authority to command and the right to expect to be obeyed were seldom at issue. Yet, in the wake of the American and French Revolutions and the rapidly expanding concept of the Rights of Man [sic], it became necessary to find some rational basis other than noblesse oblige by which to legitimize continued command and control. This had to be not only an explanation necessary for workers in order to justify their responsibility to obey but also for their managers to justify their demands of obedience. To that extent, Fayol's principles are themselves an expression of the newly rising rational–legal form of organizational rationality that Weber detailed. They are an effort to substitute the rules of rational–legal authority for the traditional authority behind the aristocratic prerogatives to expect obedience that in the past had merely been taken for granted even when breached.

What links the far-distant concern for authority and responsibility in the crumbling ancient regime to the rational–legal world of today is the underlying notion of what might be termed a just exchange, the social contract implicit in the employment contract between an agency and a worker. From the standpoint of someone assigning responsibilities, the commonsense attitude is one of "this is what I expect you to do" (take on a difficult case; hire, fire, or promote someone; initiate a new program or eliminate an old one; make a controversial statement or take an unpopular stand, etc.) "and here is how I will support you in doing it" (board or supervisory support in the face of opposition, a promotion, a resolution of support or vote of confidence from the board, etc.) From the standpoint of the person accepting such responsibilities, the understanding or explicit agreement sought may be similar: "Before I do what you request [i.e., accept this responsibility], I want to know or be reassured that there will be continuing support for my doing so, especially when I am challenged." When acceptable levels of expectations and supports are in place from all sides, we usually speak of the legitimacy of authority. It is legitimacy that distinguishes authority from the mere exercise of power. For example, to question the authority (we still often say the "right") of a police officer who has issued you a ticket for speeding will be seen as a challenge to the legitimacy of his or her authority. Similarly, any challenges to the authority of a protective services worker to remove a child from a threatening environment or of a mental health hearing examiner to issue a commitment order must be dealt with in terms of justifications of the legitimacy of the authority to act in that manner.

It would be misleading to suggest that legitimacy is the most salient characteristic of authority without examining also the variable nature of legitimacy and the process called legitimation that regulates that fluctuation. Legitimation can be defined as the social process by which the need for compliance with authority is established and maintained as, for example, through the justification of rules or standards. Legitimation is concerned with the ways to explain and justify particular institutions as we saw in the previous discussion of institutionalization (Berger & Luckman, 1966, p. 61). Legitimation, in this sense, is another key process of institutionalization. It is also a topic that has figured importantly in the perspective known as the social construction of reality. The role of legitimation in knowledge construction and our ideas about reality are explored in greater depth later in this chapter.

At this point, it is sufficient to note that steps that social administrators can take to increase the legitimacy of a particular policy, strategy, tactic, or action might include things as diverse as

- Obtaining testimonials from undisputed authority figures
- Citing legal precedents of its successful or positive effects
- Holding discussion groups to explore the intent and rationale of the policy

Such tactics need to be approached cautiously, however. A policy, strategy, tactic, or action that on its face already has sufficient legitimacy is usually better left alone than to become the subject of efforts to further improve its legitimacy. Unnecessary or excessive efforts at legitimation can easily appear to be mere rationalizations and provoke counterproductive reactions: "We thought everything was okay with that policy (or strategy, tactic, or action), but they must be worried about something.[2] Otherwise, why would they be putting so much attention into justifying it?" This is truly an important variant on the adage, "If it ain't broke, don't fix it."

The legitimacy of administrative authority has an important "until further notice" quality about it. That is, authority will continue to be authority only as long as its legitimacy remains intact. When authority is unchallenged, action based on that authority will usually proceed smoothly (the ticket is issued, the child is removed, or the patient is committed), and frivolous and insubstantial challenges to otherwise legitimate authority will be easily dismissed. Likewise, when the authority is strongly held by the person in authority and also by those from whom that authority is derived, challenges will usually be dispatched quickly (and if necessary, by force). The authority of the traffic cop says, in effect: See this badge? It is a symbol of my legal authority, and if its authority as a symbol isn't sufficient, see this gun? And if I need to, my radio will bring backup support, and they'll all have badges, guns, and, if necessary, body armor! The authority of the protective service worker says: See this warrant? It is also a symbol of my legal authority, and if that isn't sufficient I'll have to bring in the police (and their assorted means of force) with me. The authority of the mental health worker says: See this commitment order? It is a symbol of the authority of law and reason, and if its authority isn't enough to overcome your lack of reason, we will use restraints! The latter case is a particularly interesting one from the standpoint of authority, because mental illness has traditionally been treated largely as a breakdown of the ability to recognize and respond appropriately to reasonable authority.

In chapter 3, we noted that transactions in social service are fundamentally three-sided, or triadic, involving patrons, agents, and clients. The exercise of legitimate authority is another case where the importance of the three-sided nature of this relation is evident. Any real breakdowns of authority are most likely to come when at least two of the three sides recognize that the exercise of authority lacks legitimacy. "Resistant" clients can be dealt with when workers act as agents of legal authority and legislative or administrative lawmakers are in agreement. Effective handling of the same clients becomes very difficult, however, when the legal authority to handle them is not clear or when workers have no confidence in the legitimacy or justice of the law. Further, simultaneous losses of legitimacy with clients, workers, authorities, and publics would almost certainly condemn any policy as illegitimate. At that point, the law or policy might be revoked, it might be quietly ignored, or in some cases its continued observance might be a mere formality or "empty" ritual. It is also possible that the issue might revert from one of authority to one of the coercive use of power. It is not unheard of for a well-placed authority figure like a judge, teacher, parent, or supervisor in a strategic position to demand compliance with a particular rule or policy, even in the face of rather massive breakdowns of legitimacy of that policy. Every parent has probably said to their child at some point: "You'll do it because I say you will!"

In social administration, understanding the importance of just or fair exchange makes the practice of authority inherently different from the practice of power or influence, which is discussed in chapter 17. This is evident in a wide variety of settings in which employees pushed hard enough by a command-and-control structure are likely to respond: "I quit! They don't pay me enough here to put up with this. I'm out of here!" Indeed, in this context, power becomes an issue only within the bounds of just exchange. We are willing to let our bosses push us around even though we question their authority to do so only within the limits set by the financial value and other meaning that the job has for us. Conversely, the exercise of genuine authority on the job is not, as sometimes suspected, a matter of "throwing one's weight around." Instead, genuine authority grows directly out of the exercise of leadership and institutionalization (discussed in chapters 5 and 8) and only within the definite limits of legitimacy. When those limits are exceeded, everything becomes a matter of power.

Legitimate authority is most dramatically in evidence, both positively and negatively, when an authority figure becomes the embodiment or personification and dramatization or an institution, enacting or representing the values of that institution (Selznick, 1957). Thus, in an important sense, Jane Addams did not only lead and administer a settlement house. She *was* Hull House throughout her career, just as Dr. Martin Luther King Jr. became the embodiment—the human symbol—of the civil rights movement, even though he was only one of several dozen leaders important in key aspects of that movement. Another distinct aspect of authority, illustrated in the case of the civil rights movement as well as the earlier independence movement in India, is the role of nonviolent protest in engendering very powerful alternative forms of moral authority for its practitioners. Being arrested, beaten, and attacked by police dogs for their convictions conferred on the protesters something much more powerful and basic than celebrity or notoriety for their courage and the strength of their convictions. By their naked use of force against demonstrators, governmental authorities in India and the American South demonstrated in very public and dramatic ways that the policies they were attempting to enforce were unjust and unreasonable. The use of force also revealed that the government and the policies had so completely lost legitimacy, particularly among those whom the policies sought to control, that they could only be defended by coercive force. Segregation in the American South was quite literally washed away by the fire hoses used on demonstrators.

When properly mobilized and displayed, there is no more powerful weapon in the armamentarium of those working for social justice than the exercise of the moral authority of nonviolent protest against serious injustice. This is, however, a weapon to be used selectively and sparingly and with full consideration of the context in order to be effective (that is, maintain its authority). Nonviolent protest against fully legitimate authority is ordinarily a futile exercise and tends to reinforce that authority.

THREE TYPES OF LEGITIMATE RULE

According to Max Weber (1968), authority refers to "the probability that a specific command will be obeyed" and "there are three clear-cut grounds on which to base the belief in legitimate authority."[3] According to Weber, the three grounds on which authority can be based are law, tradition, and charisma.

Legislatures, courts, administrative, and other rule makers enact legal authority. In a society like ours that strives to be governed by laws and not by personal discretion, legal authority is for many purposes the highest form

of legitimate authority. Obedience to legal authority is owed not to particular persons but to the law. Enforcers of legal authority are typically bureaucrats in the Weberian sense. They are trained specialists, employed by
contract, for fixed salaries scaled by rank of office rather than amount of
work, pension benefits, and fixed rules of advancement through a hierarchy
of offices. In the best case scenario, such bureaucrats are expected to not
allow personal motives or temper to influence their conduct, and they are
supposed to enforce rules in an impartial, consistent, and predictable manner. According to Weber, public bureaucracy may be the purest example,
but other forms of legal authority are found in popularly elected officials,
various parliamentary and collegiate bodies, and professional associations.

Traditional authority in the Weberian sense always rests on belief in the
unquestionable nature of the status quo ante (the situation we inherited).
The patriarchal authority of the paterfamilas, the medieval lord, or the clan
and tribal chieftain are expressions of this pure type. In traditional authority,
administration and settlement of disputes are grounded in particularistic
considerations rather than the formal or general considerations of the law.
In its simplest form, traditional authority means that we do it unquestion-
ingly because the leader says that's the way its always been done. In the
larger sense, traditional authority was already in serious decline by the time
Weber wrote. In a more limited sense, the authority of tradition is one of
the byproducts of ongoing institutions. The weight of tradition is typically
very evident on many college campuses and social agencies:

> Every year we honor our founder at Founder's Day.

> This grove of trees is dedicated to the memory of those who fought
> valiantly against the Gypsy Moth infestation of 1911.

> This is the spot where our first President gave his immortal Ground-
> hog Day speech of 1841.

> This is how we were taught to do case records when I was a student.

As thoroughgoing modernists implacable in the face of the dwindling
authority of the larger and often negative traditions of class, race, and gender, social workers have consistently throughout the twentieth century been
reluctant also to place any importance on these modern forms of tradition.
Perhaps it was the feeling that social work had no tradition to look back on.
For whatever reasons, all forms of traditional authority have been largely
discounted in social work and social services. There are many consequences
of this. Founders of social services and past accomplishments are quietly
set aside and forgotten, along with obsolete equipment, old records, and
broken chairs (Lohmann & Barbeau, 1992). Unfortunately, the rather sub-

stantial potential for marshalling the authority of the past is also surrendered as a result. There are some signs that the social work profession may be beginning to discover the uses of the past and the authority of tradition. The National Association of Social Workers centennial observance, for example, carried with it a strong implied message: We've been around for a hundred years, and we aren't going away. This was welcome news in a profession feeling more than a little battered and bruised by events of recent decades, and it showed one of the uses of traditional authority in an organization.

Charismatic authority, according to Weber, "rests on the affectual and personal devotion of the follower to the lord and his gifts of grace (charisma)." The purest types are prophets, warrior heroes, and demagogues. In the context of social services, charismatic authority in the larger sense is only seldom seen. Genuinely charismatic figures in social services are few and far between. Mother Teresa is probably the most recent example of a category that might also include Jane Addams, the medieval abbess Hildegard von Bingen, and a few select others. The essential point of charismatic authority demonstrated by such figures might be termed complete personification. In the heyday of the settlement house movement, Jane Addams was not simply a leader of the movement. For many people, she *was* the movement—a living, breathing personification of all they stood for (Lohmann, 2000).

"Charismatic rule represents a specifically extraordinary and purely personal relationship." Generally speaking, charismatic authority is ephemeral and not long-lasting, according to Weber. It tends to give way to the routinization of charisma, in which

- Traditionalization as "the authority of precedents takes the place of the charismatic leader's creativity in law and administration"
- Disciples or followers "take over internal prerogatives or those appropriated by privilege"
- "The meaning of charisma itself may undergo a change," most notably in the crisis of successorship (Weber, 1968)

Indeed, a close study of the events at Hull House and in the settlement house movement in the United States during the decade after Jane Addams's death in 1935 shows precisely this pattern of struggle over succession, with some indication perhaps that the movement never fully recovered.

The charismatic figures in any field who make it into the history books are genuinely few and far between. However, at a lesser level, one can also see the effects of charismatic authority at the community level. We all know people whose effect on others is simply transformative: people who "light up the room," people others wish to seek out and be with, people whose actions symbolize and exemplify all that is best in an organization or community.

THE TWILIGHT OF AUTHORITY

Sociology in the wake of the English translations of Weber's work on authority has carefully tracked what Robert Nisbet (1975) termed the *twilight of authority* in a number of distinct and separate ways. In one important sense, Nisbet was concerned with the diminishing role of traditional authority in society. Some of these effects have been negative. According to Balz and Brownstein (1995), "The persistent alienation that voters now express about the political system is a force inimical to electoral stability of any sort." More recent feminist writings on the decline of patrimony, popular writings on the demise of the WASP (white Anglo-Saxon Protestant) and the "Eastern Establishment," and writings including those in social work on the rise of alternative or nonhierarchical organizations are all tracking essentially similar phenomena.

If authority is equated with domination by managers, males, WASPs, or more generally any form of hierarchy, then these writings can be read as calling for the elimination of authority as a principle of social relations. These writings may also be interpreted as calling for the replacement of particular types of hegemony, or authority supporting domination, by other more benign and acceptable (which is to say, more legitimate) forms of authority. One can, for example, accept the replacement of male domination in families without rejecting completely any concept of parental authority. One thing is clear, however. Whether one sees authority as in decline or in transition, the short-run perspective is the same in most work organizations. As a practical matter, Weber's legal-rational authority and some measure of hierarchy and the just exchange of responsibility and authority will continue to predominate for the foreseeable future in most social agencies.

Two decades ago, Alvin Schorr (1980) noted that a workmanlike reconstruction of the social compact was needed. As opposed to a "gamesmanship" view of administration where winning or surviving are seen as the main purposes of social agency administration, Schorr's reconstruction called for devotion to objectives and altruism. The essential idea here is one that is equally valid today. There is need for a consistent reworking and firming up of the basis of authority for social service activity.

CHESTER BARNARD'S THEORY OF AUTHORITY

Although Weber carefully delineated the three forms of authority, his was still a command perspective. There is little explicit concern in these three models for variations in the acceptance or response to authority. For that, we must look elsewhere. Chester Barnard is one of the acknowledged masters of American management theory, as noted previously. Yet, not all of Barnard's ideas have entered the management mainstream. According to Wren (1979), "one of Barnard's most unusual ideas was his theory of authority" (p. 341). He held what might be termed a *receiver* or *message* theory of authority. Authority, Barnard argued, is a characteristic not of people but of their messages. It can be traced directly to recipients' responses to authoritative communications or commands. Specifically, authority is "the character of a communication [order] in a formal organization by virtue of which it is accepted by a contributor to or member of the organization as governing the action he contributes" (p. 163).

In Barnard's bottom-up view, individuals will assent to the authority of an administrative directive only if five conditions are met:

1. They are capable of understanding an order.
2. They actually understand the order.
3. They believe the order consistent with the current purpose of the organization.
4. They believe the order consistent with their personal interest as a whole.
5. They are mentally and physically able to comply.

To explain further why people will obey an order they personally disagree with but do not find illegitimate, Barnard expounded the concept of a "zone of indifference." Within this personal zone, individuals would accept orders regardless of whether they actually agree without questioning the order's authority. Wren (1979) says, "When the authority of leadership (respect for the leader) was combined with the authority of position, the zone of indifference became exceedingly broad" (p. 342). In the Weberian view, rational–legal authority is a characteristic of a person by virtue of a social status (the office) they occupy. In Barnard's view, authority is literally vested in the recipient, who must accept and respond accordingly to an authority figure in order for that authority to be effective.

AMATAI ETZIONI'S THEORY OF COMPLIANCE

The sociologist Amatai Etzioni developed a plausible sequel to Barnard's view in the early 1960s in his theory of compliance. This theory also approached the matter from the receiver standpoint but with greater emphasis on the relational qualities of authority. Compliance, according to Etzioni (1961a), "refers to a relation in which an actor behaves in accordance with a directive supported by another actor's power, and to the orientation of the subordinated actor to the power applied" (p. 3). Etzioni's use of the term *power* here should be read as *legitimate power* as the preceding discussion of legitimacy should have made clear. Otherwise, authority can never be real. Without legitimacy, it is always—including such cases as parental authority—only the mask that power wears to deceive. Power in this sense means little more than the ability to get a result, so that legitimate power can be read as the acknowledged ability to get a durable or lasting result. Such power, he says, is of three basic types: coercive power, grounded in the possibility of the use of force; remunerative power, grounded in the possibility of rewards; and normative power, grounded in the possibilities of esteem, prestige, ritualistic symbols, acceptance, or affirmation.

Etzioni goes on to suggest that organizations must constantly be concerned about maintaining the involvement of participants if they are to get results: Such involvement, he says, can be of three types: alienative, or negative involvement against the will of the participant; calculative involvement, in which the participant is involved out of an expectation of gain or benefit; and moral or normative involvement, which he says can be of two types. Pure moral involvement is grounded in internalized norms and identification with the authority and social involvement; the second type "tends to develop in horizontal relationships like those in various types of primary groups" (Etzioni, 1961, p. 11). He concludes that the most effective combinations are three "congruent" types along the diagonal: alienative involvement with coercion; calculative involvement with remuneration; and moral involvement with normative rewards (Figure 16.1).

The practice implications of this model are straightforward and powerful. Literally, when people are in it against their will, you may need to force them to comply. When they are in it for the money, you should be able to buy their compliance. If they are in it out of commitment, they will comply if you give them the symbolic rewards they seek: gratitude, praise, or promise of a place in heaven, and so forth.

Etzioni's use of the term *power* in a compliance theory approach to authority is typical of such usage in much contemporary sociology and social

Figure 16.1 Etzioni's Theory of the Congruence of Involvement and Compliance

	Coercive	Compliance Utilitarian	Moral
Alienative	●		
Calculative		●	
Normative			●

(Involvement)

work, but it is also problematic. Why this is so is discussed more thoroughly in chapter 17.

MARY PARKER FOLLETT'S THEORIES OF POWER

Perhaps no one in modern management has struggled more successfully with the distinctions between authority and power than Mary Parker Follett, a management theorist and political philosopher of democracy who began her career as a caseworker. Many of her ideas still have powerful implications for social work even though her name fails to appear in most contemporary social work texts. Some of Follett's ideas allow us to link the idea of power directly with conflict, problem solving, and decision making.

Follett hypothesized that any conflict could be resolved in any one of four ways: "(1) voluntary submission of one side; (2) struggle and the victory of one side over the other; (3) compromise; or (4) integration." According to Wren (1979),

> Both one and two were clearly unacceptable because they involved the use of force or power to dominate. Compromise was likewise futile because it postponed the issue and because the "truth does not lie 'between' the two sides." Integration involved finding a solution which satisfied both sides without compromise and domination. (p. 327)

More recently, such solutions have been called win-win ones and emphasize negotiation (Fisher & Ury, 1981).

For many people, authority is associated with voluntary submission, power with the ideas of imposed solutions and domination, whereas the influence of a skilled mediator is used to find a solution that satisfied both sides without compromise and domination. According to Daniel Wren, Follett was one of the first to attempt to shift authority from position to knowledge. In a paper she did for the Taylor Society, the official body of scientific management, she said:

> If, then, authority is derived from function, it has little to do with hierarchy of position as such. . . . We find authority with the head of the department, with an expert . . . the dispatch clerk has more authority in dispatching work than the President . . . authority should go with knowledge and experience. (Wren, 1979, p. 330)

Follett's work was also an important precursor of contemporary calls for the adage that knowledge is power. Wren (1979) says that Follett "called for a new philosophy of control which (1) was 'fact-control rather than man-control,' and (2) 'correlated control' rather than 'super-imposed control'" (p. 331). Thus, Follett may have been the first to place emphasis on the role of what are currently called information and knowledge as factors in authority. Each situation, she argued, "created its own control because it was the facts of the situation and the interweaving of the many groups in the situation that determined appropriate behavior. Most situations were too complex for central control from the top to function effectively; therefore controls were to be gathered or 'correlated' at many points in the organizational structure" (Wren, 1979, p. 332).

One of the innovations that Follett sought was to encourage depersonalized power or authority through what she called "the law of the situation." Weber's solution to the same problem was that depersonalized authority was positional, located in the office or position.

> Follett sought to develop "power with" instead of "power over" and "co-action" to replace consent and coercion. When there was an "order-giver" and an "order-taker," integration was difficult to achieve. The role of "boss" and "subordinate" created barriers to recognizing the commonality of interests. To overcome this, Follett proposed to "depersonalize" orders and to shift obedience to the "law of the situation." (Wren, 1994, p. 329)

Where this is the case, Follett argued, it becomes unnecessary for one person to give orders to another. Both are, she said, guided by the situation. It might be more accurate to say that both guide themselves by their shared understanding of the situation. Although her original language is a bit fulsome, this idea itself has proved to be a durable one during the past 50 years. The practice literature of social work at all levels is filled with examples of such group process by group leaders, supervisors, consultants, and community groups. Particularly in the context of established peer relations—whether the relations of professional peers or the mutuality of fellow citizens in a community setting—domination, command and control, and giving orders to others increasingly take a back seat to the need for consensus building and being guided by the situation.

In a very interesting way, Follett's situational model of authority melds with Etzioni's third pattern of normative compliance and with at least a portion of Weber's charismatic authority. It rests in the process of individuals voluntarily taking responsibilities upon themselves without the need for either coercion or reward, simultaneous measures of individual and group self-management. Daniel Wren (1979) summarized this as: "The basis for control resided in self-regulating, self-directing individuals and groups who recognized common interests and controlled their tasks to meet the objective" (p. 332). This notion of self-regulating individuals and groups is identified elsewhere as "civic republicanism" and is a fundamentally important ideal both in the history of social work and in American culture.

As a result of this, Follett should be accorded a role as one of the sociological developers of the modern concept of social self-control. Within management, hers was a dramatic new philosophy of organizational control grounded in intelligent, knowledgeable managers and workers who share a common interest expressed through the vision, mission, goals, and objectives of the organization. This model of self-control by individuals and groups is not at all the same thing as the traditional notion of group-control, which involves the domination and suppression of individuality by the group or by a single leader. It is quite properly seen as an entirely new philosophy and sociology of organizational control and authority. Although it was first articulated in the 1920s and 1930s, it has only been more recently that concrete expressions of this model have made serious inroads into American management thinking and practice in the form of management by objectives, total quality management, process reengineering, and the like.

In laying out this view, Follett (1942) steers us on a middle course between the traditional poles of the cynical view based in profit and self-interest and the idealistic view of social service as pure altruism:

> We work for profit, for service, for our own development, for the love of creating something. At any one moment, indeed, most of us are not working directly or immediately for any of these things, but to put through the job in hand in the best possible manner . . . The professions have not given up the money motive. . . . Professional men [sic] are eager enough for large incomes; but they have other motives as well, and they are often willing to sacrifice a good slice of income for the sake of these other things. We all want the richness of life in the terms of our deepest desire. We can purify and elevate our desires, we can add to them, but there is no individual or social progress in curtailment of desires." (p. 145)

LEGITIMACY

One of the qualities associated with the idea of authority is the idea of legitimacy as a necessary quality of authoritative action. Legitimacy in this case involves conformity to recognized rules or accepted standards. Legitimation is a term for the social process by which such conformity is established and maintained, as for example, through the justification of rules or standards. Legitimation in this sense is a key process of institutionalization as that idea was discussed in previous chapters. Successful institutions are legitimate institutions.

Berger and Luckmann (1990) discuss legitimation within the context of symbolic universes or what have come to be known as *paradigms*. A paradigm is a model or scheme that organizes our view of something. In the institutional context of community social services delivered by social agencies, it is possible to identify four such symbolic universes that intersect and overlap and that are important to the process of establishing the legitimacy of the resulting institutions. We will call them simply profession, community, program, and policy.

Berger and Luckmann suggest that it is possible to identify four different levels of legitimation that should apply to any of these paradigms.

Incipient Legitimation

Merely having words for things offers the lowest level of legitimation of any object. Thus, merely being able to talk about "programs," "budgets," and "clients" makes them real and lends legitimacy to activities associated with those objects. For example, before "affirmative action" became a named policy it was not possible to view it as either legitimate or illegitimate. There were simply no words with which to adequately express either idea. Likewise, program and policy statements often begin with definitions that signal the terms and phrases that are of greatest importance.

Proverbial "Theories"

A second level of legitimation is provided by proverbs, moral maxims, wise sayings, legends and folk tales, and other examples of what Berger and Luckmann call "theoretical propositions in rudimentary form." These are based on accumulated human experience and in the context of social administration are commonly known by such labels as *practice wisdom* or *the voice of experience*. Although much is typically made by students of the great gap between theory and reality, social administration theory, like most practice theory, is only one step removed from the practice wisdom of its practitioners.

Thus, for example, the widely quoted maxim that "power corrupts and absolute power corrupts absolutely" is often used to delegitimate the idea of strong central authority (Greene, 1998). Perhaps the single most common and instructive example of legitimation by proverb in social services is the widespread use of stories, examples, and anecdotes to justify the effectiveness of social service outcomes. The way in which this practice is consistently maligned by data-oriented evaluation researchers overlooks the authority that such concrete examples, carefully chosen and to the point, have with various stakeholders and publics.

Body of Knowledge

A third level of legitimation brings us into the true domain of expert knowledge. Legitimation at this level is to be found in the explicit theories of a differentiated body of knowledge. In social science, this is the peculiar and distinctive legitimation of scientific validation, or what Abraham Kaplan (1964) called "intersubjective testability."

Thus, for example, policy practice theory and family therapy practice theory may be used to legitimate discrete activities associated with "issue mobilization" and "family narrative," respectively. Thus, full legitimacy at the third level is truly available only to those who know and understand the theory, with a kind of shadow or faith-based legitimacy granted by those willing to take the knowledge of the experts on faith.

Symbolic Universes

The fourth and highest level of legitimation is what Berger and Luckmann (1966) call symbolic universes or "bodies of theoretical tradition that integrate different provinces of meaning and encompass the institutional order in a symbolic totality" (p. 95).

This is the level of concerns for the legitimacy of things like capitalism, civil society, and the rule of law. This is also the level that we suggested in chapter 3 as being most problematic for social services, the level at which the legitimacy of the full enterprise of the welfare state and of social services in general is at issue. Social work has made remarkable strides in the past two decades at the level of creating symbolic universes for entire fields of practice like mental health and children's services. Less impressive and much less frequent have been the attempts at legitimating specific services, such as protective services, adoptions, and counseling, and specific agencies with broader publics of stakeholders. For the most part, the assorted institutions of the social work profession have appeared much more concerned with legitimating services and agencies internally to the professional and relying upon less-sophisticated devices like the coercive powers of licensure and certification.

CONCLUSION

What, then, is the nature of authority in social services and social agencies? For social services and social agencies to be viable as social institutions we need some way to draw a link between the personal behavior and the institutions as worthwhile and appropriate social mechanisms. Authority and legitimacy are the key links that forge that particular chain of connections.

Each of the approaches to authority reviewed in this chapter brings to light different aspects of the problem of authority as experienced in this context.

There clearly are cases of Weber's rational–legal authority to be found in the world of social services. To the extent, for example, that a social worker feels confident and justified to act in the face of opposition by virtue of a legislative enactment, court ruling or agency policy, one can feel and see the palpable effect of rational–legal authority. Likewise, where workers feel a desire to carry on the legacy of an agency or program, traditional authority in our second sense is at work, and where they begin to question such continuity, we begin to see the breakdown of traditions. Charismatic authority may be embodied in persons, as noted. It may also be vested in ideas like the vision of postwar social services, discussed in chapter 3. Indeed, the assorted calls for "revisioning" social services and updating the mission of social agencies are implicitly calls for more charismatic ideas that may mobilize, empower, uplift, and inspire new confidence in social services and social agencies.

It is authority that gives an executive director's memorandum its impact, or in Etzioni's sense, its power, just as it is the caseworker's legal authority to remove a child from the home. All social workers, however, do well to heed the correlations that Etzioni drew between the power of authority and its impact upon involvement and compliance. He is correct that alienative involvement may only be dealt with effectively by coercive means. This has two important ramifications. One is to avoid the trap set by the exchange perspective of seeing all relationships in social services as essentially remunerative ones. Not everyone is in it for the rewards, and even those who are may not always comply exclusively on utilitarian grounds. One of the valid points of the human relations approach to organizations that remains valid today was its attempts to escape the "iron cage" of such narrow utilitarianism. Sometimes lunchrooms can be as effective as salary increases in motivating people, and it isn't always because of the benefit directly conferred—in this case, a neat new place to eat lunch. It may also be the simple fact of the attention paid by management to worker's interests or the symbolic reward it implies of a job well done.

One of the truths of the Weberian model of authority is that a certain amount of authority rests in the office or position one holds. Smith and Raven, discussed in chapter 17, refer to this as official or positional power, but it is really more than simply the ability to get a result. It is also the ability to make the result stick or endure and for people to perceive it as real and binding.

CHAPTER 17

Power and Influence

What happens in those cases where there is not a clear, decisive exercise of authority? How can authoritative decisions be made, for example, by a coordinating committee of agency executives or supervisors who don't all agree on what should be done? What about situations where it is not clear who is in charge or who has authority in the situation, or what levels of legitimacy may be accorded any resulting decision by the various audiences involved? How can an agency operate with a female administrator whose authority is doubted and openly challenged by insubordinate male employees who question her right to give them directions and expect their compliance? And, how can a child welfare agency's actions in removing children from an abusive home or a mental health involuntary commitment retain legitimacy in the face of vocal opposition by friends, neighbors, and family members? How can a social work ombudsperson, acting alone, face down a national nursing home corporation accused of abusing the rights of an elderly resident? How can disagreements among professionals from different professions ever be resolved when they can't even agree upon shared definition of the problem?

These questions all involve similar cases of potentially inadequate authority. How can social administrators act decisively and authoritatively in circumstances in which their authority is unclear, in which the assignment of responsibilities is uncertain, or in which the legitimacy of their actions is suspect? The answer in all cases is to be found in the interrelated concepts of power and influence. It may not be a set of answers with which everyone in social work is comfortable. However, at present, a number of important administrative matters come down to exercises of power and influence.

POWER DEFINED

Power in this case can be defined as the ability to achieve a result even in the face of opposition, whereas *influence* is the effect we may have on others regardless of whether or not we intend to do so. Many social workers, influenced by ideas of consensus and cooperation, have demonstrated great discomfort with the idea of power and the related concepts of opposition and conflict. This has been mitigated to some extent recently as the concept of empowerment has come into widespread use. Though talk of empowerment of clients may increase awareness of this dimension of human behavior, it also introduces the possibility that partial understanding of the complex phenomena of power and influence will be mistaken for the whole. In clinical empowerment theory, genuine power is sometimes treated in very antiseptic ways, freed from some of its consequences, as though the possession of power were an unmitigated good in and of itself. Having power can be perceived as an unreservedly good thing by those who don't see themselves as possessing any, especially if they are willing to overlook the sometimes troublesome and vexing implications often associated with its exercise.

THE EMPOWERMENT CUL-DE-SAC

The development during the past decade of a set of practice concepts and ideas associated with the central concept of empowerment makes the already complex discussion of power, authority, and influence in administration even more complicated. In this section, we show that contemporary theories of powerlessness are—appropriately—clinical in origin and usage. As such, they are largely inapplicable to a very deep or satisfactory understanding of the role of power in social administration. Theories of *empowerment* as they have developed in social work practice and human behavior are generally concerned with bringing power to those who are powerless—those lacking or with a shortage of power. The need for this is largely unquestioned in contemporary social work, and we do not intend to raise issues with it. As the political philosopher Michael Sandel (1996) notes, the poor and powerless are often "caught in the grip of impersonal structures of power that defy our understanding and control" (p. 201). It is the case, however, that the kind of interpersonal efficacy being discussed as empowerment in social work practice is dramatically different from the exercises of political power one can expect to encounter in the governance of social service institutions.

The conceptualization of the role of power in social administration laid out in this chapter concurs to a large extent with the reconceptualization called for by Hyde (1989). Power is, indeed, not a zero-sum concept (you have it and I don't or vice versa). And power can well be an "infinite, unifying, enabling, facilitating and democratizing" (p. 155) force in social administration and in society. We stop short, however, of concurring with those who would suggest that this view of power necessarily favors either the desirability or the practicality of nonhierarchical organization. Such a notion may appear feasible in the broad context of social theory and worthy of pursuit in social reform. In the everyday context of social agencies with real contracts with real government agencies, United Ways, foundations, and insurance companies, it is an impractical idea. It is more likely to leave its advocates dumbfounded at their losses than to aid them in achieving their goals. In saying this, we bring this concept of social administration to the side of the liberal, rather than the radical, feminists.[1]

Empowerment perspectives are generally immature or narrow enough that they do not recognize the seemingly paradoxical reality that the success of empowering individuals eventually confronts the reality of getting beyond power to community as well as authority. The very idea of community and the associated concept of citizenship embraces the idea of competent or empowered individuals (Vincent & Plant, 1984). Yet many of the client groups with which social work deals are often far from the point of reaching beyond power. Social administration generally operates in the intermediate zone in which the actors are assumed to be empowered in this elementary sense, yet regularly move beyond power, through the exercise of legitimate authority and, when such authority is insufficient, through the exercise of influence.

To better understand this distinction, we need to look briefly at the concept of empowerment as it has evolved in the social work literature. According to Robbins, Chatterjee, and Canda (1998), "Empowerment theories are based on the idea that society consists of stratified groups possessing different and unequal levels of power and control over resources" (p. 91). In this context, it is virtually a definition of the situation that organizational contexts are stratified with actors in different positions possessing differing and unequal levels of power in the form of control over resources. It is also frequently the case that different self-help groups have very different ideas about empowerment (Humphreys & Kaskutas, 1995). Staples (1990) sees empowerment as the cultivation of a collective ability of relatively weak groups to develop sufficient leverage to transform institutional power relationships into a configuration more favorable to their own needs and interests.

Yet it is not primarily a recognizable political power—what the U.S. Constitution refers to as a redress of grievances, for example—that empowerment generally seeks. Empowerment is generally concerned with personal efficacy well below the threshold of such overtly political activity or active citizenship. Power, in the context of empowerment theory, refers to the ability to access and control resources and people. There is a major gap, however, between the conception of power as a resource of fully competent citizen/actors and the conceptions of its absence among empowerment theorists. The absence of power is termed *powerlessness* by empowerment writers. Those with notions of power founded in the classic perspectives can and do argue that no one capable of action can ever be completely powerless in a society as open as ours. Indeed, in one classical conception of this view, the fundamental choices are seen as the power to flee, speak up, or reach accommodation. Hirschman (1981) called these three options exit, voice, and loyalty. The challenge of empowerment is that it is usually concerned with bringing members of disadvantaged populations up to a threshold where they might be capable of exercising options such as these. This is fundamentally a clinical task.

The essentially clinical nature of contemporary social work conceptions of empowerment is evident in Barbara Simon's (1984) five basic components of the empowerment approach:

1. Construction of collaborative partnerships between workers and clients
2. An emphasis on strengths rather than weaknesses
3. Focus on individuals and their social environments
4. Recognition of rights, responsibilities and needs of clients and client groups
5. Direction of professional energies toward helping historically disempowered groups and their members

Powerlessness in this context is "the inability to manage emotions, skills, knowledge, and/or material resources in a way that effective performance of valued social roles will lead to personal gratification" (Solomon, 1976, quoted in Robbins et al., 1998, p. 91). "Empowerment theories propose that empowerment requires linking a sense of self-efficacy with critical consciousness and effective action" (Robbins et al., 1998, p. 91). Components of this theory of personal empowerment are borrowed more from liberation theology than from conventional political theory. In the liberation context, for example, Gutierrez (1973) suggested that the critical consciousness upon which empowerment is based consists of three cognitive components: identification with similar others, reducing self-blame for past events, and a sense of personal freedom. In such cases, *empowerment* is largely a process of building the self-confidence and social skill levels of the client to the point that he or she is willing to speak out and take other actions of basic citizenship.

Clearly there are important differences of degree involved here that add up to differences in kind. It is not too strong to suggest that considerations of power in social administration generally begin where empowerment perspectives leave off. As an example, Solomon's statement probably would not apply to the difficulties White House Counsel Abby Lowell was having in publicly controlling his emotions during the closing moments of his presentation to the House Impeachment Committee hearings in December 1998. One would hardly find credible the application of the term "powerless" to a White House Counsel testifying before a committee of Congress on national television. However, his was clearly a very special sense of powerlessness. His inability to prevent what he clearly felt to be an unjustified action by the committee to vote to impeach and his consequent difficulty in controlling his rage and frustration are important empowerment considerations in a social administration context but not a clinical context.

It is virtually axiomatic that professionals in official positions with organizations are seldom, if ever, powerless in Solomon's sense, except momentarily. Yet they may indeed at times be powerless to control the flow of events. It is important to recognize that although the term is the same, these are not at all the same thing. Appointment to even the lowliest positions in an organization, along with acceptance of any professional job, ordinarily carries with it certain explicit powers such as the ability to act on behalf of the agency in particular ways as well as specific access to or control over resources. Together, these explicit and implied powers make powerlessness, in the sense of inability to manage one's emotions or lacking in self-efficacy, a special disabling condition. Again, empowerment as personal efficacy is simply not what talk of power and empowerment in the context of social administration is all about.

In general, we must assume that theories of authority, power, and influence as they are used in social administration operate several orders of magnitude beyond the threshold level conception of empowerment. We generally assume in social administration that actors, including client representatives, are already empowered in the above sense and that they are possessed of an ability to function effectively in organizational settings. Thus, even with a full and complete understanding of empowerment, social administrators need to come to terms with power and conflict at a higher level if they expect to achieve positive results.

At this higher level, power may be defined in any number of different ways. In fact, one of the difficulties with the concept of power is that there are so many definitions. During the 1950s, the behaviorist school of American political scientists went so far as to reject entirely the concept of power. Part of what they were reacting to was the tradition—still very evident in social work—of expressing the laws of power in simple aphorisms like that old favorite "power abhors a vacuum" or that "power corrupts, and absolute power corrupts absolutely." Or that power only arises in the breakdown of more "normal" social relations, and in particular in the breakdown of communication and consensus. This latter view is unfortunately one of the few misleading tenants from the Mary Parker Follett legacy.

A major issue is whether power is a distinctive type of relationship or an attribute of many different types of relationship. Max Weber (1947b), whose own writings on authority are so authoritative, defined *power* as a propensity or likelihood: "the probability that one actor within a social relationship will be in a position to carry out his own will despite resistance" (p. 152). This is important because power is a concept with extremely strong potential for circular logic. For example, philosopher Bertrand Russell's famous definition of power is that it is the ability to make things happen, which leads to the simplistic view that if something happens, it is because someone in power willed it to happen, and if it does not, it is because they did not want it to happen. This approach is fraught with great difficulties. One fundamental fact of power in the present context is that the power of public and nonprofit organizations to resist meddling by individual public officials as opposed to the collective will of legislatures, for example, will typically be cast as intransigence, self-interest, or worse (Randall, 1979).

It is also extremely easy to confound the use of power with the related notion of control. Thus, one conventional definition of power is the ability to control others. There is also a strong component in the progressive tradition of seeing power as an illegitimate or improper use of influence or authority. The reasons for this are largely historical. When early twentieth-century social workers sought to deal with the abuses of industrialization, they often found those abuses defended by powerful state and local politicians ("bosses") and political organizations ("machines"). Thus, it was easy for them to interpret their own position as benevolent and reasonable and to conclude that the motives of any who opposed them must be irrational, petty, banal, and corrupt and therefore illegitimate.

Political scientist James MacGregor Burns (1978) saw power and its relationship to values as the key problem of social science. There is something of a tendency in social administration writings to see power as a natural force in human behavior. Yet, in a certain sense, power as a factor in human relationships is also a social institution. It is a human invention (what Herbert Simon calls "an artifice") and also a situational emergent. Power is not a factor in all situations, and the circumstances that lead to considerations of power, such as the collapse or weakness of authority, are themselves interesting to consider.

CLASSICAL PERSPECTIVES

One of the interesting things about social work is that it has in various ways held out alternatives to power as domination throughout the past century. Various notions put forth by Jane Addams, Mary Parker Follett, and a host of others have generally centered upon the idea of the intelligent use of influence and authority for the good of others.[2] As Addams's (1930) musings on her classical education suggest, there is something of the ancient Greek model of philanthropy in all this. The classicist Christian Meier (1998) argued that the fundamental aim of the ancient Greek aristocrat was not domination but the cultivation of excellence in himself and others. One way to bring the liberal arts more directly to bear upon social administration, as the current accreditation standards mandate, is to explore more fully this notion of professionalism as the cultivation of personal excellence. The view of empowerment noted earlier certainly fits within this framework. Viewed in this light, administrative power might also be seen as a tool for the cultivation of excellence in oneself and others.

This contrasts dramatically with most discussions of power in the management literature. Philip Selznick (1995) said that the modern social sciences are to a great extent afflicted with what he calls a "low politics" model (p. 108). This model stresses only the play of power and self-interest as opposed perhaps to a politics of character, philanthropy, and public good like that to be found in Jane Addams's and other social work writings. Political scientists and others committed to the "realism" of the low politics model have long perceived naïve idealism in Addams's writings and in social work. These and other attempts to characterize social workers in general as high minded but unrealistic suggest that striving for a politics of higher good can, indeed, fall victim both to empty high mindedness and to unfair attack. This dynamic was a factor in the progressive spirit of nonpartisan social reform in the 1890s, but it was just as evident in the pursuit of the ideals of efficiency and effectiveness in the 1990s.

MACHIAVELLI

One cannot seriously pursue this distinctive social work vision of power for long without coming to terms with the Italian Renaissance humanist Niccolò Machiavelli, whose two great works, *The Prince* and *The Discourses*, form so much of the backbone of contemporary thought on power. For Machiavelli, there are two worlds. There is a private world governed by personal morality and the world of public organization. Various interpreters have fashioned this as the distinct worlds of morality and politics, but the noted political philosopher Isiaah Berlin (1998) argued that there is more to Machiavelli than this:

> His vision is social and political. Hence the traditional view of him as simply a specialist on how to get the better of others, a vulgar cynic who says that Sunday-school precepts are all very well, but in a world full of evil men you too must lie, kill and so on if you are to get somewhere, is incorrect. The philosophy summarized by "Eat or be eaten, beat or be beaten" . . . is not what is central in him. (p. 301)

What, then, is it that Berlin sees in Machiavelli that should interest us here? The answer, it seems, only begins with Machiavelli's uncompromisingly realistic view of public power from which a great many people choose to turn away. It also embraces his uncompromising humanism and what might be termed the moral ideal of serving the community, including the exercise of power when that is necessary as the highest way of life available to humans.

> Machiavelli's values, I should like to repeat, are not instrumental but moral and ultimate, and he calls for great sacrifices in their name. For them he rejects the rival scale–the Christian principles of *ozio* and meekness—not, indeed, as being defective in itself, but as inapplicable to the conditions of real life; and real life for him means not merely (as is sometimes alleged) life as it was lived around him in Italy. . . .
>
> The moral ideal for which he thinks no sacrifice too great—the welfare of the *patria*—is for him the highest form of social existence attainable by man; but attainable, not unattainable; not a world outside the limits of human capacity, given human beings as we know them. (Berlin, 1998)

In other words, if Berlin is correct it is possible to move beyond the more cynical side of Machiavelli in the exercise of power for its own sake, or for purely venal and self-serving ends. One can see also in the exercise of power a view that also embraces the greatest possibilities of social life. We would argue that Jane Addams, Mary Parker Follett, and others among the most illustrious leaders of social work have understood this connection among power, community, and institution building in similar ways.

THE POWER ELITE DEBATE

Much of the contemporary social work perspective on power arose out of the context of an intellectual debate over the issue several decades ago. Even today, discussions of power in social work are grounded in what was at the time termed the power elite debate. Generally, social workers like most American social scientists are still largely divided into two camps: the *pluralists* hold to a view most cogently articulated by the political scientist Robert Dahl (1960) that power is widely distributed and fluid. C. Wright Mills (1956) articulated the idea of a *power elite*, a system, based on economic and social class, of power distribution operating at national and/or community levels.

The Pluralist Position

The core of the pluralist position on power is the view that the political resources that make up power are not limited to wealth and high social status. Dahl (1960) argued that political resources tend to be so diverse and widely distributed that no single elite can ever have a monopoly on them, hence, the notion of multiple or plural sources of power and the central doctrine of pluralism. A distribution of power, like a distribution of labor, is characterized by differentiation. Different power groups are influential in different issue areas. Mills (1956), the leading voice of the power elite thesis, accurately summarized the pluralist view of a system of power as "a moving balance of many competing interests" (p. 135).

Perhaps the most general update on the pluralist position was the expression of "interest group liberalism," conceived by Theodore Lowi (1969) and others as a regime in which political power is divided among multiple, competing organized interest groups.

The Power Elite Thesis

In contrast to the pluralist view, Mills (1956) wrote:

> There is no longer, on the one hand, an economy and on the other, a political order containing a military establishment unimportant to politics and to money making. There is a political economy numerously linked with military order and decision. This triangle of power

is now a structural fact, and it is a key to any understanding of the higher circles in America today. (p. 133).

Mills's power elite thesis received an incomparable boost in 1960 when President Eisenhower in his farewell address as president referred to the continuing influence of the "military industrial complex." Mills's triangle of corporate, military, and political powers was expanded by other theorists to include the mass media and organized labor. This power elite, which came to be labeled "The Establishment" during the 1960s, was a stock feature of New Left political thought and still exercises an important influence on much community practice thinking in social work, although its general political salience has declined markedly. Mills's concern was primarily at the national level. However, studies of community power by Floyd Hunter (1953) and others tended to reinforce the view of domination of community political elites as well.

It is probably fair to say that the elitists concentrated on the sources of power, whereas the pluralists concentrated on its actual exercise. One of the conventional criticisms of the power elite view by the pluralists is that "nothing categorical can be assumed about power in any community" (Nelson Polsby, quoted in Bachrach & Baratz, 1970, p. 142). In other words, it is probably not possible to definitely identify the full extent of *any* power structure at *any* time. It should be noted here that this view is closely associated with and reinforced by the limits-of-knowledge and the cost-of-information perspectives of Lindblom, Simon, and others discussed previously as well as the Berger–Luckmann perspective on legitimation processes discussed in chapter 16 and the Banfield perspective on influence discussed later in this chapter.

Closely associated with the noncategorical nature of power in the view of the pluralists is the changing nature of power structures, so far as they can be known. Again, quoting Polsby: "To presume that the set of coalitions which exists in the community at any given time is a timelessly stable aspect of social structure is to introduce systematic inaccuracies into one's description of social reality" (Bachrach & Baratz, 1970, p. 143). In other words, there may be various powerful elites in various communities at various times, but it would be a mistake, the pluralists have argued, to assume the existence of precisely the kind of fixed, unchanging controlling structure posited by Mills forty years ago.

This is closely related to a second major criticism, directed particularly at the methodology employed by Hunter's reputational method. A reputation of being "powerful" does not necessarily translate into the actual exercise of power. It should be noted, however, that within administrative settings a reputation of being powerful or for "getting things done" could, itself, constitute a form of influence as that concept is discussed below.

AGENDA CONTROL

One of the most widely practiced and well-understood forms of power among administrators is action to control the agenda of issues, concerns, and decisions under consideration in the agency. Bachrach and Baratz (Bachrach, 1980; Bachrach & Baratz, 1970) argued that power has two faces: overt and covert. It is usually the fear or suspicion of the covert, "under the table" exercise of power that most troubles and concerns agency employees. However, for skillful administrators, some forms of covert power are merely par for the course, and others are simply a temporary condition. Sometimes things are just accepted at face value; it doesn't really matter who, if anyone, is pulling the strings or controlling a situation behind the scenes. What matters here is that they are being pulled and one must respond. In other cases, such covertness is merely a temporary condition until the real power actors are unmasked, discovered, or identified.

Moreover, power may be exercised in anticipation of an event as well as in response to it. Power may be exercised, for example, by confining discussion to safe issues and avoiding controversial matters that might undermine the administrator's control.

BASES OF SOCIAL POWER

One of the most frequently cited studies of "social power" actually deals with a mixture of what we are here singling out as authority, power, and influence. John French and Bertram Raven (1968) presented five bases of "social power."

Legitimate power rests on authority of law, tradition, or charisma. *Referent* power is said to rest on identification with a reference group and a desire to be like the group or its leaders. *Coercive* power rests on the ability to punish or threaten. *Reward* power rests on power to distribute positive sanctions. *Expert* power rests on superior knowledge or expertise in particular areas.

Legitimate power, of course, is our definition of authority, and French and Raven singled out the three Weberian sources of legitimacy to make their point. Their category of referent power, as we shall see below, is not actually power at all as we are dealing with it and fits the full measure of *influence* as we deal with that term below. As Weber noted, coercive power, grounded in the ability to threaten or punish, can vary all the way from fully legitimate authority as in the case of imprisonment for crimes to fully illegitimate as in the case of enforcement by gangs or criminal organizations. Reward power, like its effect that Etzioni termed "utilitarian compliance," depends on the ability to affect the distribution of goods and services. In most instances, expert power, as with scientists and professionals, either takes the form of legitimate authority or fails as power. Failure would come if a powerful-but-not-authoritative doctor or a social worker attempted to enforce his or her professional opinion over against organized opposition.

It should be noted that these are anything but exclusive categories. The well-known problems of transference and counter-transference in traditional therapy, for example, are concerned with sorts of referent power. That referent power may be held by a charismatic worker, licensed by the state to perform psychotherapy, whose expert knowledge includes knowledge of when and how to use both negative and positive sanctions. Nevertheless, their value as ideal types for sensitizing social administrators to possible varieties of social power is substantial.

Another of the most influential modern perspectives on power in sociology and social work is that of exchange theory, in which power is seen as a fungible personal resource, akin to and exchangeable with money, status, knowledge, and other "resources" (Blau, 1967). The French and Raven perspective on the five types of social power is an exchange theory approach. Central to all exchange theory approaches to power are the concepts of reciprocity and the norm of distributive justice. This is an important connection. One of our former colleagues had a habit of presenting his ideas and proposals to others explicitly in terms of such reciprocity. Whenever he wanted anyone to do something, he would present his idea to them with an almost ceremonial phrase: "I've got something here that will make me look good, and you look wonderful!"[3] Many presenters are far less open, explicit, and direct about their attempts to influence others in an exchange perspective. Nonetheless, the classic form of attempting to influence in exchange theory is to appeal to a listener to act in a certain manner sought by a speaker because, in the speaker's view, doing so will have certain advantages for the listener or a distribution of advantages for both.

POWER AND THE POLITICAL

How and why does power arise as a factor in social administration? As we saw earlier, in the case of the empowerment discussions in social work, this is largely a matter of facilitating the self-control discussed previously of clients. In other cases, it is probably more accurate to see power as an emergent necessity in situations where authority in its traditional, rational, and charismatic forms does not reach. Power was not much of a factor at Hull House, for example, because of Addams's well-documented charismatic authority (Lohmann, 2000). Likewise, power will seldom be much of a factor in those group situations where consensus truly governs.

The political philosopher Benjamin Barber (1988) offered a very profound commentary on the emergent nature of power and "the political" in human affairs and their ability to arise in nonpolitical circumstances. He terms this phenomenon "the sovereignty of the political":

> To speak of the autonomy of the political is in fact to speak of the sovereignty of the political. For by sovereignty is meant not merely the dominion of the state over other forms of association, but the dominion of politically adjudicated knowledge, under conditions of epistemological uncertainty, over other forms of knowledge. To be sure, this sovereignty over knowledge is wholly residual: It comes into play only with the breakdown of ordinary cognitive consensus, and only where such public judgment is required by the need for common action. Where knowledge can prove itself certain, or at least where consensus is for the time being undisputed (as in the case of mainstream science, for example), or where the absence of consensus has no impact on public action (as in matters of private taste, for example), the political domain claims no sovereignty. But where scientists disagree on the public outcomes of experimental technologies (genetic engineering, for example), or where matters of taste are seen to have public consequences (the design of a national flag, for example), or where theoretical inquiry raises issues of common import (the dividing line between a fetus and a legal person, for example), the political realm necessarily becomes sovereign over the contested realms of science and taste and inquiry in which such disputes are ordinarily conducted. For at this point science, taste and theoretical inquiry are reduced to *opinion (doxa)*, and it is over opinion that sovereignty, defined by public judgment, necessarily holds sway, albeit only by default. . . .
>
> This lesson about the nature of political sovereignty can be reduced to a single priority rule: Whenever private theorists disagree on matters of public import, then the normal epistemological priority of truth over opinion is over-ridden and reversed in favor of the political priority of public over private. (pp. 14–15)

In other words, when some form of public or collective action is required and scientific, religious, traditional, and other forms of certain knowledge give way to uncertainty, the residual realm of the political will arise, and power will begin to replace authority as a dominant factor in human affairs.

Social administrators and others whose claims of legitimate authority are absent or undermined will find themselves resorting to the use of power. For decades, for example, the tobacco industry was successful at casting enough doubt on the scientific authority of the mountain of research evidence of the health risks of smoking to make it appear that the issue was a simple matter of personal preference. In similar ways, complex scientific and moral issues as diverse as abortion, evolution, and the nature of mental illness have, at various times, not been resolvable epistemologically as matters of truth and have been reduced to matters of politics and opinion. By contrast, even though there are people who believe that the earth is flat, for example, scientific authority holds on that issue. To believe that the earth is flat is not merely one opinion among equivalent, contending opinions; it is a scientifically and politically unimportant view attributed to cranks and crackpots.

INFLUENCE

The second key concept of this chapter is that of influence. Think of the effects that the mass media or the students who speak in your classes have on the development of your ideas and you can begin to come to terms with the idea of influence. Are you willing to concede that your daily newspaper or television station "has power over you"? Or are you willing to suggest that the news has no effect, whatsoever, on your view of the world? If your answer to both questions is "no," then you are precisely where most people come out with the idea of influence. To be influenced is to be subtly but voluntarily changed.

Theodorson and Theodorson (1969) defined influence as "the power to effect a voluntary change in a person's attitude or opinion through persuasive action" (p. 202). In the context of this discussion, and in light of difficulties with the concept of power already dealt with, it might be more accurate to think of influence as the *ability* to bring about such changes, rather than the *power* to. Further, it is important to note that such influence is primarily of interest in administration when such changes of attitude or opinion are associated with changes in behavior, such as voting or compliance with directives.

There has been limited attention to the importance of influence in organizations from time to time in the social work literature. For example, Albrecht, Irey, and Mundy (1982) focused on what they called "key communicators" who were viewed by their coworkers as credible information sources. Usually such influential figures were active people with strong communications skills. They tended to influence others by controlling the speed and quantity of information flow.

An example of the pure operation of influence might be the board member who says: "I was going to vote against this measure, but I really didn't understand it, and when I learned that the Board President was for it, I asked her about it. The way she explained it made me change my vote. I know she always does her homework, and I have the highest respect for her opinions on things." That isn't power. It's influence.

Power and influence are generally not seen as separate phenomena in exchange theory. Instead, influence is seen primarily as soft efforts to exercise power through verbal techniques, arguments, or persuasion. Influence in this sense is mostly a term for describing weaker, milder, and more socially acceptable forms of power. Along with this goes the highly useful idea of the possibilities of exchange between power and other values such as information, knowledge, and status as well as the rather cynical idea (contradicted by Barber above) that power is the determining factor in all human relations. To gain a deeper understanding of the possibilities of influence, however, we need to look beyond exchange theories.

In order to explore the concept of influence further, we will examine two radically different approaches to influence taken from two distinct research traditions.

Goffman's Theory of Influence

Working within a conceptual universe defined largely by theatrical and dramaturgical metaphors, the sociologist Erving Goffman (1956) put forth one of the most powerful and convincing—yet, for many people, troubling—bodies of work on influence. In a small book first published in 1956, Goffman outlined the view that people influence each other by means of elaborate symbolic devices as part of "performances" of social behavior organized and delivered much like actors on a stage.

According to Mitchell (1978), Goffman's perspective was directed, in part, at "the uncertainty, problematics and negotiation we see implicit in the course of human affairs" (p. 81). Goffman's sociology is, according to Mitchell, "an important addition and corrective to the exchange model in that he sees man's [sic] society as the result of a problematic process of the mutual exchange of utterances and support" (p. 84). The important overall point of Goffman's model for social administration is that it points out certain types of strategic interaction. Deliberate uses of self, role performances, staging of behavior ("let's sit over here so we can talk about the contract," etc.), and other performances are important aspects of social administration from a Goffmanesque view. This is so not least because of the personal representations of institutions that social administrators embody and because of the occasions they present for the deliberate exercise of influence.

Whether the reader finds Goffman's overall perspective cynical or convincing there are two particular aspects of his theatrical metaphor that we wish to note because of their importance in social administration. One is the notion of behavior as a series of deliberate or intentional performances. A distinction is made between impressions that are given off inadvertently by a social actor and deliberate attempts to manage impressions of others. Goffman saw performances and the impression management that lie behind them as the very center of efforts to influence others. By impression management he generally means presenting oneself to others in ways that are intentionally guided and controlled by the actor with the intent to focus and direct the impressions that others form. Regardless of whether one believes that all social behavior can be described in terms of performances, it is clear that most administrative behavior can be seen in these terms and analyzed by asking questions such as: What impression is she trying to leave? Who in this situation is he attempting to influence most? Why? And how?

The second aspect of Goffman's theatrical approach that can be easily and readily applied to social administration involves the differences he drew between *onstage* and *backstage* behavior and the conscious, deliberate uses that administrators routinely make of both. It follows that if there is a deliberate performance aspect to behavior, there will be times that the administrator will be onstage or in character and times when she will not. The simplest possible example of offstage behavior is what one will see in many executive offices when their occupants are working late at night or on weekends. One is likely to see people—men or women—dressed much less formally, acting much less formally, and overall behaving somewhat out of character, like actors backstage during rehearsal. Such actors will also tend to downplay the importance of their presence with statements like "I just wanted to get a little work done before tomorrow," or "I'm just trying to get a little ahead." But even in these informal circumstances, let an important stakeholder—a board president or officer, a contract monitor, or such— enter the scene and immediately our backstage actors, unkempt hair, casual clothes and all, will be back onstage. They will be performing as expected in the character of The Director or The Boss or whatever. This is not simply a distinction between formality and informality. Indeed, in many instances administrative actors will deliberately extend onstage performances to informal circumstances for deliberate effect: "Let's go somewhere comfortable where we can sit down, have a drink, and not be bothered by all these interruptions around the office. We need to talk about what to do with this issue."

Similarly, there are other forms of intentional dramatization that are carried out in very formal and very public circumstances. One would almost never expect to find a credible administrator publicly offering strong criticisms of a staff or board member or other stakeholder onstage in a public setting such as a full staff, board, or community meeting. At least, they would not do so without having carefully considered the implications, including possible legal ramifications, the probable effects of the public criticism for various audiences, and the alternatives. Even when such difficult or demanding performances are carried out in private, they may be staged and enacted deliberately for maximum effect.

One of the most sophisticated uses of the onstage/offstage distinction—but also one that can be highly dangerous if misused—is the administrative equivalent of the theatrical aside. An aside occurs when a character onstage momentarily steps out of character and looks out at the audience to offer a telling comment. The stage whisper meant to be overheard, the pause in a prepared speech or testimony to offer an out-of-character or out-of-sequence comment, the speaker who says "I'm going to put aside my prepared remarks because there is something else on my mind," and the like all represent such asides. In a very similar way, comments can be "whispered" to a trusted associate at the start of a meeting just loudly enough to ensure that they are heard by others in the room. Or, a deliberately revealed "secret" told to the office gossip can be prefaced with a statement like, "This isn't for public consumption yet, but. . . ."

Much of the successful social administrator's career is carried on in public and social settings, and much of it involves the conscious, deliberate construction of performances that will be closely observed by others. This might all be very sad and cynical were it not for a simple fact. Like the medieval courts, most others in those same situations are also performing and seeking to manage impressions and thereby exercise influence as well. Furthermore, everyone involved is usually aware of what is going on. Such mutual awareness does little to mar or detract from the effectiveness and effects of their performances in large part because of the legitimating power such performances have.

Banfield's Theory of Influence

The other perspective on influence examined here allows us to see more deeply into the process of decision making, particularly as it is carried out in circumstances of democratic governance and peer-influence in the professional social agency. A general tendency in politicized circumstances is to see untoward influences or covert power lurking behind every decision. As critics of the concept of power have often pointed out, pushing this view to its fullest extent simply reduces the idea of power to that of causation. Something happened. Therefore, someone very powerful must have made it happen, even though we can't identify exactly who it was or say for sure how she did it.

As we saw in the power elite debate above, there is also a strong tradition in the planning and administration literatures to see problem-solving activity, including planning and decision making, purely in rational terms. Results are caused. They occur only because someone somewhere intended, projected, and decided those particular results. The notion of unanticipated consequences is put forth in this context as a rather weak exception; sometimes rare things occur that nobody foresaw, planned, or intended. In actuality, such unanticipated *resultants* are often about as likely to occur as planned or projected outcomes, and anticipating the unexpected thus becomes a major aspect of management strategy. One of the most persistent reasons that things happen differently than expected is because not everyone expects the same thing. As a result, sometimes we may expect something, and the influence of someone else who expects something different prevails. In other cases, we may all expect different results and what happens may surprise us all.

The influence theory of Edward Banfield addressed this possibility and constructed a dramatically different view of decision making as a social process. The occasion for this theory was Banfield's (1986) study of a particular organization—the "political machine" in the city of Chicago, headed by long-time "boss" Mayor Richard J. Daley. It is a view grounded in the effects of interpersonal influence, a view that does not necessarily require identifiable decision makers or explicit decisions for a result to be arrived at. He wrote:

> We are apt to suppose that a "correct" or "consistent" policy must be the product of a mind (or minds) which has addressed itself to a "problem," and, by a conscious search, "found" or "constructed" a "solution." Most of our study of political and administrative matters proceeds on the assumption that all of the elements of a problem must be brought together within the purview of a single mind (whether of a person or a team) and that the task of organization is partly to assemble the elements of the problem. The more complicated the matter, the more obvious it seems that its solution must depend upon the effort of a mind which perceives the "problem" and deliberately seeks a "solution."(p. 589)

To support this view, Banfield began with the notion of critical decisions associated with Selznick and extended it to two types that he termed central decisions and social choices. *Central decisions* are made by some one individual or group to realize some type of specific intent. They are "in some sense purposeful or deliberate" (Banfield, 1986, p. 589). A *social choice*, by contrast, is "the accidental byproduct of two or more 'interested parties' who have no common interest and who make their selection competitively or without regard for each other." In this concept of a social choice, Banfield extended and routinized the concept of unanticipated consequences identified in earlier decision studies. Outcomes of social choices or problem solving can as likely be mere "resultants" as they are "solutions." Anyone familiar with administration can tell you that such social choices occur regularly. (For example, the report from one agency that "It was suddenly clear to everyone, even though we had never discussed it, that all of the principal administrators and supervisors supported getting rid of our XYZ program and moving all of the clients into other programs.")

Banfield attributed such resultants to "fragmentation of analysis," which is analysis of parts of the problem by different groups and individuals, each of which approaches it from his distinctive and limited view. Such fragmented analysis is clearly a close cousin of Herbert Simon's satisficing and Lindblom's strategic analysis:

> It may seem to common sense that because it is the product of intention, indeed of conscious and deliberate problem-solving, a central decision is much more likely to "work" than is a social choice. The social choice is, after all, an "accident"; it was not designed to serve the needs or wishes of the group, whereas the central decision was so designed. And yet, despite the presumptions of common sense, it may be that under certain circumstances the competition of forces which do not aim at a common interest produces outcomes which are more "workable," "satisfactory," or "efficient" than any that could be contrived by a central decision-maker consciously searching for solutions in the common interest. (Banfield, 1986, p. 590)

In this statement, Banfield merely made the case for administrators and decision makers to be attuned to the possible rise of fortuitous consensus. He went on, however, to make another very telling point. He suggested that no administrator can make decisions on grounds that are entirely logical. Decisions involve choices from among ranges of alternatives that are not really comparable, each of which has some desirable features. In other contexts, this is often called the apples and oranges problem. Moreover, such choices are usually made without resort to some higher value premise capable of reconciling the relative importance of these alternatives. There is no choice but to deliberately or unwittingly decide on the basis of criteria that are always open to question by those who may not put the same importance on that value (Banfield, 1986, pp. 591–92). In the absence of intersubjectively agreed-to values, there is only a single ultimate criterion and that is the distribution of influence. "The importance accorded to each alternative in a choice process depends, then, upon the relative amount of influence exercised on its behalf" (p. 592). Benjamin Barber made much the same point in an extensive quotation cited previously in this chapter.

Banfield saw a number of advantages to decisions based on the exercise of influence. Such exercises are likely to be part of broader institutions or situations in which decisions made this way are defined as legitimate. Those who see such decision making as unfair are likely to leave, seek changes in the rules, or withdraw by withholding their influence. Influence-based criteria do not emerge in a vacuum. They are likely to reflect the values and preferences of important groups such as stakeholders and the intensity with which they hold them. Finally, the nature or character of the influence exercised is often related to its perceived legitimacy in particular circumstances. Thus, influence on behalf of the common good is much more likely to be considered legitimate in a social service setting than in a business setting, for example.

At the same time, Banfield noted, the social choice process suffers from at least two inherent limitations. It can only take into account preferences and values that are expressed. Silence in influence-based decision processes is tantamount to powerlessness (Banfield, 1986, p. 595). Also, it is always possible that some result that might produce a greater total benefit will never be identified because it is not among the alternatives voiced by any of the influentials in the situation. Further, he noted, in particular cases, the distribution of influence may serve primarily to paralyze action altogether. Importantly, however, he pointed out also that "from a general standpoint, there is no presumption that 'inaction' represents a less desirable outcome than 'action'" (p. 596).

He identified four criteria for determining whether a social choice process is preferable to a central decision:

1. The complexity of the problem to be solved
2. The visibility of the factual and value elements to be taken into account
3. The presence of an appropriate "ultimate" criterion
4. The appropriateness of one or another procedural criterion (Banfield, 1986, p. 596)

Finally, Banfield noted that some processes are "mixed." A mixed process is a plurality of parties seeking their own advantage without common interaction, with a central decision maker who intervenes to (1) regulate the selection process so that "public values" or common goods are achieved, or at least not disregarded; (2) coordinate the activities of the interested parties toward an optimal solution or one in which no possible reallocation would make anyone better off without making others worse off; or (3) function as an environment to record the relative influence exercised by the competing interested parties.

> That the mixed decision-choice process . . . takes more time to produce an outcome than, presumably, a central decision process would take and that the outcome, when reached, is likely to be a stalemate cannot, of course, be held against it. Time spent discovering and evaluating the probable consequences of a proposal is not necessarily wasted; and if in the end nothing is done, or not much is done, that may be because it is in the public interest to do little or nothing. (Banfield, 1986, p. 598)

CONCLUSION

In this chapter, we examined some of the realities of power in the context of social administration. We noted that contemporary social work concerns with empowerment of client groups typically result in a level of personal efficacy well below that expected in social administration contexts. Consequently, discussions of empowerment often amount to little more than attempting to bring people up to minimal entry levels of personal power. We looked closely at lingering aspects of the power elite debate. Within organizations, social administrators are, by definition, a power elite, and it is difficult to envision organizations operating effectively any other way. Power becomes a factor, according to Benjamin Barber, in political conflicts, which are characterized by matters of shared or common interest and uncertainty.

We also looked closely at two perspectives on influence. Over the course of several decades, social psychologist Erving Goffman developed a model of strategic interaction in which both the metaphor of performances and the model of dramatic structure are used to understand human behavior. At roughly the same time, the political scientist Edward Banfield was exploring a dramatically different, but in many ways comparable, perspective on social influence as a factor in decision making. Both of them offered important insights into the nondeliberate, unintentional side of social administration.

CHAPTER 18

Marketing, Public Relations, and Advertising

Social workers everywhere are concerned that their work and the social service institutions in which they work are not well understood. They worry that because the agencies in which they work are misunderstood, people who could benefit from their services are not always aware of them. They also worry that the profession and their efforts are undervalued and unappreciated.

Leadership of the type we previously ascribed to social work administration can deal with this problem in either of two ways. One course is actions directed at social service personnel and intended to either help them cope with and adjust to these feelings of alienation or to organize effective action. Another course, which may or may not arise from such efforts, would be actions directed at enhancing the public image of the profession and of the institutions in which social workers are employed. Such efforts would involve the techniques of public relations, marketing, and advertising that are the topics of this chapter. In the 1980s, Robert Schneider suggested that social work administrators must respond to diverse audiences in representing their agencies and programs (Schneider & Sharon, 1982). Although skills in public relations, reporting, and community relations were already viewed as essential, professional social work literature then and now offers only limited conceptualizations and practice models.

Social work practitioner and student concerns with the image problems of social work form the backdrop for this chapter. We take the position that these concerns are accurately founded but that what to do about them has not been particularly well thought-out. At the core of the issue is the fact that social work and social services are not well recognized in contemporary American culture and public life and what is not recognized cannot be appreciated. Lack of understanding of the role and purposes of social work is, in fact, one symptom of the larger problem of incomplete institutionalization discussed earlier in this book. In this chapter, we examine the role of social administrators and other social work leaders in addressing this issue through the use of the tools of modern marketing, public relations, and advertising.

Part of the problem of institutionalization as we have dealt with it is very closely related to what marketing specialists call *branding*, or product identification and recognition. Calling attention to this connection is not always well received by social workers, however. The clear identification of the McDonald's corporation with hamburgers, the familiar red and yellow packaging, and the corporate symbol of the golden arches stands in stark contrast to the typical institutional ambiguity of social agencies and their vague mission statements calling for "meeting people's needs" and to a social work profession seemingly interested in nothing more clear-cut than "helping people." Certainly, there are notable exceptions to this. The crossword puzzle in our newspaper routinely carries the clue "nonprofit organization" and the answer is invariably YMCA, the four capital letters of which have become an instantly recognizable symbol in American culture.

Some of social service brand identification appears to be mere accidents of fortune. The universally recognizable Red Cross (and, increasingly, its Islamic variant, the Red Crescent) are highly visible positive symbols in every modern disaster or war. The familiar rainbow of the United Way logo owes some of its recognition to the campaign on behalf of the United Way carried on by the National Football League every fall. That adoption, however, was no accident. It was an act of pure marketing savvy. Unfortunately, there are far too few additional instances of clear brand identification associated with social services and social work. Possibly one of a hundred people in the general public who recognizes the YMCA as a charitable nonprofit might also be able to identify what the letters NASW stand for. The situation is much the same with local community agencies. The YMCA's name recognition has even benefited from a popular song frequently sung at college sporting events, accompanied by suitable hand gestures forming the letters. By contrast, the vast majority of social services remain largely unknown and unrecognized even in their own communities.

DEFINITIONS

Before we go any further, let's define a few terms. Marketing, according to Philip Kotler (1982), "is the effective management by an organization of its exchange relations with its various markets and publics" (p. xiii). Kinnear and Bernhardt (1983) defined marketing as "the performance of business activities that direct the flow of goods and services to the customers" (p. 8). As a body of knowledge in the management sciences, marketing is intended to "yield systematic insight into the structure and dynamics of market [and, Kotler could have added, nonmarket] exchanges" (Kotler, 1982, p. xiv). As a management activity, marketing involves analysis, planning, implementation, and control to "achieve its exchange objectives with its target markets" (Kotler, 1982, p. xiv). Wolf (1990) indicated that "marketing is the continuous diagnosis and analysis of the changing needs of customers, clients, and constituents and devising strategies to meet those needs" (p. 117). What all of these definitions share is a description of an interactive relationship involving a business (or agency) and its customers or clients.

As a field, public relations has traditionally been framed within a journalistic/mass media paradigm with attention to obtaining publicity in print and electronic media. Such efforts are typically directed both at the general public and at selected narrower target audiences termed "influentials," which would include the decision makers of management and planning theory. News releases, feature stories, promotional tie-ins, success stories, spokesperson tours, created or staged events (which Daniel Boorstin [1992] called pseudoevents), and teaching materials are among the familiar public relations devices. Seitel (1992, p. 6) differentiated public relations from marketing by indicating that whereas marketing and advertising have as their goals selling an organization's products, public relations attempts to sell the organization as a whole.

Advertising differs in degree from both marketing and public relations. It is principally concerned with the placement of paid messages of information, endorsement, or persuasion in various media. Display and classified ads in newspapers, magazines, professional journals and other print publications, commercials on radio and television, and various display ads on the Internet are among the most common examples of advertising. Seitel indicated that advertising differs from marketing and public relations in that the message sent is more controlled. The person doing the advertising pays for it and thus controls what is said, how it is said, to whom it is said, the medium for the message, and the frequency with which the message appears (Seitel, 1992, p. 329).

We deal with marketing, public relations, and advertising jointly and somewhat interchangeably in this chapter. In doing so, we recognize that were this a text on marketing or public relations or advertising, we would make sharper distinctions among these three approaches. Such fine distinctions are not needed or important for a general introduction to the uses that social workers may make of them.

Marketing, public relations, and advertising serve as alternative means of furthering the management objectives of improving the quality of information about social services, social work, and social welfare institutions possessed by various publics. They also serve to enhance the resource position of social agencies and ultimately to further the institutionalization of social services. Applications of marketing, public relations, and advertising to social services have received relatively little attention in the United States. Likewise, social service applications have received less attention than other nonprofit activities such as symphonies and museums, in which there may be both a clearer sense of product and a more clearly identified target audience.

Some of the ambivalence that social workers may have about these areas comes from a sense that advertising, marketing, and public relations are not always ethical fields. It should go without saying that the uses social workers make of these approaches should fit within the ethical framework of the profession. The NASW *Code of Ethics* does not have a section on advertising, but two provisions are applicable.

Section 4.06 (c) indicates that social workers should ensure that representations of their professional qualifications, credentials, education, competence, affiliations, services provided, or results to be achieved are accurate (National Association of Social Workers, 1996). That provision would certainly apply to any advertising or marketing that was done.

Section 4.07 (b) cautions against soliciting testimonial endorsements from current clients or from others who may be vulnerable. Because advertising sometimes involves the use of such testimonials, this provision would also be applicable. Both of these provisions would appear to have as much relevance to a social agency as they do to an individual social worker.

THE CASE FOR MARKETING

Philip Kotler's (1974) pioneering work on nonprofit marketing provoked growing attention to this topic, and at least one journal, *Journal for Nonprofit and Voluntary Sector Marketing,* is devoted specifically to the topic. Marketing concepts taken from business are not easily applied to social services. However, some of the key concepts and ideas of marketing can provide useful frameworks for beginning to consider the case of the social agency.

For example, market research can be used by social agencies to enhance relations with existing stakeholders and to identify new target groups that may become supporters. However, marketing techniques like market segmentation are only being actively used by a few organizations for development of successful fundraising strategies.

The Wolf definition of marketing cited above would suggest that there is or should be a strong relationship between marketing and social welfare services, although social welfare organizations likely do not call what they do "marketing." As with businesses that are going to survive, agencies that are going to survive need to periodically analyze the changing needs of those who make use of their services. Once new needs are identified, agencies need to develop ways in which those needs can be met. When agencies do this, they are more likely to use terms such as *needs assessment, program evaluation,* or *strategic planning* to describe what they are doing than to call the process "marketing." Such planning is discussed in more detail in chapter 9.

Marketing has become a concern of nonprofit organizations generally and social services specifically because at its core, the emphasis on marketing is grounded in ideas that depart from the rational person model and are consistent with the familiar social work distinction between thoughts and feelings. In a purely rational world, the distinctive concerns of marketing with performance, positioning, and product identification would be entirely superfluous. Rational consumers would be driven solely by their interest in maximizing their returns on expenditures. But our world isn't that kind of place, and people (including social services and their clients and stakeholders) respond to an assortment of rational and emotional appeals.

The contemporary concern with marketing must be seen as an effort to come to better terms with the complex, multilevel responses of clients, stakeholders, and other community members to factors of the social service situation. Within the four P's of price, performance, position, and product, the marketing discipline seeks to understand and come to terms with many of these same considerations.

Social service organizations need to engage in marketing (and public relations and advertising) for a variety of reasons. Possible clients or those who may refer clients need to know that a service is available to be able to take advantage of it. Marketing is one of the ways that they can learn about available services. Organizations need supporters and donors to be able to provide their services. Marketing represents a way to reach potential volunteers and to help persuade donors that the organization and its mission

is something that they wish to support. Marketing is also a way to persuade the public at large—those who may never be clients or volunteers or donors—that the agency engages in activities that benefit the community and that if it does not merit actual support from them, it is something that they should at least not oppose.

JUST THE FACTS, MA'AM

Perhaps because of the origins of management ideas in Enlightenment rationalism, there is a strong tendency on the part of social work managers to think of accountability problems in purely rational person terms. Thus, there are repeated attempts to marshal facts, present arguments, and engage in dialogue that will change the minds of potential supporters and opponents and increase the levels of public support for social service activities. A great many people in social work appear to believe that performance and outcome measurement by themselves will win over skeptical publics and increase the flow of resources to the field with little or no additional effort required.

Such faith in the power of rational persuasion is remarkably out of place in a profession that insists upon the equity of the cognitive and emotional dimensions of behavior. Yet social workers have done very little to develop suitable models of psychosocial behavior applicable to distinctly social administration problems like accountability. Most such efforts still proceed as if the problems of social administration should be recognized as clinical problems. Although the problem of accountability must be seen in its full psychosocial complexity, we must presently look beyond the boundaries of contemporary social work practice in order to arrive at satisfactory models for doing so. All three of the disciplines discussed in this chapter position themselves counter to rationalist assumptions and suggest important ways of approaching accountability problems.

Goffman's conception of impression management and Banfield's notions of social choice as these were presented in chapter 17 and a number of ideas laid out in other chapters together act to reinforce the viewpoints put forth by contemporary marketing theory. Herbert Simon's model of humans as creatures of finite mental ability; Charles Lindblom's conception of incremental policymaking as remedial, serial, and partial in nature; and the Berger–Luckmann portrait of social institutions may have little to do with overtly selling social services. However, they have a great deal to do with Goffman's impression management on the large, or macro, scale of public, community, and societal levels and Banfield's social influence. Together all of these perspectives reinforce the case for speaking to patrons and clients at emotional as well as cognitive levels.

THE GENERAL PUBLIC AND SPECIFIC PUBLICS

One of the key initial contributions of marketing concepts to social services comes from the process of "market segmentation," which might be said to involve identifying specific, recognizable groups in the organizational environment. If you listen closely to social workers and social work students talking, you will often hear a very undifferentiated sense of the environment as one large, undifferentiated general public often described with phrases like "society wants" and "the community needs."

One of the corollaries of Charles Lindblom's emphasis on the limits of human intelligence and Ronald Coase's attention to the importance of the costs of information highlights the importance of considering various publics. Among the members of society or a particular community, one will find strong gradations of attention, interest, and awareness, varying all the way from complete indifference to total involvement. Each of these disciplines brings slightly different techniques and approaches to the challenge, but all are committed to the general task of identifying stakeholder publics and reaching out to them with various messages. The principal reasons for doing so, we suggest, are to enhance and improve public understanding and support of social services and to engage in outreach to potential unserved and underserved client populations.

A public, according to Kotler and Andreasen (1996), "is a distinct group of people and or organizations that has an actual or a potential interest and/or impact on an organization." In this view, society and community consist of an indefinite number of separate and distinct publics rather than a single unified general will (Ryan, 1995; Westbrook, 1991). Kotler identified four primary classes of publics as potential targets of marketing efforts: input publics, internal publics, intermediary publics, and consuming publics. Each of these constitutes an additional class or category of stakeholders as that term is generally used.

Input publics mainly supply original resources and constraints to the organization. They include *donors, suppliers,* and *regulators.* Donors make gifts and donations. Suppliers are those organizations that sell needed goods and services to the focal organization. Regulators "impose rules of conduct" (Kotler, 1982, p. 49).

Internal publics in the nonprofit organization include the administration, board, staff, and volunteers of the organization. Although the assumption is often made that such internal publics will be consistently true believers in the organization and its program, the reality is that their loyalty and commitment may also need to be a target of marketing efforts at times.

Intermediary publics, which assist in promoting and distributing products and services to final consumers, are generally much less important in

social service organizations than in the ordinary business environment. There is typically no need in a service organization, for example, for transportation, warehousing, arbitrage, and such services. Likewise, there is little need in the typical public or nonprofit social service organizations for tax accountants, real estate agents, stockbrokers, and other similar intermediaries.

There are a number of unique intermediaries who take on great importance in the social service context: funding authorities, social service roundtables, and collaboratories, including what Kotler called "sister organizations." Other examples of intermediaries might include activist publics of various advocacy and cause-oriented organization and media publics. Thus, no contemporary mental health program can afford to ignore the National Association of the Mentally Ill (NAMI), and no aging program can ignore the American Association of Retired Persons (AARP).

Finally, one of the questions of central importance in applying a marketing perspective to social service organizations is: Who are the real and potential clients, customers, and consumers of the services? These persons constitute the *consuming publics.*

Seitel (1992) used a slightly different approach and indicated that the public can be classified in at least four overlapping categories. Though some of the terms differ from those used by Kotler, the emphasis continues to be on differentiating among those in the public.

1. *Internal and external publics.* Internal publics are those inside the organization such as its employees or members of the board of directors. External publics are those not directly connected with the organizations, such as consumers, suppliers, the press, etc.
2. *Primary, secondary, and marginal publics.* Primary publics can be of the greatest help or hindrance to an organization. Secondary publics are less important to the organization, and marginal publics are of the least importance.
3. *Traditional and future publics.* Traditional publics are the current consumers and employees of the organization. Future publics are the potential customers.
4. *Proponents, opponents, and uncommitted publics.* Proponents are those in favor of the organization; opponents are those opposed to it. Uncommitted publics are those with no particular point of view about the organization. (pp. 12–14)

ROUSSEAU LIVES ON IN SOCIAL WORK

Social workers often describe an undifferentiated sense of the general public, expressed with phrases like "what society wants" and "what the

community needs." This is reminiscent of the philosopher Jean-Jacques Rousseau's (1974) concept of the "general will." From this viewpoint, communities are not seen as pluralistic places that contain multiple and sometimes conflicting interests and dozens, hundreds or even thousands of public, commercial, and nonprofit institutions competing for their interest and attention. This viewpoint is in need of serious adjustment. In social administration, "public" should almost always be treated as plural.

As noted previously, social service institutions can only endure and remain vital with significant levels of community involvement and support, but high levels of public awareness and commitment do not occur naturally or spontaneously. Such support and commitment must be sought after and won. Therefore, part of an overall commitment to institution building by social administrators should also involve major efforts to increase the levels of public attention, interest, and commitment to social service institutions.

The disciplines of marketing, public relations, and advertising each bring slightly different techniques and approaches to the challenge of building greater constituent support, but all are committed to the general task of identifying *stakeholder publics,* or those people with characteristics similar to individuals and organizations who currently support a particular institution, and reaching out to those publics with messages designed to encourage their increased support and participation. Among the principal reasons for this outreach are improving the accountability position of the institution, enhancing and improving public understanding of its mission, and engaging in outreach to potential unserved and underserved client populations.

From its journalistic origins, the discipline of mass communications has fashioned this as targeting audiences who may have a *need to know* certain *messages* communicated to them through various communications *media.* This modern plural notion of publics is the theoretical core of both constituency and stakeholder theories as well as the anchor point of theories of marketing, public relations, and advertising in social services. In the circumstances of modern life and mass urban society, institutions and their publics (or stakeholders) first need to find each other before mutually beneficial relationships of support can possibly arise.

The applications of public relations, marketing, and advertising strategies, then, are premised on the assumption that such discoveries should not originate merely from one direction. Social services need not sit by quietly until discovered by their supporters. In fact, most social service institutions are not sufficiently well known or well understood by enough people that it makes sense for them to merely sit back and wait for clients, donors, volunteers, board members, professional employees, and others to

seek them out. Social service institutions need to actively pursue their discovery by potential stakeholders.

IMAGE MANAGEMENT

Along with this pluralistic concept of relevant publics, the second most important concept to arise from the cluster of public relations, marketing, and advertising that we are examining in this chapter is the concept of "image" and the associated concept of "image management." At the level of everyday personal behavior, we have already seen the way in which Erving Goffman constructed a dramaturgy of everyday behavior around the idea of impression management and the importance of certain key concepts in this approach for the institutionalization of social services.

We wish to suggest further that disciplines such as marketing, public relations, and advertising do not work directly at the level of impressions that people and organizations give and give off. The suggestion here instead is that in dealing with large publics of the type already discussed, impression management occurs through the medium of public images. We have already seen the simplest examples of this in discussion of the informal organization and the two-step flow of communication. Everything said there would apply also to relations between organizational staff members and members of various publics. Further, in the age of telephone, fax, and E-mail there is no reason to assume that the process of influentials channeling and interpreting messages must be restricted to face-to-face contact within organizational boundaries. Our principal concern in this chapter, however, is with extending similar concerns for impression management to the macro level, where those being influenced are largely anonymous and the relations are not face-to-face but one-to-many.

The topics in this chapter, and particularly the focus on image management, push further the possibility of alternatives to purely rationalist constructions of mind and mental processes that some people find very threatening. As the frequently hostile and suspicious reaction to Goffman's sociology of impression management indicates, we are talking about a subject here that arouses responses not entirely unlike the various responses to sex attributed to the Victorians. We know people do engage in image management, and we know we'd be better off if we did, but even so it doesn't seem entirely proper for social workers to talk about such things! It is easy to conclude that these tools are used only for manipulation and attempts to control. In reality, such attempts at interpersonal influence are more a correlate of democratic than authoritarian systems.

The first and most important point is that successful managers *do* engage in activities of image management, whether or not they talk about it and even whether or not they are particularly aware that that is what they are doing. Moreover, successful image management over the long term is an important component of institution building. If one expects to be dependent upon public support, it isn't sufficient merely to *be* a great, good, beneficent program or service. Relevant publics must also *see* one as great, good, and beneficent. This is a variant on the old question of whether a tree falling in the forest with no one around makes any sound. Individual acts of anonymous charity or selfless service to others are certainly morally praiseworthy. About that there should be no doubt. But we need to be equally clear that anonymous acts completely unknown to others, by their very nature, cannot generate enough of the kind of attention, interest, and commitment that are necessary to establish or continue institutional service programs.

At bottom, the method for public image management is a simple one—at least to describe. Many of the same approaches used for marketing tangible products also apply to marketing intangibles, which marketing an image is. For example, you need to identify the target market and its current beliefs and actions, establish a proposition as believable or plausible, and finally, establish the desired beliefs and action. Most Americans, for example, have never visited any Third World countries, and thus when they see images of children in squalid conditions being aided by international charities, these images are plausible whether or not they choose to act on the subsequent appeal for action (a donation).

Wolf (1990) defined image as the "sum total of beliefs, ideas and impressions that people have of an organization or the programs, services, and products it offers" (p. 121). He further indicates that a strong positive image is critical in gaining clients or an audience and essential to gaining donors and broad community support. The sense of prestige coming from an organization's image can play a major role in persuading people to serve on the organization's board, according to Wolf. He also indicates that "donors are often motivated not only by feeling that they are part of an exclusive group but also by being made to feel generous, important, and central to an organization's success or failure" (p. 126).

THE MEASURED IMAGE

Marketing research is essential to the world of commercial enterprise, and it also offers new challenges and opportunities to those concerned with the planning, delivery, and administration of public social and health services (Chisnall, 1979). Central to the nonprofit marketing laid out by Kotler is the

Figure 18.1 Familiarity Scale

Never heard of	Heard of	Know a little about	Know a fair amount about	Know very well
1	2	3	4	5

Source: Adapted from Kotler (1982).

idea of the measured image. The measured image of an organization locates where for various publics particular images fall on a continuum from awareness through interest to full commitment and support. Kotler recommends measuring the levels of familiarity, favorability, and importance displayed by key relevant publics. Leaders of nonprofit organizations, he notes, often find the measured image of their organization surprising and disturbing.

In Kotler's approach, the method of measuring images seems to involve survey research utilizing a variety of Likert-type scales to determine the familiarity of particular publics with an institution, its services and programs, and particular details of interest. In the case of social services, those details might include fee structures, eligibility requirements, and expected outcomes. Figure 18.1 shows an example of a familiarity scale. Familiarity in this scale corresponds closely with what we referred to previously as awareness. Measuring the image of an institution in the Kotler model also involves concern for what he calls "favorability", but which might also be given a more conventional name like acceptance (Figure 18.2).

Kotler then suggests transcribing the results of these two scales onto what he calls a familiarity/favorability grid. For purposes of illustration and instruction, this can be shown in preliminary form as the two-by-two grid shown in Table 18.1. Plausible strategic inferences that might be drawn from a concentration of scores in each cell of the matrix are shown.

The final two questions under consideration are how important a particular activity is to members of key publics, and how well they believe the institution performs that activity. Results of these two questions can be plotted on an importance/performance grid, as shown in Table 18.2. As with Table 18.1, possible strategic implications are shown in the cells of the matrix.

Figure 18.2 Acceptance Scale

Very unfavorable	Somewhat unfavorable	Indifferent	Somewhat favorable	Very favorable
1	2	3	4	5

Source: Adapted from Kotler (1982).

Table 18.1 Familiarity/Favorability Grid

	Favorable	Unfavorable
Familiar	An ideal informed public: they know you and like you	The only thing they know is they don't like you
Unfamiliar	They don't know you but like you	Your worst nightmare! They don't know you and still don't like you. (greatest attention here)

INFLUENCING IMAGE

Public relations, marketing, and advertising are methods that can be used to create an image for an organization or to modify images that may not be of benefit to the organization. For example, Seitel (1992, pp. 81–82) indicates that most public relations programs are designed to persuade people to change their opinion, to crystallize underdeveloped opinions, or to reinforce existing opinions.

Successful businesses often view advertising as an investment rather than an expense. That is, they believe money spent on advertising will be recovered through increased sales revenue. They perceive the need to continually keep their name and image in front of the community so that when a potential customer needs one of their products they will think of them. Though few nonprofits have budgets sufficient to advertise continually, they might do well to adopt the philosophy that advertising (and marketing and public relations) represents investments that result in achievement of a desired end.

Public service announcements (PSAs) can be one way nonprofit organizations can generate public awareness. Television and radio stations are required to devote a certain number of hours each month to such announcements. An inexpensive way that agencies can benefit from this requirement is to make use of some of the nationally produced PSAs and place a trailer or tag at the end that mentions the local agency. Thus, the national United Way advertising might have a tag at the end that mentions the local United Way agency.

Table 18.2 Importance/Performance Grid

	Important	Unimportant
Excellent Performance	Keep up the good work	Possible overkill?
Poor Performance	Concentrate here	Low priority

Locally produced PSAs can also be created. This may be easiest in radio; a script can be submitted to the station and read by one of the announcers. Producing video spots that look professional for television can be expensive and thus may not be possible for many small agencies. However, if an agency's board of directors includes someone from the media or a business person who does a great deal of television advertising, the agency may have access to expertise that can be of help in producing its own spots.

There are times of the year when local media may be more likely to run PSAs. As any insomniac knows, many PSAs run at 3:00 A.M. when relatively few people see them. However, in some media markets the first and third quarters are slower advertising times, so the media may be more likely during those times to run the PSA in a favorable timeslot when more people will see it.

Written communication is used by many agencies to influence the image that others may have about them. The written communications may take the form of pamphlets or brochures describing the agency's services. It may be a flyer that will be posted. It may be a news release. Seitel (1992) provided a three-part formula for such written communication:

1. The idea must precede the expression or thinking must occur before writing. Ideas, Seitel indicated, must relate to the reader, must engage the reader's attention, must concern the reader, and must be in the reader's own self-interest.

2. Don't be afraid of the draft. In fact, the writer should not be afraid of many drafts. Rereading and rewriting drafts often improves communication with the reader.

3. Simplify, clarify, aim. Simplifying what is written improves the chances that a greater number of people will understand it. Clarifying by eliminating unneeded passages or paragraphs will also aid understanding. And directing the writing to a particular audience will help with communication. (pp. 192–93)

Publicity in the local press is another way to influence an organization's image. However, agencies need to recognize that they have very little influence over what may appear in the press. Although they can attempt to influence the news, the reporter may take a different angle than the agency hoped. Journalists often say, "Names make news." Agencies may want to keep this in mind in developing their news releases.

Seitel (1992, pp. 334–46) offered advice with regard to newspaper coverage and television or radio coverage. For both newspaper and television, he indicated that it is important to know the deadlines that reporters may face. Television and radio often have very strict deadlines that are even more limiting than those of newspapers. He advised that news releases be sent in written format to newspapers but that television and radio are more telephone oriented; a phone call to them may be sufficient. Calling a radio or television station early in the day when staff assignments for the day are being developed can be a way to see that your event or announcement is covered. If there is sufficient time, a written press release might be sent to all media, followed by a phone call to see whether any clarifying information is needed.

Newspapers have the ability to cover stories in greater depth, so they may be more interested in detailed information or possible related stories (sidebars) than television or radio would be. Larger newspapers are likely to rewrite any release that you send to them. Smaller papers, especially weekly shoppers, are more likely to print the release verbatim. For television, it is obviously important that the story have a visual angle. There needs to be a scene or an activity or event that can be videotaped or someone who can be interviewed.

For all media, Seitel recommended making personal contact and getting to know the appropriate reporter, assignment editor, or producer. The pay-off from such a relationship may not be immediate. However, establishing a relationship of trust can result in that person contacting you when a question or issue involving the agency arises or being more receptive to story ideas that you might suggest. Treating reporters with respect is important in establishing a good working relationship. When the media has covered an event, following up with a handwritten thank-you note to the reporter and the editor or news director can be a way to further develop the relationship.

Board members may have media contacts that can be of help. We know of one board upon which a member of the state supreme court served. Through this connection, the organization was able to hold its press conferences in the court's chambers, with the justice present. The location and the justice's presence generated much more press attention than would have been created had the conference been held in the agency's offices. The justice received additional press coverage from the conferences. Though most boards may not include a member quite that prominent, other board members with media connections may be able to help the agency.

Many social service agencies overlook the possible advantages of having a representative of the media or advertising serve on the agency's board of directors. When identifying possible board members, agencies tend to focus on persons who may have expertise in the kind of service that the agency delivers or those who may be able to donate to the agency. These types of persons can be very helpful to the agency. However, the expertise that someone in advertising or the press can bring can also be of help. We know of one case in which the United Way began to receive improved newspaper coverage after the local newspaper's associate publisher joined the United Way's board of directors (they had spent several years actively courting the associate publisher to join the board).

Special events are another kind of activity that can be used to develop the image of a social service organization. Such special events may take the form of a social service fair involving a variety of agencies that serves to publicize the services that they provide and volunteer opportunities. It may be an annual event such as a five-kilometer race or a golf tournament that is sponsored by the agency. In our community, the local United Way sponsors a huge garage sale in a local parking garage that attracts thousands of people and provides an opportunity for agencies funded by United Way to publicize themselves.

Social agencies often participate with local businesses to sponsor special events. *The Guerrilla Marketing Handbook* (Levinson & Godin, 1994) encourages businesses to be involved in the community as a means of improving their images and marketing activities. Businesses are told that such involvement will be of benefit to them because customers want to give their business to people who care about them (p. 332). Thus, linking up with a local business to sponsor a special event may be mutually beneficial.

There is, in fact, often a mutually beneficial relationship among nonprofit organizations, businesses, and media that work together. For the nonprofit organization, community awareness can lead to increased funding, a larger volunteer and donor base, and increased institutional legitimacy in the community. For the business, there can be a "halo" effect that rubs off from its association with a respected social service organization. That may translate into increased sales and greater customer loyalty. For the media, involvement in the community increases readership and viewership that in turn increase the advertising revenue of the newspaper or television station.

At the same time, when establishing such relationships, administrators need to ensure that businesses are not using the image of the social agency inappropriately. We know of a business that made use of its relationship with a museum in such a way that it appeared as though the museum was selling its product. Such a relationship can raise questions about the continued tax-exempt status of the nonprofit. It can also raise questions about fairness in the community if one business but not others appears to be favored, and this can be harmful to the image of the social agency. That social agencies are at greater risk and have more to lose from such arrangements may not seem fair, but it should not detract from the fact that, properly handled, such arrangements can be very beneficial to the agency.

For a special event to have much impact on an agency's image, it likely needs to be an annual or periodic event. Woodstock aside, a one-time special event will usually not produce much of a lasting image, no matter how spectacular it may be. Annual walkathons, chili cook-offs, rubber ducky races, and a variety of other special events that benefit social services have almost become institutions in some communities.

Though social agency administrators often have not thought of sources like *The Guerrilla Marketing Handbook* or the many other publications like it as possible references, they would be well served by reading such a publication for ideas that may be relevant to their agency. Most of the publications are business oriented, so they need to be read with a sense of imagination as to how the content might apply to a nonprofit or governmental organization. For those administrators working in commercial social service agencies, the content may be applicable as written. They can be a source of ideas and suggestions about ways to influence the image of a social agency that are not a part of the usual exposure of social agency administrators.

CONCLUSION

In this chapter, we attempted to introduce some basic methods of nonprofit marketing into social administration by linking marketing to the larger problem of institutional legitimacy and by suggesting that a concern for image can be systematically used to address these issues and concerns. In doing so, we recognize the ambivalence that some may have about the applicability of such concepts to the world of social welfare services. However, we believe that they are applicable and appropriate means for an agency to accomplish some of its goals. Those goals can include informing potential clients about the services provided by the agency that may be relevant to them. They can include attracting volunteers and employees to the agency. The goals may also include attracting funding to the agency through donors or legislative goodwill. And finally, the goals should include developing a sense of community goodwill toward the agency and its mission.

Human and Financial Capital

For several decades now, the useful but vague concept of *resources* has been used to describe and categorize the topics discussed in this section. Indeed, the concept of *human resources* has become so well established that it is now commonly used to describe what was formerly known in most large organizations as "the personnel department." At schools of social work, courses in financial management and personnel management (or human resource management) are perhaps the most commonly offered courses in social administration after a general introduction to management.

This section, the largest in the book, consists of five chapters devoted to personnel and financial matters. Chapter 19 offers a general introduction to understanding the topics of personnel management. It begins with a discussion of organizational hierarchy and the division of labor, and examines job design as it relates to agency purpose, technology, employee talents, personnel policies, and staff development and training.

Chapter 20 is a further exploration of major elements of the cycle of major personnel actions, including recruitment, hiring, supervision, evaluation, and termination of employees. The emphasis here is on those topics that are typically most complex and challenging for the social administrator. Other, equally interesting topics like promotion and retirement of employees are not emphasized. Although it might be more rewarding to focus on the vast majority of successfully working employees, the reality is that human resources concerns for social administrators are often inordinately related to the more unusual situations. The adage about the administrator spending 80 percent of her time on 20 percent of the organization's employees is often correct.

Chapter 21 approaches the technical topic of financial management from the vantage point of the strategic perspectives offered in earlier chapters—an approach that has been largely ignored in much of the existing financial management literature. Particular attention is paid to the nonprofit QUANGOs (quasi nongovernmental organizations). A brief case study of Hull House shows that the multifunded agency has been part of social administration for many decades.

Chapter 22 unravels the increasingly complex web of financial inflows—revenues and public support—coming into the social agency from various sources. A key conceptual feature of this chapter is the concept of the "soft" revenue base of the contemporary nonprofit social agency and its implications for the future.

Chapter 23 is about budgeting. Although a strictly logical approach would seem to suggest that this chapter should be about financial outflows, to offset the emphasis of chapter 22, the reality is that the planning associated with budgeting makes actual expenditures a rather mundane topic in social administration. The real action in social administration is deciding where (and when) resources should be committed. What follows—the actual expenditure of funds according to the plan—is usually left in the hands of lower-level, technical personnel such as accountants and bookkeepers.

CHAPTER 19

Personnel Systems

The resources or capital available to social administrators can be characterized as three basic types: human, social, and financial. In this chapter and chapter 20, the structure and process of human resource management is explored.

Some might argue that of these three basic types of resources, human resources are perhaps the most critical if an agency is to accomplish its mission and goals. Talented and committed staff working together effectively can often overcome fiscal limitations. However, recruiting, developing, and maintaining an effective and cohesive staff can be very challenging even when almost unlimited financial resources are available. Money alone does not necessarily result in the best design of positions or the hiring of the best person for a given position.

Chapters 19 and 20 deal with agency and job design, personnel policies, staff development and training, and employee recruitment, supervision, and termination among other topics. The intent of these chapters is to provide the reader with a sense of the elements involved when creating or managing an agency personnel system. The focus in all of these areas is on how the agency's personnel resources are deployed to meet the agency's mission and purpose.

DESIGNING THE HUMAN RESOURCE STRUCTURE

In chapter 4, we discussed social administration and organizations. We focused on theories that explain why social welfare (and other) services are delivered through an organizational context and theories of what may make for an effective organization. The theories of Max Weber, Robert Merton, Chester Barnard, and Henry Mintzberg, among others, were reviewed in that chapter.

It is interesting to note that the literature on organizations focuses relatively little on the deployment of human resources within the agency. Some of the literature describes the kind of person who might work most effectively in a given type of organization.[1] However, the relationship between the mission and purpose of the agency and the design of the personnel system in that agency is rarely discussed. Yet there is, or should be, a critical nexus between these two factors.

Human resources, like financial ones, should be deployed to accomplish the mission and purpose of the agency. The jobs or positions to which employees are recruited and through which they are deployed, then, need to be designed to fit with the mission and purpose. They will influence the agency structure used, the kinds of employees needed, and the number of employees required.

All positions need to relate to the agency's mission and purpose, and each employee needs to have a sense of the way in which his or her position, no matter how menial, contributes to the mission. The oft-told story of workmen building Sir Christopher Wren's St. Paul's Cathedral in London serves to illustrate this point. The story is that a passer-by asked two workmen working on the cathedral what they were doing. One indicated that he was laying bricks. The other said that he was helping Sir Christopher build a beautiful cathedral. The most effective human resources organization will be peopled by those who are building cathedrals and who see the relationship between their job duties and what the agency is attempting to accomplish.

A few general principles about agency and position design influence the rest of this chapter:

1. Agency and job design should be determined by the mission and purpose of the agency. In deciding on the jobs required and designing those jobs, the focus should be on how each job contributes to the accomplishment of the agency mission.

2. There is no formula that can be applied to make job design (identifying the duties and responsibilities of a particular position) easy or quick. Although it may be tempting to adopt the formulas suggested by some that indicate, for example, that there should be one manager for every seven professionals or that one secretary is needed for each three professionals, agency reality is far more complicated.

3. Job design and redesign is a constant activity. It occurs not only when new jobs are created but should also occur when jobs become vacant and when an employee's performance is periodically reviewed, which is discussed in the next chapter.

4. No job is an island. No job can be designed in isolation from other jobs in the agency.

5. Job design is more an art than a science. It requires careful consideration of the agency mission, social and political environment, and talents of the job occupants.

FLAT AND HIERARCHICAL AGENCIES

One of the choices with regard to the human resources structure centers around how hierarchical or "flat" an organization may be. A hierarchical organization is one that has several layers. A flat organization is one with few administrative layers. Smaller agencies tend to be flat, whereas larger ones are most often hierarchical.

Flatter agencies are viewed as having some advantages when compared to more hierarchical ones. Flatter agencies are often viewed as being more nimble in that they can react quickly to changing circumstances because there are more sources of information about possible changes and fewer levels through which a decision must be processed to become final. In addition, flatter agencies, which permit greater employee involvement in decision making, are assumed to produce more motivated employees. Even when hierarchical agencies decide not to attempt to become flatter, they often adopt techniques that produce some of the advantages that flow from a flat organization, such as quality circles, total quality management, and others.

A traditional assumption has been that any administrator needs to have a limited span of control. The *span of control* refers to the total number of people reporting to a given administrator or manager. Some suggest the maximum span is six or seven people (Skidmore, 1995, p. 117), and thus the number of people reporting to the administrator should not exceed that number. To stay within the limit of seven, more hierarchical agencies were developed. To have only six or seven people reporting to a given administrator, the agency had to have many different levels. More recently, agency design has focused on the need to empower and motivate employees so that less control of their behavior is needed. Under these circumstances, many people can report to a given administrator because the administrator needs to exercise less control over them. Thus, a flatter organization is possible.

Regardless of the size of the agency, few agencies are successful without at least two layers. Someone needs to be identified as the "head" or "director" of the organization who has overall responsibility for goal accomplishment, and others need to report to that head about their contributions to the goal. Increasingly, however, even very large agencies are striving to become flatter, with fewer hierarchical layers.

The qualifications and assignments of employees will also influence how flat or hierarchical an agency must be. A clinical setting whose staff are largely professionals meeting independently with clients to provide therapeutic services may require little hierarchy and supervision to function smoothly. A homemaker service whose staff is largely unskilled and may operate in many different settings would probably require more hierarchy to ensure that the appropriate quality of care is provided.

Service delivery is the primary purpose of most social welfare agencies. Hierarchical agencies with their several layers of managers and administrators may have significant numbers of personnel who are not directly involved in providing service delivery. The assignments of those persons may be primarily administrative tasks, such as processing payroll and vacation forms, billing third parties for payment, responding to legislative inquiries, and so on. Given that hierarchical agencies often have significant numbers of people not delivering services, some view such agencies as "wasteful."

However, in large agencies a certain amount of management is needed to ensure that all members of the organization are moving forward toward the same goals, that there is sufficient accountability to those funding the organization, and so forth. Some social welfare agencies are striving to be flatter and to have the job design associated with flat organizations as a means of responding to the perception that many administrators equals much waste. Thus, some agencies are becoming flatter simply as a means of dealing with public criticism about the number of administrators who do not deliver services.

AGENCY DESIGN AND JOB DESIGN

The flatness of the organization also affects the design of the positions of employees. In an agency that needs to be or is intended to be relatively hierarchical, more positions will need to be devoted to various levels of management. In an agency that needs to be or is intended to be flatter, a more limited number of managers or administrators will be needed, but the jobs of many employees will include self-management and coordination tasks.

In designing positions within an agency, many start by looking at comparable agencies or the theories of organizational design and develop an organization much like those observed. Though this may be a good place to start, it is not the place that job design should end. The challenge for the contemporary social welfare administrator is to design positions that are more closely tied to what the organization is attempting to accomplish rather than to the way such positions have historically been designed.

This advice may appear to be applicable only to those fortunate enough to be able to design an agency from scratch. Nothing could be further from the truth. All agencies experience turnover in personnel. Every vacancy creates the opportunity to examine again whether the vacated position has the duties associated with it that contribute to the achievement of agency purpose. In addition, as employees' performance is evaluated, there are opportunities to redesign positions while occupied to ensure better fit between agency needs and a given employee's skills and aspirations.

JOB DESIGN FOR THE AGENCY HEAD

In the discussion about the flatness of agencies, it was suggested that every agency needs a head. Thus, identifying what the head is expected to do to achieve the agency's purposes is perhaps the best place to start with job design. Though titles differ, *head* and *director* will be used interchangeably to indicate the chief executive officer (CEO) of the agency. Is the director primarily a manager or coordinator of those within the agency? Is she primarily a fundraiser whose external communication skills are most important? Is he a change agent intended to bring significant change to an agency that may have grown stodgy and settled with the passage of time?

The governing board of the agency is the primary determiner of what the head needs to do to achieve the agency's goals and thus the primary constituency establishing the job duties of the head. In the case of a state human resources agency, that governing board may be the governor's office or whomever has the authority to appoint the agency's director. If that appointment must be confirmed by the legislative body, there is a greater possibility for disagreement about the activities on which the head is to focus. In other instances, a city council or county commission may be the governing body that determines the agency's goals and the relationship of the head's duties to them. In many instances, the governing body will be the members of the board of directors of a nonprofit agency legally charged with responsibility for managing the agency. In increasing instances, the governing board may be representatives of shareholders in a commercial or for-profit agency.

In all of the above instances, regardless of who appoints the director, there is some guidance in statute or in the agency's articles of incorporation with regard to the purpose of the agency. The design of the job of the head cannot stray too far from helping to achieve that purpose unless those purposes are formally modified through the appropriate process. However, most purposes are broad enough to cover a range of activities and to be flexible to meet the changing demands of the environment. Thus, there tends to be significant discretion in the weight attached to any one component of an agency's purpose when designing the director's position description.

That discretion may also be used to address the different needs that agencies may have at various stages of their development. Bailey and Grochau (1993) discuss the need to align leadership with the stages of organizational development and the impact that need can have on director–board relationships. For example, a new organization may need a more entrepreneurial leader than an old established organization. Significant board involvement in operations during the entrepreneurial stage of an organization could hamper the director's effectiveness.

Employees of the agency often believe that their views of the purposes of the agency should have considerable influence in the design of the director's job. Though agency life is always easier if the governing body and the agency's employees agree on agency purpose and the job of the director, it must be recognized that it is those on the governing body that have primary responsibility for what the head does. In some instances, they may seek a director who will downsize and streamline an agency even though that may not be what the employees desire. In other instances, they may want a director who will emphasize a different aspect of the agency's mission than has been emphasized in the past, even though that may not be what the employees may want, since they may be comfortable with what they are currently doing.

The hiring authority needs to make clear to the head what the duties are and how those duties relate to agency purpose. That should be clear both upon initial hiring and through the process of periodic performance appraisal (discussed in chapter 20). If there is the possibility for disagreement between what the governing board has asked the director to focus on and what the employees may believe is important, it can be helpful to both the director and the employees if the board shares its expectations with the employees. Though the director can share those expectations herself, the added legitimacy that comes from a letter from the board president or other hiring authority describing what the head has been asked to do can be of help in providing legitimacy.

Those duties should be expressed in writing. Although there will be much informal discussion about what the director is to do and even likely some discussion about how those duties might be approached, the director—both when initially hired and periodically after the initial hiring—benefits from the clarity that is achieved when expectations are committed to writing. Expressing the expectations in writing is also of benefit to the governing board in that it requires the members of the board to reach a measure of agreement as to what they believe it is important that the director do. The written description should include both the ongoing responsibilities of the head and those things that the director is to focus on for the next year.

JOB DESIGN FOR OTHER EMPLOYEES

Although it may appear unrealistic to suggest that the design of the jobs of other employees flows from that of the head, that is, in fact, what should happen. (For those who prefer nonhierarchical language, it is just as accurate to build out from that center [director] as down.) In some instances, that may mean jobs are designed to complement what the director is doing. The director, for example, may have been told to focus on external relationships as a means of improving the agency's financial base so that it can deliver more services. Because this will be his focus, he will have little time for internal management, and an assistant director or assistant to the director is needed to ensure that internal matters are attended to. Or it may be that all employees, regardless of their other duties, need to emphasize external relationships as a means of building community support for the agency's purposes. Even in a well-established agency with long-term employees, it should be expected that the emphasis attached to specific duties would change over time in response to the directions that the governing board is providing to the director.

Though areas of emphasis may change, it is important that all jobs be designed to ensure that the agency's purposes are served. If the agency's purpose is to deliver clinical services, it is expected that most employees' jobs will be designed to permit them to provide such services. Even the jobs of those who may not be expected to deliver a service, such as a receptionist, should be examined to ensure that the duties are supportive of those involved in service delivery.

As indicated above, when designing and redesigning the duties of employees, it is tempting to look at what such jobs have typically been and to design comparable duties for the new job. In many instances, designing new jobs to look just like the old ones may serve the agency well. However, just as business and industry have begun to examine different ways of arraying job duties to accomplish agency goals, social welfare agencies also need to critically examine whether the old way of doing something is still the best way.

Just as the director's duties need to be expressed in writing, the job expectations of other employees also need to be written. Personnel problems often result from uncertainty about what an employee is to do and how it is to be done. The employee has one sense of what she is to do but her supervisor has a different view. The time invested in clarifying duties and approaches to those duties can reduce the time spent dealing with problems later. Writing a job description is one of the best ways to clarify those expectations.

A written job description is also important in recruiting the best qualified applicant to the agency. The recruitment process is discussed in further detail in chapter 20. A description is important, however, not only in the initial hiring. As with the director, the job description and the employee's success in performing those tasks should be periodically reviewed and appropriate changes made following the review.

The level of detail in the job description will depend upon whether there is a civil service or union system in the agency and the degree of formality of the agency. Even in small, relatively informal agencies, personnel management would be strengthened through the use of written job descriptions that include the following:

1. Identification of the major tasks or duties associated with the job. These should be as specific as possible. They should be listed in descending order of importance. It may be helpful to estimate the percentage of time that the employee may spend on average on given tasks. It is important to distinguish among those tasks that are essential for completion of the job as opposed to those that are desired to ensure that the job description does not discriminate against those with handicapping conditions. This is discussed more thoroughly in chapter 20.

2. Identification of the way in which certain tasks are to be accomplished if the agency has expectations about this. If a case worker, for example, is to dictate notes on each case within a day of seeing a client, this should be specified. Other agency documents that are discussed below can describe those processes common to all employees such as how the agency and employee are to be identified when answering phones. The job description should focus on those processes specific to that given job or category of jobs.

3. Identification of the basic skills and education needed to complete the job and any advanced skills and education or accommodations such as working nights or overtime that may be desirable. This aspect of the description is more important in the recruitment process than it is once an employee has been hired but should still be a part of the basic job description.

Bargal and Shamir (1984) provided another example of a job description and the elements covered by such a description and also describe the process used to develop a given description. Rapp and Poertner (1992, pp. 152–53) described the process of writing task statements as a part of a job description.

In small agencies the development of a job description may be seen by some as wasted effort. It may be believed that everyone knows what needs to be done. This is not the case, and the effort is not wasted. Good human resources administration requires that the expectations of the employee be clear. Writing a job description is the best way to make those expectations clear. Abels and Murphy (1981, p. 103) indicated that where job responsibilities are clearly perceived by workers and others, workers tend to have higher job satisfaction. Rapp and Poertner (1992, p. 151) and Pecora (1995, pp. 1831–32) also discuss the importance of having clarity about an employee's job expectations.

Job descriptions also provide the basis for the employee accountability expected in social agencies by stakeholders. The job description can also be important to the agency's defense of its actions should grievances or lawsuits over employee performance or termination arise. Appendix 2 includes a sample job description to illustrate what may be included in a description.

TECHNOLOGY AND JOB DESIGN

Technology has made possible different arrangements of jobs than envisioned even a decade ago. *Technology* as used in this discussion refers to the information technology prevalent today in the modern office. Those changes have largely taken the form of reducing dependence upon clerical support as professionals are able to function more independently through the use of technology. As a result, larger portions of an agency's resources are able to be committed toward those who deliver services to clients.

Among examples of the changes technology has produced is the reliance on word processing and the ability of most employees to master word processing. With time and experience, most employees find that they can more quickly type their own memos and case notes rather than writing them out for a secretary to type. E-mail access means that much of what had previously been communicated by printed memo can now be communicated electronically. Most professionals are able to learn to type their own E-mail messages and respond to the messages of others. Voice mail boxes reduce the dependency on a receptionist to take messages. Calendar programs that allow employees access to their own and others' calendars enable them to schedule their own appointments and learn when others with whom they need to meet may be available. Web pages enable the posting of basic agency information and the answers to frequently asked questions and, for those clients with access to the Internet, may reduce the number of phone calls for routine information that need to be handled. Bookkeeping programs that enable financial analysis as well as routine record keeping may disperse bookkeeping functions differently within the agency.

Although technology can affect the jobs required and the nature of the jobs of all within the agency, there are some very real costs associated with technology. Web and E-mail access results in a cost for the agency that needs to be budgeted. A local area network that enables all employees' computers to communicate with each other is a cost item that needs to be budgeted on its creation and that has continuing costs as the network needs to be supported and upgraded. Thus, though technology may reduce personnel costs, some of the savings inevitably need to be reallocated toward the supports required for technology.

In addition to the direct costs associated with technology, there are some indirect costs as employees who may not have taken their own messages or typed their own memos previously have to accommodate these new tasks in their work days. The costs and benefits of having every professional employee, for example, do all of his or her own typing or appointment scheduling need to be considered. Sometimes the costs in terms of professional staff time devoted to clerical functions of some of the technologically enhanced approaches will outweigh the benefits to be gained.

It is important, however, to note that technology makes possible a different array of job tasks than we have traditionally associated with social welfare agencies or even other types of agencies. The design of all jobs within the agency should include an examination of what the technological changes may mean for the position. Agencies may find that their willingness to adopt technology lags behind that of their governing board whose members may have seen other agencies sharpen their focus on their primary mission through the adoption of technology. Thus, at least at present in the adoption of technology, many agencies find themselves pushed by others rather than pulling others along.

EMPLOYEE TALENTS AND JOB DESIGN

One of the overarching dictums in this chapter is that job design should be heavily influenced by agency mission. However, it would be a mistake to suggest that an effective human resources plan is simply the listing of tasks associated with fulfilling that agency's mission. An effective agency accomplishes what needs to be done best when there is a good fit between the job and the employee's talents and interests.

Part of that fit occurs when a new employee is hired or is promoted to a different job. Hiring and promotion are discussed in chapter 20. However, because neither people nor agencies are static, examining that fit and altering it is a constant process.

Job descriptions identify certain tasks that need to be accomplished. If there are specific ways in which those tasks must be accomplished, they also describe the methods that are to be used. However, even with these specifications, most social welfare positions have enough flexibility to accommodate individual differences in talent and interest. A part of the art in human resources administration comes from being able to ensure the strongest possible fit between the tasks that must be accomplished and the abilities of a particular employee. Weiner (1987), for example, discussed the need to adapt jobs to people as being as important as adapting people to jobs.

If there is a mismatch between tasks and talents, the tasks must be given the greatest weight. No agency can be successful if the only tasks completed are those that the employees have a particular talent for or interest in. When there is a mismatch, the employee must develop the needed abilities, be moved to a different position, or be terminated. However, in most instances, the match becomes more a matter of tweaking a job description to allow an employee with a particular interest to devote time to that interest when it furthers agency goals. It may be, for example, that a caseworker has a particular interest in technology and that agency goals are served by having that caseworker devote some of her time to technology design and support for the agency. Another caseworker may have an interest in training, and his job duties might include organizing in-service activities for other staff.

Though this chapter focuses on the design of the agency and positions within the agency to serve the agency's purpose, it would be a mistake to assume that means that employee talents should not be considered. Our view is not that employees are cogs in a machine. Rather, we wish to suggest that those talents be considered but that such consideration must come within the context of agency needs.

PERSONNEL POLICIES

All agencies have personnel policies, even those that may insist they have no personnel manual. The policies may differ in terms of the degree of specificity and formality with which they are expressed, but they are present in the expectations that the governing board and director have of the employees and that the employees have of each other. In some agencies, they may be verbal descriptions of expected behavior, in others they may be a series of memos describing expectations, and in still other agencies they may be codified into a formal manual given to all new employees. Agency variations with regard to the degree and specificity of formality are the result of several factors, including whether employees are a part of a civil service or union system, the size of the agency, the age of the agency, and whether the agency's personnel practices have ever been the subject of a grievance or lawsuit.

As with written job descriptions, it is our firm belief that all agencies are well served by having written personnel policies. Written policies clarify expectations and both serve to avoid personnel problems and make it easier to correct problems, when they occur. They are also an essential element in creating the sense among employees that their treatment is fair because they know what rules apply to them and to other employees.

Personnel policies are not static, and even in agencies with well-established and complete policies they need to be reviewed periodically. Changes are most often identified in response to problems or issues. Several employees, for example, may develop an interest in job sharing because of their family circumstances. A policy may need to be developed to describe under what circumstances is job sharing possible, what categories of positions are eligible for sharing, and how employees apply for sharing. In other instances, there may be concern that too much time is being spent by employees playing computer games or surfing the Internet, and policies may need to be developed that limit the use of agency resources for these purposes.

Changes also occur in response to changes in applicable laws. Several years ago, a policy dealing with sexual harassment was probably the exception rather than the rule. Today, given U.S. Supreme Court rulings about employer liability when such harassment occurs, all agencies are well served by a written policy in this area. (See chapter 26 for further discussion of sexual harassment.)

Agencies with policies should also review them periodically against a suggested list of what should be included in a policy manual. One such list, adapted from Pecora's (1995) work, is found in Appendix 3. Additional content on behavioral expectations was added because it is often such expectations that create minor sources of tension with the agency. *Creating Your Employee Handbook* (Bernstein, 1999) and comparable publications can also help in developing a personnel manual.

Agencies that do not have many written policies or have not codified their existing policies may believe that the task of developing such a codification is overwhelming when reviewing a list of possible personnel manual content. Such agencies are likely to be small or new. Unless the agency is able to devote a portion of someone's time to developing a policy manual or contract with someone to develop one, the task may indeed be overwhelming. However, the director can make use of a range of supports to make the task less overwhelming. For example, she can ask colleagues from other more established agencies if it would be possible to review and adopt portions of their personnel manual when such adoptions fit her agency. She can ask staff and board members to each be responsible for writing a section of the manual. Or she can see manual development as a task that stretches over a year or two, dealing with limited parts of the manual at any given time. If this approach is taken, it will be important for the director to be disciplined and establish a timeframe for completion and hold to that timeframe.

The governing board typically adopts personnel policies. Thus, a certain level of board involvement in the process of developing or modifying policies may be essential. The procedures to implement the policies may also be adopted by the governing board but are more often left to the discretion of the director or other appropriate administrators. A personnel manual typically includes the policies or the essence of the policies as well as the procedures used to implement the policies.

It is also appropriate and desirable for employees to be involved in the development of personnel policies. The extent to which they see the policies as clear, fair, and easy to observe will influence their observation of them. They may also identify problems in implementation that even the best board and director cannot anticipate. As with job descriptions, however, those practices that best help the agency accomplish its mission need to take precedence over employees' preferences. Employees, for example, may not prefer to work evenings on a rotating schedule, but if evenings are when the clients need to access services, those preferences cannot be respected. Though their preferences cannot determine the policies, encouraging employees to be involved in the development and periodic review of policies can do much to empower them and win their cooperation. It will also help ensure that the personnel manual is not just a tool used by management, but something that is helpful to all in the agency.

STAFF DEVELOPMENT AND TRAINING

Although written position descriptions and personnel manuals help an agency's employees know what is expected of them, staff development and training programs help ensure that employees fully understand and are prepared to meet the expectations for them. They can help employees become prepared to meet new challenges. Staff development and training programs can also be of benefit to employee morale since their existence indicates that the agency cares about them.

Skidmore (1995, p. 269) indicated that staff development is as important for seasoned staff members as it is for those new to the staff. Staff development and training is important to help ensure that neither the agency nor the employees become static. The need to ensure continued growth and development is evident from the requirement of many professional licensure programs, including those licensing social workers, that those licensed engage in a specified amount of continuing education to renew the license. Many of the agency's employees will have a strong interest in training and development programs because of the licensure requirements that they must meet.

Most small agencies have their staff participate in development activities that are external to the agency. Such agencies often cannot afford a development staff or even a portion of someone's time devoted to training and development, so external resources are the only ones that are realistically available. However, there are some ways in which such agencies might engage in internal development and training activities at a relatively low cost; some alternatives are suggested below.

Large agencies usually have a portion of an employee's time devoted to staff development and may even have a staff of several people focused on that area. They, however, also make use of external opportunities to further develop their staff.

Staff development can focus on a range of interests and activities. It may take the form of an orientation session for new employees that explains the agency's policies and practices. It may focus on the development of a new skill, such as administering a test to assess clients or learning to use a spreadsheet program. It may focus on a new approach that could be used with clients. It may be a means of preparing employees to assume a new job within the agencies. It may result in a certificate in an area or even in a degree. It is probable, for example, that some of the readers of this book are pursuing an MSW degree with the support of their agency as a means of staff development.

Agencies also vary in the forms of support that they provide for staff development and training when such training occurs outside the agency.

Some agencies may support the full or partial cost of such training, including such things as registration fees, lodging, and travel expenses. Others may not support training costs but will provide time off to participate in training, when such participation has been approved by the employee's supervisor. Still others may require that employees engage in all training on their own time and at their own expense, even if such training is related to agency purposes and the employee's position.

One of the most common forms of staff development and training is that of sending an employee to a conference or brief continuing education course. Less common when this happens is the expectation that, in return for this support from the agency, the employee will share with others relevant information learned from the experience. Expecting the employee to do so can be a way of seeing that the funds spent on development, which are often limited, also benefit others in the agency. There are several means that could be used to accomplish this. The employee could be asked to write a report on the training session, and the report could be shared with others in the agency. The employee could be asked to conduct an informal seminar for others at a brown bag lunch. The employee could be asked to make a presentation about the training in the agency's staff development and training program. Regardless of the mechanism selected, it is helpful if agencies can find a way to stretch their staff development funds by ensuring that those participating in development activities share information about what they learned with others in the agency.

Another common form of staff development in larger agencies is a formal internal program of training. In some instances, participation in a series of courses that comprise the training program results in the employee being certified in a given area. The program may make use of persons both internal and external to the agency to provide the training.

The training activities provided through such a formal program may vary. Some may focus on agency policies and be a way of providing continuing orientation to the agency and its expectations. Others may focus less on the agency and more on developing specific skills or knowledge among employees. Some activities may focus on matters that are related primarily to personal development, such as fitness or tole painting, as a way of enhancing employee morale. High-tech companies lead the way in the latter area and often provide their employees with a range of development activities that are not directly related to job expectations.

Even if an agency is too small to support its own training and development staff and does not have sufficient resources to send employees to conferences or continuing education programs, it can engage in staff development and training. There is a range of simple and inexpensive activities that even the smallest agency can use. A portion of a staff meeting, for example, can be spent on developing new skills. One agency, for example, ends each staff meeting with one staff member showing the others new techniques he or she has learned on the agency's personal computers.

Other inexpensive approaches include asking a staff member to read a relevant article in a professional journal and then lead a discussion on the implications of the article for the agency. While all staff could read the article and understand its meaning, the discussion of the article provides an opportunity for staff to learn from each other. Videotapes of television programs that may be relevant to the agency could also be viewed by the staff and discussed. And, of course, there are a wide range of professional videotapes that can be purchased or rented for viewing and subsequent discussion if the agency budget has sufficient funds.

Another way to stretch limited development and training resources is to engage in activities with other agencies that may have comparable interests. One agency's budget may not be sufficient to pay the cost of hiring a trainer on a particular technique, but the combined resources of two or more agencies may be adequate.

It is important that all agencies engage in some form of staff development and training, and there are ways that even the smallest agency can do so. Such activities help ensure that employees' skills and knowledge are current. They also help maintain the morale of employees and their commitment to the agency. Thus, they are a useful means of ensuring that the agency continues to fill its mission and purpose.

CONCLUSION

In this chapter, we argue that human resources—people and the knowledge, skill, and values they offer—are perhaps the most important resource available to a social service agency. Given the critical role that they play in ensuring that the agency fulfills its mission and purpose, the recruitment, deployment, supervision, and evaluation of those resources are critical tasks for any social administrator.

The organization of the social agency and design of the positions within that agency are essential elements of the deployment of an agency's human resources. Though there is a wealth of literature dealing with agencies, much of that literature does not address the nexus between the mission and purpose of a given agency and the personnel system of that agency. We maintain that this relationship is a critical one. The personnel system of any given organization, by which we mean the kind and number of people employed, duties assigned, and so on, and the mission of that agency must bear a close relationship to each other.

Much of this chapter dealt with position design, and some overarching principles were discussed that guided that discussion. It is argued that job design needs to relate to the mission of the agency and needs to be a constant process. That is, changes within the agency and periodic evaluations of the performance of agency employees provide opportunities to ensure that the positions of the agency are designed to help the agency achieve its purpose. Technological changes also provide an opportunity to review the duties associated with any given position.

The primacy of the need for an agency to achieve its mission and purposes influences the design of all positions in the agency. The specification of the position of the head or director usually occurs first and influences the other kinds of positions needed. Though it is appropriate that any given set of job duties reflect the talents of the position occupant, maximizing those talents or the employee's personal satisfaction should not assume the primacy that needs to be assigned to achieving the agency's mission.

The chapter also emphasized the need for written documents dealing with personnel. Such documents include position descriptions and an agency personnel manual. The focus on written documents is not intended to be fussily bureaucratic. Rather, the focus exists because communicating in writing forces clarity. Such clarity enables those external to an agency as well as those within the agency to understand the expectations of employees. It also facilitates review of the ways in which the agency's positions and personnel policies and procedures facilitate accomplishment of the agency's mission. Staff development and training were also discussed as means to ensure that employees know their work expectations.

CHAPTER 20

Human Resources

In chapter 19, we indicated that human resources are one of three basic types of resources available to an organization and are the most critical of the available resources if the organization is to accomplish its mission and purpose.[1] This chapter focuses on human resources through a discussion of how an organization proceeds to recruit, hire, supervise, evaluate, and terminate its employees.

Recruiting and hiring the best-qualified employee are critical to the success of an organization. Performing the tasks associated with this process well saves the organization funds by reducing turnover and its associated costs and results in enhanced effectiveness when the right people are hired for the right jobs. Pecora (1995) indicated that the "employment selection process is an important investment of administrative time" (p. 1829). Given the increasing legal requirements associated with this area, performing these tasks well will also help the agency avoid lawsuits and equal opportunity complaints.

Relevant to the employment process are the requirements resulting from federal statutes and presidential executive orders dealing with equal opportunity, affirmative action, and sexual harassment. All three of these areas are discussed in greater detail in chapter 26, which deals with human diversity and the concept of administrative justice. However, the implications of equal opportunity and affirmative action as they apply to the employment process are also described in this chapter.

RECRUITMENT

Chapter 19 discussed the design of positions in the organization and the need to continually reassess the skills and knowledge needed. It also discussed the importance of a position description as a means of communicating to an employee what was expected of the employee. The design and description of the position is the first step in recruiting the best-qualified employee for that position. Rapp and Poertner (1992, p. 155) indicated that developing a job description is the most important part of knowing the kind of employee needed. In many instances, a position description will already exist, but it may list only the duties to be performed and not the skills, education, and certification needed. If that is the case, those elements need to be specified before the recruitment process can occur.

In identifying the duties of a position and the qualifications needed to fill the position, it is also important to ensure that the elements identified would not prevent the agency from providing equal opportunity to all persons regardless of race, color, sex, religion, national origin, age, or disability. Many organizational policies also provide for equal opportunity regardless of sexual orientation, but this category is not covered by federal statute. People covered by the statutory provisions (and any added organizational provisions) are often referred to as members of a "protected class."

It is also important that the announcement of an available position be "posted" or advertised where it will attract the best-qualified candidates. The agency also needs to ensure that the advertising sources used will be accessible to members of protected classes. The posting of a position may take the form of a literal posting on a bulletin board, a circular distributed to those who may be qualified and interested, an advertisement in a newspaper or journal, a listing with employment or placement agencies, or a listing on a Web-based job posting site. Newspaper or journal ads are the most common form of posting, and their use can be the best way to ensure that the agency has reached the maximum number of qualified potential candidates.

How widely an announcement of a position is posted may depend on the nature of the position. The position of executive director of a large agency will likely be advertised in more sources and over a longer time period than a secretarial position in the same agency. There are likely fewer people qualified to serve as executive director than may be qualified to serve as a secretary, and thus advertising the director's position more widely and longer may help produce an adequate pool of candidates. To ensure that agencies are acting affirmatively to hire protected class persons, many agencies will advertise positions in sources targeted toward such populations, such as Hispanic or African American newspapers.

Under certain conditions, a position may be filled without having been posted or advertised. Sometimes such positions are filled through internal hiring within an organization, but occasionally someone not presently employed by the agency is hired without the position having been advertised. The conditions under which such hiring may occur include the temporary hiring of a person to fill a position while a search to fill the position permanently is under way or a reorganization of an agency that results in the movement of a person to a new position but with no actual vacancy occurring. However, those circumstances are very limited, and agencies are probably well served by posting all available positions.

Some agencies publish the complete position description when posting a position. This can be an expensive practice. It is probably better to post a brief description of the duties of the position, the complete description of the qualifications for the position, and information about where to forward applications and/or obtain additional information about the position. In the posting, most agencies will indicate that they are equal opportunity/ affirmative action employers as a means of ensuring protected class candidates that they will be treated fairly and without discrimination. A sample ad is included in Appendix 4.

In identifying the duties associated with a particular position, it is important that the job functions that are essential to the position be identified. Legally, an "essential function" is a basic job duty that an employee must be able to perform with or without accommodation.[2] A caseworker, for example, would not need to lift fifty-pound boxes as an essential function of the job, but a warehouse employee in a food bank may have to do so as an essential function. The caseworker, however, may be required to be able to travel to visit clients located at various clients' homes in a county as an essential function of the casework position.

Most jobs have functions that are not essential but are desirable. Although lifting fifty-pound boxes may not be essential for a caseworker's job, it may be identified as a marginal function that could be performed if the caseworker assisted with the food bank. Applicants would not be eliminated from consideration if they were not able to lift fifty-pound boxes because it is a marginal rather than essential function.

The qualifications for a position should relate to the duties that are essential in that position and should not unlawfully discriminate against protected-class persons. Some qualifications may be viewed as essential to the position and others may be preferred. For example, a warehouse employee would not need an MSW to perform his or her duties, but a caseworker may need such a degree. Or, the qualifications for the caseworker position may specify that a BSW is required but an MSW is preferred. The qualifications for the warehouse position should not specify that candidates must be "young" or a "boy" or use other descriptive terms unrelated to the duties of the position. The use of "young" would represent age discrimination because it is not the age of the applicants but their ability to lift fifty-pound boxes that matters. The use of "boy" would represent both age and sex discrimination because it indicates a young person is sought and suggests that only males are capable of lifting fifty-pound boxes, which is untrue.

Positions must also be posted for sufficient time to allow qualified applicants to see them and apply. Many organizations require that positions be posted for at least fourteen days before the position can be filled as a way of ensuring that sufficient time is allowed. Postings should specify a closing date for applications or specify that the review of applications will begin on a specified date and continue until the position is filled. The latter approach is sometimes selected when there is concern that there may not be enough qualified candidates in the pool; applications received after the specified review date would be given as much consideration as those received before that date. If a closing date is specified, then no applications received after that date should be considered.

Advertising a position may be sufficient for some positions to ensure that there is a reasonably sized pool of qualified candidates to consider for the position. For most positions, this is the first rather than the only step in the recruitment process. To identify well-qualified candidates, more proactive actions need to be taken. Those actions may include sending a copy of the position announcement to persons already employed in the field to whom it may be of interest. Faculty members at nearby colleges and universities are often asked to recommend qualified persons. Board members might be asked to directly contact persons whom they believe may be qualified and/ or to share information about the vacancy with colleagues who may know of qualified applicants. Calls or personal letters to qualified potential applicants can also be ways of ensuring that the best qualified people know of the position and are encouraged to apply for it.

When applications are received, it is important that there be some follow-up with applicants as a simple matter of courtesy and as a means of further informing and interesting them in the position. The follow-up should at least be a letter acknowledging receipt of the application and indicating the next step in the process. The letter might also include information and brochures about the agency and its services and about the community in which the agency is located. If the search takes longer than anticipated, a follow-up letter explaining the delay and indicating when the applicant may expect to hear about his or her status demonstrates the agency's professionalism to the applicant and ensures that applicants do not lose interest.

HIRING

Reviewing Applications

The hiring process begins with review of the applications received after the deadline for applying has been reached. Each application should be reviewed against the qualifications identified for the position. Applications that do not meet one or more of the required qualifications should be rejected, and those applicants should be notified that their application is no longer under consideration. Applicants who meet all of the minimum qualifications should be reviewed further.

Out of fairness to others and to ensure that the agency is providing equal opportunity, applications from those who do not meet the basic qualifications for the position must be rejected no matter how appealing the applicant may appear. If a basic qualification for a position is an MSW degree and an applicant who lacks that degree receives further consideration, the agency has not treated equally all other potential non-MSW applicants who might have applied for the position had they known that the MSW requirement might be waived. Since some of those potential applicants are likely to be members of protected classes covered by federal legislation, the agency may easily find itself accused of violating equal opportunity/affirmative action laws by not adhering to the basic qualifications advertised. The need to strictly adhere to the qualifications identified is part of why it is so important to consider those qualifications and their relationship to the tasks that are to be performed in designing positions.

It is usually helpful to have several different people review the applications received to ensure fairness. It may be possible for only one person to review the applications to reject those that do not meet the basic qualifications. Even that review may benefit by the involvement of more than one person. In deciding which applications merit further consideration, however, the views of several persons are almost always of help. Skidmore (1995, p. 231) discussed the various roles that directors and staff committees may play in the hiring process, and indicates that there are variations that reflect agency culture and needs.

In prioritizing applications received, several basic questions should be considered. Among them are the following.

1. In addition to meeting the basic qualifications for the position, does the applicant meet some of the preferred qualifications? A basic qualification, for example, might be an MSW degree. A preferred qualification might be two years of post-MSW experience working with adolescents.
2. Are there any gaps in the applicant's work experience that are not explained in the application or its cover letter? If so, it will be important to note them and follow up on them with the applicant and the applicant's references.
3. Does the applicant appear to have a stable employment record that reflects a progression of positions held? An applicant who changes jobs frequently merits some special follow-up with the applicant and references. Few agencies can afford to hire and invest in training an employee who will leave after a short time. Are there understandable reasons why the applicant may have changed jobs frequently?
4. Does the applicant appear to have experience in an agency like yours and/or completing the duties that are a part of the position? In some instances, such experience may be a basic requirement. In other instances, however, it may simply be a factor that makes some applicants more attractive than others.

Factors that should not enter into prioritizing the applications received are those that may represent unlawful employment discrimination. Such factors include the applicant's age, gender, race, religion, national origin, color, and disability. Pregnancy (actual or possible) is also a factor that should not be considered in reviewing applications. An applicant cannot be eliminated from consideration solely because of any of those factors. After the initial review of applications, applications from protected class candidates should be reviewed again to ensure that they received fair consideration and that their applications were not eliminated for a discriminatory reason.

When a salary amount has not been specifically identified in the position announcement, agencies are sometimes concerned about whether very well qualified candidates will be interested in a given position with the salary that the agency is able to pay. Rather than ruling an applicant out because of salary assumptions or inviting the applicant for an interview only to find that the applicant has no interest in the position given its salary, it would be better to call the applicant beforehand and discuss salary expectations. Approaching this matter relatively early in the process can save time and effort for both the applicant and the agency.

After the applications have been prioritized, the agency may wish to notify those who will not be invited for an interview that their application is no longer under review. Many agencies will notify most of the applicants who will not be invited for an interview that their application is no longer under review and delay notification for perhaps two or three applicants whose applications are highly rated but not highly enough to receive an immediate invitation for an interview. This provides a pool to turn to should the applicants invited for interviews not do well in the interviews or no longer be available.

Applicants are typically asked to forward the names, addresses, and phone numbers of three to five references with the application. Though written reference letters can be of help, telephone conversations with the references often provide more information and allow questions about matters that may be of concern. Ending those conversations with an open-ended question like, "Is there anything else about this applicant that may be important for me to know?" can often yield helpful and unexpected information.[3]

Before interviewing a candidate, it is usually helpful to check with some of the applicant's references to get a sense of potential problem areas that the agency may wish to ask about during the interview. Some reference contacts should likely be reserved until after the interview, however, so those references may be asked about things observed during the interview that were of concern.

Interviewing Applicants

Skidmore (1995, p. 231) indicated that the purpose of recruitment is to employ staff who are competent and have the ability to get along with clients and other staff members. The interview is a part of the recruitment process. Interviews are opportunities to assess the applicant's competence, to assess the fit between the applicant and the agency, and to convince the applicant that he or she should come to work for the agency. The latter facet of the interview is often neglected in the interview process.

The formality and complexity of the interview and number of interviewers associated with it may vary significantly from agency to agency. Large or well-funded agencies, for example, may bring candidates from great distances to the agency for an interview. In those instances, arrangements are more complex because transportation arrangements need to be made, hotel reservations provided, meal locations and dinner guests identified, and so on. Smaller and less well-funded agencies or rural agencies, however, are more often selecting from a relatively local applicant pool who will be responsible for their own transportation arrangements (although their costs may be reimbursed) and for whom an overnight stay or meals may not be required.

Regardless of the type of interview, it is important to realize that whatever other purposes they serve the interview arrangements also provide an opportunity for the agency to be presented as a professional place that "has its act together." That means ensuring that the applicant knows the transportation arrangements or directions to the agency, the time and length of the interview and with whom he or she will be meeting, whether to prepare a formal presentation, and other expectations.

Several people at the agency should ordinarily be involved with the interview, although the level of their involvement may vary. In large agencies, there will likely be a search committee, all of whom will participate in the interview process. In smaller agencies, there may not be a formal committee, but the applicant may be interviewed by the agency director, the persons with whom she or he would work directly, and possibly one or more members of the board of directors.

It is helpful to take applicants on a brief tour of the agency so they may see the physical arrangements and meet informally with some of the agency's employees. Such tours also provide an opportunity to observe the way in which the applicant interacts with those who would become co-workers, should the applicant be hired, and how the applicant handles new situations.

Depending upon the position, the applicant may be invited to make a presentation about a topic relevant to the applicant's past employment and the agency's available position. Representatives of other local agencies are sometimes invited to such presentations to provide them with an opportunity to meet the applicant. This is especially useful in cases where the applicant will be working with staff from those agencies.

There is a tendency to ask hypothetical questions during an interview. That is, applicants are often asked what they would do in a given situation. Increasingly, human resources specialists are suggesting that it may be more helpful to ask what an applicant has done in such situations in the past. The assumption underlying this approach is that past behavior is a better indicator of how someone may behave in the future than any response to a hypothetical situation.

If the position is a clinical one, for example, applicants might be asked to describe a situation in their work past when a client was unhappy about a service delivered or an arrangement made for the client. Applicants might be asked to describe what they did in that situation and what the outcome of their actions was. In preparing for the interview, the agency personnel should consider the kinds of situations often encountered in the position and ask about the applicant's past actions in situations like those. They may want to ask about problematic or difficult situations, but it is also appropriate to ask about more positive situations.

To further illustrate this approach, if the applicant is applying for a secretarial position, he might be asked to describe a situation in which he was given an important task to complete at the last minute. He might be asked to describe the actions taken and the outcome of those actions. Some situations that might be used apply to any position. Few job settings, for example, are without some conflict at some time. Given this, applicants for all positions might be asked to describe a situation in which they encountered conflict with a fellow employee, asked what action they took in that situation, and asked what the outcome of their action was.

Assessing the applicant's fit with the job and its expectations are also important. This can be tapped in part by asking the applicant about the things she has liked and disliked about past jobs. For example, if the position requires a great deal of travel and an applicant indicates that one thing she disliked in an earlier job was the travel required, then even though the applicant may be well qualified for the position, she may not be happy in it.

Asking about past positions may not yield as much information with relatively inexperienced applicants. This may be partly because they haven't had much work experience. It may also be that the person's experience may not reflect their present and more mature judgment. Entry-level positions attract applications from persons who have not had much work experience or experience in the field. However, even with such applicants, questions about past behaviors can provide helpful information. The applicant may describe the actions taken to deal with an unhappy customer in his job at a restaurant rather than with a client to whom he was delivering services. Regardless of the situation, the goal is to learn what applicants actually did when faced with such a situation rather than hypothetical musings about what they might do.

Interviewers for the agency should prepare for the interview by deciding what questions need to be asked and who will ask them. When an applicant interviews with several different people, often each person asks the same set of questions—What appeals to you about this job? Why do you want to leave your current job? By identifying in advance who will ask a given question and sharing information about the response to the question with all other interviewers later, more information can be obtained and repetition is avoided. At some point during the interview, the director or hiring administrator should discuss with the applicant such matters as the timetable for a decision, the salary expectations of the applicant, fringe benefits available, the probable starting date in the position, and so forth.

Interviewers should take notes on an applicant's responses to the questions. Such notes will refresh the interviewer's memory when the qualifications of all applicants are reviewed. Further, should the worst happen and an applicant complain or sue about a hiring decision, they will provide evidence of the basis on which a hiring decision was made.

Following an applicant's departure, those who conducted interviews should meet to share the information each obtained and their impressions. This may require scheduled debriefing sessions, or interviewers may just get together on their own. Notes of this discussion should be taken as well. After all applicants have been interviewed, a comparable discussion should occur to help the hiring administrator decide to whom should be offered the position.

Offering the Position

Larger agencies often have protocols for offering positions. The offer must be made by a certain person, must be made in a certain form (written as opposed to verbal), and can be made only after review by certain persons, such as the agency's affirmative action officer. Although in smaller and medium-sized agencies approval from the board of directors may have to be sought to offer certain types of positions, the protocol in those agencies is typically far less formal.

Job offers are often initially verbal. When the director or hiring administrator calls to extend an offer, the salary amount, starting date, work hours, and so on are often negotiated to the extent such negotiation is feasible. After all of the elements of the position are resolved, the offer should be extended in writing.

Any letter offering a position should specify the basic elements of the position such as title, salary, work hours, starting date, and so forth. The letter should also identify some of the major duties associated with the position and the way in which the performance of those duties will be evaluated. A copy of the full position description might be included as a way to expand upon the list of major duties found in the letter. In addition, a copy of the agency's personnel manual should be included, which was discussed in chapter 19, and the letter should indicate that the position and the employee's actions are governed by the manual. If the agency does not have a manual or is in the process of developing one, the letter should include those documents that describe the conditions of employment. (A sample offer letter is found in Appendix 5.)

Two copies of the letter should be forwarded to the new employee. One signed copy should be returned to the agency as an indication of acceptance of the offer. Having a signed copy of the offer letter in the agency files can avoid problems in the future because the signed copy indicates that the employee acknowledged and agreed to the terms of the employment.

Once an offer has been accepted, the agency should announce the hiring to other employees and, when appropriate, to the board of directors. Some information about the employee might be provided to those who were not involved in the interview process. A news release can be sent to local newspapers and other agencies. The paper may not publish the release, but if it does it will further welcome the new employee and also provide some publicity for the agency.

ADMINISTRATIVE SUPERVISION OF EMPLOYEES

The supervision of employees discussed in this section differs from that discussed in such sources as Kadushin (1992) and Munson (1993). They deal with supervision as a means of managing the provision of casework services. This section deals with the general kind of staff supervision that occurs in all organizations, regardless of their purpose. This type of supervision involves guiding and directing the activities of employees as a means of ensuring that the organization's goals and purposes are met. The supervisor is anyone who is assigned responsibility for guiding, reviewing, and evaluating the performance of a given employee. Supervision also often serves to mediate between the employee and the agency's goals, and the supervisor becomes an important linchpin in communicating those goals (Bunker & Wijinberg, 1985). The discussion here focuses on orientation of new employees, mentoring and evaluation in particular.

Good supervision begins with an employee's first day on the job.[4] The first day and the initial weeks that follow it provide an opportunity to orient the employee to the organization and the expectations of her. Given this, the supervisor of a new employee should set aside several hours on the employee's first day to provide the orientation needed.

The orientation of new employees should be both to the physical environment and to the work expectations. Orientation to the physical environment should include a tour of the space and introductions to colleagues in their workspaces. Where one obtains work supplies, where travel reimbursement and other forms are located, how one clocks in and out, where the coffee pot is located, what the office practices are with regard to paying for coffee, and where the lunch room, staff lounge, and restrooms are located should all be a part of this orientation.

Though orientation to the workspace will help the employee feel more comfortable, the orientation to work expectations is clearly more important to the employee's long-term success. This orientation should include a review of key provisions in the agency's personnel manual. Key provisions may be determined by focusing on those that most often are misunderstood by staff and that may need further explanation or those that represent the taboos of the organization.

It may be helpful to organize the initial orientation around a review of the position description applicable to the new employee. Reviewing the duties identified in that description can be a way to ensure that the new employee is clear as to what is expected. The review can also indicate to the employee the priority attached to certain duties.

This phase of the orientation should also include an orientation to some of the supervisor's specific expectations. What kind of problems should be called to the supervisor's immediate attention? Is there a time of day that is best for talking with the supervisor? Does the supervisor prefer written or verbal communication on certain types of matters? Will the supervisor and employee have regular meetings, and what types of issues might those meetings cover?

The initial orientation should be followed by a series of one-on-one private meetings between the supervisor and employee during the employee's first month or so of work. Although the new employee may participate in staff meetings, group meetings will not accomplish everything that can be accomplished in a private meeting. The private meeting will provide the employee with an opportunity to ask questions and get to know the supervisor better and provide the supervisor with the sense of the problems that the employee is encountering and ways in which the employee may be best approached. The private meeting will allow the employee to raise those questions that he thinks are too stupid or trivial to raise in group meetings. The private meeting will also allow the supervisor to provide guidance as to things that might be done differently by the employee without running the risk of embarrassing the employee by raising such matters publicly.

Some organizations formally assign mentors to work with new employees in addition to having a supervisor assigned to the employee. The mentor is someone whom the employee can approach with questions he fears are too dumb or embarrassing to ask the supervisor. Often those questions go to the organizational culture and the practices within the agency. Although many mentoring relationships develop spontaneously, during an employee's first months of employment it can be helpful to have someone identified who sees providing special assistance to the employee as a part of her duties.

Once the employee has been oriented to the agency and the job, periodic private meetings with the supervisor should continue to be held—even if the employee is doing a wonderful job. If the employee is doing well, the meetings can be used to reinforce the positive things that are being done. If the employee is struggling with some challenges, those meetings can focus on ways in which the employee might meet the challenges. The frequency with which such meetings occur may depend upon the performance of the employee, but they should occur at least once each month initially.

The meetings should be private, and the employee should be notified in advance. Supervisors sometimes believe that stopping by an employee's desk periodically is sufficient to provide the guidance needed. It is not. The employee may be more uncomfortable raising the matters in an unscheduled stop than she would be if the meeting were behind closed doors, perhaps because of concern that coworkers or visitors may overhear. The time of the meeting should be indicated in advance to allow the employee to think about those issues that she wishes to raise.

Some supervisors may view the time required to provide the kind of supervision described above as wasted. They want the employee to *do* his job and don't see the value in time spent helping the employee understand what is expected of him, recognizing positive performance, and correcting performance that is below par. To do so is to unconsciously adopt a machine model of organization, with workers as replaceable cogs in the machine. The time spent, however, represents stewardship of the agency's most valuable resources. Supervision of employees can result in the delivery of better quality services to the agency's clients because employees are better prepared to deliver the services expected of them. It can help correct minor problems in employee performance before they become major ones. It can help the agency avoid having to terminate an unsatisfactory employee and thus avoid the interrupted services and high costs of hiring a replacement that follow such termination. Thus, the time invested in supervision is of benefit to the agency and its clients.

Employee Evaluation

Supervision also provides opportunities for ongoing evaluation of an employee. In addition to the incidental evaluation provided through supervision, every employee should have a periodic evaluation of her performance that represents a summative evaluation of the performance to date. With new employees, such an evaluation might occur after six months of employment. Many agencies treat the first six months of employment as a probationary period. In large agencies and those covered by civil service or labor agreements, a probationary period is likely specified, as is the timing of the first evaluation within that period. With all employees, at least an annual evaluation should occur. In some agencies, all such evaluations occur at the same time of year. In other agencies, they occur around the anniversary of the employee's hiring.

The evaluation should be organized around the employee's position description. It should include a review of the duties specified in that description and conclusions about the employee's performance of those duties. It should also include a review of behavior that may not always be specified in great detail in the position description. That behavior may include such things as cooperation with colleagues, promptness in completing assigned work, tardiness, and so on. The employee should also be made aware through supervision of any behavior that is expected of him and thus not be surprised when such issues are covered by the evaluation.

In some agencies, both the employee and supervisor are expected to prepare a written assessment of the employee's performance and share the assessments with each other in advance of the evaluation conference. The conference is then devoted to discussing the assessments. In other agencies, no advance written materials are prepared, and only a conference is held. In all agencies, there should be an evaluation conference, and some written documentation of the evaluation conclusions should be prepared.

The evaluation conference is important because evaluation needs to be an interactive process. The supervisor needs the interaction that occurs in a meeting to ensure that the employee understands the changed behavior that may be expected of her. The employee needs to be provided with a chance to ask questions about the changes sought and to explain some of the reasons for actions that she may have taken.

Written documentation of the conclusions of the evaluation conference needs to be maintained in the agency files. The litigious nature of our society makes such documentation essential. Supervisors often view it as a waste of time, especially when the employee's performance is positive. It is not a waste of time given the critical role that it can play in protecting the supervisor and agency should a disgruntled employee file a complaint or lawsuit.

The documentation may include any notes that the supervisor prepared in advance of and during the evaluation conference. The documentation must also include some evidence that the employee was notified of the behavior expected of her. That notice could take the form of forwarding to the employee the supervisor's notes from the conference, providing they are sufficiently detailed, with a cover memo documenting such forwarding. More often, it takes the form of a memo prepared by the supervisor after the conference that summarizes the positive aspects of the employee and identifies the behaviors that need to be changed. Such a memo will often also identify a timetable for the needed changes.

Such documentation must be prepared for those employees who are doing a wonderful job as well as those whose performance needs to be improved. If written documentation of the evaluation conference is maintained only for those whose performance needs to be improved, a disgruntled employee may allege discrimination. The employee may argue that the performance of others also needed improvement, but the supervisor only noted problems with his employment because of the wish to fire him. The documentation for those whose performance needs to be improved may be lengthier, but even for the superior employee some detail needs to be maintained. It is not sufficient that the documentation for such an employee to contain only phrases like, "Wonderful job!" The documentation needs to provide some detail as to what led the supervisor to that conclusion. Such documentation should be easy for social workers accustomed to making progress notes on clients.

The discussion thus far has suggested that only the supervisor is involved in evaluation. Although it is typical for only the supervisor to participate in the evaluation conference, others may be involved in sharing assessments of performance that lead up to the conference. Such evaluation procedures are sometimes referred to as 360-degree evaluations.

The reference to 360-degree evaluations refers to an evaluation in which all persons around the employee participate. Participants may include the employee's clients or other employees she supervises, the employee's co-workers or peers, and the employee's supervisor and others who hold positions above that of the employee. The advantage of using information from all these people is that it provides a fuller picture of the employee's actions and behavior and their impact on others. For example, from the supervisor's viewpoint, the employee may be doing a fine job with her clients. Case records are complete, appointments are kept, and there have been no client complaints. The clients, however, may see the employee as someone who rushes through meetings with them and whose greatest interest is in completing paperwork. Knowledge of this will assist the supervisor in guiding the employee to establish a more open and unhurried relationship with the clients.

In conducting an employee's evaluation, the supervisor should always keep in mind the purpose of evaluation. Part of the purpose is stewardship to the agency and those who support it and benefit from its services. Clients and stakeholders have the right to expect that employees are doing the jobs that they are paid to do. Part of the purpose is also to help employees grow. Such growth comes from knowing the things that are being done well. It also comes from knowing what activities or behaviors may need to be changed and then receiving help, through supervision, to accomplish the changes that are needed.

TERMINATION OF EMPLOYEES

The termination of an employee sometimes occurs when the best efforts at hiring, training, supervising, and evaluating have not produced the desired outcomes. However, termination also occurs when an employee decides to resign or retire. Though the first type of termination will be the focus of this section, the voluntary termination of an employee's employment also merits mention.

When an employee resigns or retires, it is important that both the employee and others in the agency achieve closure. Such closure is in large part emotional closure. All parties need a chance to express appreciation for the relationships established and work performed. A cake in the office or lunch at a local restaurant is the way such appreciation is often expressed. In the case of a long-term employee, a formal marking of their departure through a reception or dinner may occur. Closure also includes learning the status of the work the employee was doing, notifying those outside the agency of the employee's departure, and perhaps even involving the employee in the training of her successor.

Involuntary departures as a result of the employee being fired or, put more delicately, terminated, are more difficult for all parties. Such departures inherently include hard feelings, the risk of litigation, and, at the most extreme, even potential physical danger for those associated with the termination. For the remainder of this section, *termination* will refer to such involuntary departures, although technically it describes both voluntary and involuntary departures.

Although involuntary terminations are relatively infrequent, they do occur. It is probable that any administrator will be involved with at least one during her career. The discussion below is relatively extensive not because of the frequency with which they occur but because of the difficulty that they present.

Unless the behavior of the employee is gross, termination should occur only after the employee has received notice (often multiple notices) that her behavior is unacceptable and has been given an opportunity to correct the behavior. Gross behavior may merit immediate termination. What constitutes gross behavior is usually defined for those employees covered by civil service or labor agreements and may not cover what the average person might define as gross. Even when the alleged behavior would be seen as gross by most, if not all—such as the rape or murder of a client or embezzlement—many agencies may be required to place an employee accused of such behavior on unpaid or paid leave until the charges of such behavior can be proved. This approach is consistent with the American legal ideal that a person is innocent until proven guilty. In such cases, actual termination occurs only after the charges have been proved.

Most terminations, however, are not for gross behavior and thus are not unexpected events. Most terminations occur after deficiencies have been called to the employee's attention, the need to correct the deficiencies emphasized, and an opportunity for correction provided. Given this, one might expect that such terminations would never be a surprise to the employee. Regrettably, this is often not the case. Underperforming employees are sometimes capable of significant self-deception and denial, and many express great surprise when their termination actually occurs. It is this self-deception that often leads to the grievances and lawsuits that follow termination.

Because of the possibility of a lawsuit or grievance, it is important that the deficiencies that might lead to termination be called to the employee's attention during the supervision and evaluation processes. Such notice is often first communicated verbally. The employee, for example, may be told that the case notes that she is maintaining are inadequate and that the agency may not be able to obtain reimbursement because of their inadequacy. The notice should include an indication of a time frame for addressing the deficiency and, ideally, a means by which it might be addressed. The employee may be told that the completeness of her notes must be improved within two weeks and provided with sample notes to provide guidance as to the kind of information that is needed. The supervisor should make a note for her records of the date on which the employee was advised of the problem and the correction specified. She should also note the date by which deficiencies are to be corrected.

If the deficiency is not corrected in the specified time or the correction proves to be only temporary, the employee should then be advised in writing of the deficiency and the time frame for correction. The written notice of the deficiency should make reference to prior verbal notification(s). Supervisors are sometimes hesitant about providing such written notification because it seems so formal. It is important that the supervisor remember that a part of her role is to protect the agency, which includes its clients and stakeholders, from unjustified complaints and lawsuits. Given the self-deception underperforming employees sometimes engage in, such written protection may be required. The initial written notice can be somewhat informal. It could be a handwritten note, for example, telling the employee that her case notes are again becoming inadequate, reminding her of the earlier discussion about the need for better notes, providing her with a new time frame for improving her notes, and inviting her to talk with the supervisor if she has any questions about what is needed. A copy of the handwritten note should be kept in the supervisor's file.

If the performance is still not improved or if the improvement again proves to be only temporary, more formal written notification should be provided. This notification should include all of the elements of the earlier written notification and also include the possible consequences if continuing improvement does not occur. Those consequences may vary depending on the nature of the offense and agency policy. The consequences may range from a negative letter in the employee's personnel file to the absence of a salary increase if improvement is not noted to an unpaid suspension and ultimately to termination. Agency policy manuals should be consulted because they may specify the range of consequences and sanctions that may be applied.

The above discussion may be taken to suggest that one verbal and two written notices must occur before an employee may be terminated. This is not necessarily the case. Sometimes, as is discussed below, the number and kind of notice that must be provided is specified. When it is not, the supervisor must exercise her best judgment. In other instances, however, the number of notices that occur before an employee is terminated depend on the seriousness of the offense and the likelihood that correction will occur. Generally speaking, a sense of fair play suggests that the employee should receive at least one notice and be given a reasonable time for correction to occur.

Some agency policies, civil service policies, or labor agreements specify an exact number of warnings that an employee must be given before termination can occur. Such provisions sometimes also specify that termination can occur only after a counseling session about the behavior has occurred followed by three written warnings that termination will occur if the specific behavior has not been corrected. With the third warning, employment may be terminated. Such proposals often offer the greatest protection to the employee and may even do so at the cost of quality of the services offered by the agency. When an agency has a choice, the quality of its services would likely be best protected by not specifying an arbitrary number of notices that must be provided but by specifying the content of the notice(s) provided and supporting the need to protect both the rights of the employee and the interests of the agency.

As a general principle, termination can occur for any behavior that is inappropriate, given the nature of that employee's duties. If a secretary's duties include maintaining the calendar of the director and the secretary fails to note meetings on the calendar or notes the wrong dates or times for the meetings, termination may be appropriate. Although the secretary may view this as a minor problem, from the director's viewpoint not keeping appointments with potential donors or the heads of other cooperating agencies may be a significant problem. One error in the calendar may not be cause for termination. Frequent errors after the secretary has been notified that such errors are not acceptable may be cause for termination. Thus, termination can occur for any behavior that is unacceptable given the nature of that employee's duties.

There may be legitimate alternatives to termination in some cases. If it becomes clear that an employee is incapable of the behavior that is expected in a position or cannot consistently demonstrate that behavior, the supervisor may wish to discuss with the employee whether another position within the agency or with another agency would represent a better fit for his abilities. Often, the employee may recognize that the job is one that he simply cannot do but does not know how to get out of the situation. Help in locating another job may be a graceful way for the employee to exit. However, when such jobs are often at a lower level or pay less, employees at risk of termination often choose not to pursue this alternative. They either deceive themselves into believing they can do what is needed or they justify their actions by telling themselves that the supervisor's expectations are unreasonable and that no one could meet them. However, supervisors are entitled to the same consideration that other employees receive, and only if several unjustified firings had occurred would it be likely that the supervisor's behavior would be subject to sanction by her own supervisor.

When a supervisor believes that she may need to terminate an employee, it is important that she notify her own supervisor of the planned action. That supervisor and others in the agency may want to review the employee's record and the notice of inadequate performance that has been provided before and actual termination occurs. In some instances, review by the director or the agency's legal advisor may occur. The director may want to ensure that the board president is notified. It may also be decided that others should be present at the meeting where the termination will actually occur.

Actual notice of an employee's termination should be provided at a meeting with the employee. The employee should be given a written notice of her termination that should describe the reasons for the termination; note in full the previous efforts to ensure that the employee's behavior was corrected; state the effective date of the termination; explain the arrangements that are to be made for the return of agency materials, such as the key to the office, agency credit card, and so on; and detail any other relevant information. The letter or memo may also specify matters that will be discussed in the meeting (use of any remaining vacation time, work site, and activities until termination takes effect, etc.) and indicate that written confirmation of those matters will be provided within a day of the meeting.

It may be helpful in the meeting to share with the employee what the supervisor plans to say about the termination to other agency employees and others who may inquire about the employee's suitability for other positions. A certain amount of bad-mouthing about the supervisor to other employees, especially those to whom the terminated employee was close, is to be expected. However, the supervisor may wish to indicate that the kinds of information disclosed would depend in part on what the employee says and does. Although the supervisor may wish to spare the employee any unneeded embarrassment, she need not have her reputation and that of the agency damaged by unchallenged inaccurate statements made by the terminated employee.

As indicated above, the agency director may wish others to be present at the meeting with the supervisor. If it is believed that the employee may be capable of physical violence, the supervisor may also wish the building's security force or local police force to be notified of the planned action and asked to be readily available, should any violence ensue. If the employee comes to the meeting with a tape recorder and asks to tape the meeting, the supervisor should either reschedule the meeting until she is able to seek legal counsel or, if such counsel is not easily available, also make a tape recording of the meeting. If the employee attends the meeting with an unexpected lawyer or other representative, the supervisor may exclude such a person from the meeting unless she is able to quickly obtain the agency attorney's presence to protect the agency's interests. In some instances, policies or labor agreements may specify those who may attend such meetings. If such guidelines exist, the supervisor should make certain that she has reviewed them before the meeting so she is aware of what may be required by them.

Conventional wisdom about termination offers some advice on when such terminations should occur. It is often suggested that an employee should not be terminated on Friday because the terminated employee may spend the weekend stewing over his termination (Finnie & Sniffin, 1984). The supervisor needs to ensure that the termination will occur when she will be available for a few days following the action. Other employees of the agency will almost certainly have concerns about the termination, and the supervisor needs to be available to reassure them that the termination of one employee does not mean other employees are about to be terminated. The terminated employee may also have questions that need to be answered, and the collection of his personal belongings may need to be supervised.

In some businesses, the termination of an employee, even when voluntary, results in the employee being accompanied from the termination interview by his supervisor to immediately collect his personal belongings and leave the building. The concern is that the employee, even if leaving voluntarily for a better job elsewhere, may damage or remove the agency's records or take proprietary information with him. Although the termination from social welfare agencies is rarely so abrupt, care needs to be paid to the damage that a disgruntled employee may do. Care also needs to be paid to protecting the employee from undue embarrassment to the extent that such protection is possible.

It may be desirable, for example, to hold the termination interview shortly before lunch so that when the employee leaves the supervisor's office, she will not have to immediately encounter her colleagues. Or the interview might be held in an office in a different part of the building so the employee will have a chance to collect herself before facing those with whom she works most closely. The supervisor might offer to collect the employee's personal belongings needed most immediately—coat, purse, and so on—so that she may leave without encountering others. It would be wise to obtain the employee's key to the agency and any of its offices before the employee leaves.

If the employee leaves the office immediately after the termination meeting, an appropriate time for her to collect her personal belongings and return any agency property should be established. The supervisor should be present at that time. Many employees will wish to return at the end of the workday so as to avoid seeing other employees. If that is the case, persons in addition to the supervisor should be available should the supervisor encounter any difficulty and, if physical violence may be a risk, the security or police force should be notified.

If there is concern that the employee may damage the agency's records or equipment or damage the agency's relationship with its clients if she continues to work until the effective date of the termination, she should either be given special tasks to complete at home, be placed on paid administrative leave, or use accumulated vacation time or sick leave until the effective date of the termination. If the agency is a large one with several buildings, it may be that the employee can be given special tasks to complete in another building, separate from her usual work group and workplace. The tasks assigned should probably not be ones critical to the agency.

The supervisor would be served well by engaging in some critical reflection after the termination has taken effect and she has been able to distance herself somewhat from the situation. Were there clues as to the problems that this employee developed that should have been evident in the hiring process? Should the timing and nature of the supervision provided have been different? Should the employee have been assigned a different mentor? Should the employee have been provided with notices of performance deficiencies earlier in the process? This is not to suggest that the supervisor is at fault when termination occurs. However, the termination can be used by the supervisor as a learning experience to further develop her skills at supervision.

Although this has been an extended discussion, let us emphasize again that its length is not due to the frequency with which the administrator or supervisor may be required to terminate employees. Its length is in part due to the infrequency of that event. Because many administrators have limited experience in termination, a more detailed discussion of it is appropriate.

CONCLUSION

The effective management of employees is a critical function for agency administrators. It is critical because qualified employees performing the duties expected of them are essential if the organization is to fulfill its mission and purpose. It is also critical as a means of providing stewardship with regard to agency resources. For most agencies, the bulk of the agency budget is in personnel costs. Thus, ensuring the effective deployment of those personnel becomes important in the wise use of agency fiscal resources.

Critical as it is, there are undoubtedly times when every agency administrator has been frustrated by the many issues, some of which are very petty in nature, associated with the administration of human resources. Is there any administrator who has not at least once expressed the hope that everyone employed by the agency would just grow up and behave like adults? Though there is no way to completely avoid those frustrations, careful attention to the hiring, supervision, and evaluation processes can help avoid many potential problems.

The recruitment and hiring of employees who have the right skills and the right attitude is the first step toward reducing those frustrations. Doing so means that some time needs to be devoted to that effort. Rapp and Poertner (1992, p. 155) compared the effort to spouse selection and indicated that in both instances, divorce is painful and costly. Thus, the administrator needs to be willing to invest the time required to do an effective job of employee selection.

Once hired, the supervision provided to the employee through orientation and ongoing conferences and consultation is important in ensuring the employee's success. That supervision needs to include periodic evaluations that are more formal in nature to provide the employee with a summative understanding of her success and those areas in need of improvement.

Even with careful attention to hiring and skillful supervision, some mistakes in terms of the fit of an employee with a particular job or agency are inevitable. Stewardship of agency resources and fairness to the employee means that the administrator needs to do her best to try to help the employee improve his performance. However, if sufficient improvement is not realized, the supervisor needs to be willing to terminate the employee's tenure with the agency, as difficult and unpleasant as that may be.

CHAPTER 21

Financial Management

Even though social workers willingly acknowledge
the importance of financial management, most students and professionals
want little to do with it. Probably no topic in the social administration pantheon generates less enthusiasm or greater dread among social work students than the two words *financial management*. As a result, a slow but
steady evolution of increasingly sophisticated financial management practice in social agencies has been going largely unnoticed by the larger profession for several decades.

Standardized financial report formats for improving accountability to
stakeholders were one of the little-noted advances of the federated financing movements of the 1920s. The concept of the community chest itself only
got widespread acclaim with the publication of the first Monopoly game in
the mid-1930s. Beginning in the late 1940s, social workers in voluntary social
agencies struggled hard to establish a sound basis for charging fees to clients
(Berkowitz, 1947; Boggs, 1949; Fizdale, 1957; Goodman, 1960; Hofstein, 1955;
Jacobs, 1952; Neumann, 1952). One of the outcomes of these initiatives was
the modern concept of the sliding fee scale,[1] which functions much like the
discounted purchase price in business albeit for different reasons. During

the 1960s, the age of grants brought wave after wave of subtle standardization in accounting and budgeting to a field long celebrated for its individualism and idiosyncrasy. In the 1970s, under the implied threat of federal standards, the accounting profession belatedly promulgated voluntary but authoritative standards for nonprofit health and welfare agencies, which have been widely adopted since that time. These standards, designated as Generally Accepted Accounting Principles (GAAP), are established for commercial and nonprofit agencies by the Financial Accounting Standards Board (GASB). They are enforced primarily through audits performed by professional members of the American Institute of Certified Public Accountants (AICPA).[2]

There have been a number of attempts in the past two decades to conceptualize the entire human service financial management process and to relate it to other aspects of social administration. In the early 1970s, the United Way of America Service Information System (UWASIS) produced a uniform model chart of accounts[3] and a comprehensive listing of program categories and embraced the accounting standards as they were published (Sumariwalla, 1976, 1989). In 1976, profit-oriented break-even analysis[4] was first adapted for use in the social agency setting (Lohmann, 1976).

What do we mean by financial management? There is still uncertainty and disagreement on this point. Lohmann (1980a) set out a five-part model of the financial management process in social agencies characterized by financial planning, fund-raising, allocation, fiscal control, and evaluation. Vinter and Kish (1985) sought to subsume the entire topic of financial management under the heading of budgeting. Sanchez-Meyers (1989) refined a three-part model characterized by (1) acquisition, (2) distribution and control, and (3) recording and reporting. United Way of America produced a financial management guide suitable for use by all nonprofit service agencies (Sumariwalla, 1989). Shostack and Compagna (1987) identified issues involved in the financing of group homes. In addition to these works cited, a number of other specific, limited discussions have appeared in print (Feit & Li, 1998; Vinter & Kish, 1985).

The focus of much of this published literature is on introducing students to the technical concepts of financial management. Yet in a very important sense, the social work educational community is currently ill prepared and largely unresponsive to the basic changes in practice being shaped and molded by changes in financial management practices associated with the managed care revolution (Lohmann, 1997; Lohmann & Lohmann, 1997). This is less a matter of mastery of the nuances of accounting, cost measurement, or financial statements than of understanding the integral role of financial and economically valuable human resources in social agency decision making.

This chapter approaches the topic of financial management from a particular point of view and does not cover all topics that might be covered under this heading. There are three principal reasons for the approach taken in this chapter:

1. Much of the existing technical literature offers a range of introductions to the technical subject matter of financial management, and there is no particular reason to review or recreate that material here. Much of the existing literature is listed in the references noted above.
2. At the same time, the overarching strategic dimensions of financial management have been largely neglected in the existing literature.
3. Just as importantly, the managed care revolution comes on top of the decline of grant funding (which we have characterized as the end of the age of grants) and the related growth of contract funding, commercial social services, and private practice. Though private donations to the "third sector" in general have grown dramatically since 1980, growth of donations to social services has not kept pace with the growth of donations to religion, education, or the arts. By 1987, for example, giving to human services was down to 8.7 percent of all household contributions, and by 1993 it had fallen further to 8.6 percent. (Hodgkinson, Weitzman, et al., 1996, p. 65)

Taken together, these developments raise serious questions about the long-term viability of some of the key financial assumptions of the social agency as an organization and institution. Most importantly, the notion that "the community" can be called upon to rise up and adequately support all existing human needs identified by professionals seems in need of serious rethinking. Perhaps social administrators should be spending less time opportunistically pursuing every available source of funding and more time devising long-term visions and strategies for shoring up the financial foundations and legitimacy of social service institutions. Continued failure to do so could, in the long run, prove catastrophic for the profession of social work as well as the institutions of social welfare.

FINANCING THE SOCIAL AGENCY

As we noted in chapter 3, social work practice has, until quite recently, been considered exclusively agency-based practice for a complex variety of reasons. Close to the core of the concept of the social agency and the underlying legal concept of agency is an explicit set of fiscal relationships between donors, clients, and financial intermediaries, including social administrators and the social workers providing services. More than anything else, it is this set of fiscal relationships, legal commitments, and contracts that defines the three-part transaction discussed in chapter 3.

Hull House: A Multifunded Agency

The folklore of social work practice suggests that the field had its origins in nineteenth-century voluntary agencies, sustained largely by private donations from assorted "mother bountifuls," and shifted essentially to public governmental support in the 1930s. The model of the "multifunded" social agency, which receives support from donations, some funds from public grants and/or contracts, and revenues the sale of products and services, is thought by many people to be a relatively recent development. It is primarily lack of awareness of the past that sustains such views. The reality is much more complicated and interesting.

In reality, the revenue base of American social welfare has long been a mixed economy of government, voluntary, and commercial activity (Hartogs & Weber, 1974; Rosenbaum, 1982; Tobey, 1925). The extent to which this is the case is demonstrated by the following reconstruction of a statement of operations for the Hull House Settlement in 1932, which was still under the direction of Jane Addams. This statement has been constructed from the records of Hull House to reflect the kinds of categories that might be used today. Financial standards in 1932 would not have produced a statement precisely like this. The year of this statement is very significant because it was the height of the Great Depression, during which, according to the conventional wisdom, virtually all private giving ceased and was replaced by the public programs of the New Deal. The statement of operations in Table 21.1, reconstructed from information in a 1932 report to the Chicago Board of Charities, shows a much more complicated picture.

Close examination of this report will reveal a surprisingly complicated financial situation. First, it would appear that the operation was cutting quite close to the bone at this point, as might be expected. The amount carried forward from the previous budget year was only slightly above one-half of one percent. It is important to note that Hull House was operating on a cash accounting basis[5] at this time and neither outstanding amounts owned to the Settlement House nor amounts owed by the Settlement to others can be reflected in the statement. As with all such cash-accounting reports, such year-end balances are largely accidental and poor grounds for comparison from year to year.

It is noteworthy that even in the midst of the Great Depression, nearly half of all of the revenues and support for the settlement house (48.83 percent) came from donations. What is equally interesting, however, is that one-fifth of the voluntary sector Hull House funds for 1932 (22.32 percent)

Table 21.1 Statement of Operations, Hull House, January 1 to December 31, 1932

		Percentages
Balance carried forward	820.31	0.69
Income		
Donations	57,952.94	48.49
Hull House operations	31,460.95	26.33
Unemployment relief	26,491.99	22.17
Endowment	30,088.11	25.18
Fees	3,446.91	2.88
Sales	4,212.24	3.52
Rents	22,987.82	19.24
TOTAL INCOME	118,688.02	
TOTAL AVAILABLE FUNDS	119,508.33	
Expenses		
H. H. program expenses	71,637.99	59.67
Losses on cash cows	20,807.07	17.33
Deficit on engine room	20,387.58	16.98
Deficit on coffee house	419.49	.35
Unemployment payments	27,618.73	23.00
TOTAL EXPENSES	120,063.79	
Operating deficit	(555.46)	.46

Note: All amounts are shown in dollars.

came from public sources and was specifically dedicated for relief of the unemployed. This was three years before the passage of the Social Security Act. Almost certainly, these were state funds, and it is just as likely that they were insufficient for the purpose (Lubove, 1968). The careful reader will note that more than that amount ($27,618.73) was actually paid out in unemployment payments, meaning that the settlement house "matched" those public funds to a small extent ($1,126.74, or roughly 1 percent). This amount alone accounts for the largest share of the deficit shown at the bottom of the report, meaning that generally the other more customary Hull House programs probably stayed within their anticipated revenues for the year.

Also of interest here is the possibility that Hull House was well ahead of its time in operating two major activities as "cash cows" or revenue-generators. However, the statement shows that by 1932, both cash cows were losing money and had become burdensome. Some time earlier, the settlement house had installed a coal-fired electric generator, which is referred to in the Hull House documents as the Engine Room, for the purpose of selling electricity to the local utility company, which was a relatively common practice at the time. Although this program had generated revenues in previous years, by 1932 the combination of falling demand for electricity and competition from other producers left the settlement house with a substantial loss ($20,387.58), equal to nearly 17 percent of all expenses for the year. In addition, the settlement house had long operated a coffeehouse for the express purpose of competing with the lunches offered in neighborhood saloons. However, by 1932, this too was running a small deficit of $419.49. Three other categories, fees for the use of facilities like the gymnasium and theater ($3,446.91), sales of various kinds ($4,212.24), and rentals ($22,987.82) to assorted tenants including Jane Addams herself generated roughly over 25 percent of the total operating budget. The net result of 1932 for Hull House was a loss of $555.46, roughly .46 percent of the total budget.

This is just one of thousands of such examples that might be provided from real social agencies. One thing it illustrates is that as early as 1932 and prior to the creation of federal social welfare programs, social agencies were making use of several different sources of funding to support their activities.

CATEGORIZING AGENCY BY FINANCES

It is possible to identify five distinct types of social agency from a financial standpoint. We will call these donatories, statutory or public agencies, nonprofit QUANGOs (quasi nongovernmental organizations), commercial QUANGOs, and genuine, market-oriented social service firms.

Donatories

Donatory is an archaic but nonetheless useful English-language word. It is used here to describe social agencies operating primarily upon donations (Lohmann, 1992). The origins of charitable donation in Western culture are religious, and it is now relatively easy to trace the actual practice of charitable donations for social services in the Judeo-Christian tradition to at least the Byzantine Empire in the fourth century. Many religiously based social service activities continue to have an important donative component, although most have become QUANGOs (see below) even while nominally maintaining their religious identifications.

In fact, many of the earliest donative social agencies in the United States were quite unlike most existing social agencies in their fiscal arrangements. For one thing, there was no federal income tax in the nineteenth century, and thus the notion of "tax-deductible contributions" was largely meaningless. There was no tax incentive to donate. Giving was on a much smaller scale both through traditional religious venues and in several emergent new types of donative organizations. One type of these new donative vehicles were local, urban neighborhood membership organizations known as "charity societies" to which members paid subscriptions that became the basis of private poor relief doled out very sparingly along with ample doses of moral advice on improving one's way out of poverty. It was largely to limit the personal (and one might add, intrusive and moralistic) nature of the assistance provided by these charity societies that a number of important social work norms like individualization and confidentiality first arose. To the extent that the archaic legal term *eleemosynary* has any exact meaning, it refers to these charity societies and their donative practices.

Another form of organization that was very common at the time was the volunteer organization, in which middle class and wealthy volunteers, many of whom were women, donated their time and energy as "friendly visitors" of the poor. Though their donations were often not of money, the time that they spent on this task certainly did have a monetary value. There is little existing evidence that any charity societies or volunteer organizations ever felt the necessity of computing the monetary value of such in-kind contributions.

Public Agencies

Many social work students, better versed in the contemporary social sciences than in social history, are inclined to see the development of social services as a linear progression from private, donatories to public, statutory agencies. However, the progression is by no means linear, as the Hull House example shows. Intergovernmental transfers between units of local government for the purpose of redistribution of resources, for example, were one of several fundamental considerations of the English Poor Law of 1601. The Poor Law, which was universally adopted as a model for local charitable relief in American states and communities, defined a minimal fiduciary relationship for these public trustees, long known as overseers of the poor, with the kind of responsibilities for public accountability evident in the newspaper reports included in chapter 12.

In general, these fiscal arrangements were individual rather than organizational arrangements, conforming to the ancient Roman concept of *patronis* or patronage. The first major organized responses in public policy began to arise after the Civil War, and even these were organizationally minimal (Skocpol, 1993). It was the Social Security Act of 1935, which for the first time embodied major programs of public assistance for families with children and old, blind and disabled people, that gave rise to the emergence of the first genuine human service bureaucracies at the state and federal level. And it wasn't really until the social service amendments of the 1960s and 1970s that major public service delivery bureaucracies emerged within that system.

Nonprofit QUANGOs

The essence of the QUANGO in human services involves the receipt by a private and typically nonprofit group or organization of public subsidies such as grants or contracts to carry out a mission that is simultaneously private and public. It is private to the extent it may be governed by a board of directors and public to the extent that it conforms to mandates of public law. The origins of such public-private partnerships are clearly discernible as far back as the colonial period in American history (Hoffman, 1934; Mackey, 1965; Morris & Morris, 1986). In fact, public purchases of service by local governments may have been common in Colonial times (Mackey, 1965; Wedel & Colston, 1988).

In terms of sheer scale of operations, however, it is clear that the modern era of QUANGOs began in earnest during the 1960s. At that time, a large number of "Great Society" programs were adopted by the Eighty-ninth Congress in an amazing burst of legislative creativity and energy and submission to President Lyndon B. Johnson's leadership (Unger, 1996, chap. 3). As a result, a host of federal social service grant programs became available to what was first identified as "the existing voluntary sector." It quickly became evident that the existing service delivery system was inadequate in scale, and, in some cases, reluctant to become directly involved with federal funding (Kramer, 1966).

As a result, eligibility for the whole range of these programs was rapidly and dramatically extended to include private community groups interested in *forming* new social agencies to operate alongside the existing agencies of the traditional voluntary sector. In some cases, such as the Office of Economic Opportunity devoted to fighting the War on Poverty, the creation of such new community groups was required in part because it was thought that existing services were too conservative and unwilling to listen to the expressed needs of those that they had been created to help. This whole initiative suggests some degree of federal coordination by some oversight agency, like the Office of Management and Budget or the Government Accounting Office (GAO) or ultimately the Johnson administration, but existing public management literature fails to provide clear guidance on this point. Ultimately, however, it is clear that it was this extension of federal funding to start-up social agencies that was behind the often-noted dramatic growth of new social service agencies during the 1960s. An entirely new revenue base for social service was created, and it resulted in creation of a new type of social agency.

Commercial QUANGOs

Most existing commercial social service providers, while espousing variants of free market and private enterprise rhetoric are, like their nonprofit agency equivalents, primarily QUANGOs. They are created expressly to be funded by public funds and committed by contractual obligation to carry out public purposes, although they may be incorporated as private, for-profit organizations. It is difficult, for example, to identify any case other than child day care where a bona fide private social service industry has grown up and is currently sustained principally by the market purchases of independent consumers. Behind the appearance of a large and growing private social service sector is the reality that most of the private sector exists only so long as Medicare, Medicaid, and Title IV of the Social Security Act public supports and others remain in place.

Commercial QUANGOs came about not because of market forces but because of social service politics at the national level. Not to be outdone by the Johnson administration's Great Society, the Nixon administration in its first term (1968–1972) took the first steps toward extending this same eligibility for federal grants, which were suitably renamed federal contracts, to a range of existing and startup for-profit or *commercial* businesses. This fact alone necessitated a shift from the language and practice of grants to that of contracts.

The transformation from the rhetoric of grants to contracts was largely completed by the first-term Reagan administration (1980–1984), which effectively dissolved most remaining differences between the eligibility of nonprofit and commercial vendors. The result was not new except in social services. Government agencies had been using private, commercial contractors to carry out aspects of public administration and policy for centuries (e.g., manufacture of military uniforms and supplies and construction of warships, roads, and bridges).

It was, however, new in social service where for at least the previous eight decades increasingly strong distinctions had been made equating nonprofit with selfless, altruistic service and for-profit with selfish (even greedy) and capitalistic business. Throughout most of the twentieth century, any idea of profit taking was seen as antithetical to the very idea of social work. Indeed, it is still not clear that genuinely private, for-profit social services within conventional market settings, in which large numbers of customers shop and compare among large numbers of vendors, or service providers actually exist on any scale anywhere in the social services universe. What is clear, however, is that what the Johnson administration's Great Society did in extending public funding from the statutory public welfare agencies to private, nonprofit social services, the Nixon and Reagan administrations broadened by extending public funding to commercial vendors as well. The resulting four-sector delivery system laid out in chapter 2 remains largely in place today.

As a result, the nature of human service organization and delivery has been fundamentally transformed in recent years in ways that are only partly documented in the social administration literature to date (Lohmann, 1995b). Although this is often portrayed as the "privatization" of social services, this is not entirely accurate. It is more as though the responsibility for the implementation of public social service policy has been placed in private hands, but the funding of social service activity has become a massive public expenditure.

Many of the most basic changes in the organization of social work practice in the past two decades, including the rapid growth of private practice and the diversification of nonprofit service delivery organizations, have been financially driven. They relate to the ongoing search for secure and predictable financial bases for social work interventions (Brown, 1991). But this search has gone on within a political economy characterized by efforts to scale back federal spending. These are just the latest chapters in the long and often stormy relationship between human service delivery and the financial resources that enable it (Hill, 1971; Pifer, 1987; Strom, 1992; Walker & Garman, 1992).

Even so, commercial service providers, functioning largely off the revenue base created by the various titles of the Social Security Act, are very much part of the contemporary social service universe. And the conventional anathema against profiting from the needs of others periodically pronounced by the social work profession has made little difference. Current generations of social work graduate students in many schools express less of the traditional public service mission of the profession and are more comfortable with the idea of social service as a business not unlike selling cheese.

Social Service Firms

To the extent that the independent and commercial practice of social work exists beyond the commercial QUANGO, it is worth noting that a good deal of it has an inherent cottage industry quality to it. Such practice is usually referred to as "private practice." Indeed, a formula for the current situation might be something like the following. If a private, commercial social work practice is a solo (one professional) venture or if it is a small group (five or fewer professionals) practice, it is more likely to be a truly private practice or social service firm operating in a market or commercial environment. Also, if it functions as a sideline or second job for those involved, there is a greater-than-average chance that it is a truly private practice. If it is a large, corporate practice engaging the services of multiple professions including social work, and particularly if it is associated with health care, the chances are greater that, entrepreneurial rhetoric aside, it is publicly funded.

The current social service delivery systems in most American communities today are essentially made up of unplanned, ad hoc mixtures of these five options: donative agencies, statutory agencies, nonprofit QUANGOs, commercial QUANGOs, and a relatively small number of genuine social service businesses.

FINANCIAL MANAGEMENT DIFFERENCES

In important ways, the demands of financial management for the contemporary social agency vary by the type of organizations. Subtle but important differences in stakeholders are an important explanation for these variations. However, the differing implications for the revenue base of service is the primary explanation.

Financial management in donatories and statutory agencies is primarily a matter of exercising good stewardship of the public and community resources necessary to conduct programs of social service. For both nonprofit and commercial QUANGOs, compliance with the terms of purchase-of-service contracts is the central concern of financial management. Managers of commercial QUANGOs must mix a concern with compliance with their fiduciary responsibilities to their investors. In some respects, purely commercial social services may be the most interesting, in part because it is least discussed.

While in theory pure-market commercial social services might be expected to be the most entrepreneurial, it is anything but clear that most social workers are interested in private practice as a way of making "big money." In general, social workers entering private practice express more interest in escaping hidebound bureaucracy and earning a decent living than in getting rich. Seiz (1990), for example, found that private practitioners placed significantly greater importance on values with an entrepreneurial orientation, whereas other practitioners valued significantly more the values associated with low-risk and social welfare/action orientations. Thus, it is ironic that commercial QUANGOs, under the pressure of a fiduciary responsibility to maximize corporate profits for investors, may need to be much more profit oriented than more purely entrepreneurial social service firms do. For the latter, independence and adequate income (forms of welfare maximizing) may take the place of profit maximization. Thus, many interesting possibilities, from conventional professional corporations and

group practices to producer cooperatives and limited dividend corporations, may be increasingly important in the future.

THE RESOURCE BASE

The concept that anchors all discussions of resources in social services is
what we term the *resource base*. This term is derived in part from the theory
of budget discussed in chapter 23. The resources necessary for social service
are either *human*, which may include both human and social capital as
discussed in earlier chapters, or *financial*, which may include physical capital or money, goods, and purchased or donated services to which explicit
dollar values can be attached.

In most general terms, the resource base of a social agency can be defined as the legacy of past financial performance projected forward into the
future. The resource base of any agency can be defined largely in terms of
its access to financial, human, and social capital. The idea of a resource
base is also directly connected to our earlier comments about the social
services as social institutions and the institutionalization process in two
important and divergent ways. On the one hand, some measure of secure,
dependable level of support and resources is a fundamental characteristic
of any successful and viable social service institution. On the other hand,
as Drucker, Gardner, and other critics of bureaucratization have been quick
to point out, leaders of ongoing institutions must continually struggle with
the challenge of institutional renewal. Any shift in the mission or objectives
of an agency or programs may also involve implications for the resource
base. New donors or purchase contracts may be attracted, existing donors
may be lost, or other funding implications may result.

Change alone is not the solution to this dilemma, however. There can be
little doubt that dramatic changes in the resource base of social services
alone have brought great changes to social services in general. Changes in
funding have brought great growth in the number and scope of available
services. However, these same changes have been responsible (just as the
critics in the early 1960s feared they would) for the virtual demise of an
independent voluntary social service sector and the rise of a third sector of
nonprofit service agencies congenitally tied to governmental funding.

TYPES OF CAPITAL

Leaving aside the large and important questions raised by the critique of
capitalism, it is important to recognize that the technical term *capital*, shorn
of most of its larger moral or political significance, is an important element
throughout modern business accounting and management discussions.

Capital, in this sense, is an important term for understanding and categorizing the resource base of organizations. The economic concept of capital is an abstract notion that generally refers to commodities used in the further production of goods and services. For our purposes, we can identify four distinct types of capital involved in the production and consumption (or, as we say here, *prosumption*[6]) of social services: financial, physical, human, and social capital.

Of these four types, *financial capital* is the easiest to understand and has a measurable operational definition in monetary terms of the agency's assets. It takes money to hire people; to rent or buy space, furniture, and equipment; and to complete all of the other steps necessary to deliver services.

Physical capital refers to tangible objects, such as physical plant and materials, and is much more relevant to manufacturing than to service delivery. Importantly, physical capital does not refer to tangible objects in general but to those used in producing services and whose cost enters into the costs of producing service in a measurable way. Very few social services are concerned with physical capital other than space and minimal equipment in anything beyond a cursory level.

Human capital refers to the knowledge, talents, and skills possessed by the employees of the organization. Such knowledge and skill can be considered organizational capital to the extent that what workers know and are able to do become factors in the organization's ability to prosume services.[7] Thus, when social workers speak of knowledge, skills, and values of professionals, they are, from a social administration perspective, focusing on the human capital of social services.

The concept of *social capital* is the most recently addressed and in many ways the most difficult to understand. James Coleman (1988), who introduced the concept of social capital, says that it "inheres in the structure of relations between actors." Two years later, he went on to demonstrate this point in a massive statement of exchange theory that makes social capital a cornerstone for understanding all social behavior (Coleman, 1990).

In Coleman's usage, social capital is not synonymous with either human or physical capital, and it surely isn't money or financial capital, although it exists in a similar symbolic realm. The concept completely subsumes and includes the kinds of influence ordinarily meant by social administration uses of the notion of "political capital." It is not lodged either in the actors themselves or in physical implements of production. In developing the idea of social capital, Coleman (1989) makes clear that he is not merely interested in restating sociological and social psychological insights in quasi-economic language: "My aim . . . is to import the economists' principle of rational action for use in the analysis of social systems proper . . . and to do so without discarding social organization in the process" (p. 95).

Perhaps the most widely and explicitly discussed example of social capital is trust (Fukuyama, 1995; Putnam, 2000). It has long been recognized that even competitive and conflictual social relations cannot be played out without a modicum of trust. Even when in conflict, you need confidence that your opponent will act in predictable ways.

Social capital is not simply an issue of trust, however. A pioneering historical study of Northern Italy by Robert Putnam identified a host of other explicit relationship dimensions. These include such additional dimensions as traditions of civic engagement, membership associations that cut across class lines and social strata, relationships of family and community loyalty, and patron-client dependencies (Putnam, 1995). It is the resource represented by these social ties wherein most authorities see the principal practical value of social capital.

Social capital is still a relatively new idea, but it has already been widely discussed and, in the process, also has been widely misread, misinterpreted, and misused according to several critical reviews (Edwards & Foley, 1997, 1998; Greeley, 1997). Its importance for social administration relates directly to the discussion of institutions earlier in this work. The process of institution building is inherently also a process of social capital formation. No social service agency or program should expect to survive without some basic measure of trust from clients and stakeholders. Likewise, alliances, crosscutting memberships, professional, family and other community loyalties, and a host of other considerations also enter into the resource base. Note that sometimes in this context the social capital of a social service institution may be referred to with such phrases as its "base of support in the community."

Although still in its infancy, the formal theory of social capital may represent a way to bring together the traditional ends-oriented concerns of social work with relationships and the seemingly disconnected means-oriented concern with financial resources. In order to further that objective even a little, two types of resources in the resource base characteristic of social service organizations are introduced and discussed in the following discussion.[8] (This discussion is based on Lohmann, 1992, pp. 76–77.)

Treasury

Perhaps the single most critical category in the resource base of most social service organizations is its liquid assets: money to purchase the skill, knowledge, and value resources required to carry out the organization's service mission. Although agencies partially or completely reliant on the donated time and expertise of volunteers do exist and typically manage to find niches within the social service community, the notion of work—as paid employment—is fundamental to the modern meaning of social *work*. And few, if any, social workers are willing to ply their profession completely for barter.

Financial resources tend to come into social service agency treasuries in two principal forms: *support,* consisting of gifts, grants, donations, and bequests; and *revenue,* in the form of various types of fees and capitation payments.[9] The difference between support and revenue is to be found in what is sometimes called *metering.* Revenues are metered by (that is, rise and fall in direct proportion to) the volume of services delivered. Support payments bear no predicable relation to service activity. An agency, for example, may receive significant donations in one year even though its number of clients has decreased. Taken together, the resulting financial resources form the financial or working capital of the agency.

Another important resource-base distinction made in social agencies, universities, and other settings is that between "soft money" and "hard money." The softness or hardness of the resource base of an organization is largely a matter of how reliable or dependable its sources of funding may be. Thus, employment in a public social service position supported by state appropriated funds may be seen as a "hard money" or dependable position. Likewise, a position in a nonprofit social service supported by an endowment would likely also be seen as a hard money position. For contrast, a grant-funded position in a nonprofit social service, backed only by a one-year grant or contract, is seen as a "soft money" position.

Ultimately, this is a central question of institutionalization. The predictability and continuity of hard money is often closely associated with rigidity, bureaucracy, and unresponsiveness on the one hand but with continuity on the other. And the uncertainties of soft money are similarly associated with flexibility and responsiveness on the one hand, but also with greater risk and lack of certainty on the other. This introduces something of a dilemma for social administrators: Rigid, hidebound bureaucracies may indeed be bad, but what happens to the client who needs grief counseling when flexible responses to greater market opportunities have transformed all the service providers into alcoholism counselors?

Repertory

What is it that money can buy for the social service agency? Because of the difficulty of this question, there has been something of a tendency to restrict our answers to the most basic: We can buy people's time. Thus, hiring a full-time social work professional may involve a forty-hour a week commitment for fifty weeks of the year with two weeks of paid vacation. Or, in a contract-based QUANGO the employment contract may be stated more explicitly in terms of the minimum number of billable hours necessary for the agency to recover the cost of the worker's salary. The human and social capital notions, however, allow us to go considerably beyond these basic time concepts into new and largely uncharted waters.

In some respects, the most critically important form of capital formation in the social agency is the establishment and creation of a repertory of knowledge, skills, and values to carry out the agency's progress. The concept of a repertory (or, if you prefer, repertoire) is a summary term that refers to the accumulated skills and abilities of the staff and stakeholders of an organization. As such, it is a form of human capital, and to the extent that the skills and abilities in question further or facilitate social relationships, a repertoire represents a form of social capital as well. The implicit reference here is to the example of a repertory theater company, where the actors in the company have as part of their skill base the ability to perform a number of different roles and productions with minimal preparation.

The repertory of any service organization is perhaps most analogous to the plant and equipment of a manufacturing firm. It represents the fixed assets necessary to carry out the tasks involved. Unlike plant and equipment, however, there is no current way to place an economic value on the repertory of a social service organization. This does not mean it is a fundamentally unimportant part of the resource base, however. It just means that it goes unmeasured.

There are two principal ways to add to the repertory of a social service: purchase or donation. This choice is, in most respects, much like the make-or-buy decisions faced by manufacturing firms. One common way in which social services organizations face a repertory issue is whether to hire a staff accountant to advise and help out with the preparation of financial reports and tax returns or to recruit a volunteer consultant or board member willing to provide such services on a pro bono basis or to contract for the needed service.

At the same time, a question of whether to engage a family therapist, community organizer, fund-raiser, hypnotist, or other program specialist is a multipart purchase-or-donation decision: Do we need someone with those skills as part of our staff repertory? (This is perhaps akin to asking does our theater company need someone able to direct Molière in French?) Is someone available? Will she be willing to volunteer? Do we minimize costs and hire her as a consultant for a few hours a week or full time? If we don't need her full-time for the task, are there other things she can do to make it a full-time commitment?

Values enter into this matter in interesting ways. A candidate for a particular position may be otherwise qualified but deemed unsuitable because of an apparent value base that allows little room for genuine respect for the particular clients of the agency: old, or retarded, or profoundly mentally ill, or terminally ill, or poor people, for example. This is a classic human capital consideration faced by social agencies. Such a judgment makes sense, however, only to the extent that the value in question is an active and important consideration in the standard repertory of that agency. That makes it a social capital concern.

The familiar social work formulation of knowledge, skills, and values goes a long way toward outlining the major categories of the typical social agency repertory. It should be noted here that close consideration of the repertory of a social agency does not need to be limited to surveying its service delivery capabilities. Indeed, one of the pioneering uses of this concept by the historian Charles Tilly and associates involved the study of changes in social protest and mobilization repertories in late medieval and early modern Europe (Tilly, 1978, 1986, 1990, 1993; Tilly & Tilly, 1981; Tilly, Tilly, & Tilly, 1975). From this perspective, the resources of community organization involve equally important repertory questions. For an agency, the critical question appears to be not what is known in general but what human and social capital—knowledge, skills, and values—are possessed by particular workers and professions and what repertories of behavior are they therefore capable of or predisposed to carrying out.

PATTERNS OF FINANCIAL MANAGEMENT

We can apply a repertories perspective, for example, to the issue of the deployment of financial management knowledge and skill in social agencies. There tend to be three dominant patterns of financial management practice in social work today. In host settings such as hospitals and nursing homes and large social agencies, specialized financial personnel with backgrounds in accounting, business, or public management tend to staff and control financial management processes, which are largely routinized. Such settings account for the largest dollar volume of human services expenditures but also represent the fewest agencies.

The second pattern occurs in small, experimental, alternative, and innovative agencies and where programs tend to be run by social workers with little or no specialized social administration training and limited financial management experience. This pattern may well account for the largest number of social service agencies, if not the largest numbers of personnel.

The third pattern is found in the emergence of private practice, where the knowledge and skills necessary to manage a private practice tend to be ignored completely by social work education. (For an exception, see Barker, 1992.) The knowledge necessary to run a private practice is essentially that of a small, service-oriented business, which is also not commonly dealt with in business school curricula, which tend to focus instead on large organizations and corporate management. Thus, anyone entering the private practice of social work today will almost certainly have to discover on their own how to manage financially.

It is possible to tie all the assorted activities of financial management together with a variety of universal and important operational tasks: reading financial statements, some familiarity with accounting and bookkeeping, and the like.

CONCLUSION

The central strategic problem of financial management in social administration is becoming increasingly apparent: There is no secure or reliable funding base for social services in the United States. Program goals dictating service to the poor and underprivileged are inconsistent with the market- or customer-oriented approaches of business, and antitax and antiwelfare calls for reductions in the size of public spending continue to undercut public support and subsidies. Meanwhile, despite major increases in volunteering and donations during the 1980s and early 1990s, eleemosynary approaches based on individual and corporate donations and foundation support continue to be inadequate to support the work to be done.

Financing arrangements are likely to continue driving the organization and its delivery of social services, at least until this impasse between purposes and means can be resolved. The realities of limited resources pull us in one direction just as the realities of social needs and major social problems pull in another, with social services caught in between.

CHAPTER 22

Financial Inflows

Focusing on the concept of capital, as we did in chapter 21, brings one issue into focus that even the most sophisticated and experienced social administrators have been unable to fully resolve. That is the limited relationship that exists in nonprofit and public organizations between financial performance on the one hand and worker productivity and reward structures on the other. Stated differently, the relationship between the measured assets of an organization and the real capital of its skill or talent base is often almost accidental. For example, an agency can have a banner year in fund-raising and be as wealthy as it has ever been and yet be serving fewer clients than it has ever served because of its employees' limited productivity due to inadequate or inappropriate training.

At least since the 1970s, the conventional wisdom in social agencies has been that the best way to resolve these problems and bring performance, productivity, and rewards into closer relation is for social services to "become more business-like." Although it has no consistent or exact meaning, this assumption has flavored the entire accountability discussion. Thus, the strategic challenge for financial management in social administration has been seen as a matter of bringing actual resource flows into greater conformity with the norms and standards of business accounting and economics. The entire thrust of recent efforts at outcome measurement, for example, can be seen within this context (Mullen & Magnabosco, 1997). Meanwhile, there has been less attention to the equally basic and troublesome question of ensuring an adequate resource base for social service activity.

In this chapter, we examine the basic characteristics of the different types of resources flowing into the social agency. From this standpoint, the assorted activities of financial management can be seen as consisting of three basic types of financial impacts upon the agency resource base:

1. *Inflows* of resources or income brought into the organization or added to its resource base or capital
2. *Financial operations* such as capital planning and investment carried out on resources under control of the organization
3. *Outflows* or reductions in the resource base

We are primarily concerned here with the inflows of financial resources, particularly donations, grants, fees, and capitation payments. Lesser attention will be paid to less important inflows that are of equal concern to the Internal Revenue Service (IRS), including membership dues, sales of unrelated goods, and investment income. In chapter 23, we shall examine the phenomena of outflows in the context of budgeting. Most social service agencies concentrate most of their time and energy on these two impacts. Concern for financial operations such as investment strategies is a highly specialized area, and social agencies engaging in financial operations with resources under their control generally do so with the aid of outside advisors or consultants (Fry, 1998). Thus, this topic will be covered in far less detail.

INFLOWS AND THE IRS 990

There is no generally accepted classification of financial inflows in social agencies or nonprofit organizations. Words such as income, revenue, earnings, and input are used in highly variable and overlapping senses. Perhaps the closest thing to a standard is the categorization used in the IRS 990, which divides inflows into five groups: contracts, gifts, and grants; program services; membership dues; sales of unrelated goods; and investment income. In the typical social service agency, the first two of these categories are generally most important, and dues, sales, and investments are much more peripheral. However, in social agencies it is also worth distinguishing between gifts and grants on the one hand and contract income on the other.

INFLOWS OR INCOME

For purposes of this discussion, we will assume that there are four principal types of financial inflows in the typical social service agency and that they tend to be clustered into two basic types. The four types are differentiated by circumstances of the financial exchange that is involved and its relation to the service delivery transaction that is being paid for. Briefly, they are

- *Donations* or gifts. These are unilateral transactions for which the donor receives nothing in exchange except symbolic rewards such as recognition and gratitude.
- *Grants* are institutionalized arrangements for handling large donations that are often received from institutional donors such as foundations or government agencies. Purpose, permissible activities or allowable expenditures, time period, or other similar features usually restrict grants.
- *User fees* or user charges. These are typically payments made by clients or family members in exchange for services rendered.
- *Third party (or contract) fees.* These are also payments in exchange for services rendered except that the person or institution paying is different from both the person or institution delivering the service and the person or institution receiving the service. Thus, the payee is truly a third party to the transaction.

These four types of inflows can be gathered together into two clusters, which, following the United Way model, we will term *support* and *revenue*. Each cluster has implications for how funds are handled once they are received. Probably the greatest differences in financial administrative and budgeting styles in contemporary social agencies are those associated with how funds are handled, which is explored in greater detail in chapter 23 on budgeting. *Support* generally refers to financial inflows generated independently of service delivery activity. *Revenue* refers to financial inflows generated as a result of services delivered.

Donations and grants are both typically support payments. They consist of relatively large blocks of funds designated for support of a specific purpose. Though some donations occur spontaneously, most result from development activities by the agency. The same is true for grant writing. Administering donated and grant funds is typically a matter of spending whatever support funds are remaining. That is, the agency administrator begins with a known and fixed quantity of support funds and expects to make expenditures that are less than or equal to that amount.

Both user fees and third-party fees are revenue funds. The amount of revenue available can vary with and be measured by the amount of previous service activity. As a result, there is never a single fixed amount available for use or to spend down as there is with support funds. The higher the level of present service delivery activity, the greater the available revenue will be in the next period.

Donations

Donations are generally subject to the will of the donor, particularly as to when, how much, why, and under what circumstances a gift may be given. This has two important impacts on the social agency dealing with donations[1]: (1) inflows from spontaneous donations can be highly unpredictable, and (2) the larger the number of individual donations received, the more predictable donations become as a source of support. The latter is a consequence of the theory of large numbers that is also an underlying dimension of statistics. Thus, much of the predictability of development campaigns arises from the fact that most campaigns set out to raise a large amount of money from a small number of donors and the remainder from a very large number of small donors.

In general there are two principal types of donations in terms of the conditions or strings that may be attached by donors. Donations can be *unrestricted*, which means that they are unconditional gifts subject to whatever use the agency may wish to make of them to carry out its mission and purpose. Most donations that are made to social service agencies are unrestricted, and thus agencies typically have great latitude in deciding what use to make of them. Existing laws in most states, however, allow donors a second option, the *restricted* donation or conditional gift given for a specific, identified purpose. Large donations are often also restricted. Donors may give a large amount of funds for a building or to fund a specific program or project and specify that the funds may be used only for that purpose. But even small donations can be restricted, and the law and ethics of fundraising require that agencies must be prepared to honor the donor's wishes or to return the gift.[2]

The earliest modern social agencies in U.S. cities, the charity organization societies, were often little more than networks of donor pools in which groups of charitable givers became members of a charity association or society and elected trustees to oversee the spending of donated funds. Donations to these clubs tended to come primarily in the form of relatively large donations from wealthy individuals who clustered together into larger networks as a way of protecting themselves against fraudulent claims by potential recipients. Thus, the emphasis on *scientific philanthropy* can be seen from a social administration standpoint as partly an effort to find more effective ways of protecting donors by restricting donations of charitable funds to the truly worthy poor (Lubove, 1965).

The basic underlying concept of charitable giving goes back thousands of years and was very widely disseminated by the Jewish, Christian, and Islamic religious traditions. Somewhat parallel religious norms and practices can also be found within the history of Asian Buddhism (Lohmann, 1995a). However, there have been a number of important recent innovations and improvement in these ancient arts, and some of these innovations arose first within social administration.

One of the greatest and most important twentieth-century innovation in social service fund-raising was the idea of federated financing. The idea is that of creating a federation or confederation of agencies in a community to seek donations that are then divided on some suitable basis among them. This idea spread widely in American cities following the success of the Liberty Bond drives during World War I. During the 1920s, the community chest as a form of federation became a familiar institution in larger American communities. The federated financing model spread even more widely to many small communities in the economic expansion following World War II. Renamed the United Funds and, more recently, the United Way, these campaigns also developed another major innovation: workplace giving, giving by workers through regular payroll deductions.[3]

In recent years, we have also witnessed the growth of a large and diverse alternative funds movement. It first arose in the early 1970s and often represented Native, African, and Asian Americans; feminist, gay, and lesbian groups; and other groups who were underrepresented and underserved by the United Way establishment. By 1998, the National Committee for Responsive Philanthropy, a national trade association for the alternative funds movement, indicated an annual growth of 30 percent since the early 1990s. Contributions to these groups totaled roughly 10 percent of United Way collections, and the alternative funds growth rate through the 1990s was greater than that of United Way.[4]

A third major innovation arising in the federated financing context was the idea of matching donations. After a series of favorable court rulings, business corporations have been allowed to donate a share of preprofit earnings to charities in exchange for suitable tax deductions. Some corporations have handled this practice by creating corporate foundations (discussed below), and others have established the practice of matching their employees' donations. When matching employees' donations, the corporations are, in effect, allowing employees to make their donative decisions for them. This practice, which now extends widely to all manner of nonprofit donations, is one of the innovations that originated in federated giving to social services.

Social services were at the forefront of donative practice in the United States throughout the first half of the twentieth century. In the second half, however, strong commitment among social administrators and social workers to the idea of public funding of a welfare state has tended to limit and restrict social service growth in this important arena.

For many existing social agencies, the full extent of support from donations comes through participation in the local United Way campaign. As is evident in Table 22.1, such contributions generally failed to keep pace with the general growth of personal giving during the 1990s. In fact, only in the last three years shown did United Way giving exceed the rate of inflation.

According to these figures, United Way donations when adjusted for inflation in the decade of the nineties were actually down 2.5 percent below giving levels at the beginning of the decade. One need only compare this with the substantial growth of donations in the third sector as a whole to see that social services have not been holding their own in the rapidly expanding field of private philanthropy (Table 22.2). Total donations to all organizations grew by more than 35 percent, from $93.3 billion to $143.5 billion, during the past two decades and by more than 11 percent, from $127.4 to $143.5 billion, in the same decade that United Way contributions remained virtually constant. Further, whether one uses actual dollars or inflation adjusted figures, it is not hard to see that social service donations today only represent a very small percentage of total giving. Contributions to United Way are probably no more than 2 percent of the total donations, and other sources of private philanthropy for social services are probably even less.

Table 22.1 United Way Contributions, 1989–1999

Year	Actual Contributions (In billions of dollars)	Contributions (Adjusted for inflation)	Change from Previous Year
1989		2.4032	2.3
1990		2.3795	−1.0
1991		2.3275	−2.2
1992		2.1668	−6.9
1993	3.04	2.1087	−2.7
1994	3.07	2.0769	−1.5
1995	3.15	2.0656	−0.5
1996	3.25	2.0701	0.2
1997	3.40		4.7*
1998	3.58		5.1*
1999	3.77		5.4*

*Preinflation growth rate.
Source: United Way of America, 1998 and 1999, multiple documents.

Table 22.2 Changes in U.S. Donations, Foundation and Corporate Grants, and Bequests by Source, 1977–1997

Type	1977	1989	1997	Change 1977–1997
Individual	78.3	102.8	109.3	+39.6
Foundation	5.3	8.5	13.4	+152.8
Corporations	4.1	7.1	12.6	+100.0
Bequests	5.6	9.0	12.6	+125.0
Total	93.3	127.4	143.5	+53.8

Note: Amounts shown are in constant 1997 billion dollars.
Source: AAFRC Trust for Philanthropy, Giving U.S.A., 1998.

Another common distinction that is also made among types of donations is between *cash* and *in-kind* donations. The meaning of a cash donation is self-evident. Actual cash or liquid assets are donated to the organization. The origins of the phrase *in-kind* are somewhat obscure, but the term generally refers to any kind of noncash donation of a valuable object or service. The range of in-kind donations is extremely broad, from automobiles to home appliances and furniture to buildings and land. One of the biggest categories of in-kind donations to organizations like the Salvation Army is donated used clothing. A general rule of thumb here is that if someone has something they no longer want and someone else is willing to accept it, then it is a suitable object for an in-kind donation. Donations of labor and services are also typically classified as in-kind.

Many people make in-kind donations in part because both cash and in-kind donations to 501(c)(3) nonprofit organizations can be tax-deductible, although deducting donated volunteer efforts is not permissible. The IRS has definite rules about the size of deductions that can be taken for in-kind donations. Independent appraisers must appraise the most valuable in-kind donations, which are those over $5,000 per item. The IRS has tried repeatedly to mandate that organizations accepting donations must set a value on in-kind donations received. In general, however, many social agencies have followed the lead of the Salvation Army, which is probably the largest recipient of in-kind donations, and refused to do so.

Donations and fund-raising practices of all types are susceptible to a number of forms of abuse, including misrepresentation and fraud. Because of close historic associations with organized religion, governments in the United States have traditionally been reluctant to subject fund-raising practices to close scrutiny. However, in recent years, this traditional hands-off attitude has changed considerably, particularly at the state government level.

One of the important developments in recent years has been the passage of state legislation regulating fund-raisers by requiring them to register and file annual financial reports in a number of states. States have also attempted to regulate practices such as telephone solicitations and to crack down on illegal telephone solicitation operations, known as "boiler rooms" (Hopkins, 1996; Pennsylvania Bar Institute, 1997; Perlman, 1996).

Another of the important developments in fund-raising practice has been the emergence of a host of sophisticated research and modeling strategies for studying donative behavior (Grønbjerg, 1993; Lindahl, 1992). Computers and electronic databases have been particularly helpful for what fund-raisers call prospect research into the incomes, giving practices, and other behavior of potential donors.

Managing Donations

An organized program to solicit donations is usually referred to today as a *development program*. Managing the development program of an agency is a highly specialized task usually assigned to a development officer or department. The staff is sometimes also called the fund-raising staff, although the term *development* is almost universally preferred today. There is a large and rapidly expanding literature in this area, and social agencies engaged in fund-raising generally do so only with the advice and assistance of experts.[5]

The reader will remember from the discussion of financial accountability that the differentiation of administrative and program costs from fund-raising costs was a major consideration of the revised accounting standards developed during the 1970s. One consideration in any social agency with a major development program is to measure and account for fund-raising costs. At a minimum, the agency needs to make certain that the investment it makes in fund-raising is raising more funds than are being spent on the development effort.

GRANTS

As noted in the previous section, commitment to a publicly funded social service state since the 1960s, which has been characterized throughout this work as the age of grants, has tended to downplay the importance of charitable donations. Just as importantly, it has tended to accentuate the importance of government and foundation grants as sources of support for social agency programs. In fact, during this period the set of skills associated with grant writing (denoted as *grantsmanship*) has become an important form of social administration practice for many (Conlan, 1984; Derthick, 1975; Galaskiewiscz, 1985; Grønbjerg, 1991; Lauffer, 1997).

Strictly speaking, a grant can be any type of unilateral transfer of wealth. Thus, in the narrowest sense, any donation given is also a grant, and in the same vein, every grant represents a donation. In practice, however, there tends to be a consistent distinction between donations as the cash and in-kind gifts of individuals and families, particularly those not accompanied by extensive restrictions, and grants. Grants are seen as the donations of donative institutions like foundations and government agencies and also as fairly restricted giving. In the case of grants, any cash or in-kind donation is accompanied by a program or accepted proposal detailing how the gift will be used. Thus, a major distinction in practice is usually drawn between fund-raising and grantsmanship.

There are a number of excellent available guides to grant-writing activity.[6] There is also a growing social science literature on the subject. Following the pioneering work of Kenneth Boulding, economists have undertaken the serious study of grant economics (Boulding, 1981; Boulding, Pfaff, & Horvath, 1972; Horvath, 1982). Sociologists have also taken up questions of the social organization of grant-related efforts (Galaskiewiscz, 1985; Grønbjerg, 1991).

There is also a critical literature that questions the efficacy of the grant funding system. A social work faculty member, Eduard Lindeman (1936), did one of the earliest of such criticisms (see also Pratt, 1974). There is, of course, much to be questioned. At the very least, the system is enormously wasteful of the time and energy of applicants. Published information on numbers of grants received and funded by federal agencies shows that less than 1 percent of submitted proposals may be funded in some instances, and 2 to 3 percent funding success rates are not at all uncommon. Though foundations are not required to publish comparable information, the success rates at many larger foundations may be comparable. Interestingly, although the current accounting standards in effect for health and human services organizations call for doing so, very few organizations calculate the full cost of grant-writing activities. In part this is because federal grant guidelines expressly disallow the costs of grant writing as a reimbursable expense from a grant. Thus, the extent of the resources expended for such a low return rate cannot be determined.

Those who make, or give, grants have begun to style themselves as grant makers, and a number of local, regional, and national associations of grant makers now exist. The Foundation Center has a number of links to grant makers and grant-maker information on its Web site.[7]

One of the effects of policy devolution in recent decades has been to open up the role of state government health and human service agencies as major grant makers. Much of what is currently written about grants is based in the federal grant experience. Only gradually will a knowledge base grounded in state and locally based experiences evolve.

Foundations and Government Grants

Public or government grants are not the only type of grant. A second form of grant-related activity is that associated with private foundation grants. A foundation, as Malcolm Macdonald (1956) once put it, is "a large body of money completely surrounded by people who want some of it" (p. 3). Once the exclusive province of the super rich, tax laws have now made it feasible for even moderately wealthy individuals and families to establish or found such trusts. As a result, there were more than 40,000 foundations in the United States in 2000, and the number is increasing each year.

Foundations tend to be of four basic types: general, corporate, family, or community.

General foundations are established by legislative statute or legal charter for the purposes of holding, investing, and giving away money. Most are established by an initial gift, often with subsequent gifts following.

By tradition, the "letter of gift" accompanying the initial financial transfer to the foundation has been an important document in establishing the scope and mission of a foundation. The missions of general foundations are usually stated in broad, sweeping terms deliberately intended not to unduly restrict disbursements by the trustees. Thus, the mission might be identified as "benefiting the poor and disadvantaged of Monongalia County" but not specify how such benefits are to be provided. How to provide the benefits would be left to the discretion of the foundation's trustees. They would be free to make cash contributions to the poor, to establish literacy programs, to create training programs, and so on as they best saw fit.

One of the most important general foundations in the early history of twentieth-century social work was the Russell Sage Foundation, established in 1907 and known for four decades as "the social work foundation" (Glenn, Brandt, & Andrews, 1947; Hammack, 1988). The Sage Foundation in its early years was an activist foundation that set a pattern followed by other foundations by operating its own programs as well as giving away money to others. It was responsible for funding the Pittsburgh Survey and disseminating Mary Richmond's work on social casework, among many other things. However, by the late 1940s, the founding generation of social work innovators at Sage had died or retired. The social work interests associated with the foundation at that time appear to have run out of ideas and initiative. The foundation was taken over and reorganized by a group of lawyers and social scientists who transformed it into the important funder of empirical social science research it is today, albeit with little surviving evidence of the former connection to social work (Glock, 1967; Hammack & Wheeler, 1994). A quick search of any library catalog under publishers will reveal the large body of work published by the Sage Foundation.

Corporate foundations are established by business corporations to give away portions of the company's assets, often for tax advantages. The Kellogg Foundation is among the largest of such foundations. Some corporate foundations are primarily engaged in giving away free products (computers, software, phones, etc.) to charitable organizations. Others use the company foundation to focus corporate giving in communities where the company has offices, plants, or locations. In a study of giving practices of twenty-six corporations in Cambridge, Massachusetts, Zippay (1992) found that most corporations use informal decision processes that rely on tradition, social contacts, and intuition to guide allocations.

Family foundations are those established by families rather than individuals. The Ford Foundation and Rockefeller Foundations are perhaps the largest and best-known examples of such family foundations. Family foundations are often also under the continuing control of family members. This may not be as idyllic as it sounds, as anyone familiar with family behavior in any division of property can attest. We are aware of one case, for example, in which the board of a family foundation in its third generation (the trustees are cousins and second cousins) is unable to make a quorum for meetings. A number of years ago, the cousins splintered into three to four factions over matters of purpose and policy, and now the operant objective of each faction seems to be to keep any of the others from gaining any advantage. So each time a board meeting is called, one or more faction stays away in order to frustrate the intentions of the others. Meanwhile, staffers try to carry on the business of the foundation, all the time worrying about getting caught in the crossfire.

A *community foundation* might be thought of as a kind of philanthropic bank alternative useful for pooling the assets of a large number of large and small trust funds to benefit a geographic area. Indeed, traditionally and in many communities today, management of a significant number of small trust funds remains in the hands of trustees who are officers of local banks. Beginning with the Cleveland Foundation in the 1920s, there are now more than 400 community foundations in the United States (Koster, Messner, Richert, Cleveland Artists Foundation, & Cleveland Museum of Art, 1996; Pogue & Newcomen Society of the United States, 1989; Tittle, 1992).

Some of the recent growth in community foundations is due to strategic partnerships and funding from general foundations (e.g., Mott and Lilly) and from corporate sponsors (e.g., Merrill Lynch) (Boris, 1999, p. 20). The general idea is to create an independent mechanism and staff for administering what may be a very large number of small and medium trust funds. Most community foundations have the capability to manage restricted funds, such as scholarship funds, and unrestricted funds. Particularly in communities where community foundations exist, agencies seeking funds may find it helpful to get familiar with trust officers in banks who control such funds.

Foundations of all types can also be categorized fairly readily by wealth. At the very top are the super-rich foundations. Less than one-fifth of all foundations in the United States hold more than 90 percent of total foundation assets and account for more than 90 percent of total grants. In general, these foundations have assets in excess of $500 million, according to Michael O'Neill (1989), and they tend to be concerned with broad national and international issues. A second type of approximately 100 large funders (those with $100 million to $500 million in assets) is often characterized by regional funding interests. Smaller foundations comprise the third type ($10 million to $100 million in assets), and with only a few exceptions, they have local community funding interests. All three types tend to have paid staff who review and process funding applications prior to review by the board or trustees who make actual funding decisions. Finally, the largest number of foundations and fourth type are the private or independent grant-making foundations with no paid staff and assets under $10 million. In many cases, they may limit their funding to a single activity such as scholarships or to a small number of agencies, and many provide only small grants (e.g., under $25,000) (O'Neill, 1989). In more than a few cases, it has been worthwhile for social agencies, in particular, to establish connections with trustees of these small, local foundations, many of which do not have full-time staff.

Government grants often entail complex and highly formalized application procedures.[8] Further, the grant-making process is usually activated by formal submission of an application. By contrast, most foundation grants begin more informally with a letter of inquiry, and only if the applicant is invited to do so will the process proceed further to the formal application stage. Indeed, many small grants from foundations are handled on the basis of letters of inquiry only, or many involve only a very simple application. At the same time, it is easy to overemphasize the differences. One knowledgeable grant writer[9] wrote, "I'm not sure that there is an easy difference between 'foundation grants' and 'government grants,' since some government grants are quick and easy, and some foundation grants are long and tedious." One possible distinction may involve the use of RFPs (Requests for Proposals). Government grant makers are under greater pressure to spend available funds and thus more inclined to clarify the kinds of proposals they seek or intend to fund.

Another of the most distinctive characteristics of grants of all types is that they seldom entail long-term commitment of any type. In particular, grant makers have generally sought to avoid any hint that they might support general operating expenses for programs and services. Cynics and critics of foundations have argued that this desire to avoid long-term commitments is the result of some underlying bureaupathology such as the desire to retain maximum bureaucratic control and to perpetuate themselves. The tendency of foundations toward self-perpetuation, long known as "the dead hand of philanthropy," becomes a major public issue and source of congressional investigation periodically. The last round of public concern in the 1970s produced the five-volume report of the Filer Commission, which is still an excellent overview of the third sector.

There is a distinctive practice theory and approach to institution building associated with the foundation practice of providing only short-term funding. It is usually identified as the demonstration grant strategy. The idea is that grants are to be provided only for initial support of innovative practices and that once the viability of these new practices has been demonstrated, other unspecified forms of financial support will be forthcoming. It is these other unidentified sources of funding that are to provide any necessary long-term resource base for ongoing social services. This sometimes produces strange responses. Indeed, during the heyday of the age of grants in the late 1960s and early 1970s, false optimism was so rampant that many serious discussions emphasized that any concern for long-term institution building was simply unnecessary. Poverty was going to be eliminated and other social problems would be resolved quickly enough that no long-term institutions would be necessary. Solving the problems would simply remove the need for such institutions. Unfortunately, this resulted in widespread adoption of a style of short-term thinking perhaps summed up by the Latin phrase *carpe diem* (especially in its connotation of "live for today") that still pervades much of the social service sector.

Whatever the reasons for it may be, the demonstration grant has a number of distinctive effects on the grants economy. One of the most distinctive of these effects is the rather stylized use of notions of innovation and change. If grant makers cannot fund operation of established, ordinary, effective service programs, then every program funded by a grant must be novel and the effectiveness of every grant-funded program must come under scrutiny. Unfortunately, genuine innovative departures from standard practice are fewer and more far between than the rhetoric of demonstration grants would suggest. Nevertheless, every grant writer knows that the language of innovation must be applied regardless of how much of a stretch it may be to label a particular activity as innovative. This has resulted in heavy doses of inflation in language with respect to terms like *innovation* and *change*. Social administrators have come to recognize that this is the case, and as a result there is often a relatively high degree of cynicism, opportunism, and, in many cases, outright deception and falsehoods associated with grantsmanship in social services.

Even though a number of social services continue to rely upon grants for some portion of their funding and even more wish they could, it is likely that the golden age of grants as a major factor in financing social service activity has passed. This does not mean that grants are no longer a force at all in social service activity. It does, however, mean that they are diminishing in importance, just as individual donations became less important earlier.

FEES

At present, the single most important source of financial inflows or income in many social service agencies is the fee or use charge levied against individual clients or their families, agents, or others. Fees for social services are currently of two basic types: (1) fees charged directly to clients, in which the principal administrative challenge consists of recording charges appropriately, billing them to clients, and collecting and processing the proceeds; and (2) fees collected under the auspices of some type of service contract with a government agency, insurance company, or some other financial intermediary or third party. In this case, the all-important challenge of complying with the terms of the contract also becomes a major consideration. We take up this topic in greater depth in chapter 24.

The single most important characteristic of all social service fees and user charges from a financial management standpoint is a quality they possess that sets them apart very clearly from donations and grants. This characteristic is usually termed "metering" and refers to the close relation between the volume of service activity and the total amount of fee revenues. When services are fee-based, the financial manager can expect that as service delivery increases or decreases the total revenue from fees will also increase or decrease.[10] The more services you deliver, the more fees you should expect to collect. Such metered financial inflows are termed *revenues* and are different in this important respect from all types of support inflows. Thus, in fee-based systems, fee revenue acts as a gauge or meter measuring the flow of services just as the water meter attached to your house or apartment measures your water usage. In fact, the more water you use, the higher usage fee you will generally pay.

An associated characteristic that is almost equally important is the retrospective nature of fees. By their very nature, one would not expect to pay in advance for other goods and services such as groceries, perhaps, or tickets to a movie. The same is true for social service fees. Though donations, grants, and other forms of support may be received in advance and the cash on hand may be spent as needed, revenues are usually not received until some time after the service has been delivered. This introduces an additional time-related complexity into the financial equation for fee-based social services: *accounts receivable*, such as unpaid bills for services rendered. Such receivables have a counterpart in the accounting concept of *accounts payable*. Accounts payable are amounts owed by the agency such as salaries for work done but not yet paid and other unpaid bills. Both receivables and payables are associated with the more or less inevitable time lags that arise between the time a service event actually occurs and the time it is paid for. In more extreme cases, fee-based social services may need to follow a common business practice of borrowing funds using accounts receivable as collateral in order to remain in operation. Unfortunately, this may also result in interest on these short-term loans becoming a significant cost of doing business.

Until quite recently, it was possible to identify five principal types of social service fees:

1. *Fair-share fees* in which each participant pays an appropriate portion of the total cost of the service
2. *Participation fees* in which the client is charged only a nominal amount to secure a minimal level of commitment
3. *Flat rate fees* in which everyone is charged a similar amount regardless of variations in the service performed
4. *Sliding-scale fees,* in which fees are raised or lowered in light of client's ability to pay
5. *Third-party fees* in which fees and charges for service to a client are paid by a third party—primarily governments or insurance companies

Recent events have brought forth two additional types: scheduled fees and capitation fees.

The idea of fair-share fees is fairly straightforward. The fee is based on some method of apportioning the cost of the service. The essential idea of fair-share fees is that payment of fees by clients be proportional to the actual amount of service used. Thus, someone who met with a grief counselor three times would pay more than someone who met with a counselor once. Sliding-scale fees are a variant of that fair-share idea based on a different notion of fairness. With sliding-scale fees, fairness comes from charging on the basis of income rather than the amount of service consumed. It might appear at first glance that fair-share fees are the most appropriate in the case of clients able to pay for their own services and that sliding-scale fees are most appropriate in cases where they are not.

The flat fee corresponds most closely to conventional notions of retail pricing. Thus, flat fees "metered" on a hourly or visit basis have a built-in fair-share adjustment: the more service you require, the higher your fee will be.

The essential idea here is to generate sufficient revenue through pricing of services to at least cover the costs of operating those services. However, pure examples of programs supported entirely by revenues from such fixed fees are actually quite rare in social services. Ordinarily, part of the full cost of services is offset by donations, grants, or other subsidies, and the flat rate fees are expected to generate the remainder. In cases where there is active competition among social service vendors, fees may also be set by the market, that is, adjusted upward or downward to reflect supply and demand and to ensure a steady flow of revenue into the agency. We know of no cases in which mental health or other social services have been advertised as on sale or at cut-rate prices.

Probably the initial form of fee in social work and one that is still around in some contexts is known as the sliding-scale fee. The central concept in sliding-scale fees is not the cost of the service but rather the client's ability to pay. This issue has been highly controversial in social work on a number of occasions. One of the central tenants of the American psychoanalytic tradition, for example, was to turn the idea of fees into a clinical principle. Clients who would not pay were labeled "resistant." Yet poor clients could hardly be asked to pay fees reflecting the full cost of services. The answer was scaling fees to some conception of the client's ability to pay, charging a diminishing portion of the full fee to a certain zero-point as clients' incomes went down, beyond which the fee would be waived completely. As an administrative issue, sliding-scale fees conform closely to the business practice of discounting. They also raise the important question of supplemental inflows. If funds to support the actual cost of services are not coming from clients, then they must be recouped from some other source if the service is to remain viable.

As we indicated above, it might appear that fair-share fees are the most appropriate in the case of clients able to pay for their own services, and sliding-scale fees are most appropriate in cases where they are not. This would also seem to be the implication of the National Association of Social Workers (1996) *Code of Ethics*, which deals fairly extensively with fees.

Section 1.13, Payment for Services, sets up some of the conditions for operation of social work as an independent profession in the medical model in a climate of multiple forms of reimbursement. It identifies three conditions governing the payment of fees:

1. Social workers should ensure that fees are fair, reasonable, and commensurate with the services performed. Consideration should be given to the client's ability to pay.
2. Social workers should avoid accepting goods or services from clients as payment for professional services.
3. Social workers should not solicit a private fee or other remuneration for providing services to clients who are entitled to such available services through the social workers employer or agency. (p. 14)

Fees are also discussed in the context of terminating clients. One of the possible causes for termination is when fee-for-service clients haven't paid. When service is terminated under those circumstances, certain provisos are to be observed: (1) financial arrangements have been made clear to client; (2) termination does not pose an imminent danger to clients or others; (3) clinical and other consequences have been addressed and discussed with client (p. 15).

Third-party fees have been in existence for at least as long as insurance programs have been available. The rapid expansion of service contracting (discussed separately in chapter 24) and the advent of managed care has led to the addition of at least two new categories of third-party fees: schedule fees and capitation payments. *Schedule fees* are fees in which standard payments are made to a third-party payee for an activity, regardless of the actual cost to the provider. *Capitation payments* are ones in which service providers are paid in advance "per head" in proportion to the size of some established client population.

It is important to note that despite movement in that direction, the revenue environment in social work created by the predominance of fee-based service is not a true market. Competition among vendors, by itself, is not sufficient to create market conditions. Even so, competition among agencies has become a major fact of life in the social services world. Boehm (1996) identifies five forces driving competition among human service organizations: (1) rivalry among existing organizations; (2) the presence of substitute services in the market; (3) the bargaining power of suppliers; (4) the bargaining power of consumers; and (5) the threat of entrance by new organizations.

In most cases rather than real market conditions, which are characterized by large numbers of buyers and sellers and prices free to move up and down with supply and demand, the social service environment can best be characterized as a state of *monopsony*. In such cases, a single buyer (in the social services cases, the federal government or appropriate state government agencies) buys services for clients from a large number of sellers. In this case, prices are not set by competition or the interaction of large numbers of buyers and sellers but by administrative fiat or bureaucratic negotiation.

The more real that federal devolution and state decision-making autonomy become, the more this pseudo-market attains a second quasi-market condition known by economists as *oligopsony* or a few buyers and a larger number of sellers. Only when the point is reached that large numbers of insurance companies, pension funds, and other buyers acting independently and competitively are involved in buying social services at prices that fluctuate with market conditions can it be said that a true social service market has been attained.

Historically, there has been only one real market affecting social service pricing, and that is the labor market, in which social services must compete or be subject to the realities of market discipline. When volunteer social service became social work (that is, paid employment) two things happened. First, tasks and assignments lost their individual uniqueness and became routinized and standardized into jobs or positions that could be described or characterized in job descriptions and thus compared across settings. Professionalization with an emphasis on standards-based training is one of the elements of this standardization. Second, comparability of positions and people allowed the entry of competitive bidding and a mobile labor force. If a worker does not receive a satisfactory salary at agency A, she can look for another job offering a higher salary. Likewise, if an agency has trouble attracting qualified employees, one of the options open to it in theory is to increase salaries. Workers and agencies are free agents in the labor market and not required to act in such an economically rational manner, but if they do not, the results are easily predictable. Social service clients and contract-seeking agencies are seldom able to vote with their feet in a similar manner in the current monopsonistic social service markets. Thus, the assorted rhetoric of competition and being business-like is mostly an ideological smokescreen rather than a descriptive reality at present.

THIRD-PARTY PAYMENTS

It is a reality that social services are increasingly delivered on the basis of decisions made by assorted third parties or financial intermediaries, rather than by the direct actions of social administrators, social workers, or clients. The third parties may be federal agencies, state Medicaid officials, or assorted private vendors such as insurance companies, pension funds, or investment groups. The one universal characteristic of third-party payments is that they are paid by someone other than the vendor of the service or the client. Payments from insurance companies, purchase of service contracts, Medicaid waiver contracts, and a host of other arrangements fall within this broad category. The third-party payment from public sources has been the single major source of revenue for the majority of social service agencies from at least 1977 to the present. Generally, public payments account for around 50 percent of all inflows (Hodgkinson et al., 1996, p. 179). It is also a principal example of the three-way transaction discussed in chapter 2. All such payments invoke a clear three-way transaction between agent (the social agency), the client receiving the service, and a patron (the third party paying the bill).

Schedule Payments

Fee-schedule payments are third-party payments paid according to a listing, schedule, or formula covering a particular service. The schedule, for example, may specify that an organization's employee may receive up to three hours of marital counseling from the agency per year and that the agency will be paid $150 for that counseling. Where such rates are set and revised realistically this procedure can go a long way to reducing the paperwork associated with fees.

A new form of fee payment that came to be known as diagnostic related groups (DRGs) hit social service and health care providers like a bombshell in the 1980s. However, there was very little comment in the social administration literature on the most novel feature of DRGs: commodification. The underlying idea is that standardized treatments with known characteristics (including cost) can be closely matched to the preferred interventions in standardized diagnostic groups or problem sets. In this way, the actual cost and pricing behavior of those services can be reliably derived and compared. Thus, someone suffering from appendicitis (standard diagnostic group) would have surgery (the preferred intervention) and be hospitalized for no longer than a twenty-four-hour period (standard treatment). Defining and computing the cost of the two service elements (surgery and hospital care) is greatly facilitated by this type of approval.

Thus, in theory it should be possible to monitor and bill for social services on the basis of assorted standard costs. We should be able to differentiate between the cost of an intake interview for an adoption, a psychotic episode, and a nursing home discharge. Billing the third party for services thus becomes a simple matter of totaling up the assorted service components much like the cash register receipt from a grocery store. The principal problem with this approach is that there really are no standardized definitions of the components of social services at present, and very little valid, reliable information is known on the standard costs of those elements that have been identified. The result is that current applications of this approach to social services often resemble nothing quite so much as a "crap shoot" with what is thought to be standardized, producing unpredictable variance among workers, units, programs, agencies, and many other unknowns. Yet implementation of such systems often proceed as if such information were known and established. One vendor may allow six home visits following discharge for a particular condition and another vendor only two, with no principle or factual basis other than short-term cost reductions governing the difference.

Although the use of DRGs in medical practice is supported by an elaborate mechanism of defined procedures and protocols together with accumulated data on standard costs, much of the most basic work necessary to make such a system work in the case of social services still remains to be done. Until it is done, there will continue to be an arbitrary and irrational quality to the system.

Capitation

The widespread development of health maintenance organizations (HMOs) in the health care industry has brought with it another, entirely new form of financial inflow for social services (Landry & Knox, 1996; Mechanic & Aiken, 1991). In theory, an HMO represents the merger of a health service provider and the risk pooling of an insurance provider. In reality, a great variety of actual practices are covered by the term. The initial interest in HMOs nationally can be dated to pioneering work done by a research group under the leadership of Paul Ellwood at the Institute for Interdisciplinary Study (IIS) in Minneapolis beginning in the late 1960s. Probably the earliest attempts to apply the HMO model, including capitation, to social services were associated with the SHMO (social health maintenance organization) studies conducted at the Florence Heller Graduate School for Advanced Studies in Social Welfare at Brandeis University beginning in the 1970s.

The idea of capitation payments (literally "per-head" payments for an at-risk population) first emerged on the national level in the context of reforms to Medicare and Medicaid proposed in the early 1970s by Paul Ellwood and the IIS staff. Borrowed from the experience of earlier HMOs such as Kaiser-Permanente, the basic idea involved a reversal of the economics of fee for service. An organization is paid a capitation fee for each member of the client population in its district or catchment area with the expectation that it will provide service to the client group whenever it needs it. Because the more service they provide, the higher their total costs will be, the organization seeking profits theoretically will have a strong self-maintenance incentive to keep the population healthy or more generally problem free. As the experience with a variety of unscrupulous HMOs has shown since that time, keeping the population healthy is not the only or even necessarily the easiest way for HMOs to minimize the need for service and maximize profits. Narrowing the definitions of service eligibility is just as effective and a good deal easier for some than the preventative health care that was a key feature of the original HMO model.

In the late 1980s a variety of interesting demonstration projects intended to bring capitation financing to mental health were announced. The Civilian Health and Medical Program of the Uniform Services (CHAMPUS) carried out a major demonstration project in the Tidewater region of Virginia (Burns et al., 1989). Hadley and Glover (1989) offered a regional capitation system for the Philadelphia area. It is probably fair to suggest that capitation is still seen largely as a possible wave of the future in social service financing generally. A survey of mental health and substance abuse providers in Massachusetts in the mid-1990s, for example, indicated that many were preparing for future adoption of capitation plans (Beinecke, Goodman, & Lockhart, 1997). Mark Schlesinger (1989) has examined ways in which special characteristics of care for mental illness may unbalance capitation plans.

The central problem with the capitation strategy as a means of financing social services continues to be a by-product of the problem of poverty. Poor clients are poor consumers, economically speaking. That is, they are by definition, unable to pay the full cost of needed services. Thus, the principle effect of any service financed by capitation alone must be systematic cost-shifting from poor to more affluent clients who end up paying not only for their own services, but also subsidizing a portion of the cost of free or reduced cost services to other, low income clients as well. Yet many social services are explicitly designed for the poor only. Thus, unless the client population is defined to include a predetermined mix of both affluent and poor clients, it is unlikely that any viable capitation plan for social services under such conditions can be developed. In cases where such shifting is not possible, some forms of supplemental support (donations or grants) must be present to make up the differences.

In some cases, clear-cut rationales for such cost shifting might be made. For example, providing free prevention services for communicable diseases like tuberculosis has an important public health benefit in reducing the risk of exposure to the disease for the affluent as well as the poor. In recent years, however, such prudent commonsense notions have been attacked in the public policy arena on two fronts. At an ideological level, the rugged individualism often associated with neoconservatism suggests a direct correspondence between assigned costs and benefits, which is extremely difficult to apply at all in cases of prevention. At a more practical level, simple free-rider behavior takes over. "Such prevention may be a good thing, but why should I pay for it? If others can be charged, I will still get the same benefit."

MEMBERSHIP DUES

One of the anomalies of all nonprofit organizations is the degree to which voluntary associations or membership organizations are still the legal and cultural norm for all nonprofit activity. At one time in the nineteenth century, many charity organizations in American cities were literally membership organizations, in which the inflows from relatively steep dues were directed into relief efforts for the "worthy poor." One of the most important explanations for the rise of the spirit of scientific philanthropy is the vested interest that such members had in seeing that the charity society's "agents" made good use of the dues paid by members (see Warner, 1894/1930; Rauch, 1976).

Generally speaking, however, this model is no longer very relevant. Social agencies tend not to have members (except in the narrow, technical/legal sense of board members.) As a result, member dues represent a totally inconsequential financial inflow in most social agencies. This need not be the case. Membership organizations of dues-paying stakeholders (along the lines of Friends of the Library or Friends of the Symphony) could be a supplementary source of financial inflows for any nonprofits and could even be designed for most public agencies. Currently, however, this source of inflows remains of little importance.

SALES OF UNRELATED GOODS

One of the most interesting and vexatious categories of inflow in many social agencies today falls under the IRS heading of "sales of unrelated goods." It might at first appear that having tax-exempt status completely prevents nonprofit organizations from engaging in unrelated inflow-producing activities, as it does many public organizations. From this viewpoint, one might expect that a nonprofit mental health agency could not own and operate a car dealership nor that a hospice could operate a shoe store if they expected to keep their 501(c)(3) certification and stay out of jail.

This is actually not the case at all. In general, the doctrine of free association largely prevents units of government (including tax authorities, contracting agencies, and grant makers) from dictating to nonprofit organizations exactly how they must limit their total activities. For the most part, they are free to determine their own missions and conduct their own affairs. Governments can, of course, dictate how their granted or contracted funds may be used. In recent years, attorneys general in some states have begun to look more closely at ways of holding nonprofit organizations more strictly to their missions. For much of the past half-century, tax-exempt nonprofits generally have had to only consider two principal concerns when deciding how widely to cast their financial nets.

First is the legal doctrine of fraud. Fraud in the social service context is almost entirely a matter of organizations appearing to be, acting as if they were, or claiming to be something that they are not. A car dealership, for example, may not claim to be a tax-exempt mental health agency or a museum and solicit tax-deductible donations if it does not have exempt status and all it does is sell cars. A tax-exempt mental health agency, however, might under some circumstances legally operate a car dealership without losing its corporate charter or its exempt status or being found guilty of fraud. The price of doing so may, however, be payment of taxes on that portion of their financial inflows. (For those who are interested in pursuing this question further, the exact circumstances are almost entirely matters of state law, and specific cases should be taken up with a lawyer and/or tax accountant.)

This brings us to the second concern: Let us assume that our hypothetical mental health agency has established a suitable legal arrangement for selling cars, and plans to transfer all the profits from car sales into supporting its mental health operations. This takes them into the IRS category of sales of unrelated goods. In a notable case decades ago, the Supreme Court held that a private nonprofit university could not extend its tax-exempt status to cover a commercial bakery it operated. The grounds for this decision established the relationship with the agency's central (and tax-exempt) mission to be the critical factor. University bakeries that bake bread for their students might in most cases be exempt. Likewise, a mental health car dealership that served to train mental patients for productive employment might also be exempt. But what about those activities that are not mission related?

Public and private universities and hospitals and at least social service agencies are able to resolve the tax portion of this issue simply by paying federal and state taxes on the portion of their inflows that are taxable. These taxes are generally termed UBITs (unrelated business income taxes). Forcing nonprofits to disclose such unrelated inflows is why the IRS treats this as a separate category. Thus, our mental health car dealership might have a net profit before taxes of $200,000, pay $50,000 in applicable taxes, and channel the remaining $150,000 net profit after taxes into its mental health services operation.

INVESTMENT INCOME

Investment income as a financial inflow in social agencies merits two quite distinct types of considerations, depending upon both the amounts involved and the degree of risk the agency may be able to tolerate. Most agencies are involved with investment questions as a relatively minor consideration, involving relatively small amounts of money and very limited risk. For example, it has been clearly established that interest-bearing checking accounts, certificates of deposit, and treasury bills are suitably safe investments for agencies. (The best—at this writing, the only—source on this is Fry, 1998).

The second set of considerations involve those agencies with endowments or asset portfolios in which investment becomes a major issue. In our Hull House example in chapter 21, for example, the reader will recall that in 1932 Hull House received roughly one-fourth of its total financial inflow from income on investments in its endowment. In such cases, the board of the social agency can only be advised to seek competent, professional help or assume the burden of risk themselves.

CONCLUSION

Social services require financial resources. Thus, any social agency that seeks to remain viable must have a workable plan for acquiring the necessary resources through some combination of fund-raising, grant writing, fee-collections from clients, and third-party contracts. A comprehensive, well thought-out program for a social agency will embrace both support and revenues.

In far too many social agencies, the agency resource development program consists of a single idea—Let's write a grant!—with insufficient consideration of issues of long-term continuation or whether the same investment of time and energy in some other form of development activity might be more successful. Thus, for example, it may be somewhat more costly in the short-run to establish a viable direct-mail fund-raising campaign than to write a grant. But over the long haul the agency might be able to establish a permanent, ongoing source of support rather than a temporary one- to three-year boost from the grant. In other cases, of course, the short-term boost may be just what is called for. The point is that unless the agency has a clear, coherent revenue plan, complete with appropriate strategies for generating support and revenue, its activities in generating financial inflows will be purely ad hoc and may even be at cross-purposes with the agency's larger mission and strategy.

CHAPTER 23

Budgeting

T he term *budget* has come to mean a plan and, in some cases, the document stating that plan. It is a plan for a program of planned or anticipated revenues and expenditures. Budgeting, then, usually refers to administrative action necessary to prepare and adopt such a plan. In this chapter, we examine the phenomenon of budgeting as both the allocation of funds already received (see chapter 22) and as part of a plan for soliciting funds, as in the case of grant writing.

The word *budget* is thought to have originally entered modern English usage from an old French word *bougette,* meaning a little bag, sack, or pouch that might be suitable for carrying coins. The British are said to have adopted the term to describe the action of the Chancellor of the Exchequer presenting an annual financial statement to Parliament (Sumariwalla, 1989).

The institutions of social agency budgeting, which are primarily the annual budget and management control through budget review and adoption, are of relatively recent origin. There have been two principal periods of intensive development of budget theory and concepts in the past century. The first occurred during the scientific management movement before 1920, and the second began in the early 1960s. For much of the rest of the time, practice has centered on actual use of the innovations developed during these brief bursts of creative change.

In the first two decades of the twentieth century, scholars and practitioners in the scientific management movement were actively involved in developing a number of key terms and concepts of modern budget theory. Frederick Taylor, the founder of the scientific management movement, is said to have "deplored the traditional post-mortem uses of accounting."[1] Many key ideas about financial management and budgeting arose by combining engineering ideas on economy with usual and customary accounting techniques. The conventional budget document showing projected income and expenditure items is typically a prospective or future-oriented format. It is usually paired with and uses many of the same categories or "line items" as ordinary retrospective or historical expenditure statements prepared by accountants.

In 1903, Henry Hess developed a crossover chart, later called a break-even chart, showing the relationships among volume of production, fixed costs, variable costs, sales, and profits as two intersecting lines in two dimensions. The same year John R. Williams offered up the idea of the flexible budget, that is, one where expenditures varied with activity. Scientific manager James O. McKinsey "pioneered in the development of budgets as planning and control aids" (Wren, 1994, p. 209). Out of Hess's crossover charts, the modern concept of break-even analysis arose. Walter Rautenstrauch coined the term *break-even point* in 1922 for the beginning point of profit: that unique combination of revenues and expenditures at which total costs and sales revenues are exactly equal. It is a concept of particular relevance to social administration planning and budgeting (Lohmann, 1976).

During the 1960s and 1970s, there was a flurry of activity that resulted in a number of permanent improvements in our understanding of budget structures and processes. Until the adoption of relatively uniform charts of accounts, the promulgation of uniform accounting standards for nonprofits, and a host of other, incidental innovations, each agency or field of service was pretty much a world unto itself with little comparability between funds, program, agencies, or service industries. The relatively standard approaches resulting from these innovations enhance our understanding of the budgeting process of various noncommercial organizations and ultimately may allow us to compare their financial performances.

THE IRONIES OF FINANCIAL MANAGEMENT

Budgeting in social administration until very recently was based completely on ideas borrowed from business and public administration and the unguided practical problem solving of practitioners. In a formulation that had a marked impact on the development of the public administration discipline, Luther Gulick included budgeting in his famous amplified version of Fayol's list of management functions described previously (Wren, 1994, pp. 184–85). The acronym that Gulick derived (POSDCORB) included planning, organizing, staffing, directing, coordination, reporting, and *budgeting* as the central functions of public administration. Budgeting as Gulick dealt with it was a very mixed bag of financial planning, accounting, and control.

Budgeting and financial reporting in human services developed largely on an ad hoc basis rather than being derived from or grounded in theory or through diffusion by the professional schools. Both theory and practice in this area remain somewhat apart from the main body of social administration theory and practice. It is probably also fair to say that many of the current generation of management scholars in social work still have only limited command of this important area. As problems arose, various ad hoc solutions to them were posed, and budget theory today in social administration is still largely a series of efforts to link these congeries of solutions-in-place and to reconstruct those practices. Still, it is possible to construct a reasonably coherent theory of budgeting in social administration that does a satisfactory job of describing actual practices.

This has produced an ironic state of affairs whereby there is widespread agreement that concern for the management of resources is and should be of central importance to the practice of social work, yet attention to the subject by researchers, teachers, students, and most practitioners remains extremely limited. During the age of grants, social work practice had reached a measure of accommodation on this issue. Grant budgets were mostly prescribed by granting agencies, and budget practice often amounted to simply following these rules. In the era of managed care, the present limitations in financial understanding could prove much more serious. In general, the rules are changing, but it is not entirely clear in some cases that new rules have yet fully evolved. One of the aspects of the age of managed care is that financial concerns, issues, and decisions have moved directly to the center of practice without much evidence of a noticeable impact on the teaching of social work (Lohmann, 1997).

Very little has ever been published about the actual budget practices of earlier social service agencies.[2] The conventional assumption that social agencies routinely received singular large gifts or grants that they allocated into various categories may be somewhat simplistic. This is, almost certainly, the system of budgeting enforced on agencies by the community chest/United Way model and the subsequent federal grant model of the Great Society period. In both these cases, the budget itself becomes part of the contract implicit in the grant. The funds are received on the expectation that they will be spent only for the known items specified in the budget.

One can derive a fairly comprehensive understanding of the range of contemporary budget approaches in social agencies from just two factors. First, there is a concern for accountability to funders and stakeholders. Second, there is consideration of the level of risk and uncertainty involved in budget decisions.

The concern for accountability in budgeting is an extension of the consideration of contract accountability discussed in chapter 12. There are implied or express contracts inherent in every grant, gift, or bequest of money or other resources, and in every employment, consulting, purchase of service, or other contract. One of the proverbial concerns of traditional social agency budget has been the search for optimal ways to clarify and solidify those agreements as a means of ensuring that agency obligations are met.

The risks or the uncertainties associated with resource acquisition and use may be any of four types:

- Risks involving *people,* especially the level of trust among the people involved, their abilities and judgments. Every person engaged in social service budgeting has had the experience of receiving advice from a grant maker on how to handle a budget item and wondered whether to comply.
- Risks involving *technology,* such as the reliability of the practice technologies used and dangers in use. Funds spent on substance abuse treatment, for example, may be inherently riskier than funds spent for Head Start.
- Risks involving *financial considerations,* such as the handling and investment of funds before their expenditure. Investing temporarily surplus funds in certificates of deposit ordinarily is much less risky than investing in stocks.
- Risks involving *market considerations,* in the case of fee-based services such as whether someone—either clients or third parties—is available to buy the service. In most cases, social services operate with such large pools of unmet needs that risks of "running out of clients" are ordinarily minimal.

Using these considerations of accountability and risk, we can identify four basic types of budgetary practice in social service agencies:

- *Allocative budgeting.* In this type, the precise amount available for allocation is known and the challenge is to allocate it or assign it to particular objects or expenditure categories. In the pure case, these allocations alone will determine the level of service presumed.[3] Allocative budgeting is a practical expression of the problem in algebra known as solution for one unknown. The one critical unknown is how much service can be prosumed with these available resources? There may be other unknowns in the situation, but from the standpoint of budget theory this one is the critical question.

- *Allocative budgeting with secondary flexibility.* In this case, the largest share of funding for the agency or program is certain. However, a small amount is flexible. This is the case, for example, when a grant supports 90 percent of a service and the remaining 10 percent is a share that must be raised by donations or some other means.

- *Flexible budgeting.* In this type, neither the precise amount of funding available nor the level of service to be prosumed are known. This is the case, for example, with all fee-paying clients who are to receive unspecified amounts of service. In such cases, various approximations must be made. In the pure case, it is not possible to establish any kind of relationship between funding and service, and this problem is unsolvable except as a set of ranges. However, there are a variety of mathematical means available for estimating at varying levels of precision that relationship. It is to the lasting credit of Henry Hess that he understood this as a problem of the relationship of the volume of production, costs, and revenues.[4] The more recent methodology of microeconomics makes handling this problem even more feasible.

- *Flexible budgeting with secondary allocations.* In this case, limited amounts of funding are certain but the largest share of funding and service levels are uncertain. It may be that the agency has some donated funds but only a fraction of the funding needed for a particular program.

Attempts at allocative budgeting probably became the core of traditional social agency budgeting with the spread of the federated funding movement sometime after 1910 and remained so into the 1970s. Community chest, United Way, foundation, and federal and state governmental grants all fit the model of allocative budgeting with contract accountability. It is as if the funder is saying, "We will give you a grant based on your proposal with its accompanying budget on the expectation that that is how you will spend the funds." Indeed, many of what are called "social service contracts" with state and local governments are still little more than grants with the added stipulation of some type of units of service measure that allows calculation of what at times is an almost mythical "unit cost" figure (e.g., a "service episode" or "an interview" of unspecified length).

Typically introducing small amounts of variable funding such as proceeds from bake sales, user fees, and the like into the allocative budget situation does not change things dramatically. In such cases, most of the funding may be certain (e.g., either you get the grant or you don't) while there is a small range of uncertainty about how to obtain some of the funds. In most cases, this uncertainty is dealt with simply because it falls within the normal range of uncertainty associated with social service efforts. If the administrator is wrong, then the most pessimistic assumptions she may have made about the variable funding turn out to be true. And if that is the case, she can scale back the overall service effort to reflect that. She can, for example, operate the program for eleven rather than twelve months or four rather than five days a week, or delay hiring the full staff for a month, or serve fewer clients, and so on. Functionally, it is when such adjustments are impractical or infeasible in a major way that we move into the arena of flexible funding, and fixed allocations become secondary in importance. For example, once the flexible funding exceeds 50 percent of total funding fixed allocations are of increasingly limited significance.

DEDICATION OF FUNDS

As we indicated above, relatively little has been published about the budgeting practices of early social service agencies in the United States. Hull House, however, yields up some interesting examples of social administration practice in the budgeting arena.[5] We have chosen to use that information here to provide some information about the budget practices of historically important social agencies and because that information serves to illustrate advances in budgeting since that time.

One of the more interesting examples of the ad hoc problem-solving approach that turned out to be a dead end for social service practice is shown in Table 23.1, based on a portion of an actual financial statement from Hull House. This approach has a certain logic to it but has since been completely abandoned.

This approach has no generally accepted name, but we call it *dedication*. It appears to have grown out of the situation in which most funds were donated for specific programs or with restrictions. Hull House accountants could only keep track of this by treating each gift, in effect, as a separate program by putting it in a separate box on a sheet filled with squares. Much of the giving at Hull House appears to have been purposeful. That is, the purposes for which the money was intended were specified in advance as a part of the donation or grant by which they are received. When most funds are received this way, the remaining task of budgeting the residual undesignated funds can fall easily into the same pattern, whereby administrators assign them to specific programs as they are received. Something like this approach seems to have been in effect at Hull House during Jane Addams's career there. Keep in mind, that in 1934—which was the year before Addams's death from cancer—fund accounting capable of tracking restricted

Table 23.1 Financial Report (by "Dedicated Funds"), Hull House, 1933

		Income	Expense	Balance	Deficit
Art school					
Balance 1-1-33	429.01	1,869.75	1,860.53	9.22	
Donations	248.00				
Sales	1,192.74				
	1,869.75				
Printing shop					
Donations	100.00	160.25	100.96	59.29	
Sales	60.25				
	160.25				
Summer outing					
Endowment income	1,200.00				
Donations	8,626.50	12,539.54	12,474.27	65.27	
Fees	1,330.61				
Special groups and					
weekend parties	1,382.43				
	12,539.54				
Boy's club and gymnasium					
Fees	353.47	4,732.77	4,732.77		
Donations	4,379.30				
	4,732.77				
Children's and mother's					
clubs					
Fees	29.46	1,948.89	1,948.89		
Donations	1,919.43				
	1,948.89				
Music school					
Balance	391.30	2,891.70	2,608.53	283.17	
Fees	815.40				
Donations	1,685.00				
	2,891.70				

funds was not yet well developed, and the Hull House financial management staff were clearly unaware of it as a developing tool, either for reporting or planning purposes.

Even if this was not the actual approach to budgeting at Hull House that it appears to be, the budgeting by dedication approach is worth some consideration by students simply because it conforms so closely to certain naïve ideas that people often bring to the budget process. In particular, it seems to represent an early attempt at program budgeting, which did not really come into its own until the age of grants. Thus, it is important to note that, in general, there are three principle problems with the approach to budgeting shown here.

1. The difficulty in keeping track of information combined with a rather confusing presentation. There is almost no possibility, for example, that the table could show how the surplus shown for the art school could be used for any other purpose.
2. The loss of discretion or decision flexibility that results from this approach, which is sometimes called *earmarking*. The table seems to suggest that each set of revenues and expenditures is a separate mini-budget unto itself.
3. The failure to account for what accountants and economists term the *fungibility* of money. Every dollar in the bank may look like every other dollar, but in the budget they remain strictly separate.

In the nonprofit and public worlds, earmarking or dedicating certain funds to certain specific purposes is certainly still a reality. Legislators dedicate particular special purpose taxes such as hunting license revenues to specific purposes such as conservation. Donors make donations only on condition that their dollars be used for some specific purpose. These limitations must be honored. Similarly, grants received for specific purposes or programs must be used for the purposes for which they were granted.

The concept of the fund entity in fund accounting is closely related to several of these problems. However, to build a complete approach to agency budgeting and the resulting budget documents around the realities of dedication is ordinarily to begin at the wrong place. Such an approach offers no easy ways to deal with unrestricted or discretionary funds other than the temptation to toss them all into some type of miscellaneous budget box and hope that you remember how you intended to use them.

The characteristic of money that accountants call fungibility[6] is also closely related to this. Once the donation from Mrs. Louise DeKoven Bowen, who was the largest single donor to Hull House during Addams's career there, was deposited in the Hull House checking account, it was impossible to keep track of exactly which dollars came from her and which from other donors. Like many other donations to Hull House, this donation was earmarked for a specific purpose. Thus, tracking of this type is exactly what the dedication approach to budgeting sought to do. Yet, subsequent budget practice has revealed the much simpler and clearer solutions of fund accounting and program budgeting, which are discussed next.

FUND ACCOUNTING AND PROGRAM BUDGETING

Modern fund accounting and program budgeting practices generally go hand-in-hand to deal more clearly and easily with many of these problems. *Fund accounting* involves system of financial records in which individual revenue and expenditure items are by purpose, program, donor group, or some other entity rather than for the enterprise (organization) as a whole. In *program budgeting,* fund groupings also often become the basis for budget allocation decision as well. In addition, accounting software based upon relational databases solves several additional problems of recording and data presentation. Fund accounting systems were developed first for governments but are also in widespread use in nonprofit agencies as well. They allow for the recording of financial transactions in ways that make possible the kind of full donor accountability that the dedication budget could only strive for. In addition, at least since the age of grants, when federal grants were often made on a program basis, budgeting by the program structure of an agency has become the norm. This is often done in matrix format with conventional line items on the vertical axis and programs on the horizontal axis, or vice versa (see table 23.1).

BUDGET BASE AND INCREMENT

The two most important terms in agency budget theory are *base* and *increment.* These terms entered the administrative vocabulary through a classic study of the federal budget process done by the political scientist Aaron Wildavsky (1967). *Base* can be defined as the legacy of past expenditures brought forward into the future as we saw in the previous chapter. One can also define the financial base in decision terms as those financial resources that will not be subject to negotiation or discussion in the current round of budget decision making. *Increment* can be defined as the unit of change in a budget, whether it is an increase or decrease. In some cases, the word *decrement* is used to indicate a negative increment. Increment can also be defined as those matters subject to decision or choice.

This, of course, introduces a minimum of two levels of considerations for decisions. Under certain conditions, the base will be accepted or recognized by all key stakeholders, and the principal matter of attention will be the increment. For example, the salaries of all existing employees may be seen as a part of the overall agency base that needs to be funded no matter what. In other circumstances, however, major disagreements and key decisions will revolve around defining the base itself. Using the employee salary example, there may be some who would argue that not all employees' salaries should be funded if the consequence of funding is to reduce the funds available for rent and utilities for the agency office. They may argue that the base funding should only be for one-half of the current employees and that any additional salary funding is an incremental decision. Thus, one person's base may be (and often is) another's increment.

MARKET-DRIVEN VERSUS BUDGET-DRIVEN ACTIONS

Everyone who engages in administration would like to believe that their actions are reasonable and justified. However, there is a difference among sectors in terms of the basis on which day-to-day actions can be justified. In the case of commercial business, where budgets have been of only limited interest or value, the justification for daily actions comes from the market. Purpose (profit), basic orientation (self-interest), behavior (buying and selling), and evaluation (the effect on the bottom line) are all tied together in this way.

By contrast, in the social service agency, purpose (goal attainment), basic orientation (service), behavior (program), and performance evaluation (outcomes) are not inherently tied together in the same way. This is perhaps the greatest difference between being a commercial business and a private nonprofit agency. In service[7] contexts in the government and nonprofit sectors, the fundamental purpose of budgeting is to link available resources to specific purposes, usually through specification or reference to a specific set of modal behaviors or a program. In an ongoing budget system, comparison of proposed future programs with previous performance by examination of outcomes, for example, becomes a primary consideration. In this way, it is the decisions of the budget process and not the market orientation that define the direction and focus of the agency. For the past several decades, well-intended efforts of business leaders to improve social services that can be summarized by the injunction to be "more business-like" have foundered on the rocks of misunderstanding this point.

FUND VERSUS ENTERPRISE BUDGETING

During the age of grants, social administrators learned that an agency with fifteen separate grants might well be engaged in fifteen separate, autonomous budget negotiations. In an age of managed care, it is possible that that same agency might have 150 provider agreements. As was discussed above, fund accounting is one way that these many separate budgets can be managed.

Though the funds are certainly important, it is also important to remember that they add up to a whole, which is usually referred to as the *enterprise*. Thus, a social agency as a whole comprises an enterprise, and it may have an overall budget of $1,780,000. That whole may be composed of ten different programs whose budgets range from $80,000 to $450,000. However, if the administrator focuses only on the specific funds and the programs that they support, there is the danger that the administrator will lose the ability to guide the larger enterprise in appropriate directions.

Enterprise is often used when referring to technology. Thus, those interested in selling an agency software packages or hardware will encourage the agency to make an enterprise decision that the same software and hardware be used for all agency programs rather than having the administrators of each program decide what software and hardware they will use. There are some advantages that come from adopting the larger perspective associated with the enterprise view; the administrator can identify areas in which economies of scale or cost savings may be realized that increase at rates greater than the rate of overall expenditure or ways in which programs can work together more closely.

THE MISLEADING THEORY OF THE ZERO BASE

One of the potential innovations that made great headway among budget theorists during the 1970s was the idea of budgeting from a clean slate, which was known as zero-base budgeting. The effort was sold as a way of overcoming the supposed limitations of the incremental approach of justifying revenue and expenditures as changes from past performance. The zero-based idea was to reexamine fully each proposed expenditure each time the budget was up for review. The principal objection to zero-base budgeting is that it has proved to be completely impractical under most circumstances. Further, there is simply no reason to believe that administrative actors ever actually think or behave in this manner or that it is practical or useful for them to do so.

To test this approach, starting at breakfast tomorrow try to completely ignore every agreement, contract, understanding, and compromise you have made previously with the people in your life. Will you drive your children to school or must they find alternative transportation? Will you report to work at 8:00 A.M. or have you decided to renegotiate a 10:00 A.M. starting time? Subject each of your understandings to complete reconsideration and renegotiation and make a formal decision of whether to continue, amend, or terminate the relationship. By about 9:30 A.M. you will probably be ready to concede the case for the impossibility of zero-base thinking as a reasonable way to proceed in human affairs. If the individuals in your life can't get from breakfast to lunch in this manner, why should there be any reason to believe that groups of individuals in organizations and communities would have any easier time of it?

Budgets are highly complex agreements under the best of circumstances, and in most instances, they involve dozens, hundreds, or thousands of separate decision points that take the form of overt agreements and compromises as well as covert "winks and nods" representing tacit understandings and unstated agreements with various concerned parties. In any given bud-

get decision, only a limited portion of the total possible issues and considerations and questions can ever be considered. Thus, the whole idea of
proceeding with budgeting from scratch is a thoroughly impractical idea.

Though impractical as a general budgeting approach, the idea of periodically reconsidering some of the base assumptions of a budget can be
helpful to an agency. To use the example used above in discussing base and
increment, although an agency may not wish to consider each year whether
each employee's position should continue to be funded, it is important to
periodically assess whether existing positions continue to be needed. The
failure to do so can mean that the agency's fiscal resources are not deployed
where they are most needed or can be most effective. Often such examination occurs only when an agency runs short of funds and is looking for
expenses that can be reduced or eliminated. The examination then occurs
in a crisis mode rather than being a part of the ongoing renewal of the
agency that ties budget to program and mission.

REVENUE, COST, AND SELF-SUPPORT CENTERS

Another of the fundamental concepts that transcend the naïve notions of
budget by dedication is that of cost. *Cost* ordinarily has two important but
related meanings:

1. *Outlay cost* is used by accountants to identify what is spent or laid
   out to acquire or purchase an object or achieve an objective. The cost
   of hiring staff, renting a facility, and equipping the facility to open a
   day care center would represent an outlay cost.
2. *Opportunity cost* is a more abstract and more widely generalizable
   notion of the same idea preferred by economists. It asks what value
   must be given up to attain an object or value (again, read achieve an
   objective). The cost of not being able to enroll more children at an
   existing day care center through expansion because the agency chose
   instead to open a new one elsewhere would be an example of an
   opportunity cost. One opportunity was forgone to allow achievement
   of another opportunity.

In both cases, cost is always relative to something definable or identifiable. We must always speak of the cost *of something*, never of cost per se.[8]
Thus, conventional models of financial management derived from cost accounting and cost analysis rely heavily upon the idea of *cost and revenue
centers*, which in the social agency correspond to some degree with the
concept of the *bougette* or purse from which the term budget originated.
Each center is a little purse, and the act of budgeting involves taking from

(revenue centers) and putting in (cost centers). For purposes of determining costs, these centers may be thought of as "magnets" to which are attached relevant or appropriate costs, and as appropriate, revenues.

As a further refinement of this basic concept, *cost centers* are those operating units or objects in which the total costs attached to the center exceed attached or equal assigned revenues. In the social agency setting, service programs not funded by fees or user charges almost always operate as cost centers. Conversely, *revenue centers* are those operating units or objects in which a surplus remains after expenditures are subtracted from revenues. In general, there are two principle types of revenue centers in social services: *earned income centers*, often referred to simply as income centers, and *support centers*, such as human resources and other administrative support activities.

The principal difference between earned income centers and support centers is a subtle but important one. Earned income or fee-based revenue centers are characterized by the "metering" relationship between service delivery and revenue-generation. The greater the number of clients who are seen, the greater the fee income will be. In support activities, no such metering relationship exists.

Human resources costs, such as fringe benefits or the cost of filling a vacant position, though related to service delivery, are separate and distinct, and there is no necessary relation between them. The number of clients seen, for example, does not necessarily have any relationship to the fringe benefits program managed by the human resources office.

In contemporary nonprofit organizations some centers are designated by a third classification that we are calling *self-supporting* or break-even centers. These are centers that are sometimes described as having to carry their own weight or to generate enough revenues to offset their costs. Thus, a settlement house might provide a café but expect that the income from the café will cover the café's costs. Thus, the café is not expected to generate revenue to support other programs nor is it expected to be supported by the revenue generated by other programs. It is to be self-supporting.

One might wonder if the goal of all social services is not to break even or be self-supporting. To answer that question, we need to remember the above discussion of the fund and the enterprise. The goal of the enterprise or the agency as a whole is to break even. Its income should at least equal its expenditures. However, the goal of any particular fund associated with a program or series of programs may be different. Some funds are expected to generate revenue, some to be support centers, and some to break even. Thus, there might be revenue centers within a break-even enterprise or support centers within a profit-oriented enterprise.

Because college examples of these types of centers are likely recognizable to the readers of this book, they will be used to provide additional illustrations. Bookstores, cafeterias, and recreational facilities of various types from bowling alleys to concert programs on many campuses are targeted as revenue centers. On the authors' campus, for example, the bookstore contract provides that the commercial organization managing the bookstore will provide a percentage of its profits to the university. Dormitories are often break-even centers. They are not expected to support anything other than their own expenses. Many continuing education courses are run on a break-even basis. If enrollment is not sufficient enough to support the costs, the course is cancelled. Classroom teaching and most administrative offices are cost centers. Faculty members continue to be paid and classrooms remain open even if enrollment in a particular course is low one semester.

The issue for any given social service organization (itself, legally a self-support center) is whether it can identify its major cost centers and whether it possesses any real or potential revenue centers that can be used to offset those costs. For the agency to survive it must ensure at the enterprise level that its revenue and cost centers are in balance. It may be possible in the short run to defer expenses to the next fiscal year and thus create a fictitious balance, but over the long run the necessity of such a balance is very real.

A fundamental consideration in assessing the costs of social services is the ability of the particular service to recover costs associated with its delivery. If a particular social service is partially or fully revenue based, it may be possible to pass the full costs of service delivery along to consumers of services or third-party contractors in the form of increased fees or charges. If the service is not revenue based but is funded by donations or grants or if its ability to raise or adjust fees is severely limited, as in the case of many membership organizations or third-party contracts, its cost-recovery ability may also be severely limited.

ONE-TIME OR RECURRING COSTS

One important distinction with regard to costs that many beginning administrators fail to make is that between one-time and recurring costs. A one-time cost is as the name describes; once the purchase is made, no further expenditure will be needed. Recurring costs are ones in which investments need to continue to be made even after the initial expenditure. The purchase of today's newspaper at a newsstand is a one-time cost. Starting a subscription to the daily newspaper today for the next year is a recurring cost.

Technology costs represent a good illustration of the difference between these two kinds of costs. Many agencies see technology investments as a one-time expenditure. Once the computers and software are purchased, no further expenditures will be required. However, technology investments are more accurately thought of as recurring ones. Computers need to be replaced every three to five years. Memory may need to be upgraded before then. Software upgrades need to be purchased. Staff must be hired to maintain the computers and local area networks used to link them together. Thus, technology is better treated as an ongoing or recurring expense than as only a one-time expense, although the amount of the expense may vary in any given year.

Social administrators sometimes fail to realize this important distinction when making personnel decisions. Sufficient funds may be available in the budget midway through the budget year, for example, to hire an additional staff member. In doing so, however, the administrator needs to realize that she has incurred a recurring cost unless the term of employment is only through the end of the fiscal year. The administrator needs to make certain that the following year's budget has sufficient funds to support the position and its fringe benefits for a full year rather than only a portion of the year.

A few years ago, many communities were dealing with this phenomenon as a result of the federally funded programs to increase the number of police officers. Many communities took advantage of that program, which generally provided funding for additional officers for a period of two years. However, many treated this as a one-time expense. Local expenses were minimal and easily manageable within existing budgets. When the two-year period of federal support expired, communities were scrambling to identify ongoing or recurring funds that could be used to continue the police officers' employment since employment most often represents a recurring rather than one-time cost. This is a familiar issue with most demonstration programs.

AGGREGATION AND DISAGGREGATION

One of the ways to begin approaching budgeting is to see it as a process of dividing projected costs into their various components and combining individual items into larger categories. In economic terms, these processes are sometimes referred to as aggregation and disaggregation. The whole is the total sum available to the agency or program, and the various parts are the categories and subcategories that combine to make the whole. In this way, projected or anticipated costs can be determined through a process of aggregating or collecting similar costs into centers or cost categories. Once a general schema has been derived, the process becomes one of aggregating individual costs into categories or modules, or disaggregating large categories into subcategories down to the level of individual expenditures.

Several of these modular approaches arose out of accounting initiatives in the 1970s and have since become standard operating procedure. For non-profit health and human services, this process involves dividing all possible expenditures among three large categories: program, administrative, and fund-raising costs.[9] A similar second set of large categories arising out of higher education may be readily applicable to social services as well. This involves budgeting by three additional categories of *personal services* or the personnel or human resources costs; *current expenses* or the usual array of nonpersonnel functional expenditure categories, such as rent or office sup-plies; and *capital expenses* or the large, periodic outlays affecting the value of permanent assets—mostly land and buildings. For the purposes of this discussion, we are treating such items as computers as current expenses rather than capital ones. However, in some state systems, the capital ex-pense category will be used to cover everything that is not consumed in a short time period. In those systems, computers and office furniture would be capital expenses.

The logic of this modular design is evident in Table 23.2. If you visualize all anticipated costs as the budget pie (baked here in a rectangular, rather than the usual round, pan) you can see that with this simple design, that pie will always be at least nine pieces. Some of course, will be bigger and some smaller. And any of them can be disaggregated or broken down into levels of increasing detail. In the typical social service agency, personal ser-vices program expenditures will almost always be the largest category, and administrative and fund-raising capital expenses, such as durable equip-ment, land, or furniture, devoted primarily to fund-raising will ordinarily be very small and quite often negligible.

A further refinement of this idea (shown in Table 23.3) is that many con-temporary social service agencies do not do extensive fund-raising and few, if any, have major capital expenditures.[10] In this case, the overall budget pie

Table 23.2 The Budget Pie (in a Rectangular Pan)

	Personal Services	Current Expenses	Capital Expenses
Administrative			
Fund-Raising			
Program			

Table 23.3 The Simpler Budget Pie (Still in a Rectangular Pan)

	Personal Services	Current Expenses
Administrative		
Program		

of such agencies is a much simpler four-part problem, involving anticipating personal services and current expense categories for administrative costs and the same two categories for program costs.

This concept of a budget pie is a useful reference point for keeping track of the whole. Everything (and we do mean everything) that is to be included within the projected costs or budgeted expenditures of an agency can be subsumed within these nine or four categories. In a certain very real sense, then, budgeting is simply a process of breaking out or detailing the contents of these categories. Such breakouts occur in two directions: anticipated revenues and support on the one hand, and anticipated expenditures on the other.

THE BUDGET TERM

Another major concept that it is necessary to understand in order to do budgets is time. Budgets are always done for specific periods of time. One of the most fundamental practices of social administration is the development of budgets for a twelve-month year. There is no real justification for this practice other than tradition and the usual and customary assumption. It is, in fact, a sheer matter of convenience and tradition that budgets are developed on this basis rather than some other time frame, such as three or five years. The fiscal year is a concept that unifies the budget year and the accounting year. That is, the fiscal year unites the period for which budgets—plans—are made and the period for which a complete set of records is maintained.

The idea of budgeting for fiscal years follows in a very commonsense way from the establishment of fiscal years. The primary purpose of the fiscal year is based in accounting. Purely on grounds of computational accuracy, accountants need to periodically close the books, reconcile all accounts, and start over in certain columns and categories in order to produce accurate financial reports and make room for future entries. By convention, it has become customary to designate one day each year to initiate the closing process, which in large organizations and governments can take months to complete. The following business day then becomes the start of the new fiscal year. And, if you are starting a new fiscal year, it probably makes sense to start with new or, as we have seen, adjusted assumptions about what is possible to do. In this more or less commonsense way, the idea of budgeting became tied to the fiscal year.

Even though almost all organizations budget for a twelve-month fiscal year, they can benefit in their planning if they simultaneously look at their likely budget status over a longer time period. Developing budget projections for the next two to five years can have several advantages. It is also a good check on the problem of recurring expenses. It encourages the agency to think about areas in which costs will be increasing. Salaries and fringe benefit costs, for example, are likely to increase because of raises, seniority, and so on. Considering those areas encourages the agency to consider how it will obtain the funds needed to cover those costs. Will it raise fees, increase services, write more grants, or lay off staff members?

Projecting budgets over a multiple-year time frame requires that the administrator make some assumptions. Though anticipating that salaries will increase is a reasonable assumption, the resignations of some highly paid staff members may mean that they will actually decrease. Thus, the actual budget in effect in three years may differ from the projected budget developed today. However, the projected budgets can be periodically refined to increase their accuracy as a predictor. The advantage that this approach has is that it encourages the administrator to actively think about and plan for the future.

The budget projections should be reviewed periodically so that they may be revised to reflect changed situations. They should be reviewed at least annually, and many agencies will wish to review them far more frequently.

One of us has been involved in using this approach for more than a decade in university budgeting involving several hundred million dollars and has become firmly convinced of its utility. In this instance, budgets are projected five years out, and those projections are reviewed every quarter. Using this approach has resulted in relatively few budget surprises because of the future orientation that it requires.

CONCLUSION

In this chapter, we introduced some basic concepts associated with budgeting. We talked about the difference between allocative and flexible budgets and their implications for the certainty one has about the availability of funds. We described the fund approach to budgeting and accounting and why it is an approach preferred to that of dedicated budgets. Thinking of both the enterprise and the fund or program has also been introduced.

Basic concepts such as base and increment approaches to budgeting and one-time and recurring costs were introduced, as were the fixed time frame on which budgets are usually based. We also introduced three kinds of centers: revenue, cost, and break-even. And we indicated that costs can be aggregated and disaggregated.

It is important that we not leave this topic without again emphasizing that budgets are plans and as such offer further opportunities for agencies to be strategic in the decisions that they make. The techniques and tools that we described are means to that end. Agencies need to be thoughtful about the plans that they make for revenues and expenditures and ensure that those plans support achievement of their goals. If budgets are a road map for how to reach a particular destination, agencies need to ensure that the destination they are planning to reach is the one that they intend.

VII

Topics in Social Administration

In this final section are four chapters dealing with additional topics of considerable importance to the contemporary practice of social administration and to the entire profession of social work. In chapter 24, we treat the important topic of service contracting and purchases of service by state and other government bodies. Contracting is a topic that dates at least to colonial times. Service contracting in the nineteenth century was conditioned by, among other things, the social differences between grand, aristocratic households for which charity was an obligation and common households, who were more likely to be the beneficiaries of local government contracts in conjunction with apprenticeship arrangements. Service contracting fell into disuse with the expanded federal public role in the mid-twentieth century. There has been a dramatic resurgence in the use of service contracting in recent decades. In this latest round, contracting is much more widely associated with state governments than with localities.

In chapter 25, we approach the demanding topic of social work ethics and its application in the area of social administration. Ethics and politics are shown to be two related facets of normative decision making. Detailed ethical codes in general, and the National Association of Social Workers

(NASW) *Code of Ethics* in particular, are shown to be of important, but limited, usefulness in social administration decision making. Also examined are aspects of John Rawls's theory of justice and other more universal ethical/political theories. Chapter 25 concludes with reconsideration of a favorite concept of economists, Paretoan optimality, and suggestions for its possible uses as a normative criterion in administrative decision making.

Chapter 26 deals with the vitally important topic of human diversity. Human diversity is shown to be a major concern of the contemporary social work profession. This concern is often most evident in social administration in regard to equal opportunity and affirmative action in employment. Chapter 26 introduces the important concept of *employment respectful of difference* and concludes with a discussion of sexual harassment in social agencies, considering both employees and clients.

In chapter 27, we examine issues of governance of social agencies through the use of boards. Three types of boards—advisory, governing, and regulatory—are said to be most important in contemporary practice contexts. This chapter outlines five principal functions for boards: governance, policy making, leadership, legitimation, and fund-raising.

The book concludes with a brief afterword.

CHAPTER

Social Administration and Purchase of Service Contracts

During the latter half of the twentieth century, the political economy of social service in the United States changed fundamentally not once but three times. In the mid-1960s, under the sway of the Great Society legislation of the Eighty-ninth Congress, the voluntary sector of social services supported largely by donations gave way to a new system of publicly funded, privately operated QUANGOs (quasi-nongovernmental organizations) and created what we have called the age of grants. But almost as soon as it was born, this age of grants began to give way to another new age of contracting for social services. More recently, the age of contracts has been giving way to a newer era of managed care in which social service contracting remains a key feature. As we shall see in this chapter, the age of grants was a remarkable aberration in public-private relations, and contracting has been an episodic feature of American social service provision since the colonial era.

In *The Social Work Dictionary*, Robert Barker (1995) defines purchase of service agreements in the following way:

A fiscal arrangement between two or more social agencies or between an agency and a government body, usually involving a contract between an agency with funds and another that can provide needed services. Purchaser agencies are thus able to extend services to their clientele, and the provider agencies can increase their budgets, extend their services, and in some cases increase their profits. (p. 307)

There can be little doubt that service contracting has become an important part of the environment of most social agencies today. In the mid 1990s, one author summed up the rise of contracting this way:

In recent years, service contracting has become an important part of financial operations in numerous social agencies, mainly in government but also in private ventures. . . . This system requires a clear understanding of what service is to be performed, the costs involved, the professional skills available, and the timetable for operation. Wise administrators weigh carefully the advantages and disadvantages of performing specific services within their own operations or offering the work to other professionals, individuals or agencies. (Skidmore, 1995, p. 93)

One of the conditions with which social work is still attempting to cope is the way in which service contracting undercut the traditional social work certainty that *nonprofit* services were essential for reasons of quality assurance. Study after study has confirmed what Kettner and Martin found in 1988: For-profit organizations have become major providers, and for-profit service delivery does not necessarily imply inferior service quality. The real challenge, however, is that neither has it been shown that market conditions and market rhetoric bring any substantial improvements in service, either in price, quality, or availability.

Purchase of service contracting constitutes both solutions and problems for social service agencies. As discussed in chapter 22, contracting for third-party fees offers one set of solutions to the problem of financial inflows for the social agency. The problem that purchase of social services by public agencies poses for social administration can be approached from a number of different disciplinary and professional perspectives. There are currently at least four distinct and largely exclusive approaches. There is one substantial and growing literature on service purchases in social work.[1] There is another completely separate tradition in public administration.[2] And there is a third to be found in the emerging field of third sector studies of voluntary association, nonprofit organization, and philanthropy.[3] Finally, there is a fourth and largely separate literature in health care.[4] The primary focus of all of these research traditions involves attempts to make sense of the contracting environment and the supposedly radical departure it represents. An actual practice literature detailing how to cope with the contract environment is still in its infancy. Therefore, the comments in this chapter must be seen as preliminary and somewhat speculative in nature.

One thing is clear. The notion of social work as a policy-based profession introduced in chapter 1 is necessary to even begin to understand the complex ways in which the social welfare roles of federal and state governments have been literally reinvented several times in the past three decades. Before the 1960s, social work was institutionally a bicameral profession with close identifications with the voluntary sector of largely donative agencies and the public sector of public welfare programs and services. In the two decades from 1960 to 1980 (i.e., the age of grants), something of an entirely new social agency closely associated with the grant-funded nonprofit organizations arose. It emerged out of public funding first by grants and later by contracts of the older voluntary sector and rapid expansion of the sector by a host of new nonprofit service agencies created explicitly as vehicles of public support. In another set of changes since 1980, the traditional voluntary social agency and its nonprofit cousin have both been moving gradually toward strictly contractual relationships with funding sources that include government. Indeed, when contracting funding sources are willing to fund independent or private practice under managed care, the entire financial basis of the traditional social agency begins to be undercut, and the prospect of a rather fundamental transformation of social service delivery arises.

Service contracting emerged in part through efforts of government agencies to respond to the perceived inefficiencies and alleged oversupplies of services resulting from public monopolies predicted or posited by public choice theory. Public choice theorists suggested that public monopolies, like state-funded and administered social services for the poor, will produce oversupplies of services of inefficient services and therefore contracting is necessary. However, the theoretical basis of this issue is pointed up by closer examination:

- Social services are always prosumed or consumed as they are produced, unlike agricultural or manufactured products. They cannot be produced and stored. They can only be simultaneously consumed. That is one of the principal reasons we do not speak of service production but instead of service delivery. In business parlance, delivery is the act of transferring produced goods to the consumers for consumption. Thus, the very idea of an oversupply of services is a practical impossibility.
- The suggestion that federal public service providers will overproduce social services is also counterfactual. There never has been a time when the federal government was engaged in the widespread pro-

duction of social services. In fact, since the Pierce veto of 1854 (discussed later) there is strong reason for believing that the federal government is constitutionally prohibited from delivering social services and therefore could not ever have possessed a monopoly. Likewise, the very plurality of the fifty states when combined with the mobility of clients makes the idea of a state-based monopoly questionable. Thus, no level of public provider could ever have established the record of producing inefficient and oversupplied social services for which service contracting is the alleged correction.

- There has never been an actual public monopoly on the prosumption of social services at any time in the past 150 years. Voluntary social services were already fully established in delivering services in most large cities when government entered the picture for the first time in the 1930s and again in the 1960s, and they continue to do so today. Any notion of such a monopoly in the past is pure invention.
- Federal social service assistance from the start had the effect of promoting competition. Since the age of grants, policy was directed variously at the small number of existing voluntary agencies; the startup of new competitors, both nonprofit and commercial; and the plurality of fifty-five state and territorial governments and thousands of local governments. Thus, the existence of a preexisting problem of inefficiency for which contracting was the solution is also largely a fiction.
- There is no evidence to be found that any credible research has ever established norms for the efficiency of social services in any form much less established the comparative efficiency of one form of service delivery over another.[5] Despite the patina of solidity, the "efficiency" of social services is a purely theoretical and some would argue fictional construct.

Thus, notions of oversupply of social services, governmental monopolies, insufficient competition, and systematic inefficiency are largely illusionary. They remain in play only because contracting for social services is very heavily ideologically based. It is grounded in the belief that, notwithstanding any evidence to the contrary, whatever governments may do can be better done by private or nongovernmental sources. The basis for this belief has, in fact, very little to do with any existing conditions of the social service delivery system and a great deal to do with the targeting of social services by conservative interest groups seeking to reduce overall federal spending.

Service contracting is not really new. It reaches very deeply into American history to the colonial period prior to the American Revolution and has been intimately tied up with the periodic emergence of antiwelfare sentiment that kept the U.S. national government completely out of social welfare until the 1930s, despite the growth of social democracies in Europe. The grounds for understanding this history fall largely outside the traditional domain of social policy history. Yet in addition to explaining the historic role of service contracting, they explain a great deal about the seemingly peculiar lack of class-based support for an American welfare state and are also closely connected to the rise of the American corporation. In order to understand this situation more fully, we need to examine that history briefly.[6]

Even though the practice of service contracting is a long-standing one, we are only beginning to connect contracting for social services to the main body of law, theory, and practice on public contracting. Limited local and state government purchases of care and maintenance of the worthy poor were very much part of the outdoor relief tradition of colonial American poor law practice. "Farming out" and "boarding out" are among the terms used to describe the process whereby town or county governments contracted with farmers or householders to support mentally ill, aged, handicapped, or other individuals. There are numerous evidences that social service contracting was a well-established practice in American communities during the eighteenth century. Wedel and Colston (1988) offer several specific examples of such early contracts. There are additional references to such practices scattered throughout the social welfare historical literature. Dorthea Dix's legislative memorials, for example, provide abundant if incidental evidence of mentally ill and/or developmentally disabled public wards maintained by local households. (For example, see the memorial by Dix reprinted in Brady, 1975.) In such cases, it is clear that what is involved is a public contract arrangement involving government and what might be termed the private household sector.

In the prevailing mercantilist political economy of the colonial era, there were, from a charitable standpoint, two clear classes of households carried over from the European tradition. In the grand households of important families like the Washingtons, Jeffersons, Masons, Randolphs, and other colonial aristocrats, household philanthropy was regarded as a civic virtue and an expectation (noblesse oblige). It was the particular obligation of the pater familias or head of the household. In this connection, Pumphrey and Pumphrey (1961, p. 45) record George Washington's instructions to his plantation manager on the dispensing of household charity. Public subsidy of the great households of the federalist class was unacceptable, less because they were opposed to such subsidies on grounds of limited government but because it was unnecessary and compromised their moral obligations, which were easily enough fulfilled. At the same time, mercantilist ideas of public subsidy did not extend to insignificant township welfare contracts. It ran more to large land grants the size of Iowa.

Colonial-era local government authorities with limited funds generally purchased indoor relief from smaller, lower-income householders who benefited economically from the practice by gaining low cost labor. The existence of such contracts as well as the fact that these vendors were predominantly smaller farmers who boarded the poor in exchange for their labor is consistent with the orientation of early American government toward mercantilism and also with the reality of scarce labor in the colonial era. Such contracts do not appear to have been overburdened by any overtly serious commitment to actually helping the poor.

The makers of the American Revolution were predominantly mercantilists in their economics rather than advocates of laissez-faire as contemporary ideologues would have us believe. In the view of Federalists like Alexander Hamilton, the role of government was neither small nor particularly limited. It was to promote the welfare of the people by using government to guide and extend business development. In the Federalist period, government contracting took a signature turn in the direction of public works that it still possesses today. The first uses of corporations in America were for public purposes like road and bridge building. Mercantilist practice extended to the use of public funds to capitalize private corporations to carry out public intent.

> "The great object of the institution of civil government," [John Quincy] Adams said in his first message to Congress, "is the improvement of the condition of those who are parties to the social compact, and no government, in whatever form constituted, can accomplish the lawful end of its institution but in proportion as it improves the condition of those over whom it is established." (Schlesinger, 1986/ 1999)

Adams—the last Federalist president—could easily have meant by this an elaboration or even an expansion of the general welfare clause of the Constitution, but he did not. Instead, he proposed only that the national government organize a system of transportation, public works, and industrial development along with a national university and a national observatory. For government to refrain from

> promoting the improvement of agriculture, commerce, and manufactures, the cultivation and encouragement of the mechanical and of the elegant arts, the advancement of literature, and the progress of the sciences . . . would be treachery to the most sacred of trusts. (Schlesinger, 1986/1999, pp. 223–34)

Reference to any sacred trust involving the poor is noticeably absent from this statement.

Laissez-faire doctrines of limited government like those held by modern conservatives were first raised in the American context, according to Schlesinger, not by the federalists who made the American Revolution nor by the rapidly expanding plutocracy, but by the Jacksonian populist Locofocos suspicious of the Federalists' use of the state and public contracting to benefit the rich. "Because the opponents of business rule feared that such intervention was, in the words of John Taylor of Caroline, but a 'slow and legal' means 'by which the rich plunder the poor,' they favored the negative state" (Schlesinger, 1986/1999, p. 227).

Anyone who lived through the abuses of public trust of the 1970s, 1980s, and 1990s must certainly have at least a modicum of sympathy for Taylor's view. Junk bonds, the savings and loan crisis, a host of tax cuts benefiting primarily the rich, and, most serious of all, the continued erosion of workers' income position should be enough to give anyone pause about the uses of government.

However, when the populist Jacksonians actually came to power they failed to practice the laissez-faire philosophy of the night watchman state that they had used to criticize the Federalists. Instead, they sought to use the powers of government to control the economic elite and experiment with a broader social democracy rather than to aid and abet business. This had the effect, according to Schlesinger (1986/1999), of provoking a sudden adoption by their opponents of the very same laissez-faire doctrines they had previously opposed:

> Businessmen were angered by the Jacksonian penchant for economic regulation and for administrative experiment. . . . They were angered most of all by his aggressive employment of [presidential] power, in the words of [Jackson's] veto of the recharter of the Second Bank of the United States, against "the rich and powerful" and on behalf of "the humble members of society—the farmers, mechanics and laborers." (p. 229)

Schlesinger (1986/1999) concluded that in the face of the political threat posed by Jackson and the populists, "businessmen began to retreat from the Hamiltonian conception of publicly guided private enterprise and to discover belated charm in the Jeffersonian proposition that government was best which governed least. . . . Laissez faire liberalism now displaced what remained of mercantilism in the business community and of civic republicanism in the general society" (pp. 230, 231). It was precisely this political dynamic that is exemplified by President Pierce's veto of the Dorthea Dix land grant bill in 1854, which would have created a national system of mental hospitals. This action forestalled the development of the American national welfare state by nearly a century.

Despite these seismic political shifts, service contracting out continued. The Yates Report (circa 1824) was, according to Walter Trattner (1999), "the first comprehensive survey of poor relief in the United States and one of the most influential documents in American social welfare history" (p. 57). It cited four main methods of public assistance in use in New York state at that time: institutional relief, home relief, *the contract system,* and the auction system.

It was not until several decades later that a viable antigovernment sentiment came to the fore. Schlesinger (1986/1999) concluded that "the victory of laissez faire came after the Civil War"(p. 232). After that war, laissez-faire doctrines of limited government interventionism were combined with social Darwinism to produce those peculiar and idiosyncratic antiwelfare doctrines of rugged individualism that have had such pernicious consequences for the American poor ever since. The local systems of contracting out remained formally in place along with the rest of the apparatus of the poor law tradition in America until replaced by the public welfare system in the 1930s. They were, however, increasingly ill suited to a rapidly urbanizing nation and dwindled into increasing insignificance as a social assistance strategy.

In the 1970s, service contracting once again emerged. This time its emergence was as an important tool of state rather than local government and as an option for subsidy of voluntary social agencies rather than farm households. This time the reappearance of social service contracting coincided with the emergence on the national agenda of the social work profession's belief in a services strategy approach to the poor. According to Popple and Leighninger (1999), the 1962 service amendments "were heavily influenced by advice from social workers and other experts who contended that providing intensive social services would rehabilitate and bring financial independence to the poor" (p. 259). This initiative, combined with the War on Poverty programs, the 1967 amendments, and Title XX brought dramatic increases in the number of social workers and a revived interest in contracting services out to a host of newly created nonprofit agencies.

The effect of this new contracting approach was for government to capitalize large numbers of new nonprofit social agencies during this period in ways that echo back to the old mercantilist doctrines. In this case, it was a new social service industry that was being fostered by government action. This capitalization of new organizations has been one of the more important consequences of contemporary service contracting. Purchases of social services by contract continued to expand gradually in the following two decades, and by the 1990s, they had became one of the most important elements in a national social service strategy.

In this new era, service contracting has taken on multiple additional dimensions. The localism of poor law mercantilism has been replaced by a system of intergovernmental transfers, government-vendor payments, and other payment mechanisms of mind-boggling complexity. The formal legal language of the Social Security Act, including Title XX and the subsequent Social Services Block Grant program, makes it clear that the primary federal social service role is fiscal, but it confuses the issue by spelling out policy objectives nonetheless.

The claims of the social service strategy were part of an ongoing struggle by the social work profession to legitimize itself and find an institutional and resource base in modern industrial society. However, the timing of the 1962 amendment could not have been worse from that vantage point. Rather than leading to decreases in the welfare rolls as promised, it immediately preceded enormous increases in public welfare eligibility during the following decade. Moreover, in many cases the rhetoric and actions of social workers were deliberately provoking such increases. The apparent failure of the service strategy to reduce the number of those receiving public aid is one of the key factors behind the accountability problem for social services that arose in its wake.

The subsequent embrace of performance contracting by the states under the successive cycles of decentralization associated with the "New Federalisms" of Presidents Johnson, Nixon, and Reagan has also had a number of unanticipated consequences. Meanwhile, gradually expanding the American welfare state became the proximate goal of the social work profession, and public purchases of services became an important means for pursuing that end. The 1962 amendments made it possible for departments of public welfare to purchase specified social services for eligible clients from other public agencies. The 1967 amendments expanded this to nonprofit and proprietary agencies in cases where state agency staff were not available to provide the needed services. But opposition to this approach was also mounting, and counter moves were not long in coming. In 1972, a $2.5 billion ceiling was placed on Title XX spending. It is interesting that Martha Derthick's (1975) somewhat hysterical title, *Uncontrolled Spending for the Social Services*, presented the ostensible rationale for this administrative cap of $2.5 billion on Title XX. Thus, for approximately the cost of one medium-range bomber, members of Congress could claim both that social service spending was out of control and that they were making serious efforts to control it. Meanwhile, medical payments through Medicare and Medicaid—wherein service contracting had been explicitly rejected as an abridgment of the "autonomy" of the medical profession—grew in excess of $50 billion, more than twenty-five times the level of social service spending.

For social services, the next two decades were largely business as usual in an incremental budget system with both marginal gains and losses and with contracting spreading continuously. By the mid 1980s, purchase of service contracts absorbed at least 40 percent of the total social service funds available in two-thirds of the American states and half of the funds in twenty-five states. Furthermore, even though the proportion of funds going to nonprofit agencies declined slightly, from 71 percent in 1974 to 66 percent in 1984, contracts with nonprofits are still the largest category of contract activity in Title XX[7] (Kettner & Martin, 1987, pp. 25–27; Wedel, 1974).

IMPLICATIONS

The resurgence of service contracting in recent decades has brought with it several important developments. Especially worth noting are the way in which service contracting has: (1) performed a kind of R & D (research and development) function for the American social service system; (2) moved social agencies increasingly in the direction of operating like small businesses; and (3) resulted in the creation of state-level political constituencies where none existed previously. We now examine each of these trends briefly.

Research and Development for Social Services

One aspect of the service contracting system that arose out of Title XX and the "new welfare" programs of the age of grants merits particular attention. This is the manner in which contracting facilitated the programmatic experimentation associated with what might be called the research and development (R & D) phase of a new national social services network. The original purchase of services arrangements of the 1962 and 1967 Social Security Acts were directed primarily at services for traditional worthy poor populations: dependent children, old people, and the blind and disabled. In rhetoric reminiscent of the nineteenth-century charity organization movement, the service strategy was intended to teach and guide the poor out of poverty on a case-by-case basis. It is clear, also, that the manifest intent of the services strategy was to catapult the poor into the middle class rather than maintaining and supporting them in their poverty.

The service strategy was naïve and ill conceived and almost immediately controversial as well. In disagreements long since forgotten, the services strategy was attacked as soon as it emerged by advocates of a more traditional income strategy against poverty and the newer opportunity strategy associated with the Community Action Program. What followed was a significant displacement of the service strategy of the early amendments. By taking advantage of growing national sentiment against institutional care, the early service strategy was refocused by the deinstitutionalization strategy reflected in the five goals spelled out in Title XX.

Social Services through the Comprehensive Annual Services Plans called for under Title XX were to be directed toward meeting the following goals: (1) self-support; (2) self-sufficiency; (3) preventing or remedying neglect, abuse, or exploitation of children and adults unable to protect their own interests; (4) preventing or reducing inappropriate institutional care; and (5) referral to or services to individuals in institutions. On this point, Gelfand and Olsen (1980) note in speaking of the continuum of care:

> As is often the case in social welfare programs, the continuum of care model resulted not from a carefully conceived plan but [became clear] only in retrospect. The increasing numbers of programs and services arising out of the fertile minds of providers in the field of aging [like other fields of service] ultimately brought about the attempts to sort them into some conceptual framework. (p. ix)

The Transition to Small Business

The complexities of contracting acted also to minimize the decision-making role of board and community and maximized the role of management and external funders. Only those engaged in contract management full time could hope to keep fully abreast the nuances and subtleties of this system. In some cases, contracting virtually eliminated preexisting board responsibilities for overall management and fund-raising in particular. Far more frequently, grant and contract management extended to the creation of completely new nonprofit corporations with no prior history of broad community support or involvement.[8]

This resulted in the creation of a large number of hybrid social service agencies—QUANGOs—in virtually every community in the United States (see chapter 21). Legally and in terms of their formal organization they look a good deal like traditional voluntary sector agencies. In reality, however, they are quite commonly controlled by individuals or small groups of professional or technical employees who function a good deal like business entrepreneurs: solo proprietorships and group practices.

Such proprietorships and group practices (solo and group trusteeships might actually be a better term) appear to be very unstable forms of organized endeavor—sometimes experiencing almost as high a failure rate as new small businesses. In particular, many of these social agencies have been under a kind of push-pull of cross pressures for much of the past two decades. The pulls come from several directions such as unmet needs, shifting priorities among available funding sources, and shifting public and professional priorities like the recent movement toward case management strategies.

Much of the push—indeed, the central financial fact of life—in the contemporary social service agency/firm is closely associated with after-the-fact cost reimbursement for services rendered. The much remarked upon profit motive pales into indifference by comparison. It is anticipating the nuances of post-service cost reimbursement, not any other type of managerial motivation, which has already transformed the typical contract-funded social agency into a virtual small business.

The reasons for this are simple and straightforward. Cost reimbursement contracts introduce the necessities of accounts receivable management and sophisticated cash management. Closely associated with this, the accompanying post-performance program (but not financial) audits by contract monitors introduce a significant element of financial risk for the agency/firm and its managers. This is not an entrepreneurial risk of not profiting sufficiently from the application of one's capital but a more basic risk of failure to cover operating expenditures with all the attendant threats of bankruptcy and liability. Finally, the fit between levels of services provided under contracts and revenues coming into the agency also introduces the phenomenon of metering not present in the grant-funded agency. When service goes up, revenue goes up, and when service slacks off, revenue does the same. When taken together, accounts receivable management, cash management, risk, and the metering of service volume by revenues are virtually a textbook definition of small business operations.

State Constituencies

A third element of the transformation wrought by the resurgent service contracting system has been the creation of state-level political constituencies for social services. As noted in earlier chapters, it is a more or less stable axiom of constituency theory that organized institutions with the best long-term chances to survive, grow, and thrive are those that successfully identify a constituency of active and influential supporters. Agencies that attempt to go it alone are less likely to achieve success in the legislative arena with budget increases and adoption of proposed new policies and in the community.

Ours is largely an age when political interests are organized around individual and group self-interest. One of the classic administrative dilemmas for public welfare and social service activities that benefit the poor has been the lack of organized constituency support. Public agency and nonprofit organization employees have frequently been constrained from political action by law and administrative regulation. State and local organizations of social workers have often shown a disinterest in public issues other than those closely related to professionalization. Poor clients are usually among the most politically inert and difficult to mobilize populations. And upper income groups, comfortable in the Darwinist assurances that the poor were already too well cared for, have often been evident mostly in opposition to social policies.

The lack of large, well-organized constituencies has not always been a problem. Initially, the social security program was sustained in Washington by a largely insider constituency of the so-called iron triangle of strategically placed bureaucrats, liberal congressmen, and expert academicians. In part because there were no comparable state-level constituencies in most states, the states were seen throughout the national welfare state era (1935–1980) as reluctant and recalcitrant partners in the American federal welfare system. Several events, including federal initiatives like the White House Conferences on Aging in 1950, 1960, and 1970 and membership drives by national organizations like AARP, are important here. Together they had the effect of galvanizing the elderly into an effective constituency for the social security program, as Presidents Nixon and Reagan both discovered in rather dramatic fashion when they attempted to cut benefits. The senior power phenomenon occurred at both the national level and in most states, transforming what had been a relatively powerless constituency into one of the more powerful organized interest groups in the American polity. Silver-haired legislatures provided older people with training in how the political and legislative process worked and made them even more effective.

In roughly the same time period, the implementation of Title XX, the Reagan-era merger of the Social Service Block Grants, and the merger of diverse state service programs into health and human services superagencies had similar effects. Together, they appear to have been generating major new constituencies of agency contractors in a multitude of different program areas—aging, children's services, employment training, health and mental health, community development, and additional fields as well. To the present, the vision of most of these contractors has been largely focused inward to the potential their own self-interest represents.

In West Virginia, for example, the potential of this constituency/coalition reactivated an all but moribund welfare conference that had been limited largely to offering an annual training conference for state Department of Human Services employees and created an association as a multiprofessional, statewide umbrella group. However, the association has yet to realize the dream of an actual statewide social services constituency group. Instead, it has been fully absorbed by the politics of interest groups, siding with some social welfare interests (mostly children) and against others (often the aged).

It is probably fair to say that most state agencies and statewide social service coalitions as well as the national social service interest groups like the National Association of Social Workers are still learning the ropes of effective constituency-bureau partnership in most areas. In an era when money talks, social services have been able to bring relatively little of that commodity to their own interest representation. Likewise, in an era of sophisticated spin doctoring approaches, naïve and earnest appeals have been much more the order of the day for social services. However, in the long run, the development of state-level constituencies may turn out to be one of the most interesting recent developments in the otherwise moribund arena of social welfare politics.

Ralph Kramer (1981) interpreted this history as a set of value-conflicts expressed as the related dualisms of self-reliance versus dependence, charity versus justice, philanthropy versus taxation, volunteerism versus bureaucracy, and bureaucracy versus professionalism. Kramer suggested that strictly political attempts at reconciliation may do little more than create a "philosophical and administrative mess" (pp. 73, 285) characterized by inefficiency, lack of accountability, and irrationality. More than two decades later, it appears that Kramer was strikingly omniscient on this point. The present contract-based system is in many important respects an irrational, inefficient mess largely lacking in accountability. Anyone who doubts the validity of this judgment or sees Kramer as excessively harsh on this point need only talk candidly to practitioners working within the present system. Works like Susan Bernstein's article (1991a), book (1991b), and much larger dissertation (1989) on purchased services in New York City document a chaotic, uncontrollable situation about which it is hard to avoid the conclusion that the system is a theoretical and administrative mess.

Yet, contracting itself is seldom seen as part of the problem. In recent years, the trend toward service purchasing by governments shows signs of not only continuing but of accelerating. Gooden (1998) notes that "government reports . . . show that purchases of goods and services at the state and local levels have steadily increased in the 1990s, especially in service areas" (p. 499). One of the consequences of this trend has been a marked blurring of the boundaries between public and private and between the business, governmental, and third sectors. "Governments increasingly need to rely on private, nonprofit, and other nongovernmental entities for delivery of services"(p. 499).

Numerous terms have been used to describe this phenomenon: Indirect government, third party-government, indirect administration, government by proxy. Jennifer Wolch (1990) termed this new realm "the shadow state." In particular, as presidential and congressional politics have accented assorted new federalisms and devolution, state and local governments have come to rely more and more on contracting for service delivery (Kettl, 1988).

There are many reasons for this—greater flexibility in changing priorities and avoiding accountability, cost cutting, alternate delivery, increasing competition, improved administrative functions such as feasibility studies, monitoring, evaluation—just to name the most obvious (Gooden, 1998). Whatever the reasons, however, this new set of institutional arrangements, whatever it is called, has brought with it increasing difficulties in identifying who is responsible for what and to whom. As Burton Gummer (1995b) noted, the increased use of contracting and other "privatization" strategies has meant, among other things, that responsibilities for planning, designing, financing, and operating services are now widely dispersed among a number of public, quasi-public, and private entities.

CONCLUSION

Purchase of service contracting as a practice of government is older than the modern social agency. It is also an issue that cannot be neatly or cleanly separated from other, larger issues of public policy and organization. In the past few decades, we have moved away from a largely voluntary, donative social services sector existing almost independently from a public sector devoted exclusively to income maintenance and support. We have moved instead to a thickly intermeshed system of public, nonprofit, and commercial service vendors subsidized by a curious and shifting blend of private and public funds. This "system"—if something this variable is truly deserving of that name—has lived up to many of the worst fears envisioned by social workers of previous generations. It has made most social agencies today effectively a part of the public bureaucracy regardless of their legal or community status.

Ethics and Administration

This chapter explores the ethical context of social administration and the special ethical demands upon social workers functioning in administrative situations. It is explicitly intended to comply with Council of Social Work Education accreditation standards by providing specific knowledge about social work values and their ethical implications as well as opportunities for students to demonstrate their application in professional practice (Commission on Accreditation, http://www.cswe.org /accreditation/frameset.htm).

A great many people in social work believe along with Chester Barnard (1938) that moral leadership is the moving creative force in organization. Among other things, this means that ethical obligations, concern for right and good, and pursuit of the good life deserve at least equal (and probably prior) consideration in social administration as such criteria as efficiency and effectiveness. The good life in contemporary society is often treated, if at all, as purely hedonistic and materialistic concern. However, the good life and the closely related notion of a life of service to others are major ethical considerations for a great many people who choose social work as a career. This makes ethical concern a major active element in the visions, missions, and objectives of social service programs.

The problem for social administration has always been discerning how such ethically based leadership is to be exercised and how ethical judgments can best be applied. As a subject matter or intellectual concern, ethics can be defined as the human concern for right and wrong, good and evil. The concern for social work ethics is usually derived from some definition or conception of the profession and speaks to the behavior of the individual social worker. Unlike other forms of ethical concern, social administration is concerned not only with rights, wrongs, and pursuit of the good by an individual professional but also explicitly with how that individual may command, lead, direct, and in other ways elicit ethical conduct from others as well. The ability of social administrators to direct the behavior of others complicates matters considerably because it treads upon the traditional distinction in philosophy between ethical concerns and political concerns.

The problem of administrative ethics is an even more complicated one. Social workers engaged in social administration practice, unlike other organizational actors, must be concerned not only with the propriety of their own conduct, but with their duty to uphold the interests of the organization. This duty is also a legal one for corporate officers. Disparities that may arise between these two ethical imperatives sometimes come out clearly and dramatically, for example, in conflicts between the ethics of board members or executives and their fiduciary responsibilities. Thus, we might take a rather extreme example to illustrate the point. Pacifist board members and executives (e.g., Jane Addams's opposition to World War I or later social workers' opposition to the Vietnam War) who voluntarily accept donations to support prowar activities may wonder if they can legitimately spend such donations on other projects in the name of a higher cause or principle. In this case the law is clear enough: they may not.

In chapter 16 we explored some of the major limits imposed by professional norms on giving orders in a social agency. This involves both what social workers may not be ordered to do and, if ordered, with which they must not comply. That is a powerful, challenging, and troubling ethical domain in the present social agency. Tremendous ethical challenges arise, for example, in an era when welfare reforms are premised on the assumption found in the language of the 1996 welfare reform act that no one has a right to expect public assistance. Therefore, restrictions on the range of choices allowed by policy and administrative decision may lawfully turn away at least some of those in need, even though doing so may be unethical for a social worker.

Equally compelling challenges are raised in the environment of managed care. Social workers in the field report repeatedly and usually covertly, because of fear for their jobs, that they are being ordered to serve only those who can pay, to terminate services prematurely, and in other ways to enforce artificial but politically popular norms of efficiency and effectiveness.

Ethically speaking, Congress and conservative backers of such harsh determinations appear to believe that they have left a moral loophole in both cases. It is, they would argue, only the morally unworthy who would be harmed, and this is due not to policy but to their own failings. Necessarily harsh determinations to turn away some in need are said to be necessitated by extreme limitations on available public funds. These proponents have yet to address the fact that this argument would seem to be refuted by the simultaneous existence of a federal surplus. They would argue also that the consequences of such harsh public judgments are more apparent than real because of the existence of a large and well-funded voluntary sector that can pick up the slack. This, of course, ignores completely the fact that the once voluntary sector is now largely captive to public funding. Thus, it is threatened by the very same forces that have abridged a 400-year-old right of the poor to public assistance and enforced the norm that only those who can afford to pay have a right to life and health. For these and other reasons, the ethical path to social administration is not a particularly easy one.

ETHICAL STANDARDS FOR SOCIAL WORK ADMINISTRATION

In conversations with social work students it sometimes may appear as though there is really only one ethical standard in social work: respecting the confidentiality of clients. Mention social work ethics in almost any conversation and the almost automatic response is inevitably some reference to confidentiality. In truth, social work ethics is a much more multilayered and nuanced topic that deals with a great deal more than this single issue. Confidentiality is very important, certainly. But so, also, are a host of other ethical concerns. In an investigation of the social work literature on ethics, Ernest Barbeau (1988) found fourteen distinct ethical dimensions discussed in the journal literature. He called these concern for the general welfare, respect for the individual person, the right of self-determination, concern for social justice, an expectation of professional competency, dignity, trust, paternalism, informed consent, confidentiality, the dignity and integrity of the profession, the primacy of client interests, truth-telling, and avoidance of harm.

THE NATIONAL ASSOCIATION OF SOCIAL WORKERS *CODE OF ETHICS*

In this section, we look closely at the National Association of Social Workers (NASW) *Code of Ethics* (1996) for those portions of the code dealing explicitly with overt and obvious administrative issues. Following that, we look more generally at the problem of ethics in the community context or, more properly, politics (or civics) in its philosophical sense.

The NASW *Code of Ethics*, which was revised in 1996, is far and away the most ambitious effort to establish an authoritative set of prescriptive ethical standards for social workers ever undertaken. The most interesting dimension of the code from an administrative standpoint is not the code itself but its role as an institution-building device within the larger context of the social work profession as a self-defining and self-regulating community. The code is merely one element in the broader context of ethical conduct as part of the profession defining itself to members, clients, and the world.

The code is ordinarily presented as the authoritative and definitive ethical guide for social work professionals, but the actual text indicates some wavering on the question of its certainty. According to the accompanying text, some of the standards are set forth as enforceable guidelines for professional conduct, whereas others are simply aspirational.

Enforcement of rules—ethical or otherwise—is always a concern in administration. The question of enforcement of the code is not clearly detailed within the code itself. It indicates that the extent to which each standard is enforceable is a matter of professional judgment to be exercised by those responsible for reviewing alleged violations of ethical standards. As a code of conduct promulgated by its members, one obvious avenue of professional enforcement is expulsion from the association and from the profession. To be deprived of the ability to practice one's profession, associate with one's peers, and earn a living is one of the most powerful sanctions to exist in civil society outside of the institutions of government.

This raises an interesting question of authority. To what extent can NASW members who are administrators use the NASW *Code of Ethics* or other expressions of social work ethics to guide the behavior of others in their agencies? There simply is no fully satisfactory answer to that question at present. Certainly, in the weak sense it can be presumed that all social workers are expected to adhere to the code and, where adopted into agency policy, other agency employees might also be expected to conform regardless of their professional status. Whether such expectations could be enforced in the strong sense, however, is unclear. Could social workers found to be in violation of the code be dismissed from agency positions? A fairly strong case can be made for dismissal on grounds that the positions they

hold required professional credentials for which they are no longer qualified. Could non-social workers not conforming with the code also be dismissed from agencies where the code was adopted as policy? This gets a
good bit dicier, but reasonable enough claims could be made on grounds
of insubordination (failure to obey stated policies) or demonstrated unfit-
ness to perform the required duties. In both cases, however, such dismissals
would quickly become legal rather than ethical concerns.

ADMINISTRATIVE ISSUES

The ethical standards identified in the NASW *Code of Ethics* are organized
under six topical headings: responsibilities to clients, responsibilities to colleagues, responsibilities in practice settings, responsibilities as professionals, responsibilities to the profession, and responsibilities to the broader
society. Limited concern for social administration issues can be found scattered throughout these six sections.

There is a special section of the code (3.07) labeled Administration and
containing four subsections. Section 3.07 (a) sets forth an expectation of
client advocacy. Social work administrators should advocate within and outside their agencies for adequate resources to meet clients' needs. It is unclear whether this is a unique responsibility of administrators or a matter
of special concern, given the administrative preoccupation with matters of
budget and resource allocation. More likely, it is an administrative expectation of all social workers, thereby offering one small additional linkage of
the type discussed in chapter 1 between the social work profession and
social administration.

The next subsection brings a distinct, if somewhat weak, ethical perspective directly into the administrative process of budgeting and resource
allocation. Section 3.07 (b) says that social workers should advocate for resource allocation procedures that are open and fair. When not all clients'
needs can be met, an allocation procedure should be developed that is
nondiscriminatory and based on appropriate and consistently applied principles. Openness and fairness are surely good things, but it is difficult to see
any genuine moral viewpoint or standard applicable in concrete cases
emerging here. The phrase "when not all clients' needs can be met" appears
superfluous from an administrative viewpoint where the assumption of
scarcity operates to suggest that it is difficult to envision any circumstance
under which all clients' needs could be met. The phrase is also ambiguous
as to which needs should be met. Is it necessary for all needs of all clients
to be met? In that case, we have the problem discussed in chapter 1 of the
open-ended nature of human needs. Or is it sufficient, ethically speaking,
to meet all of the most serious needs using some unspecified standard of

the seriousness of needs of all clients? In social administration, this is anything but an idle question.

Next, we move rather inexplicably from the issues of resources to the question of supervision. Section 3.07 (c) says that social workers who are administrators should take reasonable steps to ensure that adequate agency or organizational resources are available to provide appropriate staff supervision. Any attempt to apply this in an actual situation would require some delineation of "reasonable steps" and "appropriate" supervision. However ambiguous these terms may appear, devising such standards should in most cases be far simpler than dealing with that tricky need notion discussed above. For example, an agency policy that adopted the code might spell out as reasonable steps to ensure adequate supervision:

- Assignment in writing of all new employees to a supervisor
- Notification in writing of any changes in supervisory assignments
- Specific and general matters that supervisors must be notified of
- Any expectations for specific time requirements or frequency of supervisory meetings

Interestingly, on the assumption that appropriate supervision in this section is a resource as referred to in Section 3.07 (a), it would appear that social workers would have an ethical duty also to advocate against supervisory patterns that were adverse to clients' needs. Such a conclusion actually demonstrates two things. On the one hand, this is almost certainly a concrete expression of the kind of collegial model of organization that we found in Mary Parker Follett's theories beginning in chapter 3. On the other hand, consistently and fairly applying this standard would almost certainly require some very skillful handling because of that weasel word "need" again. Is it legitimate for a social worker to cancel an important session with her supervisor because a client needs to talk about a personal problem? The standards are completely unhelpful in answering that type of question, which is quite possibly a clear case of the conflict of client needs and accountability of the sort considered below.

The final part of this section, 3.07 (d) states that social work administrators should take reasonable steps to ensure that the working environment for which they are responsible is consistent with and encourages compliance with the NASW *Code of Ethics*. Social work administrators should take reasonable steps to eliminate any conditions in their organizations that violate, interfere with, or discourage compliance with the code. We have already dealt above with the problem presented by the reasonable standard. The code is silent on how enforcing such compliance might apply to non-social work support personnel.

Several other sections deal with explicit administrative concerns as well. Section 1.13 deals with payment for services, and Section 1.16 deals with conditions for the termination of services. Both were discussed in chapter 22. Section 1.14, "Clients Who Lack Decision-making Capacity," indicates that social workers should take reasonable steps to safeguard the interests and rights of those clients. Again, as in the earlier case, either a delineation in advance of a policy statement indicating what types of steps are reasonable or a post hoc quality control procedure to determine whether steps taken in specific cases were reasonable should be sufficient to convert Section 1.14 into a useful administrative tool.

Section 1.15, "Interruption of Services," binds social workers only to reasonable efforts to ensure continuity of services in the event that services are interrupted by factors such as unavailability, relocation, illness, disability, or death. It would seem that a useful part of any agency's policy arsenal would be more detailed specifications of such "reasonable efforts." This is especially true when assigned workers and/or supervisors are unavailable, when employees are reassigned or cannot be reached (permanently or temporarily unavailable), and in cases of illness, disability, or death of either clients or workers.

At the same time, a great many issues of central administrative concern are not dealt with in the code. What, for example, are the ethical considerations in selecting one candidate over others in hiring? What goods are most fundamental in the making of budget determinations? Is there an ethically preferred way to fire someone? Administrative ethics as situational is clearly indicated in such cases by our likely response: It all depends on the circumstances of the particular situation.

ETHICS AND (PRINCIPLED) POLITICS

Although the definition of ethics given earlier in this chapter is at first glance relatively straightforward, the topic of administrative ethics can be anything but clear-cut. Reamer (1998) notes that social work has benefited from recent advances in medical ethics. Most of that benefit to date has been restricted to individual ethical issues arising between social workers and clients. Issues involving social administrators and their relations with one another and with stakeholders or "ex officio" relations with clients as official or legal representatives of their institutions are still not well explored. However, the renaissance of interest in political philosophy following in the wake of the publication of John Rawls's *A Theory of Justice* in 1971 has provided fertile ground for the exploration of such issues. It remains to be seen to what extent social work will avail itself of this extraordinary opportunity for macro-level ethical reflection.

In general, we would endorse the position of moral citizenship that Manning (1997) defines as "the responsibility to determine right and good behavior as part of the rights and privileges social workers have as members of a community that includes clients, colleagues, agencies and society" (p. 224). All administrative acts have ethical dimensions or implications. In addition, concern for the ethical dimensions of administrative behavior is more than a simple matter of adherence to the NASW *Code of Ethics*, especially since the code is silent on many centrally important administrative issues. Thus, in social administration ethics must be seen as more than a matter of following rules of proper conduct. It should also be seen as an all-out concern for ethical choice within the good life. We do well to attend to the philosopher Charles Taylor's (1989) admonition:

> Much contemporary moral philosophy, particularly, but not only in the English-speaking world, has given such a narrow focus to morality that some of the crucial connections . . . are incomprehensible in its terms. This moral philosophy has tended to focus on what it is right to do rather than on what it is good to be, on defining the content of obligation rather than the nature of the good life; and it has no conceptual place left for a notion of the good as the object of our love or allegiance. . . . This philosophy has accredited a cramped and truncated view of morality in a narrow sense, as well as of the whole range of issues involved in the attempt to live the best possible life. (p. 3)

Ethical decision making of all types involves what Taylor (1989) calls strong evaluation. This involves "discriminations of right or wrong, better or worse, higher or lower, that are not rendered valid by our own desires, inclinations, or choices, but rather stand independent of these and offer standards by which they can be judged" (p. 4). Strong evaluations in Taylor's sense are clearly distinguishable from personal preferences. They may involve distinctions of right and wrong or of qualitative difference. They possess a distinctive universalistic quality such that preferring them for ourselves implies also that we accept them as preferences for others as well. Immanuel Kant articulated this with what has come to be known as the categorical imperative. Kant's rule is a particularly apt one for social work administration since it indicates an explicit tie between the level of individual, contingent decisions and general rules or policy. It can be stated (in English): "Act only on that maxim through which you can at the same time will that it should become a universal law."

One encounters practical expressions of the categorical imperative all the time in administrative contexts. One of the most common of these is the widespread concern for precedent. If we decide to bend our rule against workers arriving late, ever so slightly, because of one valued employee who has to come all across town in traffic from her child's day care center and is often late as a result, how will the other employees react? In Kantian terms, will tolerance for arriving late become the universal law of the agency?

Another ethical concern referred to in the NASW *Code of Ethics* with major administrative implications is the expectation that social workers practice within their areas of competence and develop and enhance their professional expertise. Particularly in an age of funding cutbacks, downsizing, managed care and billings, there can be strong temptations for administrators to make use of what they have. You need a family therapist and all you have is a swimming instructor? Why not just reassign her, retitle her, and make her a family therapist? Although this example may appear quite absurd, the mass reassignments of caseworkers and their conversion into group workers that have occurred in some agencies in recent years are very real.

In such cases, the entire ethical burden to resist such obviously inappropriate actions should not fall upon the employee who will almost certainly be concerned about losing her job if she resists. The administrator also has an ethical burden. Under the standard of moral citizenship previously identified, the administrator has an obligation to consider not simply what is most expedient and in the short-term interest of the organization but also what is in the best interest of clients and community as well.

Social administrators also have an obligation to act in an ethical manner in those instances not covered by the code. Further, social administrators and all social workers have ethical obligations to act in pursuit of social justice and to encourage others in that pursuit, topics that will be explored more fully below. Concern for the ethical worthiness of all persons involved is as important for social administrators as it is for any caseworker. According to the legal scholar Robert Dworkin (1978), the first principle of a just society is that everyone is entitled to equal concern and respect. This also serves in many respects as the first principle of ethical concern for social administration.

Administrative ethics is, in the most fundamental sense, a situational ethics without being either relativistic or purely subjective. The donation question raised above, for example, is unlikely to be an ethical concern for anyone outside the specific context of a donative organization. In that situation, however, ethical norms governing appropriate behavior are quite clear-cut. In the situation of social agencies and the triad of patrons, agents, and clients, administrative ethics is concerned with right and wrong, good and evil in the specific context of administrative action. There are those who might suggest, sarcastically or otherwise, that the very idea of administrative ethics is an oxymoron. This suggestion will usually arise from some nonadministrative workers troubled by a particular decision or other administrative action. Or, the issue might arise from within the ranks of administrators themselves, because there is a relatively strong current of opinion in some circles that management is not an ethical task at all but a purely technical one. From this point of view, administrators cannot be held to ethical standards like right, wrong, good, or evil. Social administration is seen as purely a matter of efficiency and effectiveness and considerations of right and good never enter in. On this we beg to differ. Whether approached from Barnard's view of the moral component of leadership or from the viewpoint of social administration as a key component of social work practice, the importance of ethical concerns in guiding and shaping organizational behavior should be equally clear.

ETHICS AND POLITICS

To view things in these purely technical terms is to ignore the direct relation between issues of personal conduct and the larger concerns of the profession with political objectives, most notably the pursuit of social justice. It is for this reason that Rawls's focus on justice and the debate it provoked has laid down a suitable base from which to consider the ethical issues of social administration (Rawls, 1971). Regrettably, it is beyond the scope of this chapter to attempt a systematic construction of what those issues are. We can do little more here than lay the groundwork for such consideration in work that remains to be done.

One of the first and most basic distinctions to be made in considering administrative ethics must be to draw a distinction between ethics and politics as normative concerns. An ethical concern for practice can be seen as having two major branches. Ethics is the search for right and good in individual behavior and politics is the search for right and good in the community. Taylor's comment about the good life above is a major link that ties the ethical and political together. As Aristotle (2000) noted, "The good in the sphere of politics is justice; and justice consists in what tends to promote the common interest" (p. 129).

For a great many social workers raised in the progressive legacy, the distinction is a simpler one that pits ethical professional behavior against politics as the very paradigm of unethical conduct: Ethical behavior is conscientious professional endeavor to help clients based on the best available scientific knowledge. Politics in the progressive legacy involves venal, self-serving activities often grounded in ignorance and superstition and working against the interests of clients. The phrase "it's all political" when applied to an administrative decision usually carries precisely this connotation. It is this concern exclusively with the venal qualities of administrative decision making that is the principal barrier to most efforts to deal with administrative ethics in social agencies.

The progressive legacy of perceiving the professional and the political in opposition to each other has some very real roots. In her autobiography, Jane Addams (1930) noted the political conflicts portrayed largely as a struggle of good against evil with neighborhood saloonkeepers and others. This was the fight that resulted in her decision to accept appointment as supervisor of trash collections for the Hull House neighborhood. This venal meaning of politics contrasts dramatically with the philosophical meaning dating back to Plato. In the latter sense, the term is contrasted not with professional or any other behavior as a contrast of good and evil. Instead, politics is contrasted with ethics as contrasting forms of pursuit of the good life. In this philosophical sense, ethics is concerned with the realm of good and right as it applies to the behavior of individuals, whereas politics is concerned with good and right in the context of the community. Without such a distinction, it is literally not possible to approach major parts of social administration with concepts like good and right.

This failure to distinguish ethics from politics is one of the things that gives early social workers like Addams such a patina of self-righteous and individualistic Victorian moralism. Political scientists and historians have largely recast the struggles of social workers like Addams and other progressives against local political organizations. Rather than seeing them through the eyes of the Progressives as titanic struggles between the forces of good and evil, they suggest such struggles are often between two opposing senses of the good. They represent differing forms of meeting needs as represented by the professional services of social work and the practical and quite strategic political patronage of urban political machines offering aid in exchange for votes. Edward Banfield's comments on influence in chapter 17 occurred in association with this interpretation.

If Banfield and others are correct in this latter view, the bandwidth of politics as a normative concern for good and right in the community may be broader than is conventionally assumed in social work, and the bandwidth of administrative ethics may be somewhat narrower. This is one of the important background issues in need of clarification by further examination of social service as an issue in political philosophy. However broad this philosophical spectrum, social agencies, social services, and social administration are inherently both political and ethical concerns. That is, considerations of right and wrong in a most fundamental, constitutive way are concerned with the good of the community as well as that of the individual. Further, concern for the good life is a communal as well as an individual affair.

Yet another aspect of the nature of the connection between the ethical and the political is the inherently political nature of the definition of social problems and the selection of strategies to deal with such problems. This was articulated long ago by John Dewey (1939):

> Anything that obscures the fundamentally moral nature of the social problem is harmful, no matter whether it proceeds from the side of physical or of psychological theory. Any doctrine that eliminates or even obscures the function of choice of values and enlistment of desires and emotions in behalf of those chosen weakens personal responsibility for judgement and for action.

The philosopher Richard Rorty, an avid follower of Dewey, has recently cast social policy in the twentieth century in terms of opposition to selfishness and sadism. Selfishness is Rorty's (1998) summary term for the full set of policies and practices that maintain or advance economic and political inequalities, keep the poor poor, and are opposed by policies of redistribution of wealth. Sadism is Rorty's label for policies and practices that intentionally or inadvertently inflict limitation and injury on women, minorities, and others. Dewey's comment and Rorty's dichotomy point toward a conception of an inherent ethical dimension in the definition of social problems that both an emphasis on social scientific objectivity and advancing professionalism tend to downplay.

It is often said that social work is becoming more political in the present era. Surely that statement is true in a certain sense. The increasing politicization of the profession has generally not meant that social workers are taking part in any meaningful way in the interdisciplinary discussions that are taking place across the fields of law, philosophy, and several of the social sciences in the wake of Rawls. Nothing comparable to the impressive gains in ethical insight for clinicians referred to by Reamer above should be expected for social administration until this gap is breached.

THE ETHICAL DIMENSION: THE PROBLEM OF JUST ORGANIZATION

As noted in the quote from Aristotle earlier in this chapter, justice figures in classical political theory as the principal good to which communities should aspire. Social justice is identified in the NASW *Code of Ethics* as a fundamental core value along with service, dignity and worth of the person, the importance of human relationships, integrity, and competence. However, the code doesn't identify a substantive concept of justice, although one can be inferred from it.

Social workers pursue social change, particularly with and on behalf of vulnerable and oppressed individuals and groups of people. Social workers' social change efforts are focused primarily on issues of poverty, unemployment, discrimination, and other forms of social injustice. These activities seek to promote sensitivity to and knowledge about oppression and cultural and ethnic diversity. Social workers strive to ensure access to needed information, services, and resources; equality of opportunity; and meaningful participation in decision making for all people (National Association of Social Workers, 1996, p. 5).

The impact of justice upon an administrator seeking to organize or reorganize an agency or program is captured in its most important respects by Rawls (1971). Although Rawls is concerned with the basic principles of the just organization of society, much of his perspective can also be applied equally well to smaller segments of a society like particular organizations and institutions. Rawls is probably more responsible than anyone else for the recent resurgence of political philosophy. His theory of justice sets forth a complex and demanding perspective on social justice, of which only a very small but key portion will be considered here. Although Rawls's (1971) argument has been controversial among philosophers, it is fairly clear that the overall impact of the principles is supportive of the policies of a liberal welfare state, and most people in social work have little or no trouble intuitively accepting two principles:

1. Each person is to have an equal right to the most extensive total system of equal basic liberties, compatible with a similar system of liberty for all.
2. Social and economic inequalities are to be arranged so that they are both:
   a. To the greatest benefit of the least advantaged, consistent with the just savings principle, and
   b. Attached to offices and positions open to all under conditions of fair equality of opportunity. (p. 302)

Both principles address what some have suggested is the basic structure of society. Rawls sought to support the basic fairness of the principles by using the notion of blind justice. He presented the principles as those that a rational person would select if placed behind a veil of ignorance where she was completely unaware of the personal impact the principles might have upon her life. Much of the criticism of Rawls has been directed at this assumption and suggests that this was merely a way to introduce his own bias for a welfare state.

The first of Rawls's principles is a Kantian freedom principle that projects an ideal state of the distribution of freedom that is especially important in the context of social work practice with special populations such as the poor, mentally ill, physically challenged, and others. For example, it is really this first principle of equal freedom toward which much of the recent emphasis on empowerment in clinical practice is addressed. The real measure of success in those cases is that clients with limiting conditions or life circumstances will have the same freedoms as others. The application of this principle to social administration suggests that justice is to be found in the pursuit of such equal freedom for all.

The second of Rawls's principles states a redistribution principle that at the same time rejects any norm of absolute equality of conditions. Social and economic inequalities are tolerable, it says, if they are reasonably expected to be to everyone's advantage. Some have argued, for example, that the high incomes of some practitioners of medicine would be just if everyone had access to the same high-quality health care. In the absence of such universal advantage, the redistribution principle becomes effective. Where inequalities do not benefit everyone, they should offer the greatest benefit to the least advantaged. In addition, he says, they should be attached to positions and offices open to all under conditions of fair equality of opportunity.

The controversial social welfare nature of the second principle can be shown with an example involving national health insurance. Thus, for example, publicly subsidized medical education may train physicians from throughout society with the highest scores on a fair GMAT test. And when they go into practice and some of them make some of the highest incomes in society, this may be just if it results in providing access to high-quality medical care to everyone. Or, if the care is not provided to everyone, it may be just if provided to those with lowest incomes through pro bono charity care. In this sense, action by physicians to restrict or eliminate charity care constitutes an increase in injustice in society, and action by medical schools to bias or eliminate the GMAT would similarly be unjust.

Concern for individuals, however, does not exhaust the full meaning of social justice, as the Rawlsian principles make clear. In fact, some of the knottiest ethical issues in social administration arise in situations in which concern and respect for one individual must be balanced against concern and respect for others. In social administration, a proper Kantian concern for the ethical universal is most often found in considerations of the potential precedent-making nature of a particular decision. In many cases in social administration, the concern for just treatment by employees, clients, patrons, and other stakeholders extends only to a concern for the same treatment as others. In this situation, virtually any decision is a potential precedent, and administrators do well in making their decisions to consider its universal implications. Would I feel comfortable applying the same decision to everyone?

Even if the answer is yes, that this same rule might apply to everyone, it might not be just. For example, there is the case in which a decision such as taking away sick leave or pension benefits might be equally harmful to everyone. As it happens, a rather simple premise that is widely adopted as a technical criterion by economists provides at least a partially useful ethical rule of thumb that is more widely applied by administrators than is generally recognized. The concept of Paretoan optimality or simply optimality is a technical criterion in economics for determining optimal distributions of goods and services. Optimality also offers a very appealing ethical standard useful in a wide variety of administrative situations. The basic idea arises from the work of the great nineteenth-century Italian economist-sociologist Wilfredo Pareto.

The basic idea is that an economic distribution or, in this case, an administrative decision, is considered optimal if no one is harmed and at least one person is benefited. This idea is often used by conservatives to oppose all forms of economic redistribution on the grounds that those who benefit do so unjustly by harming those who must pay. Opponents of change in organizations can also use the same argument on the grounds that no change can take place without an unjust loss to present stakeholders. Thus, one frequently encounters such justice or fairness claims being asserted in organizational decisions by administrators redistributing resources. A department that is overstaffed, for example, will almost always assert unfairness or injustice in attempting to counter administrative decisions to transfer employees or vacant positions to another unit. The underlying logic is that change should not occur so long as there is a danger of harm to anyone.

The risk for social administration is that this generally useful criterion will be discarded as unworkable if all assertions of harm are simply accepted at face value. One of the questions this should raise for the administrator is whether leaving the overstaffed department in place really does actual harm to other units in the organization. Harm or damage in such cases is almost always an empirical question and subject to testing. Such damage might be reflected in overwork, poor morale, or other factors associated with the other units' being understaffed. If there is evidence of actual harm to others, the decision to leave an overstaffed unit alone might in some cases be ethically as well as politically justifiable. In most instances, however, that will not be the case. In some instances, the social administrator may test the question with a simple A-B-A research design by cutting back on staff with the expectation of restoring them if actual damage to the unit occurs.

These examples point up an essential feature of the argument over re-distribution that has another far-reaching implication for social adminis-tration. Conservatives and libertarians often argue that some abstract prin-ciple like property rights or control over a certain budget base are absolute and cannot be interfered with without committing an injustice. Where res-toration of the pre-test conditions would not be possible or feasible, another alternative might be to compensate the losers for their loss.

Combining the Paretoan notion of harm with the Rawlsian redistribution principle can yield a very powerful ethical standard for social administra-tion. One of the most powerful aspects of Rawls's criterion 2a, like Paretoan optimality, is its focus on the distribution of benefit and harm. The essential concern in both cases is not whether anyone must give up anything but whether doing so harms them or their interests.

Thus, whether we are dealing with questions of taxation, income, or the distribution of an organizational budget base, the essential question be-comes whether a proposed change that will benefit one party will actually harm another. For example, one might ask whether a tax of $1 million for hunger relief would actually harm taxpayers. The answer is yes, it will not only harm many people but it will disproportionately harm those with in-comes below $1 million by placing a great economic debt upon them. It would not only deprive them of all of their income, it would also leave them in debt for the amount between their actual income and the tax due. Above that point, however, the amount of harm done by the tax would appear to vary directly by income. Thus, a person with a $1.1 million income will pay a proportionately greater tax than a person with an $11 million income. For the billionaire, it seems quite plausible that no actual harm will result from a tax of a mere $1 million, which is one-tenth of one percent of his or her total worth. Likewise, it is not an injustice to tax an individual or remove staff from an overstaffed department when there is no evidence of actual harm to them.

This essential administrative insight on distributive justice is uncovered by bringing Rawls together with Pareto optimality. It is just to remove un-needed or underutilized resources from a unit when there is no actual harm to the unit and when the resources are redistributed to another unit that most needs them at the time. Working administrators engage in sequential reapplications of this simple ethical rule with great frequency.

There is yet another important dimension to the use of optimality as an ethical as well as an economic criterion in social administration. Using it in this way provides an important social justice dimension to the notion encountered in chapter 5 of decision making by satisficing or incremental choice. It is optimality and particularly the idea of harming no one and benefiting at least one person that set the all-important ethical limits on this idea.

Assume, for example, that an elderly employee who really should retire wants to hold on for another two years to build up her pension just a bit more. At first glance, most social workers would probably be inclined to go along with such a plan that has clear benefit for the employee. Under the optimality rule, however, social administrators must also ask not only if there are clear benefits to the employee but also whether any harm will come from a decision to keep this employee on. Only if it is also clear, for example, that other employees will not have to shoulder additional burdens because this employee can no longer perform the work satisfactorily and that clients will not be harmed would such a decision be fully justified.

For social administrators, a part of the substantive content of social justice is supplied by appeal to process; another part is supplied by the specific behavioral sanctions of the NASW *Code of Ethics*. However, a large part of the ethical universe of social administration remains unresolved by resorts to process and code. This is particularly true in those cases where the code is merely aspirational and does not offer definitive guidance for the practice of social administration. In those instances, resorting to the guidance of Rawls's two principles of justice, Kant's categorical imperative, and Paretoan optimality will go a long way toward realizing the goal of social administration as ethically informed practice.

CONCLUSION

Social administration must be, in the most profound sense, ethically informed action. This is not merely true in the narrow sense of adherence with the NASW *Code of Ethics*, but also in Taylor's sense of strong evaluations and concern not only with the right but also with the good. In administration, concern for the ethical behavior of individuals often comes together with concern for groups and collectivities.

The terms *politics* and *political* are used in a very specific sense here that excludes a good deal of the shady dealing and arts of compromise that many people associate with politics. Because it is improbable that anyone is likely to endorse shady dealing as appropriate ethical conduct for professional social workers, this common meaning is obviously excluded here. However, in practice this issue is not nearly as easy to dismiss as all that. Political opponents have accused one another of unethical conduct from time immemorial and will likely continue doing so. Nonetheless, the words *civil* and *civic* are often used in place of political in ambiguous contexts to clarify the emphasis on principled action for the good of the community.

CHAPTER 26

Human Diversity and Administrative Justice

Justice may be described as having five qualities: It is universal, permissive, prohibitive; it commands and regulates. The way in which those five qualities relate to what is commonly described as "human diversity" has been the subject of much emotionally charged popular debate and many Supreme Court decisions. Those debates and Court decisions generally center upon the extent to which certain matters are universal as opposed to when appropriate exceptions may be made for those different from what is assumed to be the norm. The debates have also dealt with which behavior may be prohibited and/or regulated. In this chapter, the relationships between administrative justice and human diversity as broadly defined are explored.

This chapter addresses issues that often arise with regard to justice, diversity, and agency employees and/or clients. Federal legislation and presidential executive orders dealing with equal opportunity and affirmative action are described because they address those characteristics most often viewed as representing human diversity. This chapter also addresses the issue of sexual harassment. That issue was selected for special attention in part because it highlights some of the issues associated with justice. It is also an important issue, however, because changing standards with regard to behavior that is acceptable (or just) means that many social agencies need to examine their practices to ensure that they comply with court rulings as well as social work ethics and standards.

HUMAN DIVERSITY DEFINED

Social work education and practice have historically focused on issues related to human diversity. Robert Barker (1995) in *The Social Work Dictionary* defines "human diversity" as

> the ranges of differences between peoples in terms of race, ethnicity, age, geography, religion, values, culture, orientations, physical and mental health, and many other distinguishing characteristics. (p. 172)

The centrality of the concept of diversity to the social work profession is reflected through the accreditation standards applied to baccalaureate and master's programs and provisions of the *Code of Ethics* applicable to social workers. These standards reflect a definition of the essential knowledge one should have in order to practice as a social worker and the behaviors that a social worker should exhibit. The Council of Social Work Education's (CSWE) Educational Policy and Accreditation Standards (EPAS) address matters of human diversity, as does the National Association of Social Workers' (NASW) *Code of Ethics.*

CSWE's EPAS indicates that all social work programs are to include content on diversity, populations-at-risk, and social and economic justice. The NASW *Code of Ethics* identifies "social justice" as an important value undergirding the ethical principles in the code (National Association of Social Workers, 1996, p. 5). In the discussion of that value, diversity is among the topics addressed. The code includes a section entitled "Cultural Competence and Social Diversity" (Section 1.05, p. 9) and one called "Discrimination" (Section 4.02, p. 22).

The inclusion of diversity as an important topic by both CSWE and NASW speaks for its centrality to the profession. The issue for administrators is how they and their agencies might achieve justice while respecting the differences represented by the concept of "diversity."

EQUAL OPPORTUNITY AND AFFIRMATIVE ACTION

Federal statutes and presidential executive orders cover almost all of the diversity statuses identified by CSWE and NASW. In fact, the federal requirements preceded those of professional social work organizations. The impact of some of the federal requirements as they influence employment was discussed in chapter 20 on human resources, and the requirements are also discussed further below.

A range of federal statutes provides for nondiscrimination in employment and for equal opportunity. The statutes include Title VII of the Civil Rights Act of 1964 (usually referred to as the Equal Opportunity Act), the Equal Pay Act of 1963, the Age Discrimination in Employment Act of 1967, Sections 501 and 505 of the Rehabilitation Act of 1973, Titles I and V of the Americans with Disabilities Act of 1990 (usually referred to as the ADA), and the Civil Rights Act of 1991. These acts are amended from time to time by Congress, and their interpretation is frequently ruled on by federal courts, including the Supreme Court.

Federal provisions provide for equal opportunity in employment on the following bases: race, color, religion, sex, national origin, age (forty years of age or older), and disability. As indicated in chapter 20, those individuals covered by these acts are often referred to as members of a "protected class." Federal legislation does not cover sexual orientation, which is an important area of diversity in both the CSWE and NASW provisions.

Affirmative action is the result of two executive orders signed by President Lyndon B. Johnson. Executive Order 11246, signed in 1965, barred discrimination on the basis of race, creed, color, or national origin and required the creation of positive programs of equal opportunity for executive departments and agencies. The positive programs took the form of acting affirmatively with regard to those covered by the executive order. In 1967, Executive Order 11375 expanded that coverage to include women.

Affirmative action consists of taking positive steps to ensure the proportional recruitment, selection, and promotion of qualified members of groups previously excluded from employment opportunities (Pecora, 1995, p. 1830). Affirmative action must be taken by all federal contractors having contracts in excess of $10,000, and affirmative action plans are required if the contracts exceed $50,000 (Buttrick, 1985). Since many social agencies, including small ones, have federal contracts for services that exceed $10,000, these provisions specifically apply to them.

It is important to note what affirmative action is not. It is not the process of filling a quota. Those opposed to affirmative action often believe that it means that a protected class person must be hired or promoted regardless of his or her qualifications. That is not the case. Though affirmative action plans include goals for representation in the workforce of various protected classes, those persons are to be hired or promoted only if qualified. This confusion, however, has led many to oppose affirmative action and some states to pass legislation opposed to it.

Because of the changes in the relevant statutes that occur through amendment or court ruling, ensuring that organizational practices are current with the statutes' interpretation can prove difficult for any employer. The U.S. Equal Employment Opportunity Commission maintains a Web site that can be helpful to employers.[1] The site both provides the text of the relevant laws and readable discussions intended for those who are not specialists in the area of the meaning of the laws and actions required by them.

In addition to federal statutes providing for equal opportunity, many states have laws in these areas, some of which extend protection to categories of persons in addition to those covered by federal law or that establish additional expectations for the actions that employers will take. Agencies may consult their state Equal Opportunity Commission or its Web site to learn about those requirements.

Some of the federal statutes do not cover all employers. In particular, equal opportunity and ADA laws generally apply only to employers of fifteen or more and, in the case of equal opportunity, religious organizations employing persons to perform work connected with carrying on the religious organization are not covered. Many small social welfare agencies may be exempt from the provisions of the acts because they have fewer than fifteen employees and/or a relationship to a religious organization that exempts them. Other agencies may not have a federal contract or the contract may be for less than $10,000. Most agencies, however, wish to comply with the expectations even if not required to do so simply because it is the right thing to do, given the values of social work.

The above discussion should not be taken to mean that dealing with human diversity consists only of obeying federal requirements in this area. Obeying those requirements is one component of respecting diversity, but respect for diversity is much broader than that. Cheryl Hyde (1998) quotes a diversity trainer as saying:

> [It's] not just about race, it's about culture, gender, sexual orientation and so forth. One danger is that it has gotten equated with race and with people of color. When it gets skewed this way it's easy for whites to say, "I don't have a culture." But we all have cultural stories, and in human services, we need to understand that. (p. 23)

THE DEBATE ABOUT ADMINISTRATIVE JUSTICE AND HUMAN DIVERSITY

The debate about administrative justice and its relationship to human diversity centers on whether it is possible to be just and still treat people who have different characteristics differently. This debate is obviously broader than one that deals merely with the legal requirements and ethical principles in a social agency. It goes to core issues concerning fairness in the society at large. However, because of the emphasis that the social work profession has placed on issues of human diversity and societal disagreement about what is fair, the debate sometimes becomes especially pronounced in social agencies, in which the views of the agency employees may not be in complete accord with those of the general public.

The sense of what is just, especially in terms of the treatment of diverse groups, changes over time. Smith (1997) indicated that American law has "long been shot through with forms of second class citizenship, denying personal liberties and opportunities for political participation to most of the adult population on the basis of race, ethnicity, gender, and even religion" (p. 2). He indicates that forms of civic inequality often "manifested passionate beliefs that America was by rights a white nation, a Protestant nation, a nation in which true Americans were native-born men with Anglo-Saxon ancestors" (p. 3). These forms of inequality and sense of what was just have changed over time, and as such changes occurred, for example, suffrage was extended to women and African Americans.

It can be argued that the best way to assess a democratic society's views of what is just is to examine its laws and the court decisions about those laws. Thus, though it was once regarded as just that women did not have the right to vote, that is no longer the view held in American society. The Nineteenth Amendment to the Constitution reflects the changing view of what was just. Though it was once regarded as just that women be paid less than men, the Equal Pay Act of 1963 reflected a changed societal sense that the practice of paying women less was no longer just. Thus, in considering justice and diversity, it is helpful to examine the laws passed by Congress and the court decisions, especially those of the Supreme Court, to obtain a sense of what is viewed as just at the start of the twenty-first century.

Some of the federal legislation that affects practice with regard to diversity both among agency employees and clients was described above. Some of these provisions are applied to social welfare agencies through the power of the purse: as a condition of receiving federal funds, agencies are required to comply. Some provisions are relevant because they apply to all employers of a certain size, regardless of the source of funding. Private businesses, for example, do not receive federal funding but, if they are of a certain size, are still not allowed to discriminate on the basis of race, color, national origin, sex, handicap, or age. Even if a social service agency may be legally exempt from one or more provisions, most agencies choose to apply the intent of the statutes because of the consistency of that intent with the values of the agency. Thus, those statutes defining certain elements of justice within our society have great applicability to social service agencies whether or not the agency is legally required to abide by them.

There are some very real tensions between those actions that may be seen as just in the larger societal view and those actions that respect the differences that may be present among subgroups of the society. Dealing with "justice" and "diversity" is by no means easy. Smith (1997) identifies three such tensions. He indicates that the first is conflict between democracy and subgroup "authenticity" (p. 477). Democratic views hold that all group membership should be voluntary and structured so as to preserve personal liberties. However, the beliefs of some subgroups within a society may not be in agreement, and personal liberties may be less important in such a subgroup than what is best for the group as a whole. What is just within such circumstances? Is it more just to uphold the majority view about group membership or to uphold the view of any given subgroup that has a different perspective?

The second tension that Smith (1997, pp. 478–79) cites is between individual versus group equality. This tension occurs when the efforts to ensure that all individuals have meaningful opportunities to participate in public institutions such as higher education result in governmental intrusions in ways that violate the beliefs and practices of particular groups. Is the group interest in ensuring that all children have medical treatment, for example, sufficient to overcome the belief of a particular pair of Christian Scientist parents that their child should not have such care? To what extent are individuals free to differ from the group normative practice?

The third tension is over the issue of whether the government should pursue integrated or segregated equality (Smith, 1997, p. 479). Do affirmative action efforts on behalf of African Americans, for example, reinforce a sense of a separate group identity that makes true integration impossible?

JUSTICE, DIVERSITY, AND AGENCY EMPLOYEES

Agency policies and procedures sometimes deal explicitly with the rules and regulations that apply to the treatment of diversity among employees of an agency. Other times, the rules and regulations are assumed through the applicability of federal (and state) law, and the procedures to be followed are not explicitly defined. Larger agencies are more likely to have explicit written procedures than smaller ones. However, the absence of such written procedures does not mean that the statutes should not be followed. The statutes generally provide guidance in what would be considered personnel matters, such as hiring and promotion.

RECRUITMENT AND PROMOTION OF EMPLOYEES

As a means of providing social justice, agencies should ensure that their recruitment and hiring practices do not unlawfully discriminate against po-

tential employees. In small agencies, the recruitment practices are sometimes somewhat informal, and all of the actions needed to comply with
federal statute may not be spelled out or even observed. Such inattention
to required actions may put the agency at legal risk. Even if it does not,
inattention may mean that the agency is not being as just as it might be.
Some of these issues are discussed more fully in chapter 20 on human resources.

Complicating the issue of justice in recruitment is the adoption of statutes by many states that prohibit preferences based on characteristics like
gender or race. The first of these was Proposition 209 adopted by the state
of California through referendum in 1996 (Chavez, 1998). Other states that
have comparable limitations for public agencies because of referenda or
court orders are Texas and Washington. These court orders or policies often
permit equal opportunity but prohibit affirmative action.

Regardless of the state in which a social agency is located, all agencies
are required to provide equal opportunity as defined by applicable federal
laws. In most states, going beyond equal opportunity to engage in affirmative action is permissible and is seen by many in the profession as
consistent with social work ideals. In a few states, anything that creates
additional opportunities through affirmative action for those defined as
members of protected classes may violate state law.

Issues comparable to those of employee recruitment arise with regard to
employee promotion. At a minimum, equal opportunity to promotion opportunities must be provided by all agencies covered by federal statute. In
most locations, agencies may also act affirmatively in promoting protected
class members.

Whether justice is ensured only if one provides equal opportunity is at
the center of the debates that have led to the adoption of provisions like
Proposition 209. There are those who argue that equal opportunity is not
enough and that affirmative action must also occur if social and administrative justice are to occur.

As has been indicated, equal opportunity refers to allowing all, regardless
of race, color, sex, religion, national origin, age, or disability (and, in some
organizations, sexual orientation), an equal chance to compete to be hired
or be promoted. Affirmative action refers to taking the additional step of
hiring or promoting a protected class member rather than a nonprotected
class member, all other qualifications being equal, when the agency does
not have the number of employees in that protected class that might be
expected. A part of the argument for affirmative action is the assumption
that if two employees' qualifications are comparable, the employer will hire
or promote the employee most like him. Since employers have historically
been white males, additional encouragement is needed if women and mi-

norities are to be hired or promoted within the organization. The assumption is that justice is best achieved if those who have been discriminated against in the past are provided with additional help in being hired or promoted.

Debate over affirmative action often loses sight of the "equally qualified" provision associated with many affirmative action policies. It is sometimes assumed that acting affirmatively means a woman or minority is hired regardless of qualifications. That is not what is intended by affirmative action and, in fact, quotas that would result in an employer hiring minorities or women until a certain number had been hired have not been upheld by the courts. However, the assumption that affirmative action means that an employer hires the protected class member regardless of qualification is part of what has sparked the debate over the fairness and thus justice of the approach. Is it just if one's gender or race provides an added boost in being hired or promoted?

The debate has also been influenced by the argument that it is not just that those living and working today pay for the sins of the past. That argument, as applied to African Americans, agrees that the United States does have a sad history of slavery, Jim Crow laws following slavery, and racial discrimination. However, those in the workforce today were not participants in those historical events. In addition, it is argued, there have been several decades since 1964 (the year of passage of the Civil Rights Act) during which special opportunities were created for minorities as a form of atonement for past wrongs. Thus, the chances at advancement of those presently in the workforce should not be limited by practices that give someone advantages over them merely because of a personal characteristic like race or gender. Even if those special programs were once appropriate, the argument goes, they no longer are, and it is time for all to return to competing merely on the basis of abilities.

There is no doubt that equal opportunity is the law of the land. Is affirmative action also required if an agency is to practice administrative justice? Many within the social work profession would argue that affirmative action must still be an element of justice. However, that argument is losing some support within the profession and, if referenda are any indication, clearly losing support among the public at large. It is not clear what impact the loss of public support may have on affirmative action.

EMPLOYMENT RESPECTFUL OF DIFFERENCES

Another concern relevant to administrative justice and human diversity is that of creating an employment environment comfortable for employees whose backgrounds may differ from those viewed as normative. A reading of the cartoon section of any daily newspaper provides an easy illustration of some of the problems associated with creating such an environment. Cartoons like *Dilbert* or *Cathy* often illustrate some of the problems associated with responding to diversity in the workplace.

Variations in holiday practices are perhaps the easiest illustration of this issue. In the United States, the Christian observance of Christmas is pervasive in popular culture. In an agency that may employ practicing Jews, Muslims, Buddhists, and others, the observance of that holiday by the agency may result in discomfort for those employees who are not Christian.

In religiously affiliated agencies, the practices associated with the faith of the agency are expected and highly appropriate and may be a part of the way in which the agency fulfills its mission. In secular agencies, however, care needs to be taken to ensure that employees do not feel that they are expected to conform to certain practices or that their own cultural practices are not respected. With the Christmas illustration, for example, the agency might ensure that its decorations do not include any religious references and use only decorations, such as poinsettias, that have no religious meaning. Rather than calling the agency party a "Christmas party," the event might be called a "holiday luncheon."

Though holiday celebrations are the easiest example to cite of differences among employees that need to be respected, there are a range of possible differences that need attention. Some go to gender: Is the annual golf or hunting outing for agency executives something that includes women, whose recreational activities may not include golfing or hunting? A prominent woman banker told one of the authors, for example, that she had learned to golf to ensure that she would be able to participate in the links conversations that she thought so important to her business. She viewed the decision that she learn golf one of the most important that she had made in her career and one that had contributed directly to her rise in the organization. Is it just that an employee should need to alter her usual practices or interests to be successful in the workplace? Is the workplace so intolerant of diversity that someone whose recreational pursuits are not like those of others can expect only limited success?

Other differences meriting attention go to sexual orientation. Are the jokes told around the water cooler ones that would make anyone who does not have a heterosexual orientation uncomfortable? Are the implicit and explicit assumptions about an employee's sexual orientation such that anyone who does not have that orientation is made to feel uncomfortable? Or are those whose sexual orientation may differ from the norm for the agency made to feel comfortable?

One of the more difficult set of differences to accommodate and yet be just are those associated with parenting. A parallel exists between the issues associated with parenting and those associated with caring for any dependent person, such as an older parent or disabled spouse, although those of parenting are used as the example here. Although federal statute prohibits discrimination based on pregnancy, it does not address what occurs after the child arrives. How to be just in treating an employee dealing with the demands of parenting is a difficult issue and one for which there is limited statutory guidance.

There is some statutory guidance in the Family and Medical Leave Act of 1993. This act provides for up to twelve weeks of unpaid leave in any twelve months to deal with the following:

- Birth and care of the newborn child of the employee
- Placement with the employee of a son or daughter for adoption or foster care
- Care for an immediate family member (spouse, child, or parent) with a serious health condition
- Medical leave when the employee is unable to work because of a serious health condition

The Department of Labor's Web site[2] can provide further information about the provisions of the act. The act, however, deals with occasional or exceptional circumstances, not with the day-to-day issues that occur when an employee is providing care for a child, parent, or other dependent person.

There is no doubt that caring for a dependent person requires a significant emotional and time investment. Using child care as an example, children become ill and require parental time to take them to the doctor and provide home care. They may need to be taken to and picked up from their bus stop every day. Parent-teacher conferences at school are required. Poor school performance may preoccupy a parent's attention as the parent attempts to identify what might help improve the child's performance. What workplace accommodations should be made for a parent or other employee dealing with a dependent person that are fair to other employees of the agency?

Some accommodations are relatively easy to make. Holding mandatory meetings at times that do not conflict with usual parenting schedules is one such accommodation respectful of difference. Such meetings, for example, should likely not be scheduled for late afternoon when they may continue after usual working hours and pose great difficulty for the parent whose child care arrangements cover only the time up to usual closing hours.

Other accommodations are more difficult. Should a parent who cannot be at work at the usual time because of his child's school bus departure time be allowed to work different hours? If he is, what does that mean for other employees? How is justice, when defined as a perceived sense of fairness, provided in such a situation?

Parenting does produce some demands that nonparents or those parents whose children are adults do not face. The application of respect for diversity would suggest that some accommodation for those demands may be appropriate. However, the application of ideas of justice may suggest that such accommodations are unfair in that they are not universal. In situations like this, which matters most? Accommodation for diversity or the comparable treatment of all?

Barker's definition of diversity cited above is very broad and includes matters of values and culture. Providing a just work environment for these differences can be very difficult. Take, for example, the differing ways that people may be socialized to react to stress. Many women, for example, find that their most natural reaction in a time of stress is to cry. If they respond in that way, however, they may be viewed as weak or as attempting to manipulate others. The assumption is that the "normal" way to react to stress is the way many men react. A man under stress often yells or pounds the table or in some other way expresses aggression. Can the agency work environment accommodate this diversity and accept both responses?

Padgett (1993), while focusing on the research implications of various theoretical frameworks, suggested some of the differences that women administrators may pose for the work environment. She contrasted the liberal feminists' perspectives with those of radical feminists. The former she indicates emphasize equal pay, equal status, and equal opportunity. The latter emphasize women's particular experiences as a means of refining leadership and organizations. For example, radical feminists might suggest that the workplace should change so that compassion, nurturing, empowerment, and other aspects of caring become more important. Is justice served by altering the workplace so that it better reflects the characteristics often associated with women?

JUSTICE, DIVERSITY, AND CLIENT POPULATIONS

The concerns about justice and diversity as they affect clients parallel those of employees. Clients may be diverse in ways that differ from most of the agencies' employees and that also differ from most of the agency's other clients. Agencies need to find ways to accommodate and be respectful of those differences among its clients while acting in ways that are perceived as just.

Diversity and the Identification of Clients

Just as agencies need to ensure that they do not unlawfully discriminate in their employment practices, they need to ensure that they do not unlawfully discriminate when identifying and accepting new clients. Who becomes a client is defined in part by the agency mission and the agency's intake policy, which should reflect its mission. Agencies should periodically review the intake guidelines to ensure that they are not unintentionally discouraging or eliminating clients from protected classes.

The agency also needs to review its practices and environment to ensure that they are supportive of diversity. If the agency serves predominantly African Americans, for example, are all the pictures and paintings on its walls of white people? Given the focus in the Hispanic culture on family, does the agency provide an environment with play areas and other spaces that encourage Hispanic clients to make use of its services (Hyde, 1998, p. 28)? In what ways does the agency communicate to potential clients that it is interested in serving those who may differ from its usual clients and/ or from its employees?

Diversity and the Treatment of Clients

One of the more complicated areas in terms of dealing with diversity and justice is in the treatment of clients. If a client's religious beliefs or cultural practices prohibit travel, for example, on certain days, is the agency willing to change appointments to accommodate those practices? Is the agency willing to tolerate dress or even bathing customs that may differ from the usual? Even if the agency is willing to tolerate significant differences, there may be a conflict between the rights of those who are different and the rights of those who are negatively impacted by those differences. Smith cites the Amish practices with regard to education and the larger society's requirements for education as a well-known example of this conflict (Smith, 1997). The Old Order Amish do not believe that education beyond the eighth grade is required, and their right to be exempt from compulsory school attendance laws requiring education beyond this level has been upheld by the Supreme Court.

Child protective services is the area where the conflict between what is viewed as normative and diverse practices is perhaps most evident. Newspapers report daily instances where a family's practices conflict with societal norms as to the care a child should be given. If social agencies intervene, it may be that such intervention is not respectful of the diversity represented by different cultural or religious practices. If agencies fail to intervene, they are criticized for failing to provide justice to innocent children in that the children's rights are not being protected. The conflicts between justice and respect for diversity are real and not easy to resolve.

Many agencies prepare their workers to deal with diversity among clients through training programs. In her interviews with diversity trainers, Hyde (1998) found that they often had three goals for their training. The first was to help create the sense that the agency was a welcoming place where staff and clients could feel that they belonged. The second goal was to develop a culturally competent staff comfortable with diversity and able to engage in cross-cultural practice. The third was to formulate a critical analysis of the implications of diversity and the oppression often associated with it and to develop staff willing to take action to deal with oppression.

SEXUAL HARASSMENT AS A SOCIAL JUSTICE ISSUE

Sexual harassment is an issue of justice both as it relates to an employment setting and as it relates to the treatment of clients. Technically, "sexual harassment" as defined by federal statute applies only to employment settings. However, the same behavior that may exist in an employment setting may also be displayed with regard to clients. Although the behavior with clients may not be covered by federal legislation, it is covered by the NASW *Code of Ethics* and may be sanctioned behavior. This topic receives extended coverage in this chapter to illustrate some of the issues that arise with regard to diversity and administrative justice. Its coverage is also to ensure that future social work administrators are aware of the importance of this area in agency practice.

Sexual Harassment in Employment

Sexual harassment is a form of sex discrimination that violates Title VII of the Civil Rights Act of 1964. The Equal Employment Opportunity Commission's definition of sexual harassment is the following:

> Unwelcome sexual advances, requests for sexual favors, and other verbal or physical conduct of a sexual nature constitute sexual harassment when submission to or rejection of this conduct explicitly or implicitly affects an individual's employment, unreasonably interferes with an individual's work performance or creates an intimidating, hostile or offensive work environment.[3]

What constitutes sexual harassment has been the subject of many complaints to the commission and court cases during the past decade. The legal definition of such harassment is an evolving matter, given the activity in this area. The following general guidelines may be of help in describing what may constitute sexual harassment.

1. The person harassed may be male or female and may be harassed by someone of the opposite or same sex.
2. The conduct must be unwelcome. It is helpful if the person harassed tells the harasser that the conduct is not welcomed, but such notice is not required for a finding that harassment occurred.
3. The employee must have a concern that submitting to or rejecting the advances will affect his or her employment status. That is, he may be rewarded if he submits and/or may be punished if he does not.
4. The harasser may be the employee's supervisor, an agent of the employer, a supervisor in another area, a coworker, or a nonemployee.
5. The victim does not have to be the person harassed but can be anyone affected by the conduct.
6. The consequences for the employee do not have to be economic ones such as the denial of a pay increase or loss of job.

Two Supreme Court decisions made responsibility for preventing sexual harassment more than a matter involving only employees and those with whom they directly interact. Court decisions have extended responsibility for sexual harassment to employers even if the employer did not have specific knowledge that harassment was occurring. One decision in *Burlington Industries, Inc.* v. *Ellerth* (1998) held that employers are vicariously liable for supervisors who create hostile working conditions even though the employer is not directly responsible for the supervisor's action. Under certain circumstances, employers may defend themselves by demonstrating that they acted quickly to prevent and correct harassing behavior. A comparable decision was also reached in *Faragher* v. *The City of Boca Raton* (1997) Ignorance that harassment was occurring on the part of the employer is no longer an adequate defense.[4]

These decisions have meant that it is important for all employers to have a complaint or grievance process for allegations of sexual harassment. Further, it is important for the employer to indicate that sexual harassment will not be tolerated. Many employers have responded to these decisions by holding periodic required training sessions on sexual harassment attended by all employees during which the organization's stance on sexual harassment is made clear.

Many employers are also responding to these decisions by becoming far more proactive in inquiring about and monitoring situations that may provide opportunities for harassment. The increased activity is in part because of the financial cost for an employer when an employee is legally found to have been harassed. In social service agencies, one would hope that the increased activity is also the result of an ethical sense that such behavior is wrong and should not be tolerated.

It is important to emphasize that sexual harassment is not necessarily limited to what one employee of an organization does to another employee. A nonemployee may also be found to have harassed someone and the employer held liable because the employer failed to take action to prevent such harassment or address it, once it occurred. The classic illustration of such harassment often given is when a salesman or other periodic visitor makes sexually harassing comments to a receptionist while waiting to visit the receptionist's boss at the place of business.

Nonemployee sexual harassment may also occur when an agency client harasses an agency employee. Though we are unaware of any complaints that have been filed involving such a situation, it is within the realm of possibility that such an allegation could be made and be upheld, given the direction of other findings in this area. It is also possible that the agency could be held responsible for such harassment.

The best prevention against such situations is likely the education of employees as to the action that they should take when a client sexually harasses them. Though the best defense might be to educate clients as to the actions that may constitute sexual harassment and the agency's unwillingness to tolerate such actions, such education is likely not practical. It may be practical for the agency to develop a flyer provided to all clients that defines sexual harassment and indicates that the agency does not tolerate harassment of its clients by its employees or harassment of its employees by its clients. As with employee harassment of another employee, it is important that agencies be alert for the possibility of client sexual harassment of employees and take action to monitor situations that may lead to such harassment.

Sexual Harassment and Relationships with Clients

Sexual harassment was identified above as issues of social justice both as it relates to employment and to the treatment of clients. The NASW *Code of Ethics* has sections dealing with both the sexual harassment of clients and sexual relationships with clients.

The provision (Section 1.11) with regard to sexual harassment indicates that social workers should not sexually harass their clients. It indicates that social workers should not engage in any of the following with regard to clients: "sexual advances, sexual solicitation, requests for sexual favors, and other verbal or physical conduct of a sexual nature" (National Association of Social Workers, 1996, Section 1.11).

The code is equally direct with regard to sexual relationships (Section 1.09). It indicates that "social workers should under no circumstances engage in sexual activities or sexual contact with current clients, whether such contact is consensual or forced" (Section 1.09a). The code goes on to indicate that social workers should not engage in sexual activities or sexual contact with a client's relatives or others with whom the client has a close personal relationship or with former clients. Social workers should also not provide clinical services to persons with whom they have had a prior sexual relationship.

The code also addresses the sexual harassment of supervisees, students, trainees, and colleagues (Section 2.08). Because such harassment would involve an employment situation, it is covered by the provisions addressed above.

Sexual Harassment, Diversity, and Justice

The above discussion placed special emphasis on sexual harassment as an issue of diversity and justice. There are several reasons for doing so. One reason is practical. This is a relatively new area with which social agencies have had to be concerned, the definitions of acceptable behavior are undergoing significant change, and the legal and fiscal implications for agencies can be significant if violations occur. Thus, the practical reason for the emphasis given to this content is to alert social administrators to the need to attend to this area.

Another reason for the emphasis on this area is that it illustrates some of the difficult tensions that can exist when trying to be just and also respect diversity. Sexual harassment has become more important in part because of the increased diversity of the workforce. As more women are employed and as women move up the organizational ladder, sensitivity to gender differences has become more important in work life than it once was. Thus, the example of sexual harassment illustrates that definitions of *just* may change when greater diversity is introduced into the workforce.

The issue also illustrates the clash that occurs among values as changes occur. Some men would argue, for example, that pictures of scantily clad women have been found for decades in locker rooms and on garage walls. Risqué jokes have also been a part of traditional male behavior for some men. Why should they have to forego this behavior just because someone objects? Don't they have a right to engage in behavior that they find comfortable? How did traditional and innocuous behaviors such as these come to be defined as a "hostile work environment?" Do they not have a right to expressions of their diversity as a group?

Sexual harassment, then, illustrates the tension that often exists between what one group may believe reflects their diversity as a group, such as posting pictures some find offensive, and the diversity another group believes it represents, such as women in the workplace having different standards as to what is offensive. How does one find a just approach when differing outcomes are both supported by arguments of reflecting diversity? In the case of sexual harassment, the answer as to what is just has been provided in part by the Supreme Court, and the primary issue is one of practice and behaviors catching up to that which has been defined as just. With many, if not most, issues, similar clarity with regard to what is just does not exist.

CONCLUSION

There are no easy answers when it comes to questions of what is just when dealing with human diversity. Social work as a profession, however, has a long-standing commitment to dealing with issues of diversity and oppression. Thus, the commitment of the profession forces each social worker both as an individual and as a member of a community of social workers to grapple with what is just.

Societal definitions of what is just are expressed through the laws that govern that society and are interpreted by court decisions about the meaning of those laws. Since the mid-1960s, many important laws have been passed and court decisions issued dealing with what is just as it affects diverse populations. These provide a legal basis for what is just.

The social work commitment to administrative justice, however, goes beyond the requirements of law. In doing so, however, it forces social workers to deal with the three tensions described by Smith and summarized above in deciding what is just.

CHAPTER 27

Governance Issues:
Boards and Directorates

Social workers moving into social administration are faced, often for the first time in their careers, with the seemingly daunting challenges of working with boards. Without a clearer understanding of the role, scope, and purpose of board governance, they may feel they are just going through an empty set of routines that everyone goes through for no apparent reason. Our purpose in this chapter is to introduce the general subject of effectiveness in working with boards and to explore the legal, political, and organizational context for the system of board governance in effect throughout the corporate world, including nonprofit corporations. The guiding insight of this chapter is the view that the unique function of governing boards in social services is in mobilizing authority and managing the legitimacy of the social service institution.

Working with boards is one of the topics that ties social administration clearly and directly to the mainstreams of social work theory and practice (in this case, group work). It is well to keep in mind throughout that governing, advisory, and regulatory boards and committees are all groups of people. Many of the things that are taught about groups and particularly about task groups in other contexts within the social work curriculum can be brought to bear on this topic as well. Rather than rehashing material that may already be familiar here, we concentrate in this chapter primarily on the value-added dimensions. We focus on those aspects of group work with boards and administrative committees in social administration that are not ordinarily part of the regular treatment of groups. Please keep in mind that what works well with other groups can usually also be applied successfully to boards and administrative committees with a little thought and careful selection.

THE POLITICAL DOCTRINE OF FREE ASSOCIATION

The central idea of board governance is that a group made up of some mixture of stakeholders collectively assumes responsibility for determining the overall vision, mission, policy, and strategy of a social agency and its programs. This notion is very deeply rooted in American political culture and is the key link in the relation between agency and community. In a particular agency, the board's role may involve establishing programs and policies, hiring some or all staff, seeking community support or funding, or delegating some or all of these tasks to paid or volunteer staff.

The first and foremost consideration in the political theory of board governance is the doctrine of *free* association, which means in practice that groups or associations are entitled to do pretty much what they choose to do, subject only to the restraints of public law. Although this particular freedom is stated in the First Amendment and has been in practice for most of American history, the Supreme Court did not recognize it explicitly as a right of association until 1958 in *NAACP* v. *Alabama*.

The doctrine of free association applies first and foremost to organizational purpose. It is completely legal to establish an association—let's call it the Jefferson Society—to study past and present political efforts to overthrow governments. Such a group only becomes an outlaw conspiracy when its purpose shifts to actually overthrowing the government by illegal means. If it attempts to do so politically by influencing elections, the group may be a political party or an interest group. There is no test of the feasibility or realism of the group's objectives implied in the doctrine of free association. Nor is there any legal expectation of minimal efficiency or effectiveness demanded of such groups. Thus, a society to colonize Jupiter has equally as much right to form and pursue that mission as any other group has to pursue another more practical, reasonable, or feasible plan. This is one of the things that seriously complicates the issue of nonprofit accountability, even for QUANGOs (quasi-nongovernmental organizations).

Whenever there are doubts or uncertainties raised by students in this area, they are almost always traceable to this doctrine of free association.

Law and practice, for example, do not dictate what to call a governing board or even that it must be called a board. Some religious groups choose to call the governing group "elders," and some fraternal organizations choose strange or esoteric names from Greek or Arabic for their officers. In the international context, the governing group may be called a directorate. Although the term took on vastly different connotations later, the original meaning of a "soviet" in early revolutionary Russia was that of a self-governing local group. It has sometimes been suggested that "director" is the appropriate term only for commercial boards and "trustee" is the appropriate designation of nonprofit boards.[1] However, many nonprofit board members are called "directors," and doing so is entirely appropriate.

As *NAACP* v. *Alabama* and subsequent cases have clearly demonstrated, the right of free association is at least as strong as many powers of state or federal governments. Thus, in the case of social agencies, governments have often had to settle for dictating standard management practices in social services by contract, given this right of free association. *If* your agency wants to be eligible for this grant, Medicaid waiver contract, or whatever, *then* you must follow our rules and have an annual financial audit, call your governing committee a "board," include broad representation from the entire community, and call your principal paid agent "executive director." Even the much-feared Internal Revenue Service is largely restricted to a limited role: If you claim tax-exempt status, you must file an exempt tax return (Form 990). Such enforcement of norms by contract should be carefully distinguished from attempts to establish universal requirements by government law or regulation.

In sum, inconsistencies and variety in labels, functions, lines of authority, and responsibility are generally permitted in this area and are usually explained or rationalized by the First Amendment freedom of association. The extraordinary variety to be found among agencies is explained in no small part by the tradition that these are self-governing entities fully capable of establishing and changing their own missions, constitutions, articles of incorporation, operating rules, bylaws, and policies. One of the central issues in this regard involves the relative roles of board and staff in governance:

> The conception of *administration* as "the execution of organizational policies" presented by Woodrow Wilson over 100 years ago [1887], continues to present our profession with a theoretical dilemma. To what extent do human services managers participate in the policy-development process of their agencies? In social work, for example, there are some who would argue that policy development is the province of planners, and the execution of the policies and plans developed by these planners would be the province of administrators. (Weiner, 1990, p. 237)

Such dilemmas and confusions are especially prevalent with regard to board governance issues and are clearly made more complex by the restrictions imposed by the doctrine of free association.

DEFINITIONS

In the context of social service administration, the term *board* usually refers to a group or panel of people who assemble on a regular, periodic basis to discuss an agenda of issues or concerns and to make authoritative decisions for an organization or program. In the most general terms, there are three types of social service boards, depending upon the outcome of those decisions:

1. *Advisory* boards whose deliberations are purely informative and that the administrators may treat with discretion
2. *Governing* boards whose decisions are binding and authoritative for a particular organization except where they conflict with public law
3. *Regulatory* boards such as state licensing authorities and other similar bodies whose primary focus is governing or regulating the affairs of other organizations

All in all, board-related terminology can be the source of great confusion for beginners. The terms for this type of organized activity can vary widely: board, committee, and commission are commonly used, as are trustees, directors, governors, and managers, with no clear or consistent meaning. Thus, for example, one should not conclude that an advisory committee in one setting and an advisory board in another necessarily have different functions. Nor should one assume that a board of trustees is always different from a board of directors or that any two organizations using the same titles will function in the same way. We know of one organization that has more than fifty executive directors because that title is used to refer to what in other contexts are often labeled project managers or directors.

One additional distinction that novices often find confusing is the nearly universal provision in state corporation laws mandating that the affairs of nonprofit and commercial corporations are to be *managed* by a board. Legally, the board is the management of such organizations, and it may delegate various management functions to paid employees who function as what the laws usually term their *agents*. This means that, as a matter of law, the management of nonprofit and commercial social services is first of all in the hands of the board. Executives and other paid staff have the status of paid agents authorized to act only by explicit delegations of board will and intent. Actual practices vary widely within the latitude permitted by the freedom of association. It is extremely common for the powerful chief executive officer of a large commercial corporation to maintain control by recommending friendly board members and getting rid of hostile ones, and much the same has been known to happen in nonprofit social service boards. However, there is no mistaking the clear intent of the law that it is the board, and not their agents on the staff, who are in charge and who bear ultimate responsibility for the affairs of the agency.

Another of the points that every social service administrator who works with boards must understand is that nonprofit law has very deep roots in voluntary association theory and practice. As a result, state laws that place responsibility for "managing the affairs of the corporation" squarely in the hands of the board are ultimately grounded in the freedom of association. Anyone who has ever belonged to a club, association, or membership group that did not have a paid executive should understand why and how this might be. In such cases, the officers typically *do* just that: manage the affairs of the organization.

In this legal model, executives and other administrators, managers, supervisors, and staff have no independent legal status, and no distinctions are made between executives, middle management, and line workers. They are all recognized as paid *agents* of the corporation serving at the will and pleasure of the board. The extent to which this legal ideal actually describes the real performance of particular agencies, of course, varies widely. However, the nonprofit social service manager does well to remember that if any legal action ever arises, lawyers and the courts will interpret events and the facts through the peculiar lens of this model of board as management and staff as their agents. This has very clear implications for those serving on boards as well as for staff in agencies.

It is the board that is ultimately responsible for everything that goes on in an agency. Thus, the prudent executive or staff person will always make sure that board members are appropriately aware of and supportive of the activities of staff and that where necessary, the awareness and support will be tangible in the form of written resolutions, motions, or records adopted by the board. For an executive to do otherwise is to risk unnecessary legal exposure.

TYPES OF BOARDS

One of the most influential management perspectives on power and management was James Burnham's (1935/1972) influential argument that a transfer of power began occurring in the 1930s away from the capitalist/ plutocrats of the Robber Baron age to managers in business and government. Something akin to this shift may also have occurred in nonprofit social agencies since the 1960s as the economic circumstances of grants encouraged a shift of power away from board members and toward managers. Indeed, one of the most interesting characteristics of the QUANGOs discussed in chapter 3 is how many of them are characterized by a weak board/strong executive pattern. If there were no other case to be made for the model of social administrator as institution builder laid out in this work, the frequency of the strong executive alone would make such a case. There seems little question that contemporary social administrators often have wide latitude to pursue their own agendas. What is less clear is how, in the absence of legitimation by a board, their personal agendas will be made to coincide with the interests of the community. Also, one should not forget that in almost all instances boards of directors retain the legal power to hire and fire executives. Thus, should the executive's latitude exceed that viewed as appropriate by the board, the executive may find herself without a position.

In reality, the relation between boards and executives is a complex political system operating along a number of familiar dimensions. Kramer (1985) offered a political economy model of the organizational behavior of board members and executives in which the two were compared on six attributes: status, norms, roles, responsibility, authority, and power. Also affecting the decisional outcomes of their interaction, he said, are the nature of the organization, the situation, and the issue.

Governing Boards

The essential role of governing boards is to make policy, establish rules, and assume responsibility for the overall direction and activity of an organization. Governing boards generally govern in any of three ways. In newer and smaller agencies as well as those with strong traditions of democratic governance or high levels of commitment from board volunteers, board members may take a very active role in governance of the agency. One may find them initiating proposals for new programs, engaging in planning and evaluation tasks of various kinds, and generally involving themselves in the day-to-day business of the agency. In such cases, it is often very difficult to draw a clear-cut line between the governance activities of the board and agency operations or between the board of directors and the executive staff. Indeed, in some such cases that we are aware of, executive directors and other senior staff members who were involved along with other board members in creating the agency are actually voting members of the board. There is nothing inherently wrong with this pattern if it is actually working. However, it does often exact a high price from the executive director who is often caught mediating between staff and board members.

The second and more common pattern is for the board to concentrate on governance and leave the day-to-day operations of the agency to the executive and staff. In such cases, it is likely that this results in three important subtypes. In one type, the executive director is responsible for staffing the board, including such activities as preparing the agenda, copying and distributing reports, arranging for place and time, and all the myriad other details that go into a board meeting. In the second type, the executive director and the president of the board may work jointly to handle meeting preparation. In the third type, the executive director may still be responsible for ensuring that the details are taken care of, but preparation of the agenda and other substantive matters may be in the hands of an executive committee who are usually the officers of the board.

It is fairly common in the commercial world for members of corporate boards to be compensated for their service, sometimes very handsomely, to the tune of thousands of dollars per meeting. Such compensation is quite rare among social service boards, and there is some reason to believe that compensation of public or nonprofit board members may be illegal in many states. What is clear is that, in the case of public and nonprofit social services, compensation of board members for their legitimate expenses such as mileage, meals, or reimbursement for phone calls or postage is usually appropriate provided funds are available for the purpose. Any additional compensation to public or nonprofit trustees that smacks in any way of profits, dividends, or other such distributions is highly inappropriate and often plainly illegal. Thus, to pay board members a stipend as a percentage of funds they raised, for example, would be clearly illegal in most states. It is often extremely difficult to determine whether or not a particular payment to trustees is legitimate. On the question of whether a particular payment to a board member, beyond minimal expenses, is legal under particular circumstances, it is always best to seek advice of legal counsel.

One of the problems every social administrator faces in working with governing boards is how to best present information to the board in a way that will be understandable and lead to a decision. Clifton and Dahms (1980, p. 127) offered an outline of what they call issue action papers as an idealized way to present information on any issue to a board:

1. A statement of a problem dealing with situations, not people
2. A statement of the issue(s), if the problem is multifaceted and cannot be clarified in a simple problem statement, stated as a question or set of questions
3. An explanation of why the problem requires board action
4. A list of current relevant policies
5. Possible alternatives

6. The implications of the stated alternatives

7. The possible consequences of inaction

Use of this approach would likely be of benefit to a board regardless of the approach to governance that they have adopted. Boards may carefully assess each decision they make, develop an elaborate system of committees to consider and recommend actions, or merely rubber stamp any recommendation made by the staff. However they handle their responsibilities, under the law the board will retain responsibility for managing the affairs of the corporation.

Advisory Boards

In several earlier chapters, we noted the importance of communities and constituencies to the development and welfare of social service institutions. One of the most common forms for formal recognition of the importance of such stakeholders is through the creation of nongoverning advisory boards or panels. Advisory boards may exist even in organizations that have governing boards as a means of providing more stakeholder involvement in the organization. People may serve on such groups ex officio because of the office they hold, because of their importance to the community, because of particular expertise such as accounting or fund-raising that they have to offer, or for a variety of other reasons. The main point is that, as the title suggests, advisory boards are composed of people whose advice will be useful, helpful, or contribute to the overall improved functioning of the social service agency.

One of the points that can be difficult for students without substantial professional experience to grasp is the subtle, informal decision-making role played by advisory groups in both political and professional contexts. That role is perhaps best characterized as sampling or establishing a *climate of opinion* within which agency missions, strategies, and decisions can be successfully established. It may also involve the deliberate and strategic uses of influence as that notion was presented in chapter 17. For example, where a predominantly white, middle class, urban professional group is attempting to work with minority, lower class, rural, or other underclass neighborhoods or groups, such advisory bodies may be an absolute necessity. Without access to such indigenous advice, the professional group in the social agency may be so genuinely clueless that they are not even aware of the degree to which they are not aware of how their efforts are understood or, more likely, not understood by those around them. There is a large and extensive literature in social work built up over the past fifty years dealing with aspects of this issue, and it is not necessary for us to replay or summarize it here. To follow up the climate analogy, failure of professionals to seek advice in these circumstances is like sitting in an air-conditioned recreational vehicle in the middle of a desert contemplating how cool and comfortable the world is.

The social administrator working with advisory groups should not mistake the role of such groups as characterized by only one-directional advice from the community to the agency leadership, however. It is appropriate and important that there be genuine interaction and a sharing of perspectives that flows both ways. It is as appropriate for the executive to influence the advisory board and its representations to the community that it represents as it is for the advisory board to influence the executive.

Regulatory

We have included a third category of boards—regulatory boards—along with governing and advisory boards because of the growing importance of accreditation, licensure, and certification in the social work profession and social agencies. In many respects, regulatory boards resemble other governing boards. They differ from governing boards, however, in that they are concerned with governance issues across organizations.

In social work education, for example, the Council on Social Work Education is the accrediting body of all undergraduate and graduate social work programs. The council itself has a governing board that manages its affairs as an organization, establishing budgets, setting dues, operating the annual program meeting, and so on. The accreditation activities, however, are the primary domain of a separate and semi-independent body, the Commission on Accreditation, which establishes standards, accredits programs, and also accredits the site visitors who visit and investigate programs on site. The council's concern is the quality of social work education. Such education is offered by other organizations rather than by the council itself.

Of increasing importance are state licensure boards, which are regulatory in nature. In social work, those boards typically identify the qualifications that one must have to legally call oneself a social worker. The members of these boards are often appointed to their roles by a state's governor or some other public official.

BOARD FUNCTIONS

Discussions of nonprofit and public boards tend to center on the discussion of at least five major roles: governance, leadership, policymaking, legitimation, and fund-raising. Nancy Axelrod (1994) elaborated on those basic five functions and identified nine basic responsibilities of nonprofit boards:

1. To determine the organization's mission and purpose
2. To select and support the chief executive
3. To review executive performance
4. To plan for the future
5. To approve and monitor the organization's programs and services
6. To provide sound financial management
7. To enlist financial resources
8. To advance the organization's public image
9. To strengthen its own effectiveness as a board

Since each of Axelrod's responsibilities can be subsumed under one of the major roles, the discussion below focuses on the five major roles.

Governance

There has been an ongoing debate for some time now over the function of social agency governing boards in the nonprofit or voluntary sector.[2] On one side, we have had advocates of an updated version of the traditional perspective outlined in chapter 3 and discussed in chapter 12 on accountability. From this view, which draws its strength from classic American civic republicanism, an active role of board members in governance is seen as an expression of democracy and community. On the other hand, a traditional elitist posture probably is traceable to pre-Jacksonian Federalists such as John Adams but currently is closely tied to models of professionalism. That view expresses great concern for and suspicion of board autonomy and is generally supportive of administrators having the upper hand.

One of the most widespread and influential models of board governance from the first position is John Carver's (n.d., 1990; Carver & Carver, 1997; Oliver, 1999) model of board governance in which the board is given the major role in policymaking for an agency or organization but leaves the details of implementation and operations to the administrator. An equally eloquent and forceful statement of the second position was recently set forth by Steven R. Block (1998). Block's position rests directly on three key assumptions. First, board members should not be expected to know how to operationalize the concept of board effectiveness. Second, an effective board of directors is an outgrowth of an executive director's leadership and ability to skillfully and sensitively facilitate each board member's involvement to use their strengths, skills, and community connections for the purpose of achieving mutually agreed upon organizational objectives. Third, board effectiveness results directly from the skillful use of management tools to improve board commitment and participation. In Block's view, then, the critical variable in effective board activity is the skill and initiative exercised by the managers who nominally report to the board but who actually control it.

Like Block, our principal concern in this chapter is not with consideration of board issues from the vantage point of board members but from the vantage point of executives charged with working with boards of various types. However, our comments are premised on the desirability of professional social administrators taking board governance seriously and working to develop and enhance the ability of boards to carry out their assigned responsibilities.

One of the things that the polarity of the Carver and Block perspectives does is focus attention on the question of board effectiveness or competency. Tom Holland and Douglas Jackson (1998) identified six dimensions of board competency that seemed to capture the elements essential to effective governance:

1. *Contextual.* The board understands and takes into account the culture, values, mission, and norms of the organization it governs.
2. *Educational.* The board takes the necessary steps to ensure that members are well informed about the organization, the professions working there, and the board's own roles, responsibilities, and performance.
3. *Interpersonal.* The board nurtures the development of its members as a group, attends to the board's collective welfare, and fosters a sense of cohesiveness and teamwork.
4. *Analytical.* The board recognizes complexities and subtleties in the issues it faces, and it draws upon multiple perspectives to dissect complex problems and to synthesize appropriate responsibilities.
5. *Political.* The board promotes, develops, and maintains healthy two-way communications and positive relationships with key constituencies.
6. *Strategic.* The board helps envision and shape institutional direction and helps ensure a strategic approach to the organization's future.

Leadership

Board membership is generally recognized as a formal position of leadership in most organizations. Such formal leadership is an interesting example of an "until further notice" phenomenon: others will usually give board members the benefit of the doubt, considering them to be leaders of the organization unless and until they prove themselves unworthy of this designation.

In the modern social agency, the executive is often well placed strategically to impact the leadership of her board in a number of ways both directly and indirectly. The executive director who signals to everyone involved by her actions that the board isn't really very important and her views are the ones that really matter may get a temporary rush or heady sense of power from this. However, in the process she may also be cutting off an important resource that can be of great help to her in carrying the load of managing.

Often, those invited to serve on a board have established themselves as leaders in other arenas. The fact that they are recognized as leaders can produce some conflicts of ego and direction among board members. It can be difficult, for example, for the high-powered business executive who is used to leading in her business and in other settings to take a back seat to the board president and other board officers or long-term board members. Often special assignments on the board can be found to satisfy the various needs of board members to exercise their leadership abilities.

Problems can also occur when long-term board members object to any new directions or changed approaches on the grounds that the direction or approach does not represent the way things have been done in the past. Leadership can sometimes be devoted to maintaining the status quo rather than preparing to meet new challenges. All boards are well served by bylaws or other rules that limit the number of terms that someone may serve on the board before being eligible for reappointment. Although some strong and positive leadership may be lost as a result of such a rule, the organization as a whole generally benefits from such a policy.

Policymaking

Clifton and Dahms (1980, p. 128) included a list of thirteen specific areas in which governing boards can initiate policy:

1. Bylaws of the organization
2. Personnel policies (salaries, fringe benefits, job descriptions)
3. Administrative policies
4. Budget and finance (fund-raising, planning for funds, grant terminations)
5. Program priorities
6. Program goals and objectives
7. Board goals and objectives
8. Needs assessment
9. Research and evaluation (annual reports, program results, program adjustments)
10. Community relations, public relations, and education

11. General operations
12. Coordination of services
13. Evaluation of the executive director

This list should be seen as a guide only. The areas in which a board can establish policy are only limited by the laws of the state in which the board is incorporated, the articles of incorporation of the board, and any bylaws or similarly binding documents adopted by the board or the membership of the organization. The list is illustrative of areas in which a board may establish policies but is not intended to suggest that these are the only areas in which a board may act.

Legitimation

As noted in previous chapters, legitimization and institution building must be ever-present concerns for the social service manager. Because of the legal doctrine of board governance introduced above, savvy social service administrators concerned with enhancing the authority and legitimacy of their actions generally find it appropriate to adopt a permanent stance as *serving* the board in the same sense, perhaps, that legislators and city counselors are public servants.

This stance involves several related actions and attitudes:

1. Presenting and defending agency policy as board action and not an administrative invention
2. Not acting to undercut or undermine the legitimacy of board action, for example, with "nods and winks" to outsiders in order to indicate that the board didn't really come up with this on its own
3. Providing the board with the information that it needs to take action rather than withholding certain types of information from it

No single role is probably more worthy of attention in the practice of social administration than the importance of governing and advisory boards in legitimizing administrative actions. One of the important and easily neglected roles of both advisory and governing boards is that of ratification of actions already taken or contemplated by professional staff. Novice social administrators often ask, "Do I have to take this to the board?" as if to do so were a punishment somewhat akin to staying after school or paying a parking ticket. In a properly functioning agency-board relationship, this question cannot be answered except by considering two additional questions: Is it legally necessary or prudent to do so? and Is there something to be gained by doing so? If the answer to the first question is yes, or even maybe, it's ordinarily a good idea to raise it with the board or at least discuss it with the chairperson. In most cases, matters of legal import such as purchases of property, offers and acceptances of major contracts, potentially litigious issues, and so on should be handled by formal resolution or written motion; at the very least, care should be taken to ensure that any actions taken are reflected in the minutes of the meeting.

What busy administrators sometimes have trouble accepting is the importance of the second question. Even where it is not legally necessary for the board to approve an action, decision, strategy or policy, savvy administrators may seek board advice and approval because of the additional legitimacy that board consideration can add. This dimension, which we call *ratification,* can be a very powerful tool when properly used. In those cases where executive or professional actions may be controversial or where staff, clients, or other agencies affected by an action may be reluctant to accept it, it can be very persuasive to be able to make them aware that this isn't just the executive's idea alone. Being able to say, "I talked this matter over with members of the executive committee of our board and they thought it was a good idea," can at times be very persuasive to others. And with a little bit of practice, such actions can usually be introduced to the board in a manner satisfactory to everyone. Even executives jealously guarding their power or worried about giving away too much authority to the board can usually preface the introduction of such items with statements such as, "This next item doesn't require board action, but I wanted to make you aware of it and get your thoughts on it anyway." Only rarely will a board respond, "Oh yes, this does require our formal action, and here's how we order you to handle this." In most cases, board members, like most people, will be flattered that they were asked for their advice and will be impressed with the good judgment of the person doing so.

Fund-Raising

One major consideration is the role the board is destined to play in fundraising. An elite board, which has direct access to a sizable number of people of wealth, need not be very large, but a middle-class board that is going to engage in extensive fund-raising probably can never have too many members, although a smaller executive committee of key members may be essential if it appears to be too large.

In some communities, those who may be expected to contribute financially to agencies on whose boards they serve are often remarkably straightforward about that expectation. Shelby White (1999), a volunteer and board member in New York City, for example, indicates that when she is asked to join a board she likes to be told what is expected of her financially. She reports some of the annual financial expectations of board members with various organizations at the end of the 1990s. They range from $5,000 per year for the Omaha Symphony to $100,000 for New York City's Lenox Hill Hospital. She describes joining a board as being like a mating game and indicates she will often only join the board of an agency where she's volunteered and so has some awareness of the agency and what it does.

Most social agencies are not in the fundraising league that White is describing and may not have the same kinds of expectations (particularly financial) that she describes. However, in many agencies that expectation gets translated as board members being expected to sell a certain number of raffle tickets (called "give or get") or in other ways engage in activities that help the agency raise funds. Describing those expectations to a potential board member when that person is asked to join the board will help ensure success in the mating rituals that make up board recruitment.

In the age of grants, many community social service boards became extremely inactive with regard to fund-raising. Today, however, with national voluntary contributions increasing annually such agencies are missing opportunities to add to their budgets and thus further extend their services.

STRUCTURAL ISSUES: COMPOSITION/MEMBERSHIP

Another major consideration in both advisory and governing boards is composition of the board or the types of members to seek out, recruit, and encourage. In the case of strong boards of either type, of course, this will not be up to the administration. Board members themselves will determine whom they will ask to join them. In recent years, however, many social service boards have been relatively weak, and issues such as board recruitment are left entirely to agency executives.

Another important issue is the age of board members. Peter Drucker (1992) says

> All my life I've been opposed to age limits. But when it comes to boards, I have reluctantly come around to the idea that it is best to limit membership to two terms of, say, three years each. After that you go off the board. Three years later you may come back again. But at age seventy-two or so you go off and stay off the board. (p. 159)

Although the idea that board members may lose their effectiveness is not entirely without merit, the notion that one can identify a chronological age at which this occurs should be approached with great caution.

One of the most fundamental concerns in board composition is the issue of what to do about agency critics and opponents. Obviously, it is much easier to make a place for such voices in an advisory group rather than on the governing board. However, the legitimacy of the agency may be increased if at least a few of its critics are asked to serve on the board so that their voices may be heard. If it is feared that their presence on the board may be too disruptive, such critics could be asked to serve on a board committee as well as on an advisory group.

STRUCTURAL ISSUES: RECRUITMENT AND SELECTION

Most organizations tend to recruit and select board members with prior experience from among those already known or active in the organization. According to the Hartogs–Weber (1974) study of board members, two-thirds (66 percent) had prior experience on another board before joining the board on which they served at the time of the study. They found also that the vast majority (83 percent) of board members were recruited to serve, about one-third (34 percent) expressed a strong prior interest in the organization, and nearly half (44 percent) had at least moderate prior interest (p. 21).

It is easy to forget that joining a board is a complex process of relationship formation. Even as a board is selecting a new member, that member is also selecting a new organization to associate with. Hartogs and Weber reported that prospective board members engaged in a variety of activities prior to joining a board. About half (51 percent) visited the organization, determined the time and place of meetings (48 percent), met with the executive (48 percent), talked with the president (46 percent), identified other board members (36 percent), made private inquiries about the organization (35 percent), or determined the financial status of the organization (18 percent) (Hartogs & Weber, 1974, p. 23). This, when combined with the findings that high proportions had prior knowledge of the organization and prior experience as board members, is strongly suggestive of the conclusion that most board members are fairly well informed about the boards they are joining. It also suggests that when they are not informed that they take steps to become better informed. Before accepting board service, a very high proportion (83 percent) of prospective board members also determined whether regular attendance was an obligation of board members, three-fourths (76 percent) determined whether they would be expected to serve on committees, two-thirds (67 percent) asked about specific time commitments and/or asked about expectations to engage in fund-raising (62 percent) or whether they would be expected to make a financial contribution (52 percent) (p. 25).

The vast majority (81 percent) of new board members reported that they accepted board service because of a strong interest in community service.

More than a third (37 percent) reported prior positive experience with the organization's services, and nearly half (42 percent) had had some prior association with the organization, including financial contributions, volunteering, or serving on committees (Hartogs & Weber, 1974, p. 27).

STRUCTURAL ISSUES: SIZE

One of the principal questions involving boards is the matter of size. There may be a relationship between board size and the availability of volunteers for board service. At any rate, the Hartogs–Weber (1974, p. 4) study found that the average size of boards in the New York metropolitan region was thirty-four members. In our experience, this is significantly larger (in fact, twice as large) as boards typically found in small cities and rural areas, which tend to range more in the vicinity of twelve to eighteen members.

In many instances, the size of advisory boards and panels will be entirely up to the administrative group receiving the advice. In other instances, the size of the advisory body will be regulated by the policy or rule creating the advisory body. Thus, for example, aging agencies that make extensive use of advisory groups generally follow the "rule of forty-five." That is, advisory panels may have up to forty-five members.

The major consideration in determining the appropriate size of advisory groups is probably the type of advice the group can offer. Expert panels where advice is sought on the basis of the expertise of the panelists are generally small. A panel of forty-five lawyers, for example, aside from being entirely unaffordable, would never be workable because the likelihood that forty-five lawyers could agree on anything is almost nil. By contrast, if what is sought is what is sometimes called "the pulse of the people" or public opinion, the problem is very similar to public opinion survey. The theory of large numbers and the binomial theorem suggest that both size and random selection are important in such instances.

To some extent, the size of governing boards is a matter of fashion. Early in the twentieth century, smaller boards composed of members of community elites were commonly used and recommended. After World War II, when representativeness became a greater consideration, board size increased accordingly. In many respects, the profile of the Board of Directors of the Hull House Association is an indicator of these trends. It may also be a measure of the perceived power and authority of the board. In the forty years from its creation in 1895 to Jane Addams's death in 1935, for example, the Hull House board was never larger than seven people. In the following two decades, the Hull House board increased to eighteen, then twenty-four, then forty-two.

KEY BOARD ROLES

Discussions of nonprofit and social agency boards routinely include considerations of the role of the board in the agency as an organization and institution, but there has been very little consideration of the roles of individual members within the board as a group. Certainly, one should expect to see officers such as the president, vice president, secretary, and treasurer and others involved in official or ex officio leadership roles within the board by virtue of their elected or appointed positions.

In most circumstances, new board members will not begin as president. Instead, there will be a definite progression from less demanding positions to positions of increasing responsibility. Being a committee member before becoming committee chair is one such customary progression, and being vice president or serving in some other office before becoming president of the board is another customary practice. Indeed, some organizations explicitly provide for multiyear presidencies, with the expectation that the first year will be an orientation and training period designated by labels such as "president-elect." Organizations of volunteers without staff support and membership organizations sometimes also have co-presidencies or other co-officers in which two people share a board office and divide the workload between them. This works well for co-treasurers, for example, when one person is responsible for collecting and depositing dues and another is responsible for paying bills. Perhaps the longest standing example of sharing of positions is the use of separate corresponding and recording secretaries in many membership organizations.

Informal group roles that often emerge in actual board meetings may include the official or self-appointed *historian* who is usually a long-term board member whose first contribution to any discussion is likely to be, "I remember when we faced this same situation a number of years ago." Although it is fairly common in many other types of boards, an official board role of historian is fairly rare among social service boards.

Also to be found in many organizations is the *conserver*, whose primary interest is usually in maintaining the status quo or in keeping things as they "always" have been. This role is not to be confused with the political conservative whose ideological agenda may involve a great deal of change of the way things have been. Political conservatives on social service boards sometimes, in fact, function as *zealots* or as enthusiastic or even fanatical advocates of particular ideas or causes. The notion that social services should be operated in a more business-like manner, for example, is sometimes sound advice and in other cases the rallying cry of board zealots.

Another board role adopted at various times by various board members is that of the staff or client *advocate*. This is a board member who strives to measure or test all issues and topics discussed in terms of their implications for staff or clients. A particular example of this role that also sometimes arises is the board member who functions as the *patron* or personal protector of the director or some other particular staff person. Professional school faculty who serve on the board of an agency directed by a former student are often suspected of and sometimes even succumb to this role. It is usually a good idea to routinely screen board candidates for their preexisting relations with other board members and staff for this reason. It isn't necessary or even possible in rural, small town, or other cases that every board member begin with complete anonymity and with a completely clean slate. But it is usually a good idea to find out about such prior relationships so that they can be taken into account in board functioning, however.

One could go on identifying many other roles found in the relations of board members. Sometimes one will see the *cheerleader*, for instance, who takes it upon herself to increase morale, enthusiasm, or "team spirit" on the board. Or, the *big brother* (not of the Orwellian kind) may take personal responsibility for seeing that new board members get properly oriented. Two other role players sometimes found on boards, masquerading as big brothers, are signs of trouble for the executive who has to work with them. First, there are the *faction leader*s who, in sharply divided boards, may be seeking out new board members primarily to recruit them to their particular faction. Even more problematic but less frequently seen is the sexual *predator*. This is the (usually male) board member who routinely "hits on" new board or staff members, using his official position on the board to improve his social life.

Division of Labor of Board Members

Part of the legacy of social agency boards and committees is the notion that such bodies should be *self-constituted*. That means that once the members of the board or committee are established they should be free to go about their deliberations in any manner they find acceptable. Thus, for example, some board presidents may insist upon conducting business using formal parliamentary procedure from *Robert's Rules of Order*, whereas other presidents may be equally insistent upon operating purely by unstructured discussion and consensus. In the latter case, the executive director and perhaps the secretary need to be particularly mindful that decisions and actions with possible legal ramifications are properly recorded in the minutes.

Perhaps the biggest worry in this area for social administrators working with boards is the inevitable concerns that will arise about imbalances in workload among board members. This can be an area where an excess of social work clinical skills may be called for. For example, there may be a situation in which one or more board members are each convinced that they are carrying the entire burden of responsibility while everyone else on the board is shirking their responsibilities and letting the burden fall upon them. For some people such martyrdom seems to come easily and periodic venting sessions to allow them to express their frustrations may be all that is necessary to keep them relatively happy and working hard for the cause.

In other cases, the problem can be a much more complex one that, if not dealt with, can lead toward the development of factions within the board and other negative effects. This can be particularly traumatic in cases where two or more board members are convinced that they alone are contributing. In one case we know of, the board was almost equally divided three ways. One faction was supportive of a member who felt that her efforts in fund-raising for the organization were misunderstood and unappreciated. Another faction downplayed the role of fund-raising and emphasized the service mission of the organization. Finally, there was a group of nonaligned members whose primary interest was in not provoking either faction. The division in this case was not over ideology or issues but merely over who was making the greater contribution to the agency's mission. To the best of our knowledge, the division is still going on.

Interactions with Executive and Staff

The alignment between the executive and the board as the two key leadership elements in social agencies is a perennially important consideration (Bailey & Grochau, 1993). Following the business model of management does little to resolve the matter and may, in fact, complicate it. Strategic theorists such as Kenneth R. Andrews, for example, see business chief executive officers as "architects of organizational purpose" in ways that are clearly impossible for most social service executives (Moore, 1992, p. 8). In theory, at least, it is the board and not the executive who should establish the goals and mission of the organization and lay down its principal strategies, although this is usually done with input and advice from the executive.

Nonetheless, it is useful to think of the management of social agencies in terms of a partnership or collaboration between board and professional staff. Even if there are personality conflicts between various board members and members of the staff, keeping everyone focused on the mission of the agency and the ways in which each contributes to that mission can sometimes overcome the conflict.

LEGAL ISSUES

There are a host of legal issues, some of them relatively straightforward and others relatively arcane, that can arise in the context of board discussions. However, one of the issues that is a nearly universal legal concern but that does not often arise in social work discussions is the matter of "self-dealing" by trustees. The legal notion of self-dealing refers to practices by which a board member acts in ways that serve or appear to serve their own financial interests.

Both the Internal Revenue Service, which controls nonprofit agencies' tax-exempt status, and many state attorneys general have taken a serious interest in this issue. Thus, a grocer serving on the board of a women's shelter who is also the supplier of groceries for the shelter may be guilty of self-dealing. Usually, with ordinary commercial services such as banking, insurance, or accounting, this issue is relatively straightforward, and bankers, accountants, lawyers, and others are familiar enough with the law and conventional practice to avoid the practice.

Unfortunately, some of the most common occurrences of potential self-dealing today arise when social service professionals serve on boards, and such issues are often not even recognized by those involved. The staff member of another agency that receives referrals from a social agency while serving on the agency's board, for example, might be accused of self-dealing at some point. If both agencies are nonprofit or public agencies, probably the strongest accusation that could be mounted would be a charge of unfair competition from another competitor. However, if the board member were a professional engaged in private practice and received referrals from an agency while serving on its board, the charge would be much more serious. It does, indeed, appear in that case that the professional may be serving on the board as a way of generating referrals and income for his or her own practice. This is the very essence of self-dealing, and such cases should be avoided.

INITIATING A BOARD-DEVELOPMENT STRATEGY

A continuing concern on the part of most people who write about boards is about their effectiveness, and one of the responses to this challenge has been an ongoing need for board development activities. A 1989 study of Canadian nonprofit executives by Brudney and Murray (1993) for example, found that three quarters of them reported undertaking some intentional efforts to improve board performance and that from their perspective, such efforts proved worthwhile.

Board development should be seen as much more than simply a limited training program to teach board members how to behave in meetings. For one thing, any major changes in board composition, roles, or activities should not be undertaken without an underlying strategy, including at least an outline of definite goals to which the changes are directed. The first step in any board development strategy is assessment of the current situation. Such an examination should take account of the leadership, environment, and needs of the program.

Most board development strategies will do well to heed the principle of differential leadership. Keep in mind that different agencies need different leaders at different points in their history. In the early years, leaders with a strong, lively imagination or a high tolerance for ambiguity may be needed. Later on, some of these people may become bored with the lack of challenges and just stir up trouble, whereas others who are more comfortable with the concerns of ordinary day-to-day operations may come into their own. At other stages, board members with strong financial sense, an ability to recruit volunteers, high levels of tact and diplomacy, or some other particular set of traits may be needed. Very few people have all of the good qualities necessary. The differential demands of leadership are one of the principal factors that lead to the necessity of board turnover.

Changing environmental circumstances and the particular needs of the program are also important to consider. Thus, an agency in transition from a largely grant-funded environment to a contract environment and then to a managed care environment, which many social agencies have been seen in the past fifteen years, will almost certainly find that different kinds of board members and different ranges of skills among board members are called for in these different environments.

Ideally, board members themselves will see and understand the need for this. If not, the executive staff may find themselves in the rather delicate position of having to guide and direct such transitions. One of the principal effects of both the age of grants and the transition toward contracts in the Nixon–Carter–Reagan years was to shift the board strategies of many agencies. The age of grants meant that there was less emphasis on board members as leaders and definers of agency mission. Boards frequently were called upon merely to ratify already completed agreements and to play almost no role in fund-raising. The devolution to local communities that began in earnest in the Reagan years meant more attention to and need for community influentials to serve on social service boards as well as much greater reliance upon fund-raising by the board.

Likewise, at times the agency's program may need to evolve in entirely new directions. Just as you would hire new professional staff to facilitate such an evolution, it may also be necessary to consider new types of board members. Perhaps the clearest examples of this involve efforts to incorporate concerns of social justice in social services. A board insisting upon greater diversity in its client groups and among its employees should hardly expect that its initiatives would remain strongly legitimate if the board itself is composed entirely of middle-aged white males from the business community. Some communities have board recruitment fairs to help diversify their boards through outreach.

Board development on this scale takes time as well as careful thought and planning. In the best of circumstances, major board development activities would be undertaken jointly by the executive director or group and key leaders such as an executive committee from the board. The generous use of group techniques, total quality management, process reengineering, strategic planning, and other tools and techniques may also prove helpful. The planners should try to move carefully and deliberately without too much reversing of direction.

A board training program should first seek to socialize new board members to their responsibilities. Handbooks and orientation sessions can be used for this purpose. All board members should be aware of their rights and prerogatives as board members as well as their obligations and potential liabilities. At the very least, board members should be informed about the existence of personnel and other policy manuals and how they can gain access to these materials if they wish to examine them and whether they are protected by board insurance. The Hartogs–Weber study found that two-thirds or more of new board members received lists of other board members, copies of annual reports, statements of purposes, and program descriptions of the organization. However, slightly less than half received descriptions of board members' responsibilities (Hartogs & Weber, 1974, p. 29).

Socialization of new board members involves more than simply information sharing, however. The Hartogs–Weber study (1974, p. 31) found that in their first month of board membership, half of all new board members met with the executive director or toured the organization, and three-fourths of all new board members were asked to accept a committee assignment.

CONCLUSION

Though the existence of the social agency board is probably a result of legal requirements, its function and potential helpfulness extends far beyond those narrow legal provisions. Boards may be of one of three types. Regardless of the type, however, they play an important role in the governance, leadership, policymaking, legitimation, and fund-raising support of the organization.

Because boards are composed of people, the social administrator can face some issues of personalities and roles in dealing with board members. However, the benefits that can be gained from having access to the accumulated experience and wisdom represented by board members makes dealing with those issues a worthwhile activity.

Afterword

$\mathbf{A}$t the very beginning of this work, we noted that a full understanding of social administration was the work of a lifetime. In the previous twenty-seven chapters, we introduced the reader to most of the key topics important to the practice of social administration today. A great deal more might be added, but now it is up to students and their instructors to add it.

There are no readily available answers to the paradox that social administration poses for the social work curriculum today. Social administration is, as we said at the very beginning, the highest and most encompassing form of contemporary social work practice. Yet, in most social work curricula, coursework in this area is shoehorned into one or at most two or three courses. As a result, most of what practicing social administrators know about management, leadership, decision making, and institution building they must learn on their own or on the job.

This text is not intended to teach everything there is to know about social administration or everything one needs to know in order to practice it. No one book can do that. What we have tried to do throughout is introduce students to the range of topics and issues of greatest concern in the contemporary practice of social administration.

Some students (and some faculty) may be distressed that we have not included more "how to do it" material in this book. Certainly there is an abundance of exercises, games, and "how to do it" manuals on the market. Our reason for not including more of this material is simply that, in its fundamentals, social administration is not about specialized methods, memorized techniques, and other such things that are readily conveyed as "how to do it" exercises. As each class of case and group workers who get promoted into managerial positions quickly learns, real administration is fundamentally about the exercise of leadership, vision, moral certainty, good judgment, and a concern for building lasting and effective social service institutions. For social work professionals who have learned and understand this, mastering the assorted methods and techniques of management as they come along is a suitable subject for lifetime learning. For those who have not, no array of skills and techniques can ever turn them into effective administrators.

We've given you the basic map of the field. The rest is up to you.

How to Write a Memo

MEMORANDUM

To: The Reader

From: The Authors

Re: Writing memos

Date: Undated

One of the standard skills of administrative practice is the ability to write appropriate memoranda or, as they are known everywhere, memos. In this memo, we attempt to spell out some of the standard features of memoranda along with tips for writing good memos.

The term *memorandum* signifies a written record of something to be remembered or referred to for future action. Memoranda are generally recognizable by a number of stylistic features, which are demonstrated in this memo. For example, so that virtually no one will miss the point, true memos (including this one) frequently have the word *MEMORANDUM* centered in capital letters at the top. This is purely a secretarial school convention and by no means a universal practice. Much more universal is the appearance of the addressee (To), recipient (From), subject (Re), and date items in the left-hand margin, each followed by a colon. A fairly standard feature of memoranda that sets them apart from other forms of communication, including letters and reports, is the absence of paragraph indents.

One of the most universal features of the text of memos is an introductory or lead paragraph that tells the recipient the purpose of the memo. Memo introductory paragraphs also often incorporate a brief background statement or history of the events leading up to the memo. Thus, the following paragraph might have served as a substitute for the introductory paragraph above:

> The authors and publisher of this book agree that this book should contain a chapter on administrative communication that includes an example of a communication to the reader written in memorandum format rather than the more conventional trade-book prose of the rest of the book. This memo is that example.

This alternative heading would be most likely to be used in legal, conflict, or other situations where clarification of authorial intent is critical.

In some cases, where there are contested issues, the introductory paragraph may confront or embrace the issue directly, as in this alternative lead paragraph:

> Some of the readers of this book may be uncertain that there is any value to spelling out the details of how to write written memoranda. As authors of this book, we believe that there is value in such an approach, and we hope in this example to convince you, the reader, of our position.

Note: There is a paradox or perhaps irony associated with writing good memos that also frequently applies to administrative reports. Unlike book or article authorship, which is a relatively esoteric skill, limited to a relative few at any given time, authorship of memos is extremely widely distributed, and most people who write memos eventually come to believe they are pretty good at it. With that belief comes the further viewpoint that might be termed the *best practices illusion:* Because they are good at writing memos, they have discovered or developed the best way of writing them, and others should follow their good example. Many of the references to poor writing skills directed at student interns, new employees, and junior officials are, in our experience, the result of failure to comply with that best practice, not necessarily the result of actual poor writing skills.

In our case, of course, this is no illusion, and any memo practice that corresponds with ours is an example of good memo writing!

Sample Job Description

POSITION: CASE MANAGER

General description: The occupant of this position is responsible for managing cases involving elderly at-risk residents living at Lakeside Manor, with the goal of maintaining the greatest degree of independence possible for each elderly resident and avoiding nursing home placement.

Lakeside Manor is a church-affiliated nonprofit social welfare agency providing townhouse and apartment living for older people. Meal and housekeeping services are available to older residents. The goal of Lakeside Manor is to provide a safe environment that will facilitate the continued independence of its older residents.

DUTIES

Essential Tasks

40% Identify services needed by each resident that will help maintain his or her independence. This is to be accomplished by interviewing each resident privately in his or her unit at least once every three months. An assessment of that older person's needs and possible resources available to meet those needs is to be filed in the case record within one week of the interview.

15% Identify resources available in Lakeside Manor and the local community that might be used to meet the needs of older residents. To accomplish this, the case manager is expected to participate in the Social Services Forum and other organizations and programs that will provide information about local services. The occupant is also expected to meet with representatives of other agencies and organizations to learn more about their services.

15%   Arrange for older residents to receive services provided in the community. Assist the older person in enrolling as a client if appropriate. Arrange for transportation for the older resident as required.

12%   Create and maintain a resource database of local social services that may help meet the needs of residents. This database is to be available to other employees of Lakeside Manor for their use. The database is to be updated as new information is obtained. The accuracy of the content in the database is to be reviewed at least annually.

5%   Provide liaison with the family members of older residents as to the services that may be needed. Meet with family members when requested or as seems appropriate. Return phone calls from family members within twenty-four hours.

2%   Identify new programs or services that Lakeside Manor might offer to facilitate independence. Suggestions are to be shared with the executive director or at the weekly staff meeting.

2%   Suggest changes in existing programs and services at Lakeside Manor that might facilitate independent living. Suggestions are to be shared with the executive director or at the weekly staff meeting.

2%   Assist in providing holiday coverage at Lakeside Manor, when assigned on a rotating schedule.

3%   Other duties as assigned by supervisor or executive director.

Marginal tasks

4%   Drive the Lakeside Manor van to provide transportation services for residents when needed.

EDUCATIONAL AND SKILL REQUIREMENTS

- BSW from a CSWE-accredited educational program required. MSW preferred. Must be a certified social worker licensed to practice in the state. Previous experience working with older people and/or coursework dealing with social gerontology preferred. Previous case manager experience preferred.
- Must be capable of maintaining electronic case notes and database on Macintosh computers.

- Must provide own transportation to travel from Lakeside Manor to attend community meetings and visit local social service agencies. Chauffeur's license or willingness to obtain such a license desirable.

REPORTING RELATIONSHIPS

The position reports to the assistant director for resident services and through that position to the executive director. Case manager participates in a weekly staff meeting of all those reporting to the assistant director for resident services.

Typical Table of Contents for a Social Services Agency Personnel Manual

Introduction
  Organization philosophy and mission
  Major organizational goals and objectives
  Organizational programs or types of services

1. Employment
  Hiring authority
  Nondiscrimination and affirmative action policies and safeguards
      (includes safeguards as mandated by the Equal Employment
      Opportunity Commission, affirmative action, and the Americans
      with Disabilities Act)
  Types of employment (full-time, part-time, temporary, volunteer)
  Probationary period procedures
  Maintenance and access to personnel records

2. Working hours and conditions
  Work schedule and office hours
  Flexible time/job sharing
  Overtime or compensatory time
  Types of absence and reports

3. Salaries and wages
  Wages and salary structure and rationale
  Paydays

Deductions
Raises (merit and cost of living) guidelines and rationale
Compensation for work-related expenses
Employee access to current salary schedule

4. Employee benefits
Leaves of absences
    Vacations
    Holidays
    Sick days
    Personal days
    Family Leave Act leaves
    Maternity leave
    Paternity leave
    Unpaid leave of absence
    Other excused absences
Insurance
    Social Security
    Medical insurance
    Life insurance
    Disability insurance
    Unemployment insurance
    Workers' compensation
    Pension or retirement plans

5. Employee rights and responsibilities
Employee responsibilities
Employee rights

6. Performance and salary review
Procedures
Timing
Use of probation periods or suspension
Promotion policies and procedures

7. Staff development
Orientation of new employees
Planning process for in-service training and related activities
Educational programs and conferences

8. General policies and procedures
Outside employment
Office opening and closing
Telephone

Travel
Personal property

9. General office practices and procedures
Office coverage
Smoking
Use and care of equipment

10. Termination
Grounds of dismissal
Resignation
Retirement
Release
Reduction in force

Appendixes
Organizational chart
Salary ranges by position
Equal opportunity guidelines on sexual harassment
Conflict of interest policies
Personnel evaluation procedures and forms

Source: Adapted from Cox (1984) and Wolfe (1984).

Sample Advertisement
for Case Manager Position

Below are two sample advertisements for the case manager position. The first of these is the kind of ad that might be mailed to other social agencies or schools of social work. The second is the kind of ad that might appear in the local paper.

AD NO. 1

> **Case Manager**
> Lakeside Manor
>
> Lakeside Manor seeks a case manager to work with its older residents to enable them to maintain their independence. Lakeside Manor is a townhouse and apartment complex that is home to 140 residents living in 110 units and is affiliated with the United Methodist Church. Lakeside Manor's goal is to provide residents with a safe and secure environment that will facilitate their independence as long as possible. The case manager plays a critical role in linking Lakeside Manor's residents to the services that they need to maintain their independence.

Position duties

The case manager will assess the needs of residents and link residents with services that will meet those needs. The case manager will be responsible for identifying services in the community that may be needed by residents. He or she will advocate for new or modified services that Lakeside Manor might provide. The case manager will also provide liaison with the families of residents.

Qualifications

A BSW degree from a CSWE-accredited program and licensure as a social worker in West Virginia is required. Preferred qualifications include an MSW degree, previous experience in working with older people or coursework in social gerontology, and previous case management experience.

The starting salary for the position will be between $27,000 and $35,000, depending upon the qualifications of the applicant hired. Health insurance and a retirement plan are provided. Employees have twelve days of paid vacation. Employees are expected to work on some holidays on a rotating schedule.

Application process

Candidates may apply by forwarding a letter of application, copy of their resume, and the names, addresses, and phone numbers of five references to Ms. Melissa Supervisor, Assistant Director for Resident Services, Lakeside Manor, Cross Lanes, WV. The review of applications will begin on March 10 and continue until the position is filled.

Further information about Lakeside Manor and this position may be found at *http://www.LakesideManor.org* or by calling 800-555-0193.

Lakeside Manor is an equal opportunity/affirmative action employer.

AD NO. 2

Case manager for Lakeside Manor. Identifies services needed by older residents and links residents with available services. BSW degree and WV license required. MSW preferred. Salary between $27,000 and $35,000 depending on qualifications. For further information and application information, call 800-555-0193. EO/AA employer.

Sample Offer Letter

April 4, 2001

Mr. Andrew Employee, MSW
112 Floradale Dr.
Ashland, KY

Dear Mr. Employee:

I am pleased to offer you the position of case manager at Lakeside Manor. As we discussed in our phone conversation, you will begin this position on April 16. I am pleased that in our conversation you indicated your willingness to accept this position. The other members of the Lakeside Manor staff and I are looking forward to you joining us.

Your salary in this position will be $34,000 annually. You will be paid twice each month. You will also be reimbursed for the expenses associated with moving to the Cross Lanes area for up to $1,200. Please contact Ms. Lisa Johns at 800-555-0193 for information about allowable moving expenses and how reimbursement for your costs may be obtained.

Fringe benefits for the position include health insurance. Lakeside Manor will pay 90 percent of the premium for the insurance and the remaining 10 percent will be deducted from your check. The employee's contribution to Social Security will also be deducted from your pay. You will also be covered by a private pension plan. Lakeside Manor will contribute an amount equivalent to 7 percent of your annual salary to the plan; an amount equal to 5 percent of your salary will be deducted from your pay and be applied to the plan. We discussed the fringe benefits provided at Lakeside Manor when we met on March 25. I am enclosing a more detailed description of those benefits. If you have any questions about the benefits, please contact me.

Our goal at Lakeside Manor is to keep our residents living independently outside of a nursing home as long as is possible and feasible. In your position as case manager, you will play an important role in helping us achieve that goal. You will identify services needed by residents to maintain their independence and where those services may be available. Both Melissa Supervisor and I discussed your position description with you at the time of your interview. Enclosed is another copy of that description.

You will be a probationary employee at Lakeside Manor for the first six months of your employment, or until October 16, 2001. Your performance will be formally evaluated by Ms. Supervisor at the end of your first, third, and fifth months of employment. After your probationary period ends, your performance will be evaluated annually. After your annual review has been conducted, a salary increase for you will be reviewed. Enclosed is a copy of the Lakeside Manor Personnel Policies Manual, which describes probationary status and other personnel policies and procedures.

Your immediate supervisor will be Ms. Melissa Supervisor, with whom you met on March 25. You will participate in weekly staff meetings run by Ms. Supervisor in her position as Assistant Director for Resident Services. Ms. Supervisor will meet with you at 8:30 A.M. on April 16 to provide you with an orientation to Lakeside Manor and the duties of your position.

I have enclosed a copy of this offer letter. As an indication that you understand and accept the terms of this offer, please sign one copy and return it to me by April 10.

I am pleased that you will accept this offer and look forward to working with you at Lakeside Manor.

Sincerely,

Christine Johns, MSW
Executive Director

Notes

Chapter 1   Social Administration: An Overview

1. It might be noted that the continuing influence of policy devolution makes national resource issues somewhat less central today than they appeared in 1978. This is, however, a matter of degree rather than kind.
2. The title of Slavin's 1978 book, *Social Administration: The Management of the Social Services,* is a reflection of the ambiguity over the terms *administration* and *management.* Though the term *management* has become the more popular summary term in recent years, we believe there is value in restricting it to more technical and internal organizational perspectives and in distinguishing management from other identifiable aspects of social administration, such as leadership, policy making, and institution building.
3. Many major decisions made by social administrators involve issues of social policy, and much of this component of social administration fits together easily with existing and emerging policy practice models. However, to avoid additional confusion and because we highlight slightly different aspects of administrative decision making from those of greatest concern to policy practice writers, we choose not to refer to this component of social administration as policy making. Students and instructors who choose to speak of policy making will not go far astray. Does social administration thus equate or reduce to social policy? No, in the very explicit sense that social policy is concerned not only with how policy is made in and for organizations but also for nonorganiza-

tional policy (e.g., policies affecting individuals directly, such as tax policy) and with the substance, content, and implications of policies made.

4. Weber's (1947, 1968) model of bureaucracy, which is discussed in detail in chapter 4, was part of a critique of modern society. He was concerned that modern humans were trapped in an "iron cage" of rationality from which Weber saw no escape. This view would almost certainly apply to the efficient, effective delivery of social services by professionals working in formal organizations to provide (albeit more effectively, perhaps) the types of assistance that were the traditional province of family, friends, neighbors, and other "natural helpers." Wilensky's (1965) model of organized social service as a product of the social forces of urbanization and industrialization and Etzioni's (1969) model of the emergence of social work and other occupations as "semi-professions" have also had major impact on the self-definition of social work as a provider of organized social services.

5. In general, we prefer the term *commercial* to the frequently used but less concise *for-profit*.

6. Recent work in social history keeps pushing back the boundaries of our understanding. Brodman (1998), for example, is one of a number of recent works that deal extensively with administrative issues in medieval charitable institutions, some as early as the twelfth century and earlier.

7. For a more complete discussion of these and other curriculum questions regarding the role of administration in social work curricula, see Skidmore (1995, pp. 7–13).

8. All writing about social work must eventually encounter the problem of a generic label encompassing the many varieties of working face-to-face with individual clients. The adjective *direct* practice is unacceptable, for reasons noted later in the chapter. In general, we shall refer to such efforts as *clinical.*

9. Addams was president and head resident of Hull House from its founding until her death in 1935. She gave up the treasurer position after ten years.

10. In defining *administration in social work,* Barker (1995) states, "For social work administrators, implementation of administrative methods is informed by professional values and ethics with the expectation that these methods will enable social workers to provide effective and humane services to clients" (p. 8). This definition fails to offer any insight into why in a pluralistic world social agency administration should be informed by the values of the social work profession or where the expectations of indirect practice arise from. Once that question is examined more closely, it becomes obvious that there can be nothing at all indirect about such concerns.

11. Among the definitions of *indirect* in the *Random House Dictionary* is "devious, crooked, not straightforward." For a more positive slant on indirect clinical practice, see Johnson (1999).

PART I   The Ecology of Social Administration

1. For an article that treats the weaknesses of the indirect practice notion but approaches the issue very differently than the approach taken here, see Johnson (1999).

Chapter 2   Social Administration and Community

1. This approach is indebted to Max Weber's (1958) simple but accurate definition of a city as a population settlement with a market. Weber's concern was essentially comparative and sought to embrace all the communities of human history. Because our approach is considerably more limited, we believe we are justified in adding in additional dimensions.

2. The notion of proximate objectives is an important feature of the strategic theory that figures large in this work.

3. One sign of this resurgence is the publication since 1994 of the *Journal of Community Practice.*

4. For a more thorough introduction to the history of social administration and its community component, see Austin (2000).

5. For fuller discussions of some of the essential work in community studies, see Germain and Gitterman (1996, Pt. 3) and Robbins, Chatterjee, and Canda (1998, chaps. 2–4).

6. For a thorough and systematic restatement of Warren's structural–functional view of communities and the place of community service delivery systems, see Netting, Kettner, and McMurtry (1993).

7. The four-sector model of community presented in this chapter closely follows that presented in Lohmann (1992).

8. In one well-known definition, Robert Payton defines philanthropy as the private pursuit of public goods.

9. The term *commons* is generally preferred to the more ambiguous *third sector* for reasons spelled out in Lohmann (1992, 1993). The term is not intended to suggest that all forms of third sector organization conform in all respects to the ideal type of the commons, but rather that the archetype of the commons (voluntary participation of individuals pursuing common, joint, or shared purposes, with common or shared resources, experiencing a sense of mutuality, community, or communion and feeling bound by an indigenous sense of justice) exercises a strong normative, or moral, constraint on all activity within this sector. Thus, nonprofit social services or educational or health administrators acting in an excessively entrepreneurial manner will, at some point, come under criticism for being "too commercial."

10. Exchange theory here refers to a body of conceptual and theoretical approaches to personal behavior and social organization grounded in an economic metaphor of production and exchange. Traceable ultimately to the economic theories of Adam Smith, modern social ex-

change theory was developed by George Homans (1961) and came into social administration through the organizational theorizing of Peter Blau and colleagues (1967). Less clearly articulated models of social exchange emphasizing the tit-for-tat qualities of interaction and norms of reciprocity have long been part of the administrative conventional wisdom. Also important is the dualistic nature of exchange theory that divides most reality into matched pairs of concepts (e.g., buyers and sellers, production and consumption, gains and losses, burdens and benefits, etc.).

Chapter 3   The Social Agency

1. Gulick and Urwick (1937) defined the management function of organizing as "the establishment of the formal structure of authority through which work subdivisions are arranged, defined and coordinated for the defined objective" (p. 12).
2. Republicanism in this sense is no more associated with a particular political party than is democracy.
3. The English language is rich with expressions for this condition: thinking for yourself, maintaining your independence, getting along on your own, etc.
4. Though this point may seem obvious, indeed self-evident, to some readers, it is important to note that it has not always been thus. Office-based service delivery is, in fact, a relatively recent phenomenon. It may have rendered at least some older forms of institutionalized residential care obsolete. For example, orphanages and mental hospitals have generally been in decline in the face of community-based services. Moreover, the impact of forces as diverse as the growth of private practice, managed care, and the Internet all have major potential for undermining the social work office as it has been known in recent decades.
5. Portions of this section were published previously in Lohmann (1996).
6. The very idea of an "outside world" only makes sense in the context of an office-based conception of the social agency. The distinction it implies makes little sense to the street-based community organizer, for example, who is always "on the outside."
7. Students may not be aware of the range of other options for nonprofit organization under the tax code, but there are nearly a dozen options in addition to (c)(3) charitable organizations defined under section 501(c). Three of the most relevant of these that are also tax exempt are 501(c)(4), social welfare organizations (e.g., civic leagues, United Ways); 501(c)(6), business leagues (trade associations, like the National Association of Social Workers); and 501(c)(7), social clubs or membership organizations. For a very useful summary of all the nonprofit tax categories, see the Internal Revenue Service Web site at www.irs.gov /prod/bus_info/eo/eo-types.html.

8. The term *prosumption* here refers to the simultaneous production and consumption of an economic good or service. It is a unique characteristic of some types of service (including most social services) that the producer of the service and its consumer must be co-present with one another in order for the service to occur. Such services cannot be either produced or consumed independently. They cannot be warehoused or transported or inventoried. They can only be prosumed. Since the late 1960s, the notion of service delivery has been used to connote many aspects of the idea of service prosumption.

9. In the theory of the commons, common goods are set forth as a third category of goods along with public goods (which either benefit everyone or they benefit no one) and private goods (which can be "alienated"; benefiting from them means in part that others are not benefiting). Thus, the interstate highway is a public good in that either we can all drive on it or no one can. In contrast, your driveway is a private good, in that you can "alienate it" or restrict its use to whomever you choose. Church, synagogue, and mosque parking lots are often common goods, in that any member of the congregation planning to enter the sanctuary can park there, but others, including members seeking to park for other reasons like going shopping or going to work, cannot.

10. As we saw with the quotations from Arthur Dunham (1958, 1970) and Sue Spencer (1970), earlier social administrators unfailingly defined community in this triadic manner: a commons, as it were, of patrons, clients, and professional agents of community who are engaged in pursuit of a common good. The earlier chapters of Jane Addams's (1930) *My Twenty Years at Hull-House* and, just as important, histories of the Toynbee Hall in London, which served as Addams's model for Hull House, are very revealing here.

11. Jane Addams, in particular, has often been the target of such criticisms.

12. The term *office manager* is a somewhat ambiguous one. We are not speaking here of the lead clerical person or chief clerk, but rather the professional in charge of a freestanding area or district office.

13. The nondistribution constraint refers to any legal or ethical prohibition of inurement or distribution of any form of profit or capital gain to board members or stakeholders. Reimbursements for legitimate out-of-pocket expenses are, of course, allowed.

Chapter 4   Social Administration and Organization

1. Further discussion of the importance of legitimacy is taken up in connection with the discussion of authority in chapter 16.

2. More recently, some economists have sought to add economies of scope to concern for scale economies. Scope economies are those that occur when the production of a particular product reduces the production costs of a similar or related product. Thus, it could be argued that in

the social agency, co-production of resource directory information and discharge planning, for example, tends to lower the cost of both.

3. However, one should carefully avoid concluding that all problems of support and opposition can be reduced to matters of technology. There are also the intractable problems of ideology to be considered. In cases like abortion policy, for example, it is not arguments over technology (e.g., how best to carry out abortions) but fundamental issues of ideology (whether or not abortion is acceptable) that divide supporters and opponents of any particular position.

4. Peter Drucker claims that Woodward's insight had actually been discovered some time earlier. Charles R. Walker of Yale found very similar things about the role of technology in studies of workers, work, and work groups in the 1940s (Drucker, 1974, p. 273). Even if this is so, it remains the case that Woodward was the first to receive widespread recognition for work in this area.

5. For further discussion of this classification scheme, see Schmid (2000).

6. Ferdinand Tönnies (2001) is important in community theory, and Georg Simmel's formalist sociology of social groups (Ray, 1991) is behind the triadic model of exchange noted in chapter 2. For the most part, however, Weber is the major German source in management theory, which is primarily reliant on French, British, and American sources.

7. For a more detailed discussion of Barnard's place in management theory, see Wren (1994, pp. 335–45).

PART II   Elements of Social Administration

Chapter 5   Leadership and Decision Making

1. This list is taken from among those listed in the biographies section of the latest edition of the *Encyclopedia of Social Work.* The list purposely errs on the side of caution and includes only people with significant periods of administrative experience. Charles Loring Brace was the chief executive of the Children's Aid Society of New York for almost forty years. Addams was a leader of the settlement movement for more than forty-five years. Leaders primarily identified as philanthropists, reformers, or educators are not included unless they have clear administrative credentials. Obviously many more names belong on the list as well.

2. The tension is sometimes described as the conflict between tough and tender or hard and soft. Administrative realism often has some of the hard-edge cynicism of film noir.

3. A good introduction to Follett's ideas on management and leadership is found in Graham (1995).

4. As a matter of historical interest, the use of the male pronoun "his" applies universally to all people regardless of gender in the work of pioneering female scholars like Follett.

5. Interested readers might begin with James M. Burns's (1978) fascinating volume *Leadership*.

Chapter 6 The Processes of Management

1. For some of the early writings on railroad and factory management, see Wren (1997).
2. Wren (1979, pp. 229–33) offers an excellent discussion of the origins of this question for those who are interested. He traces the problem to differences in two translations of Henri Fayol's term (*gouverner* as distinguished from *administrer*) from the original French. According to Wren, Fayol intended management (*gouverner*) to be the more general term as the overall function of conducting an enterprise toward its objective by making the best possible use of all the resources at its disposal and designated administration (*administrer*) as only one of six essential management functions: (1) technical, as in production and manufacturing; (2) commercial, or buying, selling, and exchange; (3) financial, or the search for and optimum use of capital; (4) security, or the protection of property and persons; (5) accounting, or financial reporting; and (6) administration, or planning, organizing, command, coordination, and control. Obviously, the multiple homonyms involved between the French and the English complicate this question enormously. *Gouverner* looks very much like the English term *governor; administrer* resembles the English *administrator;* and there is apparently no French homonym for the English *manager*, even though that English term comes closest to Fayol's intent. However, because of the hundreds of variable usages of these terms since Fayol, the task of sorting out any exact meaning has been rendered impossible. All anyone can do in this context is to state the meanings they associate with particular terms and attempt to be consistent in their use of them. Any attempts to argue that one or the other is the proper term, or that one is subordinate to the other, must deal, among other things, with nearly a century of similar (and unsuccessful) efforts at clarification.
3. Since a human relations study of worker performance at a Westinghouse plant in Hawthorne, New York, concluded that the action of studying assembly workers resulted in an increase in their morale, any instance in which social research intrudes upon behavior being observed or changes eventual outcomes can be referred to as a *Hawthorne effect*.
4. This interpretation comes from Perrow (1972).

Chapter 7 Management Models

1. For a detailed intellectual assessment of Drucker's contributions to management thinking, see Beatty (1998) and Guy and Hitchcock (2000).

2. The quartet refers to psychiatrists, nurses, psychologists, and social workers.

3. This approach has produced a vast outpouring of work. A selected list includes Association for Systems Management (1971), Carroll and Tosi (1973), Chakraborty (1976), Coppa & Avery Consultants (1982), Deegan (1977), Granvold (1978), Humble (1970), Jun (1973), Laczko (1993), Morrisey (1970, 1976), Musgrave and Elster (1974), Odiorne (1965), Olsson (1968), Raider (1977), Remion (1995), Ryan (1976), Santora (1982), Siegel and U.S. Civil Service (1978), Spillane and Levenson (1978), Tarter (1974), Tosi et al. (1976), U.S. Office of Personnel Management (1985), Varney (1979), and Wiehe (1974, 1978).

PART III   The Processes of Institutionalization

1. See also the brief discussion in Hasenfeld (2000, pp. 99–100).

2. Lester Ward first introduced the notion of social telesis. Ward was the first American sociologist who also had a strong interest in social reform. For Ward, social telesis refers to "the conscious control and direction of social development by the human mind" (Martindale, 1960, p. 71).

3. Advanced students wishing to pursue this point may wish to take on Karl Popper's two-volume *The Open Society and its Enemies* (1966) and his earlier *The Poverty of Historicism* (1957).

Chapter 8   Policy, Institutions, and Strategic Action

1. That these three assertions are related is a principal point of chapters 1 and 2 of this work.

2. During the 1960s, there was an explicit national-level debate of the most effective ways of dealing with poverty. Most economists and remaining members of the old left generally supported an income strategy on the grounds that poverty was primarily a matter of lack of money, and therefore the wisest course of action was to increase the incomes of the poor. Tax deductions and credits, money payments, and food stamps are all examples of such an income strategy. Advocates of a services strategy in social work and elsewhere argued consistently that the problems of the poor began with the lack of money, but were more complex than the income strategists would acknowledge. Certainly, the poor needed increased incomes, but they also needed assorted social services to assist them in dealing with the daily challenges that poverty presented. Like most issues in American social policy, this one wasn't so much settled as it was set aside.

3. Initially, the community mental health centers approach was adopted by the Kennedy administration as a full-blown strategy for approaching

the problems of mental illness at the community level. Independent living for the mentally ill, which was a major feature of deinstitution-alization a decade later, was a major feature of this model.

4. In the Economic Opportunity Act, and the earlier Grey Areas Project, the theory that what the poor needed most fundamentally was oppor-tunities to escape poverty represented a completely new, third theory of poverty. The issue was neither money nor services, but instead the opportunities represented by education, training, and eventually affir-mative action.

5. A great many of such proposals still fall within the postwar incremental welfare state paradigm dominant in the second half of the twentieth century and call for incremental additions to the service cafeteria backed up by federal financial support.

6. Again, as we saw earlier, a reductionist interpretation of the social ser-vice triad, in which social workers may either be interested in their clients or in professional development, but not in both, is the key to this interpretation.

7. These comments are certainly not original with the authors. The prob-lem is well understood, and the leadership of the National Association of Social Workers and the Council on Social Work Education has made efforts to address the problem of an up-to-date vision for social work and social service. The CSWE Millennium Project is just one of several such ventures that could be cited. The point is that a new vision for the field is, at this writing, only slowly beginning to evolve.

8. It might be possible to identify at least a dozen other perspectives on strategy in addition to Quinn, who was chosen in large part because of the affinity of his ideas to those of Lindblom, Simon, and others. The question always in a work of this sort is whether to present brief sum-mary comments on a number of perspectives or to concentrate in depth on one perspective. Because of the relative novelty of strategic thinking in social services, we thought the latter was the wiser choice in this case. A number of summary overviews have been published (see Moore [1992]).

9. The present federal policy on grants to nonprofit community organi-zations is largely spelled out in OMB Circular A-121 and the standard forms accompanying any federal grant application.

10. It is tempting, but misleading, to place the burden for the relative anonymity of crisis services and other community mental health insti-tutions on the professional responsibility to preserve confidentiality. However, a great many community institutions (including the public schools) are highly recognized in communities while preserving the confidentiality of crucial participants.

11. One of the interesting aspects of institutions in this sense is the bridge that they offer out of the morass of self-interest. With genuine institu-

tions (e.g., Grand Central Terminal or Sesame Street or thousands of more limited local examples), people tend to express interest and concern whether or not they stand to benefit directly.

Chapter 9 Administrative Planning

1. This is actually a simplified version of a definition offered in the early 1960s by Yeheskel Dror (1963). The full definition is "preparing a set of decisions for action in the future directed at achieving goals by optimal means." Planning, in Dror's sense, had four principal facets: environment, subject matter, planning unit, and form of the plan.

Chapter 10 Implementation

1. *Tarasoff* v. *The Regents of the University of California* was decided by the California Supreme Court in 1976 and dealt with the duty of therapists to warn both local authorities and a potential victim about a patient's threat to harm a third party.

Chapter 11 Operations

1. Max Weber made this one of the universal characteristics of organizations in his ideal type of bureaucracy.
2. See www.datawarehouse.org and www.datamining.org.
3. For a discussion of Gantt's contributions to management theory and practice, see Wren (1994, pp. 134–41).

Chapter 12 Accountability

1. See Greenlee (1998) for a current perspective on this issue.
2. Governments also use business accounting data as the basis for determining the taxes owed by businesses.
3. The cost of goods sold is a standard business calculation of how much it costs the seller to make or purchase the products sold. The cost of goods sold is deducted from total sales revenues to determine the level of gross profit. The cost of goods sold represents the direct costs of production—that is, the costs that can be directly attributed to the production of that particular good.
4. Ferdinand Braudel (1986) says, "When Luca Pacioli published his *De Arithmetica* in Venice in 1496, he was summarizing what had long been known about double-entry bookkeeping (it had been used in Florence since the late thirteenth century). When Jacob Fugger visited Florence, he studied double-entry bookkeeping there and brought the technique

back to Augsburg with him. One way or another, it ended up by spreading to a large part of trading Europe" (p. 555).

5. Many of the governments of Europe, for example, had little idea of where they stood financially for much of the period from 1500 to 1800. See Kennedy (1987, especially pp. 73–86).
6. This section is excerpted from Lohmann (1995a).
7. See Anthony (1978) for a discussion of some of the issues involved.
8. Much of the theory of nonprofit accountability arose from the British Statute of Charitable Uses, adopted by Parliament the same year as the Elizabethan Poor Laws, 1601.
9. The philosopher of science Abraham Kaplan distinguishes "logic in use" from "reconstructive logic," which is how people may reconstruct the process of what actually happened both before and after a problem-solving episode. This is the essential problem of decision-making practice that concerned Herbert Simon, Charles Lindblom, and others discussed earlier in this book. Can we create models of how people actually make decisions or policy, rather than relying upon the models of enlightenment rationality for how eighteenth-century French philosophers in the wake of Rene Descartes thought they ought to?

Chapter 13   Program Evaluation

1. The reader is referred to a research methodology text for a fuller discussion of the methods used to evaluate programs. Specialized reviews of this area, such as Wholey, Hatry, and Newcomer (1994), provide more detailed discussions of methodology.
2. The remainder of this paragraph and the next two paragraphs are a modified version of content appearing in Lohmann (1991).
3. The complete survey results may be accessed at http://www.omb watch.org/www/ombw/gpra/aspen/.
4. The plan may be accessed at http://aspe.os.dhhs.gov/hhsplan/intro .htm#contents.
5. The reader is referred to any of the many available texts on research methods for a more complete discussion of the issues of validity and reliability.
6. See Campbell and Stanley (1963) for what is viewed as a classic discussion of experimental and quasi-experimental design.

PART IV   Communications and Information

Chapter 14   Administrative Communication

1. A reference public is any collection of persons, who may or may not be known to one another, who are not members of an organization but who make matters of organizational communication their concern.

2. Foundation documents are documents (such as articles of incorporation and the original by-laws) instrumental in creation or founding of an organization.

3. Lawyers in administrative law frequently refer to such memoranda as "contemporaneous notes." They commonly have an advantage over unassisted mental recollections in hearings and such because they were made at or close to the time of the events described or recalled, and thus have a presumed greater likelihood of accuracy.

4. A communication event is defined here as a deliberate or planned occasion for convening a group whose primary purpose includes some form of expected or anticipated communication (someone communicating something for some deliberate purpose or reason with some more-or-less expected result).

5. For applications to social administration, see Elshtain (1996), Quinn (1996), Taylor et al. (1996), and Yankelovich, 1999.

Chapter 15   Administrative Information Systems

1. This is precisely the sense in which the Declaration of Independence speaks of "unalienable" rights: the right of free speech can be exercised by anyone without "alienating" it or removing or denying it from others.

2. www.ecommerce.gov/emerging.htm.

3. *Government Technology Review,* June 1998, p. 11.

4. This section is adapted from Lohmann and Lohmann (1995).

PART V   Empowerment

Chapter 16   Administrative Authority

1. Perhaps the ultimate statement of this view came from the American railroad tycoon George F. Baer, who said in 1889, "The rights and interests of the laboring men will be protected and cared for, not by labor agitators, but by the Christian men to whom God in his infinite wisdom has given control of the property interests of the country." In fourteenth-century Europe, such an assertion of authority from a bishop or church leader might have gone unchallenged. The unsuccessful efforts of nineteenth-century capitalists to abrogate for themselves the authority of divine representatives, must be seen, however, as one element in what Robert Nisbet (1975) termed "the twilight of authority." It may have been this sense of the problematic nature of authority in the industrial age that led Max Weber to his classical consideration of authority, discussed later in the chapter.

2. "They" in this case is the ubiquitous paranoid administrative "they" one hears commonly in organizations, an indefinite pronoun referring to

sinister and diabolical forces somewhere further up in the organizational hierarchy.

3. This work appeared in German following Weber's death in 1922 and was first translated into English by Hans Gerth in 1953.

Chapter 17   Power and Influence

1. See the discussion of this issue in Hasenfeld (2000, pp. 106–8).
2. Some of this is evident in the early chapters of Jane Addams's *Twenty Years at Hull-House,* and the other side comes out in Addams's conflict with the "low politics" of the neighborhood saloonkeepers.
3. There is, of course, a wonderfully ironic ambivalence in the latter phrase of this statement that should not be lost on those who are prone to cynical and conspiratorial interpretations of power in particular. The wording of the phrase "and you look wonderful" could mean "and my idea has even more advantages for you than it does for me" or just as likely is the possibility that it is a completely unrelated compliment tacked on as an afterthought: "Oh, and by the way, even though this has nothing to do with what I'm proposing, you're looking wonderful today."

PART VI   Human and Financial Capital

Chapter 19   Personnel Systems

1. Anthony Downs's (Downs & Rand Corporation, 1967) model of five ideal types of organizational role performers is an example of this literature.

Chapter 20   Human Resources

1. Human resources can be divided into two basic types of human capital. There are the personal skills repertories of individuals called human capital and the social relationships or social capital. See chapter 21 for a further discussion of the forms of capital.
2. *Accommodation* is related to the provisions of the Americans with Disabilities Act and is discussed more fully in chapter 26.
3. In some instances, references may be reluctant to provide more than confirmation that a candidate was employed by their organization and the dates of employment. Such responses are more often found when checking on the references of someone who has worked for a commercial business, and are intended to avoid a lawsuit about the nature of the reference provided.
4. Sources like Perlmutter, Bailey, and Netting (2000) provide very practical information about supervision.

Chapter 21   Financial Management

1. The sliding fee scale is one in which the fee charged for a particular service varies, usually in accord with the consumer's or client's ability to pay. Thus, a client with an income of $20,000 may pay only a fraction of the amount for the same service paid by a client with an income of $100,000.
2. See www.aicpa.org for further information.
3. A chart of accounts identifies the categories in which financial data will be reported and drives all the financial records of the organization.
4. Break-even analysis focuses on the ability of the organization to break even, a condition in which its income equals its expenditures.
5. A cash accounting reporting system reports only the cash actually received and/or paid out at the time of the statement. An accural accounting system would report both amounts that were due to be paid out and amounts that were owed and due to be paid to the organization.
6. *Prosumption* is a coined term that describes the delivery of social services in which the act of production occurs simultaneously with and is inevitably linked with the act of consumption. Additional aspects of the prosumption of services are described in chapters 23 and 24.
7. The issue of the way in which social services are simultaneously produced and consumed, or prosumed, is discussed in chapter 3.
8. Collections, a third type also discussed by Lohmann (1992), are less important in social service organizations than, for example, in churches and museums and will not be discussed here.
9. A capitation payment is a fee based on assumptions about the average cost to an agency to deliver a service. A firm, for example, may contract with an employee assistance program (EAP) to pay a fee of x dollars for each employee who receives services, regardless of the cost of service for any particular employee. The assumption is that there will be some lost cost cases on which the EAP makes more than the cost of the treatment and that they will be balanced by some more costly cases on which it makes less than the cost of service delivered.

Chapter 22   Financial Inflows

1. Nonprofit donatories are the type of organization most likely to deal with donations. Although donations are not unheard of in public and commercial QUANGOs and even commercial corporations, it is important to note that only donations to 501(c)(3) tax-exempt nonprofits would be legally tax deductible.
2. For this and other fund-raising questions, Kelly (1998) is an excellent source.
3. See Brilliant (1991) for more on these developments. The United Way web site is located at www.unitedway.org.

4. For more information, see the National Committee for Responsive Philanthropy Web site at www.ncrp.org.

5. See Kelly (1998), Sharpe (1988), Hopkins (1996), Howe (1991), Huntsinger (1987), Mixer (1993), Murray (1991), Rosso et al. (1991), Rose-Ackerman (1982), Booth, Higgins, and Cornelius (1989), Baer (1992), Lindahl (1992), Burlingame and Hulse (1991), Turner (1995), Christian (1992), and Chang and Tuckman (1994).

6. See, for example, White (1975), Lauffer (1997), and the forty-eight-page guide on program and proposal writing published by the Grantsmanship Center, which is available through its Web site, www.tgci.com.

7. http://foundationcenter.org.

8. See OMB Circular A-102 or A-122 (http://www.pr.doe.gov/omb2.html) and Standard Form 424 (http://www.acf.dhhs.gov/programs/ofs/grants /form.htm) for current application information.

9. Michael Wyland, E-mail to ARNOVA-L discussion list.

10. When all clients (or third parties) are paying fixed and comparable fees, this increase (or decrease) will be directly proportional to the amount (hours) of the service increase (or decrease). When some portion of clients are paying sliding-scale fees, both the portion of the new services supported by sliding-scale fees and the portions of fees paid will have to be taken into account.

Chapter 23   Budgeting

1. The historical discussion in the rest of this section is from Wren (1994, pp. 209–10).

2. This is not the same as suggesting that nothing is known. Although details may be sketchy at times, there are some interesting exceptions. For example, Brodman (1998) provides a fairly detailed discussion of the financial management of medieval hospitals and related facilities in medieval Catalonia from the eleventh to the sixteenth century.

3. Prosumption, as noted in an earlier chapter, is the simultaneous production and consumption of services. By their very nature, social services are consumed by clients simultaneously as they are produced by workers. There can be no gap of the type, which in goods production is the concern of transportation, arbitrage, storage, or inventory. (Try producing one unit of service this afternoon for a client who is coming in tomorrow, so that you can take the day off, and you get the idea. It can't be done.)

4. What most American economists don't appear to understand is that the conventional microeconomic equations invoking supply and demand, although allowing more precise calculations, do not address the central issues and concerns of budget decision making. That may explain why budget decision makers are often willing to forego the greater accuracy of microeconomic models for the greater relevance of the break-even models derived from Hess's discovery.

5. We are aware that using examples from Hull House will be provocative for some social welfare historians. Our answer to them is twofold. (1) The concern here is with the Hull House organization and not the persona of Jane Addams. There has been remarkably little attention to the administrative or organizational concerns of Hull House at this level. (2) Although we agree completely that attention to other, less-celebrated turn-of-the-century social agencies would be equally interesting, the fact is also that information on such agencies is often difficult to come by and less complete than the remarkably thorough financial records in the Hull House archives. Further, as our carefully chosen examples illustrate, there is little of the hagiographic in this presentation. Hull House is an excellent example of both the best and the worst of financial practices in early social agencies.

6. For a simple demonstration of the basic idea of fungibility, take the coins out of your purse and the bills out of your wallet and spread them out on a table. Now, identify where you got each one from and for what reason. The fact that you cannot (no one can—or would want to) is what is expressed by the idea of fungibility. Money is fungible. That is, there is a fundamental break between the events and activities associated with income (or inflow) and those associated with its expenditure (or outflow). This critical arena in which inflows are translated into outflows is the arena of budgeting, and it is characterized in a fundamental way by decision making.

7. Even the word *service* means significantly different things in these two contexts. In business, the term is generally defined in terms of economic function, whereas in social services, the term ordinarily refers to a range of activities engaged in.

8. See Lohmann (1997) for a more thorough introduction to cost concepts.

9. For definitions and a further discussion, see Lohmann (1980).

10. It needs to be noted, however, that not monitoring fund-raising costs would be a breach of usual and customary accounting practice for nonprofit organizations.

PART VII   Topics In Social Administration

Chapter 24   Social Administration and Purchase of Service Contracts

1. See, for example, Gibelman (1981), Judge and Smith (1983), Kettner and Martin (1985a, 1985b, 1986, 1987, 1988, 1990, 1993a, 1993b, 1995, 1996a, 1996b), Leeman (1978), Malka (1990), Poertner and Rapp (1985), Richter and Ozawa (1983), Wedel (1974), and Willis (1984).

2. See, for example, David (1988), DeHoog (1984, 1986, 1990), Dudley (1990), Kettl (1988), MacManus (1992), Rehfuss (1989), Ross (1987), Salamon (1989), and Savas (1987).

3. See, for example, Deakin (1996), Ferris (1993), Grønbjerg (1991, 1993), Nowland-Foreman (1998), and Smith and Lipsky (1992).

4. See, for example, Davidson, Schlesinger, Dorwart, and Schnell (1991), Milligan (1998), Schmid (1993), and Vandeven (1996).

5. For example, an investigation of local government contracting by Boyne (1998) concluded that "claims that empirical studies find 'consistently' and 'without exception' that contracting is more efficient than municipal supply are demonstrably untrue." Only about half the studies located make such claims, Boyne argues, and the vast majority of those are methodologically flawed and raise serious doubts about their reliability. In the case of social services, the results are even more stark; there simply are no studies of the comparative efficiency of social services.

6. This discussion is based primarily on Arthur Schlesinger Jr.'s work *The Age of Jackson,* which is widely considered one of the classic works of American history. Schlesinger (1986/1999) himself summarized many of the key points in a shorter and more recent essay.

7. Note also, however, that this apparent decline could be due to differences between the Kettner–Martin and Wedel samples.

8. Writers in the traditional social administration literature were always well aware of the changes taking place in the nature of voluntary agency organizations and governance as a result of the entry of government. They just weren't entirely sure what to make of it. See, for example, an early article by Brown (1934). See also Vasey (1958). A later article by Kramer (1967) shows greater certainty about the nature of the changes that were taking place in the social agency, although such terminology as "voluntary sector" was maintained.

Chapter 26   Human Diversity and Administrative Justice

1. See http://www.eeoc.gov.
2. See http://www.dol.gov/dol/esa/fmla.htm.
3. See http://www.EEOC.gov/facts/fs-sex.html; last modified on January 15, 1997.
4. See http://www.shrm.org/hrnews/articles/062698.htm to gain access to the syllabus for each case. See also http://oyez.nwu.edu/cases/cases .cgi for a summary of the Burlington Industries and other gender discrimination cases.

Chapter 27   Governance Issues: Boards and Directorates

1. On the original incorporation certificate for the Hull House Association, for example, the word "Directors" is crossed out with a single line and the word "Trustees" is written over it in ink. See Lohmann (2000b) for more on this point.

2. Although the discussion addresses governance in governing boards, it should not be forgotten that advisory boards also participate in the governance process except that their role does not generally include decision-making powers. They offer advice instead.

References

Abels, P., & Murphy, M. J. (1981). *Administration in the human services: A normative systems approach.* Englewood Cliffs, NJ: Prentice Hall.

Adams, J. L. (1986). *Voluntary associations: Sociocultural analyses and theological interpretations.* Chicago: Exploration Press.

Adams, P., & Nelson, K. (1995). *Reinventing human services: Community- and family-centered practice.* Hawthorne, NY: Aldine de Gruyter.

Addams, J. (1930). *Twenty years at Hull-House.* New York: Macmillan.

Addams, J. (1964). *Democracy and social ethics.* Cambridge, MA: Harvard University Press.

Addams, J., et al. (1893). *Philanthropy and social progess.* New York: Crowell.

Albrecht, T. L., Irey, K. V., & Mundy, A. K. (1982). Integration in a communication network as a mediator of stress. *Social Work, 27*(3), 229–34.

Alexander, C. (1965). *Trends in social work practice and knowledge.* New York: National Association of Social Workers.

Alinsky, S. D. (1946). *Reveille for radicals.* Chicago: University of Chicago Press.

Alinsky, S. D. (1989). *Rules for radicals: A practical primer for realistic radicals.* New York: Vintage Books.

Alwon, F. J. (1980). Response to agencywide crisis: A model for administrative action. *Child Welfare, 59*(6), 335–46.

American Association of Fund-Raising Counsel. (1998). *Giving USA* (pp. v). New York: AAFRC Trust for Philanthropy.

Anthony, R. N. (1978). *Financial accounting in nonbusiness organizations: An exploratory study of conceptual issues.* New York: Financial Accounting Standards Board.

Anthony, R. N., & Young, D. W. (1984). *Management control in nonprofit organizations* (3rd ed.). Homewood, IL: Dow Jones.

Applegate, J. S. (1988, December). Leadership: A dimension of clinical social work practice. *Social Casework, 69*(10), 640–43.

Aristotle. (2000). *Nicomachean ethics.* (R. Crisp, Ed.). New York: Cambridge University Press.

Association for Systems Management. (1971). *Management by objectives.* Cleveland: Author.

Atherton, C. R. (1990). Adam Smith and the welfare state. *Arete, 15*(1), 24–31.

Auletta, K. (1999, August 16). Hard core. *New Yorker,* pp. 42–69.

Austin, D. (2000). Social work and social welfare administration. In R. J. Patti (Ed.), *The handbook of social welfare management* (pp. 27–54). Thousand Oaks, CA: Sage.

Austin, D. M. (1983a). Program design issues in the improved administration of human service programs. *Administration in Social Work 7*(1), 1–11.

Austin, D. M. (1983b). The political economy of human services. *Policy and Politics, 11*(3), 343–59.

Austin, D. M. (1985). Administrative practice in human services: Future directions for curriculum development. In S. Slavin (Ed.), *Introduction to human services management.* New York: Haworth Press.

Austin, D. M. (1989). The human service executive. *Administration in Social Work, 13*(3/4), 13–36.

Austin, M. J. (1988). Managing up: Relationship building between middle management and top management. *Administration in Social Work, 12*(4), 29–46.

Austin, M. J. (1989). Executive entry: Multiple perspectives on the process of muddling through. *Administration in Social Work, 13*(3/4), 55–71.

Axelrod, N. (1994). Board leadership and board development. In R. Herman (Ed.), *Handbook of nonprofit leadership and management* (pp. 119–36). San Francisco: Jossey-Bass.

Axinn, J., & Stern, M. (1988). *Dependency and poverty: Old problems in a new world.* Lexington, MA: Lexington Books.

Bachrach, P. (1980). *The theory of democratic elitism: A critique.* Washington, DC: University Press of America.

Bachrach, P., & Baratz, M. S. (1970). *Power and poverty; theory and practice.* New York: Oxford University Press.

Baer, S. H. (1992). Fund raising and public relations: A critical analysis, by K. S. Kelly. *Public Relations Review, 18*(4), 394–96.

Baghadi, M. K. (1975). *Protestants, poverty and urban growth: Organization of charity in Boston and New York, 1820–1865.* Unpublished doctoral dissertation, Brown University.

Bahrdt, H. P. (1966). Public activity and private activity as basic forms of city association. In R. Warren (Ed.), *Perspectives on the American community: A book of readings* (pp. 78–85). New York: Rand McNally.

Bailey, D., & Grochau, K. E. (1993). Aligning leadership needs to the organizational stage of development: Applying management theory to nonprofit organizations. *Administration in Social Work, 17*(1), 23–45.

Balz, D., & Brownstein, R. (1995). *Storming the gates: Protest politics and the Republican revival.* Boston: Little, Brown.

Banerjee, V. (1979). Planning and evaluation: The roles of the public and voluntary sectors. *Child Welfare, 58*(4), 229–36.

Banfield, E. (1961). *Political influence.* Glencoe, IL: Free Press.

Banfield, E. (1970). *The unheavenly city.* Boston: Little, Brown.

Banfield, E. (1986). Influence and the public interest. In P. S. Nivola & D. H. Rosenbloom (Eds.), *Classic readings in American politics* (pp. 588–99). New York: St. Martin's Press.

Barbeau, E. (1988). *Content, method and sufficiency in ethics in six master's in social work curriculums: Perceptions of students and faculty.* Unpublished dissertation, West Virginia University.

Barber, B. (1988). *The conquest of politics: Liberal philosophy in democratic times.* Princeton, NJ: Princeton University Press.

Bargal, D., & Schmid, H. (1989). Recent themes in theory and research on leadership and their implications for management of the human services. *Administration in Social Work, 13*(3/4), 37–54.

Bargal, D., & Shamir, B. (1984). Job description of occupational welfare: A tool in role development. *Administration in Social Work, 8*(1), 59–71.

Barker, R. L. (1992). *Social work in private practice.* Silver Spring, MD: National Association of Social Workers.

Barker, R. L. (1986). Supply side economics in private psychotherapy practice. *Journal of Independent Social Work, 1*(1), 16–21.

Barker, R. L. (1995). *The social work dictionary* (3rd ed.). Washington, DC: National Association of Social Workers.

Barnard, C. (1938). *The functions of the executive.* Cambridge, MA: Harvard University Press.

Barry, B. (1992). *Strategic planning workbook for nonprofit organizations.* St. Paul, MN: Wilder Foundation.

Baumheier, E. C. (1982). Productivity in human services. *Journal of Health and Human Resources Administration, 4*(4), 451–64.

Beatty, J. (1998). *The world according to Peter Drucker.* New York: Free Press.

Becker, G. S. (1976). *The economic approach to human behavior.* Chicago: University of Chicago Press.

Bedger, J. E. (1974). Cost analysis in day care and head start. *Child Welfare, 53*(8), 514–23.

Beinecke, R. H., Goodman, M., & Lockhart, A. (1997). The impact of managed care on Massachusetts mental health and substance abuse providers. *Administration in Social Work, 21*(2), 41–53.

Below, P. J., Morrisey, G. L., & Acomb, B. L. (1987). *The executive guide to strategic planning.* San Francisco: Jossey-Bass.

Berger, P. L., & Luckmann, T. (1990). *The social construction of reality: A treatise in the sociology of knowledge.* New York: Anchor Books. (Originally published in 1966)

Berkowitz, S. J. (1947). Reactions of clients and caseworkers toward fees. *Social Casework, 28*(4).

Berlin, I. (1998). *The proper study of mankind: An anthology of essays.* H. Hardy & R. Hausheer (Eds.). New York: Farrar, Straus and Giroux.

Berman, E. M. (1995). Implementing TQM in state welfare agencies. *Administration in Social Work, 19*(1), 55–72.

Bernstein, L. (1999). *Creating your employee handbook: A do-it-yourself kit for nonprofits.* San Francisco: Jossey-Bass/Pfeiffer.

Bernstein, S. R. (1989). *Playing the game of contracted services: Administrative, ethical and political issues for the nonprofit agency manager.* Unpublished dissertation, City University of New York.

Bernstein, S. R. (1991a). Contracted services: Issues for the nonprofit manager. *Nonprofit and Voluntary Sector Quarterly, 20*(4), 429–44.

Bernstein, S. R. (1991b). *Managing contracted services in the nonprofit agency: Administrative, ethical and political issues.* Philadelphia: Temple University Press.

Berry, E. (1992). *Gifts that make a difference: How to buy hundreds of great gifts sold through nonprofits.* Dayton, OH: Foxglove.

Billis, D. (1992). Planned change in voluntary and government social service agencies. *Administration in Social Work, 16*(3/4), 29–44.

Binstock, R. H., & Ely, K. (1971). *The politics of the powerless.* Cambridge, MA: Winthrop.

Blais, A., & Dion, S. (Eds.). (1992). *The budget-maximizing bureaucrat.* Pittsburgh: University of Pittsburgh Press.

Blake, R. R., & Mouton, J. S. (1964). *The managerial grid.* Houston: Gulf Press.

Blake, R. R., & Mouton, J. S. (1978). *The new managerial grid.* Houston: Gulf Press.

Blau, P. M. (1956). *Bureaucracy in modern society.* New York: Random House.

Blau, P. M. (1967). *Exchange and power in social life.* New York: Wiley.

Blau, P. M., & Scott, W. R. (1962). *Formal organizations: A comparative approach.* San Francisco: Chandler.

Block, P. (1987). *The empowered manager: Positive political skills at work.* San Francisco: Jossey-Bass.

Block, S. R. (1998). *Perfect nonprofit boards: Myths, paradoxes and paradigms.* Indianapolis: Simon & Schuster.

Blum, S. R., Feldman, S., & Heller, K. (1991). Responsibilities and training needs of mental health administrators [Special issue: Education in mental health administration]. *Administration and Policy in Mental Health, 18*(4), 257–69.

Boehm, A. (1996). Forces driving competition in human service organizations and positional competitive responses. *Administration in Social Work, 20*(4), 61.

Boggs, M. (1949). Administration and casework aspects of fee charging. *Social Casework, 30*(8).

Boisot, M. (1995). *Information space: Framework for learning in organizations, institutions, and culture.* London: Routledge.

Bombyk, M. J., & Chernesky, R. H. (1985). Conventional cutback leadership and the quality of the workplace: Is beta better? *Administration in Social Work, 9*(3), 47–56.

Bonney, N. L., & Streicher, L. H. (1970). Time-cost data in agency administration: Efficiency controls in family and children's service. *Social Work, 15*(4), 21–31.

Boorstin, D. J. (1992). *The image: A guide to pseudo-events in America.* New York: Vintage Books. (Originally published in 1961)

Booth, A., Higgins, D., & Cornelius, R. (1989). Community influences on funds raised by human service volunteers. *Nonprofit and Voluntary Sector Quarterly, 18*(1), 81–88.

Boris, E. (1999). The nonprofit sector in the 1990's. In C. T. Clotfelter & T. Ehrlich (Eds.), *Philanthropy and the nonprofit sector in a changing America* (pp. 1–33). Bloomington: Indiana University Press.

Boris, R. M., & Fiedler, F. E. (1976). Changes in organizational leadership and the behavior of relationship- and task-motivated leaders. *Administrative Science Quarterly, 21*(3), 453–73.

Borkman, T. J. (1999). *Understanding self help/mutual aid: Experiential learning in the commons.* New Brunswick, NJ: Rutgers University Press.

Boulding, K. (1981). *A preface to grants economics: The economy of love and fear.* New York: Praeger.

Boulding, K. E., Pfaff, M., & Horvath, J. (1972). Grants economics: A simple introduction. *American Economist, 16*(1), 19–35.

Boyne, G. (1998). Bureaucratic theory meets reality: Public choice and service contracting in U.S. local government. *Public Administration Review, 58*(6), 474–82.

Brady, J. P. (1975). *Classics of American psychiatry.* St. Louis: Green.

Brager, G. A., & Specht, H. (1973). *Community organizing.* New York: Columbia University Press.

Braudel, F. (1986). *The wheels of commerce: Civilization and capitalism, 15th–18th century* (Vol. 2). New York: Harper & Row.

Braybrooke, D., & Lindblom, C. E. (1963). *A strategy of decision: Policy evaluation as a social process.* Glencoe, IL: Free Press.

Briar, S., & Blythe, B. J. (1985). Agency support for evaluating the outcome of social work services. *Administration in Social Work, 9*(2), 25–36.

Brilliant, E. (1991). *The United Way: The dilemmas of organized charity.* New York: Columbia University Press.

Broadhurst, B. P. (1978). The Johns Hopkins University: Training center for social scientists. *Journal of the History of the Behavioral Sciences, 14*(3), 213–22.

Brodman, J. (1998). *Charity and welfare: Hospitals and the poor in medieval Catalonia.* Philadelphia: University of Pennsylvania Press.

Broskowski, A. (1987). Goldfields and minefields: Changing management technologies and resources. *Administration in Mental Health, 14*(3–4), 153–71.

Brown, C. W., Powell, L. W., & Wilcox, C. (1995). *Serious money: Fundraising and contributing in presidential nomination campaigns.* New York: Cambridge University Press.

Brown, D. (1991). *Human universals.* Philadelphia: Temple University Press.

Brown, G. S. J., & Kornmayer, K. (1996). Expert systems restructure managed care practice: Implementation and ethics. *Behavioral Healthcare Tomorrow, 5*(1), 31–34.

Brown, H. M. (1991). Medicaid reimbursement in a time of budgetary crises. *Journal of Long Term Care Administration, 19*(2/3), 20–26.

Brown, R. H. (1989). *Social science as civic discourse: Essays on the invention, legitimation and uses of social theory.* Chicago: University of Chicago Press.

Brudney, J. L. (1987). Coproduction and privatization: Exploring the relationship and its implications. *Journal of Voluntary Action Research, 16*(3), 11–21.

Brudney, J. L. (1990). *Fostering volunteer programs in the public sector: Planning, initiating and managing voluntary activities.* San Francisco: Jossey-Bass.

Brudney, J. L., & England, R. E. (1983). Toward a definition of the coproduction concept. *Public Administration Review, 43*, 59–65.

Brudney, J. L., & Murray, V. (1993). Do intentional efforts to improve boards really work? The views of nonprofit CEOs. *Nonprofit Management and Leadership, 8*(4), 333–48.

Brudney, J. L., Hebert, F. T., & Wright, D. S. (1999). Reinventing government in the American states: Measuring and explaining administrative reform. *Public Administration Review, 59*(1), 19–30.

Bryson, J. (1994). Strategic planning and action planning for nonprofit organizations. In R. Herman (Ed.), *Handbook of nonprofit leadership and management* (pp. 154–83). San Francisco: Jossey-Bass.

Bryson, J. M. (1995). *Strategic planning for public and nonprofit organizations: A guide to strengthening and sustaining organizational achievement* (Rev. ed.). San Francisco: Jossey-Bass.

Buchanan, J. M. (1969). *Cost and choice: An inquiry in economic theory.* Chicago: Markham.

Bunker, D. R., & Wijinberg, M. (1985). The supervisor as a mediator of the organizational climate in public social service organizations. *Administration in Social Work, 9*(2), 59–72.

Burlingame, D. F., & Hulse, L. J. (Eds.). (1991). *Taking fund raising seriously: Advancing the profession and practice of raising money.* San Francisco: Jossey-Bass.

Burnham, J. (1972). *The managerial revolution: What is happening in the world.* Westport, CT: Greenwood Press. (Originally published in 1941)

Burns, B. J., Smith, J., Goldman, H. H., Barth, L. E., et al. (1989, Fall). The CHAMPUS tidewater demonstration project. *New Directions for Mental Health Services, 43*, 77–86.

Burns, J. M. (1978). *Leadership.* New York: Harper & Row.

Buttrick, S. M. (1985). Affirmative action and job security: Policy dilemmas. In S. Slavin (Ed.), *Managing finances, personnel and information in human services* (Vol. 2, pp. 230–37). New York: Haworth Press.

Buttrick, S. M., & Miller, V. (1978). An approach to zero-base budgeting. *Administration in Social Work, 2*(1), 45–58.

Campbell, D. T., & Stanley, J. C. (1963). *Experimental and quasi-experimental designs for research.* Chicago: Rand McNally.

Capoccia, V. A. (1981). Social planning orientations: Exercises in compliance or planned social change? *Administration in Social Work, 5*(2), 37–46.

Caputo, R. K. (1988). The tao of evaluation: Deriving good from flawed methodology. *Administration in Social Work, 12*(3), 61–70.

Caro, F. G. (Ed.). (1971). *Readings in evaluation research.* New York: Russell Sage Foundation.

Carroll, S. J., & Tosi, H. L. (1973). *Management by objectives: Applications and research.* New York: Macmillan.

Carroll, S. J., Paine, F. T., & Miner, J. B. (1977). *The management process: Cases and readings* (2nd ed.). New York: Macmillan.

Carver, J. (n.d.). *Empowering boards for leadership: Redefining excellence in governance* [Audio tape]. San Francisco: Jossey-Bass.

Carver, J. (1990). *Boards that make a difference: A new design for leadership in public and nonprofit organizations.* San Francisco: Jossey-Bass.

Carver, J., & Carver, M. M. (1997). *Reinventing your board: A step-by-step guide to implementing policy governance.* San Francisco: Jossey-Bass.

Cass, R. H., & Manser, G. (1983). Roots of voluntarism. In B. O'Connell (Ed.), *America's voluntary spirit* (pp. 11–22). New York: Foundation Center.

Chakraborty, S. K. (1976). *Management by objectives: An integrated approach.* Delhi: Macmillan.

Chambers, D. E. (2000). *Social policy and social programs: A method for the practical public policy analyst* (3rd ed.). Boston: Allyn & Bacon.

Chang, C. F., & Tuckman, H. P. (1994). Revenue diversification among nonprofits. *Voluntas, 5*(3), 273–90.

Chavez, L. (1998). *The color bind: California's battle to end affirmative action.* Berkeley: University of California Press.

Chin, R., & Benne, K. D. (1976). General strategies for effecting changes in human systems. In W. G. Bennis (Ed.), *The planning of change.* New York: Holt, Reinhart and Winston.

Chisnall, P. M. (1979). The contribution of marketing research to health and welfare programs. *Administration in Social Work, 3*(3), 337–48.

Christian, J. (1992). *Marketing designs for nonprofit organizations.* Rockville, MD: Fund Raising Institute.

Clifton, R., & Dahms, A. (1993). *Grassroots organizations: A handbook for directors, staff and volunteers of small community-based nonprofit agencies* (2nd ed.). Prospect Heights, IL: Waveland Press.

Clifton, R. L., & Dahms, A. M. (1980). *Grassroots administration.* Prospect Heights, IL: Waveland Press.

Cloward, R. A., & Ohlin, L. E. (1960). *Delinquency and opportunity: A theory of delinquent gangs.* Glencoe, IL: Free Press.

Cloward, R. A., & Piven, F. F. (1975). *The politics of turmoil: Essays on poverty, race, and the urban crisis.* New York: Vintage. (Originally published in 1974)

Clynch, E. J. (1979). Zero-base budgeting in practice: An assessment. *International Journal of Public Administration, 1*(1), 43–64.

Cnaan, R. A., & Rothman, J. (1986). Conceptualizing community intervention: An empirical test of "three models" of community organization. *Administration in Social Work, 10*(3), 41–55.

Coase, R. (1937). The nature of the firm. *Economica, 12*(16), 386–405.

Cohen, M. B. (1979). Long term care and cost control: A critical analysis. *Health and Social Work, 4*(1), 60–88.

Cole, L. (1996). *Frustration is your organization's best friend: Measuring corporate culture change.* Conway, AR: LifeSkills.

Coleman, J. (1988). Social capital in the creation of human capital. *American Journal of Sociology, 94,* 95–120.

Coleman, J. (1990). *Foundations of social theory.* Cambridge, MA: Harvard University Press.

Commerce department releases IT report. (1998, June). *Government Technology,* p. 11.

Commission on Accreditation. (1994). *Handbook of accreditation standards and procedures* (4th ed.). Alexandria, VA: Council on Social Work Education.

Conlan, T. J. (1984). The politics of federal block grants: From Nixon to Reagan. *Political Science Quarterly, 99*(2), 247–70.

Coppa & Avery Consultants. (1982). *Management by objectives: A guide to periodical articles on evaluation, planning, budgeting, management of MBO.* Monticello, IL: Vance Bibliographies.

Cottrell, L. (1976). The competent community. In B. H. Kaplan, R. N. Wilson, & A. H. Leighton (Eds.), *Further explorations in social psychiatry* (pp. 195–209). New York: Basic Books.

Council on Social Work Education. (1997, Fall). Changes to the Handbook of Accreditation Standards and Procedures. *The Reporter.*

Covey, S. R. (1997). *The seven habits of highly effective people: Restoring the character ethic.* Thorndike, ME: Hall.

Crowell, E. (1976). Cost concepts and cost analysis skills for program administrators. *Journal of Social Welfare, 3*(2), 15–25.

Cultip, S. M. (1965). *Fund raising in the U.S.: Its role in American philanthropy.* New Brunswick, NJ: Rutgers University Press.

Dahl, R. A. (1960). The analysis of influence in local communities. In C. R. Adrian (Ed.), *Social science and community action.* East Lansing: Institute for Community Development and Services, Michigan State University.

Dalton, M. (1950). Conflict between staff and line managerial officers. *American Sociological Review, 15,* 342–51.

Darnell, D. K. (1972). Information theory: An approach to human communication. In R. W. Budd & B. D. Ruben (Eds.), *Approaches to human communication* (pp. 156–69). Rochelle Park, NJ: Spartan.

David, I. T. (1988). Privatization in America, *Municipal Yearbook.* Washington, DC: International City Management Association.

Davidson, H., Schlesinger, M., Dorwart, R. A., & Schnell, E. (1991). State purchase of mental health care: Models and motivations for maintaining accountability. [Special issue: Law, psychiatry, and mental health policy]. *International Journal of Law and Psychiatry, 14*(4) 387–403.

Davies, G. (1996). *From opportunity to entitlement: The transformation and decline of great society liberalism.* Lawrence: University Press of Kansas.

Davis, R. C. (1951). *The fundamentals of top management.* New York: Harper & Row.

Deakin, N. (1996). The devils in the detail: Some reflections on contracting for social care by voluntary organizations. *Social Policy and Administration, 30*(1), 20–38.

Deegan, A. X. (1977). *Management by objectives for hospitals.* Germantown, MD: Aspen Systems Corp.

DeHoog, R. H. (1984). *Contracting out for human services: Economic, political and organizational perspectives.* Albany: State University of New York Press.

DeHoog, R. H. (1986, Winter). Evaluating human services contracting: Managers, professionals and politicos. *State and Local Government Review, 18,* 37–44.

DeHoog, R. H. (1990). Competition, negotiation or cooperation. *Administration and Society, 22*(3), 317–40.

Demone, H. W., Jr., & Gibelman, M. (1984). Reaganomics: Its impact on the voluntary not-for-profit sector. *Social Work, 29*(5), 421–27.

Derthick, M. (1975). *Uncontrollable spending for social service grants.* Washington, DC: Brookings Institution.

Dewey, J. (1939). *Freedom and culture.* New York: Putnam.

Dickey, B., McGuire, T. G., Cannon, N. L., & Gudeman, J. E. (1986). Mental health cost models. Refinements and applications. *Medical Care, 24*(9), 857–67.

Donnison, D. (1961). The teaching of social administration. *British Journal of Sociology, 13.*

Downs, A. (1957). *An economic theory of democracy.* New York: Harper.

Downs, A., & Rand Corporation. (1967). *Inside bureaucracy.* Boston: Little Brown.

Dror, Y. (1963). The planning process: A facet design. *International Review of Administrative Sciences, 29*(1), 44–58.

Drtina, R. (1982, Summer). Financial indicators as a measure of nonprofit human service organization performance: The underlying issues. *New England Journal of Human Services, 3,* 35–41.

Drucker, P. (1990). *Managing the non-profit organization: Principles and practices.* New York: HarperCollins.

Drucker, P. (1996). *Landmarks of tomorrow: A report on the new post-modern world.* New Brunswick, NJ: Transaction.

Drucker, P. F. (1954). *The practice of management.* New York: Harper.

Drucker, P. F. (1964). *Managing for results: Economic tasks and risk-taking decisions.* New York: Harper & Row.

Drucker, P. F. (1974). *Management: Tasks, responsibilities, practices.* New York: Harper & Row.

Drucker, P. F. (1987). *Concept of the corporation* (2nd rev. ed.). Mentor Executive.

Drucker, P. F. (1992). *The age of discontinuity: Guidelines to our changing society.* New Brunswick, NJ: Transaction.

Drucker, P. F. (1993). *Concept of the corporation.* New Brunswick, NJ: Transaction.

Drucker, R. (1973). Low cost social work on a private practice basis. *Social Casework, 54*(3), 147–53.

Dudley, L.-S. (1990). *Contractual governance: Theory and practice in circular A-76.* Blacksburg, VA: Institute for Government Research.

Dumpson, J. R., Mullen, E. J., & First, R. J., with the assistance of Harder, W. P. (1978). *Toward education for effective social welfare administrative practice.* New York: Council on Social Work Education.

Dunham, A. (1958). *Community welfare organization: Principles and practice.* New York: Crowell.

Dunham, A. (1970). *The new community organization.* New York: Crowell.

Dworkin, R. (1978). *Taking rights seriously.* Cambridge, MA: Harvard University Press.

Edelman, M. (1971). *Information and cognition.* New York: Academic Press.

Edson, J. B. (1977). How to survive on a committee. *Social Work, 22*(3), 224–26.

Edwards, B., & Foley, M. W. (1997). Social capital, civil society and contemporary democracy. *American Behavioral Scientist, 40*(5).

Edwards, B., & Foley, M. W. (1998). Civil society and social capital beyond Putnam. *American Behavioral Scientist, 42*(1), 124–39.

Elkin, R. (1985). Paying the piper and calling the tune: Accountability in the human services. *Administration in Social Work, 9*(2), 1–13.

Elkin, R., & Molitor, M. (1984). *Management indicators in nonprofit organizations: Guidelines to selection and implementation.* Baltimore: University of Maryland Press.

Elshtain, J. B. (1996). *Democracy on trial.* Boulder, CO: Westview Press.

Emery, F. E., & Trist, E. L. (1966). The causal texture of organizational environments. *Human Relations, 18,* 21–31.

Epstein, W. (1981). The theory and use of ad hoc advisory committees: A case example in the federal government. *Journal of Applied Social Science, 5*(2), 66–82.

Erikson, E. H. (1959). Growth and crisis of the healthy personality. In *Identity and the life cycle: Selected papers of Eric H. Erikson.* New York: International Universities Press.

Erve, M. van der (1993). *The power of tomorrow's management: Using the vision-culture balance in organizations.* Oxford: Butterworth Heinemann.

Etzioni, A. (1961a). *A comparative analysis of complex organizations: On power, involvement, and their correlates.* Glencoe, IL: Free Press.

Etzioni, A. (1961b). *Complex organizations: A sociological reader.* New York: Holt, Rinehart and Winston.

Fanon, F. (1963). *The wretched of the earth: The handbook for the black revolution that is changing the shape of the world.* New York: Grove Press.

Feit, M. D., & Li, P. (1998). *Financial management in human services.* New York: Haworth Press.

Ferris, J. M. (1993). The double-edged sword of social service contracting: Public accountability versus nonprofit autonomy. *Nonprofit Management and Leadership, 3*(4), 363–77.

Fiedler, F. (1967). *A theory of leadership effectiveness.* New York: McGraw-Hill.

Finnie, R. A. J., & Sniffin, P. B. (1984). *Good endings: Managing employee terminations.* Washington, DC: College and University Personnel Association.

Fischer, J. (1973). Is casework effective? *Social Work, 18*(1), 5–20.

Fisher, R., & Karger, H. J. (1997). *Social work and community in a private world: Getting out in public.* New York: Longman.

Fisher, R., & Ury, W. (1981). *Getting to yes: Negotiating agreement without giving in.* Boston: Houghton Mifflin.

Fitzsimmons, J. A., Schwab, A. J., & Sullivan, R. S. (1979). Goal programming for holistic budget analysis. *Administration in Social Work, 3*(1), 33–43.

Fizdale, R. (1957). A new look at fee charging. *Social Casework, 38*(2).

Flynn, J. P. (1992). *Social agency policy: Analysis and presentation for community practice* (2nd ed.). Chicago: Nelson-Hall.

Follett, M. P. (1942). *Dynamic administration: The collected papers of Mary Parker Follett.* New York: Harper & Row.

Follett, M. P., & Graham, P. (1995). *Mary Parker Follett—prophet of management: A celebration of writings from the 1920s.* Boston: Harvard Business School Press.

Fraser, W. J. (1989). *Charleston! Charleston! The history of a southern city.* Charleston: University of South Carolina Press.

French, J. R. P., & Raven, B. (1968). The bases of social power. In D. Cartwright & A. Zander (Eds.), *Group dynamics* (pp. 262–68). New York: Harper & Row.

Frieden, B., & Morris, R. (1968). *Urban planning and social policy.* New York: Basic Books.

Friedmann, J. (1959). Introduction to the study and practice of planning. *International Social Science Journal, 11*(3), 327–39.

Friedmann, J. (1973). *Retracking America: A theory of transactive planning.* New York: Anchor Doubleday.

Fry, R. P. (1998). *Nonprofit investment policies: Practical steps for growing charitable funds.* New York: Wiley.

Fukuyama, F. (1995). *Trust: The social virtues and the creation of prosperity.* New York: Free Press.

Galaskiewiscz, J. (1985). *Social organization of an urban grants economy.* San Diego: Academic Press.

Gantt, H. L. (1916). *Work, wages and profits.* New York: Engineering Magazine Company.

Gelfand, D. E., & Olsen, J. K. (1980). *The aging network: Programs and services.* New York: Springer.

Germain, C. B. (1991). *Human behavior in the social environment: An ecological view.* New York: Columbia University Press.

Germain, C. B., & Gitterman, A. (1996). *The life model of social work practice: Advances in theory and practice* (2nd ed.). New York: Columbia University Press.

Gibelman, M. (1981). Are clients served better when services are purchased? *Public Welfare, 39*(4), 26-33.

Gifis, S. H. (1991). *Law dictionary* (3rd ed.). New York: Barrons.

Gilbert, N., & Specht, H. (1977). Quantitative aspects of social service coordination efforts: Is more better? *Administration in Social Work, 1*(1), 53–61.

Ginsberg, L. Social workers and politics: Lessons from practice. *Social Work, 33*(3), 245–47.

Glazer, N. (1978, Winter). Should judges administer social services? *Public Interest, 50,* 64–80.

Glenn, J. J., Brandt, L., & Andrews, F. E. (1947). *Russell Sage Foundation: 1907–1946.* New York: Russell Sage Foundation.

Glisson, C. (1989). The effect of leadership on workers in human service organizations. *Administration in Social Work, 13*(3/4), 99–116.

Glock, C. (1967). *Survey research in the social sciences.* New York: Russell Sage Foundation.

Goffman, E. (1956). *The presentation of self in everyday life.* Edinburgh: University of Edinburgh Social Sciences Research Centre.

Goffman, E. (1969). *Strategic interaction.* Philadelphia: University of Pennsylvania Press.

Goffman, E. (1986). *Stigma: Notes on the management of spoiled identity.* Englewood Cliffs, NJ: Prentice Hall.

Gooden, V. (1998). Contracting and negotiation: Effective practices of successful human service contract managers. *Public Administration Review, 58*(6), 499–508.

Goodman, N. (1960). Are there differences between fee and non-fee cases? *Social Work, 5*(4), 46–52.

Graham, P. (Ed.). (1995). *Mary Parker Follett: Prophet of management.* Cambridge, MA: Harvard University Press.

Granvold, D. K. (1978). Supervision by objectives. *Administration in Social Work, 2*(2), 199–209.

Gray, B. K. (1905). *A history of English philanthropy: From the dissolution of the monasteries to the taking of the first census.* London: Cass.

Greater New York Fund of United Way (1978). *The impact of government funding on the management of voluntary agencies: Research report.* New York: Greater New York Fund of United Way.

Greeley, A. (1997). Coleman revisited: Religious structures as a source of social capital. *American Behavioral Scientist, 40*(5), 587–95.

Greene, R. (1998). *The 48 laws of power.* New York: Viking.

Greenlee, J. (1998). Accountability in nonprofit organizations. *Nonprofit Management and Leadership, 9*(2), 205–10.

Greenlee, J. S., & Trussel, J. M. (2000). Predicting the financial vulnerability of charitable organizations. *Nonprofit Management and Leadership, 11*(2), 199–210.

Greider, W. (1981, December). The education of David Stockman. *Atlantic Monthly,* pp. 27–54.

Grønbjerg, K. (1983). Private welfare: Its future in the welfare state. *American Behavior Scientist, 26,* 773–93.

Grønbjerg, K. (1991). Managing grants and contracts: The case of four nonprofit social service organizations. *Nonprofit and Voluntary Sector Quarterly, 20*(1), 5–24.

Grønbjerg, K. (1993). *Understanding nonprofit funding: Managing revenues in social services and community development organizations.* San Francisco: Jossey-Bass.

Gross, M., Warshauer, W., & Larkin, R. F. (1991). *Financial and accounting guide for not-for-profit organizations.* New York: Wiley.

Guetzkow, H. (1950). Interagency committee usage. *Public Administration Review 10*(3), 190–96.

Gulick, L., & Urwick, L. (Eds.). (1937). *Papers on the science of administration.* New York: Institute of Public Administration, Columbia University.

Gummer, B. (1995a). Reinventing, restructuring, and the big bang theory of organizational change. *Administration in Social Work, 19*(3), 83–97.

Gummer, B. (1995b). Social planning. In R. Edwards (Ed.), *Encyclopedia of social work* (19th ed., Vol. 3, pp. 2180–86). Washington, DC: National Association of Social Workers.

Gummer, B. (1996). Total quality management: Organizational transformation or passing fancy? *Administration in Social Work, 20*(3), 75–95.

Gummer, B. A. (1979). A framework for curriculum planning in social welfare administration. *Administration in Social Work, 3*(4), 385–95.

Gutierrez, G. (1973). *A theology of liberation.* Maryknoll, NY: Orbis.

Guy, M. E., & Hitchcock, J. R. (2000). If apples were oranges: The public/nonprofit/business nexus in Peter Drucker's work. *Journal of Management History, 6*(1).

Haber, S. (1991). *The quest for authority and honor in American professions, 1750–1900.* Chicago: University of Chicago Press.

Hackman, J. R. (1986). The psychology of self-management in organizations. In R. O. Perloff & M. S. Pallak (Eds.), *Psychology and work: Productivity, change, and employment. The master lectures* (Vol. 5, pp. 89–136). Washington, DC: American Psychological Association.

Hadley, R., & Hatch, S. (1981). *Social welfare and the failure of the state.* London: George Allen & Unwin.

Hadley, T. R., & Glover, R. (1989). Philadelphia: Using Medicaid as a basis for capitation. *New Directions for Mental Health Services, 43,* 65–76.

Hairston, C. F. (1981). Improving cash management in nonprofit organizations. *Administration in Social Work, 5*(2), 29–36.

Hairston, C. F. (1985). Using ratio analysis for financial accountability. *Social Casework, 66*(2), 76–82.

Hall, M. D. (1981, Winter). Financial condition: A measure of human service organization performance. *New England Journal of Human Services, 2,* 29–34.

Hammack, D.C. (1988). *The Russell Sage Foundation: Social research and social action in America, 1907–1947—Guide to the microfiche collection.* Frederick, MD: UPA Academic Editions.

Hammack, D.C., & Wheeler, S. (1994). *Social science in the making: Essays on the Russell Sage Foundation, 1907–1972.* New York: Russell Sage Foundation.

Hanlon, A. (1978). From social work to social administration. In S. Slavin (Ed.), *Social administration.* New York: Haworth Press.

Hansen, M., & Evashwick, C. (1981). Hospice: Staffing and cost implications for home health agencies. *Home Health Care Services Quarterly, 2*(1), 61–81.

Hansmann H. (1981, January). Reforming nonprofit corporation law. *University of Pennsylvania Law Review, 129*(3), 503.

Hansmann, H. (1987). Economic theories of nonprofit organization. In W. W. Powell (Ed.), *The nonprofit sector: A research handbook* (pp. 27–42). New Haven, CT: Yale University Press.

Hardina, D. (1990). The effect of funding sources on client access to services. *Administration in Social Work, 14*(3), 33–46.

Harriman, L., & Straussman, J. D. (1983). Do judges determine budget decisions? Federal court decisions in prison reform and state spending for corrections. *Public Administration Review, 43*(4), 343–51.

Hartogs, N., & Weber, J. (1974). *Boards of directors: A study of current practices in board management and board operations in voluntary hospital, health and welfare organizations.* Dobbs Ferry, NY: Oceana.

Hasenfeld, Y. (1980). Implementation of change in human service organizations: A political economy perspective. *Social Service Review, 54*(4), 508–20.

Hasenfeld, Y. (1983). *Human service organizations.* Englewood Cliffs, NJ: Prentice Hall.

Hasenfeld, Y. (1984). The changing context of human services administration. *Social Work, 29*(6), 522–31.

Hasenfeld, Y. (1985). The administration of human services. *Annals of the American Academy of Political and Social Science, 479*(1), 67–81.

Hasenfeld, Y. (1992). *Human services as complex organizations* (7th ed.). Thousand Oaks, CA: Sage.

Hasenfeld, Y. (2000). Social welfare administration and organizational theory. In R. Patti (Ed.), *The handbook of social welfare management* (pp. 89–108). Thousand Oaks, CA: Sage.

Hasenfeld, Y., & English, R. (1974). *Human service organizations: A book of readings.* Ann Arbor: University of Michigan Press.

Hasenfeld, Y., & Schmid, H. (1989). The life cycle of human service organizations: An administrative perspective. *Administration in Social Work, 13*(3/4), 243–69.

Haynes, K. S., & Mickelson, J. S. (2000). *Affecting change: Social workers in the political arena* (4th ed.). Boston: Allyn & Bacon.

Haywood, T. (1995). *Info rich/info poor: Access and exchange in the global information society.* London: Bowker-Saur.

Heffernan, J. (1991). Efficiency considerations in the social welfare agency. *Administration in Social Work, 15*(1/2), 119–31.

Heimovics, R. D., Herman, R. D., & Coughlin, C. L. J. (1993). Executive leadership and resource dependence in nonprofit organizations: A frame analysis. *Public Administration Review, 53*(5), 419–27.

Hersey, P., & Blanchard, K. H. (1977). *Management of organizational behavior: Managing human resources* (3rd ed.). Englewood Cliffs, NJ: Prentice Hall.

Hertzman, M., & Montague, B. (1977). Cost analysis and alcoholism. *Journal of Studies on Alcohol, 38*(7), 1371–85.

Hill, W. G. (1971). Voluntary and governmental financial transactions. *Social Casework, 52*(6), 356–61.

Hirschman, A. O. (1981). Exit, voice, and loyalty: Responses to decline in firms, organizations, and states. Cambridge, MA: Harvard University Press.

Hobsbawm, E. (1998). *Uncommon people: Resistance, rebellion and jazz.* New York: New Press.

Hodgkinson, V. (1993, March 3). *Giving and volunteering in the United States: Summary.* Paper presented at the 1993 International Conference on Fund Raising, National Society of Fund Raising Executives, Atlanta.

Hodgkinson, V., Weitzman, M., Abrahams, J. A., Crutchfield, E. A., & Stevenson, D. R. (1996). *Nonprofit almanac 1996–97: Dimensions of the independent sector.* San Francisco: Jossey-Bass.

Hoffman, M. E. (1934). *History of the West Virginia poor law.* Unpublished doctoral dissertation, University of Chicago.

Hofstein, S. (1955). Fee payment in social work counseling. *Social Casework, 36*(7).

Holland, T. P., & Jackson, D. K. (1998). Strengthening board performance: Findings and lessons from demonstration projects. *Nonprofit Management and Leadership, 9*(2), 121–34.

Holloway, S., & Brager, G. (1977). Some considerations in planning organizational change. *Administration in Social Work, 1*(4), 349–57.

Holoski, M. J., & Feit, M. D. (1990). A proposed cost-effectiveness method for use in policy formulation in human service organizations. *Journal of Health and Social Policy, 1*(3), 55–71.

Homans, G. C. (1961). *Social behavior: Its elementary forms.* New York: Harcourt, Brace.

Homans, G. C. (1968). Social behavior as exchange. *American Journal of Sociology, 63,* 597–606.

Hopkins, B. R. (1991). *The law of fund-raising.* New York: Wiley.

Hopkins, B. R. (1996). *The law of fund-raising* (2nd ed.). New York: Wiley.

Horvath, J. (1982). Grants economics. In D. Greenwalt (Ed.), *Encyclopedia of economics.* New York: McGraw-Hill.

Howe, F. (1991). *The board member's guide to fund raising: What every trustee needs to know about raising money.* San Francisco: Jossey-Bass.

Huczynski, A. (1993). *Management gurus: What makes them and how to become one.* New York: Routledge.

Hughes, E. C. (1936). The ecological aspects of institutions. *American Sociological Review, 1*(2), 180–92.

Hughes, E. C. (1939). Institutions, Part V. In R. E. Park (Ed.), *An outline of the principles of sociology.* New York: Barnes and Noble.

Hughes, S. (1999). *To go forward, retreat!* Washington, DC: National Center for Nonprofit Boards.

Humble, J. W. (1970). *Management by objectives in action.* London: McGraw-Hill.

Humphreys, K., & Kaskutas, L. A. (1995). World views of Alcoholics Anonymous, Women for Sobriety, and Adult Children of Alcoholics/Al-Anon mutual help groups. *Addiction Research, 3*(3), 231–43.

Humphreys, K., & Rappaport, J. (1993). From the community mental health movement to the war on drugs: A study in the definition of social problems. *American Psychologist, 48*(8), 892–901.

Hunter, F. (1953). *Community power structure: A study of decision makers.* New York: Anchor.

Huntsinger, J. (1987, September). What to do after all of your donors are dead. *Fund Raising Management, 18,* 37–45.

Hyde, C. (1989). A feminist model for macro-practice: Promises and problems. *Administration in Social Work, 13*(3/4), 145–81.

Hyde, C. (1998). A model for diversity training in human service agencies. *Administration in Social Work, 22*(4), 19–33.

Ilchman, W., & Uphoff, N. (1968). *The political economy of change.* Berkeley: University of California Press.

Jackson, P. (1982). *The political economy of bureaucracy.* London: Allen.

Jacobs, T. C. (1952). Attitudes of social workers toward fees. *Social Casework, 33*(5).

Janssen, B. (1993). *The reluctant welfare state: A history of American social welfare policy* (2nd ed.). Pacific Grove, CA: Brooks-Cole.

Jansson, B. S. (1979). Public monitoring of contracts with nonprofit organizations: Organizational mission in two sectors. *Journal of Sociology and Social Welfare, 6*(3), 362–74.

Jansson, B. S. (1990). *Social welfare policy: From theory to practice.* Belmont, CA: Wadsworth.

Jenkins, S., et al. (1988). *Ethnic associations and the welfare state: Services to immigrants in five countries.* New York: Columbia University Press.

Johnson, L. (1998). *The new workplace: Transforming the character and culture of our organizations.* Waltham, MA: Pegasus.

Johnson, W., & Clancy, T. (1991). Efficiency in behavior changing social programs: The case of in-home child abuse prevention. *Administration in Social Work, 15*(1/2), 105–18.

Johnson, Y. M. (1999). Indirect work: Social work's uncelebrated strength. *Social Work, 44*(4), 323–34.

Judge, K., & Smith, J. (1983). Purchase of service in England. *Social Service Review, 57*(2), 209–33.

Jun, J. S. (1973). *Management by objectives in a government agency: The case of the Social and Rehabilitation Service.* Washington, DC: U.S. Department of Health Education and Welfare Social and Rehabilitation Service.

Kadushin, A. (1992). *Supervision in social work* (3rd ed.). New York: Columbia University Press.

Kahn, A. J. (1969a). *Studies in social policy and planning.* New York: Russell Sage Foundation.

Kahn, A. J. (1969b). *Theory and practice of social planning.* New York: Russell Sage Foundation.

Kahn, A. J., & Kamerman, S. B. (1977). *Social services in international perspective: The emergence of the sixth system.* Washington, DC: U.S. Department of

Health Education and Welfare Social and Rehabilitation Service, Office of Planning Research and Evaluation.

Kakar, S. (1970). *Frederick Taylor: A study in personality and innovation.* Cambridge, MA: MIT Press.

Kamerman, S. (1983). The new mixed economy of welfare: Public and private. *Social Work, 28,* 5–9.

Kaplama, V., & Varoglu, A. K. (1997). "Learning to learn" as a tool of total quality management (TQM) in educational institutions. *Turk Psikoloji Dergisi, 12*(39), 81–97.

Kaplan, A. (1964). *The conduct of inquiry: Methodology for behavioral science.* San Francisco: Chandler.

Karn, G. N. (1982, December). Money talks: A guide for establishing the true dollar value of volunteer time, I. *Journal of Volunteer Administration,* pp. 1–15.

Karn, G. N. (1983, March). Money talks: A guide for establishing the true dollar value of volunteer time, II. *Journal of Volunteer Administration,* pp. 1–19.

Katz, D., & Kahn, R. (1966). *The social psychology of organizations.* New York: Wiley.

Keener, T., & Sebestyan, D. (1981). A cost analysis of selected Dallas day care centers. *Child Welfare, 60*(2), 81–88.

Kelly, K. S. (1998). *Effective fund-raising management.* Mahwah, NJ: Erlbaum.

Kennedy, P. (1987). *The rise and fall of the great powers: Economic change and military conflict from 1500 to 2000.* New York: Random House.

Kettl, D. (1988). *Government by proxy.* Washington, DC: Congressional Quarterly Press.

Kettner, P. M., & Martin, L. L. (1985a). Issues in the development of monitoring systems for purchase of service contracting. *Administration in Social Work, 9*(3), 69–82.

Kettner, P. M., & Martin, L. L. (1985b). Purchase of service contracting and the declining influence of social work. *Urban and Social Change Review, 18*(2), 8–11.

Kettner, P. M., & Martin, L. L. (1986). Making decisions about purchase of service contracting. *Public Welfare, 44*(4), 30–37.

Kettner, P. M., & Martin, L. L. (1987). *Purchase of service contracting.* Beverly Hills, CA: Sage.

Kettner, P. M., & Martin, L. L. (1988). Purchase of service contracting with for-profit organizations. *Administration in Social Work, 12*(4), 47–60.

Kettner, P. M., & Martin, L. L. (1990). Purchase of service contracting: Two models. *Administration in Social Work, 14*(1), 15–30.

Kettner, P. M., & Martin, L. L. (1993). Performance, accountability, and purchase of service contracting. *Administration in Social Work, 17*(1), 61–79.

Kettner, P. M., & Martin, L. L. (1995). Performance contracting in the human services: An initial assessment. *Administration in Social Work, 19*(2), 47–61.

Kettner, P. M., & Martin, L. L. (1996a). The impact of declining resources and purchase of service contracting on private, nonprofit agencies. *Administration in Social Work, 20*(3), 21–38.

Kettner, P. M., & Martin, L. L. (1996b). Purchase of service contracting versus government service delivery: The views of state human service administrators. *Journal of Sociology and Social Welfare, 23*(2), 107–19.

Kettner, P. M., Moroney, R. M., & Martin, L. L. (1990). *Designing and managing programs: An effectiveness based approach.* Newbury Park, CA: Sage.

Kidneigh, J. (1950). Social work administration: An area of social work practice? *Social Work Journal, 31*(2), 57–61.

Kingson, E. R., Larson, R. E., Peterson, C., & Rivelois, K. (1986). Estimating the cost of continuing disability reviews. *Administration in Social Work, 10*(2), 79–90.

Kinnear, T. C., & Bernhardt, K. L. (1983). *Principles of marketing.* Glenview, IL: Scott, Foresman.

Knapp, M. (1991). Cost. *Administration in Social Work, 15*(1/2), 45–63.

Koontz, H., & O'Donnell, C. (1974). *Essentials of management.* New York: McGraw-Hill.

Koontz, H., & O'Donnell, C. (1978). *Essentials of management* (2nd ed.). New York: McGraw-Hill.

Koster, M., Messner, B., Richert, S., Cleveland Artists Foundation, & Cleveland Museum of Art. (1996). *Cleveland's artistic heritage: Symposium presented by the Cleveland Artists Foundation at the Cleveland Museum of Art, March 30 & 31, 1996.* Cleveland: Cleveland Artists Foundation.

Kotler, P. (1974). *Marketing for nonprofit organizations.* Englewood Cliffs, NJ: Prentice Hall.

Kotler, P. (1982). *Marketing for nonprofit organizations* (2nd ed.). Englewood Cliffs, NJ: Prentice Hall.

Kotler, P., & Andreasen, A. R. (1996). *Strategic marketing for nonprofit organizations* (5th ed.). Upper Saddle River, NJ: Prentice Hall.

Kramer, R. M. (1966). Voluntary agencies and the use of public funds: Some policy issues. *Social Service Review, 40*(1), 15–26.

Kramer, R. M. (1973). Future of the voluntary service organization. *Social Work, 18*(6), 59–69.

Kramer, R. M. (1981). *Voluntary agencies in the welfare state.* Berkeley: University of California Press.

Kramer, R. M. (1985). Toward a contingency model of board-executive relations. *Administration in Social Work, 9*(3), 15–33.

Kuechler, C. F., Velasquez, J. S., & White, M. S. (1988). An assessment of human services program outcome measures: Are they credible, feasible, useful? *Administration in Social Work, 12*(3), 71–89.

Kuypers, B. C., & Alers, M. B. (1996). Mapping the interpersonal underworld: A study on central roles and their scripts in the development of self-analytic groups. *Small Group Research, 27*(1), 3–32.

Laczko, F. (1993). The state and social welfare: The objectives of social policy, by T. Wilson, D. Wilson. *Ageing and Society, 13*(Part 1), 126–27.

Landry, C., & Knox, J. (1996). Managed care fundamentals: Implications for health care organizations and health care professionals. *American Journal of Occupational Therapy, 50*(6), 413–16.

Lang, J., & St. John's University. (1988). Unequal access to information resources: Problems and needs of the world's information poor. In New York Department of Library and Information Sciences, *Proceedings of the Congress for Librarians.* Ann Arbor, MI: Pierian Press.

Lauffer, A. (1978). *Social planning at the community level.* Englewood Cliffs, NJ: Prentice Hall.

Lauffer, A. (1979). Social planning in the United States: An overview and some predictions. In F. M. Cox, J. L. Erlich, J. Rothman, & J. E. Tropman (Eds.), *Strategies of community organization* (3rd ed., pp. 292–304). Itasca, IL: Peacock.

Lauffer, A. (1997). *Grants, etc.* Thousand Oaks, CA: Sage.

Leeman, W. A. (1978). Third-party purchase of voluntary agency services. *Child Welfare, 57*(8), 497–504.

Leiby, J. (1991). Efficiency in social service administration: Historical reflections. *Administration in Social Work, 15*(1/2), 155–73.

Levinson, J., & Godin, S. (1994). *The guerrilla marketing handbook.* Boston: Houghton Mifflin.

Lewin, K., & University of Michigan, Research Center for Group Dynamics. (1975). *Field theory in social science: Selected theoretical papers.* Westport, CT: Greenwood Press.

Lewin, K., Lippitt, R., & White, R. K. (1939). Patterns of aggressive behavior in experimentally created social climates. *Journal of Social Psychology, 10,* 271–99.

Lewis, J. A., & Lewis, M. D. (1983). *Management of human service programs.* Monterey, CA: Brooks-Cole.

Lindahl, W. E. (1992). *Strategic planning for fund raising: How to bring in more money using strategic resource allocation.* San Francisco: Jossey-Bass.

Lindblom, C. (1977). *Politics and markets: The world's political-economic systems.* New York: Basic Books.

Lindblom, C. A. (1959). The science of muddling through. *Public Administration Review, 19*(1), 79–88.

Lindeman, E. C. (1936). *Wealth and culture: A study of one hundred foundations and community trusts and their operations during the decade 1921–1930.* New York: Harcourt, Brace.

Littler, C. R. (1982). *The development of the labour process in capitalist societies: A comparative study of the transformation of work organization in Britain, Japan, and the USA.* Exeter, NH: Heinemann Educational.

Lohmann, N. (1991). Evaluating programs for older people. In P. K. H. Kim (Ed.), *Serving the elderly: Skills for practice* (pp. 259–77). New York: Aldine De Gruyter.

Lohmann, R., & Barbeau, E. (1992). The executive director as keeper of the past. *Administration in Social Work, 16*(2), 15–26.

Lohmann, R. A. (1976). Break-even analysis: A tool for budgetary planning. *Social Work, 21*(4), 300–307.

Lohmann, R. A. (1979). The principles of organizational inaction. *Bureaucrat, 8*(2), 87–89.

Lohmann, R. A. (1980a). *Breaking even: Financial management in human services*. Philadelphia: Temple University Press.

Lohmann, R. A. (1980b). Budget-making, financial management and human services administration. In S. Slavin & F. Perlmutter (Eds.), *Leadership in social administration*. Philadelphia: Temple University Press.

Lohmann, R. A. (1981). *Planning for aging services: Implications of recent amendments to the Older Americans Act*. Paper presented at the annual meeting of the Gerontological Society of America.

Lohmann, R. A. (1984). Resource development as executive leadership. In F. Perlmutter (Ed.), *Human services at risk* (pp. 93–108). Lexington, MA: Lexington Books.

Lohmann, R. A. (1987). Private social services in a welfare society. *Journal of Independent Social Work, 2*(2), 7–20.

Lohmann, R. A. (1989). And lettuce is non-animal: Toward a positive economics of nonprofit action. *Nonprofit and Voluntary Sector Quarterly, 18*(4), 367–83.

Lohmann, R. A. (1991a). *Crisis response services in north central West Virginia: A resource inventory*. Unpublished manuscript.

Lohmann, R. A. (1991b). Social planning and the problems of old age. In P. Kim (Ed.), *Serving the elderly: Skills for practice* (pp. 209–32). New York: Aldine De Gruyter.

Lohmann, R. A. (1992). *The commons: Perspectives on nonprofit organization and voluntary action*. San Francisco: Jossey-Bass.

Lohmann, R. A. (1993). Farmers and ranchers. *Nonprofit and Voluntary Sector Quarterly, 22*(3), 271–73.

Lohmann, R. A. (1995a). Financial management. In R. Edwards (Ed.), *Encyclopedia of social work* (Vol. 2, pp. 1028–36). Washington, DC: National Association of Social Workers.

Lohmann, R. A. (1995b). The Buddhist commons in Asia. *Voluntas, 6*(2), 140–58.

Lohmann, R. A. (1996). The social work docuverse: A challenge for the twenty-first century. *Tulane Studies in Social Welfare, 20*, 107–25.

Lohmann, R. A. (1997). Managed care: A review of recent research. In R. Edwards (Ed.), *Encyclopedia of social work* (19th ed., 1997 Supplement, pp. 200–214). Washington, DC: National Association of Social Workers.

Lohmann, R. A. (1999). Has the time come to reevaluate evaluation? Or, who will be accountable for accountability? *Nonprofit Management and Leadership, 10*(1), 93–102.

Lohmann, R. A. (2000a). Lindblom County: How diversity influenced philanthropic sufficiency. In D. Fauri, S. Wernet, & E. Netting (Eds.), *Cases in macro social practice*. Boston: Allyn & Bacon.

Lohmann, R. A. (2000b, July 6). *Charismatic authority and the board of the Hull House Association, 1895–1935*. Paper presented at the International Society for Third Sector Research, Dublin, Ireland.

Lohmann, R. A., & Lohmann, N. (1995, April). *Nonprofit community service and the hidden cost of information technology*. Paper presented at the Nonprofit Technology Conference, Michigan State University.

Lohmann, R. A., & Lohmann, N. L. (1997). Management: Cost measurement. In R. Edwards (Ed.), *Encyclopedia of Social Work* (19th ed., Vol. 3, 1997 Supplement, pp. 214–29). Washington, DC: National Association of Social Workers.

Lohmann, R. A., Locke, B., & Meehan, K. (1984). A model for human service planning. In *Proceedings of the 10th National Institute for Social Work in Rural Areas.* Columbia: University of Missouri School of Social Work.

Lowi, T. J. (1969). *The end of liberalism: Ideology, policy and the crisis of public authority.* New York: Norton.

Lowi, T. J. (1995). *The end of the Republican era.* Norman: University of Oklahoma Press.

Lubove, R. (1965). *The professional altruist.* Cambridge, MA: Harvard University Press.

Lubove, R. (1968). *The struggle for social security, 1900–1935.* Cambridge, MA: Harvard University Press.

Macdonald, D. (1956). *The Ford Foundation: The men and the millions.* New York: Reynal.

Mackey, H. (1965). The operation of the English old poor law in colonial Virginia. *Virginia Magazine, 73,* 29–40.

MacManus, S. (1992). *Doing business with government.* New York: Paragon House.

Maddox, D. C. (1999). *Budgeting for not-for-profit organizations.* New York: Wiley.

Malka, S. (1990). Contracting for human services: The case of Pennsylvania's subsidized child day care program—Policy limitations and prospects. *Administration in Social Work, 14*(1), 31–46.

Mangham, I. L. (1986). *Power and performance in organizations: An exploration of executive process.* Oxford: Blackwell.

Manning, S. S. (1997). The social worker as moral citizen: Ethics in action. *Social Work, 42*(3), 223–30.

Maor, M. (1999). The paradox of managerialism. *Public Administration Review, 59*(1), 5–18.

March, J., & Simon, H., with the collaboration of Guetzkow, H. (1958). *Organizations.* New York: Wiley.

Martin, L. (1993). *Total quality management in human service organizations* (Vol. 67). Thousand Oaks, CA: Sage.

Martin, L. L., & Kettner, P. M. (1997). Performance measurement: The new accountability. *Administration in Social Work, 21*(1), 17–29.

Martin, P. Y. (1985). Multiple constituencies, dominant societal values and the human service administrator: Implications for service delivery. In S. Slavin (Ed.), *An introduction to human services administration* (2nd ed., Vol. 1, pp. 72–84). New York: Haworth Press.

Martindale, D. (1960). *The nature and types of sociological theory.* New York: Houghton Mifflin.

Martinez-Brawley, E. E. (1990). *Perspectives on the small community: Humanistic views for practitioners.* Washington, DC: National Association of Social Workers.

Marx, K., & Engels, F. (1967). *Capital: A critique of political economy.* New York: International.

Maslow, A. H. (1959). *New knowledge in human values.* New York: Harper.

Mayadas, N. S., & Duehn, W. D. (1977). Performance contracts in the administration of social work education. *Administration in Social Work, 1*(4), 443–52.

Mayer, R. (1972). *Social planning and social change.* Englewood Cliffs, NJ: Prentice Hall.

Mayer, R. (1985). *Policy and program planning: A developmental perspective.* Englewood Cliffs, NJ: Prentice Hall.

Mayers, R. S. (1989). *Financial management for nonprofit human service agencies: Text, cases, readings.* Springfield, IL: Thomas.

McCready, D. J., & Rahn, S. L. (1986). Funding human services: Fixed utility vs. fixed budget. *Administration in Social Work, 10*(4), 23–30.

McGregor, D. (1960). *The human side of enterprise.* New York: McGraw-Hill.

McKay, A., & Baxter, E. H. (1980). Title XIX, title XX and catch XXII: Cost analysis in social program evaluation. *Administration in Social Work, 4*(3), 23–30.

McMaster, R., & Sawkins, J. (1996). The contract state, trust distortion and efficiency. *Review of Social Economy, 54,* 145–67.

McNeely, R. L. (1985). Gender and job satisfaction during budgetary retrenchment. *Administration in Mental Health, 12*(4), 233–45.

Mead, G. H. (1934). *Mind, self, and society from the standpoint of a social behavioralist.* Chicago: University of Chicago Press.

Mechanic, D. (1998). *Mental health and social policy: The emergence of managed care* (4th ed.). Boston: Allyn & Bacon.

Meier, C. (1998). *Athens: A portrait of the city in its golden age.* (R. Kimber, Trans.). New York: Metropolitan Books/Henry Holt.

Mencher, S. (1967). *Poor law to poverty program: Economic security policy in Britain and the United States.* Pittsburgh: University of Pittsburgh Press.

Merton, R. K. (1940). Bureaucratic structure and personality. *Social Forces, 18.*

Merton, R. (Ed.). (1952). *Reader in bureaucracy.* Glencoe, IL: Free Press.

Merton, R. K. (1957). *Social theory and social structure* (Rev. & enl. ed.). Glencoe, IL: Free Press.

Meyer, D., & Sherridan, M. (1985). Toward improved financial planning: Further applications of break even analysis in not for profit organizations. *Administration in Social Work, 9*(3), 57–68.

Miller, D. C. (1970). *Handbook of research design and social measurement* (2nd ed.). New York: McKay.

Miller, K., Fein, E., Howe, G. W., Gaudio, C. P., & Bishop, G. (1985). A parent aide program: Record keeping, outcomes and costs. *Child Welfare, 64*(4), 407–19.

Milligan, C. (1998). Pathways of dependence: The impact of health and social care restructuring—The voluntary experience. *Social Science and Medicine 46*(6), 743–53.

Mills, C. W. (1956). *The power elite.* New York: Oxford University Press.

Mintzberg, H. (1973). *The nature of managerial work.* New York: Harper & Row.

Mintzberg, H. (1979). *The structuring of organizations: A synthesis of the research.* Englewood Cliffs, NJ: Prentice Hall.

Mintzberg, H. (1994). *The rise and fall of strategic planning: Reconceiving roles for planning, plans, planners.* New York: Free Press.

Mitchell, J. N. (1978). *Social exchange, dramaturgy and ethnomethodology.* New York: Elsevier.

Mitroff, I. I., Mohrman, S. A., & Little, G. (1987). *Business not as usual: Rethinking our individual, corporate, and industrial strategies for global competition.* San Francisco: Jossey-Bass.

Mixer, J. R. (1993). *Principles of professional fundraising: Useful foundations for successful practice.* San Francisco: Jossey-Bass.

Moore, J. I. (1992). *Writers on strategy and strategic management: The theory of strategy and the practice of strategic management at enterprise, corporate, business and functional levels.* New York: Penguin.

Moreno, J. L. (1956). *Sociometry and the science of man.* New York: Beacon House.

Moreno, J. L. (1960). *The sociometry reader.* Glencoe, IL: Free Press.

Moreno, J. L., Jennings, H. H., Whitin, E. S., & National Committee on Prisons. (1932). *Group method and group psychotherapy.* New York: Beacon House.

Morgan, G. (1997). *Images of organization* (2nd ed.). Thousand Oaks, CA: Sage.

Morris, R. (1964). *Centrally planned change: Prospects and concepts.* New York: National Association of Social Workers.

Morris, R. (1985). *Social policy of the American welfare state: An introduction to policy analysis* (2nd ed.). New York: Longman.

Morris, R., & Binstock, R. (1966). *Feasible planning for social change.* New York: Columbia University Press.

Morris, R., & Morris, S. (1986). *Rethinking social welfare: Why care for the stranger?* White Plains, NY: Longman.

Morrisey, G. L. (1970). *Management by objectives and results.* Reading, MA: Addison-Wesley.

Morrisey, G. L. (1976). *Management by objectives and results in the public sector.* Reading, MA: Addison-Wesley.

Mullen, E. J., & Magnabosco, J. L. (1997). *Outcomes measurement in the human services: Cross-cutting issues and methods.* Washington, DC: National Association of Social Workers.

Munson, C. E. (1993). *Clinical social work supervision* (2nd ed.). New York: Haworth Press.

Murray, V. (1991). *Improving corporate donations: New strategies for grantmakers and grantseekers.* San Francisco: Jossey-Bass.

Musgrave, G. L., & Elster, R. S. (1974). *Management by objectives and goal setting.* Monticello, IL: Council of Planning Librarians.

National Association of Social Workers. (1996). *Code of ethics.* Washington, DC: Author.

National Institute of Mental Health (1972). *Cost finding and rate setting for community mental health.* Washington, DC: Government Printing Office.

Nelson, W. (1992, October 6). A reason to have fund raisers: Stingy rich people. *Chronicle of Philanthropy,* p. 41.

Netting, E. F. (1982). Secular and religious funding of church-related agencies. *Social Service Review, 56*(4), 586–604.

Netting, F. E., Kettner, P. M., & McMurtry, S. L. (1993). *Social work macro practice.* White Plains, NY: Longman.

Netting, F. E., McMurtry, S. L., Kettner, P. M., & Jones-McClintic, S. (1990). Privatization and its impact on nonprofit service providers. *Nonprofit and Voluntary Sector Quarterly, 19*(1), 33–46.

Neugeboren, B. (1991). *Organization, policy and practice in the human services.* Binghamton, NY: Haworth.

Newkhalm, J. B. (1981). Computerizing and integrated clinical and financial record system in a CMHC. *Administration in Social Work, 5*(3–4), 97–111.

Newman, W. H. (1951). *Administrative action: The technique of organization and management.* Englewood Cliffs, NJ: Prentice Hall.

Newman, W. H., & Wallender, H. W. (1978). Managing not-for-profit enterprises. *Academy of Management Review, 3*(1), 24–31.

New state laws and proposals in Congress seek to curb charitable solicitations by telephone. (1991, May 21). *Chronicle of Philanthropy.*

Nisbet, R. A. (1975). *Twilight of authority.* New York: Oxford University Press.

Niskanen, W. (1968). The peculiar economics of bureaucracy. *American Economics Review, 58,* 293–305.

Niskanen, W. A. (1998). *Policy analysis and public choice: Selected papers by William Niskanen.* Northampton, MA: Elgar.

Non-profits in Nevada get rights to hold lotteries. (1991, October 8). *Chronicle of Philanthropy.*

Nowland-Foreman, G. (1998). Purchase-of-service contracting, voluntary organizations, and civil society: Dissecting the goose that lays the golden eggs? *American Behavioral Scientist, 42*(1), 108–23.

O'Neill, M. (1989). *The third America: The emergence of the nonprofit sector in the United States.* San Francisco: Jossey-Bass.

Odiorne, G. S. (1965). *Management by objectives: A system of managerial leadership.* New York: Pitman.

Oliver, C. (Ed.). (1999). *The policy governance fieldbook: Practical lessons from boards implementing the model.* San Francisco: Jossey-Bass.

Olsson, D. E. (1968). *Management by objectives.* Palo Alto, CA: Pacific Books.

Osborne, D., & Gaebler, T. (1992). *Reinventing government: How the entrepreneurial spirit is transforming the public sector.* Reading, MA: Addison-Wesley.

Ostrower, F. (1997). *Why the wealthy give: The culture of elite philanthropy.* Princeton, NJ: Princeton University Press.

Otten, G. L. (1977). Zero-based budgeting: Implications for social services? *Administration in Social Work, 1*(4), 369–78.

Padgett, D. L. (1993). Women and management: A conceptual framework. *Administration in Social Work, 17*(4), 57–75.

Page, W. J., & St. John, D. (1984). The CEO and general counsel. *Public Welfare, 42*(3), 10–18.

Pancoast, D. L., Parker, P., & Froland, C. (1983). *Rediscovering self-help: Its role in social care.* Beverly Hills, CA: Sage.

Parkinson, C. N. (1957). *Parkinson's law, and other studies in administration.* Boston: Houghton Mifflin.

Patti, R. (1983). *Social welfare administration: Managing social programs in a developmental context.* Englewood Cliffs, NJ: Prentice Hall.

Patti, R. (Ed.). (2000). *Handbook of social welfare management.* Thousand Oaks, CA: Sage.

Payton, R. L. (1988). *Philanthropy: Voluntary action for the public good.* New York: American Council on Education.

Pecora, P. J. (1995). Personnel management. In R. L. Edwards (Ed.), *Encyclopedia of social work* (19th ed., Vol. 3, pp. 1821–36). Washington, DC: National Association of Social Workers.

Pennsylvania Bar Institute. (1997). *Fundraising regulations for tax exempt organizations.* Mechanicsburg, PA: Author.

Perlman, S., & Bush, B. H. (1996). *Fund-raising regulation: A state-by-state handbook of registration forms, requirements, and procedures.* New York: Wiley.

Perlmutter, F., & Adams, C. (1990). The voluntary sector and for-profit ventures. *Administration in Social Work, 14,* 1–13.

Perlmutter, F. D. (1990). *Changing hats: From social work practice to administration.* Washington DC: National Association of Social Workers Press.

Perlmutter, F. D., & Wilkerson, A. E. (1988). Alternative social agencies: Administrative strategies [Special issue]. *Administration in Social Work, 12*(2).

Perlmutter, F. D., Bailey, D., & Netting, F. E. (2000). *Managing human resources in the human services: Supervisory challenges.* New York: Oxford University Press.

Perrow, C. (1972). *Complex organizations: A critical essay.* Glenville, IL: Scott, Foresman.

Perrow, C. (1973). The short and glorious history of organization theory. *Organizational Dynamics, 2*(1), 2–15.

Peter, L. J., & Hull, R. (1969). *The Peter principle.* New York: Morrow.

Pifer, A. (1987). Philanthropy, voluntarism, and changing times. *Daedalus, 116*(1), 119–31.

Piven, F. F., & Cloward, R. A. (1971). *Regulating the poor: The functions of public welfare.* New York: Pantheon Books.

Piven, F. F., & Cloward, R. A. (1979). *Poor people's movements: Why they succeed, how they fail.* New York: Vintage Books.

Piven, F. F., & Cloward, R. A. (1982). *The new class war: Reagan's attack on the welfare state and its consequences.* New York: Pantheon Books.

Piven, F. F., & Cloward, R. A. (1988). *Why Americans don't vote.* New York: Pantheon Books.

Piven, F. F., & Cloward, R. A. (1993). *Regulating the poor: The functions of public welfare.* (Updated ed.). New York: Vintage Books.

Poertner, J., & Rapp, C. A. (1985). Purchase of service and accountability: Will they ever meet? *Administration in Social Work, 9*(1), 57–66.

Pogue, R. W., & Newcomer Society of the United States. (1989). *The Cleveland Foundation at seventy-five: An evolving community resource.* New York: Newcomer Society of the United States.

Poister, T. H., & Streib, G. (1999). Performance measurement in municipal government: Assessing the state of the practice. *Public Administration Review,* 59(4), 325–35.

Popper, K. (1957). *The poverty of historicism.* Boston: Beacon Press.

Popper, K. (1966). *The open society and its enemies.* Princeton, NJ: Princeton University Press.

Popple, P., & Leighninger, L. (1997). *The policy-based profession.* Boston: Allyn & Bacon.

Popple, P. R., & Leighninger, L. (1999). *Social work, social welfare, and American society* (4th ed.). Boston: Allyn & Bacon.

Prasad, S. B., & Sprague, D. A. (1996). Is TQM a global paradigm? In S. B. Prasad (Ed.), *Advances in international comparative management* (Vol. 11, pp. 69–85). Greenwich, CT: Jai Press.

Pratt, G. (1974). The demonstration grant is probably counterproductive. *Social Work,* 19(4), 484–85.

Prentice-Dunn, S., Wilson, D. R., & Spivey, C. B. (1985). Assessing the cost of behaviorally oriented residential treatment: Predictive program factors. *Child Welfare,* 64(2), 137–42.

Price, J. L., & Mueller, C. W. (1986). *Handbook of organizational measurement.* Marshfield, MA: Pitman.

Pring, G. W., & Canan, P. (1997). *SLAPPs: Getting sued for speaking out.* Philadelphia: Temple University Press.

Prottas, J. M. (1981). The cost of free services: Organizational impediments to access to public services. *Public Administration Review,* 41(5), 526–34.

Pruger, R. (1991). Efficiency and the social services [Special issue]. *Administration in Social Work,* 15(1/2), 5–44.

Pumphrey, R. E., & Pumphrey, M. W (1967). *The heritage of American social work: Readings in its philosophical and institutional development.* New York: Columbia University Press.

Putnam, R. (2000). *Bowling alone: The collapse and revival of American community.* New York: Simon & Schuster.

Putnam, R. D. (1995). *Making democracy work: Civic traditions in modern Italy.* Princeton, NJ: Princeton University Press.

Quam, J. (1995). Bertha Capon Reynolds (1885–1978). In R. L. Edwards (Ed.), *Encyclopedia of social work* (19th ed., Vol. 3, p. 2605). Silver Spring, MD: National Association of Social Workers.

Quinn, J. B. (1980). *Strategies for change: Logical incrementalism.* Homewood, IL: Irwin.

Quinn, J. J. (1996). The role of "good conversation" in strategic control. *Journal of Management Studies,* 33(3), 381–94.

Radin, B. A. (1998). The Government Performance and Results Act (GPRA): Hydra-headed monster or flexible management tool? *Public Administration Review,* 58(4), 307–16.

Raider, M. C. (1977). Installing management by objectives in social agencies. *Administration in Social Work,* 1(3), 235–44.

Randall, R. (1979). Presidential power versus bureaucratic intransigence: The influence of the Nixon administration on welfare policy. *American Political Science Review, 73*(3), 795–810.

The Random House Dictionary of the English Language (Unabridged ed.). (1967). New York: Random House.

Rapp, C. A., & Poertner, J. (1992). *Social administration: A client-centered approach.* White Plains, NY: Longman.

Rauch, J. B. (1976). The charity organization movement in Philadelphia. *Social Work, 21*(1), 55–62.

Rawls, J. (1971). *A theory of justice.* Cambridge, MA: Harvard University Press.

Reamer, F. G. (1993). Near- and farsightedness in social work education. *Journal of Social Work Education, 29*(1), 3–5.

Reamer, F. G. (1998). Ethical standards in social work: A critical review of the NASW code of ethics. Washington: National Association of Social Workers Press.

Reddin, W. J. (1970). *Managerial effectiveness.* New York: McGraw-Hill.

Rehfuss, J. (1989). *Contracting out in government.* San Francisco: Jossey-Bass.

Reid, R., & Non-Profit Network. (1987). *What does marketing have to do with fund raising?* Arcadia, CA: Non-Profit Network.

Reimer, F. G. (2000). Administrative ethics. In R. J. Patti (Ed.), *The handbook of social welfare management* (pp. 69–85). Thousand Oaks, CA: Sage.

Reiss, H. (1991). Introduction. *Kant: Political writings* (2nd ed., H. B. Nisbet, Trans., pp. 1–40). Cambridge: Cambridge University Press.

Remion, G. (1995). Bases, objectives and dimensions of social development. *Scandinavian Journal of Social Welfare, 4*(4), 290–97.

Rhoads, J. L. (1981). *Basic accounting and budgeting for long-term care facilities.* Boston: CBI.

Rice, G. H., & Bishoprick, D. W. (1971). *Conceptual models of organization.* New York: Appleton-Century-Crofts.

Richan, W. C. (1983). Social work administration under assault. *Administration in Social Work, 7*(3/4), 9–19.

Richter, B., & Ozawa, M. N. (1983). Purchase of service contracts and the functioning of private agencies. *Administration in Social Work, 7*(1), 25–37.

Rifkin, J. (1995). *The end of work: The decline of the global labor force and the dawn of the post-market era.* New York: Putnam.

Robbins, S. P., Chatterjee, P., & Canda, E. R. (1998). *Contemporary human behavior theory: A critical perspective for social work.* Needham Heights, MA: Allyn & Bacon.

Robert, H. M. (1999). *Webster's new world Robert's Rules of Order: Simplified and applied.* New York: Webster's New World.

Rogers, E. M., & Shoemaker, F. F. (1971). *Communication of innovations: A cross-cultural approach* (2nd ed.). New York: Free Press.

Rorty, R. (1998). *Achieving our country: Leftist thought in twentieth-century America.* Cambridge, MA: Harvard University Press.

Rose-Ackerman, S. (1982). Charitable giving and "excessive" fund raising. *Quarterly Journal of Economics, 7*(2), 193–212.

Rosenbaum, N. (1982). Government funding and the voluntary sector: Impacts and options. *Journal of Voluntary Action Research, 11*(2), 14–21.

Rosenberg, G. (1980). Concepts in the financial management of hospital social work departments. *Social Work in Health Care, 5*(3), 287–303.

Ross, C., & Joelson, J. B. (1986). Holding accountability systems accountable: Is what's good for the goose good for the gander? *Journal of Applied Social Sciences, 10*(2), 156–75.

Ross, T. (1987). *Privatization in America.* Washington, DC: Touche Ross.

Rossi, P. H., & Freeman, H. E. (1985). *Evaluation: A systematic approach* (3rd ed.). Beverly Hills, CA: Sage.

Rosso, H. A., & Associates. (1991). *Achieving excellence in fund raising: A comprehensive guide to principles, strategies and methods.* San Francisco: Jossey-Bass.

Rothman, J. (1977). Three models of community organization practice: Their mixing and phasing. In F. Cox, J. L. Erlich, J. Rothman, & J. E. Tropman (Eds.), *Strategies of community organization* (pp. 20–38). Itasca, IL: Peacock.

Rothman, J. (1996). The interweaving of community intervention approaches. *Journal of Community Practice, 3*(3/4), 69–99.

Rousseau, J.-J. (1974). *The essential Rousseau: The Social Contract, Discourse on the Origin of Inequality, Discourse on the Arts and Sciences, The Creed of a Savoyard priest* (L. Bair, Ed.). New York: New American Library.

Ryan, A. (1995). *John Dewey and the high tide of American liberalism.* New York: Norton.

Ryan, E. J. (1976). *Management by objectives in perspective: A comparative study of selected federal experience with the fiscal year 1975 program.* Washington, DC: George Washington University.

Salamon, L., & Anheier, H. K. (1998). Social origins of civil society: Explaining the nonprofit sector. *Voluntas, 9*(3), 213–48.

Salamon, L. M. (Ed.). (1989). *Beyond privatization: The tools of government action.* Washington, DC: Urban Institute Press.

Salamon, L. M. (1992). *America's nonprofit sector: A primer.* New York: Foundation Center.

Salancik, G. R., & Pfeffer, J. (1974). The bases and use of power in organizational decision making: The case of a university. *Administrative Science Quarterly, 19*(4), 453–73.

Samuelson, R. J. (1995). *The good life and its discontents: The American dream in the age of entitlement, 1945–1995.* New York: Times Books/Random House.

Sandel, M. J. (1996). *Democracy's discontent: America in search of a public philosophy.* Cambridge, MA: Harvard University Press.

Santora, J. C. (1982). *Management by objectives (MBO): A selected periodical guide, 1960–1981.* Monticello, IL: Vance Bibliographies.

Sarri, R. (1971). Administration in social welfare. In R. Morris (Ed.), *Encyclopedia of Social Work* (Vol. 1, pp. 39–48). New York: National Association of Social Workers.

Savas, E. S. (1987). *Privatization: The key to better government.* Chatham, NJ: Chatham House.

Schilling, R. F., Schinke, S. P., & Weatherly, R.A. (1988). Service trends in a conservative era: Social workers rediscover the past. *Social Work, 33*(1), 5–9.

Schlesinger, A. M., Jr. (1988). Affirmative government and the American economy. In *The Cycles of American History* (pp. 219–55). Boston: Houghton Mifflin.

Schlesinger, A. M. (1999). *The cycles of American history.* Boston: Houghton Mifflin. (Originally published in 1986)

Schlesinger, M. (1989). Striking a balance: Capitation, the mentally ill, and public policy. *New Directions for Mental Health Services, 43*, 97–115.

Schmid, H. (1993). Non-profit and for-profit organizations in home care services: A comparative analysis. *Home Health Care Services Quarterly, 14*(1), 93–112.

Schmid, H. (2000). Agency–environment relations: Understanding task environments. In R. Patti (Ed.), *Handbook of social welfare administration* (pp. 133–57). Thousand Oaks, CA: Sage.

Schneider, R. L., & Sharon, N. (1982). Representation of social work agencies: New definition, special issues, and practice model. *Administration in Social Work, 6*(1), 59–68.

Schorr, A. (1980). The social compact. *Journal of Applied Social Sciences, 4*(2), 115–27.

Scott, W. R. (1995). *Institutions and organizations.* Thousand Oaks, CA: Sage.

Seidenberg, G. R., & Johnson, F. S. (1979). A case study in defining developmental costs for quality assurance in mental health center programs. *Evaluation and Program Planning, 2*(2), 143–52.

Seitel, F. P. (1992). *The practice of public relations* (5th ed.). New York: Macmillan.

Seiz, R. C. (1990). *Entrepreneurial personality traits, value systems, and the private practice of social work: An ecological model for practice setting choice.* Unpublished dissertation, University of Texas.

Sellers, C. (1991). *The market revolution: Jacksonian America, 1815–1846.* New York: Oxford University Press.

Selznick, P. (1949). *TVA and the grassroots: A study in the sociology of organizations.* Berkeley: University of California Press.

Selznick, P. (1957). *Leadership in administration.* Evanston, IL: Row & Peterson.

Selznick, P. (1995). Defining democracy up. *Public Interest, 119*, 106–10.

Sharpe, R. F. (1988, April). What to do before your donors are dead. *Fund Raising Management,* pp. 40–48.

Sheridan Associates, Zimmerman Associates, & Independent Sector. (1988). *Study of cause-related marketing.* Washington, DC: Independent Sector.

Sherraden, M. (1991). *Assets and the poor: A new American welfare policy.* Armonk, NY: Sharpe.

Sherraden, M. W. (1986). Benefit-cost analysis as a net present value problem. *Administration in Social Work, 10*(3), 85–98.

Shostack, A. L., & Campagna, G. P. (1987). Financing group homes. *Public Welfare, 45*(4), 38–42.

Siegel, A., & United States Civil Service Commission, Organizational Psychology Section. (1978). *Management by objectives: Guidelines for managerial decision making.* Washington, DC: Civil Service Commission Personnel Research and Development Center, Organizational Psychology Section.

Simon, B. L. (1994). *The empowerment tradition in American social work: A history.* New York: Columbia University Press.

Simon, H. A. (1997). *Administrative behavior: A study of decision-making processes in administrative organization* (4th ed.). New York: Free Press. (Originally published in 1947)

Singer, L. (1998, July). Welfare puzzle tests state ingenuity. *Government Technology,* p. 34.

Skidmore, R. A. (1995). *Social work administration: Dynamic management and human relationships* (3rd ed.). Boston: Allyn & Bacon.

Skocpol, T. (1993). *Protecting soldiers and mothers: The political origins of social policy in the United States.* Cambridge, MA: Harvard University Press.

Slavin, S. (1978). *Social administration.* Binghamton, NY: Haworth Press.

Slavin, S., & Perlmutter, F. (Eds.). (1980). *Leadership in social administration: Perspectives for the 1980's.* Philadelphia: Temple University Press.

Smith, A. (1981). *The wealth of nations.* New York: Viking Penguin.

Smith, P. B., & Peterson, M. F. (1988). *Leadership, organizations, and culture: An event management model.* London: Sage.

Smith, R. M. (1997). *Civic ideals: Conflicting visions of citizenship in U.S. history.* New Haven, CT: Yale University Press.

Smith, S. R., & Lipsky, M. (1992). *Nonprofits for hire: The welfare state in the age of contracting.* Cambridge, MA: Harvard University Press.

Solomon, B. (1976). *Black empowerment: Social work in oppressed communities.* New York: Columbia University Press.

Sorensen, J. E., Hanbery, G. B., & Kucic, A. R. (1983). *Accounting and budget systems for mental health organizations.* Washington, DC: Government Printing Office.

Spencer, S. (1970). *The administration method in social work education* (Vol. 3). New York: Council of Social Work Education.

Spergel, I. A. (1977). Social development and social work. *Administration in Social Work, 1*(3), 221–33.

Spillane, R. R., & Levenson, D. (1978). *Management by objectives in the schools.* Bloomington, IN: Phi Delta Kappa Educational Foundation.

Staples, L. H. (1990). Powerful ideas about empowerment. *Administration in Social Work, 14*(2), 29–42.

States progress toward digital nation. (1998, September). *Government Technology News,* p. 22.

Stern, D. (1991). Efficiency in human services: The case of education. *Administration in Social Work, 15*(1/2), 83–104.

Stoesz, D. (1989). Human service corporations: New opportunities for administration in social work. *Administration in Social Work, 13*(3/4), 183–97.

Stogdill, R. M. (1974). *Handbook of leadership: A survey of theory and research.* New York: Free Press.

Stokes, M. (1997). *The market revolution in America: Social, political, and religious expression, 1800–1880.* Virginia: University Press of Virginia.

Strom, K. (1992). Reimbursement demands and treatment decisions: A growing dilemma for social workers. *Social Work, 37*(5), 398–403.

Strom, S. H. (1992). *Beyond the typewriter: Gender, class and the origins of modern American office work, 1900–1930.* Champaign: University of Illinois Press.

Suchman, E. A. (1967). *Evaluative research: Principles and practice in public service and social action programs.* New York: Russell Sage Foundation.

Sugarman, B. (1988). The well-managed human service organization: Criteria for a management audit. *Administration in Social Work, 12*(4), 17–27.

Sumariwalla, R. D. (1975). *Budgeting: A guide for United Ways and not-for-profit human services.* Alexandria, VA: United Way of America.

Sumariwalla, R. D. (1976). *UWASIS II: A taxonomy of social goals and human service programs.* Alexandria, VA: United Way of America.

Sumariwalla, R. D. (1989). *Accounting and financial reporting: A guide for United Ways and not-for-profit human service organizations.* Alexandria, VA: United Way of America. (Originally published in 1974)

Sundel, H. H., Zelman, W. N., Weaver, C. N., & Pasternak, R. E. (1978). Fund raising: Understanding donor motivation. *Social Work, 23*(3), 233–36.

Swift, L. B. (1934). *New alignments between public and private agencies.* New York: Family Service Association of America.

Taintor, Z., Widem, P., & Barrett, S. A. (1984). *Cost considerations in mental health treatment.* Washington, DC: Government Printing Office.

Tannenbaum, R., & Schmidt, W. H. (1973). How to choose a leadership pattern. *Harvard Business Review, 51,* 162–64.

Tarter, J. L. (1974). *Management by objectives for public administrators.* Washington, DC: National Training and Development Service.

Tasi, H., Hunter, J., Chesser, R., Tarter, J. R., & Carroll, S. (1976). How real are changes induced by management by objectives? *Administrative Science Quarterly, 21*(2), 276–306.

Taubman, S. (1991). Efficiency in clinical practice. *Administration and Policy in Mental Health, 18*(5), 313–24.

Taylor, C. (1989). *Sources of self.* Cambridge, MA: Harvard University Press.

Taylor, J. R., Cooren, F., Giroux, N., & Robichaud, D. (1996). The communicational basis of organization: Between the conversation and the text. *Communication Theory, 6*(1), 1–39.

Terrell, P. (1979). Private alternatives to public human services administration. *Social Service Review, 53*(1), 56–74.

Terry, G. R. (1972). *Principles of management* (6th ed.). Homewood, IL: Irwin.

Terry, R. W. (1998). *Authentic leadership: Courage in action.* San Francisco: Jossey-Bass.

Theodorson, G. A., & Theodorson, A. G. (1969). *A modern dictionary of sociology.* New York: Crowell.

Thompson, J. (1967). *Organizations in action.* New York: McGraw-Hill.

Thompson, J. A., & McEwen, W. (1958). Organizational goals and environment: Goal setting as an interaction process. *American Sociological Review, 23*(1), 23–31.

Tilly, C. (1978). *From mobilization to revolution.* Reading, MA: Addison-Wesley.

Tilly, C. (1981). *As sociology meets history.* New York: Academic Press.

Tilly, C. (1986). *The contentious French.* Cambridge, MA: Belknap Press.

Tilly, C. (1990). *Coercion, capital, and European states, AD 990–1990.* Cambridge, MA: Blackwell.

Tilly, C. (1993). *European revolutions, 1492–1992.* Oxford: Blackwell.

Tilly, C., Tilly, L., & Tilly, R. H. (1975). *The rebellious century, 1830–1930.* Cambridge, MA: Harvard University Press.

Tilly, L., & Tilly, C. (1981). *Class conflict and collective action.* Beverly Hills, CA: Sage, in cooperation with the Social Science History Association.

Tittle, D. (1992). *Rebuilding Cleveland: The Cleveland Foundation and its evolving urban strategy.* Columbus: Ohio State University Press.

Tobey, J. A. (1925). *The Children's Bureau: Its history, activities and organization.* Baltimore: Johns Hopkins University Press.

Toffler, A. (1990). *Power shift: Knowledge, wealth and violence at the edge of the 21st century.* New York: Bantam Books.

Townsend, R. (1970). *Up the organization.* New York: Knopf.

Trattner, W. I. (1999). *From poor law to welfare state: A history of social welfare in America.* New York: Free Press.

Trecker, H. (1946). *Group process in administration.* New York: Women's Press.

Trecker, H. (1965). *Social work administration.* New York: Association Press.

Trecker, H. (1971). *Social work administration* (Rev. ed.). New York: Association Press.

Trecker, H. B. (1961). *New understandings of administration.* New York: Association Press.

Tropman, E. J. (1977). Staffing committees and studies. In F. M. Cox, J. L. Erlich, J. Rothman, & J. E. Tropman (Eds.), *Tactics and techniques of community practice* (pp. 105–11). Itasca, IL: Peacock.

Tropman, J. E., Johnson, H. R., & Tropman, E. J. (1992). *Committee management in human services* (2nd ed.). Chicago: Nelson-Hall.

Tuckman, H. P., & Chang, C. F. (1991). A methodology for measuring the financial vulnerability of charitable nonprofit organizations. *Nonprofit and Voluntary Sector Quarterly, 20*(4), 445–60.

Tullock, G. (1965). *The politics of bureaucracy.* Washington, DC: Public Affairs Press.

Turner, J. B. (1995). Fund raising and philanthropy. In R. Edwards (Ed.), *Encyclopedia of Social Work* (19th ed., Vol. 2, pp. 1038–44). Washington, DC: National Association of Social Workers.

Unger, I. (1996). *The best of intentions: The triumphs and failures of the Great Society under Kennedy, Johnson, and Nixon.* New York: Doubleday.

Urwick, L. (1943). *The elements of administration.* New York: Harper.

U.S. Bureau of Labor Statistics. (circa 1925). *The cost of American almshouses.* Washington, DC: Government Printing Office.

U.S. Office of Personnel Management, Office of Performance Management. (1985). *Management by objectives in performance appraisal systems.* Washington, DC: Office of Personnel Management Workforce Effectiveness and Development Group, Office of Performance Management.

Van Hayek, F. A. (1947). The decline of socialism and the rise of the welfare state. In C. I. Schottland (Ed.), *The welfare state*. New York: Harper & Row.

Vandeven, W. P. M. M. (1996). Market-oriented health care reforms: Trends and future options. *Social Science and Medicine, 43*(5), 655–66.

Varney, G. H. (1979). *Management by objectives* (2nd ed.). Chicago: Dartnell.

Vasey, W. (1958). *Government and social welfare: Roles of federal, state and local governments in administering welfare services*. New York: Holt.

Vincent, A., & Plant, R. (1984). *Philosophy, politics and citizenship: The life and thought of the British idealists*. New York: Cambridge University Press.

Vinter, R. (1959). The social structure of service. In A. J. Kahn (Ed.), *Issues in American social work* (pp. 242–69). New York: Columbia University Press.

Vinter, R., & Kish, R. (1985). *Budgeting in not-for-profit organizations*. New York: Free Press.

Volland, P. J. (1980). Costing for social work services. *Social Work in Health Care, 6*(1), 73–87.

Walker, R., & Garman, E. T. (1992). The meanings of money: Perspectives from human ecology. *American Behavioral Scientist, 35*(6), 781–89.

Waring, S. P. (1991). *Taylorism transformed: Scientific management theory since 1945*. Chapel Hill: University of North Carolina Press.

Warner, A. G., Queen, S. A., & Harper, E. B. (1930). *American charities and social work* (4th ed.). New York: Crowell. (Originally published in 1894)

Warren, R. (1956). Toward a reformulation of community theory. *Human Organization, 15*(2), 8–11.

Warren, R. (1963). *The community in America*. Skokie, IL: Rand McNally.

Warren, R. (Ed.). (1966). *Perspectives on the American community: A book of readings*. New York: Rand McNally.

Warren, R. L. (1971). *Truth, love, and social change, and other essays on community change*. Chicago: Rand McNally.

Warren, R. L. (1977). *New perspectives on the American community: A book of readings* (3rd ed.). Chicago: Rand McNally.

Weber, M. (1947). *The theory of social and economic organization* (A. M. Henderson & T. Parsons, Trans.). New York: Free Press.

Weber, M. (1948). *The Protestant ethic and the spirit of capitalism* (T. Parsons, Trans.). New York: Oxford University Press.

Weber, M. (1968). *Economy and society: An outline of interpretive sociology* (G. Roth & C. Wittich, Eds.; E. Fishoff, Trans.). New York: Bedminster Press.

Wedel, K. R. (1974). Contracting for public assistance social services. *Public Welfare, 32*(1), 57–62.

Wedel, K. R. (1976). Government contracting for purchase of service. *Social Work, 21*(2), 101–105.

Wedel, K. R., & Colston, S.W. (1988). Performance contracting for human services: Issues and suggestions. *Administration in Social Work, 12*(1), 73–87.

Weiner, M. (1990). *Human services management: Analysis and applications*. Belmont, CA: Wadsworth.

Weiner, M. E. (1987). Managing people for enhanced performance. *Administration in Social Work, 11*(3/4), 147–60.

Weisbrod, B. (1988). *The nonprofit economy.* Cambridge, MA: Harvard University Press.

Weiss, C. H. (1972). *Evaluation research: Methods of assessing program effectiveness.* Englewood Cliffs, NJ: Prentice Hall.

Weissman, H. H., Epstein, I., & Savage, A. (1983). *Agency-based social work: Neglected aspects of clinical practice.* Philadelphia: Temple University Press.

Wernet, S. P., & Jones, S. A. (1992). Merger and acquisition activity between nonprofit social service organizations: A case study. *Nonprofit and Voluntary Sector Quarterly, 21*(4), 367–80.

Wernet, S. P., Hulseman, F. S., Merkel, L. A., McMahon, A., Clevenger, D., Coletta, A., & Leeds, V. (1992). The fee-for-service schedule: A new formula. *Families in Society, 73*(2), 109–15.

Westbrook, R. B. (1991). *John Dewey and American democracy.* Ithaca, NY: Cornell University Press.

Westoby, A. (1988). *Culture and power in educational organizations: A reader.* Philadelphia: Open University Press.

White, O. (1969). The dialectical organization: An alternative to bureaucracy. *Public Administration Review, 29*(1), 32–42.

White, S. (1999, September). The board game. *Town and Country,* p. 148.

White, V. P. (1975). *Grants: How to find them and what to do next.* New York: Plenum.

Wholey, J. S., Hatry, H. P., & Newcomer, K. E. (1994). *Handbook of practical program evaluation.* San Francisco: Jossey-Bass.

Wiehe, V. R. (1974). *Management by objectives in mental health services* (Rev. ed.). Ann Arbor, MI: Masterco Press.

Wiehe, V. R. (1978). Management by objectives in a family service agency. In S. Slavin (Ed.), *Social administration* (pp. 276–82). New York: Haworth Press.

Wildavsky, A. (1967). *The politics of the budgetary process.* Boston: Little, Brown.

Wilensky, H., & LeBeaux, C. (1965). *Social welfare in industrial society.* New York: Free Press.

Willis, D. (1984). Purchase of social services: Another look. *Social Work 29*(6).

Witkin, S. L. (2001). Valediction: Howard Goldstein. *Social Work, 46,* 105–6.

Wolch, J. R. (1990). *The shadow state: Government and voluntary sector in transition.* New York: Foundation Center.

Wolf, T. (1990). *Managing a nonprofit organization.* New York: Simon & Schuster.

Woodward, J. (1965). *Industrial organizations: Theory and practice.* London: Oxford University Press.

Wren, D. A. (1979). *The evolution of management thought* (2nd ed.). New York: Wiley.

Wren, D. A. (1994). *The evolution of management thought* (4th ed.). New York: Wiley.

Wren, D. A. (1997). *Early management thought.* Aldershot, U.K.: Aldershot Publishing.

Wresch, W. C. (1995). *Disconnected: Haves and have-nots in the information age.* New Brunswick, NJ: Rutgers University Press.

Yankelovich, D. (1999). *The magic of dialogue: Transforming conflict into cooperation.* New York: Simon & Schuster.

Young, D. A. (1973). Case costing in child welfare: A critical step toward increased accountability in social services. *Child Welfare, 53*(5), 299–304.

Young, D. W., & Allen, B. (1977). Benefit cost analysis in the social services: The example of adoption reimbursement. *Social Service Review, 51*(2), 249–64.

Zelman, W. N., DelPizzo, L. E., & Sorenson, J. E. (1987). In pursuit of survival: Managing revenues. *Journal of Mental Health Administration, 14*(2), 44–51.

Zimbalist, S. E. (1977). *Historic themes and landmarks in social welfare research.* New York: Harper & Row.

Zippay, A. (1992). Corporate funding of human service agencies. *Social Work, 37*(3), 210–14.

Zucker, L. G. (1988). *Institutional patterns and organizations: Culture and environment.* Cambridge, MA: Ballinger.

Index